NOT IN VAIN

Mothers Share their Journey through their Child's Life and Loss
to the Drug Pandemic

BOBBIE R. ZIEMER

Not In Vain: Volume 1

The publisher assumes no responsibility for errors, omissions, or contrary interpretations of the subject matter herein. Any perceived slight of any individual or organization is purely unintentional. Information not meant to replace medical or legal advice.

Cover Design by: Jody L. McLain
Publisher: Madison Victoria Publishing, LLC
Print Book ISBN: 9798689344195
Ebook ASIN: B08JS1L23C
1st Printing Oct. 31, 2020

100% of the Amazon/KDP proceeds from both the ebook and paperback for Volume 1 are being donated to the #NotInVain nonprofit to continue supporting the grieving mothers of this pandemic

Contents

May these stories give you hope and understanding that you are not alone. May they provide guidance you seek, help you avoid decisions you may regret, and provide direction in the abyss led by the mothers who have walked this painful journey.

You can't change what you don't know.

Madison

FOREVER 22

Dedicated in loving memory of *MADISON VICTORIA CROSS* eldest daughter of *BOBBIE ZIEMER* and mother of *KINSLEY RANEE*.

Madison committed to fighting for her life by agreeing to a long-term (one year) rehabilitation program after her family joined in together with an intervention. She flew from her home in Ohio and voluntarily admitted herself into a medical detox center in Sun City West, Arizona on October 7, 2017.

Three days after her admission, Madison collapsed and died. Her cause of death was "septic pneumonia." There is an active lawsuit preventing Madison's story from being shared within this book.

"As long as I can, I will look at the world for both of us.
As long as I can, I will laugh with the birds,
I will sing with the flowers.
I will pray to the stars for both of us."

Foreword

We never think that OUR CHILD will be labeled an "addict." From the moment of their birth we taught them love, compassion, sharing, hope, manners, patience, and so many more qualities to live by only wanting them to flourish as an even better version of ourselves. When we learn that our child has been using drugs, our minds seem to immediately flash back to our own youth when we drank or maybe even smoked marijuana. Unfortunately, these experiences do not compare to the reality of what's ahead.

This book is filled with over 160 real-life stories from grieving mothers through their initial discovery of their child's drug use, to the devastating end of their journey. They have shared what they learned, the emotional ups and downs, "enabling," "tough love," and "unconditional love," the affect within themselves and their family, as well as what they wished they would have known or even done differently. Now it is our combined effort to help educate others.

In the following chapters of the book, we will include stories from around the globe from those who have suffered loss. We're very optimistic that this first volume will set the stage to spread awareness of the disease of drug addiction and the devastation of the precious lives lost that are Not In Vain.

We believe that these real-life stories will not only further awareness, but also may in some way help provide comfort and navigation so that those struggling know they are not alone.

By sharing these stories, others will see many of the same struggles and situations mamas have lived as well as resources we have found along the way. Here is our opportunity to share the painful experiences mamas have endured to help and guide those on the same journey.

This book sadly cannot bring our child or children back who were tragically lost due to the drug pandemic; nothing can. But perhaps these stories from real mamas that have survived loss can help you understand and guide you through the most challenging situation that anyone could possibly have even considered: Your child lost related to the drug pandemic. There are over 200+ lives lost a day to drugs! Whether it be "prescription drugs:" Oxycontin, Percocet, hydrocodone, Xanax, fentanyl, or "street drugs:" heroin, crack, cocaine, meth, synthetic fentanyl…never did we think or consider the possibility that our child would ever be exposed to any of them. Why? Desperation, fear, ignorance, lack of experience, social support, societal stigma? All of this leaving us confused and following whatever advice we can get with no way of knowing where or what resources could help with what happened to your child and that your family has forever changed because of it.

I've been inspired to share the stories of these grieving mamas who started out just like many others; however, have had a child or children that lost this battle. My hope is that these honest stories help educate, forewarn, and hopefully even save lives in knowing what we didn't know…In sharing the biggest heartbreak of our lives…In showing that if you are struggling, you are not alone and we are here not by choice, but we now try to save others from ever joining this "life sentence" of grieving mamas.

Nobody wants to talk about it when it's happening to them. Or how families are completely lost when fighting this disease. My hope is that this book will open eyes and doors in creating awareness as well as resources and support to help your children and your family.

From an idea, inspiration, rough drafts, editing, combined hard work and dedication, and finally, publication, this book intends to help all families regardless of where they are with friends, family and coworkers through Prevention, Education, Hope and Healing. You are not alone. Thousands of families are in your exact shoes.

Prevention and Education for the families who have not experienced drug addiction around how easily this can happen to someone they love.

For the families who are struggling with this right now. The only true "rock bottom" is death, so where there is life, there is still Hope.

Also, Healing for the families who have lost a loved one to know they are not alone and the person you lost very much mattered.

This book will not provide you with "professional" guidance, however you will be able to see a small view into this painful journey that these grieving mothers of this pandemic now carry as a life sentence.

In conclusion, this book is devoted to all the precious children we have lost and to the mamas who are struggling to survive this devastating loss; to the families still fighting for the lives of their children. May these stories give you hope, insight, and may God give you strength to never give up.

Acknowledgments

I am grateful to so many people. To name them all is impossible, to name a few is a privilege. First and foremost I thank my family, my friends and colleagues who were and continue to be part of my process of surviving, healing, and living.

Next most importantly, thank you to all of the mothers who took the time to painfully write and contribute their stories. It's incredible to see this beautiful act of kindness as those that are brokenhearted standing up to protect a world of strangers in effort to save even a single one from this tragedy.

My sincerest of gratitude to all of the mothers of the #NotInVain support group as I honestly held onto many of you to survive the loss of my daughter Madison, without the support from the #NotInVain group I don't think I would have.

Special thanks to Pj Champion Sallie for starting the support group #NotInVain, and for the tireless hours she, Cathy Williams and Tina Stephenson Baack as well as for the pages, groups moderators, past and present. It is no easy task being strength for others dealing with their own grief and life challenges.

Sincerest gratitude to our volunteers, editors, journal writers, formatters, and all of the incredible talent donated to this massive and emotionally intense project:

Amy May, Lisa Bolton, Yvonne Carpenter, Sandy Gearlds, Cathy Lawley, Elizabeth Costello, Olga Martin, Jodi Mclain, Lisa Montagano, Danielle Moreau, Angee Cannon, Pj Champion Sallie, Rebecca Dettorre, Gloria Atcheson, and CJ Anaya.

Finally...Lord I thank YOU. Thank you for asking me to do this. I've listened and continue to listen and trust where you lead me.

Preface

From the day I found out I was pregnant with you, my life immediately changed. My body was no longer just my body. Any and all plans I had been redirected to now caring for the little person growing inside of me. First things first to scheduling a doctor's appointment with my OBGYN. Of course, they confirmed my pregnancy and not long after, another visit for an ultrasound. You were so small and the shape of a peanut, so that is what we called you for the first few months.

As you grew in my belly I took my daily prenatal, tried to eat nutritious foods, paid attention to my activities, signed up to receive weekly emails showing your development and of course studied the book "What to Expect while You're Expecting" like it was my only job.

Then came the day that you left my body to enter the world. There was nothing that sounded nearly as sweet as the sound of your first cry. I felt immediate unconditional love and an overwhelming need to protect you swearing that I would never allow anything to hurt you. I remember I couldn't stop holding you and staring at you. I've never loved anything so quickly or with so much passion.

The day I brought you home, I was so nervous and wanted to make sure I was doing everything the right way. The hospital had sent home paperwork and one pager that included how to bath you as a newborn. With these instructions lying beside you, I organized Q-tips, wash clothes, baby wash and lotion following the directions step by step until you had your very first "bath€". The next book that became my bible then became "What to Expect the First Year".

Next were the toddler years with first steps, potty training and so on. Of course, there are books that serve as guides to this as well. As you grew, my job as your mama also grew. I had to keep your surroundings safe and make sure to keep you out of harm's way. I was the helicopter mama in who I allowed you to be around as well as inspire you to become your own person by finding group activities and sports to involve you in. I took you to every doctor's appointment, made sure you had all of your immunizations, took time off work to care for you when you were sick, let you snuggle with me when you just needed some cuddles, made cupcakes and desserts together for your classmates and never missed a parent-teacher conference. There was nothing more important in my life than you and in providing you the best life I could possibly make for you.

As a mama, I also needed to be a role model in showing you love, patience, friendship, guidance, forgiveness and being genuinely you for whoever you would become in this world. Most of all it was my job to always protect you, guide you, hold you, hug you and wipe away your tears when you felt hurt.

Your ability to make friends was incredible as was your fiery spirit to also be a protector and defender of those who needed a friend. I couldn't be any prouder of the person you grew to be. Of course, your teenage years you pulled away in efforts to do all that I had taught you in making your own decisions and being a dependable friend and reliable young woman. Even when it came down to getting your first car. I remember your excitement in experiencing your freedom now as a beautiful young woman. As your mama, it was still my job to protect and guide you which I would continue to do as the years passed.

This is what we do as mamas.

Unfortunately, there was not a book that could guide me through the most challenging situation that I had not even considered. Drugs. Not the drugs that were around and popular when I was in my late teens or early 20's such as alcohol and marijuana, but "prescription drugs" that included OxyContin, Xanax, Valium nor the "street drugs" like Heroin, Meth, Fentanyl that in my mind were only in the darkest parts of town or only being used within the neighborhoods that were the worst in the area. Never did I think or consider any possibility MY CHILD would ever even be exposed to those things. Nor would I ever expect the introduction of drugs within my family would lead to the battle of my life to save my child's life, however I could. Desperation, fear, ignorance, lack of experience, social support, societal stigma all left me confused and following whatever advice I was given. There was no way of knowing where or what resources could help with what was happening to my child and that our family would change forever; worst yet it would change almost everything about my child to feed the addiction.

This book will not provide you with "professional" guidance, however you will be able to see a small view into this painful journey that the grieving mothers of this pandemic now carry as a life sentence. I've been led to share the stories of these beautiful mama's who started out just like other mamas however have lost this battle and our babies. With over 160 stories, my prayer is that they help educate, warn and even save lives in knowing what we didn't know. In sharing the biggest heartbreak of our lives. In showing that if you are struggling, you are not alone and we are here not by choice, but now to try to save others from ever joining this "club".

Nobody wants to talk about what is really happening or how lost the families are when fighting this disease. Prayers that this book opens both eyes and doors in creating awareness as well as programs to help our children and support the families.

We dedicate this book to all of the incredible children we have lost and to the mama's who are struggling to survive this devastating loss; to the families still fighting for the life of their children.

Not MY Child

My kids are little
They are around here some place…
This teen that lies and manipulates.
She must be someone else's kid.

Not my oldest who makes A's and B's.
This young lady who only wants to please the crowd.
Not my little one who sings "Trust and obey."
This gal who wrote such filth in a notebook.
Not my daughter who can write circles around Frost.
This adolescent who harms her sister like a vile enemy.
Not my darling who kisses and says, "I love you, sissy, night." This
young woman who was violated…
Not my child who won the bible memory award.
This 14-year-old who just overdosed.
Not my girl who brings so much pleasure and pride to life
This is Not My Child.

My kids are little.
I just saw them a moment ago.
This adolescent who fears her older sister.

1

She must be someone else's kid.

Not my cutie who worships the ground her sister walks on.
This girl with so much anger and hurt built up.
Not the little one who has a million hugs each day.
This child who talks back disrespectful to me.
Not my sensitive doll, "You are the bestest mommy in the world." This
kid that can't focus on the real world.
Not my child playing house with me.
The gal who just got a detention for fighting.
Not my gentle natured one: "Don't kill the ant, mommy."
This 11-year-old that doesn't want to eat.
Not my healthy, happy, pudgy toddler.
This is Not My Child.

My kids are little.
These are not my children.
This is not my life.

I made sure my children wouldn't turn out like those kids.
I kept them my first priority after God, faithful in church, a Christian
school, good influences, read and memorized the Bible together, prayed,
family films, worked from home, every penny going into the family…

Then a nightmare…
A violation of innocence in the midst of perfect planning.
Nothing has been the same since.
Trying to rebuild beauty from ashes…
Almost succeeding.
Then the unthinkable happens again.
I spent years going back and forth trying to save their lives, only to lose
my baby.
Dead with a needle in her arm.
My oldest in recovery.

I'm raising both their babies.
I just turned around a minute ago.

Where did my children go?
Where did my life go?
Are you glad they are not your children?
Are you glad this is not your life?
Is it a relief to bask in my pain?
Don't turn around…
You could be the next one saying…
Not My Child.

PJ CHAMPION SALLIE
Toledo, Ohio

What to Expect When You're Grieving the Death of Your Child

Over the next few days, weeks, months and first several years you will feel like you're in a horrible nightmare; an unreal dream way beyond even the most lucid dream you've ever felt. You'll want so badly for someone to wake you up. Somehow, at the same time, you'll be aware that you're not dreaming.

Life will feel like it's stopped and that you, as well as everything around you, is moving in slow motion. The noise around you will sound distant or muffled. The air you breathe, when you do breathe, will feel heavy and without oxygen. Your mind will seem to have gone "offline" at times and scramble at others when you're flooded with thoughts that will not make sense. This is temporary.

There will be many moments when you do try to speak that you'll forget what you want to say, or you'll be told that you've already said it yet don't remember doing so. The term for this is "brain fog". Get used to using this phrase as well as saying it in replace of what you don't remember. Memory issues seem to be a big one for many, but not all. This symptom, although extremely frustrating, will slowly resolve itself. You'll find moments when it returns and those moments you should celebrate. This will also help reassure you that this state is not a permanent one.

The people who come around you will be polite and truly DO want to help you, they just don't know what to say or how to make anything better. Do be honest, there really isn't anything they can do or say that would. Just remember, they love you and even when they say things that feel hurtful, they don't mean to. This will tie back to the "grief fog" as you won't remember much about who visited or who you talked to during the early months anyway. This feels like a mixture of what amnesia and Alzheimer's would feel like if struck by them at the same time, although, you will be acutely aware that you have no control over it. I'm certain this is the brain and body's way of somehow going into survival mode because it's too much to bear.

You will find yourself catching your breath, both day and night, almost as if you've been holding it. You'll cry harder than you ever knew you could as your heart and soul both feel this intense loss at a level that has no human words to describe. There is a sound that will come out of you as you cry, one that is inhuman, almost like the howling of a wounded animal, when you do allow yourself to absorb this new reality. It's a terrifying sound that rips into the heart of whoever hears it.

Sleep won't come easy, even more difficult than when you were worried about your child being out with "friends" and all the fear that came with any unknown phone number calling you praying it wasn't "the call". When you can sleep, you'll awake startled as though someone has jumped out and scared you. This is just your mind realizing that this nightmare is your new reality. Your heart will literally and physically hurt...anxiety and panic attacks come in waves with every memory or flashback and these too can keep you from sleeping or even trying to rest. Try to get rest anyway and do your best not stay in bed. Challenge yourself daily to sit outside or even take a walk as your mind, spirit and body needs this.

Eating will either become something you either forget to do or overdo and personal hygiene doesn't seem to matter as you feel as though you are dying from the inside out. I've described this feeling as though my soul was dying. In reality, a piece of it truly did.

If you're anything like me, you will fight with everything you know and have inside to try to have a sense of normalcy, however you must truly be patient with yourself, the process, and those around you as there is no timeline in which things will resume as normal. It will be a new normal and will feel empty more days than it doesn't.

This agonizing event will take its own time as well as present you with twists and turns. Like the waves of the ocean, they are hard and fast in the beginning and gradually slow and lighten only with time; although the storm will return on occasion raging when you least expect it. Just know that just as a hurricane demolishes everything in its path, the sun will eventually return.

There is nothing you can do to rush this type of grief nor check a list of the "stages" after losing your child. Just as this loss broke the natural cycle of a parent outliving their child, this level of pain breaks the cycle of grief.

This will be the most painful event of your life. I promise you however you can and will survive this; although on many days you will question your strength to do so. It is critical that you ask when you need help as well as ask for it, and that have reliable people around you for support. Find a support group either in your community or online that you feel safe and comfortable speaking in or sharing. Although many things will change in your world now, just take one thing at a time and remember, it's okay to take your time. There is no limit to this pain just as there was no limit to the love you felt for your child.

There are no words I can say to lighten your heartbreak. If I could, I would without being asked. This is what I'm trying to do within this book; save a mother or family from even knowing how we feel. We do not send invites to join this club for a reason. We have more than enough members already.

Madison's Mom,

BOBBIE ZIEMER
Lewis Center, Ohio

Joseph

FOREVER 19

Every addict was once a little child, and quite the child Joseph Abraham was. He made an impressive entrance into this world, almost being born in the parking lot of the hospital. He was barely able to hold on for my doctor to get there; no epidural for me of course! He made himself heard as his little voice screeched over everyone in that birthing room! Welcome to the world Joe. Little did I know, his demeanor was established well before I held him in my arms for the first time; he proceeded to live his life just as he had come into this world, fast and furiously.

Joe was a funny kid. As a little boy he loved superheroes and he frequently dressed as Robin or Spiderman or a Power Ranger, especially around Halloween, when he would take on the persona of each character. When asked his name, he simply replied with that superheroes name without hesitation, leaving the questioning party with a flabbergasted grin. Halloween was his absolute most favorite holiday right behind Christmas. One Christmas, Joseph insisted that he was going to go visit the Grinch up at the North Pole. He was adamant about going and even had packed his bag while wearing his gloves and hat and big coat. When Joe got something in his mind, there was no stopping him. He was stubborn and insistent, with a heart of gold.

Joe adored his big brother Matthew from the get go. Matthew, three-and-a-half years older, was the best brother around. Matthew never got impatient with his little brother and he was always Joe's biggest cheerleader. They always got along and never fought. They were each other's best friends. Life seemed just perfect through pre-K and elementary school and even into middle school. Matthew and Joe were thriving in their environments. They both excelled in school, participated in soccer and baseball, played the piano and had lots of friends, including one another.

I remember thinking how fortunate I was to be able to raise my boys in an upper middle-class neighborhood with good schools. As a teacher, I was able to take my boys to school with me for several of their elementary years. We were together a lot of the time. My husband worked retail and then owned a small business, so between the two of us, our boys were always taken care of. Our family and our life were good. We wanted for nothing. Reflecting back now, I had no idea what was ahead of us. I never imagined our lives would be thrown into such turmoil and my husband and I were ill-prepared for what was about to happen.

Joe began playing baseball as a young boy, and really began excelling at the sport in middle school. Although he was an incredibly talented athlete, he was very self-conscious about his weight. Around the age of eleven, he already weighed 150 pounds. Joseph was smart, athletic, handsome and had a steady stream of girlfriends; one in particular stole his heart. Joe appeared to have it all and seemed comfortable in his own skin. But suddenly things began to change. One of his best friends developed brain cancer and passed away within the year and then another classmate drowned in Lake Lanier. He lost faith in God and began cutting himself to alleviate the pain he was feeling. I remember the day I came home from work and he was sitting at his desk sobbing, his head in his hands, wondering why everyone was dying. I truly believe this was a turning point for Joe; the trauma of these losses on his sensitive heart became more than he could handle. In his own words:

"I am Joseph Abraham. I go by Joe, Big Joe, Abe, Big Abe etc. My life consists of baseball, family, God, school, fishing, and my social life. I have been playing baseball since I was seven, that surprisingly isn't that long, but last year I played on the Mountain View Bears eighth grade team, and we ended up ranking seventh in the state. In addition, I played with the varsity summer ball this summer. It is my passion. I'm a Christian, who enjoys the outdoors, from fishing to white water rafting. Lastly, my social life, our ninth grade class, is probably the class with unbreakable friendships. We all grew up fairly close, went to the same elementary school and have lost some extremely close friends, two in four months to be exact. Ansley from brain cancer and Carlos from a drowning in Lake Lanier. This is a big part of my life because there isn't a day I wake up wishing they experienced what I do. There is a pink and grey ribbon on my book bag to honor Ansley."

The summer before he entered high school, we caught Joe and his friend drinking beer. After speaking with him and his friend about it, we attributed it to normal teenage rebellion. When we later discovered he was smoking marijuana and was continuing to drink alcohol, our concern grew. He got into trouble when he and a group of his friends had a party and social media got hold of it. As a result, his baseball coach put them on probation and his girlfriend broke up with him. Joe was devastated at this and sunk into depression. He found that smoking pot took the pain away. The pain of the death of his two friends, the pain of losing his girlfriend, the pain from the social media posts. As parents we knew we needed to act, but we didn't know exactly how. Our first thought was to have him attend therapy with a private counselor. We felt that this would be a good step and we thought it was, but his struggles continued.

In retrospect, I know now, that a switch was flipped in Joe's brain. His tendency toward addictive behavior and his use of substances indicated this, however as his parents, we wanted to believe it was just normal adolescent experimentation. So, we continued with traditional private therapy and we moved forward with life as we had always known it: school, baseball, family time. Trying to keep hold of what we always knew and not diverting from the expectations and dreams we had for both of our boys. But the snowball effect of addiction was going on in the background of our lives; it had begun to discreetly rear its ugly head, creeping up on Joe and ambushing him before anyone realized it.

It's a sneaky disease and everyone who loved Joe or cared about him was affected. It was a confusing and terrifying time. Joe continued to play baseball and excelled as a freshman, even playing on the varsity team. The pressure of playing and trying to keep up with the big guys may have contributed to him trying to be cool. Drugs would alleviate his self-consciousness and one day I came home and caught him in the family room surrounded by some of his older teammates. I just froze, not knowing what to do. Thankfully everyone left, but Joe evaded my questions and denied my suspicions. This was just the beginning. When he was fifteen, he got his wisdom teeth out and was prescribed oxycodone for the pain. I think this medication may have furthered his journey down the road of addiction and his discovery of prescription medications and the use of other pills to find that feeling he so desperately sought.

The next four years we battled and persevered through many hurdles and nightmares. Our hearts ached as we desperately searched for answers and what to do. This part of the story is so incredibly painful that I cannot even begin to share what our day-to-day lives looked like and felt like. Suffice it to say that our family was barreling down this path, the snowball effect was in full force, and we were hanging by a thread. The constant barrage of problems included car wrecks, police visits to our home, night upon night of sneaking out of the house, broken bones, felony charges, fighting, punching walls, destroying property, things from our home going missing, quitting high school, running away from home, calls from jail, and the list goes on. We lived as firefighters, putting out constant fires, trying to pick up the pieces and rebuild as quickly as we could before the fires returned.

As Joe's parents, we didn't know what to do. I spent hours upon hours researching treatment facilities and options. But when your son is self-medicating over and above his prescription medications, it wasn't long before psychiatrists refused to treat him any longer. I looked into interventions and sought help at local recovery centers. Each time I ran into obstacles. The biggest hurdle of them all: how to get Joe to agree to go. So, we continued with AA meetings and NA meetings, setting boundaries and putting out the imaginary fires, in hopes that we could help him to get back on track.

Joe had landed in some legal trouble. His dad and I knew that the trouble he was in was a result of drug use, but the charges did now indicate that. As a result, he had some pending court dates. Sadly, these dates kept being postponed and postponed. It was frustrating to have this hanging over our heads. However, in the midst of these postponements, Joe's life seemed to settle down. He continued to smoke marijuana, but his goals seemed to come back into view. He aspired to go out west and work over the summer and he was interested in attending technical school. He held a steady job and was earning money. He was so excited to buy the fishing kayak he had been longing for and was beginning to gain some confidence and self-esteem. This went on for about nine months and then in the fall of 2016, his past came knocking. The court summons arrived. Almost immediately, Joe's stress levels began to rise and an increase of drug use was set in motion. I could tell that it was more than smoking pot. His personality changed; he became angry very quickly and would sleep for long periods of time.

On October 12th I came home from work with balloons and a cookie cake in hand. It was Joe's nineteenth birthday. Part of me knew that there would be no need for any fanfare whatsoever, but the Mama's heart within me wouldn't have felt right not celebrating his birthday. I walked in the door at four in the afternoon to find Joe passed out on the family room couch. When he awoke, he was disoriented. Upon seeing the balloons and cookie cake, he realized what had happened. In that moment reality hit, because for the first time in his young nineteen years, he had missed his own birthday. He was upset and sad. We sat with him and talked to him in a way that resonated with him at last. He finally heard the pleas we had been making for almost two years.

Sunday, October 16, 2016, Joe flew to Pennsylvania to be admitted into a thirty-day treatment facility. He only agreed to go after he had a chance to say goodbye to his friends which meant an all weekend bender. I'll never forget the extremes we had to go to in order to get him on that plane. It was like walking in slow motion. My husband and I just stared at the opening to the gate as he walked down the ramp to board the plane. We didn't move until we were certain that he was on that plane. There was no turning back.

As a parent of a child with substance abuse disorder (SUD), you always carry hope within your heart. This hope always led me to believe that there was no hurdle that we could not overcome. For me, it was not a matter of if, but when we would get through this and come out on top with a bright future in sight. Joseph finally agreeing to treatment and getting the help he needed was a huge step, one that I felt cautiously optimistic about. I had never been away from him for longer than a week, nor had he been away from home for very long, so it was very difficult to see him go.

We spoke to Joe regularly via phone and he seemed ok-ish. Some calls he was more optimistic than others. As the thirty days were coming to an end our anxiety levels began to rise again. What next? We trusted the folks at the treatment facility and knew that it was too soon for Joe to come home, but we were caught in a financial trap, especially with the insurance limits. The treatment facility was wonderful though. After realizing that our insurance did not cover his treatment, they issued Joe a scholarship for his time there.

The next step is one I will question in my mind for the rest of my life. The decision was made with all the best intentions from a family that was trying to do the best thing for their son as he worked through recovery. We found a sober living home in Asheville, North Carolina. There is a big recovery community there and we felt good about having Joe closer to home and in a beautiful environment. The cost was pricey but we were determined to make it work. In retrospect, I wish I had known more about the sober living option. Things started out pretty well, but began to stall out as time passed. I'll never forget the phone call after Thanksgiving. Joe told us about some guys from the group that were drinking off campus. He assured us he was going to take some leadership in the situation and we believed him.

We got the call after New Year's Eve that Joe had been cited for underage drinking. He got in a fist fight with another guy in the house and he got kicked out of sober living. I'd wished someone had told me that relapse was part of the process. Somehow, I wasn't prepared for that news. Amidst the turmoil and trying to find another place for Joe to live, he got picked up by the local police for failure to maintain his lane. Combined with the charges up in North Carolina, he was in violation of his probation. We were advised by his new house manager to let him sit in jail up in North Carolina where we knew he was somewhat safe and alive. Shortly thereafter, he was transported back to Georgia and my son proceeded to sit in jail for the next three months. This time we had no choice. On Mother's Day, May 14, 2017, I received the best present I could ever have. My son. I embraced him and hugged him after the longest period of time we had ever been apart.

Sadly, relapse came again. I had twelve days with my son. I wish I had known those would be our last. Would I have spent them differently? Probably. We had the most amazing conversation after Joe went on a college visit. We sat outside until nearly eleven p.m. talking, sitting side-by-side and I told him I loved him and he told me he loved me too. We woke up the next morning and both readied for work. I had an extra spring in my step that day. I'll never forget it. That feeling of hope had returned, and I believed life was back on track for all of us.

I would never see my son alive again.

On the morning of May 26 of 2017, I held Joe in my arms for the last time. My feisty, sensitive, handsome, intelligent nineteen-year-old son, my baby.lifeless and cold. I instinctively grabbed a nearby blanket, trying to warm him and protect him. My body covering his as I sobbed and pleaded from the core of my being. Sounds coming from within me that I never knew could exist. In the early hours of May 26th, Joe made a fatal mistake. Purchasing what he thought was a small amount of heroin, just enough to get him through the night. But fentanyl came into play. An instant killer. I truly believe that Joe never knew what hit him. We learned later that morning that his close friend and our neighbor also passed away on that same dreadful morning. Same dealer. Fentanyl.

I never ever thought I would lose my son to this beast. Our lives are forever changed. Somehow, I am still standing after three years. I don't know how. But through Joe's life and death, I have found my voice. The voice that stayed silent for all those years. Silence is not the solution. I know that Joe's story has saved so many lives; some I know about and some I do not. I am so proud of you son.

Always in my heart.

Joe's Mom,

KATHI A.
Lawrenceville, Georgia

> *The Lord is close to the brokenhearted*
> *and saves those who are crushed in spirit.*
> *Psalm 34:18*

Branden

When I found out I was pregnant, I could not stop smiling... I was happy and felt my dreams had come true! My Beautiful boy Branden was born on December 24, 1991, and he was perfect! He was such a good baby, always happy and smiling, sleeping thru the night at two weeks old!

He loved Barney the dinosaur and anything to do with cars and trucks. His first word was car, car. When Branden was about 10 he started Go Karting with his step dad, Jeff. He was VERY GOOD and went on to Win GRAND NATIONAL CHAMPI-ONSHIP FOR THE PACIFIC NORTHWEST!! We were very proud and happy. He had Earned it!

Because I was Branden's mom, he was the joy of my life. When he started kindergarten, his teacher noticed he was hyper and couldn't pay attention. We then found out he had ADD or Attention Deficit Disor-der. We put him on Ritalin so he could get through school. This went on almost all the way to high school. He could not function without his prescription; always argumentative, occasionally aggressive, defiant towards rules and authority. Looking back, I know he also had ODD or Oppositional Defiant Disorder. He was never diagnosed with ODD but the signs were there. When Branden started high school, he began drinking and smoking pot. He started selling marijuana and making cash under the table; when that wasn't enough, he started selling Oxycontin for forty dollars each.

When he started dealing out of our house, we had to kick him out. He promised to stop but never did. Once, when we got home from NA, or Narcotics Anonymous, there was a car sitting two houses down from us with the driver sitting in the car. It seemed suspicious due to Branden's previous activities so I walked up to the driver and asked him what he was doing there. He said he was just sitting there and wouldn't leave. I threatened to call the police. The driver tried to pull into a neighbor's driveway; I got in my car and chased them off. My son took a turn for the worse when he got hooked on Oxy pills; he was selling anything he could plus stealing from us and anyone he came across. When he owed the drug dealers money, they would come to our house and bomb our car with bombs they had made from about a dozen M80's taped together. My car windows got blown out on three occasions.

When my step-daughter Kelsie was going to get married, Branden called me the night before, leaving me a voicemail that he was going to die. I was so beyond wild trying to find him; no one could. We went to the wedding and pretended all was ok. I made it through the day when my heart was shattered. I did find him a couple days later, thank goodness! By then, Branden was so into the drugs nothing I said made a difference. He asked me to pick up his truck one day, and I came to find his license was expired and he had no insurance. When we got home, he tried to grab the keys out of my hand. I started yelling and my husband came flying around the passenger door and pulled Branden off of me; they fell backwards and Branden tried choking his stepdad Jeff. He turned sheet white! I was terrified; I pulled Branden off and he ran into the house. As I got Jeff up, we realized his ankle was broken. I called the police and drove Jeff to the hospital. Branden was beyond wild, hallucinating and aggressive now that he was on heroin. He couldn't afford Oxy's anymore.

When I let him back home, he was so angry all the time. I found needles and spoons and foil wraps everywhere! It was insane; when I asked him to leave, he threw our microwave across the living room. He was told he would not be allowed in our home again until after rehab. Branden went to multiple rehabs, jail on many occasions, and still fought us every step of the way. He broke our hearts with worry for him. I love my son with every ounce of my being so when he decided to go this last time in September of 2016, I drove him to the airport, praying he would make it. He was in detox, rehab, then sober living in California for five months and I decided to visit him! Above is the last picture I have of him, my beautiful Branden.

Branden lost his life on January 17, 2017, when he bought heroin and used it in the bathroom of a grocery store. My heart is shattered; my son was only twenty-five years old and had so much to live for. I found #NotIn-Vain about a year into my grief journey and they have been my hope and my lifeline. I have been able to help other mamas and give them love, compassion, and advice. They are my family now and I love my sisters in grief. I am also blessed with a wonderful husband and family.

With the Support and Love from my Hubby Jeff and Family, I Thank God for them Everyday.

Hugs and prayers from Branden's Mama.
Blessings to you, Madison's mama,
Thank you.

ALICE A.
Rockford, Washington

Nicholas

My story begins on July 24, 2019. My son Nicholas had come to live with my husband and myself. It was good for a while, until that night. Nicholas had finished one of the many programs he needed to get his drivers license reinstated. We came home from his program, and we were about to go out shopping. He went into his bedroom for no more than five minutes when I heard him sniff in. I instinctively knew it was his nasal spray Narcan.

As soon as I found out Nicholas was addicted, I wish he had kept Narcan with him at all times. He came out of his room and sat down. Nicholas immediately began to turn blue. We called 911 and rushed him to the hospital where my son refused any treatment.

I know he felt embarrassed. Without any medical intervention, we came home and he began a tiring night feeling sad for what he had done. Later that night, I went into his room around 10:00 pm. I kissed Nicholas goodnight and went to bed.

He never woke the next day. It was truly the worst day of my life; July 25, 2019.

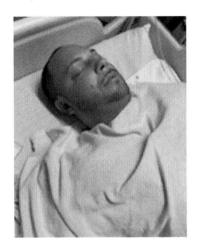

Nicholas's Mom,

BRENDA A.
Windsor, Connecticut

Cody

FOREVER 26

Cody had a traumatic birth and was in NICU until he was ten days old. He turned blue shortly after birth and was rushed to the NICU and placed on CPAP for five days and antibiotics for ten. He was always a little slower at meeting developmental milestones. He repeated first grade twice and at the end of second grade had a year of individual special classes. He was being promoted to the third grade but couldn't read at a first grade level. I then made the decision to home school. He had also been diagnosed with ADHD and dyslexia. We chose to not treat the ADHD with medication.

Cody had the hardest time with fine motor skills, so his handwriting was that of a kindergartner and even as he got older looked like a first or seconder grader. When we started home schooling, he only qualified for help with his speech and no other resources because he wasn't in public school. He wasn't athletic and the sports he tried were quite obviously not his thing. But he loved swimming and did well on the swim team.

I didn't suspect Cody "Free-Hugs" had autism until a few years ago. I knew he was hyper. I knew he hated change. I knew he was socially awkward. I knew he was developmentally delayed. But no one else seemed to think there was anything wrong. Two years ago, I was a travel nurse for five months in Iowa at the Center for Disabilities and Development and had the opportunity to share my concerns with the doctors there. My suspicions were confirmed.

The problem is, how do you tell a young adult who was raised his entire life like he was everyone else that he has autism? How do you have that conversation? I chose to not have the conversation. Last year before Cody came to Utah, he asked me if he had autism. When I told him that I thought he did it was like his whole world fell apart. He came to Utah before the tests were able to be done in Georgia. This past April, Cody had testing and was diagnosed with autism spectrum disorder-mild severity, severe depression, severe anxiety, along with ADHD and dyslexia. The psychologist believed that Cody's drug use stemmed from his need to self-medicate. It started with marijuana and progressed to harder drugs to continue to keep it at bay.

I'd gotten a lot closer to Cody that year. He loved me fiercely and knew I loved him. But he shared that he'd questioned God for a long time as to why he had been born. He shared his theory of how he came to be. He said as God was putting him together, God went to the backroom and grabbed a box of spare parts and put them all together and that is how he came to be.

The real Cody felt he was broken. He felt no one loved him beside me. He felt no one would ever know he was gone. He wanted the pain of life to go away (but he also said he would never intentionally take his life). When he was in a group, his anxiety was at its worse. He usually didn't talk much in a group and was most comfortable one on one. He started using marijuana because it made it easier to be with friends. He craved friends but making friends was very difficult for him.

I'm sharing this to raise awareness for those who hide their pain and struggles with a front that is very hard to see through. Don't be afraid to say "I love you" to someone that you love. Let them know that they are loved before you lose the opportunity to say it again. Life is short and we aren't promised tomorrow so hold your loved ones tight and hug them a little longer.

I loved him so much and as I am grieving the loss of such an amazing person, I have been blessed as others share their memories with me.

Cody had his faults, but I chose to sweep them under the rug and focus on the good.

He had an amazing work ethic. He took pride in his job and when he was done cleaning his area, it looked good. I smile as I remember him talking about closing at his job. He took his time and deep cleaned the work area because it had been a disaster, and if he was closing and putting his name on cleaning an area, it was going to be clean.

I smile as I remember him telling me about the compliments about the bathrooms at work never looking cleaner then when he cleaned them.

He was polite and respectful. He didn't fit the typical profile of an addict. He didn't have the best vocabulary (my ears would hurt often, lol), but he did try to not cuss around me. He valued people and always took time to help others.

He was honest and even when it got him in trouble, he believed in telling the truth. A couple weeks before he was to leave for Georgia, we went in to see his probation officer (PO). He was told he had the right to a probable cause hearing in Utah to answer to the charges against him. The charges were presented by his PO about his failure to comply with his probation. His PO had written down the things Cody admitted to doing. It took a little bit for Cody to understand that he had the right to a hearing to say whether or not the charges were true. Cody's response was, "They are true, I told you those things. Why would I say they aren't true? That would be a lie. He ended up waiving his right to the hearing.

The typical drug addict steals to support their habit. Not Cody. Yes, he was once caught trying to steal duct tape from Walmart. And a certain cell phone because it was said to interact with fidget spinners a few years back. But he wasn't one to steal. I recall leaving my mom's ring on my dresser back when I lived in Georgia, working in the float pool and working in the NICU. I came home the next day to find the ring missing. I went to Cody and told him my mom's ring was missing. He got up and said he would help me find it. He followed me about fifteen seconds after I left his room. In my room he looked under the dresser and handed me my ring. I know my ring hadn't been under the dresser (I had looked earlier). I believe he had a change of heart when he realized how much that ring meant to me. I never had anything missing from that point on and my landlord has said that he hadn't either.

He tried to help others feel good about themselves and get them to smile. I believe because he often felt sad and unloved, he didn't want others to feel that way. He was always giving out "Free Hugs."

My heart is heavy, and a lot is on my mind. I may be blundering through this through my tears, but I need to write.

Cody and I moved to Utah for a new start. He struggled with addiction and this was his chance at starting over. It wasn't long before he sought out the drugs. He had no job and no money. I asked him later how he got it. He replied that the first purchase was free. He promised tomorrow to no longer use. He tried but the hold that addiction had on him was too strong.

He had a plane ticket to leave for Georgia on the day he passed away. He also got paid the day before. He was partially packed. He had every intention of going back. He knew jail awaited him. He told me on that Friday: "Maybe they can help me while I'm in there."

Friday evening, Cody "Free-Hugs" and I went to Joe's Crab Shack. That was our favorite place to eat here in Utah. There isn't a Panera Bread here which was always our go-to place, so this was our new place. We ordered the Arctic Pot for two. The meal was wonderful, and we had a good evening together. His phone was down and so was mine. We knew the next day he was going back without me. On the way home he was laughing and kept rubbing his belly and saying, "Happy belly."

He came to my room and got on the bed to talk to me before I fell asleep. This is common. He loved to get and give hugs and he would talk to me as our dogs licked his face. He would get up and leave once he had enough of having his face licked.

I believe in my heart that his death was due to an unintentional overdose. He knew every time he used that it was a possibility, but the addiction hold was stronger than his desire to not break my heart. I've thought about his last day on earth and I know he thought he had many more. He told me a few months back he wasn't afraid of dying and actually welcomed it, but he had no plan to end his life.

Addiction rips families apart. It takes brothers from their sisters, children from their parents, and parents from their children. It touches their aunts and uncles and grandparents. Friends and coworkers are touched too. There is an addiction epidemic in America.

Cody had a beautiful soul. He had a smile and hug for anyone that wanted one. He loved to laugh. He was my baby and he knew he was my favorite son. And then he would laugh and remind me that he was my only son.

On August 22, he shared a picture on his Facebook profile. Although he admitted to thoughts of dying, he was adamant about not intentionally ending his life.

I'm 47 years old. My mom passed away three years ago. She had Alzheimer's and I knew she didn't have long to live. Until my mom passed, I had lived forty-four years without experiencing someone close to me dying. My grandparents had died several years back but they lived on the other side of the States from me, so we were never close.

Losing Cody "Free-Hugs" was and is so very hard. I'm back in Utah now and although I don't have family here, I have amazing friends and my work family and Cody's work family. And I've always been an online person. My online family is incredible. I say "family" because family isn't about blood, it is about love and support and even not having personally hugged some of my dearest online friends, I can feel their love and prayers.

In a world where people say that we are losing real connections to people because of social media and that there is so much fake out there, we all got real.

Addiction is an ugly epidemic that is taking over our country. I have never used illegal substances. I drank a little way back twenty years ago; never really liked it. Now I'm allergic to brewer's yeast so I definitely won't drink. I don't even smoke. I have never even tried it. It gave me a headache just from standing near someone smoking. But I have been addicted to online games on Facebook. I know that draw can be strong and so hard to break.

Addiction hurts so many. Not just the person addicted but those who love them. I've thought about the rest of this story for some time now. I need to share what I experienced up until the moment of finding Cody. I'm letting you know the content is heavy.

Stop reading if you don't think you can handle it.

I went to bed about ten thirty Friday night on September 6. I was prepared to take Cody to the airport the next day. I slept ok that night and woke up around six a.m. I sent Cody a text with his itinerary for his flight. No response and the text message was green. Usually iPhone to iPhone is blue. About two hours later, I sent another text. It was green and there was no reply. About twenty minutes later, I got up to shower and stopped by his room. The door was locked, the TV was on, and the light was on. I knocked and called out. Yet still no response. Cody has always been hard to wake up. I took my shower, got dressed then knocked on his door a little harder and called out a little louder. I walked outside to see if I could see into his room. The blinds were down but the window was open and the window screen in place. I also called his phone. It went straight to voicemail. My concern level is now on high alert. I knew something was very wrong and I needed to get in there.

I went upstairs to tell my housemate my concerns. I told him I thought we could pop out the window screen easier and cheaper to replace then to try to break the door down. He agreed and got a screwdriver. He got the screen off and lifted the blinds. Cody was face down on the floor at the foot of his bed.

I'm taking a pause to breathe. If this is too much for you it is ok to stop reading now. I'll put another break in here.

The nurse in me kicked into overdrive. I climbed through the window and was by his side within seconds. I was on his left side. I could not feel a pulse and he was cold to touch. I called out to my housemate and he was on the phone with 911. Cody was lying partially on his right arm; it was purple what I could see. I rolled him over. He had vomited a little; it was in his mouth and a little on the floor. His face was purple, and his upper chest was purple. He was so cold. I didn't do CPR. I knew as a nurse that he had been gone a while.

This memory will stay with me forever. This is the cost of drug addiction. It affects more than the user. My biggest fear has always been that I would be the one to find him gone. My message today is not for the other moms. It is for those struggling with addiction. Get help. If you can't afford it, find a church with a free program. I'm willing to guess that you have someone that you love very much, like your mom.

Please get help and determine that you are going to get clean and stay clean.

Don't let your addiction take you away and leave your mom to find you gone. Don't do this to her.

I am highly allergic to caffeine. I had to give up chocolate because it had caffeine. Anyone that knows me knows that I love chocolate. But when I cheat and eat chocolate, I get a five-day headache. So, when I am tempted, I ask myself, "Is it worth the five-day headache?" And I know it isn't and I walk away without eating the chocolate.

I do realize that chocolate addiction is not the same as drug addiction. But I do believe that when you put it in perspective it can be useful. When you are tempted to use, ask yourself: "Am I ok with this being my last time? Am I ready to die? Am I ok with my mom finding me? Am I ok with my child finding me?" If your answer is, "No I'm not," then you need to seek help.

My prayers for those who knew and love Cody. If you are struggling with addictions please seek help. The next time you use might also be your last.

There is no class you can take to prepare you for grief. It is something you have to experience personally. There is also no perfect way to grieve.

You can overcome this, but not alone. Counseling, treatment, a good support system, and God.

I'm praying for you.

Cody's Mom,

GLORIA A.
Terra Haute, Indiana

26

Garrett

Garrett was a beautiful breastfed chubby baby. His family called him "Fluffy" when he was little, and some still do. Garrett was an easy baby and he had an older brother, Phillip. Phillip was three-years-old and Garrett was only nine-months-old when we were forced to move back to my hometown because their father found a new girl. I did my best in being a good momma but stuff happened and I'm often ashamed of the choices I made. Did I cause my son to die on June 18, 2016, from a drug overdose? Lord I pray not, but I feel responsible in so many ways. I knew he was selling weed and I told him, "I'm not stupid, I can see what's up." It seemed to stop, but little did I know that my Garrett, my beautiful boy, was now hooked on pills.

He told me about a month before he died that one of his friends who moved back to town was doing heroin. "Oh my God," I plead, "Please son, never do that. Please let's get you help." We were going to

AA and a recovery place. High or drunk it didn't matter; we were trying. The very last AA meeting, he got a call that his best friend had been found dead in his mother's bathroom. That night he was leaving on a cow truck with a reformed addict; Garrett tried to get out of leaving but he went. He came back home and after a trip to the lake with his dad and others, it was the same shit. We were trying to quarantine him with me. He left on a Thursday night and his younger brother informed me many of his hats were missing. He said, "I know Garrett sold them for dope." He's pissed and I get that. My oldest son was also there telling me to kick Garrett out until he stops using drugs. I said no, I wouldn't do that to any of them. Garrett came back later on Thursday night, grabbed a few things, and said it was probably best if I assumed he was going to stay with his dad, and he left for the night. I said, "Give Momma a hug," and that was the last hug ever.

The next day I had driven my mom and aunt to their brother's funeral about an hour and half from our town. They barely had my uncle in the ground when I looked at my phone at about noon. I learned that my baby Garrett was in the hospital, brought in about four-thirty a.m. on Friday due to a drug overdose. I can't remember the drive or the walk from the parking lot to my son. He was on a ventilator. I stayed the four nights in the waiting room. I'm still confused on days and times but I know the doctor was planning on taking Garrett off vent a couple days later to see if he could breathe on his own! I was with Garrett when the induced coma was slowly lifted. I saw him cry just before; oh God my baby Garrett was waking up, still with a vent. I was in his face; I was so happy.

I said, "Son, do you see me, it's Momma" He blinked; I asked for a smile and he gave me a crooked one. The nurse asked him to give her a thumbs up. He did. She asked him to squeeze her hand; he did! I was so happy. I was asked to leave the room while they took the vent out. I've done this waiting before with my mom and it was always ok, so I waited alone. I felt like it was taking too long. About an hour and half later, a doctor and a nurse called me into the hall and said they were not sure what went wrong but they had to re-vent and give Garrett a chest tube! They said they would try again tomorrow. What the fuck happened?

Garrett was gone after that. They finally sent my son, my beautiful Garrett, to a bigger, better hospital like I had begged for all along. I

28

spent the night in the bed with my Garrett and the next day we had him sent to the hospice floor. His dad and I had to make the most gut wrenching, god-awful choice to take him off the vent. He died hours later surrounded by his friends, family, and Momma in his bed.

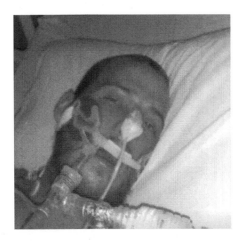

Garrett's Mom,

TONYA S.A.
Farwell, Michigan

Chase

FOREVER 21

To tell my son Chase's story, I must start at the beginning, with my story. Look at my picture, what do you see? You see the face of an addict. Be careful when you judge another; be careful when you say not my child and especially not me! My story doesn't start like you imagine an addict. I did come from a broken home, with a father who drank a lot. I lived with him until age ten, then was thrown to live with a mother I had never met. But I knew right from wrong. I was a straight "A" student, never did anything wrong through high school. I didn't even drink at the prom. So where did I go wrong? How did it happen?

A lot of us ask that question about ourselves or our kids. I definitely didn't wake up one day and decide to be an addict! I didn't even wake up that day, knowing I was going to do drugs. I was twenty-two years old, had a great job, and was dating a good-looking guy, but a "bad boy." However, I had no idea how bad; one day we drove somewhere to meet his friend and before I know what's happening, he hands me a pipe and lights it. Wow the rush, I didn't even know what I was doing. Turns out I was smoking crack. This went on a few months here and there until I wasted a $1,500 bonus check in a weekend and I realized whoa, I may have a problem. I told him we had to quit and he agreed. A few days later, he wanted to do drugs. I said no and we argued; he hit me. I had his fist, bruised, on my chest. He left my house and I never looked back! I walked away from him and that life.

Then I got married. I led a normal life for twelve years, had two beautiful children, Chase and Mallory. They were born in Memphis, we attended church, they were dedicated, life was normal. In 2000, we moved to Florida. Eventually, our marriage fell apart after he lost his job. But I had a great job and I continued to give my kids everything they wanted or needed. Until...

Now I'm thirty-five. I have a great job, a car, taking care of my dad. two great kids, eleven and seven, both gifted and making straight A's. I was the skinniest, and to me, the best looking I had ever been in my life. So, it happens again, I meet the "bad boy" and we start dating. One day I come home from work and he's smoking in the bathroom, and again...here try this, and boom, here I am again. But this time, I really developed a crack addiction.

One day turns into every other weekend when the kids are gone, then turns into every weekend, then every day. Then the unthinkable happens; I find out I'm pregnant. In April 2008, I lost it all, as I had a baby born with cocaine in his system; lost my kids to their dad, who moved them back to Memphis 1,200 miles away, and my baby Jordan (by my addict boyfriend) was snatched from my arms to go live with his grandma. I got fired from an awesome job, my car got repossessed and I got arrested twice in the same week.

Now let me tell you this scared little girl (well not so little, I was 36) had never been in trouble in my life, didn't grow up doing drugs or around drugs. Who did I get myself involved with and how did this happen? My house was raided and turned upside down like a bad scene from *Cops*. My baby's father went to jail for four years and I had to start from nothing and get my baby and life back! I live with a lot of regret and wonder if I am to blame for Chase becoming an addict. When I put it all down in 2008, I walked away for good. I worked to get myself together again. Did every class, every drug test, everything CPS required and got my son back in less than a year. They told me it would be a minimum of a year. And I did it all on my own.

Now that you know the backstory, let me tell you my version of what Chase went through. Did he see me high? Probably, as he told his dad I had slurred speech, but generally he had a mother that couldn't wake up to take him to school because I had been up for three days over the weekend. When his father took him away, I was devastated, as I am sure he was too. He moved away in the end of his sixth-grade year. I read in one of his journals from rehab that he took his first Xanax at a party in seventh grade. So, this is where I blame myself; I should have seen the signs. I should have known what to look for in his behavior. His father, however, had no idea about drugs. He was taking good care of both Chase and Mallory. I spoke to them often. They had a stepmother they hated. In the beginning she was nice to them, then she just put up with them.

I think Chase's beginning usage was a typical teenager experimenting with drugs. Let me add though, that was then, and now it's just not safe for kids. So, a few times Chase would call and ask me for money and I was working a serving job at night, so I was usually busy when he called and I never acknowledged the urgency with which he was asking me for money. I didn't recognize the signs. Me being the absent parent 1,200 miles away, wanting my kids to love me again, had gotten him a prepaid card and I could immediately transfer money to him. If he called and said he was going to a movie with his friends, it never crossed my mind that he was lying! Never once did I think my kid was doing drugs! See I wasn't there to check his backpack, check his phone messages, or search his car. I suggest doing all of these things, even if you don't suspect your child is doing drugs, just to know what they are up to, who they are with, and if they are lying to you. During the years, I only saw Chase and Mallory for a couple of weeks in the summer. This was before Chase started driving or had a job, so I think he had only experimented a bit and could make it through my visits without drugs.

In 2013, Mallory came to see me for the summer and asked if she could stay! My dream come true, at least one of my kids wanted to come back home. Chase didn't want to move during his senior year and leave his friends' looking back, maybe I should have made him. Maybe he didn't want to leave the lifestyle, but I know he was upset Mallory left him alone with the evil stepmother. If I had known about the drugs that early, maybe I could have helped him stop before it got too bad. Getting him away from friends could have helped early on.

Chase had two car wrecks; still not a clue as I wasn't there and was given the impression that he's just an awful driver. Of course, later I find out he had nodded out, both times, and was lucky to be alive. Ok, let me now get to when we find out about the drugs...I get a late-night call that Chase got pulled over for a broken tail light. Well they run his license and he had a warrant for his arrest. What? A warrant? For what? So, he stole a donation jar at Kroger, swiped his debit card and got some gum and cash back, grabbed the jar, and walked out. They figured out it was him from video and his swiped card transaction! With that, had a warrant issued. Still, at this point, he's saying he was stupid, he just wanted money to go out with friends and they went to eat and a movie. It was about $100.

Me, not buying his story at all, tells his father I'm sending him for a drug test. I call around, find a place in Memphis and pay for it over the phone. So, now the truth comes out! Opioids in his system and further testing proves heroin! What? Not my son! How did this happen? It's April, senior year, I had literally just bought four plane tickets to go to his graduation in May. His father calls the insurance company and takes him to the facility to detox. I call his school; this is such a popular occurrence among the students that they have a protocol in place! I think "What?" Seriously, they just acted like it was no big deal. This was 2014, they will call the facility, his teachers will send all his work over and he can try to catch up. If his scores are good enough, he can still graduate with his class! I am thinking we have a problem, if the school is used to this! So, now the truth comes out, everything's out on the table, and he's not going to school much this year, therefore it's going to take a miracle for him to catch up his grades. He does a lot of schoolwork during his thirty days at the facility, but he winds up failing one exam. This will keep him from graduation. We still fly to Memphis and only get to visit with him a couple hours at the facility. A very good friend of his named Kyle overdoses and dies while I'm there visiting with him. He wasn't allowed to leave for the funeral and I don't think he ever got over that. He even had Kyle's initials tattooed on his arm, in his memory.

When he gets out of rehab, his father's wife won't let him come home, so he goes to live with his aunt and uncle. A month or so goes by and everything is fine, but then his aunt tells me he's acting different again. I overnight a drug test and he failed. He agrees to go to rehab again. This time the insurance company can get him into a facility in California. We start talking to them at 2:00, and he flies out that night. I looked them up, it looks like a great facility, and turns out we have a very good friend whose son went there and is now working there. He spent thirty days in detox and black out. Then he moved into inpatient IOP, followed by outpatient, and finally sober living. We knew he had a court date in November and this was July. His dad thought he was going to go do the sixty-day treatment and then be home. I tried to explain to his father that he wasn't going to the doctor to get well; this wasn't a broken arm. We were going to fight this the rest of our lives. That's what drugs do; it's a daily struggle. It changes your brain; it changes your thinking. While he was at the facility in California, I explain to his counselor that he was on probation for that theft charge. My second piece of advice, if your child is in any trouble at all, make sure that you follow up with the court system, it is very important. I told his counselor and I thought they were talking to his probation officer. I also thought his dad was talking to his probation officer and that everyone knew he was in treatment. It is very important when they are in any trouble with the law that they follow the rules.

Chase spent seven months in California and was doing really well. Then one night he and some other boys went on a road trip to Tijuana and smoked some weed. This was a few days before Chase was to return to Memphis for his court date. In his mind he had six months probation that was supposed to end in November, so he just thought it ended. Turned out it didn't end; he didn't listen to me and the judge acted as if he didn't care Chase was in treatment and we didn't have permission to send him out of state. He ordered him to return for a court hearing. As soon as he lands in Memphis, his dad had been instructed to take him to the probation office to drug test. Of course, he tests positive for weed, now gets a violation of probation charge as well as the theft charge and a court date set. I fly to Memphis to go to court with him and get him out of that state and away from his friends, as soon as we go to court. I was going to pay the restitution for what he stole, pay his court fines, and get him out of there. His public defender told him he could choose drug court and have all of his charges dropped. Please, please, please, do not ever let your child, who is an addict, choose drug court and be forced to stay in the same city, with the same friends. I begged him to take the misdemeanor and come home with me. I did drug court and it is very, very hard. He chose to do drug court.

I bought Chase a $1000 car so that he could get back-and-forth to his meetings at court once a week and to drug test. He was going to stay with his cousin during his drug court. It only took him one week to fail, to get a title loan on this piece of crap car and nod out at the wheel again. This time it's jail or rehab through drug court. He spent thirty days in a small county jail outside of Memphis until the drug court counselor offered him a rehab program. Now this will not be some nice, beautiful facility that insurance pays for. This will be the state-run, drug court facility. First, they send him to Jackson, Tennessee. I don't really remember what happened there, but they literally set you out on the street with all of your belongings if you fail a drug test. Don't forget Mom is 1,200 miles away; it's not like I can come pick him up. I called the drug court counselor and this time they send him to rehab in Nashville. He does well there for about two months. He's in sober living and has a job. I'm thinking he finally has this.

At this point he's nineteen and not in school. His grandmother had set up a college fund, which had to be cashed out because he wasn't in school. He got $10,000; he spent $7,000 on a car. He even told me that was the most adult thing he had ever done. I was so excited he was doing well. The kids and I drove to Nashville on a long weekend to see him. We got to Nashville and we're supposed to meet him early Saturday morning. He didn't answer the phone; kept calling, no answer. When he finally did pick up, he said he was with a friend in Jackson. Then he said his car was wrecked. I figured out he had used again and I was not going to see him, after driving all that way. He spent a few months avoiding drug court and finally called and asked if I would come get him. Of course, I did. I figured it's only a misdemeanor charge. I'll figure it out later. I need to save my son. If I bring him with me, I will know what he's doing, when he's doing it, where he's doing it, and who he's with. I will take him away from his friends, his familiar places, and his way to get drugs. But, let me tell you, an addict will find a way to get what they want, even in a new place, not knowing anybody.

Chase did well at my house or so I thought for about six months and then I started to notice the signs. He would stay up all night. He was working with me at the restaurant I owned, and he literally fell asleep standing up at the grill. I asked him what was going on and he denied it, then I looked at his arms and saw the needle marks; there was no denying. He and his friend, who had come to live with us, admitted they had started using and promised to stop. I watched him and helped him try to detox at home. We bought Suboxone off the streets, whatever it took, I wasn't going to give up.

He went to Memphis for Thanksgiving in 2016 with his sister and when he returned, he asked and made the calls to go to rehab. The rehab got him a flight and sent him to West Palm. Oh, if only I had known then what I do now. It's illegal for them to buy the flights; they were only after the insurance money. He did thirty days in detox, then on to sober living, where we went to visit and buy him food and essentials. His sister gave him $30 of her money to get a rail pass to look for a job. He walked to a store that night and found someone to buy drugs from. So again, detox at another facility for thirty days, back out to sober living. This cycle just kept going. I believe thirty days is a joke! I believe, and told his counselor, that if he couldn't find a job fast enough for the sober living rent that he would relapse, just to go back to a safe place, detox, where you are fed and taken care of and don't have to support yourself, much less stress. This went back and forth. The South Florida area is a horrible place for these facilities and sober homes; they scam the insurance companies and provide easy ways for you to relapse so they can get more money.

Why didn't I know these places were a scam? Why didn't I research further before sending my baby somewhere I expected to be safe? Chase got out of the last detox and called me on Monday, May 15. Our last conversation was, "Mom, it's so hard to be an adult, I need to find a job I like." The next Tuesday, he took a cab to get his last paycheck from his previous job. I spoke to him every afternoon after work, if he wasn't in blackout. Wednesday at three p.m., I called and his phone went straight to voicemail, so I began to worry. I called his new sober living; he checked into it on Monday but didn't show up for eleven p.m. curfew Tuesday night. "What? Why didn't you call me!?!?" He hadn't even filled out all his paperwork there. Make sure you, as a parent, are always on the paperwork, so that you are allowed to find out about your adult child or you will be told nothing because of HIPPA laws.

So anyway, I get on the computer when I get home to check his call log, as he's still on my phone plan. I can see every number called or texted! This is great information in the situation. No call activity since midnight, never showed up to sober living. I start calling hospitals. I call sober living to see how many area hospitals there are to call, as I don't know the area. No luck. Next step, retrace his steps and call every number he last called. Many friends, a girl from Memphis that said they talked for an hour and she and her boyfriend offered for him to come live in the country with them. Next, call a number I recognize from the night of relapse. I searched the numbers on Facebook and put faces with names, including the dealer! "Where is my son?"I asked. Just some mumbling and I said, "I know you sold my son drugs, where is he?" He just hangs up. Next number is a cab driver, not a lot of English. He says, "Yes, I remember your son, I took him to Walmart, then to a hotel.' At Walmart, he purchased a backpack, needles, spoon, and water. He was having one last night of fun before coming home. He had already contacted a friend in Clearwater and texted, "I need to come home, I will pay you $100 to come get me." Why didn't he call me???? I would have rushed down there. The cab driver texted me the name of the hotel and I began calling. The desk clerk told me Chase was there and had been all day. She only saw him come out for ice, but that when he checked in; he had been badly beaten. I called the sober living manager and some of the guys at the house and they were going to go try to talk to him. I then called the police to do a well check.

Called the hotel back, they had no phones in the room. Why didn't I beg her to take a phone to him? I should have talked to him! I found him and I couldn't reach him! I waited patiently for the police to call me back. At nine-thirty p.m., I called the hotel again. The clerk says, "Whatever they are about to tell you, I believe your son was a good kid." She hands the phone to the officer. The officer verified all of Chase's information from his driver's license, so I think he's getting arrested, then those unimaginable words, "I hate to tell you this over the phone, but your son…" and I screamed, I dropped to my knees, I couldn't breathe; he continues to say, "The local police are being sent to you" and I'm just screaming.

Looking back, my thoughts are he owed the dealer money before his last week of detox. When he got out and got his check, he went to pay him and was beaten and given a fatal dose of straight carfentanyl. When my son Chase died in May 2017, I just wanted to get high, I wanted to escape, I wanted to run from the pain! But first of all, I was scared as fuck because the shit isn't safe. Second, I remembered his face, once, when I didn't wake up to take him to school, as I had been up for three days. That face of disappointment is engraved in my mind forever. I could never do it again and I know it wouldn't help. I've come too far to ever go back. Why do you need to know all this? Because you all need to know that you are not alone; you don't have to face addiction or loss alone, it does happen to anyone. While I cannot change the past, I can do my part to help every addict that asks for help and help every mom that needs support from this awful tragedy of losing a child. I will continue to fight for change with insurance and rehabilitation centers. Thirty days is never enough to change a behavior and help someone so deep in opioid addiction.

The decisions need to be out of the insurance companies' hands and in the doctor's control. These centers need better monitoring and our kids deserve to be treated with the respect that any other patient receives. My son Chase was a good kid, I was a good mom, we both made mistakes, I made it out, he was poisoned. I am forever changed and forever broken. I wish that no other mom has to go through this. I tell my part of the story for the  many moms that blame themselves also and so you know there is hope and a way out.

Chase's Mom,

Tina B.
Dickson, Tennessee

Jake

I'm really not sure where my story begins, because I feel like I'm living someone else's life and I'm just going through the motions. Jake passed away on May 31, 2020. He left behind an eight-year-old daughter and a one-year old son. He also has two brothers. I found out that Jake was doing pills and heroin about five years ago. He lived an hour away from me. We convinced him to move in with his brother who only lived five miles away.

Jake had his ups and downs, but he held down a job and he had custody of his daughter. He was the most amazing father ever. His daughter is very wise beyond her years because he was always working with her. He eventually got his own place and was doing well. Then, he was introduced to meth. That's when he went downhill. He went partying one night at his girlfriend's house and we found out he was arrested the next morning. He was charged with attempted rape and several other charges. To sum it up, he spent six months in a prison, lost his job, his house, and his daughter. When he got out, he moved in with me and my husband. He got a new job and was trying very hard. He got his daughter every weekend.

In March of 2019, it was late at night and I went by his room and I heard him breathing what sounded like a death rattle. I tried to wake him up and I checked his breathing. My husband said he had a hard week at work, and he was probably exhausted. I stayed with him to make sure that he was still breathing through the night. I searched his room and I didn't find anything. I couldn't get him up for work, so I called him off. When he finally came to, I talked to him about rehab. He did admit to me that he was doing drugs to help him with his pain. A week later he overdosed. We called the squad and I did CPR until they got here. They gave him four doses of Narcan and brought him back. The same thing happened three days later. We got him into a rehab, but he was not able to go because of financial and insurance issues. He decided to go stay with his other brother an hour and a half away and get a fresh start in a new area. He was staying clean and doing so well. We talked every day.

On September 2, my husband and I went to visit both my sons. It was our tenth wedding anniversary. We don't get along with my other son's wife. We picked Jake and his daughter up, we took his daughter to her mother's house, and we went to my sister's house to stay the night. Sometime during the night her rent money came up missing. Jake denied it and we searched him and our car and could not find it. We stopped and got gas and coffee and we got back in the car and I immediately told my husband to get him to the hospital. We got him there and he had a massive seizure. To sum it up, he was on life support for three days. He had taken a bunch of gabapentin and Kratom.

The hospital set him up for rehab, but again the same financial and insurance issues prevented him from treatment. He did go to outpatient counseling for a while. He got a new girlfriend and through many struggles they got their own place. She was straight and they were really good for each other. She has three of her own kids, too. It wasn't long before they were engaged. I really thought that he was going to be okay. I knew he was drinking occasionally, but I didn't think he was doing anything else.

On May 26, I got a call from his fiancée that Jake had overdosed. His fiancée has some nurse's training and she was able to do CPR and get him breathing on his own. Jake and his fiancée came up to my house the next day. Jake had agreed to get help. He was scheduled for outpatient treatment to start on June 1, which was a start, and we were looking into a residential type treatment for him, which he agreed to. I gave his fiancée the two doses of Narcan I had, with hopes she would never need it. I also talked to both of them about the drinking and how that's what triggers his opioid use. That was the last time I saw my son.

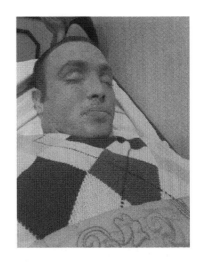

On May 31, I got a call from my other son. He was gone.

I am still very proud of Jake. There is more to this story, but I am still waiting on toxicology reports and it is still under investigation, if that's what you want to call what the sheriff's department is doing.

Thank you for listening, and I hope and pray for all our kids that laws and treatment centers get changed.

Jake's Mom,

KRIS B.
Convoy, Ohio

Jesus

FOREVER 26

My son Jesus was always against drugs so when he started, I was really surprised. He hadn't been using very long when he was diagnosed with something called methamphetamine induced schizophrenia.

I couldn't believe it; he was one of my babies. What was happening to him? There were nights I would hold him just so he wouldn't hurt himself, and we would both cry. Those damn voices told him he was no good, he was worthless, and that we didn't love him. Jesus took his own life on September 27th 2016, knowing he was leaving his two boys behind. I visit with his boys often and they are being well taken care of.

Jesus's Mom,

GINA B.
Mesa, Arizona

> *The righteous perish, and no one takes it to heart;*
> *the devout are taken away, and no one understands*
> *Â that the righteous are taken away to be spared from evil.*
> *Those who walk uprightly enter into peace;*
> *they find rest as they pass in death.*
> *Isaiah 57: 1-2*

Chance

This all still feels so unreal. Like a horrible nightmare that you cannot wake up from; one that continues to haunt you every minute of every day.

I will never forget the first time I held him and his first little cry. He was so loving and sweet. I already had two daughters and had grown up with three sisters, and without a fatherly figure present when I was younger, life was difficult. So, this baby boy was a whole new world for me. At times I can still feel the warmth of him in my arms.

He rarely talked until his third birthday party. It brought him so much happiness that he never stopped talking about it. I'm sure others grew tired of hearing of it, but it seemed to open up a whole different little person. He then began to wait until we were all eating, and he would entertain us with his stories. Sometimes I had to tell him to stop so he could finish his plate, although, I never tired of hearing them. Once, when he was really little, we went to Florida for a vacation and booked a large charter fishing boat. Whatever you caught,

44

the deckhands would keep to serve in the local restaurants. Chance caught a large redfish. He wanted to throw it back and cried when he found out they were going to keep it and eat it. He was so tender-hearted.

Another time while living out in the country in New Mexico, we had some type of bird that resembled a seagull. They were able to fly but spent a lot of time on the ground. He asked me if he could keep them. I told him yes, never believing that he could actually catch even one. He proved me wrong and caught two, then tried to stick them in a small empty aquarium. I had to convince him that it would be better to let them go, and they might die if he kept them. I loved his determination.

When he was about six, he wanted a small Chipmunk .22 rifle. So, we took a hunter's safety class to prepare him to handle a gun properly. He wasn't quite to the reading level needed to take the test so one of the instructors read the questions to him. He made 100% and outscored me. Around that same age we had gone to a gun shop which had multiple bullets lined up inside a glass case on display. Chance went to each and described what caliber they were. The store owner argued with him about a particular one, but Chance was adamant. The owner pulled it out to prove that he was right, but he wasn't, Chance was.

I loved his enthusiasm for life and when he wanted to learn anything, he immersed himself in it. He worried about others, even giving his allowance to a drunk on the corner or buying food for someone that was hungry.

Chance went to live in Las Vegas to be close to his dad after high school graduation, while his sisters and I lived in New Mexico and Texas. Being so far away, we didn't quite see the signs of addiction and were conflicted if it was actually drugs or mental illness or both. Or perhaps we chose to ignore them. We may have been spared watching him slowly lose his life but for that we face mountains of guilt. We will always miss that sweet little boy and a part of our hearts will never be whole again.

The pain that we struggle with now is that he will be remembered for the dark years, those riddled with drugs and mental health issues. For putting his friends and family through what eventually became emotionally exhausting. Everyone wants to know the dark details. Those will not haunt us anymore. We just want to know why. Why he was cheated out of the life he could've had, and the wife and children he so desired and deserved.

I know this book is not only created to preserve the memory of our loved ones but to reach out to others to help them through their journey or perhaps to persuade someone to decide this isn't the life to follow. May God bless all the loved ones left behind and those struggling with the path that we have already walked. I had always heard that there is nothing worse than burying your child and I can now tell you that there are no truer words. Unfortunately, I know this from experiencing the worst pain in my lifetime.

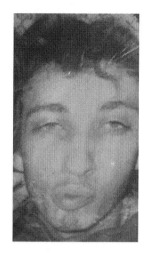

My heart will remain forever broken.

Chance's Mom,

SHERRY B.
Montgomery, Texas

Colin

FOREVER 23

The night Colin died, I knew it was his time. I went to bed and whispered to myself, "He is in your hands God, whatever you choose, I accept." I awoke on Saturday morning, December 23, 2017, and walked out to the kitchen at approximately ten-thirty a.m. Colin had a peaceful expression on his face, eyes closed, blanket hugging his body as he rested in my "happy chair." I would sit in that chair in the evenings to relax and always felt happy, hence my happy chair. My daughter Claire, soon to be twenty-one on December 28, 2017, was lounging on the couch watching television. As I walked through the dining area toward Colin, I knew he was dead. Claire looked at me as I laid my hand on Colin's forehead. He was cool. Claire stood up and just looked at me...we embraced. I do not recall what we said or did. I just knew he was gone, and I had to go into action to inform authorities and family.

I am a school social worker. I am sitting in my office at the local high school. My cell phone rings. It is a call from Colin: "Mom, you have to come get me and take me to the hospital. I am sick from heroin. I am really sick."

My thoughts were, *Fuck!! This cannot be happening!!!*

My words were, "Colin, pack a bag, I am taking you to the hospital, you need to go inpatient. Just pack a bag, and I will be home in twenty minutes to pick you up. Everything is going to be okay. You are going to be okay."

The hospital I took Colin to is an established drug and alcohol treatment center. Some of my colleagues have gone there for alcohol treatment. We are sitting in the waiting room, not saying much. What is there to say? Finally, an intake worker calls us in. We discuss his using history which of course he has minimized. She lays out his options. She recommends inpatient right then. I concur. He is twenty-years-old; his own guardian. Colin refuses inpatient. He is feeling very sick at this moment, chills, cramps, sharp-like electrical zaps shooting through his body. I am secretly praying he will change his mind. Of course, he does not. I decided to take him to a non-specialty hospital ER. My hope is that the ER can at least monitor his vitals and give him something to ease the electrical shocks until he is stable. Six hours later, I am driving us back home. I am feeling overwhelmed by this. I am feeling angry. But anger is not an emotion I connect with. So, I go into problem-solving mode.

I divorced the kids' father in 2004 due to his alcoholism. Their father died from cirrhosis in 2008. Colin decided he was not going to be addicted to alcohol like his father, so he chose other mood-altering substances. Is one substance any less painful to families than the others? I do not think so. We all know people who have lost a loved one from alcohol, crack, opioids, etc. It is painful no matter what the person took. Back to problem solving. Of course, I did not problem solve this. I was relieved Colin was alive. I had long talks with him and told him he would have to seek intensive out-patient treatment. But wait, he was scheduled to leave for Italy in three weeks as part of a college course. The trip was paid for, the itinerary was set. Only Colin knew if he could handle the rigor of overseas travel for ten days. NOT! He did not go; he lost the money he had paid for the trip. I was so disappointed and ashamed. How could my son, who comes from an average family, had been an A student throughout school, and was a wiz with history and politics be so lost? The truth is, it does not matter what type of family a child has, the economic level of the family, the skin color, the race, the level of faith, the IQ of the child, or any other factors we tend to make judgements on. A child from any family can become seduced by the mood-altering substances of opioids.

It all started August 2013. I am driving Colin, nineteen-years-old and Claire, seventeen-years-old, home from the oral surgeon. Both had their wisdom teeth taken out. I dropped them off at the house and headed to the pharmacy to fill the prescriptions for pain the surgeon issued. Norco enters our lives. I wish I had paid more attention to the warnings of drug task forces about how painkillers can be the gateway to opioid abuse. I was totally blind to the prospect that either of the kids would embrace the feeling of the Norco. Claire said she took one and did not feel any different, therefore she tossed her bottle in a tote in her bathroom. Colin never mentioned how he felt on Norco until two years later, while we were having one of our bi-weekly prison visits. (Yes, I will get to that period soon enough.)

Life continued through the fall of 2013, winter and spring of 2014. Claire was in high school; Colin was attending a local college and working at Jimmy John's. He had a nice girlfriend and two close friends. Were there overt signs of his using drugs? Prior to him calling me to take him to the hospital in the spring of 2014, I was aware that he was smoking pot and cigarettes. On two occasions, in the middle of the night I woke to use the restroom. The first occasion, I found Colin passed out on the toilet. The second occasion I found him standing in the bathroom, his back toward me, and he was swaying with his eyes closed. He did not hear his name, so I touched his shoulder which roused him. He came to and I directed him to his bed. I went to bed with a troubled feeling, not sure what to think. I knew he was on something but what could it be? The next morning, he of course had no recollection of the incident. I was in complete disbelief that it could be anything so strong as heroin. I told him he had to stop whatever he was using, or he would die. Still, I had no idea what he was using.

Then, the frantic call from him to take him to the hospital in the spring of 2014. From that event began the rollercoaster ride of addiction that we all have endured. It would be another year before I realized how serious his addiction was. I was in total denial of his use. I was raising the two kids myself, working full time trying to hang on to any scraps of normalcy I could. I was lonely, having been divorced for 10 years, and their father's death in 2008 had left a hole for all of us. In 2011, my life blew up. The seven-year relationship I had been in tanked, leaving me with financial disaster and emotionally raped. In 2012, my house went to foreclosure. No one had any idea how sad and alone I felt. The last thing I needed was to have a son who was a drug addict. I needed a "break." It was this type of thinking that I believe lent itself to my denial of his use. I needed some peace and wanted to begin to enjoy life again. I had so much shame from losing my house, that the shame that comes with having a child addicted to drugs was going to be too much for me. So, I minimized. Just like an addict minimizes their use, I minimized.

August 2015 I was not going to be able to minimize any longer. Claire and I had gone on a two-week cruise with her father's family. Colin chose not to join us. He would continue working and manage the house. Upon our return, the neighbors shared there had been a series of house break-ins in our neighborhood. I thought nothing of it. Phone calls with my sister and three of my friends revealed that while we were on our trip, Colin had hit each of them up to borrow money. He told them I left no food and there were bills to pay. WTF??? They all reported he was acting strange yet were convinced he needed the money, therefore they loaned him some. Hard-core confrontation about his behaviors while I was on the cruise proved to be needed. Either go to inpatient treatment or move out of my house. He chose to go to treatment. The next day he conducted a phone intake for an in-patient program and was scheduled to be admitted two days later.

The day after that, I had just come home from grocery shopping. It was approximately six p.m. Claire was working as a waitress and I assumed Colin was out with his girlfriend. He had left the house at one p.m. for a therapy appointment. I just poured a glass of wine, sat down in my "happy chair" and clicked the TV on to catch the news.

"Put your hands up!!!!"

I jerked my head toward the front door and saw figures dressed in black flowing through the entrance and dispersing into the kitchen and front room. Guns, black, helmets, yelling. It was all a blur. I thought someone was playing a joke on me. NO. Within seconds reality kicked in. I knew this was no joke but could not understand why they were there. It felt like I was in a movie, something like *Pulp Fiction*. I stood up, hands in the air as an officer approached me. He took me to the front room, placed a chair facing a wall and had me sit facing the wall.

"We arrested your son earlier this afternoon when he was coming out of his therapy session. He is in jail. We have been following him for the past two weeks. He has been breaking into houses in this neighborhood."

What the fuck???? My heart stopped. My mind was in disbelief. For the next two hours, the SWAT team tore the house apart looking for stolen property that had been reported. Vents were unscrewed and taken off, not replaced, drawers were dumped onto beds, ceiling tiles in the basement were removed, totes of seasonal clothing were dumped onto the floor. The attic, garage, and shed were ravaged the same. In the end, they found some drug paraphernalia but no stolen property. The officer talking to me indicated that one of Colin's friends had reported a handgun had been stolen from his brother. He was certain Colin had stolen it the last time Colin was at their house. It turns out, Colin had stolen a number of guns from the houses in the neighborhood and had sold them. Again, what the fuck? What has happened to my son? During the two weeks I was away, he became a "runaway train."

What can I say to you mothers who are reading this? Each and every one of us has a different experience but the same outcome. We are forever kindred by the loss of our child to this opioid epidemic. The addiction journey with Colin did not last more than four years. What was just as trying were the years between thirteen years of age until his active use at seventeen years of age.

Colin would say to me, "If my mind is going to be like this forever, I do not want to live."

He was referring to the negative thought patterns he experienced about himself. The self-hatred, self-loathing, the propensity to measure himself against others and feel as though he was not enough. Where did this thinking come from? In reality, we as humans all have experiences of self-doubt and insecurity. For Colin, his thoughts and experiences were magnified by a hundred.

I would tell him, "Your brain does not stop growing until you are twenty-four-years old. Please give your brain time to mature, please do not interrupt its development with drugs."

Again, he would state, "I do not want to live like this." Hence, the four years before turning seventeen involved therapy, diagnosis of anxiety disorder and severe depression, medications (some were effective for periods), more therapy, and suicidal thoughts with one hospitalization. More therapy. Then, Norco was introduced to him after oral surgery and the game changed.

Take note: painkillers can lead to drug addiction. Colin fell in love with the feeling that Norco provided. Colin began to buy hydrocodone, oxycodone, Norco's. Anything he could find on campus. Once the supplier (college girl) has you as a regular, she suggests snorting heroin; it works the same as the painkillers but cheaper. Hence, the addiction is in full force. I stated before, Colin became a "runaway train" during the two weeks I was on the cruise. He broke into four houses, stole guns, watches, money. He stole guns from our family gun safe that had been given to him by his father and grandfather. He sold everything on the street. He probably should have been dead based on the areas I was told he sold the items.

To the mothers who have had a child in prison, you understand the mixture of emotions and feelings triggered by their incarceration. Initially, it is shame and embarrassment. Eventually, it becomes a reality that is keeping your child safe, structured, and alive. I believe God's hand in Colin's life was to have him incarcerated so Colin could develop a relationship with Jesus, and that he did. Aunt Bridget sent Colin a devotional journal by Sarah Young, *Jesus Calling Enjoying Peace in His Presence*. For one and half years, Colin wrote in the journal while he was in prison. I have his journal now. I get comfort reading his entries, seeing how he began to understand he was not alone in this world and that faith can heal your negative feelings, or at least guide you during those dark periods. Colin's journey has strengthened my faith. I believe Colin's incarceration was God's way of preparing me for his death. There are so many excerpts from his journal I want to share with you, but that is not practical. Here are some that many of our children I am sure could relate to:

- February 26, 2016: "I am worried that I will not be able to succeed in life and I will be a failure and be alone. Relapsing is also a big worry for me. My biggest worry is that I will not be able to overcome my depression and anxiety and will live a lonely, depressing life eventually ending in suicide. Please remove these worries from my mind God."

- February 27, 2016: " Have to deal with my own sadness and loneliness and feelings of inadequacy without drugs now which is very hard for me."
- February 28,2016 journal prompt, Stop judging and evaluating yourself for this is not your role. Above all, stop comparing yourself with other people. This produces feelings of pride or inferiority, sometimes a mixture of both. I lead each of MY children along a path that is uniquely tailor-made for him or her. These are ways I secretly judge and compare myself to others: "I compare my body with others, I compare my intelligence with others, I compare my level of confidence with others, money or material possessions, my life experiences." I am beginning to understand the only source of real affirmation is God's unconditional love."

I had the best conversations with Colin during our visits. For the first time in four years, I felt like I was meeting my "real son." He was able to identify with his feelings, positive or negative, and not let them determine his value and worth. He was less anxious about his life and seemed to have a new sense of hope about his future upon his release. He had developed a better sense of self and would relate this to his developing relationship with Jesus. Please do not think that I thought he was cured. I was thrilled that he had begun to develop an understanding of how his faith could help him navigate life's challenges. However, I was fully aware that once out of the predictability of prison life, the demons of day-to-day life for this twenty-three-year-old male would surface.

In order to cope with him being incarcerated, I joined M.O.S.S. Mothers of Incarcerated Sons Society, Inc. It was on this Facebook group page that I did not feel alone. I had some friends whose child struggled with addiction, but not to the extent that Colin took his. I knew no one who had a child incarcerated. The shame I felt was crippling. I had to repeatedly tell myself that his actions were not because of my mothering. He made his choices and the results were his to deal with. Still, it is our nature as mothers to analyze and pick apart how we may have had a hand in our child's addiction. I also had the loving support from my therapist who has mothered me through all my adult life tragedies. In the end, prison provided a respite for Colin, Claire, and me. Colin was safe. Claire and I did not have to daily wonder about his safety nor the drain of emotional energy his presence created in our family.

It is August 16, 2017. Claire, Alyssa (Colin's girlfriend), and I arrive at the prison at 8:15 a.m. We are waiting in the stark foyer as we had dozens of times over the last two years. I looked at the guards I had come to know. I wonder if they take bets on which inmates will be repeat offenders. I turn my head to see Colin come through the security doors. He looks so healthy. He is lean, strong, and buff. He is smiling like I never saw him smile before. He is truly happy. We are all joyful, yet it is awkward as we get in the car and begin the two-hour ride back to Livonia. The transition from being incarcerated to former living is not easy for the individual returning, nor for the family. Fortunately, Colin spent some days of the week at Alyssa's.

During those days, I felt a sense of normalcy. On the days he was at the house, I was tense and often suspicious of how he was coping with life. This was his "do-over" chance to create his life with a new sense of trust he had in Jesus that was absent before. He told me he did not want to go back to that way of life. I suggested he get treatment, because he had not had any drug treatment while in prison, and now the hard part of living would begin. He agreed and started out-patient drug treatment. No, he did not go back to using during the first three months. Hell, maybe he did, and we did not pick up on it.

This part of our story is very hard for me to draw on. I am struggling with this and cannot stop tearing up as I type. Colin got a good job in a trophy store and registered for classes to begin in January 2018. He continued to work out at the gym, participate in family gatherings, and visit with friends he made while in prison. He even enjoyed the family Thanksgiving gathering we held at our family's up north home. This was surprising to me as he often avoided social gatherings due to his anxiety. It seemed as though we might make it.

The Monday after Thanksgiving, I received a call from Colin in a panicked voice at 12:30 a.m.

"Mom, can you come get me? I totaled my car."

The next day, once I was in control of my emotions, I told Colin he had to go to inpatient treatment or move out. I should have insisted he leave that day. The holidays were here, Colin had been gone for the last three years. The mixture of thoughts I had. On one level I knew he needed treatment if he was going to make it. On another level, I wanted my son to be home for this Christmas.

"Can't I go to treatment the day after Christmas?" he asked.

I was eager to follow the traditions we had initiated when the kids were young therefore anticipating the season, yet I had a sense of trepidation that it would really come to fruition. It did not. "He's in your hands God; whatever you choose, I accept."

If you are a mother, and your child is actively using: Find a balance between tough love and loving support. Your child needs your support if they are willing to accept it. If you are a mother who has lost your child...you did all you could with what information you had. It is not your fault that your child chose to use drugs. If you are a child actively using, perhaps reading this in a treatment facility; I beg you to go back and read Colin's excerpts. He thought he was the only one struggling with his thoughts. YOU ARE NOT ALONE. There are thousands of you out there thinking you are the only one struggling. Please accept help from family, friends, or strangers. People want to help. You can receive support that will alter your journey and the young people coming up behind you. Remember if you are thirty years or younger, your brain is not fully developed. Especially if you have been using drugs since you were a teen. But your brain can rewire and develop, only if you seek the support. Finally, seek to develop a relationship with Jesus. Colin finally did and I truly believe Colin is with Jesus as I write this.

This was not easy to write. There are incidents that were left out for the sake of time and length. There are moments that perhaps have blurred since they occurred. Even some of the trying moments such as the SWAT team coming in my front door seem to pale in comparison to missing Colin. The writing of this story occurred in July 2020, at the height of COVID-19. If Colin had lived to experience this pandemic, I

55

am certain he would have been miserable and out of his mind with angst. He struggled with unpredictability and loss of structure. Working from home and on-line college classes would have been impossible for him to adapt too.

This tribute to Colin was written by his godmother. It captures the essence of my son:

"You entered the world on August 22, 1994. A beautiful baby boy with dark hair and big brown eyes. The first few months were difficult for you and your parents due to severe colic.

Eventually, you grew out of it and enjoyed playing and building with your Legos. You loved to fish and hunt with your dad and Grandpa Ed. You enjoyed splashing in the pool and playing with your sister, Claire. Your quiet nature allowed you to be more introspective than most young boys your age. Good times and experiences filled your days, but challenges of darkness were there as well. Your sensitive personality provided a close bond between you and your dear mother, Renee.

The twinkle in your eyes and sweet smile captured the love of your life, Alyssa. The inner struggles you held were known only to a few, but those that loved you best always knew.

On December 23, 2017, your struggles and pain came to an end. We will miss you with every breath we take. Our sadness and grief are overwhelming to bear. We take comfort in knowing you are now resting in peace."

In loving memory from your Godmother, Anna.

Colin, I love you more.

Colin's Mom,

RENEE B.
Livonia, Michigan

Sarah

Sarah was my first born, my only daughter. My three sons followed her. My story is like so many other stories. Her dad and I divorced when the children were young. She spent the rest of her life trying to get her dad's attention. She was diagnosed with bipolar in her early twenties, but by then she had been dabbling in drug use for several years. She was beautiful and had a heart of gold. She loved babies and eventually had three of her own. Her drug use just continued to grow. She was very overwhelmed with life and just could not seem to find peace. She would often tell me that her mind just never quieted down. She had difficulty sleeping. She was always on the go, even in her early teen years. I always tried to make her happy because I knew she had such a void in her heart. She adored her siblings dearly as she did her children. She just did not fit in. She was shunned because of her drug use, this is often the case, because of the behavior that comes with addiction.

I did not really come to terms with my child being an addict until about four years before her death. I just "didn't see it" that way. I always knew that she had mental issues she grappled with for most of her life; she was not perfect, but she loved her family. The addiction stole so much from her and us. She did go to a rehab for about seven months before her death. She came home to a drug court program and was making progress at first. Then about four months in, the same old behaviors began to slowly surface. She was falling into the same old trap, old people, old places. We found her on March 29, 2018. Too far gone to even use Narcan. I had just spoken with her hours before. Now I am without my daughter, her children without a mother, her siblings without their oldest sister. I understand addiction as a disease, something I did not understand then at all, but wish I had.

I started a group in honor of my girl called S.A.R.A.H. - Seeking Action Raising Awareness & Hope. We have held a vigil on August 31 for International Overdose Awareness Day to honor those lost to addiction. To remind the world that their lives mattered, that they lived, and loved and were loved, that the addiction will never stop our love for our children, mothers, fathers, brothers, sisters, friends. God loves all of us, and it is in that I find my strength to continue. I am now raising her children, as so  many of us parents are having to do. I will remember the beautiful things about Sarah; I will love her until I see her face again!

Sarah's Mom,

RENEE B.
Houma, Louisiana

Kerri

FOREVER 26

Where to begin? My daughter was my whole world. She was my best friend. If there was anything I did right in this life, it was her. I have made that statement to people who know what she died from, that the medical examiner ruled her death an accidental overdose. They don't understand how I can still say that because of how she died. I have even had someone close to me who lost a child tell me that their child died from a disease and mine died from a choice. Addiction is a disease, not a choice. An addict does not wake up one day and decide today is the day they will become an addict. That is what so many fail to understand.

Throughout Kerri's battle with addiction, I have learned so much. Addiction can happen to anyone. It doesn't choose because of race, age, class, or status. It doesn't discriminate. It claims countless lives every single day. And it is getting worse every single day. We need to stop the judgements and to understand and face addiction for what it is. An epidemic. My daughter was one of the countless lives lost by this horrible disease. I miss her more and more every single minute of every single day.

Someone once told me that I didn't die, my daughter did. Well, they were wrong. The day she died part of me died. But if sharing her story can help just one person then she would want that. That's who she was, who she still is because she is still with me. She lives on through me, in my heart, in my memory and in all that I do. In all that I can do to make sure her life and death matter. So, let me tell you about my beautiful angel.

Kerri Elizabeth was born on August 14, 1992, at 3:27 p.m. She was twenty inches long and weighed seven pounds nine ounces. She was named after my "cousin" Kerri (Lynn), who died when I was thirteen and she was twelve. The "Elizabeth" was in honor of my grandmother. However, the name Elizabeth was also the middle name of both her grandmothers! Kerri was my "Rainbow Baby". When she first arrived into this world, I was terrified that I would lose her as I had her brother before her. I slept in the living room, in her bedroom, and on the couch with her. She came to work with me since I was a preschool teacher. We were together every day, all day, and I wouldn't have had it any other way.

She slept through the night at six weeks old and I didn't because I checked on her probably every five minutes to make sure she was breathing, still deathly afraid of losing her. I was overprotective to a fault. I knew that but it didn't matter. She was my whole world then and always would be. Kerri was joined by her brother, Kevin, three years later on August 23, 1995. My world was complete.

She took her first dance class at three, joined drama classes at eight. She loved marine biology and after watching *Free Willy* wanted to become a marine biologist. She was a Brownie, then a Girl Scout. Kerri had a way of making everything look like the most spectacular thing you ever saw. She made you feel like you were seeing something for the first time no matter how many times you saw it. Her awe and wonderment at things never ceased to amaze me. Kerri's enthusiasm and joy were contagious to anyone she came in contact with even at a young age. As was evident to even a security guard at a concert when he let a five-year-old little girl sit on top of a fence to hear her favorite song. And as a tour bus left that stadium, that very same five-year-old little girl had a van full of adults believing the musician was waving to HER as his tour bus pulled away!

My daughter didn't embarrass easily but when she did, she did it well! There is a cathedral in NYC with nuns, still in shock, I'm sure, that can attest to that!

Kerri loved school and when I say loved I mean LOVED! She was a straight "A" student. One year she got off the bus upset that summer break was about to start and asked me, actually begged me to let her go to summer school. She hated to fail at anything! When she was in middle school, she received her first "D" in Spanish. She was devastated and completely broke down. Everything mattered to Kerri and failure was never an option. It devastated her that her addiction was something she "failed" at. Not only did Kerri hate to fail at anything, she also hated to be wrong about anything. I taught sign language so I would go and teach some basics in my children's classes each year.

One year, Kerri decided to "help" her classmates pass their spelling test by fingerspelling all the words to them while the teacher wasn't looking. Everyone got an "A." Kerri never did understand that it was considered cheating and made quite the argument against it. Anytime she felt she was right she was always ready to back it up! One of the things about Kerri was that she wanted to hear the other side and she wanted to hear why she should believe their points. She was fair that way. I loved watching my daughter's mind at work! That mind of hers was truly amazing. She was innovative and inspired. She was creative until her disease took that from her too. Long before it took her life.

Kerri loved to be in charge. The first time I noticed this she was three and it was at her first dance recital! Even at that age she was a natural born leader.

She loved to read. She enjoyed singing, acting, bossing her brother around, and helping others. She was empathetic. She always believed she could fix everyone's problems. She loved everything about Harry Potter! She could write a poem, essay, or short story without batting an eye. She loved her pets: the dogs, cats, and her bunny! She was an environmentalist. She participated in Habitat for Humanity in high school.

If there was a cause that she cared about, she was all in! If she saw something that she thought was wrong, she would let you know! I think the first time she did that she was only two years old!

She had the biggest smile and the most infectious laugh! She had the best sense of humor and I miss that laugh so much. She was sarcastic and brutally honest, sometimes too brutal. She spoke her mind and she could really hold a grudge! She used to argue with me when I would remind her of the expression that you get more bees with honey. She would just laugh at me and say, "Yes, but a fly swatter works better."

But if she was your friend, she was your friend no matter what. My daughter would give you the shirt off her back. My beautiful girl loved fiercely and if you were lucky enough to be on the receiving end of her love, you were one of the luckiest people on this earth. Family was something Kerri valued more than anything. She loved her family and nothing was more important to her than it. She fought for it, she fought within it. She hated knowing she let her family down. She used to tell me that all the time. She hated that her addiction caused her to do that.

Kerri knew she could do anything she wanted to at one time. She knew she could take the world by storm at one time.

But my daughter was fighting a demon that was stronger than all of us put together, stronger than she was. God knows she tried to fight it and only God knows how hard. My daughter had a DISEASE and that disease is called addiction. She battled it, she won some battles, she lost others. She was recovering sometimes and sometimes she wasn't. She fought her final battle and lost on January 25, 2019.

She was in and out of rehabilitation facilities. She struggled for a few years with it. She had life-altering events happen, but those would have been her stories to tell, and so I am not going to share those stories. She struggled with depression and anxiety. We had our times when we struggled to get along, where we didn't like each other. But love each other we did. We fought, boy did we fight, at times. But in the end, we had a relationship that I only ever thought I could dream about having with my daughter. If someone had told me when she was sixteen, seventeen, or even eighteen that we would have been as close as were in the end, I would have told them it was impossible. We could tell each other everything. Someone once told me they couldn't believe how close we were and how they envied our relationship. We talked or texted every night. We could be on the phone for three minutes or three hours. Never did we hang up without saying, "I love you more," more than once. She was my saving grace. She hated me at times but I never doubted how much she loved me. One of the last things she said to me was how much she loved me and how much she would always need me. She told me she always knew that no matter what she did I always had her back. But it was never easy.

When I first learned of her addiction, we had just lost her step-sister and I felt like she did it for the "shock factor." At the time, we were in the process of not quite rebuilding our already shaky relationship due to her father's and my divorce eight years earlier. The accusations she made, the things she said were more devastating than I could ever possibly describe in writing. No loss; not Kerri Lynn's, not my grand-mother's, not my divorce after twenty years of marriage, and if I am being honest, not even losing my step-daughter or my son; nothing pierced my heart like this. Learning she was an addict, learning she blamed me and the viciousness of her words was an indescribable pain. I just couldn't believe my baby girl could turn on me in this manner. She called to tell me she was going to a rehabilitation facility. She wouldn't tell me where. There was very little contact and when there was it was nothing but accusations and anger.

Then she briefly cut off all contact. I read on Facebook that the facility she was in was in another state. I began to basically read about her life online. I didn't even know if she was still using! I didn't know what drug or drugs she used. I felt like my baby girl was lost to me. So, I sat and cried myself to sleep most nights. Mother's Day that year came and my phone rang. It was Kerri and when I started to cry, I will never forget that conversation or how it was the best gift she could have given me, the best gift I have ever or will ever receive.

She said, "Mom, why are you crying?"

I said, "Because I didn't expect to hear from you."

And she said, "Mom, I love you. You're my mom and no matter what I will always love you."

And our healing began. We started to communicate. Sometimes it went well, sometimes it did not. There were more accusations but there were also healing conversations. Her step-dad and I drove to Florida to visit family and we had our first face-to-face meeting since I learned of her addiction. We talked for hours and she shared things with me that I had been unaware of, things that occurred while I was lost in my own grief about my divorce.

I will blame myself for not seeing, not knowing, and not being there for her. I have been told it is not my fault, that nothing I could have done would have changed the outcome. But I am the mother of an addict. I am her mother. I was supposed to keep her safe. I was supposed to protect her. I failed her. And that is my legacy. It doesn't matter how many times I hear it or how many times I read about it. I am a grief counselor so I know it; I tell that to others who are grieving and who blame themselves. It is not their fault. But for me, Kerri's mom, I believe deep in my heart and soul I should have been able to save her, to stop her from making that choice. So, I don't know if I ever will believe my very own words. That is what this disease has done to me. It has taken my daughter and it has broken me. I will bounce back one day. Kerri would expect nothing less from me. Right now, though, that day seems far, far away.

My final time with my beautiful precious daughter was nine days before she left this world. Kerri came and spent a week with us in mid-January. She spent time reconnecting with her grandparents. We had the time of our lives. I am so very grateful for that week. I didn't know at the time it would be some of my last memories with her. We stayed up many of those nights until the early hours of the morning talking. Good, quality time just talking. Heartfelt talks, cleansing talks, promises that would later be broken. She was in good spirits.

We spent two days at Universal Studios. We made some wonderful memories that I will be forever grateful for! I am thankful for every single moment with her. I was so happy to have my daughter back. But my heart was heavy and I kept pushing it away. I had spent the last few years waiting for "the call" people telling me I would be "putting her in a pine box" or that she was an addict and that I needed to face the reality. But here she was. She sounded good, looked great. She was talking to me about everything. She cried, she laughed. She played her favorite music in the car.

I thought, *Record those sounds and her laughter in your brain.*

She looked at me and promised me she wasn't going anywhere and I thought, *Freeze this moment.*

I look back now and every once in a while, I catch myself wondering: Did she know? Did she know these would be my final memories with her?

The day she left I didn't want her to go; it was more than I was just going to miss her. It was a feeling that I just can't explain. She left most of her stuff at my house because she was planning on coming back in three months and she would just bring more stuff with her. As she turned for one last wave and ILU sign, which was always "our thing" from the moment she was old enough to do it, the strangest thing happened. All around me the airport seemed to freeze. For just a second all I saw was Kerri standing there with that beautiful, infectious smile, holding up the sign for I Love You and yelling "I Love You" at the same time. Every fiber in me shouted, DO NOT LET HER GET ON THE PLANE!

I knew it was the last time I would see her. Then the moment was over. Everything was moving again. She waved, blew me a kiss, and walked away. I shook off the feeling. For the next eight days we would talk and/or text. She would tell me over and over how much she wanted to be there with me, about how she planned on moving down with me and how she knew she could always count on me. And we made a plan! But, on the ninth day after she left, just a little over twenty-four hours after our last conversation, after the "I love you's" and "Talk to you tomorrow's," at 1:15 a.m. On the 24th, no indication, no feeling of impending doom, the damn call came on January 25 around 5:11 a.m. Just a little more than **TWENTY-FOUR** hours after I spoke to her for the last time, my daughter was just gone.

I remember not being able to breath, or sleep or eat. I remember just wanting to see her, hold her, to hear her laugh and say, "I love you more." I wanted someone to tell me it was all just a nightmare and I waited to wake up from it. When everything was "done," I was angry. Not at Kerri, not even at God. But at everything and everyone else. I wanted answers. I wanted to know why. I wanted to understand. It was just easier to be angry. If I was angry then I didn't have to face that she was gone. But the anger caused health issues. It caused strains in relationships. It caused memory loss and anxiety. I was unable to do my job. The job I had been doing for over thirty-five years and was really good at, but could no longer do!

Then one day, even when you don't want it to and whether you are ready or not, it happens. The grief becomes unbearable. I found myself unable to stop the tears. I screamed. I even tried to yell at her to come back. They say the first year is the hardest. Well, the second year is harder. Oh, and everyone goes on with their life. Meanwhile, support, if there was any, is also gone. In most cases individuals want to support you but find it hard because they don't know what to say or how to act around someone who has lost a child, no matter what the child's age. It's not the "normal order of things." So, we are told to "move on." No one understands there is no moving on from the loss of your child.

When your child has lost his or her life to addiction, due to the stigma attached to addiction and the lack of understanding, the support is even less. I personally have experienced the "just move on already" from so many. The "it was her choice." The "she was an addict, so it was going to happen." And my all-time favorite, "Well, what did you expect?" Unfortunately, until awareness is raised it will continue to be this way.

In fifth grade, my kids attended the DARE program - Drug Abuse Resistance Education. Think about that. Fifth grade. That was it. Why? Why wasn't this education required in junior high or high school? As a parent, I was never brought in to be told what my children would be taught as they got older. I was naive enough to think if I raised my kids "right" they would not use drugs. All I had to do was tell them that drugs were bad, right?

We just had to be "good parents." Our children were raised by parents who loved them more than life itself. They had rules and consequences. My daughter went to college, maintained a 4.0 GPA while working full time and commuting back and forth every day. She was in a sorority, received her BA in forensic psychology. She mentored others. She had an incredible talent when it came to writing and speaking. She could do anything she put her mind to.

But one day she made a choice. A bad choice, an awful choice, a choice that would change her world, change her brain, change her life and in a few years take her life.

Education. Empathy. Understanding. We shouldn't shame. We shouldn't be hiding our heads in the sand. We need to open everyone's eyes to what it really is and what needs to be done from here to stop the needless, endless deaths that are occurring each and every single day! Not a day goes by that I don't learn about someone else who has succumbed to their addiction. But those are not the only deaths due to addiction that I learn about. I also learn about the deaths of those left behind and I understand. I have been there. When Kerri first died, all I wanted to do was be with her again. But I knew that there were others who needed me here too. I also knew that if I did something to myself, she would never forgive me. That was my daughter.

I know the pain of missing her every single second of every single day. I understood the mother who was diagnosed with cancer and said she is not afraid to die and counts down the days until she can be with her daughter again. I know why the mother took her own life because she just couldn't live without her child. The pain of losing your child is overwhelming. It takes your breath away. It takes every ounce of energy, of strength and courage to just get out of bed each day, knowing your child is not here anymore. Addiction doesn't just affect the addict. It affects everyone who loves them.

I read the stories from families who have watched and continue to watch as their family members struggle, parents and spouses who are suffering as her father, brother, and I do each day, to make it through another day without their loved ones, especially their children. Those raising their grandchildren because their children are no longer here. There is one baby born every fifteen minutes suffering from opioid withdrawal and in the past two decades children placed in foster care due to their parents' drug abuse has doubled.

I think of all the things Kerri will never get to do: have children, get married, follow her dreams, and help all the people she planned on helping. She touched so many lives as was evident the night of her service. Although I am devastated at what I have lost, it saddens me even more at what she has lost. Her life, her opportunities. It breaks my heart that her father will never walk his daughter down the aisle or how we will never hold our grandchild. It hurts that she will never watch her own children grow up. But one of the things that hurts me more is worrying about my remaining child. My youngest son. Not only did he find his sister, he tried to revive her and his last memory of her will be that. She promised me that she would never do that to him. But he now grieves his only sister, only sibling. They were so close. She would have

67

moved Heaven and Earth for him. I grieve for him as well as her. I grieve for what he has lost. For his pain.

I think it's important to say I am not ashamed or embarrassed by her death. My daughter was an addict. There was no reason. No one to blame. Addiction can happen to anyone. Kerri would want you to know that.

Years ago, Kerri wrote an essay that, at the time, I never dreamt would become what I would read at her memorial service ten years later. As I reread it periodically now, it's almost as though she did know what life had waiting for her.

Two thoughts stand out the most: *"Almost as if, once one has lost the inno-cence of childhood, they begin to realize that things are not always going to work out the way they would like them too, or have that cliche happily ever after' ending we all would like it to have,* and *maybe the innocence of childhood is nothing more that the ignorance of life. As we get older, the events that have occurred in one's life put life itself into a new perspective."*

There is so much more I could add to Kerri's story. I could add more details about her times in rehab, how it didn't help and the things she was exposed to. The times she made me feel so guilty because I wouldn't enable her by sending money or renting her a car or when I did send her $20 for gas so she could get to work, it terrified me for doing it. I could describe the first time she overdosed, or the time she saved someone who overdosed in her arms and the effect that had on her. I thought that was her turning point. I could share how a few times when I saw her, I was terrified by her appearance but that final time I saw her brought me hope and fear. However, my point of sharing what I have is to share who she was and how addiction is not "picky" at who it chooses to affect. My goal, our goal, is that Kerri's story will help you, the reader.

My daughter taught me to never stop fighting. Her death, as she said herself, was an "event that occurred in my life that put life itself into a new perspective." Her future, my future, our future, will never be the one we always dreamt about. We will never have large family gatherings with her. I will never see her raise her own family or see her obtain the rest of her dreams and goals. I will never again hear her voice or laugh. I will never hear her "pearls of wisdom" and she will never ask me what

I think of something again. I will never again sit outside and talk to my daughter at three a.m., just because.

But Kerri still needs me. She needs me to help her spread awareness and help another mother, father, brother, sister, or grandparent from feeling this pain. To maybe help another person to think twice before choosing to use. To help others understand that no one is immune and to open the eyes of others. Education is a MUST. Empathy and understanding are what we need. Support one another. Kerri's life mattered. Kerri's death matters just as much. She did not choose to be an addict. She did not choose to die. It **WILL NOT** be in vain. This is for her. It has always been for her and her brother and it always will be.

Kerri's Mom,

LISA B.
Lady Lake, Florida

Tara

FOREVER 27

As a child, I remember learning about leap year and thinking to myself what it must be like to be born on February 29 and only getting to celebrate your actual birthday every four years. Little did I know, Tara, my fourth and youngest child, my only girl, would be born that beautiful, unusually warm spring-like day in Claremore, Oklahoma, on February 29, 1992. Being my youngest and only girl and born on such a special day is a true sentiment to the joy she would bring our whole family.

Tara was a beautiful girl who loved her life. She had three older brothers and could definitely "hold her own." She was smart, funny, and everyone's friend. She loved to sing and play tennis, enjoyed gymnastics, and was a cheerleader for four years. One of my fondest memories was when she and her three brothers acted out the entire *Grease* movie for me in our living room. It was priceless.

Things started to change for Tara when she was seventeen years old. She got pregnant with her daughter. Tara was small and petite, and the pregnancy was rough for her. After the birth, the doctor told her she had a slipped disc in her back, so she started on pain pills. She then started abusing the pills and that led her to losing custody of her daughter. She got very depressed which pushed her to using more pills. It's true, depression feeds the addiction; the addiction feeds the depression. A vicious cycle. Tara's new love interest would introduce her to a "cheaper more affordable" addiction...heroin.

We tried very hard to help her through this; sometimes we thought she was better, but this grip on her, it was too strong.

Tara met a new man who was also an addict, but was on the right track of getting clean, and working a good job. They got a nice home and things were looking good. She was able to get off the needle and started going to the methadone clinic. Although she was still going to the clinic, she became pregnant with their son. After several years, I was finally seeing my girl again, the girl she was before. I could sleep again. She was happy.

In February 2019, my daughter got to have the beach wedding she always dreamed about. We all flew to Florida; I was so happy for her, she was a beautiful bride.

A few months later, she would go to rehab. Her husband relapsed, depression returned, and she also relapsed. She went into a ninety-day in-house program where she thrived. Her graduation day was a happy celebration.

She tried very hard to make her meetings; she was being told to do this, go there, you're not doing this, you need to be doing that.... etc. She was extremely overwhelmed. She came to my house and cried to me. She said she wasn't able to make her meetings because she was being pulled by her husband's family to do so much. They felt like if they kept her busy, she wouldn't have time to relapse. This was two days before...before that day. That day, December 19, 2019. I was at Sam's Club shopping with my mother, buying baking supplies for Christmas, when I got "the call." The call I feared for years, the call that changed my life forever.

The drive to the hospital was torture. Telling the doctors to "unplug" was the worst thing I could ever imagine saying. I sat with her holding her hand, kissing her forehead, saying goodbye to the love of my life; my heart was broken. And then she was gone.

If I could offer any advice to anyone who has a loved one who is going through this, take them to their meetings and try to keep them from stress; stress is a trigger. Don't tell them what they need to do and what they should be doing. Take them and guide them. When they are using, the world they are in is a different one. When they get clean, they are overwhelmed. They don't want to relapse; they have to learn to live in a world without drugs and it could be overwhelming and scary.

Tara didn't want to die; she had just gotten a new lease on life and had a lot to live for. As do so many others.

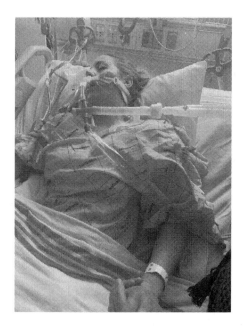

Tara's Mom,

SANDRA B.
Tulsa, Oklahoma

Alex

FOREVER 28

Where do you begin when you find out that your child is an addict? I think all of us as parents know the teenage years are the most vulnerable, the most impressionable. The first time I was ever told that there was any sort of paraphernalia, was by my son's father; his wife had found paraphernalia going through my son's things. Of course, you don't want to ever believe that; she and my son did not get along. So, the resolution was for him to come home and stay with me. It wasn't long after that it was evident. Something was seriously different. Alex was a hard worker, he was great academically, held two part-time jobs, but he was always broke. Then he began to lose weight.

I work night shift so there were times that our paths would cross. When Alex and his brother, Nick, moved in with my husband and myself, Alex made new friends and soon began getting into trouble. We were about to move from the area because after my husband came home from his deployment, he got a job which would take us out of the situation. I thought it would be a fresh start; my thoughts were, "If I can just get him away from this area and these people, he'll be OK."

Of course, we have all gone through it, we know it doesn't take long for them to find like-minded individuals to befriend. My husband was still in the reserves and he would often go away for training. He was gone one time for about six weeks and when he came back, he noticed a lot of his things had disappeared such as lawn equipment and other things that could be pawned for money.

I think one of my biggest breaking points was the day I walked into his room to ask him a question. And there it was right in my face, all the paraphernalia, and he was startled into consciousness. I told him at that point that he had to go, one of the hardest things a parent ever has to tell their child. Alex and his brother were both attending college classes, so Alex's brother would pick him up from where he was living with friends. Then the day came when Alex's brother said, "Mom, he's very sick," and I told him to bring Alex home. Being in the medical field, you always want to rationalize and think you can fix it. Alex would do so well, he would go so long, he would gain weight, he would look wonderful, and then out of the blue he would just disappear. Alex didn't drink; sometimes he would have a beer while swimming in the pool, but he could never hold his liquor, so he wasn't really big on drinking, it was always pills.

Then he started seeing a psychiatrist. Mind you, this particular physician was covered under our military insurance and was giving him medication for ADHD, which I always thought he had when he was very young, but I never gave him medication for it, I just kept him busy. Then Alex said he was having trouble sleeping because his ADHD medicine kept him awake. He started with the prescription medications, which began the barter system. Watching your child eat food and passing out asleep in their plate, waking up in the middle of the night to check on your child, just to make sure you can see their chest rising. Unfortunately, Alex didn't win his battle against his demon. The last time I spoke to my son was Thanksgiving evening. As I was getting ready to walk out the door to work, he told me he was going to make pies and we would do our Thanksgiving the next day. I was elated we were going to continue to decorate for the holidays. And he was excited he had a new job. He was getting all of his office clothes out of the closet and pressing his shirts.

When I came home on a Friday morning, my dog was in Alex's room and barking and the sound was not a normal bark; the door was locked. Then this sudden chill ran down my spine, and I became frantic. I unlocked the door and there he was. I didn't even see the syringe on the floor, I just ran over to pick him up. He was beyond resuscitation. He looked as though he dropped something and was going to pick it up while sitting on the bed. That is when my whole world changed. It was like everything was in slow motion. I've had the opportunity to meet other mommas who lost their child through the Facebook support group #NotInVain and listen to their stories, and it means so much to be able to share with others who understand.

My son's name is Marcus Alexander, a.k.a. Alex. He was born on the day it snowed in Florida in December, 1989, and he passed away in November 2018. Some days are better than others when I have to work and take care of family, but there are just some days I can't get out of bed. It's somewhat surreal; we love our kids, we miss them, and would do anything to have been able to cure them and have them here with us, but then I feel relieved that he's not fighting his demons anymore.

I just wish as a mother that I could've protected him from this terrible demon, and his so-called friends. I'd like to thank everyone for allowing me to share my story. God bless us all on this journey and in this new life that we have to live in; that's what it seems like, a terrible nightmare from which you just can't wake up. Alex has been gone for twenty months, but it seems like yesterday. I think reading his autopsy and toxicology report was probably one of the hardest things I had to do. Fentanyl and benzodiazepines, a.k.a. Xanax, were found in his body.

Alex wasn't married and he had no children. I know some of the mothers here have grandchildren. Oh, what I wouldn't give to have just a small piece. I would want to look at Alex's child every day, especially if he had a child with beautiful pacific blue eyes like his. But I get to look at his photo every day and I talk to him every day. When I'm frustrated, he helps me find things like my garden gloves when I'm in the garage. He came to me in my dreams only once; he didn't say anything, he just smiled. Somehow that made me feel that was his way of letting me know it was OK and he was OK.

I have a friend that told me the Lord only keeps you here on this earth until your job here is complete; then He brings you home. Alex had the kindest heart. I would come home and find strange people in my house. He brought home a man who got a job telemarketing, but he was homeless. Alex told me that everybody at that job was making fun of him because he wore the same clothes. He let this man sleep in my Florida room and as I walked out there and saw a strange man sleeping on the floor, it about scared me to death. We let him stay for about a week, put a roof over his head, some hot food in his belly until he got his paycheck.

That is the kind of man my son was; that's the legacy that I share with others. Alex would give you the shirt off his back; he would even take food out of our pantry to take it to people that had no food to eat. He would let people wash their clothes in our washing machine because they had no place to wash their clothes. He was a gentle soul, with a kind and compassionate heart. He is forever loved and missed.

Alex's Mom,

LISA B.
Melbourne, Florida

Shannon

FOREVER 31

Shannon is my angel daughter. She was born in 1987. She was the cutest little girl, spoiled rotten, and she knew she was cute!!

In her late teens/early twenties, she started taking pills. She OD'd on pills but survived. I believe then a boyfriend introduced her to heroin. That began her struggle. For years she was in and out of rehab and she went to prison for forging prescriptions. I thought prison might wake her up. It did for a short while.

The heroin use intensified into a full-blown habit. She was in and out of rehabs and jail. She had many abscesses on her hands that required surgery. She met a man who genuinely loved her and did well with him, but she always went back to the neighborhood and streets that eventually killed her.

She went from a beautiful girl to walking the streets with sores all over her. She was estranged from her family due to the heroin use. She stole, she lied, everything that goes with addiction. The last time I saw her she looked awful and it did not go well. That I will live with forever. I was just so done.

I now realize Shannon's life was a living hell. The end of February 2018, I got a call she had been taken to the ER by "three men" and was dropped off. She had a fever of 104 degrees, was delirious, sick, etc.

She was admitted to the ICU and diagnosed with sepsis and endocarditis, which is a heart valve infection due to IV drug use. She had been sick for several days to a week but continued using heroin during that time.

I later found out the house where she was living continued giving her the heroin. I believe they were trying to kill her instead of calling an ambulance to help her. She was put on a ventilator two days after admission and passed after seven days. She had simply waited too long to get treatment and her body had had enough; I believe God also knew she had had enough.

I had gone home after seeing Shannon and got a call not long after that she was dying and to come quickly. I hardly remember the drive but after I got there, I remember everything, even what I was wearing. I hate that top now. They were doing CPR on her when I walked in. I had never seen that, and it was heart wrenching to see them try to save my beautiful girl.

I watched them try to bring her back three times. I was told it would continue to happen and after the third time, I could not put her through it any longer. She passed away and her family was with her.

Also with her was the man mentioned above; he still loved her through it all. He went every day to the hospital. I am so glad she experienced that kind of love and not just a "drug buddy." He asked to put a ring he had bought her, but had never given her, on a chain to be buried with her. Of course, we said yes.

Once heroin got a hold of Shannon it never let go, never. I know she tried and wanted a different life. She loved rides in the country, going to outdoor country concerts, and Ohio State. When she was trying to stay clean, she was meticulous about her hair and makeup.

I talked to her about doing makeup, she was so good at it. Well, heroin would not go away. I was not easy on her at times and I hope she knows why; I believe she knows why. I live to see my precious girl again. Shannon Nicole February 17, 1987 to March 5, 2018.

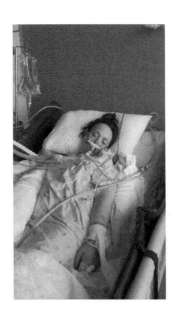

Shannon's Mom,

LISA B.
Dayton, Ohio

> *"I am worn and tattered but I endure.*
> *God does not want me to suffer,*
> *He gives me strength and wisdom from*
> *my suffering and carries me through my burden."*

Christopher

FOREVER 31

Where do you begin to tell your child's story of addiction? I was one of those clueless mothers, who didn't even know my son was an addict, much less he had been an addict for fifteen years. I knew Christopher, nicknamed "Biffy," smoked marijuana, but I never dreamed that could be an addiction. Then I learned he was taking pain pills, never dreamed again he was an addict, as I didn't know exactly how many times he was running to the ER to get scripts for pain pills.

Then one day, my older son texted saying, "Mom, I just found out Biffy is shooting up."

"What do you mean shooting up?"

So, he explained it to me. He said my son was shooting up heroin. "WHAT THE HELL? Why is he shooting up heroin, Nick?"

I was told, "Because meth was getting too expensive."

I thought, *OH MY GOD, he was using meth too, WHAT THE HELL is going on here?*

So, off I go to find Chris. When I found him, I went off! I was like, "Why, why is my son using these hard drugs and why haven't I known about this?" Well, of course I heard, "I am not Mom. Nick is crazy. I only tried it a time or two and didn't like it, so I don't do it anymore. I've been staying with a good friend, who is a Christian. He's been studying the Bible with me and I don't even think about pot anymore, Mom."

"Ok that's good, you stay on that track son. You know I love you to the moon and back. You do know that you can come to me about ANYTHING Chris, right?"

"Yes, Mom I know and I love you, too."

I leave to go home and I am just in another world, wondering why is he even doing this crap? I call his dad asking him all kinds of questions, only to find out that Chris had apparently OD'd one night. His dad's girlfriend had kept going into John's bedroom telling him, "Hey man your son has OD'd and he needs you to get up to help him. Take him to the ER, call 911 or something." He tells me that he told her, "Tell him just go to bed, sleep it off." She said, "Dude, he can't do that man. Do you realize your son could die?" Well, thank God for her because she called 911. They got there and administered Narcan. He came to and was ok.

So, yea, he tells me, "He's ok, but your son has a problem."

"EXCUSE ME, my son, he's your son too man and you are very much at fault for this crap, John. You have bought their drugs; you have paid the dealers off, so they wouldn't shoot up your house. You have even given them drugs to do chores for you. So, this crap is on you!! You have made those two boys what they are turning out to be! How does a father buy his sons crack, meth, heroin, whatever the hell type drugs they want? What the hell is wrong with you?"

"I'm sorry, but I am not going to have dealers coming to my house threatening to shoot me or my house, Sheryl!"

Well, then don't be buying their drugs you idiot!! Needless to say, through more investigating, I found out this wasn't the first time Chris had OD'd and 911 needed to be called to administer Narcan. This was the fourth time. Then I find out he had been incarcerated and had a pending court date. He also had another case of being arrested for having a syringe with a substance in the syringe. This was the fourth time for the same charge, becoming a felony. I go to court with him and the judge lets him walk out without jail time.

A few nights later my daughter calls me in the middle of the night telling me Christopher just left her house after beating on her door. She said, "Mom, your son has to be on some type of drugs."

She said he came by to warn us that the entire street was on fire. Businesses, houses with Satanic symbols in a lot of the windows everywhere. She said she tried getting him to come in, but he said he needed to go warn people. She told me which way he was heading down Washington Street. I got up, got dressed, and went out looking for him. I found him, got him in the car, and asked him what was going on.

He said, "Mom, don't you see it?"

I said, "See what Chris?"

He said, "Look around, Mom it's on fire, can't you see it?"

I said, "Son, there's nothing on fire anywhere."

He said, "Yes, it is, Mom." Then he said, "OMG they have gotten to you; you are one of them, you have succumbed to the other side."

"Chris, what are you talking about son? I have not succumbed to anything; there is nothing on fire."

He said, "Do you not see the Satanic signs in the windows? Look right there. The Dollar General store has a Satanic sign in the window."

I said, "No it does not, Chris. What have you taken, son?"

He said, "Nothing, I haven't had anything."

"Chris, It's apparent you have taken something. What the hell did you take?" So, I texted my daughter, told her to call 911, tell the officer I am taking him to get something to eat at Burger King next to Kroger's on West Washington Street, and to have someone meet me there. He needs help, I feel he's taken some type drugs. An officer showed up, and of course, did nothing.

So here I am with a son who's higher than a kite and I don't know what to do. I brought him home with me to stay. He spent the night, so I talked him into spending more time with us. I asked him the next day, would he be willing to go to a rehab to get help? And he agreed. I called every place I could find. No insurance, no help, sorry ma'am. After the second night, he began to get sick. Constantly taking hot baths, just lying in the water several times a day and all night long. He was freezing. Here I am thinking he's got the flu or just getting sick; here I am waiting hand and foot on him freaking out because he's so sick. Little did I know he was going through withdrawal. I am still begrudgingly pleading with every rehab facility I can call to please take him to get him help. Why is it only if you have insurance that you will be able to be admitted? Are you telling me if you don't have insurance you don't matter?

So, I finally find a place who will take him and will help him get Medicaid to pay for it. We went to pick up clothing and were headed to the Salvation Army for men. I run to grab him cigarettes, snacks, and anything they will allow me to bring to him. They tell me he can't talk to me for a certain amount of time because he will be in detox and classes. I could not take it anymore after four days; I call to ask if I can just check on him, to see how he's doing, only to find out he had walked out less than twenty-four hours after arriving! Are you serious, he did not even give it twenty-four hours? The counselor said, "No ma'am, I really thought he was going to be one of the ones who made it through. He talked the good talk in my office."

I went looking for him, but no one knew where he was. I was searching the streets for several days trying to find him, no luck. I didn't even know who his friends were to be able go over to check to see if he was there or if they knew anything. I just started stopping people walking down the street he was living on to see if they knew him. Luckily one guy said, "Yea, that's Biffy, I know him. He's over so and so's house, over on such and such a street. I can call over there for you."

"Yes, PLEASE do tell him his mother is looking for him, I need him to call me as soon as possible. Thank you so much."

He calls me several hours later only to apologize for walking out and said, "They were just so damn strict." Please, in less than twenty-four hours you came to that conclusion? No, you just don't want the help. He ends up getting arrested that evening, and goes to jail. I find out his court date, attend, and the judge gives him five days. The judge asks him if anyone is in the court room with him.

He said, "Yes, I see my mother."

The judge asks me if I would like to say anything; of course I said yes. He tells me to come up and take a seat on the witness stand so I did. I began to cry, beg, and plead with my son, telling him he has a problem; he needs help badly! He rolls his eyes. I say I'm sorry and that I see him rolling his eyes. I say he knows he has a drug problem and seriously needs help; how he went to rehab, left less than twenty-four hours later only to go back out and get arrested again for the very same thing! I ask what is it going to take to get him to wake up? I ask him how many times he's OD'd and how long is he going to allow Satan to have this control over his life? Well, he would not talk to me. Even when he got out of jail, he didn't talk to me.

Then he was homeless, living in an old camper my ex had. It was the dead of winter, he had no heat, no nothing. I went over to see him, and it ripped my heart out. I began to run over there every chance I could to take him hot meals, hot coffee, begging him, pleading that he go to rehab. Nope, he wasn't doing it, no matter how many tears I shed. The drugs turned my loving, sweet, baby boy into something I've never seen. It wasn't long before my ex tore that camper apart to try get him to leave to go into rehab.

That did not work because now he had chosen to live in a dog house! Are you freaking serious? You are allowing drugs to have this hold on you so that you now live in a dog house? WHYYYYYYYYYY? I don't know how someone could allow something to have this much control, but of course I didn't understand how bad addiction really is. How hard it was to shake it, get clean, and stay clean. On and on — he ended up getting another charge for possession of an illegal substance. I found out his court date and had several people in my family write letters to the judge requesting he place Chris in a court-ordered drug rehab to get the help he so desperately needed.

I get to court, and hand in the letters as court started. They finally get to my son's case and the judge asks again if he has someone with him in the courtroom. He said, "Yes, I see my mother and grandmother."

The judge asks me to stand, asks me if I have anything I would like to say to the court. I answered, "Yes," and he told me to come take a seat in the witness stand, so I did. I began talking. It wasn't long before the tears start pouring down. I asked the judge if he could possibly help us in getting him into a court-ordered rehab facility. I said jail time is not going to help him, he will not get the help he needs. Even Chris pleaded with the judge to help him get into rehab, but it didn't do any good. The judge refused to help him. Instead he gave him nine months in Duval work release.

For two months, I picked him up every day and took him to look for a job. When he found one, I took him to work, until one day he was busted buying a cigarette, which was considered contraband in there. They could smoke, but cigarettes were not allowed in their facility. So, that meant he was shipped to Marion County jail to finish his sentence. As soon as they got me set up for visitations, I visited him every week until he was released. Oh, how I wish I could even have those days back now. Our visits were monitored, but at least I was getting to see him, he was doing so good. My six foot, four inch beanpole was now gaining weight for the first time in his entire life. He was working in their kitchen, so he was getting to eat a lot of meals. His release date was September 2, 2018; that was the best night, when I saw my baby boy walk out the jail doors.

Little did I know my time with my son was extremely limited now. I got two good days with him, then I became ill. I myself am on pain meds for a chronic pain disorder and I had run out of my morphine. Unfortunately, my doctor had called them into the wrong pharmacy before he had to have surgery, himself. This pharmacy wanted six times the amount I normally pay. We are on Social Security with no prescription insurance, so I could not afford to pay that amount. So, here is his mother going through withdrawals. It was the worst six days of my life or so I thought then. I was deathly sick. I could not take it anymore. I caved in, borrowed the money, and got the medication I needed. The only thing my son wanted was a homecoming dinner, a cookout with the family. He wanted some of Momma's famous BBQ ribs. I go to the store, grab everything; I am planning on having this cookout. I invite the family over for it, but it poured down rain for the next several days. Chris ended up leaving on September 12, saying he wanted to go for a walk, get some fresh air. He took a bus downtown to a place he had stayed before. It was a group of guys who were recovering addicts. They help recovering addicts find jobs, give them a place to stay, help them with so many things.

My son was now nine months clean and sober. My husband dropped him off at the bus stop. While he was waiting on the bus, one of Satan's demons rode by on her bike. What I heard was that she was an old girlfriend and she had invited him over to sit, talk, chill, and have a bonfire. He told me this when he called me at 8:15 p.m. that evening, saying, "Mom she is talking about God, quoting scriptures out of the Bible. She knows all the words to songs on K-Love. I just want to hang out with her as I haven't been around anyone but inmates for nine months, besides you and Pops. I will be ok, don't worry about me, Mom. I'll be back first thing in the morning to go to work with Pops. You can even drug test me too if you want to!"

I said, "Oh, trust me, I will because you sound funny now, Chris."

He said, "Oh we just had a couple beers that's all."

I said, "Nope not buying it, you don't sound like you do when you're drinking, this is totally different, Bud."

"I promise Mom, it's just beer."

"Ok, I will see you in the morning, I love you so much Bud."

"I love you, Mom."

The next day; it's now 2:30 p.m. I went into the kitchen and told my husband I was worried.

"I haven't heard from Chris, heck I don't know where he's at, who he's with, who he hung out with before, nothing. How do I know he's not dead?"

WHY on earth did this even cross my mind? I no more than get those words out before I get a call. I usually don't answer unknown numbers, but this one I did. There was a gentleman on the other end asking me if I was the mother of Christopher.

I say, "Yes," and he tells me he is the chaplain at a hospital and that my son is in his ER. He's very sick and I need to come. He says he got my number from his old records. I ask what he means by sick but he says he can't go into details over the phone. I asked him if Chris is high and he says I really need to get to the hospital as soon as possible.

I head to the hospital. I start making calls telling others in the family where I am going and what's going on. I arrived at the hospital, told them who I was, who my son is, and that the chaplain called me. They tell me to have a seat, that the chaplain would be with me shortly. I don't know, it could have been five minutes or fifteen, but it felt like several hours, until the chaplain came over and asked me to follow him. He takes me to this room and begins to tell me just how sick my son is. They've been working on him since picking him up at the scene. His heart keeps stopping!! I am screaming, crying, I can't stop. He asks me if there someone I can call to come be with me. I ask him to call my husband. When my husband arrives, we are taken upstairs and told to wait in the waiting room. Eventually they come out to get us, saying two people were allowed to go back. I said I know I am going back and feel since his dad is here, he needs to go back as well. We can take turns.

Mamas, I was NOT prepared to see what I witnessed. My son was hooked up to every machine there was; so many different bags of stuff running in him. I totally lost it! I stayed, I was not leaving his side so others came in and out. Later they told us we all had to leave for an hour. Everyone else left for the night. I came home, showered, packed a bag; I was not leaving that hospital for anything. Those hours were the longest ever! It was a roller coaster all night long. He would do so good, then bad. Then it happened; his heart stopped beating! They asked me to leave the room. I said no way in hell am I leaving, you cannot make me. I am not sitting in the waiting room forever waiting for you guys to come back out and me not knowing what's going on! Besides, if my son doesn't make it, I want him to know Momma was there with him, he was not alone! So, they ended up getting him stabilized. They talked to me about sending him over to another hospital to be placed on this new life support that will allow his body to heal and do all the work for him. I agreed, let's do this, I want my son.

Lifeline picked him up, I met them at the hospital only for the doctor to come back out an hour later to tell us he does not see any hope for my son. His kidneys and liver shut down. He ran a brain scan. You could not even see the lobes, as his brain was so badly swollen. It was only a matter of time before his brain stem would close and his brain would basically burst. He said, however, I could keep him on life support; he could live that way, but become a vegetable. He said we only had a matter of time to decide, so we called the rest of the family to the hospital and had a meeting. One of my sons tells me not to be selfish and keep him here because I can't let go; it's not fair to him. So, needless to say I could NOT take it if I allowed him to be in more pain. So, we decided to let him go.

They gave us some time with him to say our good-byes, then they called the chaplain in to pray with all of us. During this time when he was praying, my son's heart rate was up over 100. Then it came time for them to remove everything. I could NOT do it. How could I tell someone to remove everything, let my son die? My daughter told the nurse to do it as she was holding me, sobbing herself. I could NOT bare to watch. Just as they removed everything, my daughter told me later that I grabbed ahold of him and held him so tight, telling him how much I loved him. I played the song, *Dancing in the Sky*. I began to hear the death rattle. I started screaming at them, telling them to stop, do something, stop letting him drown in his fluids, how cruel are you people. Then we noticed my son had a tear roll down his face. He did NOT want to die; he wanted to live, but Satan had such a horrible hold on him with the drugs.

But let me end with this Mama's PLEASE, even if you feel like you can't handle anymore with your addict child, I am begging you please don't turn your back on them. Everyone turned their back on my Chris and I was the ONLY one he had left in life!

After he passed away, I found a small note in his stuff that he had written to me when he was in jail. It said, "I'm sorry," at the top in big letters. Then it said:

"Dear Mother,

I'm sorry for not understanding the sacrifices you gave. I was more of an enemy who only misbehaved it was nothing you done that made me this way. It was my own faulty actions that more than paved this way so when I say that I'm sorry that I really want to say is I love you so much. And I can finally say I've opened my eyes cause your love made way to a broken heart that was lost with no way. I love you.

Chris."

Chris' Mom,

Sheryl B.
Indianapolis, Indiana

> *"Why?" A mother asked God.*
> *"Why have you closed his eyes?"*
> *God replied, "So he could see a million miles."*

Dominic

FOREVER 24

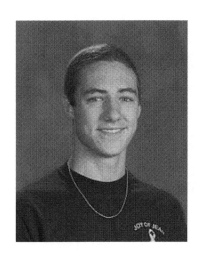

My beautiful Dominic was my youngest child and the only child of my ex-husband. He was born on November 25, 1994, in Toledo, Ohio. He had bright blue eyes and a smile that touched everyone's soul.

A moment I never spoke about until after I lost him occurred when he was an infant. I was looking at him in my arms after I finished feeding him. A voice in my head said that I would not have him for very long. I know now that was God trying to prepare me. I felt like a horrible mother; how could I have this thought about my own perfect baby? When Dominic was six years old, he got an infection in his brain stem while he had the chicken pox. He was pretty much in a vegetative state for weeks. He could no longer talk, eat, or move his body. I watched him in his hospital bed with tears streaming down his voiceless face. Thankfully, after too many spinal taps and so many tests, they found a medication that helped heal him. I told myself this is what God was trying to prepare me for that day when he was an infant, and my baby beat death. Dominic's father and I divorced when he was two. I was a single mom with three children.

My son and I talked about what may have led him to using substances resulting in his addiction. I believe the pain inside of him he was trying to escape started when he was about eight years old. He said that the counselors he worked with also think it went back to this same trauma. He would always tell me that no one made him take the path he took, and he didn't like talking to people, even if it meant healing for him. Dominic was in the middle of a long custody battle between me and his father after I attempted suicide while he was at his dad's one weekend. While I was getting help, his dad filed for custody on an emergency basis, which was granted. Dominic's stepmother was addicted to cocaine and used the money to care for him to support her habit. He was dressed in ripped, dirty clothes and denied the same basics his stepbrother had.

I fought for many years to get him home. This meant that Dominic had to meet with attorneys and be in the painful position of choosing between parents that he loved. I think this killed him inside. He did come home for good when he was twelve. He was introduced to marijuana first in junior high. Dominic had his heart set on going to a private Catholic high school. I worked multiple jobs to make this dream come true for him. He told me this is where his drug use really increased. Some of the students had an almost unlimited access to money from their parents and he was introduced to different drugs. Dominic loved playing basketball, football, hockey, and golf. He was on a swim team for years and eventually worked as a lifeguard for the city pools. He played CYO basketball and football for many years. He finished his senior year at the local high school because he was close to failing at the Catholic high school.

He complained about being sick a lot of the time. I took him to so many doctors and specialists. I did not know that his sickness was due to drug use. My heart ached seeing him so sick, being angry at the doctors who said they did not know what was wrong with him. I felt so helpless. I started noticing small amounts of cash come up missing, which I thought was me not remembering where I left it. Once or twice, my prescription of Klonopin was missing, and Dominic would offer to help me look for it. In 2013, one of the vascular specialists said that he would need major surgery to repair damage to his intestine. He was on high amounts of morphine and other pain medication for a long time in the ICU. A week or two after he came home, Dominic was extremely sick and throwing up non-stop. I was afraid he had internal bleeding from the surgery and took him to get help. He was having extreme withdrawals from all the medications he was given. I believe this intensified his need for drugs.

Most of the time, Dominic was able to hide his addiction. He loved to spend time with his nephews. They loved to get rides on his shoulders, horseback rides, and wrestle on the floor. His blue eyes sparkled when he was with them. Dominic was an extremely hard worker and loved to help people, especially his momma bear. When we were in the car together, he would roll the window down and hand cigarettes, food and/or money to people he saw that were homeless. The last couple years of his life had grown into a constant struggle and addiction that had a strong grip on him, one he would never break free from, unfortunately. The instances of money being withdrawn from my checking account increased. His father also had the same thing happen. Dominic would deny taking any money. His hygiene got worse and worse. Eventually, he started having episodes of nodding off mid-sentence. When I would ask him what was going on, he would say he was only tired. A couple of times, his legs gave out and he could not walk, so I called 911 and he was hospitalized. It was his body breaking down due to drug use. He would still deny using anything and because he was now over eighteen, no one would let me know if anything showed up in his system.

The first time I know of him overdosing, he came home, went to his room, and collapsed behind the door. My daughter and I worked together to pry the door open. He was laying up against the door unresponsive. She called 911 while I cried, screamed, and tried putting water on his face, desperately trying to wake him. After they revived him, he calmly denied using anything stronger than marijuana. I often slept on the floor in front of the apartment door so I would know if he tried to sneak out. He would not go to counseling or speak to anyone about his drug use. He told me I was crazy so many times, I started doubting myself. I knew if he did not get help, I would lose him. I followed him around, trying to catch him using. I went through his belongings constantly, hoping to find evidence I could confront him with, and then he couldn't deny it any longer. We had a few incidents with our cars. I am so thankful that the accidents he got into never resulted in anyone getting injured; that was all God!

I had to make the very painful decision to throw him out twice. Both times, he went to live with his father who I believe was in denial for years. Dominic eventually got into trouble with the law. He stole checks from his girlfriend's mom to get cash. He was so deeply into using at that time, I asked them to please file charges on him. I knew if he stayed out on the streets, he would die. He was charged with theft and spent time in jail. The nights he was in jail were some of the first times I had slept through the night in many months. It is something I could never imagine saying. At his hearing, the officer I contacted told the judge there was room for Dominic at a nearby center and he was moved there that day. This would be his first time receiving treatment and he did well for about four months. I was so hopeful and proud of him. He was proud of himself too.

One day, I got a call from them saying my son was in custody for using drugs and violating probation. When I got to talk to him, he said the new roommate he had was using in their room and he started using with him. From then on, he spent so much time in and out of either jail or the correctional treatment facility. I spoke to him on the phone almost every day and visited him once a week. When he was incarcerated, he put weight back on and looked like my beautiful boy again. He tried other treatment centers and sober living residences, but he started using again after a noticeably short time.

My oldest son and my daughter went through so much watching the slow progression of drugs on their brother and what it was doing to me. For a long time, I tried fighting this on my own, underestimating the depth of its hold on him. They both tried to talk to me about how afraid they were that their brother would die and begged me to do something. I had not been around this before, I did not recognize the early signs of what was really going on, and I didn't know how to handle it. Dominic was always a really loving person. He and his sister were close, but he did not want to talk to her about drugs. They would cuddle on the couch and watch movies or play video games together. They talked, laughed, and just loved being together. Dominic always wanted a closer relationship with his older brother and struggled to keep him from seeing his addiction. He loved to climb on his big brother's lap and mess with him, even into his twenties. His cousins Jamie and Leila brought out the glow in his eyes while he embraced them in one of his big bear hugs.

For years, it was just Dominic and me. During his addiction, I told him often that I loved him from the very depths of my soul and would not be able to live without him. He told me, "Don't worry, Momma Bear, that won't happen." When he would get down on himself, I told him I hoped one day he would see all the beauty I saw in him every day. When I would ask him if he was high, he would say, "Can't you just love me, Momma?" Then he would put his head on my lap or on my shoulder. I often replied I knew for sure that I loved him so much more than he loved himself. When I told him how worried I was through all of this, I never heard him say that he was done and never wanted to use again; he always said he was going to show me instead of telling me.

Dominic was my best friend, the person who I talked to daily, laughed and cried with. Even in his darkest days, he met me at the car and carried all the groceries in the house, fixed things when they broke, and always just wanted to be with me. He was proud of being a momma's boy. In March of 2019, he asked me to drop him off at his probation officer's. The next call I got was the all too familiar collect call from an inmate at the county jail. He had violated his probation and was being sent back to the correctional treatment center. We still talked on the phone during this time, but he called me less than he had before. I went to see him once a week, but he didn't talk as much during our visits. He always wanted to see me, but I was worried. It felt like this time he was giving up.

His father and I picked him up on July 31. He looked so healthy and went home with his father to live. I had been doing events with a local support group for addiction and Dominic wanted to start going out in the community with me. I could tell that he was using some kind of substance again shortly after his release, but he denied it. It felt like we were back doing this old familiar dance again. A few days before he died, he called me and said he was walking over to see his brother and spend time with his nephews. He sounded happy, said he loved me and would see me after work. My oldest son called and said Dominic was so high that he kept falling and was displaying behaviors we had not seen before. He got him into the car and took him to his dad's. Dominic's dad had him call me when I got off work. The last words I said to my son on the phone were, "I don't want to speak to you right now, put your father on the phone."

I never got to speak to him again. I sent him a text two days later letting him know I got the job promotion he told me he knew I would end up getting, but no reply. On Tuesday, September 3, 2019, I got a call from the hospital that my ex-husband drove himself to have surgery and they would not let him drive home. I tried to call and text Dominic, but he never answered. After work, I picked his dad up from the hospital and drove him home. As we sat in the parking lot, I told his dad I ran Dominic's court record and saw that he had tested positive for drugs. I remember watching the curtain in their living room blow in the wind knowing Dominic was inside. His dad was not aware of the positive drug test but was going to talk to him about it when he got into the apartment. Around eight p.m. that night, I got a call from my ex-husband. He told me that Dominic was gone. He found him lying dead on the floor in the apartment after I dropped him off, and he had prob-ably been gone for hours. He tried to revive him and called for help, but it was too late.

If I had the opportunity, I would do so many things differently, starting with my suicide attempt that I believe set all of this in motion. My poor beautiful son was hurting so much inside from a very young age. I asked him if he wanted me to stop fighting for custody of him so he could stay with his dad, but he always said no, he just wanted to come home. He just wanted to be home with me and his siblings. Now, I must figure out how to live the rest of my life without him. Dominic was so much more than his addiction. He was loving, generous, and beauti-ful. When his struggling and pain stopped that day, mine would lead me down this lonely road that all of us who love them fear. Every day, I try to see the beauty in my family and the world around me. But I also know I am one more day closer to holding my baby boy again, this time forever.

Dominic's Mom,

CATHY B.
Toledo, Ohio

> *"We are afflicted in every way,*
> *but not crushed; perplexed, not driven to despair;*
> *persecuted, but not forsaken; struck down, but not destroyed."*
> *2 Corinthians 4:8*

Shawn & Jessica

FOREVER 22 & 26

 My story is a story of the most devastating loss.....twice. My two beautiful children were taken by the disease of addiction. Shawn is my middle child and Jessica is my youngest and only girl. Growing up in Paramus, NJ, they were always close. Shawn was born on April 8,1990 and was a charmer from the start. He was such a love and was always funny, witty, and charismatic. We nicknamed him "Ferris Bueller" because like the character in the movie, the whole town knew and loved him.

Shawn was a natural athlete. He was a talented baseball pitcher and held the strikeout record. He loved doing tricks and stunts while skateboarding and bike riding, professional wrestling and anything that required him to be a daredevil. Shawn was always naturally smart in school. Shawn began lifting weights when he was 21. When he hurt his back, he was prescribed Oxycodone over and over by a doctor. He immediately became addicted.

When the doctor saw that there was a problem, he stopped the prescriptions and turned my addicted son out on the streets. My once carefree, loving son became angry and withdrawn. He found heroin to satisfy his withdrawals. It was cheap and so easy to get. Shawn sold his TV, our laptops and anything else he could find to pay for the drugs. We sent him to an inpatient rehab for six weeks and I got my lovable, happy Shawn back. He was only home for three days when his brother, my son Nicky found him unresponsive in our house on September 30, 2012. It was the day before Nicky's 24th birthday. Our Shawn was gone. He was twenty-two years old.

Jessica was born on July 3, 1992. I got my girl and she was the love of my life from day one. Oh, how we loved her birthday because it was always a celebration! Jessica was known for always having the longest hair. I cried when she got her first trim when she was ten years old!

Jessica was also a natural athlete. She was a talented gymnast and head cheerleader. You could always find her doing triple flips and handstands wherever we went. We travelled to different states to support her in all her show-cases. My Jessica had the biggest heart. She was always the one who would jump to help anyone. She and I were inseparable. We always sang "You Are My Sunshine" to each other.

Everywhere we went she would always hold my hand and always called me "mommy" or "mama". Jessica was twenty when we lost our Shawn and because of the tremendous loss of the brother she adored, she suffered from PTSD, anxiety, and depression. She was so sad all the time. Her therapy sessions were twice a week and even with prescribed antidepressants, Jessica began self-medicating. She started snorting heroin. For the next six years, I literally lived and breathed to help her. My beautiful girl was disappearing before me.

It's so heartbreaking to look into your child's eyes and see the most unbearable pain. She cried how badly she wanted to stop but at the same time the drug use hardened her. Jess was in several inpatient rehabs and after everyone, I tried to show her new beginnings and how amazing her life could be. She had a beautiful loft apartment and a new Jeep, but the addiction always pulled her back. Jess got a DUI, had her license revoked and moved out of her apartment. After she came home from a six-week rehab in Laguna Beach, California, one of her closest friends overdosed and died. Jessica relapsed. She snuck out on the night of September 8, 2018 and was sold fentanyl. I woke up to find her and the Jeep missing. We searched tirelessly for her. The police found her two days later in the Jeep right where she was sold the fentanyl that poisoned her. Jessica was 26 years old.

Despite evidence on her phone, my beautiful Jessica never got any justice. Her murderer was never even questioned. My two beautiful children with the most beautiful souls are gone. Their lives have been stolen from them. There will be no loves of their lives, no weddings, and no children. Addiction destroys the entire family and then returns to bury them.

Shawn and Jessica's Mom,

LAURA C.
Paramus, New Jersey

Hannah

FOREVER 20

Hannah Renee was born January 22, 1996, in Corydon, Indiana. She always loved the outdoors and animals. As a child, she wanted to be a veterinarian, but that changed as she got older and she decided she wanted to become a nurse, like her mother. She was an excellent student in school, always on the honor roll every year. She had planned out her entire high school schedule when she was in seventh grade. Her goal was to be third in her class, because then she would not have to give a speech at graduation. She knew exactly what classes she was taking each year, up to graduation. But those plans changed.

By the time Hannah's senior year came, she had become a different person; one we really didn't know. She missed most of her senior year because she "didn't feel like going," in her words. But she still managed to graduate with a cum laude medal around her neck. She missed graduating with honors by one class because she decided not to take it her senior year. She only had two classes to take that year. She was eighteen, what could we do?

Hannah started working at the age of fifteen and worked throughout her high school years and then worked full time after graduation. She loved what she did, working in a nursing home as a CNA. She rarely missed work and would go in extra to help out. She helped with activities during special occasions because she loved her job and her residents.

Hannah sounds pretty normal, but she had one thing that most don't have, and that was an addiction to heroin. She was what they call, "a functioning addict." She went to school, held down a job; she had to, to support her and her boyfriend's addiction. He was not able to work and be an addict at the same time, so it became her job to support both of their habits.

Hannah's addiction caused her to lose many friends. Addicts have a very tight social circle because they don't want everyone to know about their addiction. She closed herself off from friends and family, from the ones who cared the most about her. But she didn't see it as love and caring, she saw it as trying to control her life, trying to tell her what to do. She knew we would be disappointed, so she didn't want us to know. What an addict doesn't know is that, yes, we will be disappointed, but all we want for them is to be alive and sober.

As a parent, I felt shame at first. I thought we had raised her to be a better person. She had always made the right decisions, but now she wasn't, so we must have done something wrong. But what was it? Did we give her too much? She was the spoiled one, our baby. Did we not do enough for her; did we work too much; not spend enough time with her? Did she feel loved? All of these things run through a parent's mind when they find out their child is an addict. But the truth is, we do love them as much as we possibly can. We can't be with them at all times and everyone makes mistakes, right? Isn't that what they say? The problem with this mistake is that she paid for it with her life.

Hannah first OD'd in May of 2014, ten days before she graduated from high school. This first time we didn't know about, because she was eighteen and the hospital did not have to call us. The next time she OD'd was in January of 2015. We probably wouldn't have known about this time either, but Hannah and I worked at the same place. When the

ER doctor called in for her, they called me because I happened to be the one on call, so I was expected to go into work. I first had to go to the hospital to check on her, then go to work, and work all night while worrying about her at the same time. This is when we realized she had a problem. And to think she was going to go to work and take care of residents after using heroin.

We started Hannah in counseling, but she didn't like it and stopped. Our problem was that she was eighteen and we couldn't force her to do anything. She would agree that she had a problem, but wasn't willing to do the right things to help her stop.

Hannah tried several times to kick her habit herself, but it never lasted more than a few weeks. The problem is that it's not the drug they crave so much anymore, it's the sick feeling they get if they don't have it that they are trying to get away from. She would tell us that she felt like she was going to die without it. That's how sick it makes you feel. The withdrawal feeling is worse than taking the drug could ever make her feel. She knew that it could kill her, but without it, they want to die. She always said that she was careful and nothing was going to happen to her.

Hannah also spent her time in jail. In 2015, she spent three days a week, for ten weeks, in jail in Louisville, Kentucky. They had allowed her a work release. We thought this might actually help her because she said it was the scariest place she had ever been. But we found out since then that she had been scared before. We heard from friends that she had been chased down the streets of Louisville by a dealer that she and her boyfriend had tried to cheat. He chased them with a gun and he probably would have shot them if he had caught up with them. Somehow, they were lucky and he didn't.

When Hannah's grandmother passed away on March 29, 2016, Hannah took it hard, but we didn't realize how hard. The first day of visitation at the funeral home, Hannah didn't show up and we didn't hear from her. I was so mad at her for not caring enough to even show up. As we were leaving the funeral home, I checked my phone which had been on silent, and I had missed calls from Hannah's boyfriend. As I was getting ready to call him, he called me. Hannah had OD'd again and was at the hospital.

When we got to the hospital, we learned she was alert, but had hit her head and had stitches. They were going to release her, but my husband and I decided that the best place for her was in jail, where we would know that she was safe. We made a few calls and were able to get her arrested at the hospital. I will never forget the person that I saw when she learned that she was going to jail. She cussed at me, yelling and screaming, in the middle of the ER. I was heartbroken that my daughter could talk to me like this; this was not the daughter that I knew. As parents we knew that we were doing what was best for her at this time, but having her arrested would mean that she would miss her grandmother's funeral the next day. As I watched them handcuff her and put her in the back of the police car, I thought to myself, how can it get any worse? But it can and it did.

Hannah stayed in jail for sixty-two days, until we believed that she could do it this time. She could stay clean, that's what she kept telling us and we wanted to believe her. We bailed her out on June 1, 2016. We believed what she told us; that this time would be different; she could do it. She was so happy to be home and we were so happy to have her home. The next few days we just spent time together. We went shopping and out to eat. We celebrated her best friend's birthday, the one friend that was clean or so we thought. We didn't let her out of our sight. After the eighth day, we awoke to realize that she had left during the night and when she returned, she wouldn't tell us where she had been.

On June 10, 2016, Hannah and I spent all day texting back and forth to each other about recovery places. I would find one and tell her to look it up, but she always had a reason that it wasn't the right place for her. I thought we were having a good day, but what I didn't know was that she was also texting her old buddies, trying to find a hit. I came home from work and she asked if she could go to her best friend's house for just a little while. I thought it would be good for her to have someone else to talk to. She told me that she loved me and I said the same as she was leaving the house at 4:00 p.m. At 4:54 p.m., I received a call from her friend who was crying uncontrollably and I couldn't understand her, but I knew that something was wrong with Hannah. I hung up and jumped in my car and went to her house, which was just about three miles away.

When I arrived, there were so many police and an EMS ambulance in the driveway that I had to park by the road and run to the trailer.

They were bringing Hannah out on a stretcher and doing CPR on her. She was pale and had vomit all over her. As a nurse, I knew it was bad. They wouldn't let me ride with her, so I jumped in my car and went to our house and picked up my husband and we went to the hospital. When the ambulance arrived, they were still working on her. She was placed on a ventilator because she was unable to breath on her own. After what seemed like an eternity, we were allowed back to see her. It's hard to see your child with so many different tubes coming from every-where. She wasn't responding to anything, so they wanted to send her to another hospital in Louisville, Kentucky, for further testing. They told us to go ahead because the ambulance would be traveling fast and we wouldn't be able to keep up.

We left the hospital and ran home to get a few things because we knew it was going to be a long night. When we got to the hospital, Hannah wasn't in her room and the hospital didn't know anything. We waited and we waited. Finally, here they come with her. The EMT explained to us that as they were pulling out of the parking lot her heart had stopped beating again and they had to take her back in and revive her. During the next four hours, her heart stopped two more times. They had already talked to us about the damage to her brain being caused by the lack of oxygen. They didn't think that she would come out of this and that she would be in a vegetative state for the rest of her life. My husband and I had to make the hardest decision we had ever made in our lives and that was, if her heart stopped again, no CPR would be performed. We would let her go. The machine kept her going through the night and we never left her side.

In the morning, we asked for Hannah to be checked again for any signs of a change in her condition. We hoped that a miracle would happen and she would pull out of this. She had all kinds of doctors looking at her at various times, so we knew she was getting the best care possible, but that didn't matter. The doctor came in that afternoon and told us that there was no change; that it was with 99% certainty she was in a vegetative state which would never change; she would never wake up. So, once again we were faced with yet the hardest decision of our lives. Do we continue like this or do we turn her ventilator off and let her go in peace? We talked and prayed and made the decision to turn the machine off. She would not want to continue this way and we couldn't be selfish and keep her with us. She was never really ever coming back to us. So, on June 11, 2016, at 4:18 p.m., she took her last breath, with her family by her side. Approximately twenty-four hours from when she had taken her last hit of hell.

What we have found out, since Hannah's death, is that her best friend was using and she is the one who had given her the drugs. They had shared the same drug, but Hannah didn't make it. She never woke up. One of the last texts from her friend before she picked Hannah up was "I don't want you to die," referring to her finding it on her own. How ironic that this is one of the last things that she said to Hannah and it became a reality in her own home. Something she and her boyfriend will have to live with for the rest of their lives. They did try to give her CPR until the ambulance got there, but it didn't make a difference. They couldn't revive her. It was too late.

What we have been through, since Hannah's death, has been hard on all of us. We had to go home without our daughter. She would never walk through that door again and say, "Hi Mom." There was a funeral to plan, decisions to be made, what she would wear for the last time, what jewelry to put on her—because you want to keep everything that was hers, but you want her to leave this earth with the things that also meant the most to her. What music to play? Who would be pallbearers? So many things to think about in just a short amount of time.

Something that all of you must know is that Narcan does not always save your life. It is capable of bringing you back to life, but don't count on it. It had saved Hannah twice before, but this time it didn't. It was too late; she had been without oxygen to her brain for too long. So, don't think that there is a "safety net" out there for you, because it has to be used quickly or it won't work.

You also have to ask yourself, "Do the people I am with know how to use it? Will they be able to use it on me or will they panic and leave me to die because they are scared of the consequences?"

The circle of life is not for parents to bury their children. Parents are supposed to go before their children. Holidays and birthdays are now spent visiting the cemetery. Everything reminds us of her and we laugh or cry and sometimes both.

This is Hannah's story; don't let it be your story also. The only way you are going to survive this drug is to never use it. There are people who survive, but they are the lucky ones. It's not going to be that way for everyone. It only takes one time to die from using these drugs, and that is what happens to most of them. Please don't let it happen to you.

Hannah's Mom,

BARB C.
Corydon, Indiana

Forrest Jerry

FOREVER 25

My baby boy Forrest aka Jerry was born in August 1991, in Elkins Park, Pennsylvania. He was my first born. He was the third to be named Forrest in the family, and enormously proud of his name. Jerry was such a joyful, happy little boy. When his little sister was born two years later, he could not stop hugging and kissing her. They automatically brake best friends and were inseparable. He was such a lovable sweetheart. They always had a lot of fun on our block. Good memories in our first home.

My husband and I decided to move out into the pinelands to a bigger house, because there was more room and had the best schools for our children. We thought it would be a great life for the kids growing up. They both met lots of friends and they all loved to go riding on their quads. It was that kind of town. He also did well in school, played all the sports. Jerry was growing up as a kind young man. In high school, he was also into body building with a good friend of his. I think this is when the drugs started. He and his friend began with steroids.

Jerry ended up in a fight one night and dislocated his shoulder. That is all it took for it to keep popping out in any kind of incident. He ended up needing surgery. In the meantime, he was hanging with a couple other guys and spending some weekends at their house. At that time, I never noticed anything different about him. When it was time for his shoulder surgery, I stayed with him in the hospital. He was begging for more pain meds and acting agitated and aggressive. That is when I found out he was using heroin because he said he was going to leave the hospital bed and go get some off the street. That is when it all began. That night he came home, and we realized the next morning that he had shot up most of his pain meds. When we found the rest and would not give him anymore, he got overly aggressive. I was so scared of how he was acting; he was not in his right state of mind. I called 911 and that was his first time spent in jail.

So much has happened and it is hard to put everything in the exact timeline, but I will tell you that from that beginning, our lives were turned upside down and in hell, worrying and watching every move, trying everything we could to save our baby boy for approximately seven years until Jerry's passing at the age of twenty-five. Now it is a worse hell from losing the beautiful soul of our baby boy. Through those years it was rehab after rehab. It was from one jail to another. It was everything stolen from personal to anything that was not nailed down. I called a crisis center on him at least twice because he wanted to end it all; he hated me for that, of course, but when he sobered up, he knew why I did those things. He hated his life and what he became. He tried so many times and would do wonderful in rehab. The counselors would always tell me what a sweet, kind kid he was. But the devil would always reappear and show his face.

My son and I would have many heart-to-heart talks. I always kept it real with him and he did as well. Jerry would say to me, "Mom, you would be much better off without me ruining everyone's life."

Of course, I would tell him how much we all loved him and we would do anything to help, but that is always how he felt because he would feel defeated by that devil. I also put him in jail once, thinking I would know he would be off the streets and alive. It was horrible visiting my son in jail. One time he called me with a broken jaw; he had his friend call because he could not speak. That was horrific. Another time when he was in rehab I flew from New Jersey to Florida to find him on the streets after a counselor called and said he left. It was a lot of stopping our lives and dropping what we were doing to help him stay alive.

One morning Jerry proceeded to tell me that his friend OD'd in the passenger side of his car. My son woke up, but his friend did not. Jerry took him to the hospital, but it was too late. How devastating is that! You would think that would make you want to stop using, but no, he continued. We ended up calling 911 at least three times because of him overdosing in our house. Who knows how many times it happened elsewhere? It was a constant worry. When he would use the bathroom, that was just the worse, hearing him shut the door and worrying that he might be shooting up. We just never knew and prayed for him to come out. When he would leave the house, I would go through all his things. We would find needles, empty bags, rolled up cotton, spoons, empty water bottles, etc. He started losing jobs.

Jerry worked on and off for his father. He was exceptionally good at his job. Jerry knew the business would be handed down to him and his sister. He was a smart, good looking kid that could have accomplished it all. That still was not enough for him; he felt defenseless against the power of this drug. I would kick him out of the house until he would go back to rehab, then invite him to return home after. It was such an emotional and exhausting roller coaster ride, but I would NEVER EVER give up on him. He said to me once when he was sober, "Mom, I wouldn't be alive if it wasn't for you." Talk about having your heart ripped out in a million pieces time after time. But that was our life.

My husband and I, after twenty-five years of marriage, decided to divorce. It was not all the commotion with Jerry that caused our divorce, but it certainly did not help. We did not see eye-to-eye on some things regarding Jerry. So, we ended up selling everything including our house. I ended up moving to Florida to our condo in Pompano Beach. Everyone went their separate ways. Jerry ended up staying in New Jersey renting a room in a five-bedroom house. It was not even a couple of weeks later that I received that dreaded phone call. It was a Monday morning, and the three of us (my ex, my daughter, and I) knew Jerry had a court date.

We were all texting and calling him to make sure he was up and ready. My ex happened to be down here in Florida with me at the time. My daughter was the only one in New Jersey. We all had a horrible feeling. She drove to his house and saw his truck still there. She called one of the roommates for the combination to get in the house. My poor daughter had to go up to the third floor to find her best friend in the whole world hunched over his television set, stiff and the color blue. She called me frantically after she called 911. After we both calmed a little, I called my best friend who worked right around the corner to hurry and go be with my daughter, who was all alone. That is how that nightmare happened.

I am crying as I write this. It has been three years and it feels like yesterday; the pain and its void never go away! The grief comes and smacks you dead in the face when you are least expecting it. There is not a day that goes by that I do not think of Jerry and miss the hell out of him. No parent should ever have to bury their child. Yet this drug epidemic has not slowed down; it is disgusting! There is so much that has happened to our family and its dynamic during those seven or so years, but this is just a glimpse into the ugly and heart-shattering world of addiction!

Do not ever think for one moment that because of the neighborhood you move to, thinking it is a wonderful place to raise your children, that you're safe from this devil! Do not ever think, "Not my child!" Do not ever think because you are of a certain age, race, gender, or anything else for that matter that this devil cannot find you! He is  out there just looking and hooking more and more prey!! God Bless EVERYONE!

Jerry, I love you more than you will ever know!

Jerry's Mom,

Yvonne C.
Tabernacle, New Jersey

Chynna

My name is Angela Lawson and I am the Mother of an Angel.

My daughter, Chynna, was born in July 1991 in Cincinnati, Ohio. She was so incredibly beautiful at birth. Her color and complexion were the combination of milky white and pink. Her skin was so soft and delicate, like a China doll. And that is why we chose her name. From the time she took her first breath, she screamed independence and strong will. As a child, she never accepted the word "no," regardless of the situation. Her strong will and independence refused to let her quit anything she tried. She was like that until the day she died.

Chynna was a hippie through and through. By the time she hit adolescence, she loved the 60's, 70's, and 80's, and everything those decades were about. She loved all types of music, but the Grateful Dead was one of her favorite bands. Chynna loved collecting crystals and learning everything she could about them. She made jewelry in her free time, every chance she had. She was an avid reader, and anyone who knew her will say they never saw her without a book in her hands. She read books from every genre. Chynna was incredibly passionate about everything she did in her life! But unfortunately, that included meth and heroin.

We started noticing a change in her behavior when she was a freshman in high school. Her choice in boys and the company she kept were rapidly leading her to spiral downhill. Every time she got into trouble at school or during extracurricular activities, she was with the same people. None of them cared about the consequences of their actions or behavior, including Chynna. We found out she began binge drinking at the age of fourteen, because she had a seizure on the bus ride to school one morning caused from withdrawals. After that, she was hospitalized several more times during the course of her high school career, for alcohol poisoning and liver damage. By the time she was twenty years old, her liver damage was irreversible.

After realizing she was causing catastrophic damage to her liver, she white knuckled detox. But after several months of doing really well, she was introduced to a forty-three-year-old man that took complete control of every aspect of her life. He was controlling and abusive, physically, verbally, and emotionally. Chynna's self-worth was gone, and her interests in anything she loved faded away along with her self-worth. We racked our brains trying to figure out how she got to this rock bottom.

She admitted she never had a reason that she was consciously aware of that played a part in her addiction. She wasn't abused sexually, physically, mentally, or verbally growing up (that we are aware of) except for the abuse from her boyfriend. She was a well-rounded, happy child. She excelled academically, although she was very hard on herself when it came to grades. We just couldn't figure it out. Something had to be there in her subconscious. She was diagnosed with depression in high school. So, we knew that much.

By age 21, Chynna and her boyfriend were introduced to bath salts. Two years of abusing that caused her to drop out of college, lose her job, her apartment, and relationships that she had with family, as well as friends that she had known literally since preschool. She became homeless, had no income, and was living in her car. She cut all ties with me and her father, as well as her siblings. We found out she was using meth and how serious her addiction was after her boyfriend had a heart attack caused by both meth and bath salts. My husband and I felt so stupid and naive, after finding out how bad her addiction truly was. Bath salts eventually became too difficult to find on the streets. So, meth became her primary drug of choice.

After a few long months, day in and day out of hardcore meth use, she needed a way to pay for her habit. So, Chynna and her boyfriend robbed a church and the home of a church's deacon, taking anything and everything that wasn't nailed down, including the donation safe. They were both convicted of several misdemeanor and felony charges and sent to jail. Chynna's boyfriend went to the state penitentiary for five years, because of his prior history. Chynna's sentence was much, MUCH lighter because it was her first offense. And as sickening as this sounds, her father and I found a sense of relief knowing she was in jail. It was easier to breathe, and we didn't worry about her as much. She got clean in jail. It was awesome, and I could finally sleep. She was released from jail after serving several months of her sentence and placed on probation.

At the age of twenty-three, although clean, Chynna was now a convicted felon. She was doing really well once released from jail. But, seven and half months later she gave birth to a stillborn baby girl on the toilet, in the basement of her boyfriend's parent's home. She told no one she was pregnant and swore she didn't know herself. We never saw a baby bump; she was having regular periods and had no other signs or symptoms of pregnancy. Our granddaughter, Madalynn, was born an angel on April 4, 2014. Needless to say, that tragic incident was a major trigger and Chynna immediately relapsed. She couldn't get her hands on any meth at that time, so she started doing heroin.

By this time, I was constantly angry at her and her addiction so I started the "tough love" approach. It was the HARDEST thing I had to do thus far in her addiction. I struggled with sticking to my "bottom lines" every second of every damned day! My husband and I couldn't stay on the same page, so he kept sabotaging everything I did in regard to my tough love approach. He bought her cell phone after cell phone, snuck her cash when she asked for it, and told me I was throwing our child to the wolves.

When he finally realized his actions were helping her slowly kill herself, he jumped back on the wagon with me. He realized I wasn't throwing her to the wolves; that in all reality, she was calling the wolves to herself. We then did a family intervention. She was asked to go to a long-term rehab and continue on to a sober living facility. We begged her to go and told her that her choices were life and family or the streets, her addiction and ZERO help from us in any way, shape or form. She chose meth and heroin.

What most people don't understand about this disease (and it may sound really selfish) is that it's harder on the family of the addict than it is on the addict themselves. Even though they love their families and know it's hurting them on every level imaginable, addicts have only one worry: where and how will they get their next high. The need to avoid being dope sick is not a choice! Withdrawals can also kill an addict. While they worry about finding their next fix, parents and loved ones worry about where they are on a minute to minute basis. Are their bellies full? Do they have a place to lay their heads at night? Are they in jail, are they safe, are they being taken advantage of? Are they sick, hurt, or worse? Are they laying in the morgue waiting for their parents to identify their bodies? It is relentlessly looking at your phone for a missed call or text. But at the same time, every ping you hear from a text or every time the phone rings, your heart drops into the pit of your stomach and you don't want to look because it may be THE call every parent fears. So many layers....SO MANY LAYERS!!

Chynna was far into the grips of this monster by the age of twenty-three and she desperately needed help. Her father and I felt so sad and angry. Angry at ourselves for feeling like we failed her and so incredibly sad for Chynna. She just couldn't stop. It was killing her slowly. We tried so many times to help her. Two days before Thanksgiving in 2017, at the age of twenty-five, Chynna was rushed to the hospital. Her body was swollen from head to toe and she was struggling to breathe. We received a call from the ER and after speaking with several doctors, we were told she was in end stage, terminal congestive heart failure. She had blood clots in her lungs as well as fluid buildup in her lungs and around her heart, suffocating her heart and drowning her. We were told that Chynna had maybe a year to live, if she continued abusing her already fragile body. The meth alone had caused too much damage to her heart. But if she managed to get and stay clean, her prognosis would be a bit better.

She was twenty-five-years-old, but her mentality was that of a fifteen-year-old due to constant meth use. After several days in ICU and three weeks in a step-down unit, Chynna was released from the hospital with a cardiac vest and a cocktail of medications that she would have to take every day for the rest of her life. The vest had to be worn 24/7 (except when showering). She went into cardiac arrest three times and that vest saved her life every single time! We brought her home with us knowing she was too sick to be alone. After several weeks in our home, unbeknownst to us; she called a dealer to meet her at the corner of our subdivision. When she walked back into our home, she was so high we had to make her leave. There is no worse feeling than having to kick your very sick child out on the street. We not only had our sanity to maintain, but our youngest daughter and our two-year-old grandson were living here. We felt uneasy knowing a dealer knew where we lived and needed to protect our grandson as well as his mother and ourselves. Let me tell you this....having to choose between your children is extremely difficult!! And that is a gross understatement. Especially when one is so sick.

Once again, Chynna found someone on the streets to cling to. He gave her as much meth and heroin as she asked for and needed. She prostituted to make money for him. It was gut wrenching to know my beautiful, intelligent daughter was selling her body and living in an old truck with her new "boyfriend." It was cold and getting colder every day. The truck didn't run. They had no running water, no toilet, no heat....NOTHING. At one point, her new boyfriend was arrested at a Marathon gas station while trying to steal money from a customer as he exited the store. He had several prior drug-related offenses, a warrant, and violated his probation. So, he was sent to jail for the remainder of his sentence. Chynna found herself alone, again, and reached out to us asking to come home.

We agreed she could on the condition she let us find her a bed in detox and transfer to a six-month rehab program out of state. Unfortunately, by this time, Chynna's heart condition was deteriorating which made her a "liability." So, most facilities wouldn't accept her. And the ones that were equipped to help her were so expensive that we couldn't afford them. We were devastated. We couldn't afford to save our daughter's life and it broke our hearts. So, we tried to help her in other ways, as long as she did random drug tests and complied with her treatment plan for her CHF and other various drug-related illnesses. Knowing Chynna's history with taking off, we told her if she left, she couldn't come back.

Well, she did leave. And again, ended up in the ICU two weeks later. We found out about this hospital stay after we got a call from a young man we didn't know (and still don't know who he is to this day) saying Chynna was found unconscious in the bed of her truck and was taken to the hospital. What we found out had unfolded that evening was horrible!! It made me physically ill. Chynna owed a dealer money. So, he took her cardiac vest as collateral until she paid him. It was of no value to him otherwise, because it was specifically fitted for Chynna. He left, and she found some "friends" to use with.

After binging on meth and heroin with these friends, she passed out and they left her there. Her so-called friends left my daughter unconscious and unresponsive in the bed of her snow-filled truck. Swollen so badly she gained ninety pounds in fluid weight from CHF and had sores on her feet from injection sites that were infected, some infected clear to the muscle. The same friends made her give them a blow job in return for a sandwich. The same friends that knew she was on death's doorstep, but offered her meth and heroin anyway. It's not solely their fault; I'm angry at their addiction and the choices their addiction and disease forced them to make. I'm angry that my daughter's life wasn't important to any of them! Including Chynna herself.

After stabilizing Chynna as well as they could, she remained in the hospital for a week. She was offered hospice and palliative care upon discharge. She turned it down. For the third and last time we brought her home with us. Her meth psychosis was so bad she was beyond paranoid. She wore two pairs of binoculars twenty-four hours a day. She swore drones were following her and snipers were hiding around every corner of our home. She didn't sleep and sometimes she stood in a corner and stared at the wall for what seemed like eternity. It was the HARDEST thing to watch. Two weeks later, Chynna left our house for the last time. By this time, her ex-boyfriend had been released from prison.

On Saturday, February 9, she went to her aunt's home, called her ex-boyfriend, her daughter's father, to pick her up, and left with him. At 4:12 a.m. on Sunday, February 10, 2019, my husband woke me up telling me Chynna was gone. Both of us had missed the fifteen to twenty phone calls from other family members and the hospital. Why we were sleeping so soundly was beyond us, we never did when Chynna was actively using. We were always on edge. But not that night. We raced to the hospital, thinking they had the wrong Chynna, she was fine. She was just at the house. SHE WAS FINE!!

The walk from the car into the ER seemed like miles. There is NOTHING that can prepare a mother for what I saw next. My beautiful daughter, laying on a gurney, the open end of an intubation tube still in her mouth. Her eyes half open, blood had pooled to her backside already because she was gone for several hours by this time. Vomit still in her hair and caked in her ears. And her skin was cold and pale. I went to hold her and was told I couldn't touch her because she was a coroner's case. Screw that!!!! Nothing was keeping me from holding my child's hand or kissing her forehead one last time.

It is not natural for a mother to bury her child. It's just not the natural course of life. I am supposed to go before her. Chynna died of acute fentanyl and heroin poisoning at the age of twenty-seven. I'm pissed off! I'm angry my child's life was unfinished and snuffed away from her. I'm angry because for seven years, addiction stole my daughter's hopes and dreams. I'm angry because her life was more than her addiction. I'm angry we were robbed of a future with her! And I won't lie, I'm angry at her for robbing herself of a future with us! I'm angry that my daughter is reduced to ashes and is sitting in an urn in my family room! I'm angry that all I have left of my daughter's life on this earth are pictures. However, I am grateful for the pictures, as they are memories of her life. I am just angry at everything. I wouldn't wish this paralyzing and suffocating pain on my worst enemy.

If I could go back and change anything, I'd change the way I let myself get consumed with worry every second of every day for seven years. Which in turn caused me to neglect the needs of my other children. It sounds horrible when you have a sick child who needs you so badly, but it's the truth. I don't sugar coat my feelings about this disease and what it did to our family. The brutal truth is the only way to open closed minds! A lot of mothers would say they would change the way they handled their child's addiction in terms of enabling them. But I won't say that because enabling her was part of my learning process and

I did my best to help her. It's a double-edged sword; if you enable them you feel guilty, if you use tough love you feel guilty. There is no winning and the only positive side to addiction is the sobriety and long-term success in their sober life. And again, as selfish as this sounds, I'm angry I didn't put myself first sometimes. I'm angry I let her addiction turn me into a raging bitch. And I'm angry at myself because I judged addicts until my daughter became one. I'm angry I added to the stigma of this disease.

I AM ANGRY AT EVERYTHING THAT ADDICTION IS! And everything it does to not only the addict, but to the families of the addict!

To parents reading this...I don't care if you're a millionaire, middle class, or live paycheck to paycheck. Addiction doesn't discriminate! I had that "not my child" mentality and now my daughter is dead! We must end the stigma attached to this disease. It is vitally important to educate those who are ignorant to how addiction affects the chemistry of the brain.

Addiction is NOT A CHOICE! No one wants to be an addict. My daughter despised being an addict. She didn't wake up one morning and say, "I know what I want to do with my life, I want to be an addict!" No one chooses that life. Please educate yourselves on addiction and pay attention to any and all changes in your  child's normal behavior. It may save their life one day!

My name is Angela, and I am the mother of an Angel. Taken by the disease of addiction at the young age of twenty-seven! Thank you for reading our story. If it helps just one family avoid the pain of losing their loved one to addiction, that means Chynna's death, although tragic, had a purpose. An unfinished life.

Chynna's Mom,

Angela L.
Cincinnati, Ohio

Latasha

FOREVER 29

My daughter's name is Latasha May; she was twenty-nine-years old when she died August 28, 2018. She left behind a ten-year-old boy and an eight-year-old girl. She's in heaven now with her twins. She started using about two years before she died; she went down really quick. We would find her in the bathroom a lot.

I could never imagine life being like this; we are left with Latasha's children and many unanswered questions. We can't wait to see Latasha again up in heaven. We will all miss her no matter what. She was a great sister, a great daughter, and a perfect mother. She made up her mistakes quickly and easily. She did a lot for her children and had to do what she could. That's all that really mattered to her, her two children.

So many young lives are being lost, taken too soon with this heroin. We never thought the day would come that I would get that call early morning. They asked me my daughter's birthdate. I thought she was being arrested again. Eight hours later, nobody came and talked to me. Finally, I got hold of the sheriff's department; they said someone will call me right back. The Lucas County Morgue called instead. I will never forget that day. All we have left of Latasha are the happy memories and the ashes that were left behind. We will carry the ashes all the way until the end and we'll see her again in heaven.

Latasha's Mom,

ROBIN C.
Toledo, Ohio

Zachary

FOREVER 24

Zach was so much fun as a kid. His smile and laugh were infectious. As a baby, he was a grandpa's boy. He would wake up in the night and cry and cry no matter what I did, until Grandpa came out and rocked and sang him back to sleep. I was still a kid myself. I thank God I had such wonderful parents. They helped me raise him. We all loved him dearly. He always had lots of friends. We always had kids at the house for dinner. I called them his strays lol. If a kid didn't have dinner to go home to, he brought them to our house.

As a teen, Zachary quickly became the life of the party. Always making an entrance. I would come home from work to a house party and have to kick everyone out lol. What I wouldn't give to come home to that now. He played sports in high school, basketball and football. He was so tall, six feet one inch. He kind of just quit after we moved. It was a bigger school so he wasn't playing as much. Things went downhill from there.

By the time Zachary was out of school he was drinking and smoking weed which I didn't like, but didn't read too much into it at the time. I drank and smoked a little once in a while. I really wish I hadn't now. Maybe I would have paid more attention. His behavior got worse and worse. The fun kid I once knew wasn't there anymore. He started using cocaine. First time I saw it in his room I dumped it on the floor. He laughed and said, "I'll just get more." That's when I started really getting worried. Then came the pills which quickly turned into "Perc 30's." Those get expensive. So, next was heroin. From there, my beautiful boy was gone. And I had an angry nineteen-year-old begging me for money.

It is the most horrible thing a mother can go through up until his death. To watch your child whom you love so dearly transform into someone you don't know. Something ugly had taken him over. He was nineteen when that rollercoaster started. He was living with my mom and dad for a while. It got so bad they had to kick him out. We tried tough love. That was a mistake. He ended up homeless and sleeping in abandoned houses or in a park. I would get him food sometimes. He would call my mom and have guys in the background yelling at him and threatening to kill him if he didn't get their money. It was all fake but of course, she would go running to him with $500. Of course she would, that's her grandson.

My timeline may jump around from here because it's all become such a blur. At his lowest, Zachary called my mom for a ride. She never went to see him alone anymore so my dad went with her. When he got in the car, he started begging for money. They never carried cash anymore. None of us did. They were stopped at a light and he grabbed my mom's purse and took off running. Knocked my mom down when she got out of the car. I said ok, ENOUGH! You don't mess with my mom! So, I knew he had a warrant for driving under suspension which would be three days in jail. I called him and told him to meet me at McDonald's and I'd give him some money. Then I called the police and told them to meet us there to arrest him. They were a little surprised but did it. So, I had three days to get him a bed in a treatment facility. After fifty or so phone calls, I finally found one who could take him as soon as he got out. Of course, he was pissed at me for having him arrested. But he admitted that I probably saved his life and he agreed to go.

So here we go, round one of treatment. Things calmed down; Zachary was doing well. He moved to sober living but got kicked out for getting drunk on his 21st birthday. So, he came home and soon spiraled out of control again. Shot up in his ankle and it got infected. If he had waited one more day to call me, they would have had to amputate his foot. Twenty-one, with one foot. I put him in his old room at my mom's and bought some suboxone off the street so he wouldn't drive them so crazy. Then it was back to rehab. Thank goodness I had good insurance.

On to round two. He called one day for advice, that was different. There was a treatment center in West Palm Beach that would pay for his plane ticket if he came to their facility. I thought it might be good to go somewhere where you don't know anyone. Try again. I was kind of happy he was looking for help on his own. So, to the airport we went. I was really sad to see him go but so hopeful. Well, little did I know, Florida was booming with treatment centers all in it for the money. He bounced around Florida for four years. Got sucked into treatment life. Had gotten addicted to detox. Get clean, go get high. It's like getting that first-time high all over again. He was very up and down the whole time he was down there.

We and Zachary's three sisters went down to Florida, Christmas of 2015. He had been clean for a little while and it was just so nice seeing him and being able to have normal conversations, laughing and goofing off. My parents had retired at this point and were living in Florida about four hours from him. We were all at their place. The first night, me, the girls, and Zach went down to Longboat Key to the beach. Two of my girls had never seen the ocean before. We had so much fun; the girls running and splashing in the water, me and Zach standing on the beach in the moonlight talking and laughing. This is my most cherished memory. The next day the whole family went to the beach to take some family photos on Christmas Day. My brother and his family were there too. Afterwards, back at Mom and Dad's, we were having dinner. Zach and the girls sat at the "kids" table with their little cousins. Zach had them all laughing so hard I think they barely ate. My mom and dad and I were so happy just watching them laugh. It was like we had our Zach back. Then we all went our separate ways. That was the last happy memory I have of him so I hold on to every single detail of those few days.

I saw Zachary one more time before he was gone. The treatment centers had caught on to how charismatic he was. He would brag that he could sell water to the ocean. He started getting paid thousands of dollars cash from several facilities to recruit people into their centers, which included getting them high before they went. It was all a big insurance scam. It was just all bad from there.

Zachary called me one-night begging to come home. Said he would die out there. I could tell he was really messed up. I worked nights so I was at work. I told him to sober up and call me in the morning. Oh, how I wish I had just bought a plane ticket right then. It was the last time I talked to him. He was dead by morning in the sober living house. I waited up for his call and was just about to go to bed when my phone beeped. It was a text from his best friend that he was in a coma, but he did not know which hospital, so I started calling around. On the third hospital call, my mom called. She was his emergency contact because she was in Florida and well, she is his grandma. They were very close. She told me what she knew, and my oldest daughter and I jumped on an airplane. Mom and Dad picked us up and made the four-hour drive to West Palm Beach. We finally got there at 11:30 pm. I had been up almost forty-eight hours when I saw my very big, baby boy on life support. It was heart wrenching seeing him like that and he had so many friends there. The nurses made them all leave when we got there so we would have some time with him.

Oh, my goodness. I cannot even describe the pain in my heart that was just beginning. Over the next four days, we met ALL of Zachary's friends. There was even a girl who had moved down there from back home. She used to babysit my girls. She and Zach had just bumped into each other. I learned a lot from his friends. The stuff Mom doesn't get to see. They talked about how he would drop everything if someone needed help with something, whether it was help not using or just anything totally random, he was there. He had a heart of gold. Always looking out for others. My daughter and I got really close to some of them and still talk to and check in on them. On day four, there was zero brain activity and no hope of recovery.

We decided it was time. We only had a few of his closest friends there. Only one ended up staying which is completely understandable. She waited in the hall as they turned off the machines. I had seen it done on TV but whew, I was not prepared.

The four of us surrounded him, holding on to him, and my dad said a prayer. They had told us it would take about three minutes. We watched him breathe for sixteen minutes. Heart of gold. Longest sixteen minutes of my life. What people don't talk about is the color change in the skin. It really threw me. I was not ready. But when would I be? It went from pink to yellow to grey and that was it. He was gone. My beautiful boy was gone. The pain is so...there are no words for your heart shattering into a million pieces. My Zach was gone.

Zachary "Binx" forever 24, January 9, 1993, to May 26, 2017. If love could have saved a life, you would have lived forever.

Zachary "Binx" Mom,

Jennifer C.
Delaware, Ohio

Jeff

FOREVER 39

Jeff was born in May 1979 in Memphis, Tennessee. We were so excited and so in love with our second-born son. I brought him home on Mother's Day that year to our home in Horn Lake, Mississippi. This past Mother's Day fell on what should have been his forty-first birthday. At first, all I could do was cry because now all I have are his ashes instead of a card, hug, or phone call. But Eric and Sissy had us and her parents over and it ended up being a wonderful Mother's Day. Eric is my oldest son and Sissy is my daughter-in-law.

When Jeff was a small child, he followed his older brother, Eric, around everywhere that he could. He was four-and-a-half years younger than Eric. He loved Eric and always looked up to him. Jeff thought he should be able to do anything that Eric did. So that created a problem when he got a little older and he wanted to hang out with Eric and his friends. At this time, I was in a marriage that should have been over a long time ago and it created a lot of tension in our home. I spent too much time trying to make it work but to no avail, so it ended in a divorce. Drugs and alcohol played a big part of that at the time.

My boys so longed for a relationship with their dad that they never really got. My husband stayed gone A LOT. One time when Jeff was living us, after he had been paid he called his dad and wanted to take him to a Grizzlies game and out to eat. His dad's response was I really don't care for the Grizzlies. So, when he and Jeff hung up, Jeff was about in tears and said all he wanted to do was spend some time with him. That really hurt Jeff. And it really made me hurt for him too.

Then as Jeff got a little older, he started hanging out with some of Eric's friends. One of Eric's friends even taught Jeff how to drive a stick shift when he was fourteen-years-old. Of course, I knew nothing about it, but by this time I was divorced from their dad and I was working two jobs and would try to be home by ten p.m. I decided to go back to school and still had to work full time, trusting my two boys to stay at home alone at night. Of course, there was no adult supervision. They assured me that everything was fine and when I got home at night my house was clean. They would be in bed or they would be watching TV. This was way before cell phones. So, I would call periodically to check on them. Too much alone time for kids is not a good thing. They can get into a lot of situations they shouldn't even know about.

Our small town was riddled with drugs, but I didn't realize that for a while. And I never thought my kids would ever do drugs or even give them a second thought. Boy was I blind to the truth.

Jeff loved playing basketball in the neighborhood and played football in high school. He was such a gifted athlete and could play both sports with ease. I went to every game of his that I could. Then he started not showing up for football practice and got kicked off the team.

I could see Jeff becoming less and less enthusiastic about school and becoming depressed. I took him to a therapist, and he diagnosed him as having ADA, but he also said that Jeff was good about saying what you wanted to hear. Jeff was already smoking pot, but I had no idea. Jeff became a great manipulator. After the last session with the therapist, the therapist told me he thought I needed to watch him.

But Jeff was always popular with all the kids and teachers at school. He and Eric both were very well mannered. And Jeff used it to his advantage. He was very kind to everyone. He treated all the kids at school the same. On weekends all the kids would gather at my house. There would be a lot of them in my front yard. What I didn't know was they were all smoking pot. I would go out and talk with them, but I didn't stay out there the whole time. By this time Eric had graduated high school and was working nights. Soon Eric moved to Louisiana to be with his girlfriend, Sissy. They later married.

Jeff and I had some really hard times because he wanted to go and do as he pleased and I said NO, but he would leave anyway. He and I argued a lot. Of course, he thought he was always right!! I missed Eric terribly because I could talk to him about Jeff. And I know Jeff missed him too.

One night I found out that Jeff was smoking pot. So, I checked him into a juvenile rehab. A lot of his friends came by to check on me and see how he was doing in rehab and of course none of them knew he was smoking pot and they were all innocent. By this time, I knew better. All of them were smoking it and some were doing harder drugs.

This would end up being the first of many rehab stints. This rehab only lasted two weeks. I thought oh boy he will be changed. Because I kept thinking not my child. My child could not be a drug addict. Of course, the day he got home from that rehab he was already back with his same friends.

After all this, I found out Jeff was skipping school all the time. So, I went to the school and talked to a counselor. Jeff decided he wanted to quit school. So, he did. He did get his GED a few years later.

Everything with Jeff was out of control. I didn't want anyone in my family or friends to know what was going on with him because I was so embarrassed. I thought no one would understand and they would think I was a bad mother. Jeff was very headstrong. But then he would always tell me he was sorry and didn't mean to hurt me. Of course, this would become a pattern. I wanted to believe him but deep down in my heart I knew I couldn't.

When I married my husband Robert, he got Jeff a job interview with the trucking line he worked for and Robert's boss called Robert and said Jeff tested positive for cocaine. Cocaine? Talk about a shock! I knew he was in trouble and so were we. I almost lost my mind, it was all I could think about and no one to share this secret with! All of his drug use took a big toll on my health because I just knew I would be getting a call any minute that he was dead!! I would wake up in the morning with my teeth clenched and my hands were in tight fists.

Robert got transferred to Jackson, Tennessee. Jeff was living with Eric and Sissy and their baby back at our old house in Horn Lake, Mississippi. And Sissy was really rooting for Jeff to get straightened out; she would tell him he could beat this for the rest of his life. But they couldn't put up with him doing drugs, so Robert and I made him move to Jackson, Tennessee, with us. Jeff and Robert got along really well. Well, that is most of the time until his drug use got so bad and we couldn't believe anything he said.

Robert got Jeff a job interview at another truck line, and he did well there! He could always find a job and keep it while using drugs but would eventually end up losing his jobs because of the drugs. It seemed that every time something good would happen to Jeff, he would self-sabotage. It was almost like he didn't think he deserved good things to happen to him. I hated seeing my boy going through all of this, because he could be so loving and fun.

Over the years the drug choices changed, and addiction took control of him totally. But Jeff was a charmer and very handsome and got away with more than a lot of addicts would have. I just wanted so badly for my son to be free from all of this! And live life.

He was in a really bad car wreck with his first wife and eleven-day-old baby boy. A work truck hit them and if his wife had been driving, it would have killed her. Jeff had to be cut from the car and air lifted to the hospital. This started Jeff on the road to painkillers.

I knew Jeff was doing street drugs before he even got married. Even his girlfriend knew before they married. But now a baby was involved so I became an enabler because I was so afraid that Jeff's baby would grow up and never know his daddy. He and his first wife divorced over his drug use. She could always tell because she would come home from work and he would be sitting there reading his Bible.

The preacher where we were going to church even took Jeff to a Teen Challenge Event at another church. It seemed like nothing was going to work with him. I never felt so alone in all my life. I loved Jeff with all that I am, but the pull of the drug was too powerful.

So, then Jeff came to live with us at our house. I didn't want anyone to know he used drugs. I even didn't want my best friend Kathie to know. We have been friends for forty-eight years now. But I was too embarrassed for even her to know. So, for many years we didn't talk or didn't talk much because of me and my little dirty family secret. I ended up telling her and going to stay with her in Mississippi to get away from everything and all she's ever done is love me and love Jeff. No judgement from her ever. And we are even closer now than ever before. And for that I am so very grateful to God.

But again, because of the stigma, well, I just couldn't tell others. Because Jeff always knew how to get to me. Naturally, he was kind and loving but when he would leave, every time he would end up calling me for money that he owed drug dealers. It would be anywhere from $20 to $500. Drug dealers would come to my house. I lived in fear knowing that they knew where we lived. I would eventually give in for a while. Then Jeff started going to church with us. Everyone there loved him as he was known at the church to be very loving to addicts. Everyone there knew he was an addict and tried to help. But the drugs had too strong of a hold on him. He would even cry and ask me why God didn't take this off of him like he does some people. I just told him to keep praying. I stayed on my knees a lot in prayer for him. I finally knew it was out of my hands and it was time to step out of God's way.

I tried the tough love approach and told Jeff he couldn't come in the house. This would happen over and over again. He would blow my phone up and finally I would start getting afraid that something would happen to him and I would talk him into going into rehab. Yes, this led to several stints in rehabs all over the country. He also had stints in jail and two times in prison for all drug-related and nonviolent crimes. Jeff could make friends anywhere. The guards and a lot of inmates all liked him. That always amazed me because he could talk to anyone and become friends with them. I couldn't understand why he would want to keep using when he could be helping people.

I took Jeff's son with me to visit his daddy every weekend on visiting day at the prison. The first time we went to visit him, I was overwhelmed at how huge the prison was and all I could do was cry! His son would be so sad, and I was too every time we visited him and left.

Jeff's drug addiction lasted twenty-two years. And in twenty-two years there was more using than not. There is way too much to write here. He led a terribly sad life. Don't get me wrong, there were months in between that were good and happy. I felt bad for the life he lived and sad for the life he didn't get to live. He did have some good moments too. It seemed like he developed a habit of staying clean for four months and then go at it again until he would hit a brick road.

Jeff was very loving with his son and could get down on his level. He could do that with all kids and they just loved him. His nephews and niece loved him because he was so much fun to be around. Jeff was kind, loving, handsome, and he knew Jesus as his Savior. If someone needed help, he would do whatever he could to help them, he loved all people, and he had a great sense of humor. Oh, how he loved music! It was great therapy for him. He would always be singing. And he was loud and off key. I wish I could hear him sing one more time! He could make people laugh so hard that they would literally beg him to stop because they were hurting from laughing so hard.

When my boys' dad died in 2017 from cancer, it was a big blow to both of them but especially Jeff because he had questions that would never get answered and that really bothered him.

Jeff moved to Nashville to go to rehab. But before he moved, he lived with his girlfriend and he kept using. He would even go through detox at her house or mine, which is very dangerous to do on your own, but he would do it to get clean. But it just didn't last. The heroin pull was just too strong. By this time, he was living in Nashville and working.

While living in Nashville, Jeff overdosed who knows how many times. And he did in Jackson, too. But in Nashville, he did a lot of over-dosing. He would be lucky that someone would find him and call the ambulance and bring him back. He had fentanyl in a lot of the heroin. December 21, 2018 would be his last time using.

I had a gut feeling when I found that black bag. It was Jeff's but at the same time I wanted to believe him. You can never trust an addict because their whole life is based on lies, first and foremost, to them-selves. I knew he had been using for a while because he came and stayed the weekend at our home. When he was getting ready to leave he was looking for something, I don't even remember what he was looking for, but he asked me if I would help and I started looking too. Well, he had this big overnight bag and I thought I would look in it this one more time. That is when I found this small little black bag with a spoon, cotton, and something that looked like wax and a syringe in it.

My heart hit the floor. I felt like I had been hit in the gut. I was shaking uncontrollably all over. I thought my child would never inject himself with anything. And you couldn't see any marks on him showing that he did. When he came back in, I held that bag in my hand and asked him what it was and he said, "I really hate you found that because it's not mine," and he went on to explain that it belonged to a friend of his and he needed to get it back to him. I gave it back to him and I said if you are lying about this and you keep this up you are going to die. He said as he was leaving, that he really wished I hadn't found it.

He did marry his girlfriend and they all moved to Nashville, but the marriage was so up and down because he just kept using. That's when he did his last two stints in rehab. His wife had to put him out and they both eventually agreed he go one more time to rehab, which he did, and go to sober living and stay for six months. Then he started going home on the weekends and back to sober living on the weekdays. When he was home on the weekends, their marriage became good and strong. Or that is what we all thought. Then I saw his mother-in law's name on my phone. I knew something was wrong because she never called me.

Anyway, my husband had been taken to the hospital the night before because he lost all muscle use and fell onto the bathroom floor. So, when I answered the phone I said, "Please don't tell me anything bad about Jeff because Robert is in the hospital and I just can't take anymore." She said she would come by in just a minute. Eric and Sissy were staying with us at our house so I told Sissy something bad has happened to Jeff but I am not sure what it is. His mother-in-law came over to tell me Jeff was dead. However, Jeff's wife had already contacted Robert not knowing he was in the hospital and told him the news. He didn't want me to be alone when I was told, so Robert had called Sissy who then told Eric. I was in the house, just walking out of the bathroom and Eric was standing there waiting for me. He grabbed me and told me Jeff was gone.

I said, "Who is gone?"

Eric said, "Momma, Jeff is dead." I was devastated.

When Jeff's mother-in-law got there, I told her I already knew and just fell apart. I couldn't believe my boy was dead. And that I would no longer get hugs, sweet texts, or talk to him ever again!

I was devastated beyond belief. He died in front of a Verizon store on December 21, 2018, about five p.m. according to the coroner. According to an employee at Verizon, his truck had been running since the day before and when the employee looked in his truck the next day, he saw Jeff was dead. The coroner wouldn't let us see him because it was right before Christmas and he was very busy. And since Jeff died in public, with no witnesses, he had to have an autopsy done on him. All I wanted to do was touch my boy one last time.

At first someone told us it was a heart attack. But I kept calling the office where the death certificates come in for weeks and nothing.

Finally, the lady answered and she said, "Yes, the death certificate is here, but all I can do is read the cause of death and I will send you a copy." When she read the cause of death was from "Acute Heroin Toxicity," I couldn't believe what I was hearing. I started shaking and felt that punch in the gut because he was living at the sober living house and I had thought he was doing great. When we had his Celebration of Life service, we didn't even know that he had died from a drug overdose.

But now Jeff is gone and he left behind a nineteen-year-old son, a wife and her kids, a stepfather, a brother and sister-in-law, other family members, and a lot of friends who miss him greatly, and a mother who mourns him every day.

Jeff overdosed so many times but he was lucky because someone always found him in time to call an ambulance to come and administer Narcan on him to bring him back. But not on December 21, 2018, in his running truck parked in front of a Verizon store. That was his last and final time to use heroin.

I know he is at peace now. I know he doesn't hurt anymore, but we do!! I started grief therapy. I know the drugs are so much more potent than five years ago. People need to quit spending so much time on their phones; stop their children from spending so much time on their phones and spend time with each other. Hold your children accountable to you the parents. Interfere in their lives. You are their parents, not their friends.

We are living in scary times in this country. Now drug addiction and drug overdoses are at an all-time high. And fentanyl is being put into every drug there is out there. Most of these kids think they are getting the drugs they are wanting but they are dying by the hundreds every day because they are getting drugs laced with fentanyl or straight fentanyl. The drug dealers know they are going to kill them and they don't care.

If you are the family of an active user, don't give into them but always let them know how much you love them, that they matter, and they are important! Just keep stressing that to them. And you go get yourself some help so you don't lose yourself to addiction because if you don't, you will lose yourself and your sanity.

If drugs and alcohol run in your family, your children may have inherited the genes that make them more susceptible to becoming an addict if they ever try drugs.

Never say, "Not My Child." Drug addiction knows no boundaries. It doesn't matter how much money you have or don't have, and it doesn't matter the color of your skin or your age. It is from the Devil and drugs are out to kill, steal, and destroy. And they will if they can get a hold of their next victim. None of our kids wanted to be addicts nor did they want to die!

And at this alarming rate of over-doses a whole generation will be destroyed; a generation that had a lot to offer to our society. And don't be ashamed of your child if they are using drugs! Drugs are everywhere and it takes us all working together to fight against it!

And now they are starting to charge some of these drug dealers with murder, as it should be. But that is a small amount in this vast society in which we live. Now all we have left are his ashes and memories.

Jeff's Mom,

GAYLA C.
Memphis, Tennessee

Brett

FOREVER 33

Our story isn't unique. We raised our son Brett in a middle-class family. His dad a CHP officer and I was a stay-at-home mom that earned extra money with a daycare business. Brett was born on the 4th of July, 1986, in Palm Springs CA. On the day of his birth, the Statue of Liberty had an unveiling after a two-year restoration project. We always thought that this would be something special for our son to celebrate. He was a beautiful nine pound eight ounces baby. He did everything early, crawling at five months and walking at nine months. We always thought that meant he was a "go-getter." With every birthday came fireworks that he thought were just for him until he was about five years old.

When Brett started school, he was shy. He never drew attention to himself and was very quiet. When he graduated to first grade, his teacher noticed he was falling behind and asked that he be tested, and subsequently he was put in a resource program. They advised that he be put on medication for ADD. We declined, after consulting with his pediatrician. Brett stayed in the resource program until fifth grade, when he apparently was doing well enough to graduate out. He was around eleven years old at this time. In California when you are in sixth grade it's called middle school.

At this age, you're going to school with sixth, seventh, and eighth graders. Here he met a few kids a grade or two ahead and was introduced to alcohol. We only discovered this because he got caught stealing a bottle of Creme de Menthe from a nearby market. Thinking this was him experimenting, and following older influences, we disciplined him. We just thought he was doing it younger because kids were doing everything younger these days. It was around this time we also found out he was smoking. We were finding it very difficult to stop him from doing these behaviors so we started restricting his time. He started acting out more. Cutting school, and staying away from home.

When Brett was fifteen, he was very angry and sad. So we found a behavioral health specialist and they admitted him to the hospital for depression. When Brett was released, he was angry at us and ran from home. During the next two to three years, he was in and out of the house. He stopped going to school and started using meth. When he was almost eighteen, he made a choice to get clean. Without any outside help, he decided to stop. Brett was successful and moved back home. He went back to school, got his GED, and started working with a friend doing carpentry. He seemed to enjoy it and he was very good at it.

For the next eleven years, he worked, moved into a house, bought two cars, and seemed to be doing well. We knew he was drinking, but he was living his life so we stayed quiet, for the most part. He began working as a gutter installer and dating a new girlfriend. He let her and her two children move in with him. We started seeing the pressure build. She didn't work and he was taking care of everything. It was at this time he fell off a ladder at work. He was transported and subsequently misdiagnosed. He had been hobbling around on a broken ankle and broken foot, for nine months.

During this time, the doctor was writing pain prescriptions. One after another. Brett's dad had even gone to many appointments with him and explained to the doctor that he had been an addict and this

136

was going to be a problem. The doctor continued to prescribe pain pills without regard for his predisposition for abuse. Finally, they did surgery to correct the misdiagnosed break, but by this time Brett had been abusing his prescriptions and so was his girlfriend. He was also smoking heroin. Finally, he lost his home and moved back home with us. By this time, the girlfriend had left and his car had been repossessed.

While he was out one evening, we got a call from a police officer that he had been pulled over. They asked if we could come get his truck. They could have towed it, but chose not to, to give him a break. Upon arrival, the officer informed us that our son had needles and other items to shoot heroin. We were shocked!! Brett was crying in shame and taken to jail. When he was released, he told us he could stop. Having stopped before, we believed him. Looking back, I feel so naive.

Fast forward several months of watching Brett struggling—we chose to place a 51-50 on him. In California, that is a seventy-two hour mental hold. He stayed for three days and when he was released he decided to live in his car so he could continue with his addiction. He received a large settlement from the work injury and we watched him spiral into full-blown addiction, living in hotels where he could continue the drug life.

When the money ran out, he began a crime spree of stealing to feed his habit. It finally caught up to him and he went to jail. He made a plea and after two months in jail, he went to rehab. He spent thirty days in rehab. That is what was required and then he left. He was out about a month when he relapsed and over dosed and ended up in the hospital. So he went back to rehab. He wasn't ordered to stay so he didn't. This was in August of 2019.

Brett decided to go into a methadone out-patient treatment program. He was told by the doctors to continue using until they were able to increase his dose enough to keep him "well." He was doing this when on December 7, 2019, he was driving his truck at a high rate of speed in the rain and crashed his truck. He was ejected from his vehicle. The autopsy report said he died instantly from his head injuries. The report also said he had heroin and meth in his toxicology report.

Our hope was always that Brett was doing better. He was trying to conquer this beast. We always hoped he could do it again. He had been clean for eleven years. Truth is, it's a daily battle. We had no idea how hard he was fighting. We loved him through everything. Our ignorance of this disease helped in it defeating him. At least that's how we feel. Knowledge is power!! But sometimes it comes too late.

I see things now that I didn't recognize when we were in this battle. Our son is not suffering anymore, we are, including Brett's sisters who watched their brother go down a path that they couldn't understand. We all felt so powerless to stop any of the choices he made. To love someone so much and to not have any control over the outcome of this journey has to be the worst feeling to accept. So we console ourselves with knowing he's not suffering anymore. It doesn't take the deep loss away. It doesn't help with the day-in-day-out pain of his loss.

As Brett's mother, I will always remember him before he became an addict. The beautiful child they handed me that July 4th morning. All the hope I had for him. He didn't have to be a famous author or a successful doctor or an architect, though he could have been. I would have been satisfied with a happy life. Maybe a wife and kids. And in the end, I'd just be happy with him alive. Drug free would be a bonus. I know we're not in this suffering alone. In some ways that's comforting. In other ways, I think, how is this epidemic going unchecked? Until it becomes personal,  it will continue. So we must share our stories and help to share awareness.

Brett Ross July 4, 1986 to December 7, 2019

Loving son and brother, Uncle Buba to his nieces and nephews.

Brett's Mom,

JOLENE C.
Grass Valley, California

Cortney Ann

FOREVER 42

Where to begin?

Cortney had always been a high achieving person and intellectual. I always thought this was a blessing, but it turned out to be a curse. She was a popular student, but I noticed in twelfth grade she changed her friends, smoking marijuana. She ended up getting thrown out of school. However, she did get her GED immediately. Of course, it didn't stop there, the drinking started. At some point, a couple of years later, I realized she was a full-blown alcoholic. What followed were several car accidents, jail, rehab, then more jail and rehab. Nothing worked. It was never ending.

They say many alcoholics and drug addicts suffer from mental health disorders. Cortney was no exception. She was diagnosed with OCD. She was also a cutter. Eventually, she got into other drugs. Crack, pills, and occasionally heroin, but liquor was always her drug of choice. There were any years of dysfunction, and I was obsessed with her disease. I would have gone to the ends of the earth to get her better. It was twenty years of trying. I can tell you it is all consuming when you are trying to save your child from herself., but you can't.

Then there was Christmas night, December 25, 2019, she made that fatal mistake of thinking she was going to do heroin, but instead of heroin, she got pure carfentanyl. There was no heroin in her system. I am sure she died instantly. I found out the next day when that dreaded knock on the door at seven a.m. produced two police officers. Hope was gone.

I am unable to live with the pain. I should have done more. I think every grieving mother feels the same. She was smart and beautiful and caring. She just couldn't care about herself. I am not the same person since her death. Just a shell of my old self. I grieve for the life she never had and the person she will never be. My daughter was murdered by drug-induced homicide. I am sure she didn't think she was going to die. The dealer ended her life and destroyed me.

Cortney Ann's Mom,

SHARON **D.**
Strongsville, Ohio

Devin

FOREVER 26

The year was 2008. My son Devin worked at a small restaurant in our small community in Oklahoma. He took a fall one evening on a wet floor and developed a staph infection near his elbow. Doing what any mother would do, I took him to our local hospital. The infection tested positive for MRSA and Devin received antibiotics and his first prescription of opioids. Over the next several years, staph would appear on different areas of his body. With every trip to the doctor, he received more opioids. In 2013, he went through a surgery that would eliminate it for good. A drain tube was inserted for three weeks and pain medication prescribed. As a mother, you trust that a doctor has the best interest of their patient.

Devin used heroin for the first time in 2015. The pain of watching your child go down the dark road of addiction is almost unbearable. Devin didn't want that life. In 2016, he came to me and said, "Mom, I need help." My main goal was for him to get as far away as possible so he could focus on his recovery. He went to a treatment facility out of state for thirty days. When he got off the plane from treatment, I remember thinking to myself, "He looks worse than when he left." Devin had been prescribed Suboxone. He would soon begin using again, within ten days of being home. Devin attended another thirty-day treatment program, and this time everything was different. Our family was able to visit, attend family therapy sessions, and Devin was taking his recovery very seriously. I attended his graduation and was asked to speak. I hold on to the memory of that day. Everything seemed perfect. Devin came to live with me, his brother, and Devin's son, who was six-years-old at the time. Devin enrolled at a tech school to become an EMT and he excelled. He rekindled his relationship with his girlfriend, and they would soon be expecting. Devin was a mental health tech. He absolutely loved working with teenagers. He told me he related to their troubles. He was excelling at his place of employment and received employee of the month in March 2018. On May 24, 2018, a police officer and chaplain came to my door at six a.m. to give me the most devastating news. My son relapsed, after having a significant time in recovery, and had passed away, alone. The day our world changed forever. Devin's son, who was eight-years-old, was crushed. His daddy was gone, after finally having him back. His fiancé was left alone with their five-and-a-half-month-old daughter. They had dreams and goals that were shattered.

Devin was a sweet soul. He was very talented. He was a black belt in Tae Kwon Do (he didn't like anyone to know that). He had the best vocabulary. I was constantly asking him what words meant. Devin didn't want to leave us; he wanted to be better, but addiction won and he has left us heart-broken forever. He fought and fought hard. Forever in our hearts, Devin.

Devin's Mom,

ANGELA D.
Tulsa, Oklahoma

Jeff

FOREVER 40

There were two sides to Jeff. There was Jeff the Addict and there was the Jeff we loved. Those of you who love an addict know exactly what that statement means. The most difficult part was that both Jeffs resided in the same body. I often didn't know which Jeff I would encounter so I had to prepare myself in advance.

If Jeff the Addict was the one that was present, my heart had to be hardened in an effort to protect the love that I had for him. If my beloved Jeff was present, then I could exhale and enjoy his presence. It was difficult for all of us to constantly be on guard. I know that while under the influence of drugs, Jeff shared with some of you stories about being abused, unwanted, and unloved. None of those things were true. The stories that were told came from an addict that, in his pain and bewilderment, was trying to justify his choices. Addiction causes one's mind to be altered in a way that truth becomes a lie and lies become truth. We all have heartbreaking memories of Jeff the Addict but, to contrast the heartbreak, we also have many memories of Jeff as he truly was.

Those memories are brought to mind with a smile, a chuckle, or even a hard-to-catch-one's-breath laugh.

The first memory that I have of the beginning of Jeff's sense of humor was when he was almost a year old. Television wasn't watched back then as it is now. There was much less to watch. We watched Sesame Street and Mr. Rogers and then spent our days playing with toys, making cookies, washing dishes, and going for walks. We loved to sing along to music made especially for children and varieties of other music.

There was always music playing while we were at home or while in the car. One morning, Jeff and I were playing with his toys, one of which was plastic eggs that came apart in halves. The purpose was to put them together, but Jeff found another purpose. He bit the edge of the egg which caused the rest of it to flip up over his nose. I laughed SO hard when he did this that he continued. His response was to laugh into the egg which made his laugh sound funnier and caused us to laugh harder. The laughter resulting from a moment of pure goofiness was one of many to come.

One of Jeff's favorite foods when he was around a year old was a banana. Before we realized that giving him smaller pieces were a necessity, he'd take the piece that I gave him and slowly shove the whole thing into his mouth. I think he liked the texture and liked the fact that he didn't have to really chew each bite. As he shoved, his cheeks began to bulge out and his mouth could no longer close. With his banana filled, deformed, chipmunk-like face, he'd smile, and the banana would ooze from between his gums and few teeth. There were times, while laughing, I'd have to dig part of the banana out of his mouth so that he could actually swallow. Although his banana eating folly caused us to laugh, to prevent his laughter from causing him to choke, I learned that one bite-sized piece was all he'd get at one time.

As a child, Jeff was very sweet and affectionate. He loved being held in my arms and rocked until he'd gotten so big, he couldn't fit anymore. His legs would hang over the chair and I'd get lost somewhere in his height, but we didn't care. When he was a teenager and taller than I was, it amazed me that he'd have his arm resting on my shoulders when I'd walk with him in the mall or out in public somewhere. Most teenagers keep their mothers at arm's length at least, but, for whatever reason, Jeff didn't.

Because of his gentle nature, small children and animals were drawn to him. I had a daycare in our home for a few years and the kids would fight over who got to sit next to Jeff. While teaching in a summer program, he spent some time assisting me with the students. I remember one troubled boy who latched onto him the moment Jeff entered the room. It was Jeff that motivated him to complete the academic activities that this boy hated doing. He loved Jeff's tattoos and really looked up to him. No one else was able to get through to this little guy, but Jeff did. As our boy grew from a baby to a young child to a young man, his love and concern for others began to deepen and become almost painful for him.

When he was thirteen, Jeff began to change as all teenagers do, but in more extreme ways. We began to see evidence of drugs in the house and, as time went on, the effects of the drugs began to change our son into someone else. He found ways to escape into places that were caused by such extreme amounts of mind-altering chemicals that it's truly amazing that his life didn't end long before now. God had a plan for him and for us with him.

For many years, I prayed and prayed and hoped and hoped that Jeff would be healed. God shared with me that He would save Jeff and that He had a purpose for him.

I clung to Bible verses like Isaiah 49: 50: "'Surely thus says the Lord, Even the captives of the mighty man will be taken away, and the prey of the tyrant will be rescued; for I will contend with the one who contends with you and I will save your sons.'"

And John 10: 28 & 29, "I give eternal life to them, and they will never perish, and no one will snatch them out of My hand. My Father who has given them to Me, is greater than all; and no one is able to snatch them out of the Father's hand."

I shared my belief with Jeff that God had created him to do something very special here on this earth. In fact, my last text to him was to that effect. Although these verses sustained me, their purpose, God's purpose, was not the same as my desire for Jeff, but their meanings are now clear. He was never meant to be healed here, but I believe as promised, that Jeff's heart was never snatched out of God's hands and he is now safe with his Heavenly Father.

Although Jeff is no longer here to cause us to laugh, or to feel his sweet hugs nor can we look into his blue eyes that revealed so clearly his kind soul, God created two beautiful daughters through him. They are a reflection of his kind, sensitive, loving, humorous, talented heart. They are the best of him, and he lives on through them. There was a time, actually two times, when Jeff shared that he was going to have a child.

My response to God was to ask, "What are You doing?" Now I know the answer. God took the beauty of our son and bestowed it onto Morgan and Izzy. They are his purpose. He took the tortured soul of our boy home to be with Him, healed him, and now the beauty of our boy lives on through his girls.

Twenty-two years ago, in the winter of 1997, while struggling through the heartbreak of Jeff's choices, I wrote a letter to him. It was actually an assignment while I was a student at MSU. Little did I know at the time that I was writing the letter for his memorial. In fact, it's eerily prophetic. In God's infinite wisdom, He was preparing me way back then for this day and it's so appropriate that I'd like to share it with you.

To My Son

I consider the title of "mother," which was bestowed upon me from the moment I conceived my first child, the most important title I will ever hold, while being a mother can be the most painful. The following represents the opportunity to express my feelings as a mother to you, my prodigal son.

From the moment you were conceived, you were a miracle. We were told that we were not to be blessed with children of our own and yet through us, you were to be ours. God's plan for your existence overshadowed the wisdom of man.

As you developed within me, I often spoke to you. We spent all of our time together, as you were a part of me. Your existence comforted me and through God's infinite wisdom, you gave purpose to my life.

When you were born, the joy of seeing you for the first time and holding you in my arms was such that cannot be put into words. Your sweet way of communication was welcomed as I could not wait to hold "my little." Your sweet presence made life for me more important as I began to see my responsibilities with new eyes. It was because of you that I chose to give my heart to the God who created me and who so lovingly blessed me with you.

As you grew, the love I had for you deepened. My heart's ears were touched by the sweet sound of my precious boy saying, "Ah loo" (I love you.) for the first time. I taught you about our Heavenly Father and we often sang songs, which were a demonstration of your faith.

God made me strong through you. He taught me what unconditional Love meant by demonstrating it through you. He taught me about forgiveness, and He taught me how to let go of those I hold dearly in my heart.

From the moment you were born, I have had to slowly let go of you. You are not and never been my possession. You were merely given to me for a time to love, to care for and to teach until you could care for yourself on your own. I have visions in my mind of days when I left you at pre-school while you stood at the window and watched me go. I have visions of you walking backwards as you set out for school, waving to me until I could no longer be seen. My heart wanted to run to you and hold you to myself, but my mind understood the necessity of letting you go. I waited with anticipation for you to return, for it was with welcome, not possessiveness that I could hold you close.

Now that you are grown and considered an adult, letting go of you has not become any easier. My heart still longs to run to you, to protect and shield you from the pain that will result from your choices. But my mind knows that my protection is insufficient. So, I leave you in the hands of the God who created you, who made you a miracle in my life and will wait for you to come home.

I love you,
Love, Mom

One of the many ironies of this letter is that instead of me waiting for Jeff to come home, he'll be waiting for me. Each day that passes brings me closer to that day and God reminds me that not only will I be with my Savior, I will be welcomed into Heaven by my son. Although I will treasure each moment that I have on this earth with my loving husband, our beautiful, precious daughter, Jeff's daughters, and my wonderful family, as I'm in no hurry, knowing that I will see Jeff again gives me great comfort. The Jeff that I look forward to seeing will be the beautiful, sweet, healed Jeff that he was created to be. Jeff is no longer a prodigal son, as he is safely home with his Father. God has answered my prayers.

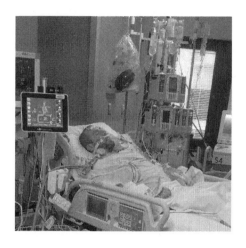

Jeff's Mom,

SHERYL D.
Eaton Rapids

Amandee

FOREVER 23

My Amandee was a happy-go-lucky, friendly, and caring child. She was a sensitive soul and always put others before herself. She danced, played soccer, and had friends. Her brothers and sister were her world, she would do anything for them. She went to a private catholic grammar school until the 8th grade. She felt she didn't fit in from probably the fifth grade on. Everything snowballed from that point. She began cutting herself and experimenting with recreational drugs, and by 12 to 13 years old she was probably an alcoholic. She had a few friends that had died and had a hard time dealing with it and turned to heroin by 18.

That was truly the beginning of the end. Mental hospitals, rehabs, police, fights, deceit, and lies all followed. The heartbreak is unimaginable. The drugs took hold and never let her go, only in brief moments of sobriety could you see her shining through. We tried tough love, all love, and a mix of both, and nothing worked.

The hardest thing in life I ever had to do was admit MY love couldn't save her. She was swallowed up in the lifestyle of getting her next fix, nothing else mattered. God said enough and took her home after over a decade of struggles, two weeks before Christmas 2018. The police came to my door, and we will never be the same.

These are real children with real families, and the stigma needs to go!

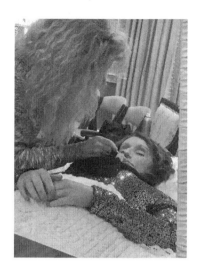

Amandee's Mom,

ELAINE H.D.
Wakefield, Massachusetts

John

FOREVER 31

I have three children. My daughter is the oldest at thirty-seven, my middle son is thirty-four, and my youngest son, John is forever thirty-one.

John grew up being called little but grew to be six feet tall. John played baseball, basketball, and football. He also loved skateboarding. He wanted to become a chef and boy could he cook. He was very outgoing and he enjoyed riding motorcycles with us. We did everything together.

My children and I were all so close. John was my rock and I was his. John hated his sister so much because she used heroin; she's been using for fourteen years now. This makes it real hard to try to understand why he did it.

John had a heart of gold and always looked out for and helped anyone. He fought his addiction for seven years. He thought he knew what he was doing and only people that didn't know what they were doing died. He was smug and thought he was invincible. He was in and

151

out of jail, rehab, and detox. Every time he was in a facility, even jail, I knew he was safe.

I have saved his life countless times. I have brought him out of seizures from smoking too much crack at least three times. I have brought him back with CPR at least four or five times from heroin. Watching your child laying there and trying to save them is so heart breaking. This disease is so exhausting; we lose sleep because of worry, and I would stay up all night and day just to watch him, so he didn't die. I can tell you they have to want to get clean and until they want to, they won't. I really thought that when my daughter saw her brother John in a coffin that she would stop.

John had a year-and-a-half clean. He accomplished so much in that time. He was so proud and happy; I had never seen him so happy and proud of himself and really enjoying every day. He had gone to rehab and came out being the real John again. He was happy and ready to take on the world. He got a great job and got his license back, which he hadn't had since he was eighteen. He had an appointment to get the Vivitrol shot five days after he died, and his license came in the mail on the same day.

No parent should ever have to bury their child. Losing my child is the worst hell on earth; I never thought pain like this existed. I'm still praying for my daughter and anyone else struggling. I guess this addiction was stronger than John was and stronger than me. Life will never be the same. I will forever long to see him, hug him, hear his voice, and I will miss all that could have been (all the nevers).

John has been in Heaven for one year, two months, and two weeks now and the pain has not gotten easier. It still seems like yesterday. When I close my eyes at night, I see him lying in the hospital lifeless and cold, with me in disbelief, then the vision of him lying in the coffin comes next and I remember how numb I was. There isn't a day that goes by that I don't cry and I still spend many days in bed  feeling like I failed him even though I did everything I could. He left behind his beautiful ten-year-old daughter on the same month as her birthday. We need to remember they always walk beside us.

John's Mom,

DEBBY D.
Plympton, Massachusetts

> "The righteous perish, and no one takes it to heart;
> the devout are taken away, and no one understands
> that the righteous are taken away to be spared from evil.
> Those who walk uprightly enter into peace;
> they find rest as they pass in death."
> Isaiah 57: 1-2

Brittney

Why my daughter? How could this happen to our family? It's the question I go over in my head every day. Brittney was born in February, 1996, in Long Island. Brittney was my only daughter and she was the middle child. She has two amazing brothers. Brittney grew up in a middle-class suburban town. We moved to the Hudson Valley when Britt was only three-years-old.

Brittney made so many friends in school throughout the years. She played all kinds of sports in school (softball, soccer). Soccer was her favorite. She also rode horses at the young age of four. She learned equestrian style and won many competitions in her younger years. Brittney also took ballet and jazz lessons for many years and enjoyed being involved in the shows. Brittney was very artistic; she drew many pictures. She had a very nice singing voice. She had a big passion for music and animals. Her favorite animals were dogs. She loved all three of our dogs. Punkin, a rescue bulldog, was her favorite. We were lucky to have Punkin for three years; she passed away two months after Brittney. I still have our other two family dogs from her childhood. Rudy is seventeen and Madison is fourteen; they are Jack Russell Terriers.

Thank goodness for all the wonderful memories I have with my daughter Brittney; they are cherished forever in my heart. Britt always loved life and then life took an unexpected turn when her grandmother passed away from cancer when Britt was only thirteen-years-old. This was a turning point in my daughter's life that altered the happiness she once felt. She never seemed the same after that day. There was a sadness to her that never went away. She became rebellious like a lot of teenagers do. Time moved on and a few years went by, then another unfortunate life-changing event happened. Her dad and I split up and ended up divorced. It rocked our family dynamic to the core.

Then Brittney started dating a boy and got into a very serious relationship with him at the age of seventeen. She met him in a small neighborly town called Walden where we lived. He lived in the village of Maybrook. What I didn't find out, until some time had passed, was that this was the boy who introduced her to a nightmarish world of drugs which turned her life, and all our lives, upside down. I never knew life could be so horrific and scary. I didn't want to know any part of this world. The day I found out my daughter was addicted to heroin I was so scared, ashamed, and lost. I couldn't believe this had happened to my beautiful daughter Britt. I knew as her mom I would do everything I could to help her fight the battle of addiction. I was committed to see her have a life of feeling good about herself and help her along the journey of recovery.

In the beginning, Brittney was willing to do anything to stop the drugs. She went into rehabs both near and far with the help of an interventionist. She went to psychiatrists, counselors, inpatient, outpatient, Narcotics Anonymous, Alcoholics Anonymous. We had so much hope and I never stopped believing she would beat this addiction.

Unfortunately, Brittney couldn't get off this horrifying roller coaster ride of drugs; lying, fighting, getting arrested, crashing her car, hurting herself, and hurting the ones that loved her the most. Even with overdosing five times, I truly believed that every time she completed a program she was healed. I found out later that some people call this "false hope." You want to believe with all your heart and soul that your loved one is going to be okay, that this nightmare will be over, and she is not going to die. I wanted so much to have my daughter back to the sweet loving girl she was, not the heroin addict that would do anything to get her fix no matter how much pain and hurt it would bring to her family or to herself.

It's with much sadness and a heavy heart to say my beautiful daughter's journey to recovery didn't happen. On a rainy stormy summer night, my daughter overdosed for the last time. I was the one who found her. I was so distraught and overcome with fear. I called 911 immediately and the paramedics showed up within minutes. The paramedics were able to get a pulse after 4 Narcan doses, two of which I kept in the house. The next few hours at the hospital were full of intense and surreal pains of crying, anger, praying, and a feeling of sorrow that overcomes you to the point that you are numb.

The next morning, my daughter Brittney passed away from a heroin/fentanyl overdose that she could never recover from. According to the autopsy, the fentanyl in her system was three times the legal limit. My worst nightmare became a reality. My daughter will be Forever 22. I know I can't bring her back!!! Yet I know her spirit lives on with me!! I feel her presence watching over me and my boys all the time.

The reason I am here today telling you our story is to make sure her death will not be in vain. This tragedy can happen to anyone and will keep happening until more is done to make sure addiction is treated as a disease. There is so much that needs to be done in the fight against addiction. We need to help change the way addiction is being viewed in society, and "Break the Stigma."

Thirty days is not enough time in a rehab for someone to break active addiction. We need detox and treatment that are regulated in every state. We need healthcare reform. Healthcare reform's purpose is to increase the number of insured and to increase the quality of care while trying to stabilize or reduce costs. Emergency rooms in every state have to be the first step to help someone with addiction realize that their lives matter and they have to go into rehab immediately; people who are addicted should not be sent out into the streets after a few hours. I pray there can be more done to help everyone who is losing someone to addiction or has lost someone to addiction.

My daughter, Brittney, left me a note in a small prayer box that I had shipped to her when she was in a rehab in Arizona. I found this note from my daughter about two months after she passed away. This is what she wrote:

Life doesn't make sense. Where do I go from here? Decisions are what make the unknown possible.

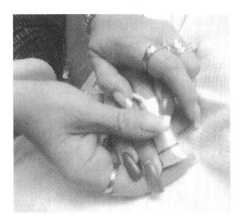

Brittney's Mom,

KAREN D.
Southfields, New York

Max

FOREVER 20

My beautiful Max loved to hike, camp and travel. He loved his brother and border collie Sky with all his heart. Max had just turned twenty when we found him on his bedroom floor dead from and accidental overdose from a Fentanyl laced drug.

He had struggled with dyslexia, speech & Math from age 5. He refused his IEP in HS when he started to self-medicate with illicit Xanax.

He struggled with body Dysmorphic Disorder, anxiety/depression that led to his fears, doubts and insecurities. My heart is a burning hole that will never be filled.

"Loss brings a very complicated kind of pain.
It's ever changing and has a fierce stronghold.
You change.
Most days it's Impossible to participate in anything
or even concentrate.

There is no place to escape grief.
There is no safe haven.
Only a lingering memory and a void."

Max's Mom,

MARY D.
Andover, Massachusetts

Wesley

FOREVER 29

My son Wesley was the second of my three children born a total of three-and-a-half years apart. He was born a day early, and died way too early.

Wesley was a beautiful child. He had thick, white blond hair and tanned so easily. Other mothers would stop me on the street to compliment me about how good looking a toddler he was. He was also very smart and physically gifted. He and his brother took his training wheels off his bike when he was two years old because he didn't want to look like a baby. He was the first kid in T-ball who could hit the ball over the fence and he did it most every game.

He started wrestling at six and won every match by a pin the first year. He usually cried while he was pinning the other boy and when they were supposed to shake hands after he was declared the winner, Wesley would hug the other boy to make him feel better. In his second year, he went to the National Wrestling Competition and scored in the top ten for his age group. He went on to also play football. A big boy, he always started at center and nose guard and his team always won the league championship. He made good grades and was especially good at math. He was just a sweet, smart, good-looking kid. Everyone loved him, but he loved his family more than anything.

I always told my children that I had them for each other, not for me. If I'd had them for me, they would have been three or four years apart so that each one would be independent before the next one came. Not me...I had them one right after the other so they could experience each stage of their life together and be best friends. And they were. They were always there for one another and always loyal, but Wesley took it to a whole other level. He was the most thoughtful, loving person I have ever known. Wesley wanted for nothing and led a charmed life surrounded by friends and family who loved him.

As with nearly 80% of Americans who become addicted to heroin, Wesley didn't want or choose to become addicted. While playing a pick-up football game with friends in college at WVU, Wesley hurt his knee. He went to the family doctor and was prescribed hydrocodone and oxycodone for the pain. Then he was prescribed these drugs over and over again in higher dosages. Wesley, like millions of others, had a predisposition for the disease of addiction. His father is a lifelong alcoholic who has never sought recovery.

This began in about 2007. By 2010, Wesley was addicted to opioids and was doctor shopping to keep up with his habit. It was heart breaking to try everything you could think of, but nothing worked. You think if you can just get him into treatment, he'll be all better. Wesley completed five rehab programs at about $30,000 each, multiple intensive outpatient treatments and halfway house stays. Each time he would remain sober for a time, but the disease would grab ahold of him again. As a mother, there is nothing in the world you would not do or sacrifice to save your child. At one time, I even tried the "tough love" approach and threw him out of his sister's apartment at school, leaving him basically homeless. It broke my heart picturing him walking the streets with his possessions in a trash bag.

By the summer of 2013, Wesley had aged out of all insurance coverage and could no longer afford pills so his dealer introduced him to heroin. He had hit his rock bottom and finally agreed to go to Faith Farm, a free, nine-month, Christian, men-only program in Ft. Lauderdale where his friend JoJo had been begging Wesley to come for several years. He spent his twenty-seventh birthday in detox then checked into Faith Farm and saved his life. Wesley thrived at Faith Farm and we finally knew he was safe. He devoted his life to Jesus and loved the impact he was able to have on other addicts. He worked In-Take and began to be known by the entire South Florida recovery community as someone they could turn to and he would help them. He played first base on their baseball team and they won the championship every year he did. He became very humble there and no longer cared if the designer label clothes he wore were second hand. He had pride in his appearance and the work he was doing to save others, while giving God the glory.

My husband has been in law enforcement well over twenty years and I was a magistrate for twelve. We like to believe we've impacted peoples' lives. But the outpouring of love and appreciation we got after Wesley's death was phenomenal. We had no less than fifty people reach out to us and tell us how Wesley had saved their life when they were at their lowest. He was an amazing man and still deeply missed by so many.

When Wesley graduated Faith Farm in May 2014, he chose to remain there and teach classes and work. It was home for him. In January 2015, he could not be hired on as a full-time employee, so he ended up leaving. At the same time, my husband had been transferred to Brunswick, Georgia, to be a firearms instructor at the Federal Law Enforcement Training Center. Soon after, Wesley begged me to let him come move in with me. He said he was being approached by dealers dropping heroin into his pocket trying to lure him back as a customer. He knew he wouldn't make it in that environment so he moved into our rental and would help me remodel the house we bought.

Wesley was skilled at construction and had worked for me and my mother many times in the past. He did beautiful work and was great company for me in a place where I knew no one else. It was a real gift to have him work side-by-side with me every day at twenty-eight and see he had returned to the sweet, loving man I had always hoped he would become. He told everyone he was a "Momma's boy" and didn't care what they thought. Every morning he'd bound through the kitchen door with a "Hey Momma" and a big hug. He picked our church to attend and would go to services and bible study with my husband and me each week. He had finally met a lovely girl and she was talking of moving to the area so they could be together.

The night before he died, he came to the house so excited about the positive interview he had doing maintenance work for a landlord nearby. He was expanding his business and would soon be able to support himself with it. After dinner, he was telling me and my husband that he wanted to build a dock in our backyard over our lake. He wanted to marry his girlfriend Krystle there, then have the reception in our yard. We had completed most of the renovations on the house, but he promised to come the next morning and help me paint the front door. He told me, "I love you, Mom." Then, "I love you, Rich," and went home.

When he didn't show up in the morning, I started to worry. I called and texted with no answer. My husband called and I asked him to stop by and check on Wes. I left our home at the same time. I was on the phone with Rich when he entered the house, called out to Wes, then found him dead on the floor just outside the bathroom. I hung up and called 911, but we both knew it was too late.

My worst nightmare had come true. Just when things were going so well, he made a poor choice and he's gone...forever. No marriage, no grandchildren, no starting his own business. All the hopes and dreams I had for my amazing boy were gone. The only thing that gets me through is knowing that he had been saved, and that he died in his home knowing how much he was loved.

The Orlando Drug Task Force did an amazing job. They used his phone to set up a controlled "buy" and arrested the defendant within days. He had been arrested repeatedly under the state code and got off with a slap on the wrist. He had a very swift business on an online website. He openly offered heroin for sale and included his phone number. In all the texts between him and my son, they discussed my son buying heroin. He admitted to agents that he knew he was selling pure fentanyl to his customers. Fentanyl is 50 to 100 times stronger than heroin. My son's death certificate reads "Homicide" because he was never told the drugs he was buying would kill him. I take comfort that the medical examiner said he died instantly.

My life will never be the same. I tried exercising to relieve the grief, but my heart gave out. I say it literally broke. In one year alone, I accrued over $1.3 million dollars in medical bills due to the stress of losing my son. I haven't been able to work, and am now disabled. I have been seeing a grief counselor for five years, every other week to help me cope. The opioid epidemic is killing 144 people each day in the US. This person was responsible for at least four deaths in just a few months time. This isn't including the overdoses that didn't end in death, and the other time periods when he killed others with his trafficking.

This is my Victim Impact Statement that I wrote and read aloud in court during the sentencing phase of my son, Wesley's murder trial. The defendant charged with Trafficking Resulting in Death or Serious Bodily Injury and Conspiracy was sentenced to twenty years in federal prison. I am now forever in the club, the one no parent wants to be in but you cannot get out of. My beautiful son is dead. I  would have traded places with him in an instant, but we don't get to choose. I will love and miss him every day until we are together again. I don't wish this journey on any parent, ever.

Wesley's Mom,

KRISTY D.
Brunswick, Georgia

Alicia

FOREVER 31

My daughter, Alicia Anne. Born on July 8, 1986, in Grand Rapids, Michigan. My first love.

I was in awe of her the first time I laid eyes on her. I can't believe she was my baby. She was so beautiful, and she looked like a little Indian baby. I remember telling her father to make sure there's a wristband on her hand, because I'm not letting this one get away. She was voted the most beautiful baby in the hospital. I knew this was going to be the beginning of a wonderful adventure with this tiny human.

Alicia was a joy as a child, always well-behaved and just the cutest little thing. I used to go shopping at the mall and I would dress her up and proudly walk her around as she was sitting in her stroller, looking around for compliments. I didn't brag about her because I didn't need to.

I received so much attention because she was so adorable. At six-years-old, her grandmother enrolled her in dance school and that would be the biggest part of Alicia's life. The next twelve years she participated in lyrical, jazz, ballet, and tap and would compete throughout the state of Michigan.

During her school years, she was always a pleasure for her teachers. She always had good grades and participated in many activities. These were the best times, but also some of the darkest. I left her father when she was a baby because I found out he had a severe cocaine addiction.

After many chances, I decided to leave him, for the sake of our child. I ended up pregnant with my second daughter, Justine, and later married her father who was an alcoholic. Even though Alicia excelled as she was growing up, she was hiding the fear of her stepfather and how he treated me physically and mentally.

Alicia was in a gifted class, two years in a row, for her high honors. She participated in cheerleading, track, and singing. She definitely was the highlight when it came to the boys. Alicia was very popular and spoiled. I did everything I could for my girls, being a single mom. We lived in an apartment, but I made sure my girls had nice clothes and all the things a girl would need. I always supported my girls when it came to their school activities. I wanted to give them more than what I had growing up. My girls were enrolled at a higher-rated school in the area. I wanted what was best for my children.

As Alicia was reaching graduation, she started to change and the last three months before the event, she didn't seem to care about things like she used to. She did cheerleading during her last year of high school and she stopped dancing. Since she was already eighteen-years-old, she wanted to do what young adult children want to do. Alicia was more of a follower and she just wanted to have fun and go with the crowd.

She had many friends and five of her best friends were on some kind of medication, whether for anxiety, depression, or ADHD. I remember Alicia coming home one day and telling me that she needed to be on pills. I asked her why.

She replied, "Because I need it for my anxiety."

I said, "So you're just going to diagnose yourself, because all your friends are on pills." I believe this was the start of her nightmare.

In her young adult years, she worked at different places and she was slowly developing bad habits. Like most young adults will do (I did it myself), she would start experimenting with marijuana, pain pills, and other types of pills. The pills were always given to her; they were never her own prescriptions. Sometimes she didn't control her drinking.

Alicia met a new boyfriend and moved in with him. She started to dabble and try drugs. She took the drug GHB with her boyfriend and something went terribly wrong and he left her in the bathtub.

Thank God he kept calling my youngest daughter's phone. He lied and said he was at an interview. My daughter decided to go check on her. She broke through the sliding glass door and found her. Alicia was rushed to the hospital and put on a respirator for over thirty hours. The local police were at the hospital questioning me.

I had no idea what was going on and wondered, *Why are they doing this?*

The detective told me, "If your daughter dies, her boyfriend will be charged for leaving her in the bathtub."

I didn't realize how serious this was. My daughter came through and actually ended up sticking up for him, because she claimed that she made the choice and I shouldn't blame him. My youngest daughter and I were not very happy with Alicia at the time.

Not long after that, they both moved into another apartment. Her boyfriend was being watched by the local drug force team; he was dealing drugs and after the investigation, they realized Alicia never took part in that, so only he ended up going to jail. Later she ended up leaving the boyfriend. As her mother, I'm thinking...this was a great decision on Alicia's part. I was satisfied!

It wouldn't be long after this that Alicia found another boyfriend. He was about five years younger than her, with definitely the same traits as the prior boyfriend. He was a charmer and I worried like any mother does. The mother's instinct came over me; I always felt like something bad was going to happen to her. I did not jive too well with this boyfriend. He never worked, always leeching off others and didn't have any type of transportation. There wasn't any income he contributed to their relationship.

After the first year with this man, I started to see my daughter become a different person. It was hell watching my beautiful daughter physically and emotionally changing. She wasn't communicating with her family like she used to. Our circle was being broken and the last four or five years, I had to bail my daughter out of jail a few times. Most of the charges were minor. I knew she still took pills and I'm sure she did other drugs. I was glad she was still working during this whole time.

It was about 2016; I feel my daughter is finally growing up and wants to get away from the boyfriend. She had enough of the toxic relationship. During this time, she had to go to court for inhalant charges.

Again, I didn't realize the severity of what she was involved with. I didn't know that she got hooked on methadone, another drug that was given to her by a friend which caused her to get to the point where she needed to go to a clinic on a daily basis. This was all new to me, so I am still learning and just trying to support Alicia as she struggles with this new addiction.

Alicia's anxiety grew during her adult years. It had been developing since she was a child. She watched her dad, stepfather, and boyfriends all battle their own demons. All of these men in her life that were supposed to take care of my child and love her were nothing but one failure after another.

My daughter was always quiet and would never openly talk about her feelings. She kept things bottled up in her mind; the distance from her father and how she was mistreated by the stepfather (years later, I found out my bastard husband did something sexual to my girl).

The few times I bailed Alicia out of jail, she always cried and told me how sorry she was. She was embarrassed and ashamed. I always hugged her and told her I loved her, and we would get through this together. One of my biggest mistakes was talking to a friend that works at the courthouse. She went back to talk to the judge, so my daughter would only get probation.

Later, I realized that was probably the worst thing I could ever have done. I should have talked to the judge myself. In fact, the judge's daughter was my youngest daughter's good friend in high school. Alicia would have been put in rehab during her jail time. But I did what my daughter asked, giving in to make her happy.

By the end of 2017, Alicia is slowly coming back. She is looking and sounding good but is no longer working. She is living at her grandparents and still struggling with her anxiety. In October 2017, Alicia was severely burned on her arm. She told me that she took three sleeping pills and woke up to the electric heater burning her arm.

At Thanksgiving that year my daughters, my father, and I are enjoying the holiday. Alicia returns to her grandparents and said she was having a bad anxiety attack. I was going to go pick her up, but she never answered her phone, which was a bad habit of hers. I would not see or hear from her for about three to four weeks. I became worried because she was scheduled to have a skin graft on her arm.

I had this feeling that she had gone back to her boyfriend. Sure enough, I was right. I went with her to get her skin graft and then didn't see her during Christmas. I had another one of my motherly instincts; I had a feeling she was pregnant and that was why she was back with the boyfriend. I was right again. We both had a long talk and I expressed how disappointing this was. This was not a good time. I cried and her sister cried. We were scared for Alicia because she wasn't ready.

As a mother, I had to be there for her. I told her I would support her in any way because I wanted her to be happy. She looked so good and I really thought she was on her way to recovery and changing her life. She was living about forty-five minutes to an hour away, so I didn't get to be part of her journey during her pregnancy. She left a message for me in February and she sounded sad. She wanted to tell me something after the boyfriend leaves for work. I called her back, but she did not answer.

Fast forward to April/May 2018. The last thirty-six hours with my daughter, Alicia. It was Sunday, April 29, 2018. Alicia decided she's going to come over and spend the weekend with me so we could decorate the bottles for her baby shower. She is now five months pregnant. I tried to talk her out of it because it was kind of chilly. I told her come the following weekend.

Alicia said, "No, I'll spend both weekends with you, if I have to."

We went shopping at Walmart. She returned some clothes, while I went grocery shopping. I later found her in the shoe department and stood in the aisle, staring at her. I don't know why. She looked up at me and yelled that she was going to take longer, and I could just leave. She seemed a little snotty towards me, so I stood there and continued to look at her. I was a little hurt by her mean behavior. I decided to pay for my groceries and leave. At home, I had just finished putting away my food when Alicia calls me.

She asked me, "Did you really leave me?"

I replied, "Yes."

Then she asks me, "Are you going to pick me up?"

I said, "Yes." We both ended up giggling.

I picked Alicia up and she tells me that she wants to get her ears pierced at the mall but she does not want to go to any other stores. She knows how I like shopping. I agreed, but I needed to go to Charming Charlies to buy a purse. We went to the Icing store.

The piercing was $60, and I complained about the price. I told Alicia that she needed to pay $15 and I will pay for the rest. She picked some cute white clear stones. We went to Charming Charlies and I found a purse and we went home. We ate dinner and sat around for a bit.

Around eight p.m., Alicia decided she wanted to take a bath. I was laying on my couch falling asleep. Then, I realize the water was running for a while. I'm thinking, is she taking a shower? I go to the bathroom and call out Alicia's name about three times. No answer, so I went to my toolbox and grabbed a tool to poke through the hole of the doorknob. Alicia was laying on the floor. She was breathing, she had a pulse, she just was not awake. I saw my GHC needle (vitamin B shot) sitting on the sink.

I immediately went to the living room and grabbed my cell phone to call 911. I explained what was going on, that Alicia was snoring lightly and had a pulse. The dispatcher asked if she was breathing irregularly and said I needed to start compressions.

I did over 130 compressions. I was getting tired and nervous at the same time. The first responders finally came, and they did not take over the compressions. I had moved to the living room, while there were four to six people already standing in my apartment. I started searching in her phone and purse for clues to whatever it was she took and wondering why at the same time.

At this point, Alicia is awake and a first responder and/or police officer said in a snotty tone, "Your mother just saved your life." I don't know what was being said between them as I was still searching for clues. I am just glad she is awake.

The Ottawa County Police Officer asked me what I was doing. My response was, "I want to see what my daughter took." Asshole asks me where she is staying and I replied, "She doesn't live here, she is visiting with me." He wanted to know where her belongings were, and I pointed to her bags that were sitting on the floor in the living room. He finds a bag of weed. I told him that she bought that for her "sweetie," being sarcastic. Then he makes a comment about her pile of clothes that had tags on them. His comment was, "She must have stolen these."

I told the asshole she did not because we went shopping earlier that day. He then makes a comment that he will be contacting CPS. The female first responder asked us what hospital her preference was and Alicia and I both gave her the same answer. I called my daughter, Justine, to tell her what happened, and she said she was on her way to come get me to go to the hospital.

We get to the hospital and find that Alicia is not even there. I asked the guard to please tell me the truth, even if she is there and doesn't want to see me. I want to know where she is. The guard guaranteed me that she was not there. Justine and I called around and Alicia was at another place. We go there and we had to wait in line to see her.

When we finally see her, I started asking questions. I asked Alicia why. This isn't something you just decided to do at five months preg-nant. She was getting irritated with me and told me I could leave if I wanted to. I told her I would stop asking her questions. I told her that I loved her and I'm sorry. It's getting late and Justine had to take care of Noah (my grandson).

She left to get him and came back to bring me to my car. I was so exhausted and nerved up, I didn't think to grab Alicia some clothes.I get back to the hospital and a nurse tells me that she has been discharged. I start asking Alicia questions again.

Supposedly, a social worker talked to her while I was gone and recommended a 180-network program (been there before). She got snotty again and said she should just kill herself. I told her that it wasn't fair to say that to me knowing that my twin committed suicide. We both calmed down, made it home, she went to bed, and I laid on the couch.

April 30, 2018, Monday morning. I was planning on going to work because I had to get things situated with not only Alicia but for myself. I recently found out that I have a hole in my heart. I figured, I better take care of both issues with FMLA papers and have a discussion with my boss about what to do next.

My plan was to go in at 5:00 a.m., take care of my team and go from there. I woke up late. It's around 5:30 a.m. I heard some commotion going on outside and I got up to look out the window and there was an ambulance.

I said to myself, "What the heck, is this ambulance day at Brook Meadow Apartments?"

Then it hit me. I ran into my bedroom, no Alicia. I checked the bathroom and the second bedroom and no Alicia. I ran outside, a man was sitting in his car and asked me if I was looking for a young woman. I told him I was, and he told me she is in there...pointing to the ambulance. I went to the back side of the ambulance and I looked right at the first responder. Amazingly, it's same lady that was with us hours ago.

I asked her, "What the hell is going on? Did she do it again?"

The lady looks at me with disgust and tells me she did. I hear Alicia saying she is cold as she is squirming around. The first responder asks what hospital would you like her to go to and

I replied, "Are you going to get it right this time? Try the hospital like I told you last night." I then asked why no one came to my door to tell me about my daughter.

She replied, "Well, I don't know, I thought she came from upstairs." I thought that was an odd response, like that mattered?

I say to her, "That's funny, you remembered her? I would have thought since you both (meaning her partner) were just here, the social worker."

It came out that Alicia had started her habit a year prior and had OD'd before. I was mixed up with dates and said, "Are you sure, because I brought her in myself a year ago and it was for an inhalant."

My mind was not working right, as I was completely exhausted. It was two years prior when Alicia did that. At first Alicia tried to deny it, but the social worker confirmed it was an OD. Well, she then told us there was a program for pregnant women in Alicia's situation, and typically you need a doctor's referral. But she was going to help us. I looked at Alicia and told her this was it. This was her calling and she was going to get the help she needed. She agreed and we were on our way, downtown, to the clinic.

My windshield got cracked by a rock on the way. The nurse spent an hour with her. Alicia came out and she's so tired. She made a comment that didn't make sense. She said she did not want to go through the hell of being on methadone or Suboxone. She also asked for a bus schedule.

I turned and looked at her with a strange look, because I knew she was out of it. Alicia refuses to take a bus anywhere. We went home and folded her new clothes.

I said, "Alicia, don't worry about that right now. You are so tired. That's not important right now."

We decided to go to the pharmacy together and get her prescriptions. We were told that we had to wait about twenty minutes. I am driving around wasting time and at the same time I am talking to a lady about getting my windshield fixed. The woman on the phone is driving me nuts and at the same time, Alicia is nodding while I'm talking on the phone.

I yelled at Alicia, "Are you alright?"

We get her meds and go home. Justine is coming back with her dogs and Noah to visit Alicia. I'm a nervous wreck, just waiting for them to get there because she is so tired. I'm tired, stinky, and we both need to rest. Alicia is sitting outside looking up at the sky with her face towards the sun. Justine gets here and they take a walk to the play area. I take a quick shower. Then, I make dinner. Alicia doesn't like my chicken tacos and is throwing it all up.It's now eight p.m., so we both decide we are going to bed.

In the middle of the night, Tuesday morning, I wake up to a noise around two-thirty a.m. Alicia is in my Nike sweats going through my bottom drawer. I ask her what she is doing.

She says, "Putting on your pants."

I said of course it would be my Nike pants. We both giggle. She said she needed to go to the bathroom.As she is sitting on the toilet, we are having small talk and she tells me, "I'm constipated."

Half an hour has passed, she is kind of nodding and I tell her she is so tired to just go to bed. She gets up and goes to bed. I lay back down on the couch, but I couldn't sleep. I get up to get things ready for Alicia before I attempt to go to work again, to get things straightened out. I set Alicia's phone alarm for her to get up at 10:30 a.m.; I wrote her a note and placed it on the bathroom door.

I wrote, "Alicia, Stay Strong. I love you. Keys & pills are by the TV." I laid down next to her to listen to her breathing. It was a different snore than the other night. I'm wondering to myself, "Is my girl going to get through this?" I held her hand, kissed her, and left. I sent a message to my team lead that I was on my way. A few hours later, I told my other team lead that I didn't feel right. She told me to go home. I told her I planned on doing so, after I talked to the boss.

At around ten-thirty a.m., I'm talking to Justine on the phone, who says she is going to drop off a strawberry smoothie for Alicia to have when she wakes up. I told Justine to call me when she gets there.

I kept calling Justine but she didn't answer. After three attempts, she answered and said, "Alicia's dead."

I'm in shock and I'm thinking I left my baby. I now have to plan a funeral for my beautiful daughter and her unborn baby girl, my grand-daughter, Braylee Anne. We did this and three days later my daughter is laying in a casket, ready for her funeral.

Nobody wants to go to a funeral, but I probably had the most compliments anybody ever could have. It was beautiful; it was all about her and Braylee. The pastor told her story. My youngest daughter, Justine, and I both spoke at her funeral. We couldn't give her the baby shower and we were going to make damn sure she was going to leave this earth being proud of us. I don't know how the hell we pulled it off.

I'm sharing this story because I want other mothers and loved ones to know what signs to look for. There were many signs that I missed. People don't understand addicts and how their minds work. They made the choice, or they just want to get high, but that wasn't the case with my daughter. I didn't go through all the bad stuff like other families have been through when their loved ones are battling addiction; how they lie, steal, and continually batter you physically, mentally, and emotionally, stripping from you what used to be.

My daughter didn't have a chance to go to rehab. Yes, a lot of people are probably wondering how my daughter OD'd three times in thirty-six hours. Believe me, I searched high and low during this whole time. The cops and I failed to find the drugs which were two feet away from my bed. The aftermath was horrific.

We found the drugs, two days later, and they had me bring them to my other daughter's house, and they took two more days before they came to pick them up. Come to find out it was almost pure fentanyl and we all could have died from having contact with this s***. The detective took my daughter's phone for six weeks and returned it saying there's nothing they could do, because I erased the message, even though I gave them the phone number.

Amazingly, I downloaded an app that recovered all her old messages. I just didn't know that this would lead to a beautiful young woman's life coming to an end so early. Alicia never had a chance to be a mother. She always loved others and never received love in return. You find out things after somebody dies when people come forward and tell you the truth.

I found out how the boyfriend knew she was on heroin; how he gave her s*** during the last hours; about how he said she deserved to die and that he didn't want her to go to rehab because he wouldn't be able to watch the baby grow in her stomach.

That's how much of a sick f***** he is. I found out her grandfather found his diabetic needle on the floor after she moved out. Her grandparents are AA sponsors and they didn't bother to tell anybody what they found? That her high school friend introduced her to heroin, to help make her feel better.

My daughter Alicia died from an unintentional fentanyl overdose that was administered through her nose. Her life is gone because of something she snorted through her nose. My beautiful, talented, smart, kind, soft-spoken, loving baby girl is GONE. May 1, 2018 .

Alicia's Mom,

AMALIE E.
Wyoming, Michigan

Jason

FOREVER 27

Dear Jason,

You brought so much joy to our lives!

From the instant we found out I was pregnant, love grew in our hearts. And this miracle came into our lives, a perfect, sweet little baby boy that inspired us in so many ways!

I remember that your dad and I could not get enough of you and would argue about who got to hold you. People would warn us that babies shouldn't be held too much, or they would be spoiled. Not true. You were calm, content, and happy.

You continued to amaze us every day. You were sensitive, yet brave and adventurous. And absolutely crazy smart. You were like a walking little sponge that would absorb everything.

And it never stopped. Year after year you grew smarter with a witty, unique sense of humor. And our hearts were filled with pride and love.

I remember the first week of kindergarten when the teacher called me in for a meeting. She wanted to let us know that you could not be in that class because you were so far ahead of the other kids. She was impressed with your vocabulary and mature behavior for your age. She proceeded to tell me about the time she had the kids sit in a circle and played a game to observe their capabilities. They had to throw a little bag at each other and name the part of the body it landed on, such as hand, leg, foot, head etc.

When it was your turn and the bag landed on your chest, you confidently said "pectoral muscle." They then convinced us that you should be tested to be placed in the Gifted Program. Well, that year you were not only placed in the Gifted Program but were moved ahead to first grade, plus attended second grade English classes.

When I think back, maybe it was not a very smart decision on our part. You may have been pushed too hard, too early. It was like you did not fit anywhere and you tried too hard to please. At times it seemed that you were more comfortable in an adult world than a child's one.

Six years later, we were blessed with another wonderful little boy. Your brother Jesse was born. Jesse grew up watching your every move and loving you like a superhero.

You and your brother filled our hearts with joy, and we continued to motivate you to explore and learn. Since our family is a melting pot, our goal was to have you know both sides of our heritage. We are blessed with an adventurous family who embraced this and generously shared their love and resources.

We made incredible memories on trips to Iceland and Brazil. Uncle Don, Ruthann, and Jara led the way on expeditions through the woods, the beach, diving lessons, skiing and, most importantly, through sharing their experiences and stimulating your curiosity.

Berta and Kristjan welcome you many times and taught you about Icelandic culture and nature. You also went on a youth mission trip to Honduras with our beloved priests, Father Harris and Father Vargas.

Family has always been a big part of your life. Uncle Brian encouraged a passion for football, especially the FSU Seminoles. You were privileged to have spent time with Uncle Danny, who has also left us. Remember when you got a pet snake and I absolutely would not live under the same roof with that creature? It was Uncle Danny who fostered the snake for you.

When you were ten-years-old, you spent the summer with Vovo Cyra (Grandma Cyra), exploring Virginopolis (a small town in Brazil) with cousins Ana and Flavia. You visited farms, milked cows, rode horses, and met and played with many cousins. To our surprise, you came back not only speaking Portuguese but had adapted your sense of humor to Brazilian culture. Though Vovo Cyra has visited us many times in the US, she cherishes that time she spent with you.

When it was time to go to high school, you did not seem to find a place for the perfect, well behaved, smart little boy you had been. All you wanted was to be like everybody else. You struggled, and we did not see it. All we saw was this handsome, charming, intelligent young man with nothing but success ahead of him. What we also did not realize was that out there, there were monsters preying on confused adolescents.

You graduated with honors and were awarded prestigious scholarships to go to college. But little by little, you pulled away. And the monsters would not leave you alone. As you started to mature, you fought them. And we fought them with you with unconditional love. The burden was dark, heavy, and lonely. We had amazing support from family and friends who were always by our side offering love with no judgement. My brother Leo and his wife Jackie have walked this journey with us.

This past year, things started to clear up and we finally had you back. Our Jason was home, whole. We enjoyed and shared Thanksgiving, Christmas, and my birthday with family and friends. You were surrounded by love, laughter, and joy. Every day, Mom got to kiss you good morning and good night and tell you that she loved you. Dad loved played golf with you on Sundays. And life was normal again. Through all the suffering you had endured, you had become a strong, resilient man. And as always, we were so proud.

But the fight was not over, and the monster came back to hound you. This time God said: "Enough."

You can have his body, but his soul is mine.

Jason you are in heaven now, in peace and free. We love you and will miss you forever.

Mom, Dad, and Jesse

That is the letter I wrote and read at my son's funeral service.

Jason was twenty-seven years old when he accidentally overdosed from heroin and fentanyl after ten-and-a-half months being clean and sober from it all including alcohol and cigarettes.

So, the remaining question is, How did we get here?

It was a long ten years journey with some periods of peace. We found out Jason was using drugs shortly after he turned eighteen. One Sunday morning, we were awoken by the knock of the police on our door. Jason was caught stealing from unlocked cars in our own neighborhood. Jason received a five-years probation. We went to family counseling and thought that things would get better.

In between all of this, Jason's best friend Gene accidentally overdosed on pills and Xanax and died. On the day of the funeral, all the friends got together and went to the beach for Gene's celebration of life. That's when another friend had an accident and became paralyzed.

Jason then asked for help and went to a sixty-day rehab. Before he got out, they recommended not to bring him home (big mistake) so he could be accountable for his mistakes. Jason started working with my brother and we were renting a room for him in one of my brother's friend's home. While he was in rehab, he became friends with another young man who had family issues and no place to stay. So, Jason would let his friend come and sleep there sometimes.

One week, Jason had been missing work, saying that he was sick. So, I decided to stop by with the intention of taking him to a doctor. When I got there, Jason told me that he woke up and found his friend dead from an overdose. They had both used pills the night before. Jason got sick during the night, threw up, and went back to sleep. When I got there, he went to get his friend up and realized he was gone. I believe this was just too much for him to handle. Using drugs was the only way to deal with all the pain and chaos.

After this experience, he fought really hard to stay sober. Jason worked in our business with his dad for over six years. During that time, he had periods of sobriety and mostly managed to function well. He would ask for help when it would start to get out of control. He was in detox, rehabs, and halfway houses many times.

He overdosed at least eight times before. Most of the overdoses occurred while he was in halfway houses.

Jason loved family and he truly enjoyed all the holidays. No matter what was going on, we made sure to take a break from any drama and enjoy the holidays together.

I could go on and on, but the truth is Jason so very much wanted to be well. Addiction is a horrible, unforgiving, relentless disease. I wish I knew more about drugs. I have never done any type of drugs in my entire life. I have not even tried marijuana. If I did, I would perhaps have recognized the signs earlier or before he got to the hard drugs.

I would recommend to every parent to learn about drugs before your children do. Have a well-informed conversation about all types of drugs. Do not just say that drugs are bad. Back it up with facts and discuss it. Do not protect and shelter them from the reality. Do not over-react when they tell you something that they did wrong. If they are afraid of your reaction, they will start lying. As parents, we convince ourselves that our kids are perfect. And they are. However, pay attention to their personality. It is true that we love all our children the same. But they are not the same. Pay attention to unusual behavior and follow your gut.

I hope Jason's story will help save someone.

Jason. My beautiful boy. Forever loved and never forgotten.

Jason's Mom,

MARIA F.
Boynton Beach, Florida

Delaney

The pain of losing a child is like no other pain a person can feel. However, when a mother loses a child to drug addiction, I feel the pain and loss are even worse. We don't get the sympathy from the world or even our own family, in many cases, as that from a child who dies of any other disease. Our child's death is attached to a stigma, loneliness, and immense guilt. After all, it is a mother's most important job to protect her child from harm. How could I have failed so miserably?

Over and over in my mind I ask, "How the hell did I get here?" Only another mother who has been through this nightmare can truly ever understand.

I don't know exactly when my daughter Delaney started using heroin, but I'll never forget the day I figured it all out. I think I may have been in denial for many months and I'm ashamed that I didn't figure it out earlier, especially since I work in the medical field. Because she didn't have needle marks and was capable of holding a job, etc., I just blew off the innuendos and other telltale signs; plus, my husband at the time convinced me her behavior was normal and "all the other kids were doing the same crap."

So, two nights in a row, I found a piece of my old jewelry on the kitchen counter. Knowing that they were hidden in a safe box, I didn't understand how they got out and when I confronted my daughter, she admitted to taking out a gold baby bracelet because she "thought it was a hoop earring."

When I tried to explain to her that she had no right to be taking my stuff, both she and my husband made me out to be the bad guy. My ex-husband went as far as to say, "She just wants to be like you, what's the big deal if she wears your jewelry?"

A few minutes later when I went to return the bracelet to the box, I realized all my valuable jewelry was missing. I opened each little box that should have held diamond rings, pearl necklaces, and gold earrings and found them all to be empty. My world as I knew it came crashing down. At that point I knew it must be true, that my daughter had a major drug problem and was selling my jewelry to support her habit. Of course, she lied and totally denied that she was using drugs and my ex-husband said that he had a long talk with her and I'm just blowing it out of proportion, blah, blah blah.

After months of fights and lies, we finally convinced her to go to rehab. On September 11, 2013, she went to her first of many rehabs for twenty-eight days. At the time, we didn't tell anyone. My ex and I depended on each other to get her through this. He told me to tell no one as everyone would judge us for being bad parents. I don't know exactly what was going through his mind, but I remember feeling so humiliated. The feelings of guilt and failure as a mother were over-whelming.

We never cried so much in our lives, but we were also so happy and full of hope, dropping her off at this big old mansion in the middle of nowhere in Pennsylvania. It had an excellent reputation for treatment of drug and alcohol abuse. It was the go-to treatment center for NYC cops, firefighters, and their families. Unfortunately, back then the rehabs weren't prepared for the opioid epidemic and her treatment was basi-cally the 12-Steps used for alcoholism. As we know now, that simply just doesn't work for an opioid addict.

When Delaney first went to rehab, she was only snorting heroin (hence the reason she had no needle marks) but shortly after her first rehab stint, she started shooting up...needless to say, things went from bad to worse. Over the course of the next two years, things at home became unbearable. I used to call my home, "The House of Horrors." I literally had one of the nicest homes in the whole town. From the outside, we looked like an upper middle class, successful, loving family, but the inside told a totally different story.

My ex-husband and I always disagreed on how to raise the kids and that part of parenting responsibility only got worse. We had several loser boyfriends living in the house, kids hanging out in the garage, doing things they shouldn't be doing, and of course Delaney up all night and sleeping all day. Without fail, I got woken up in the middle of the night, due to one ordeal or another. Every light would be left on and the kitchen a mess...forget about her bathroom or bedroom. I used to tell her squatters had more pride of ownership. Needless to say, I had to keep my bedroom locked and any valuables around the house hidden at all times. Our lives were in turmoil.

After participating in outpatient therapy, she started getting the Vivitrol shots. The closest clinic was over an hour away and we thought things were going well, but she was somehow able to still do the drugs and get her shots, which on one occasion almost killed her. She had stopped going for her Vivitrol treatments for several months, but then my ex-husband convinced her to start them up again. He drove her to the clinic and even though she tested positive for heroin the doctor gave her the shot along with several prescriptions to get her through the acute withdrawal, which he knew was inevitable. They drove off and my ex stopped at the first drug store he could find to fill the many prescriptions.

Within ten minutes, Delaney's boyfriend at the time came running into the store to tell her dad that she was really sick. When her dad came out to the truck, he found her convulsing in the back seat covered in vomit and diarrhea. But instead of bringing her to the ER, he drove her to a motel, cleaned her up, and stayed the night. His rationale for that was he didn't want to get the doctor into trouble for giving her the Vivitrol shot while she was using…that's how desperate we were for his help.

A few days later, she told me she never ever wanted to go through that again and swore to get sober, but within days she was using again. It came to a point that I just knew in my gut that this situation was not going to end well, and I started changing up my prayers. I used to pray every night and begged God to make her clean and sober. Please! But after so many years of unanswered prayers, I remember one night I said, "God, if she is going to die of a drug overdose, please have her do it soon."

The pain of watching my child suffer from this disease was so debilitating. What kind of mother prays for that? Who asks God to take their child from them? But I loved her more then I loved myself and if it took away her suffering, then I could live with that. It didn't make it hurt any less in the end, but I feel that she is safe and pain free now.

Throughout this whole ordeal, I was working part time as an LPN and going to nursing school, which included classroom and clinical to get my RN. In 2015, I got my nursing license and was able to finally take care of myself. After almost thirty years of marriage, I left. I truly believed at the time that it was the best thing for everyone. My kids were all adults and I could no longer condone their behavior. My marriage and relationship with my kids was truly toxic and I could no longer handle it.

Looking back, I remembered thinking that I needed to show my girls that they could work hard and be self-sufficient, if they tried. That they don't have to be controlled and abused by men.

Two weeks later, Delaney overdosed for the first time. She was revived with Narcan and brought to the ER. With the help of the social workers, she was placed on the psych ward for a few days and then transferred to another rehab. If I remember correctly, that same scenario happened again a few months later. Once when she was locked away and sober, she actually told me the story about the first overdose. She said when she woke up on the floor surrounded by EMTs, she realized she had peed her pants. She knew she was going to the hospital, so she convinced them to let her go to the bathroom, clean up, and change her jeans. While she was doing all that, she took the last of her stash and shot up again...no one being the wiser.

One of the arguments that my ex and I used to have was over the fact that he was constantly enabling the kids. Always supplying them with money, cars, luxury drug dens, and always getting them out of legal trouble. After the last overdose, my ex finally agreed that I was right and instead of trying to keep her out of the legal system, he needed to get her into it.

At the time, we both felt it was the only way to save her life. She had gotten caught with heroin and was put on probation, but then tested positive while on house arrest; so, after almost three years of trying to help her, she was finally put into jail. She agreed to a two-year drug rehabilitation program, which started out with the county jail (time already served), then state prison, boot camp, rehab, and finally sober living in a halfway house, until she was well enough to come home for good.

Although the jail and prison kept her clean, they did little to help her once she got out. It was also very upsetting to see your child in such a place, but we all agreed it was for the best. When she went to boot camp, I think they finally started helping with her rehabilitation, but I also remember thinking she still had not 100% convinced me she was going to try her hardest when she got out.

In the first rehab, they teach you that once you become sober, you are at the age that you started doing drugs or alcohol. So even though Delaney was twenty-two at the time, I remember thinking she was acting like she was sixteen. She still had a long way to becoming the woman that I knew she could become if she tried. After boot camp, she was sent to a rehab in Reading, Pennsylvania. It has since closed down because of several overdoses and deaths of people in the program. We knew this rehab had a bad reputation, but it was state mandated, so we told her she had to be extra strong. Unfortunately, she wasn't, and she had gotten caught doing drugs there on two occasions (I believe), but instead of sending her back to prison, they just extended her rehab for another two weeks.

After that, she went to a halfway house in Williamsport, Pennsylvania. Again, we thought she was doing OK. She had gotten a job at a local hotel and was attending mandatory NA classes. I'm not sure exactly what happened over the course of the last week or so, but from what I gathered, Delaney started using again and got caught by the counselors at the halfway house. Someone told us that she was crying on the phone and wanted to be picked up, but the counselors told her to stay at work.

The next morning, I saw that I had a missed call from the halfway house and a voice mail that indicated that Delaney never came home the night before. When I called the counselors, they told me that when she gets picked up, she will be going back to jail. Because Delaney was still considered a ward of the state, I asked if we would be notified once they found her, but the counselor didn't know. I went on to call the Williamsport Police Station and asked the same thing. I asked if someone could go to the hotel and look for her. I told them that she had a drug problem and she may need help, but they wouldn't go. No one could answer my question regarding if we would be notified once she was found.

I called my other daughter and told her what was going on and asked if she knew anything, which she didn't. A few hours later, my daughter called me back, crying hysterically and said Delaney was dead!

I asked her how she knew, and she said that the girls in the halfway house were posting RIP on Delaney's Facebook page. I could't believe it, because the counselors or the police never called me, but when I called the halfway house, they confirmed it was true. I was hoping that it was all a mistake, but they said she had her license on her, so it wasn't necessary for me to identify the body.

That night my ex, our two other children, and I went to the hotel to see if we could feel her there and see the place where she died. The desk clerk was indifferent but very cooperative. He showed us the surveillance video of Delaney walking into the lobby bathroom at 7:53 p.m. on June 30, 2017, approximately twelve hours before she was found. He told us that a random hotel guest saw her on the floor in the next stall and alerted him. He said when he found her, that her face was in the toilet; however, the coroner said that was not true and that she was sitting up with the needle still in her hand.

She explained that she most definitely died right away and that there was nothing anyone could have done. She suspects that because she hadn't been using that much since she was locked away that her body couldn't handle the larger than usual dose. According to the coroner, she only had heroin in her system and there was no fentanyl. However, she had additional bags of heroin in her purse, one which contained carfentanyl, which apparently is an elephant sedative.

The dealer who sold her that bag is in jail because his stash resulted in over fifty other overdoses that weekend, in which three people died. Unfortunately, they don't have enough evidence to arrest the drug dealer that sold her the drugs that killed her and the one other person that was a witness to that crime is now dead, as well.

When it came time to write her obituary, I knew instantly I wanted to do it. When I sat down, the words just flowed. It was so easy to describe what an amazing person she was, but sadly had a drug problem. I didn't hide the cause of death and I also included a poem that Delaney had written just a few months before.

Delaney Marie of Selinsgrove passed away on Saturday, July 1, 2017, in Williamsport, Pennsylvania, after a long and hard battle with drug addiction.

She was born in Nyack, New York.

If there was one word to describe Delaney, I'm sure everyone would agree that it would be "funny." Delaney loved to laugh and make people laugh. She would always make jokes, stupid remarks and facial impressions, which would get those around her roaring even in the most serious of moments.

Delaney was also known for her love of Oreo cookies. This addiction started in the third grade during her special reading class. Every time she read a sentence correctly, she received an Oreo. Needless to say, Delaney loved to read and read often. However, even with no books around Delaney could be found eating Oreo cookies by the dozen. While holding three to four cookies at a time, she would dunk them into a big glass of milk to soften and shove them all in her mouth at once. Ironically, at twenty-three years old she never had a cavity.

She loved social networking and was usually found posting selfies on Facebook. She was absolutely beautiful and had a singing voice to match. Another one of Delaney's hobbies was writing. When she was younger, she would often write silly stories about her family or her beloved pets, including her many dogs, cats, rabbits, squirrels, horses, and even a llama.

Delaney would also write in her journals or on just random pieces of paper; some were private but some she would share. She forwarded one of her last entries to her sister, which depicts the pain and suffering that she was enduring throughout this horrific drug epidemic that has affected so many families in this country. Her soul is finally at peace.

Sadly, for us, but lucky for her, God was listening and answered her prayers. Now she is no longer in pain and is flying free.

After her obituary was published, it instantly went viral and millions of people read it. To this day, we get messages from people telling us how it has helped them in recovery.

Shortly after, I was asked to speak at an opioid symposium in Washington DC, and actually met with Surgeon General Jerome Adams, which was an amazing experience. It really gave me hope that the world was getting together to find a solution to the drug epidemic. Sadly, three years later it's still such a major problem.

I participate in other drug aware-ness projects on occasion, but these days I mostly just keep to myself. I think about my daughter every single day and hold onto the belief that we will see each other again someday. It may sound silly, but to make myself feel better I equate her death (and all the deaths of our children) to that of soldiers going off to war for their country. It's the War on Drugs. They've risked their lives to help save millions of others; their deaths were Not in Vain!

Delaney's Mom,

Bridget F.
Selinsgrove, Pennsylvania

Samuel

FOREVER 27

My story of a child with addiction is a little different in that Samuel didn't get prescribed opioids for a surgery or for pain management of any kind. Unfortunately and honestly, I have to put together pieces. I don't know exactly how Sam got to the point of using heroin and meth. I never asked him about it. I didn't know he was to that point until it was too late for him to talk about it.

I believe Sam's drug use started as a fairly young teenager. It was just plain old peer pressure. I homeschooled my boys from about second grade on. I felt it was the "table" thing to do. I was in a marriage that wasn't the best. There were signs of my ex-husband having the "addictive gene," in that alcohol was a more powerful force than fatherhood was—at least at that time. We had already moved a couple times and I didn't want the boys to continually be changed from school to school. Ultimately, that marriage ended in divorce and I continued, as a single parent, homeschooling until the boys reached high school level. At that point, it was a whole lot more involved than I wanted to tackle, so I enrolled them in high school. And here is where I second guess myself every day!! Did me putting them in "mainstream" school steer them towards the unexplored? Did the fact that they didn't deal with peer pressure up until high school drive them to try to impress? Did they not know how to say "no?" Had I not equipped them for the "real world?"

At some point, Sam tried marijuana. At this time, I, as well as his father, did not really look at pot as being anything but a social drug. I had smoked weed in my earlier years and didn't really put it in the same category as a hard drug. I really didn't consider it a "gateway" drug. So consequently, I didn't really come down too hard on his smoking pot every now and then. Oh, if I could only go back to that time. This is the time I believe peer pressure and the wrong "friends" came into the picture. Sam got mixed up with the wrong crowd and I believe he must have started with trying pills along with pot. This is where a LOT of the unknown comes in for me. I can only assume and look back on things that are plain as day now! Then, I either chose to turn a blind eye or ignore it in hope that I was looking at it all wrong.

In Sam's later teen years, he shifted to IV use of drugs: heroin! His dad and I found out and quickly tried to get him into some sort of treatment. Of course, the lack of affordable resources for us at that time, about ten years ago, was a big stumbling block. By his choice, Sam ended up on methadone. I honestly didn't know much about his choice. He had done the research and came up with this as his way of "getting clean." He actually educated me on this form of treatment. This worked very well for him for many years.

Sam started educating and teaching himself the ins and outs of knife making. Long story VERY short. He ended up becoming a worldwide known self-taught knife maker. His knives were sought after around the globe. He had thousands of people that followed his adventures in this knife making world. At some point, he decided for multiple reasons that he could begin the process of coming off the methadone. He started decreasing the dosage of his daily amount of methadone. He did it precisely and methodically, so that I really felt like he was doing it the right way. I even encouraged him. (Sadly so.)

I really don't know when the shift happened, but Sam was not strong enough to beat the withdrawals of methadone. He also had a new girlfriend that we found out later, along with her mother, were actually dealers!! That sure didn't help matters any. I started noticing his lack of communication, and he was asking for money for materials for his knives. He wanted me to use my PayPal account to help with his money flow from customers. In some of his knife-making videos, his hands were shaky. I attributed all this to withdrawing from the methadone. How wrong I was! He was dope sick from needing his next dose of heroin or meth.

Looking back, there were soooo many signs! Did I ignore them and try to tell myself that it wasn't what it was? YES!! I wanted to believe that it wasn't true. Well, to bring the story full circle, Sam had some trouble with the law in Idaho. He was arrested for a felony possession of methamphetamines. He had to go back and forth for court, and by this time, was so deep into the drugs, he missed court dates. He ended up having a bondsman on the hunt for him. This was his ultimate demise. He ended up in prison in Idaho for almost a year. He got sober, as much as one can, in prison. We had high hopes for him. He completed a rehab program in prison and was released with strict stipulations to my care back in North Carolina. He of course had rules he was to adhere to.

Sam arrived here in North Carolina on July 16, 2019. He stayed here with me and my husband. We had plenty to keep him busy and had laid the groundwork for a transition back to the county where he could be close to his shop and close to transportation for his business. We knew he was overwhelmed by this transition and knew he felt he had a long uphill climb. We had no idea just how overwhelmed he was! On July 25, I dropped him off to stay with his dad for the weekend. The next day, he had plans to hang out with an old, sober friend, at least that's what we thought. July 26th was the last anybody heard from him.

My last message from Sam: "Everything is fine."

We found him under a bridge four days later. He had overdosed that July 26th night, likely just because his tolerance was low and his system couldn't handle it. As of this writing, I still don't have the autopsy report. It really doesn't matter. I don't have my son. That's what matters! So many takeaways from this story! I wish more than anything that I knew then what I know now. So many regrets, so many things I would change. But none of that matters. What matters is what I do with what I know now. I will do my son proud and not let his death be in vain. I will hopefully help others to not have to experience the loss of a child. And I will help my remaining son to NOT travel the same road! I am better equipped to help him and hopefully watch him travel the road to recovery.

Samuel's Mom,

LISA F.
Waynesville, North Carolina

Joseph

I had been dealing with Joe's addictions for the past eight years or so. He would take anything. Joe's addictions had taken his looks and his self-esteem. He could not tolerate anyone who was critical of him and when on Xanax, everyone was his enemy.

About four years ago, Joe got high and went downtown with his friends and was so high, he lost them. He subsequently broke into a church in his bare feet and pajamas, was busted and thrown in jail. I was relieved. I knew he would die if he kept going the way he was. I was ready to let him sit in jail and hopefully get clean.

My ex, his dad, would have no part in that. All the way from Oregon, he bailed this kid out and where else would he go, but to me. He came home and continued his use. I could not put him on the street. I thought I could protect him, if he was home. He was busted a few more times after that for DUI and sentenced to drug court and probation.

Joe did well the first few months and stayed clean and sober. Little by little, he would start to drink on the weekends, knowing he would test clean if he had to test on Monday. One of his friends introduced him to Kratom. It has the same opioid addiction properties and when it was hard for him to get that, he went to Tianna.

COVID-19 hit and all support from the system stopped; no more AA meetings, no testing, no probation other than Zoom. His addiction was raging. On June 2, 2020, Joe reached out to his old dealer and arranged to purchase seven Xanax bars. I found this out after his death when I was finally given access to his e-mail through Google. I reset his Facebook password and found the whole deal. I was working in my office that day, a room right next to his. I saw him that morning and he seemed okay. I always knew when he was on Xanax; he had a look. I thought he was doing okay, so I paid no attention to the bang I heard on his wall while I was working.

He was a gamer and often had outbursts during gaming. I got off work and saw his door was open and his van was there. My husband asked where he was, and I figured he just took off with a friend. I walked into his room twice, trying to see what he might have taken with him. The second time I saw his wallet and noticed a crushed-up substance and a dollar bill on his desk.

I was madder than a hornet and was ready to confront him when he came home. Around nine thirty p.m. when I knew he had to go to work, I texted him and did not get a delivered message, so I called him. Straight to voicemail. I decided to go into his room and look for his phone.

Twice I was in his room, once right at his desk. I did not see him crumpled on the floor, at the wall next to his desk. He was cold and blue in the face, as his face had been on the floor. I knew he was dead.

This image never leaves my mind, ever. Why didn't I get nosy and gripe about the bang? I lost my Babyloo and even though we will never admit to our kids that we have a favorite, he was mine. He is survived by three older brothers and one younger and a host of friends and family who loved him.

Joseph's Mom,

TRACY F.
Huntsville, Alabama

Anthony

Anthony was a true and loyal friend. After Anthony passed away, a few young men told me stories about how they were shy or kept to themselves and how Anthony reached out to them and became their friend. Anthony tried to fit in with the good kids but was shunned on many occasions. So, he began to change to a group that accepted him. They started smoking marijuana in eighth grade and started taking Oxycontin in twelfth grade. Anthony always wanted to have friends and he was very loyal to them.

I do believe Anthony had some issues, although throughout his life I took him to four psychologists and the only diagnosis he got was ODD, Obstinate Defiant Disorder.

Anthony was very intelligent, never had to study and always had above a 3.5 GPA. He liked to make people laugh and he joked around a lot. He got into Penn State, main campus in State College, Pennsylvania, based on his SAT scores and his GPA. In his sophomore year, he joined the fraternity Alpha Sigma Phi.

During the Christmas break of 2009, he told us he was addicted to Oxycontin. He said he could detox at home and would just take more time before returning to Penn State. This was the first time we had heard any of this. He promised he wouldn't use anymore. Looking back at this, we were very naive and did not understand the disease of addiction.

He returned to school in January, 2010 and began using again. When he came home at the end of the semester, we sent him to a relative's house for the summer, away from his addicted "friends." The whole time we kept in touch. He was passing urine tests, and everything seemed to be going well. Anthony wanted to go back and finish college at the main campus. Once again, we did not understand the disease of addiction and let him go back in the fall of 2010.

We found out in the beginning of 2011 that he was using again and pulled him out on a medical leave. This time we sent him to a rehab in Florida. It was a twenty-eight day inpatient treatment.

When he returned everything seemed fine. He had a friend pick him up to go to NA meetings. He would show us a chip for being clean for a certain amount of time. We thought he was clean, therefore we let him return to Penn State in 2012.

At some point he switched to heroin because it was cheaper. Anthony had periods of time where he actually was clean. During those times, he would tell us things he had lied about in the past. One thing he told us was that he had never gone to the NA meetings, he was just taking the chips and still using. In the beginning of 2012, two of his best friends came to our house and told us he had switched to heroin and was injecting it. Because of their courage, we had more time with Anthony. We went up and picked him up and left everything there. We just had to get him home.

We were then referred to an inpatient rehab facility in Pennsylvania. We didn't have insurance, so they only kept him about five days, just long enough to detox. He was diagnosed with depression, but we were never informed of that. Once again, when he came home he said he wouldn't use anymore. He stayed home that summer, worked and seemed to be doing fine. In the fall, he enrolled at the Abington campus, about thirty minutes from home, since we refused to let him go back to the main campus. He had totaled his car, so my husband drove him to school in the morning and he hitched a ride home with one of his classmates or sometimes took the bus.

What we didn't know was that he had made a copy of his dad's car key and was sneaking out in the middle of the night to go to Kensington, also known as the "Badlands," to get heroin. At some point, he and his "friends" added cocaine to the mix. He had been on Suboxone in the past and while on it he did not use. But he did not take it all the time. He overdosed May 23, 2013, in our basement, but one of the boys came and got me. I called 911. He was given Naloxone, which saved his life. In the ER the nurses tried to give him another Naloxone shot, but he fought them and wouldn't allow it because he wanted to enjoy what was left of his high. That's how powerful of a hold heroin has on its victims. Less than an hour earlier, Anthony had almost died, but he still wanted the drug. Because his heroin usage had depressed his breathing so much and allowed fluid to collect in his lungs, Anthony developed pneumonia.

We then tried Vivitrol. This is a shot a doctor gives every twenty-eight days. When he got his shot, it worked. He found a way around it and didn't take it every twenty-eight days, as prescribed. He would wait until about thirty-two days, get high, wait a couple more days, then get the shot. Then one day he said he wasn't going to get it anymore. We did the hardest thing we had ever done and said he could no longer live with us if he wasn't getting the Vivitrol. We were all crying. At some point, he had gotten another car, which he packed up with clothes and left. He was out of the house for nine days, living in his car and shooting heroin. Every day we worried. He finally agreed to get the shot. I said I would meet him at the doctor's and only after getting the shot could he come home.

In the summer of 2013, Anthony and the other boys robbed a drug dealer thinking that a drug dealer wouldn't go to the police. Well, the boy's mom did, and a warrant was issued. Months later, Anthony was stopped in Kensington for possession of heroin, and when they found out about the warrant in Bucks County for the robbery, they sent him to Bucks County Prison. We refused to bail him out despite his constant pleas because we felt at the time that prison was where he needed to be and at least he was clean.

After he had been in prison for a month, we hired a private criminal defense attorney, who was able to arrange for Anthony to be released on his own recognizance, on the condition that he immediately go to an inpatient rehab facility. By this time, we had insurance, but once again, the recommended program was only twenty-one days. I begged the facility to keep him, but they said that's all insurance pays for. After the twenty-one days, they sent him to a sober living house. The person in charge was the recovering addict who had been there the longest. Anthony was told to go out for eight hours a day and look for work. The first day he called me and told me he was passing corners where dealers were and where he used to buy drugs. We went and picked him up and brought him home that night.

This time he said HE wanted to stay clean. All the other times we had made him go to rehab, but this time was different. HE wanted to be sober. He started cooking dinner for the family and hanging out with his younger brother, Nick, which he never did before. They would go to the movies, go to the gym, and various other things brothers do. I said, "I finally have my Anthony back." We felt like he had won. He looked good, acted fine, and was not argumentative and agitated as he was when using. He got a job at Passanante's Food Service in Bensalem, Pennsylvania, which he really enjoyed. He was doing well. He bought a pure-bred boxer that he named Caesar. He was saving to move out on his own.

We told him none of the boys he had hung around with in the past could come over again and he should find new friends. This lasted about four to five months, then one day he said, "Phil is coming over."

Anthony said he was the only person he knew who was clean. In fact, Phil was not clean and still using. Phil was with Anthony the entire night and morning when he died. Phil said he didn't have any idea what happened, but he did find time to steal Anthony's debit/credit card from his deceased body and proceed to spend $2,500.

I found my son's body. What an awful thing for a mother to go through. We are broken. Anthony received four years' probation for the robbery. We think he wanted to get high "one more time" since he had received a letter from his probation officer, who was coming to our house the following Thursday. He knew he would be urine tested.

Anthony is not defined by his addiction. He was a loving son, brother, grandson, cousin, and friend. There is no greater pain than for a parent to bury a child. When my child died, I lost someone I would die for.

We love you always and forever Anthony. Love, Mom, Dad, and Nick

Anthony's Mom,

VALERIE F.
Warrington, Pennsylvania

Morgan

Unfortunately, my story is not an uncommon one. My incredible son, Morgan, passed away from an overdose of fentanyl, heroin, and Xanax July 11, 2019, just weeks after his twenty-seventh birthday. He was extremely handsome, had tons of friends and always had a wonderful girlfriend. He felt most happy and at peace riding through the woods on an ATV or dirt bike.

He was in a motorcycle accident and the doctor put him on Oxycontin for pain after his surgery. This is where his fatal spiral began. Let me be clear. He hated his addiction, and he did not want to die. Being a drug addict embarrassed him. He would hide and withdraw from the world so people wouldn't see him in that condition.

Morgan liked the way the Oxy made him feel. When he couldn't find more, he ran into someone he used to ride with who told him he could help him out. This "friend" brought him to an inner-city house where the mom was so messed up her six-year-old son injected Morgan with heroin for the first time. They told him he could stop whenever he wanted and that being hooked on heroin was a cheap way to get high. Morgan said that first shot was better than sex and he was forever trying to find that euphoric feeling again. It turned him into a soulless zombie. He wasn't Morgan when he was on that stuff.

There were many rehabs all over the country where Morgan tried to find his way back to being who he once was. I always made sure the rehab handled dual diagnosis. I strongly believe mental health is always a high contributor to addiction. He had overdosed a couple of times through the years and we brought him back with Narcan. He would go through sober periods where we naively thought he was going to stay that way. He just wanted to be himself again. He would be on Vivitrol shots or Suboxone, but it was hard to find a doctor to provide these meds in our rural area. I would even drive him to a city close by and get it off the streets for him. Anything to keep him sober.

I was never angry with Morgan for being an addict. I knew he couldn't help himself. He had a horrible disease. I paid for his rent, food, car, etc., all of his expenses when I knew he couldn't help himself. I am proud of the fact that he was never homeless or hungry. I paid the bills, so he didn't have access to cash while he was using. I knew he couldn't be trusted. He had sold the watch my father left him and anything of his own that was of value. It was a hurricane of emotions, chaos, and hard reality for seven years. I never thought he was going to die because I was fighting too damn hard to keep him alive.

The week before Morgan passed, someone was leaving packets of heroin on his doorstep. He was in a great place, so he kept flushing them. He was about to start a new job working for the elevator union. He was so excited for this new opportunity in his life. He was looking for apartments away from all the familiar triggers and toxic people he had come to know.

This person who left heroin on his doorstep came again. I am assuming Morgan was nervous about starting his new job, which led him to shoot up that fatal last time. I am sure he had no clue the heroin contained fentanyl.

I can hear him now as he was shooting up saying, "Oh shit, I'm screwed."

He knew the consequences of fentanyl. A week before, his friend's little brother died from it and he said to my daughter, "You can't mess with anything containing fentanyl."

But how do you know it's in there!?! You have to go by the dealer's word. Morgan knew who was leaving him the drugs, but he never told me. I look at this as murder. If you are selling drugs laced with this chemical, you are killing people. They are the bad guys, not the users.

If I can help one family save their child's life in any way from what I have experienced or learned, then Morgan's death will not have been in vain. We need to crush the stigma, make mental health readily available, and find a way to let users know fentanyl is in their drugs. The most important thing we need to know is that they need to be showered with love. We don't know how long we will have them in our lives. I am the one in recovery now. It will take me my lifetime to heal the big hole that is in my heart, the shape of my boy Morgan.

May the passing of our children be #NotInVain.

Morgan's Mom,

ELISE F.
Delmar, New York

Ashley

My baby girl was born June 9,1995, in Queens, New York. Did I know twenty-three years later she would die in the same hospital? My story begins with this beautiful, blond haired, blue-eyed little baby. She was loved by so many. She had such a great imagination and my dream for her, in a perfect world, was for her to be successful.

I divorced her father when Ashley was only four. Her father was an addict and I wanted more for us, so I left him. I met an amazing stepdad for her, and I also made her a big sister three times. Ashley went to Catholic school her whole life. She was an awesome soccer and softball player. The friendships she made were overwhelming. When Ashley turned nineteen, she wanted to experience life on her own, so she got an apartment and that is where my life turned upside down.

I was unaware of her daily activities, which consisted of taking opioids and smoking weed for breakfast. One afternoon she called me after nursing school saying she got into a fender bender. I ran to the scene. I made excuses to everyone. Little did I know that she nodded off at a red light.

A few months went by. I asked her to move back home, so I could help her with her depression. I knew she suffered from mental illness, due to the cutting she did all over her body for years. I started finding more cuts and she was passing out all over the house. I just did not want to accept that my daughter was doing this to herself.

In 2018, she came to me, after we buried her grandmother, telling me she had been shooting heroin three times a day and she had had enough. I decided not to tell anyone and put her in a detox program. I was embarrassed and didn't want to explain that my perfect daughter was a drug addict.

After a few days Ashley came home, and I started seeing the same signs. I went through her room and found a bag of Xanax and oxycodone. The way she reacted, I could not have taken them away. She said she needed a pill a day to stay alive because it helped with her depression. Again, I was so clueless and I was afraid to ask for help.

I would find her passed out in her car, her room, even in the shower. But she woke up and functioned every day. Then I got a call: "Your daughter Ashley has been arrested and she will be locked up until tomorrow." I ran to see her handcuffed to a hospital bed.

I screamed, "Why are you killing yourself like this?"

She was so high; she didn't even know what was happening to her. When she came home I said, "How come you're still high?"

She said, "Mom, I shoved the bag of Xanax in my private area, because I would not have been able to sleep in jail."

That was the final straw. I opened my mouth and decided to put her in rehab for a month.

Ashley came out of rehab on April 1, 2019. I seriously thought that was it. She was going to be all better. She was sick, so she went to the doctor. They gave her meds and my life would be normal again.

Well, that didn't happen. She went off to work one night and I waited up for her. She came home. We spoke. She said she loved me. I told her I loved her too and we went to bed at two a.m. I woke up at six thirty a.m. and found her overdosing in her bed. I called 911 and by the time they came, she had stopped breathing. I didn't know how to do CPR. They restarted her heart and off to the hospital.

I arrived a little after for the doctor to tell me they didn't think she was going to make it, but that they were keeping her on life support to run brain activity tests on her. Four days of hell. I lost my girl forever.

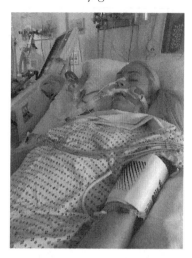

I had to make the decision to shut the machines off and let her go. My heart, my life, was destroyed on May 2, 2019. I knew I had to stay strong for my sons. My oldest boy had just started in the marines, but he came home immediately and asked if he should bring his dress blues. I couldn't even bear to answer him. My legs gave out and I just lost it.

My other son said, "Mom, please don't donate her organs, because for the rest of my life, I don't want to imagine that people who pass me in the street might have my sister's heart." My youngest son wouldn't leave her bedside.

I had a beautiful funeral for my daughter. The line was wrapped around the corner three times. I made sure to let everyone know addiction and mental illness are very real. I asked the priest to speak about it at her funeral.

Ashley's Mom,

Kathy F.
Queens, New York

Terry

FOREVER 26

Terry was born December 20, 1987, after twenty-eight hours of labor. He was our second child. We were thrilled to have another boy, so our first born would have a best friend for life. We truly had no idea how short that friendship was going to be or how difficult life without Terry would be. When Terry was four weeks old, we found out he had a hole in his heart, an atrial septal defect (ASD). He was asymptomatic and we were just waiting for the hole to close. Terry was an easy baby and truly always happy. When Terry was seventeen months old, his doctors felt he needed a heart catheterization…first opiate exposure.

When Terry was two years and seven months old, he was scheduled for open heart surgery to correct his ASD. His surgery went amazingly and this, of course was his second opiate exposure…this was the beginning of the end. Terry had several surgeries during the next twelve years and each time the doctors prescribed pain killers. Even in the hospital he was given pain meds while sleeping. I, being a nosy mom, asked why he needed pain killers when he was not crying, and he was asleep? The answer was, "Well, we do not want to be chasing pain, do we?" I was naive; I believed they knew best and by the time Terry was sixteen, he came to me and said he was scared. He thought he was addicted to pills. I quit my job and put him into treatment. I believed the answer to getting off pain pills was by way of other pills and away we went. After Terry was "better" per his drug treatment specialists, we felt secure. Knowing nothing about this disease, we thought we were done.

Terry continued to go to school, play sports, live at home, and have many jobs. Terry had many of the symptoms and behaviors of addiction, but we really knew nothing, we just kept living. When Terry's longtime girlfriend broke up with him, he never seemed to have any money, even though he was working all the time. We got scared. Just as we started chatting with his brothers and asking more questions, Terry came to me and told me he needed to tell me he was addicted to heroin. I told him he was funny, then I looked at his face and knew he was not kidding. I begged him to go for help; he told me he had and I foolishly believed him.

My husband and I started to drug test him, no notice, just wake and go. He never argued, he was happier, gaining weight, spending more time with family, and never failed a test in eleven months. Three hundred dollars per test, four or five tests a week, over $74,000 of our savings gone, but I still had my boy. I talked to him every day; he never left the house without saying he loved me, his dad, brother, and new nephew. He had a million friends, did everything for everyone. He was a great person, with a smile that lit up the world. He was gentle, an old soul, as we called him. He was my best buddy, my favorite middle child. We were as close as a mother and son could be. Terry was a wiseass and funny.

We lost Terry on October 1, 2014. He was twenty-six and he is missed by all that knew him. I am so lost without him that I am changed forever. I am meaner, more argumentative, and suspicious of everything, I am told by everyone. I have lost a piece of my heart and my soul is in limbo. It is so hard to believe that he is never going to smile at me or hug me; he gave the best hugs. I will never hear him say, "I love you

Mom," again. I am mad at myself for not knowing enough. I am distrustful of the police because they cannot seem to find his killer.

I hate my life most days. I pray to not wake up, because I was not a good enough mom to save this boy of mine. I feel selfish for missing him so much, that I want my pain to end and I am sure my husband, children, and grandchildren do not understand. It is different for a mother that loses her child. I have lost friends because I have a child that died of heroin toxicity, which of course translates to me being a very bad person. I have people tell me it is time to move on and forget the bad things and just keep happy thoughts. I have asked people, which of their children could they lose, and then still be able to explain to me how to get over it...I have spent countless hours daily on the internet reaching out to other moms like me just so I can fit in. I have walked, ran, swam, cried, and drank to try to feel better, nothing fixes it.

My oldest son started the Terry Fritz Memorial Foundation. He has hosted one golf outing a year since we lost Terry; he has raised over $100,000 and donated every penny. He speaks all over, he tells our story in hopes of educating people. We are all trying our best to communicate, educate, and rehabilitate.

We want to change laws. We need to end the stigma and remind people that mental illness is a real disease and that addiction is not a choice but an

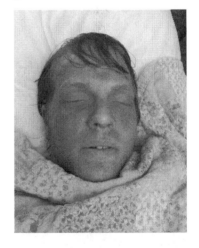

affliction. I lost my son before I had the chance to save him or the knowledge I needed to fight for his life. I want people to know he lived, he loved, he mattered, and that his life was good, and he did not die in vain.

Terry's Mom,

EILEEN F.
Delafield, Wisconsin

209

Patrick

FOREVER 25

I awoke on the morning of October 20, 2016, with thoughts of my upcoming trip to Jersey. In ten days time, Patrick and I would be in full hiking mode. We hiked every fall together, calling it our "hikes for life." Patrick was an addict struggling to stay clean. We walked in nature pushing ourselves to go farther than we had ever been before, in hopes of pushing away the demons for good. I sent Patrick a text that morning, he did not respond, but hey, he's a twenty-five-year-old kid and what kid doesn't ignore texts from their mom from time to time. Little did I know that in a few short hours, my world would come crashing down. I received a phone call from my oldest son, Jesse, telling me Patrick had overdosed. He's going to be okay right? We have been here before. "It doesn't look good, Ma."

My heart stopped; they were on the way to the hospital. Many frantic "what's going on" phone calls between the family. And then, the tearful call from my daughter, Wendy, en route to the hospital, "Mom, he didn't make it." Those five words will haunt me all the days of my life. My world went black. I'm 800 miles away and my baby is gone. Gone as in not coming back, ever. October 20 was an ordinary day for Patrick. He woke up early and took his dad to see the doctor. They stopped for breakfast on the way home. He was talking to his dad about his new job and his girlfriend, Allison. He was happy. He made a list for his dad of fruits to be picked up at the store for juicing. He went home, his dad went to work. His dad, Ken, got a call that Patrick was late for his new job. Ken came home to check on him and discovered a horror no father should ever find: his unconscious son on the floor of his bedroom. At that same moment, Patrick's brother, Tim, and his son arrived home. Hearing the desperate shouts from above, Tim raced up the stairs to start CPR and mouth to mouth. Jesse arrived to help Tim. The police arrived, then the ambulance, all trying, in vain, to revive my precious boy. Everyone raced to follow the ambulance to the hospital. Narcan had been administered. It was too late. Patrick was gone. Patrick struggled with substance abuse since at least 2010, when it was brought to my attention. He was addicted to anything he took. It began with marijuana, moved on to Oxycontin, and when that became too expensive, heroin came on the scene. Patrick became someone we did not know. He lied, begged, borrowed, and stole. Pawn shops became his best friend. They became mine, as well, to go and buy back what he stole, only to have it stolen again. He was desperate.

Outpatient became his source of sanity and rebirth, only to have the demons back knocking louder at his door. He had many close calls with death, scaring him straight for a short while, or so he would say. You can't always tell if they are high, because the addict becomes so good at hiding it. Hiding everything. We finally got him a bed for inpatient treatment. The family had high hopes that this stay would finally help him. Patrick refused to go saying, "I'm clean. I'm going to meetings. I have a sponsor. I can do this. I got it, Mom." And he did, for over a year, no heroin. We were all so proud of him; we talked about his future, his recovery process, about choosing life. But Patrick still had the need to self-medicate. He had so many things, health wise, bothering him. He suffered from severe anxiety and was prescribed Xanax, in low doses. It wasn't enough. He used loperamide, an over-the-counter anti-diarrheal medication that contains opiates. He totally abused those by the hundreds. He hid it well from everyone. Over that last summer, he turned to alcohol to the point where he signed himself into detox, once again, to stop his drinking. Again, he overcame the demons leading us all to believe that maybe, just maybe, this was a signal for a brighter future. Sadly, this was not meant to be. Something triggered a need that nothing and nobody could fill for him and he turned to his old reliable. Only this time, it was not heroin, but deadly fentanyl. Fentanyl and Xanax took our Patrick from us. If love could have saved Patrick, he would have lived forever. Patrick had a unique perspective on life, always seeing the good in everything. He loved deeply and was kind-hearted, going above and beyond to help anyone in need. His addiction did not define who he was as a human being. His life mattered, he mattered. Looking at him you would never know he was a tortured soul. Family parties would find him surrounded by his niece and nephew playing in the backyard. He loved kids, animals, old people, young people, his girlfriend, everybody and everything. His family was his everything. He never had a bad thing to say about anybody. The most important thing that Patrick taught me in life was positivity. He could take anything negative and turn it into a positive thing. So, I will take the negative aspect of his passing and honor him by turning it into a positive, by speaking out, ending the stigma, pushing for education at the grade school level and helping others who need guidance with addiction, overdose, and loss.

The hardest thing I have ever heard was that my child passed away. The hardest thing I have ever done is to live every day since that moment. This moment is for you Patrick, in loving memory of you. God Bless.

Patrick's Mom,

KATE G.
Boonton, New Jersey

Amber

FOREVER 34

In the midst of trying so desperately to save my middle daughter, Kristin, from various drug addictions and countless overdoses that spanned over a thirteen-year period, I was clueless to the fact that addiction had snuck up behind me and sunk its teeth into my oldest daughter, Amber. And just like that, in less than a year, I would be burying "The Other Daughter."

Amber was the oldest of my three daughters. Her father and I divorced when she was four. He remarried and had two sons, making her the oldest of five children. Even though I remarried when she was young, to a wonderful man, it still didn't change the fact that to her, she was from a "broken home."

Amber was always a character, the life of the party, an abundance of laughter, always active with so many childhood friends.

It's always easy to say, "Not my child." I was one of "those" moms. Amber went to a Christian school, was brought up in the faith, involved in every sport available and too many to count. She had a happy and safe upbringing, loyal friends, family who supported and loved her dearly, and yet this monster called addiction was still able to grab ahold of my beautiful, strong-willed daughter and we buried her on September 20, 2017. No parent ever expects to get "that call." It's numbing, heart-stopping, takes your breath away, and makes you wonder where in all of this did YOU go wrong?

The only signs we saw were that she was sinking into a depression from a recent hysterectomy in December 2016. When the pain pills became too hard for her to obtain from the doctors who had already prescribed an over-abundance of them, she turned to buying harder pain meds from the street, which eventually included heroin. This put her into even a deeper depression and someone we hardly recognized or knew.

Amber thought snorting it instead of actually injecting it wasn't the same in her mind as "using" and that it was safer. She wasn't using to get a high at this time; she was using to just get herself off the couch and try to take care of her two young children. Even though her use of heroin was only a few times, her last dose was laced with a lethal amount of fentanyl. Amber's hysterectomy was December 2016 and she lost her battle less than a year later.

Early morning, September 20, 2017, I received "the call." It was from Amber's father telling me to sit down. I thought for sure it was a call about Kristin, as she had just overdosed two weeks prior and we almost lost her. When he told me it was Amber, I thought, without a doubt, he was mistaken. He had uttered the wrong daughter's name. My mind, nor heart, could not grasp that it was indeed my Amber. She was gone in the blink of an eye.

Amber was always hard to read as an adult. She kept so much to herself. She was a proud person; wanted you to think she could make it on her own, no matter what. I don't know if she felt like it was a burden to ask for help, that she'd let us down, or that it would put her addiction into the light, such as her sister's was. I do know my guilt is, that as her mom, I should have known my daughter better and reached out despite the walls she built. I will truly live with that the rest of my life. I mean, we are moms, right? If not anything else, our job is to protect our children. If you do have a gut suspicion that something is wrong, it probably is, so don't ignore it. Don't wait for them to come to you; address it and discuss it head on. Get it out in the open, so at least there's an open dialogue.

Things I've learned on my journey of battling addiction alongside my daughters and having to watch one lose her battle: While trying to save them, with all that's in you, remember until it is actually THEIR choice, you will be fighting a losing battle. They have to want to make a change and get sober.

Unconditional love is always needed no matter how much it feels they break you, remember they feel even more desperate and broken.

Provide them pathways, light the way, show them hope; they must take the steps, sometimes you can walk beside them, but the hard part they must go alone. Be there when they return.

In all the darkness, sadness, and guilt that comes with fighting your child's addiction, remember these were their choices.

When you have other children not involved in addiction, be mindful of their successes and life's milestones. Their lives matter too.

I am guilty of this. My youngest daughter Kassandra did everything right. I believe she made a lot of her good choices based on what she saw her sisters do. Her life took a backseat to all the drama because of the addictions.

While I was busy spending years putting all of my energy into one daughter and trying to save her life, I lost my oldest to an unexpected overdose and my youngest was affected more than I ever realized.

Moms, sometimes we think we are superheroes, but we are not. We try our best. We raise them well and still our children are affected. All we can do is prepare our children with the best tools possible to be good and decent humans. Then, when we are the unlucky families that tragedy strikes, find strength in one another.

For thirty-four years, I felt like I was hanging on to the tail end of a shooting star that was trying to defy gravity...Heaven's pull defied all laws, and away she went.

Missing your laughter. Missing you all the time.
We are but a family of many left behind
who belong to this wretched club where statistics mean nothing,
where natural order has been demolished,

and words like fate, heal or plans are hollow and laughable.

We were robbed, her siblings and friends were robbed, her children robbed.
There is no healing from this. Time doesn't heal all pain despite what they tell you.
This kind of aching is in your soul and it takes you to a new place of existence where
you must pick up your broken heart and carry on in pieces.
Three years.

Amber's Mom,

SANDY G.
Indianapolis, Indiana

216

Blair

FOREVER 37

My first son Blair was born in Hammond Louisiana when I was 16 years old in 1981. He was the first grandchild and nephew in our family. He was so cute and adorable. He was healthy and always active. The only negative issue we had was once he was about 6 months old, at times when he would cry, he would lose his breath and we would have to try several things to get him to catch his breath. This lasted until he was 2 years old. A doctor suggested a brain scan and the result was simply, "He has a temper". Nothing more was done.

Blair was very happy growing up. We were poor but he never knew that. He started kindergarten at age 4. He was already very smart and had no problems learning. I literally hardly had to help him with any homework ever. When he was 6 ½, he became a big brother. He loved having someone else to play with. He would read books and entertain his little brother. They became close even though they were 6 years apart in age.

All through school, Blair continued to amaze me with his grades, awards, and recognitions he was receiving each year. I remember the day he came home from school in the sixth grade and told me very casually that he won the 6th grade Spelling Bee at school and he now had to go to the Parish Fair to compete against others from different schools who won their grade also. I was so proud of him and just still not understanding how my son was so smart when I was not when I went to school. He won with the word "Calendar". I will never forget that word. At the parish Spelling Bee, I could tell he was nervous being in front of so many people. He went 3 rounds until he missed a word. He received a dictionary with his name on it. All throughout school he maintained A's & B's. Always on the honor roll. In 6th grade. He brought home his first "C" and I began to cry. (I know that seems silly now). He felt bad that I cried. His teacher talked with me about how hard the subject was and that a "C" was not bad at all.

When he started the 7th grade, he was a member of the "Just Say No" club. They did various things throughout the year to raise awareness for drug abuse. He was a very likeable guy and he got along with everyone. He was small for his age though but that did not bother him. He played baseball and basketball and was always the smallest on the team which made him quick.

In 8th grade, he was awarded an Upward Bounds scholarship. He was able to attend Southeastern University for the summer. He was able to live on campus and take college classes. He also took part in a "Showtime at the Apollo" talent show. He was a comedian. So cute and seemed so comfortable. He did a really great job. He came in 2nd and we were all so proud of him. He enjoyed it.

When Blair was 14, his dad and I begin having marital issues. I was a stay at home mom and was so glad I could do that. I was able to help at school functions and both my sons enjoyed that. When he was 15, I noticed his eyebrow and a shaved mark in it. When I asked him about it, he said his friend dared him to do it. I believed him. I was told by him years later that it was part of a gang initiation.

I started seeing odd behavior from my husband and stumbled across pills in odd places. My husband had been abusing pain medication. There were pills hidden in so many different places. It was unreal all the things I started realizing. I found out much later that this had been going on for many years. After 2 years of trying to get him clean through doctors, psychiatrist, in patient treatment and counseling, I finally realized I had to get on my own so my kids would not be exposed to this. Before leaving, I had to get a job for the first time at age 30, and I needed to get my GED. I started working on it but was unable to finish it before things got too bad, so I had to leave and live with my Mom. In our court case, my husband was granted custody of both of my sons. I had no money and he had a lawyer. That broke my heart. I could do nothing. As time went on, I knew what they were being exposed to. Swapping pills was a "family" deal with my in-laws. Everyone would go to several doctors and would share medications. Something I learned after the fact. I continued to work on my GED and I would call Blair and ask him to help me understand English for one and more subjects. It did not make sense to me and it was so natural for him. I loved being able to have his help. It took me over 2 years to finish. I do not think I could have passed it without his help.

Soon after, I got a call that Blair was taken to a juvenile detention center and his dad was in jail also. Blair had skipped school with a friend, and they went down to the police range nearby our home and stole cameras, VCRs, and other things. I could not believe it. I had to be in court the next day with Blair. When I saw him, they had shaved his head and I lost it. He had beautiful hair. He looked scared and so different. The judge let him come home with me and told him he could have no contact with his dad. That did not last very long. I was presented an option for Blair to go to a Boot camp. I said yes please; however, when they mentioned it to his dad, he said no way. He never wanted anything to happen to his kids. I then found out that his dad had discarded all the stolen items by throwing them in a river. He was an accomplice. It did not surprise me.

When Blair was in his Junior year, his dad moved them to a different town which was farther from me and meant my kids had to go to a different school. Blair had already taken his senior photos and I was getting excited to see him graduate. About 3 months after moving, he ended up dropping out of school. I was devastated and tried to get him to go back. He had started having an attitude. His dad told both my sons so many lies about me and they both had different attitudes towards me. I knew Blair was using but when it started, I do not really know.

Eventually, my sons moved in with me. Blair attained his GED on his first attempt. Things were good. I brought Blair to his first treatment center when he was 17. It was 30-day program 4 hours away. The next day, I got a call from Blair, he said that they were mistreating him because he knocked a lamp off a table. He was not going to get any supper. I was very angry about this and called the office. I began to fuss with the lady on the phone and she was trying to tell me that people in Blair's situation lie all the time. I just refused to believe he was lying to me. They were going put him out at 9:00pm that night so I had to go back and get him.

Things seemed to be good for a while. He got his first job and even walked to work when needed. He eventually got fired because he stole some pills from the owner. He later got his girlfriend pregnant, but they never married. They both were not making good choices. He became a father at the age of 18. The grandparents raised his son.

As time went by there were good times and bad. Blair once again lived with me and it was Thanksgiving time and he wanted to visit his dad's parents. He was close to them even though they were enablers. I told him that I did not think it was a good idea. He was doing so well, and I did not want him to be around temptation. He talked me into it. He got to be a good talker and I guess I wanted to believe he could visit and not be tempted. He came home later that night high. I have no idea what pills or other substance he took. My younger son thought it was funny and started videoing him as he walked around the house. I was very upset, and it made me uncomfortable. Eventually, he ended up back with his dad. Blair was able to get another job and ended up in jail, after he wrecked a company vehicle under the influence. He was in there for 1 1/2 years about 6 hours away. His first time ever. When he was released, he went to live with his dad and things were up and down.

Blair eventually came to me and wanted help. I took him to the hospital, and they put him in The Tau Center. It was an inpatient treatment center. He did very well there. I think he stayed there about 3 months. We were able to bring his son to visit him. When he got out, he stayed with me. Once again, he was able to get a good job, but he would always end up with the wrong crowd as well as the bad influence from his dad's side of the family. He would get into fights regarding drugs with people he did not know. I once noticed scars on the back of his head. He said some guys attacked him with num-chuks over a long time ago. I think this may have caused him some brain damage. He told me he stayed in the hospital when that happened, but I do not recall ever being told about it before.

Through the next few years, he was in an out of detention centers for various drug related things. His dad always seemed to help him get out sooner somehow. I also brought him to several treatment facilities, and I do believe that he tried to get clean and followed programs. It just seemed like back in the real world, he could not function without falling back into his old habits, which landed him back in jail.

12 1/2 years ago, my present husband met him for the first time when we went to visit him in a detention center in Monroe Louisiana. It was the only time I visited him there since it was so far away. We stayed in touch via phone calls. The grandparents of his son wanted him to give up his right as a parent and he would not agree to that. It made him sad even though he knew it would be for the best. Once he was released, he came to live with us. We helped him all we could. He was always able to get a good job. He picked up HVAC and electrical skills quickly. He worked and gave me his check. I would pay his probation fees and other bills. He saved enough to buy him a car. He was doing so well. Within a few months he started dating a girl. They wanted to move in together. We begged him to wait, stay with us and save more money but, in their minds, they were in love and wanted to be together. He was happy and so they moved in together. This girl convinced him to sign his rights as a parent away. I know he did not want to do that. She did not want him to have to pay any child support. Things were good for a while. His girlfriend became pregnant. They continued to do well. Blair became a dad again at age 30. He had an instant bond with his daughter. I do think it caused him stress as well. Eventually his relationship with his girlfriend started to get strained. He had told me that she had high standards as far as clothes and how she should be treated. I saw it with my own eyes, so I knew he was telling the truth. They were up and down constantly. He again was on and off with a job too. They would split up and get back together over and over. His drug use was

becoming a big issue again. He drove around under the influence with his daughter in the car. Even with all that, they ended up getting married in 2015 after Blair stayed sober for one year. It was still stressful for him and again, drugs were becoming a big part of his life. His wife would call me asking me to come get him. I could hear him yelling in anger in the background. I always told her to call 911, but she would not.

Through the years he had reached out to his younger brother, who also would get high with him. His brother would go get him and bring him places and help him. It put a strain on his marriage too and his wife left him. My younger son was able to get his family back. Blair continued to spiral out of control. On several occasions I have put him up in hotels, buy him phones, clothes, and food. I no longer felt safe with him staying in my home. My husband would take him places and bring him food as well. Same for his brother. It seemed to bean endless cycle.

One day I specifically remember he had called me for help. He had posted a goodbye message to his daughter on Facebook earlier. When I brought him there, they asked him if he was suicidal and he said no. I did show them the post so that they were aware. While waiting for the doctor to come in to see him, he was like a caged animal. He was ranting and raving and would not sit down. Constant pacing and he was just getting angrier as time passed. After about ½ hour, I was about to lose it myself. I began to secretly pray for God to calm him down. Over and over I would pray the same things. It took 5 minutes and he finally calmed down. The doctor sent him back to the Tau Center for inpatient treatment. He was not happy with that. I think he just wanted some meds to make him feel better. He reluctantly went to treatment and was not happy with me. He did to want not to see me. He wanted to see his wife. I took her to see him 2 days later and I went in the room with her in case he changed his mind. There was a social worker there too. When Blair came in and saw me, I could see the hate he felt for me. He started telling me mean things. I ended up leaving the room so he would calm down and visit with his wife. After he left the room, the social worker called me back in and told us that he needs to stay there for a while so if he calls to come get him, tell him he has to stay there. I thought we were all on the same page. Well he called his wife the next day and she went and got him. I was so angry with her. After that, I guess I had hard feelings towards her.

As time went by, they ended up building a 2-story home. It was beautiful. Blair had another great paying job with a company truck and credit card. Eventually, the marriage began to be strained again. Blair would come visit with is daughter by himself every now and then. He knew we did not care for his wife that much and I am sure that was hard for him, but he understood why. Once again, he got into an accident under the influence after being sober for about 8 or 9 months. With that came information that linked him to misusing the company credit card. He had bought some electric tools at 2 different stores and sold them for drug money. That was the end of that job. Back in jail for a few months. He was no longer allowed to talk to or see his daughter. Blair loved to draw. He drew his daughter some amazing pictures. He would often draw or doodle. He was very good at it. He would write letters to her also.

Eventually he got out of jail and again was staying with his dad. He was going to a Mental Health clinic that provides people mediations. One day his dad dropped him off and was unable to pick him up. He started talking with this older lady in her 60's. Blair is 36 years old at the point. She ends up bringing him home that day and next thing I hear from my younger son is that Blair is now living with this lady in an apartment. He stayed in touch with his brother. Even the older lady would text my younger son and tell him things he did not want to know. As time went by, she came to love Blair. They did have a physical relationship. He stole from her and they were also into swapping pills with others. He wrecked and totaled her car. She also had told my younger son that Blair was doing things for money. Things that you do not want to hear. (I later found letters from this woman after his death that confirmed this). Eventually he was arrested while living with her for a drug charge. He was in jail for about 13 months. He contacted me and I would as usual, put money in his phone account to stay in touch. He asked me to help find out when he could get out. I called and/or wrote letters to his probation officer, court appointed attorney, judges, and the jail itself. I wanted to try to get him in a drug program after his release. It was like hitting a brick wall. I didn't' want him out. I felt he was safe, had a roof over his head and food to eat. I did manage to get them to send him to a different detention center where there was a drug program. It was a 90-day program and he completed it and was released. My husband and I were looking for facilities that could help him and he could stay at prior to his release. We came across Cenikor. They had a center near my office. I bought him everything he needed to enter the program. I got his teeth fixed because I knew he was self-conscious about it. He stayed there for 3 months and then he left. His brother picked him up and brought him to his dads. He said it was degrading and all they did was work you 7 days a week and treat you badly. He ended up at his dad's again. Once there, they had a physical fight and his Dad put charges on him. (Something to do with drugs). He was in jail once again for about 3 months. We were able to talk on the phone and I did go to his court appearances. When he got out, we offered to help him once again. There were 2 places we had. One was Cenikor and one was a church run organization. He chose to go back to Cenikor. He really became aware of how hard they are on everyone once again. After about 2 months, He ended up getting kicked out after refusing to go to work because it was hot and there was no water to drink on the job and the AC was broken at Cenikor itself. He called me and told me this and I told him that I was sorry, and I do not have anywhere else for him to go. He said he understood, and he was just calling to let me know in case I tried to call. I asked him to let me know where he ended up, knowing it would be his dads. He said he would. I had about 2 hours before I got off work and I was going through feelings of guilt. Since Cenikor was close, I was going to go ride the roads to see if I could find him. When I got off work, he was sitting in the lobby and his belongings was by my car. I was so happy to see him. I took him home and fed him good. My husband had called that church organization and they had an opening, so we took him the next day. It was not in a good part of town and the building was old. I told him he did not have to stay there but he would have to find somewhere else quickly. He agreed to stay but I knew he was not happy. He only stayed 3 days and called me once again to tell me he was leaving. He just said it was too hard for him there. I once again told him I did not know how else to help him. He mentioned to me that going to his dad's would be the worst place for him. I agreed and asked him to let me know where he ended up. He did end up at his dad's. He called me and told me he was working in another city. I found out few days later that it was a lie and he was with his dad.

On Saturday June 15th, he called to ask if I could work on his resume and get it printed for him. He was ready to get back to work. I told him yes so, his dad brought him over. He was not familiar with using the internet. I could tell he was very restless and under the influence of something mildly. The next morning, he called my husband and asked if he could bring him to church so he could see his daughter and then go to the park afterward. My husband said of course. Blair's dad dropped him off that morning. He was so handsome. I first saw him standing outside my back porch. He had his back to me, and he looked so nice. I had a thought, "Take a pic", but I did not. Then he came inside, and I told him how nice he looked. He always did dress nice. He has a sense of fashion. After he had spent time together with his daughter and wife, he came back to my house to pick up some clothes. We were just about to leave when he showed up. My mom was here, and she got to see him too. He told us he had a wonderful visit. I could tell he really did not want to leave. I feel guilty for leaving in a rush.

One week later, on June 23rd at 7:30 in the morning, my youngest son called to tell me Blair had died. His dad could not wake him up. It was ruled and accidental overdose. I learned at the funeral from his uncle whom he and his dad were staying with, that he had taken Blair to the emergency room 2 nights before he died because he found him unresponsive in the bathroom with a mouthful of his heart medication. The hospital treated him and offered him a place to get help, but he refused to go. They could not make him since he was 37.

Blair was a joy to me as he was growing up. He became a very smart intelligent person. He was caring and loved to give and get hugs. He had a sense of humor and could always make us laugh. He loved his kids, niece, and nephews. Aunts etc. He was kind and caring. He loved family events, even though he missed many throughout the years due to being in detention centers or treatment. He always told me Happy Mother's Day even if it was late by phone, text, or letter. I miss all the things that made my son so lovable. I am grateful for the memories I have. I wish I would have known when this all started for him. Was it due to my actions? I wish I would have known more about this disease and how to help him better. He so hated living that kind of life but was unable to break from it. His life matters to me and I will keep his memory alive until I no longer can.

Forever in my thoughts and prayers. My love never stops.

Blair's Mom,

Monica G.
Denham Springs, Louisiana

Robbie

FOREVER 21

Every parent has the same reaction when they find out that their child/children are addicts. Never in a million years did I think this would happen to our family. When I found out our son Robbie was doing drugs, my heart sank and I cried. How could this happen. We're a good family. He played four sports and is a wonderful person. Always smiling and wanting to help people and make friends. Drugs robbed my husband and me of our son. My son is an addict and when he is using he's not my sweet loving son that always gave hugs.

Robbie's personality changed completely. It seemed like in a flash it happened. Robbie started using pot first and then it escalated. Anyone who says that pot is not a gateway drug is delusional. Talk to us and we can tell you otherwise. It may not be for everyone, but let me tell you, it most certainly can be. Watching my son spiral out of control was absolutely heart wrenching. I had no control. I was mad at myself because I felt I wasn't strong enough, but I was with my husband's help. I was mad at Robbie. At first my thinking was, he is picking the drugs and those people over me and his dad. He robbed me of his senior year of high school. The school asked him to leave because of his behavior as a result of the drugs, and it was terrible. I was supposed to be there with his dad for senior night at the hockey game, take pictures on prom night. We are grateful that he did graduate, but it was because he was tutored at home. We were robbed of seeing him walk with his class to get his diploma.

Then my feelings became fear. Where is he? Who is he with? What is he doing? Why isn't he home? Robbie wasn't at family gatherings when his addiction got worse. We would argue a lot. I was angry with him and we would yell. Then I tried to avoid any arguments at all cost because I had become afraid of my son. A mom's worse feeling is being afraid of her child. Drugs altered his personality so much that he would get enraged and I was actually afraid to be in the house by myself with him. I know it was the drugs but it's the most horrifying feeling to be afraid like that. Never in a million years did I ever think my child would frighten me. I had to get a restraining order on my son and it is something that I will never forget. Drugs robbed him of his common sense and ethics at times. Thank God for my husband Steven because he was the buffer and tried to keep situations from happening and protected me. My son cornered me in my home office and wouldn't let me leave the room; he was mad at me because I wouldn't give him money. The only way I got out of the room was because my husband Steven came home from work and banged on the door to get it open. That was one of the most terrifying moments of his addiction journey for me.

The lying and sneaking around doesn't stop. Pretty much anything he said we took as a lie unless otherwise proven. From the moment we realized what road he was going down, we told family and friends. We didn't shy away from talking about it and making it known. We asked family and friends to not enable his addiction and behavior. Easier said than done. We did have a couple of family members who were enablers. Fighting with them was also stressful on top of dealing with Robbie's addiction. Family and friends were extremely supportive and still are.

Society has its head in the sand for so long. The shame and stigma attached to addiction needs to stop. Addicts are people too. They are not low-lifes. Addicts are from all walks of life and society needs to get on board with treating addiction for what it is, a DISEASE!!! Though a lot of addicts start with opioids, our son and others like him started with what people think is a harmless drug, pot!! Pot as well as other drugs are being laced with all sorts of drugs.

Fentanyl is what took our son from us. Robbie thought he was getting heroin but it was straight fentanyl. I am thankful that at times Robbie asked for help for his addiction and other times we had him sanctioned. As a parent of an addict, it takes a lot of strength and working together, being on the same page to get through this terrible journey. Treatment facilities have a lot to learn and correct. While Robbie did stay at some facilities that worked well with him, others didn't seem to want to deal with him. You see, besides being an addict, Robbie was also bipolar and had ADHD, so facilities would say that they couldn't control him. Well, he can't be the only person like this, so why aren't there more facilities focusing on the dual diagnosis and why don't they have more staff that can help difficult patients?

There needs to be consistency across the country with how facilities operate. There needs to be stricter regulations with licensing treatment facilities and more help from the government with funding. Our mental health care system is horribly broken and needs to be changed, and again be consistent across the board. Some facilities failed our son and that makes me angry. When families go through the addiction journey with a family member, everyone needs to be on the same page. Do your homework and investigate facilities the best you can. Ask for help if you need it. Robbie did go to some facilities that were very good, but again dual diagnosis came into play and some couldn't handle that. Addiction is not one sided. There are usually two sides to this disease.

Addiction makes or breaks a relationship within the family. Thankfully, my husband and I were almost 100% on the same page. One thing you have to do is talk things through and be in agreement for the direction you need to take to help your addict. One of the things that happened to me emotionally is that I would shut down sometimes and not communicate. When this would happen, I would go to therapy. There is absolutely 100% nothing wrong with being in therapy. Again, another stigma that needs to end. Addiction is a very emotional road that we've been traveling. This is a road that we never in a million years thought we would be traveling.

During this new journey we are traveling, we have been blessed with meeting a group of wonderful Angel Parents. Yes, Angel Parents. That's what we are. We are the parents of Angels, our children that have lost their battle with addiction. Team Sharing is a national group of parents who have lost a child and/or children to this terrible disease of addiction. We have state chapters and even though we may not have met in person, we have been able to create bonds as a result of this journey. We support, encourage, and help find help for families and addicts in recovery. We've seen success stories of recovery in this group. It is a group no one wants to belong to but one that only members understand: the emotional ups and downs, and the effects of this journey that we now call our new normal life.

Robbie was the prayer that God answered for us. You see, I couldn't get pregnant due to medical reasons. From the start, Steven always said we would adopt if we couldn't have our own. So we started the process and after seven and one half years, God answered our prayers and we received a call from the adoption agency that they had a beautiful baby boy for us, a blond, blue-eyed healthy baby boy. We fell in love the minute we met him; he was this precious bundle of joy for us and instantly we became a family. As Robbie grew, he had a harder hold of my heart with each passing year.

Robbie was full of energy; he always wanted to be outside and play with balls and bats, hockey sticks and pucks, anything outside. He was a typical boy that got dirty and had fun. Robbie loved people and had an infectious personality and smile, a sparkle in his pretty blue eyes, and he was the giver of the most awesome and world's best hugs. Everyone he encountered fell in love with him. Robbie always gave me a hug and kiss no matter where we were or who was there. Robbie was a literal person. He took everything literally, which was both funny and not so funny at times. He was full of love and laughter. Robbie was a wonderful son, grandson, nephew, and fierce friend to teammates and friends. Robbie stood up for the underdogs. He was friendly to everyone and touched many lives.

There are so many wonderful stories of our precious son. One of my favorites and also his grandmother's (my mom) was when he was about four or five, he dressed up like a Viking for Halloween, with a blond braided wig, Viking helmet, chest plate, and play sword. When we walked into my parents' house, my mom started laughing because he was so cute. Robbie got mad and asked why she was laughing. When my mom said because he was so damn cute, he got even madder and yelled, "I'm not cute, I'm a mean Viking!" There are many stories like that. One year, Robbie received a sled for Christmas and tried to sleep on it in bed.

Joy, love, and laughter were always part of our family life. Sports were a very important part of Robbie's life. Hockey was his first love followed by soccer. Freshman year, he played baseball and football. Our Robbie was a multi-sport athlete and was a multi-positional player. Robbie was our world. We traveled and went on many trips as a family or with sports families. Always on the run. The title of "Mom" is one of the best titles I have.

No child is perfect, and of course Robbie was no exception. When Robbie started using pot, his dad noticed immediately because his personality changed so drastically. Dealing with that was heart wrenching. Between his junior and senior year for half of the summer, I didn't know where he was a lot of times. Pot had taken a hold of my baby and there were times I didn't recognize him. Where had my sweet Robbie gone? Pot brought the drinking and then eventually the harder drugs. I had sleepless nights, crying myself to sleep wondering where he was and who he was with. Was he ok? Was he in trouble? When we said what was happening out loud, our son is an addict, it tore through my very heart and soul. I thank God for my husband Steven because without him I would never have been able to go on. Steve is my rock and the glue that holds us together.

Robbie's addiction continued to get worse and we would later tell others his story and say that we had no choice but to section him numerous times to go into rehab. Thankfully, Robbie realized probably deep down that he needed help because he would call Steven and ask for help. As parents of an addict, we become a force to be reckoned with when it came to helping our son get the help he needed and wanted. Robbie would end up going to numerous facilities for rehab. As a mom of an addict, I felt relieved and guilty when he was in a facility, relieved because I knew my son was safe and I wouldn't hear the phone ring in the middle of the night, and guilty because I felt this way. Addiction is as mean and unforgiving a disease as any other disease. It can bring families closer or completely destroy them. I am truly blessed that God gave me my husband, family, and friends because I wouldn't have arrived where I am without them and I wouldn't have the strength to move forward.

Robbie hugged me and gave me a kiss good-bye the afternoon before he died. Robbie didn't live with us off and on while in addiction. He was at the house with a few friends, and later that day he would say good-bye to us; little did we know it was the last time. It was the last time he would give me the world's best hug, kiss me, and say, "I love you, Mom." October 19, 2015, will always be the worst day in my life. Steven had to wake me up and say that our son, our precious, loving Robbie was gone. He was dead. I remember screaming and crying. Then I was numb. Nope, this was a bad dream. We went to the hospital and the doctor eventually brought us to the room where Robbie lay. He wasn't going to wake up. My baby was gone. He was sleeping peacefully, that's what I told myself. I sat next to him and cried, "Why did you leave us?' He was so cold. I just cried and kept running my hand on his head. How are we going to live without him? Little did we know that same night in a room down the hall, another mom was there with her daughter who overdosed and lived that night, but later lost her battle. We would later meet this mom through Team Sharing.

We had to call family and friends and tell them that Robbie lost his battle with addiction. He was gone. Now, what do we do? How can I live without my only child? This was not supposed to happen. Parents don't bury their children. Children are supposed to bury their parents. Robbie was supposed to grow up, go to school, maybe fall in love and get married. I was supposed to dance with him at his wedding. We would watch him become a dad and have a grandchild/grandchildren. What now? I didn't know what to do. Steven would help and hold me over and over as I cried and screamed about this new life. THIS NEW LIFE SUCKS WITHOUT OUR SON!!!!!!

A strong relationship is definitely helpful when dealing with addiction and communication is key. Family and friends need to be educated on addiction if they don't already know. Everyone needs to be on the same page and needs to communicate. Ultimately, the parents need to have support and if family and friends can't or won't support them, they need to step aside.

We need education and to hold accountable people who are responsible for either manufacturing the drugs (saying no harm of addiction will happen) and the dealers. They need to pay for their actions with jail time. If we don't hold people accountable and if we don't stop the stigma by talking about this disease, then we are screwed. We need to get communities involved in education. Our children need to be involved and need to know that it's okay to speak out about drugs. We need to give our children the tools to help them talk about this disease and what they can do as the next generation to help find a solution and end the stigma.

Life after losing Robbie hasn't been easy. It's a struggle most days to just get up. There are days that I cry all the time and just want to stay in bed. We were robbed of our son's life. It sucks and it's not fair. How do you move forward? Not easily, that's for sure. I am blessed with a husband that keeps me putting one foot in front the other on days I don't want to. I'm blessed that he lets me cry when I need to and just holds me. He laughs with me with I think of something funny Robbie would say or do and I tell him. Family and friends talking about Robbie helps also. I can't imagine living this life if everyone just stopped talking about and remembering Robbie.

Yes, my beautiful son died and he's no longer here, BUT that doesn't mean he never existed. He is still our son and part of our life; just now he is our Angel. When asked how many children I have, I say I have a son who is an Angel. Talking about my son helps me heal and move forward. If you don't talk about my son, it hurts me worse than what I am already feeling. I don't want pity. I want to celebrate my son's life, and family and friends sharing stories and memories helps. Holidays will always and forever be changed; this is just a fact. How we deal with them is another story. I have in the beginning stayed in bed and refused to have the holiday. Steve, again my ROCK, lovingly now kicks me in the ass as a gentle push to remind me that Robbie would be pissed as hell if I stopped celebrating holidays. He will always be with us as long as we believe and you can be damn sure I will never stop believing.

One of the things I have found that helps me with my loss is writing. I write as a result of dreams that Robbie has talked to me in. I have also discovered through a game that Robbie and I would play that I have been able to help other Angel Parents. That's what we are, Angel Parents. When Robbie was small and not in a very good mood, I would ask him to give me five happy words before he got out of my car. Before he got out, he would be smiling. So I decided to do something like this with Angel Parents. Through Team Sharing, I write a daily (or as many days as possible) message to the parents. Sometimes it's a happy word, an observation, or just a thought. I find my writing helps me heal and move forward, and at the same time, I help other parents cope and move in a forward direction. I post my positive message to twelve Facebook pages devoted to moms and dads to help them, even if it is just bringing a smile to their face for the day.

Talking helps me heal. When you ask about Robbie, it brings a smile to my face. It comforts me when people acknowledge Steven and I as a couple who have lost a child. An observation I have made is that sometimes it seems that everyone talks about the moms, but dads have lost the child as well. Now if the dad isn't in the picture, then yes, it's the mom, but what makes me mad is when everything revolves around the mom. Yes, I lost Robbie but so did Steven. We are partners in this loss. Please remember that.

Support groups are very important to cope and learn to live a whole new life without our child. Supportive family and friends; you need them. You need positive in your life and not toxic or negative. You need to remove the negative barriers to move forward. Deep breaths and one step at a time. Put one foot in front of the other and never stopping talking. I move forward because I need to keep Robbie's life and memories alive and need to stay alive. I push forward to help parents who might not be able to voice what they are thinking. I guess I can be their voice until they find it.

Family and friend gatherings can often end up with tears and laughter as a result of stories about Robbie. Some we've heard and some we haven't. We try and celebrate Robbie's life. On his birthday, Steven and I take the day off and go to his favorite restaurant, Hooters, and have lunch or dinner. We place his prayer card on the table and talk about him. We bring balloons to his grave.

This new journey has shown us much sorrow but has also shown us joy and success when we meet those in recovery. It makes us happy to see them working whatever program and be successful. You see, just because Robbie wasn't able to beat this disease, there is always hope and success in others.

If you are struggling with addiction, please seek help. If you are a family member of an addict, educate yourself on this disease. Be supportive but not enabling. Support groups are important. Communicate, communicate!!

Robbie's Mom,

Lois G.
Massachusetts

Kyle

FOREVER 34

I'd like you to meet the sweetest, kindest person ever, Kyle. He was an Eagle Scout. He was a welder by profession. He lived at home with us. He was our middle son and a mama's boy. He told me when he was three years old that he "was never getting married, never having children and was living with Mama the rest of my life."

Then three years ago, drugs entered his life. My thirty-four-year-old son, Kyle, was murdered two months ago. Just for being nice and giving someone a ride. Even the sheriff said he was in the wrong place at the wrong time. I know he could have said "No" to that person that asked him to take them out there. He had a car and they didn't. He was never one to say no. He wanted everybody to like him.

I know he is in heaven and happy and safe. I'm so sad that we never got a last hug, or I love you. He just couldn't resist these people when they called. I believe we were starting to get our relationship fixed but needed more time. He never liked me calling and texting. He wanted his own life. I wish I hadn't listened.

I tried to tough love him and we had some bad fusses in the past. A couple of weeks before he was shot, I think we were beginning to heal. We were talking and enjoying each other's company just like always before the drugs and users and bullies came into his life. I am so heartbroken that he left like that. He never liked to see me cry.

I wonder what he would say now. He abandoned his welding work and those good friends for younger addicts. I miss him so bad.

Kyle's Mom,

CATHY G.
Baxley, Georgia

Elena

FOREVER 19

Elena flew into our lives upon the wings of an angel in January of 2000. We adopted each other on the day she was born. She was worshipped by all of the family, who had waited so long to be blessed with this perfect, little human being, our only child. She was a cautious little girl whose family was her world. Her sense of humor was apparent right from the beginning.

She shared her beautiful smile and extraordinary sense of humor and made us laugh every single day. She loved animals of all kinds, from dogs and cats to lizards and fish, while enjoying playing the violin, cheerleading for the junior football league, playing softball, socializing, and making friends within all groups at school. She was most comfortable around her family nucleus and never strayed far from Mama.

Both separation anxiety and stranger anxiety hovered over her during the early years. Elena suffered her first full-blown panic attack at the age of seven, after falling from a jungle gym at summer day camp and breaking her elbow. She later told us, once she could truly verbalize and explain it, that she believed the doctors would cut her arm off because it was broken. Intensive therapy at that tender age helped her to fight her daily anxiety and she seemed to prevail until it reared its ugly head once again in the later middle school years.

Teenage Elena had a fierce appreciation for the arts and nature: a constant love of music, paintings by Van Gogh among many others, poetry, and astronomy. She enjoyed capturing and editing her own photographs. An obsession with social media during middle school led to pressures of acceptance by her peers and feelings of low self-esteem. She found herself slowly ousted from long-term friend groups and began her never-ending search for inclusion.

The transition to high school did not go well for Elena. School anxiety reappeared with a vengeance, and it became a daily battle to get her there. Once again, it appeared to us as the anxiety we had seen before and intensive therapy was reinstituted, along with medication for the first time, mainly to get her to attend school. The medication was never taken regularly because Elena did not like the feelings of disasso-ciation that she believed the medication brought on. Dosages were adjusted, different medications introduced, but the right combination to ease her symptoms of anxiety and depression was never found.

The self-isolation became a constant; yet social media was still an obsession. Elena wasn't one to let too many people in. You had to earn her trust for her to open up. She was very spiritual in her search for inner peace, decorating her room with soft lighting, special healing stones, potted Zen gardens and self-help books. She began smoking marijuana in either eighth or ninth grade and managed to hide it for a while. She was smart as a whip, yet was always satisfied with average grades, so we didn't see the decline at first. The friend groups became ever changing, but coming home drunk a few times during high school seemed to be just "what teenagers do."

During early junior year, it was strongly suggested by school coun-selors that Elena attend an outpatient program in place of the indi-vidual therapy, where she could attend school within a smaller group setting to help her manage her daily fears and the disruption of wanting to leave school shortly after she got there, when she could get there.

Mandatory drug testing took place at this program. Elena was failing every test for marijuana and Xanax use and was recommended to attend an inpatient rehabilitation program.

The age of consent in our state is fourteen, so we battled with getting her to agree to admission at sixteen. Elena spent her seventeenth birthday in rehab and fought it all the way at first, running away twice into the woods and trying to find a house, so she could call me to come and get her. Once she finally accepted the treatment and began to accept the help, she was discharged within ten days due to loss of health coverage. The rehab recommended a long-term program which Elena refused, and we unfortunately could not afford. She was returned to the regular high school setting by her choice and her addiction began to slowly grip her.

The drug use progressed to opioids, which became her ultimate drug of choice. Our family suffered another blow when her beloved aunt was diagnosed with breast cancer. Elena worried constantly that her aunt may not make it and accompanied her to many chemotherapy treatments and provided constant comic relief, often refusing school so she could support her through hospitalizations and surgeries. Thankfully, her aunt persevered; however, Elena's grades in school continued to plummet and she had completely lost the motivation for trying to make up the mounting schoolwork that loomed over her. She ended up dropping out in senior year to avoid all the makeup classes she would need to take to graduate.

Her dream had always been to attend cosmetology school. Her plan was to work and eventually get her GED. We didn't feel comfortable with her driving and neither did she. She had a learner's permit and seldom drove. We drove her back and forth to the jobs she had and to friends' homes to ensure her safety, performed random home drug testing, and instilled an ever-present list of household rules. The rules were broken again and again, with the sincerest of apologies that she wanted to make us proud and turn it all around.

Throughout all of these difficulties, Elena and I spent countless hours texting while apart, sharing jokes, going out to dinner and getting ice cream, visiting Nanny and her aunt in the next town, weekly mall trips, and nightly walks along the beautiful paths near the Hudson River to see the New York City lights from the New Jersey border. Elena was the first person to jump into my car when I received a call that my older sister had jumped from her apartment balcony after struggling for years with substance abuse and mental illness.

My sister, tragically, passed several months later. A few months later, we received a call that my mom was non-responsive, and Elena and I drove together to my mother's house and learned of her passing. Elena suffered especially hard with this loss and experienced a profound grief for the Nanny that she had shared the most amazing bond with through the years. This loss proved to be the ultimate devastation of her life.

She finally agreed to attend another rehab program after a family intervention, but only for thirty days. She spent her final Christmas in rehab and was released just before her nineteenth birthday. She chose not to continue with a sober living program, saying that she couldn't be far away from her family, but she began attending meetings in an outpatient program. She decided to move to my mother's home in the next town and make her Nanny's room her own, so that my surviving sister wouldn't be alone in the house and she would be within walking distance to a job that she applied for.

The final downhill slide happened so swiftly. The weekend prior to her passing, we opened the family beach house together and talked of the fun we would have during the summer. Sunday was spent relaxing together and barbecuing with family, sharing a perfect day and many laughs. That final Monday, Elena began a job in a factory that produced makeup. On Tuesday, she set up an appointment to receive a Vivitrol injection and was excited about the future. She worked full time for three days and on Wednesday evening we joked about how exhausted she was putting in full days of work. We were making plans for that weekend and she seemed very happy. We were in constant communication on that final night and the last text she sent me was "Love you, night-night."

I was awoken very early that Thursday morning by a telephone call saying that Elena was unresponsive and to come to my sister's house. I sped to the house, repeating, "Please, Elena, please Elena, please," the entire way there. Upon entering, I received the devastating news from the police officers that Elena didn't make it. She had overdosed on a combination of substances, unknowingly including fentanyl, less than twelve weeks after leaving rehab, at the tender age of nineteen. Her first overdose became her last. Drugs robbed her of her future dreams, of the beautiful life she could have had. Several friends came forward after her passing and spoke of how she had convinced them to get help and had called 911 more than once for a friend. Elena saved everyone she could, but in the end could not save herself.

My dedication to my child's hopes and dreams will never cease where life ends; it is forever, through eternity. I will spend each day on this Earth honoring my beautiful girl and telling her story, in the hope that it will save just one life.

Elena's Mom,

JANET G.
Milford, New Jersey

Sean

FOREVER 23

It was a beautiful spring afternoon March 2,1996, that marked the sunrise of Sean's life. He was born in Bend, Oregon, surrounded by family and friends anxiously awaiting his arrival. He arrived healthy, happy, and loved. This is where our adventure began, in a small-town hospital, surrounded by love and excitement.

My daughter Amanda, who was six, finally had the little brother she had been waiting for and Dan and I had just experienced the birth of our precious son. Sean's Grandma Joyce was there, she watched over Amanda and helped her hold the new baby. By the smiles on their faces, I could tell they were in love — we all were. It was a beautiful day, the kind of day that changes your life forever.

That night when all was quiet and I was alone with Sean, I just felt so happy. He was mine and I was his. Many people who knew Sean felt that kind of connection to him throughout his short life. It was his gift. The name Sean means "Gift from God." That is how we see him.

Sean was an easy-going child. He was happy and playful at home. He was also painfully shy in public. I thought it was just his personality. In hindsight, this should have been my first clue that something was going on in his head. Even though shy in group settings, Sean made friends easily. He talked to the kids that were left out and he introduced them to each other, creating a group of his own. They have stayed beautifully connected to this day.

Sean was a huge Harry Potter fan as a young boy, and learned to read early. Grandma Joyce and his sister, Amanda, would take turns reading the books out loud to him, until he mastered reading them on his own.

Sean never went to a babysitter. Grandma Joyce watched and cared for him while we worked. They had a very tight bond; he was lucky that way.

Sean did all of the things young boys do. He rode his bike, played with friends, teased his sister, and insisted she play with him.

"You owe me playtime this weekend," he would demand.

So, there she was playing Harry Potter for hours. He had a way of wrapping her around his finger.

Once he said to her, "You have too much perfume on."

She replied, "You smell like cookies and dirt."

The term stuck in our household. Sean loved it!

His dad taught him to fish and play guitar. They enjoyed astronomy together. He was in tae kwondo, wrestling, basketball, swimming, and the all sports club. He even played the trombone one year in middle school.

He loved camping and water sports. Sean was also a gamer. He spent a lot of time on his computer. He did lots of things and had lots of opportunities.

We played games, went on magic picnics, and made up stories. We went to the beach. We searched for leprechauns and went on a hot air balloon. We loved the fun we had.

His dog, Bear, was his greatest companion. She looked out for him and he watched over her. Sean had rescued her when he was in middle school. I believe she knows more about Sean than I do. A boy and his dog is a beautiful thing.

Sean had a very sensitive spirit. He was kind and gentle. His humor, quick wit, and flare for the dramatic made him endearing. He loved deeply and he was deeply loved.

Slowly all of Sean's hobbies, interests, and possessions disappeared. His connections to the people who loved him became strained. The monster of addiction had him gripped tightly in its grasp and anyone who dared to stand up to the monster would become forever scarred. Some of us would never be the same and Sean would pay the ultimate price.

I do not know how the monster first reached for my son. I wish I knew the moment he came under attack. There was no big event, no one thing that stands out. I can point to things in our lives that were not ideal, but lots of people experience these things without becoming addicted. My guess is the genes of addiction are hereditary; my father died from the effects of lifelong alcohol addiction. Sean had surgery to repair a hernia when he was eleven months old and was sedated with opioids. The combination of those two things may have been the perfect set up for the monster to get in. Sean once wrote, "Was I born addicted?" Well, he was not born addicted, but he had a vulnerability from the beginning.

His personality was gentle, tender, and shy. It made it hard for him to do some things like going to school. While he made friends easily, he was also targeted by some kids, because he was bigger than them.

He was also sensory sensitive. He did not like loud noises or chaos. He didn't like rough textures. His clothes needed to be soft on his skin and without buttons. He liked routines and needed warning if there was going to be a change in his routine. I never clued in that this might be a disorder of some sort. I just thought he was particular and sensitive. We adjusted life to fit these needs and kept moving forward. I never saw the monster coming. He left plenty of clues. I missed them all and it took my son. In middle school, Sean was caught with marijuana. The principle called and I had to pick him up. He was expelled from school. I took him to our family doctor, and I was reassured it was a teenager thing. This happened again in high school, again marijuana. After Sean graduated and had been living with his dad, I was told that he was using heroin and the family was doing an intervention. Sean had pawned his dad's prized guitar. He refused to talk to me about any of it. I did not even know people in our area did heroin. This was the beginning of the monster shutting us out.

I believe Sean's addiction spanned most of his life. I asked him once when he first used drugs. He told me that when he was ten, he stole some pills from a family member who had just had surgery and it made him feel good. For the first time in his life, he felt comfortable in his own skin. He said from that moment on he sought different drugs. I asked him what made him even think to take the pills at such a young age and he said he wanted to know what they did. He was never clear with me about it. I had no clue this had ever happened. How do you not know your child took pills at such a young age? I wish I knew the answer. It never crossed my mind. By the time I knew of it, Sean was a poly drug user. That means he used everything. We never had a chance. The monster remained hidden for many years before it showed us its ugly head. We fought the monster the best we could. I took Sean to a local Suboxone clinic and got him started on medication-assisted treatment, but it was all new to me. I was still naive about substance use disorder. I thought they could fix him. I did not understand any of this. I thought addiction was a choice. I had moved two hours away for work. Sean was living with his dad and grandma. They stood up to the monster every day. They lived the day to day struggle of addiction with Sean. They tried everything and they saw more than I ever did.

Sean overdosed twice to my knowledge. The first time his dad found him and got him breathing again. Sean was rushed to the hospital and put on a ventilator in ICU. The call from his grandma came saying, "Come quickly, they do not know if he is going to make it." I called Amanda and she rushed to the hospital. I jumped in my car and headed over the mountain, unsure if I would see my son alive again. Sean survived this overdose. When they took him off the ventilator, he was angry. I wanted to take him back with me for treatment, but he refused. The monster's grip closed tighter. We asked the hospital for help, to send us a social worker, give us resources or force him to treatment; no help was available. I watched him get in the car with his dad and grandma as they left the hospital. I could feel the power of the monster as it consumed our son.

His dad and grandma worked hard to get him a bed in rehab, but as it so often happens, by the time a bed was ready, Sean was no longer willing to go. His dad and grandma were on the frontline of the battle with Sean's addiction. I was a long-distance ally in the battle, and I believe his sister, Amanda, was the one most in denial. It was too hard to believe that she could not protect her little brother from the monster and being shut out broke her heart. We all fought for him, each of us in our own way. I believe each of us changed our personal strategies many times. We all loved him deeply and we all took turns being the hero and then the victim. None of us knew how clever the monster of addiction really is. One thing that remained constant — everyone's unconditional love for him. The effects of addiction, on our family, has been life altering for each of us. It is difficult to speak for everyone involved, but I will do my best. Our grief is still fresh and raw. We were each weary and tired from the long battle when the monster delivered its fatal attack, leaving us all in shock and horror at the news that Sean had been taken from us.

On the cool, fall evening of September 11, 2019, Sean said good-night and I love you to his grandma...and sometime after midnight on September 12, for a reason that none of us understand, he went into the bathroom and injected a lethal dose of heroin and fentanyl. The monster had won. Sean lost his life and long battle with the monster. His dad went to find him, early in the morning, for work and found him in the bathroom. He tried to save him, but it was too late.

I awakened that morning, got my coffee, and headed out to the porch. I settled in and picked up my phone to see I'd missed a call from Dan. I noticed a message saying, "Call me, we lost our son." The sound that came out of me was not recognized, by me, as my own voice. I have heard others who have lost children describe the death scream. It is an out of body experience...I was literally looking down on myself sitting there screaming. I spoke with Dan and got the details and we cried together. Then it was my job to tell Amanda...How do you do that? We are never prepared for this, even though we know the risk is always there. I called Amanda and told her. It was a horrible experience. She denied her brother's death, she would not accept it. She hung up with me and went straight to Sean's house. The police would not let her in. She called me back and told me Sean had died and Grandma Joyce

247

was crying. My heart shattered a second time that morning. My son was dead, and my daughter was broken.

I am often asked what I would do differently, and I feel like my answer is everything. I feel like I got it all wrong. We did not understand addiction. We were not educated on the subject any further than, "Just Say No." There was no real effective support for Sean or his family. Then there is the stigma. We must have been horrible parents. We must not have loved him enough or disciplined him enough or tried hard enough. So on and so forth. I still do not see anything that has changed. We do not have effective education and treatments in place to stop this epidemic. I believe the thing we all did right was to love him each and every day. He always knew we loved him and that brought us some peace. Each of us would have done anything to save him.

To the family with a loved one in active addiction, I would say...seek support and educate yourself about addiction. Believe that this is a disease and it can kill your child. Join groups and help the community to end the stigma. Help build effective support and services. Fight the stigma of addiction and know your child deserves to be treated for this disease. What would I shout from the roof tops about addiction? It is not your fault. Getting trapped in blame and shame only help the monster to keep you isolated and defeated, while it comes for your child.

What would I say to a parent who says, "Not my child?" First, I would warn you, I said that too, and I was so wrong. We were a regular family. Dan and I were divorced, but we raised Sean together and I think we did a great job. We were from an average, small town, surrounded by friends and family, middle class, good schools, with regular, old traditions. We were just like you, until the monster grabbed our youngest child.

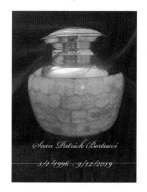

Sean Patrick Bertucci
3/2/1996 - 9/12/2019

Sean's Mom,

KIMBERLY G.
Bend, Oregon

Keaton

Keaton was the kid who always tried to make everyone laugh. He gave the impression of a "tough guy" but had a heart of gold. He made us grandparents when he was seventeen years old, and I thought then that was the scariest time of my life. Keaton and Xalene, my grandson Bryson's mom, had their ups and downs, as anyone would becoming parents at the ages of sixteen and seventeen. Keaton hit a rough patch when my grandson was a baby, hanging out with the wrong crowd and using drugs.

At that time, we made him leave our home (the hardest decision of my life) until he could show that he was going to clean up his act and take responsibility for his son. That lasted six long months. By the time he changed his ways and came back home, his girlfriend, Bryson's mom, had found a new boyfriend. Keaton, of course, was devastated. However, after a year and a half, they found their way back to each other. In December 2017, he asked Xalene to marry him. They had talked about having a summer or fall wedding in 2019, but I talked them into waiting until 2020. I had a lot going on in 2019 including my youngest graduating high school and leaving for college in the fall. I felt it would be too stressful to plan a wedding along with everything else. I now regret this to this day! Their wedding was planned for October 3, 2020. We had been making plans and buying things for the wedding all along, but began planning full force in January of 2020. The week my son passed, we had just booked the outdoor ceremony at a beautiful park near us, bought a whole bunch of decorations, wood flowers that we were going to dye and put together ourselves, and took Xalene to try her dress on to make sure it still fit since it had been well over a year since we found her dress. The thought of seeing his face light up when she came walking in that dress made my heart swell.

Two days later, I got the phone call just after six a.m. on Saturday, January 18. HE WAS GONE! We later found out that he had used cocaine as a recreational drug. This time though, it turned out there was no cocaine. They didn't find any in his system. It was pure fentanyl. There has been an investigation and no leads as to who sold it to him. After six long months, I have decided it is time for me to do something. I have learned that this is happening a lot! I can't sit back and let this happen to another mother. I am pained every day that my son will not be marrying the love of his life this year, and my grandson who adored his dad and vice versa will grow up without his dad.

This could have been prevented! Some-thing needs to be done to stop these people from murdering our children!! For anyone that thinks this can't happen to them, you're wrong. To anyone that knows what it's like, I'm sorry. Please know that are so many people that have gone through the same thing. We are all here for you! We need each other more than ever and to make our voices be heard, so that their deaths will not be in vain.

Keaton's Mom,

TARI G.
Onalaska, Wisconsin

Brian

FOREVER 34

It's been a year and a half since the death of my precious son. I remember figuring out the truth of why my son was acting the way he did. Several times I found him slumped over, in his car, when I came to visit him. He would awake and say he was tired. Other times, he would go missing for a few days at a time. I filed a missing person's report several times, with endless nights of searching, and I would always find him in the end. I started to scramble for advice at every angle; it was frustrating. He would have to be willing to get help. He was ashamed. He did attend detox, twice, but did not go to rehab because he would say, "I can do this myself."

At that point, I needed more help. With my friend and father, we would sit and try to figure out our finances on how to have an intervention that would cost thousands and then how to send him to rehab, which again would cost in the thousands. Trying to put it all together,

Brian would be the one, ultimately, to make the decision to go to rehab. In the past, this wasn't going to happen, but every time this was being arranged, he would seem to get better. It was a back and forth battle, draining me of all my energy, as a single mother, working full time. It would become too late for that help.

The coulda, shoulda, woulda will haunt me the rest of my life. The emptiness is so final, nothing can heal my soul, I've learned to live with it, hiding my deep sorrow and loss. I would find this online grief group Not In Vain; I would read the heart-breaking stories and this would make me feel not so alone.

Brian's Mom,

Elizabeth H.
Olympia, Washington

Eric

FOREVER 36

This story is about my son Eric. He was successful in his life; he had a great job as a concrete pump operator, had his own apartment, drove a nice car, and had many friends. Drugs and alcohol were never a part of his life.

In 2010, he was hit by a car while out riding his motorcycle. He ended up in the hospital in intensive care for many injuries; he had multiple surgeries and skin graphs, many months of physical therapy, but a broken back is something you really can never come back from. Pain meds became his lifeline; he could not function without them and was trying to get back to work and life. Because of a lawsuit from the accident, he had plenty of money to supplement the pain meds that he needed more and more of.

As with all good things, it came to an end in 2012; Eric lost his job and license, his apartment and girlfriend; he had hit rock bottom, but still had to live with chronic back pain. Soon, he sold his vast collection of Jordan shoes and autographed picture collection. He moved in with me. I did not know that he was breaking into houses to support his habit; he also stole everything of value in my home. He ended up in jail and I couldn't have been more heartbroken.

The next several years after jail were a cycle of rehab stints and struggling with alcoholism to mask the pain. Slowly he lost all his friends and family; he still lived with me and I was his main caregiver. I took him to rehab, called the ambulance for him numerous times, and even took a leave of absence from work one summer to care for him. I just wanted my old Eric back, the Eric with the biggest heart, the funniest and smartest person I knew. He struggled to get clean constantly.

In December 2019, Eric went to rehab for the last time. When he got out, he was sure he would stay clean and had things he was looking forward to. On January 29, 2020, he wanted me to pick up a pizza for us for dinner. We ate dinner together and his last words to me that night was to make sure he was up for his doctor appointment at ten thirty the next morning. On January 30, 2020, I woke up early and got ready for the day. As I stood in the kitchen, I heard his alarm going off. I looked at the kitchen clock and it was 9:25. It made me think about him because his birthday is September 25, 1983. I walked down the hallway to his room, annoyed that his alarm was still going off, not knowing my life would be forever changed the moment I opened his bedroom door. I later found out that after I went to bed, he left the house and met up with someone who said that they had "Perc" what they had was fentanyl! Things will never be the same again, I will never be the same again. So many years of trying to get his life back were over. I will miss my son, Eric, every day of my life.

Eric's Mom,

GAIL H.
Swansea, Massachusetts

Travis

My son was born in 1983 at 10:09 a.m. What a wonderful moment that was. He did not live a rich life! I was a single mother. I feel like I was doing and did the best I could, since I did not get any help from his dad.

He played football in school, loved skateboarding, hanging out with friends, and listening to his music. During football season in tenth grade he hurt his back and neck. Well, this is where it all began with pain medicine.

After he graduated and turned eighteen, he went to live with his dad (drugs and alcohol). His dad was an addict. I thought for sure my son would make good decisions, even though he was now living with an addict. He started smoking marijuana with his dad and drinking, but he really did not care for alcohol. He started dabbling with Xanax and many other different pills to kill the pain. Later, it would lead to heroin. My son struggled for fifteen years in and out of jail, detox, and rehab centers. OD'd at least twenty times, involving hospital stays and horrible phone calls in the night. I now have PTSD from the dramatic episodes.

The last year he was in and out of jail and the week before his passing, he called me and told me that he couldn't do this life any longer and surrendered to the Lord. I was so happy. He was reading the bible every day.

His court date came on a Thursday. He got out of jail with time served on May 7, 2020. I talked to him on Saturday. He sent me a Happy Mother's Day message on Sunday, through a text that will be my forever contact with my son.

Wednesday, May 13, 2020 at 3:40 p.m., a sheriff pulled into my drive, walked up to my porch, and told me my son was no longer with us. Ever since then I have been in a fog.

Everything is so raw. I am taking this new life that I have to live without him day by day and that's how my life will forever be, forever changed.

Travis's Mom,

Dora H.
Crawfordsville, Indiana

Taylor

My daughter, Taylor Renee (aka Buggie) is the middle child of my three, beautiful daughters. As a child, Taylor was such a momma pot. It still brings a smile to my face and a warmth to my heart remembering her as a small child, who adored her mother, as I so adored her. When I would take her to daycare she would hold onto my leg and beg me not to leave her. Telling me daily that she was going to "cry on her mat for me." I remember her many attempts to sleep over night at a friend's house, only for me to get a phone call in the wee hours of the night, from parents asking me to come and pick her up, as she was crying uncontrollably. I would pick her up and with tears streaming down her face she'd say, "Mommy, I'm just so homesick and want to be with you." It was not until she was in middle school that she was finally able to spend the night over at a friend's house, without me having to go and get her.

Taylor loved her older sister, Autumn, and tried to as she put it,

257

"clone her every move." She would follow her around and want to be with her all the time. There is a six-year difference between Autumn and Taylor. Autumn always played with Taylor, let Taylor hang out and tag along with her and her friends until her teen years. Taylor is only eighteen months older than her younger sister, Kira. Taylor was always very protective and very close to Kira. As a child she spoke for Kira. When I say she spoke for her younger sister, I mean literally spoke for her and answered all questions I would ask Kira. Kira hardly even spoke until she was three or four years old. I thought something was wrong with her and even sought medical advice. The doctor told me that she had a case of "sibling syndrome." I had never heard of such and inquired. The doctor laughed and said that everything was ok, that she did not need to speak because her big sister had it all under control. Taylor loved and protected Kira to the end. There isn't anything that she wouldn't do for her. The bond they shared is unmatched, by any I've ever seen.

Taylor was such a loving and kind child. Always a protector. Never liked to see anyone else hurting. Always concerned for others and would do anything for others. She had a gift for prose, art, and poetry. Creativity had always been an essential part of her. She was very smart in school. Taylor never had to study and always received straight A's. Taylor was also daddy's little girl. She loved her daddy as a child, or so I thought.

When Taylor was nine years old her father and I split up. He had promised to continue to be a part of the girl's lives, which could not have been farther from the truth. Once we split up, he never called, saw them, sent birthday or Christmas cards or gifts, nothing. He was gone and no longer a part of the girl's lives. I begged him to contact the girls and to see them, to no avail. He saw them one time in nine years. I never realized how much pain and anguish that caused my kids, until it was too late.

When Taylor was thirteen, life began to get exceedingly difficult in our house. What I thought was natural teenage attitude, turned out to be much more. I had walked into my daughter's room, after a heated argument, to find my daughter cutting herself. The shock and hurt that rushed me was overwhelming. I immediately sought the help of a psychiatrist and started family therapy.

For the next five years of her life, we would do inpatient and outpatient therapy and weekly family therapy with weekly psychiatrist appointments. Taylor was diagnosed with bi-polar disorder. We tried medications that seemed to eventually get things, somewhat, under control. This chapter of our lives was difficult on everyone. I am sure my other daughters felt left out or possibly even abandoned as so much of my time was spent seeking help for Taylor. It was exhausting and in the long run it didn't even matter. When Taylor turned eighteen, she quit going to school and quit taking all her medications. Thus, began the even more horrible downward spiral.

Taylor fought two powerful demons in her life: addiction and bipolar disease. Taylor sought out anything to ease her pain. This is when she slowly and painfully became an addict. She began to indulge in many different drugs to cope with life and to ease the depression that she felt daily. Eventually she would find her drug of choice, heroin. She wrote and explained it as, "A deafening, quiet storm rush, breathing only when absolutely necessary. I nod into a bright, soft, warm ocean. I am not sad, I'm not happy, I just am. My mind isn't screaming with worry, regret or shame. I can breathe if I want, I can stop and be gone. There is power in my pain now. I found the wholeness my aching mind and heart so badly craved."

At this point in Taylor's life, she became my gypsy child. In her younger years she couldn't even spend a night away from home. Now she was a free spirit, running to different places looking for new friends, adventures and seeking a sense of peace, that always eluded her. She would be gone in different states for months at a time, then come home, stay for a while and then be off again. Seeking a place to find that she could escape her addiction and bad choices. Only to find the same environment in each new location. She had sought refuge in California, Texas, Pennsylvania, Arizona, Michigan and Florida. While home in Florida, in 2016, she was going to make her attempt at yet another rehab facility. The day that she was to go to rehab, she OD'd. I rushed to the hospital, hundreds of miles away, to be by her side. To see my baby in this state was unbelievable. Tubes down her throat, black eyes and lifeless. As she clings to life, all I can do is ask myself how did we end up here? She recovers, this time. Enters rehab and within a few short months is off living her life on the run again. The worry, countless nights of sleep, unanswered phone call and texts - the whole time praying and hoping that you don't end up getting "the call."

Four months before my beautiful baby lost her battle with addiction, she called me from Arizona. "Mom please come and get me. Fly out and drive my car back home or I'm going to end up dead." I booked the flight that evening and was on a plane the next day. I drove us home, I was saving her, so I thought. The drive was good for us. We connected again. She wanted better for her life. She didn't want to be in this world of addiction anymore. She promised me that I would not have to bury her.

We made it home and within a week, she is back on the same cycle. I know, by now when she is bingeing and doing drugs. She ignores my phone calls and texts. Finally, four days later, I received a call from Taylor. She has been arrested for possession of cocaine and heroin. This is her first and last time ever being arrested. She was so scared. She hated being in there. As hard as it was not to rescue my baby, I would not bail her out.

You see, worry is the only thing I know when it comes to my Taylor. At least now, I knew she was safe from herself. I could actually sleep at night. I knew where she was. We spoke daily. We wrote each other. She was reading her Bible daily and reconnecting with God. Released in the beginning of November she was optimistic about her future, adamant that she would never end up back in jail. She started to make plans for her future. She was positive about her new future. I was hopeful that she would remain sober.

Our last day together was Thanksgiving of 2018. In three short days, my Taylor would overdose and die. Our last day together was an amazing day. I am forever grateful for the memories I have of that day. She helped me in the kitchen (which she never did before), we cooked, we laughed and seeing her play & cut up with her nephew are memories that I will forever cherish.

Taylor took off the following day, while I was at work. I couldn't get ahold of her. The worry and gut-wrenching feeling, I had in my stomach was something that I had never experienced in the past. I pleaded with her two sisters to get ahold of her. To let me know that she is okay. She finally spoke to Kira on Saturday and promised that she would be coming home the following day. Tomorrow came but she did not make it home. She would die in a hotel room, in West Palm Beach, on November 25th, 2018 with two "friends" that did nothing to try and save her. Taylor had two units of Narcan in her car. The "friends" cleaned up all the drug evidence, stole her purse and all her personal belongings before they called 9-1-1. I can tell you that I was not prepared for "the call", that I had unintentionally thought I may receive, previously.

The next week is a total blur to me. No mother ever expects to plan their child's funeral. My two daughters did an amazing job, preparing everything. They did the memory boards, the video, the memorial cards.... everything. I was of no use. I was inconsolable. When my baby Taylor died, I died with her. Her father failed her yet again, by not even attending her funeral.

December 3rd, 2018, I put my daughter Taylor Renee to rest. My only solace is I pray, that she is finally at peace. That she has no more depression, pain or hurt. However now, I am the one that is inflicted with heartache and depression, from the loss of my baby, that I will carry until the day I die.

After Taylors death, while going through her personal belongings and journals we found out just how truly traumatic my daughter's life had been. Reading one of her many journals, that she wrote while in one of her many rehabs stays, I stumbled on her pain that she held inside since a child. She wrote of the abuse that her own father inflicted on her as a child. His disgusting, foul actions that she carried with her for the rest of her life. Why didn't she ever confide in me? Why couldn't she include me in her torture? How did I not know? I failed her by not recognizing that pain that tortured her since childhood. Her father never responded to the need Taylor harbored to try to reconcile the harm he had done to her. He refused to participate in therapy sessions. He didn't even come to her funeral.

Taylor was beautiful and always loved. She wasn't a desperate young woman living on the streets or scorned by her family. She was loved and I tried to help her overcome the effects of the torture that haunted her. I blame myself, as any mother might do. I am so blessed to have been her mother and I'll always treasure the twenty-three years that we shared. The world is a better place because she was in it. My life will never be the same. The heartache and emptiness, I feel, is a constant for me now.

My daughter, Taylor Renee died on November 25th, 2018 from an overdose. I died on November 25, 2018, of a broken heart.

Taylor's Mom,

DAWN H.
Sebastian, Florida

Matthew

FOREVER 31

Matt became a dad at sixteen; he was a great dad. I think he was twenty when I found out he was using heroin, but "he could beat it no problem." The next eleven years had many ups and downs. The worst was dealing with a county agency, talk about people treating you like trash. There were a couple times when he was doing great, on the Suboxone program, good job, but it still killed him that he was forced to sign his parental rights away. His wife had a third baby who died of SIDS and that was the beginning of the end.

Matt died in his rented room which was close to his job. They found him on a Wednesday, so that's the official death date, but most likely he died on Sunday. I saw him on Tuesday, he gave me a hug and a kiss and a "I love you, Mom." I never saw his body or got to say goodbye, something I'll regret forever.

Matt was a kind, gentle, loving, funny man and I love him beyond words. Matt was a liar, a thief, he would steal meds, money, your car, your credit card, and badger you 'til you wanted to punch him. Matt was two different people in the same body, but he was my baby boy and I will love and miss him 'til I take my last breath.

Matthew's Mom,

Barbara H.
Bensalem, Pennsylvania

Austin

At thirteen, my son got into trouble at school for smoking weed. He went to rehab for three months and then went back to school. He was targeted by the school staff as "a bad kid." They never gave him a break, and he was always being accused of different things. I was always going down to the office and getting him out of trouble, because he wasn't doing anything wrong. He figured if they were going to accuse him of doing drugs, he might as well use.

Austin had a job. He was also smoking and selling weed. He was very popular and everyone in our town knew him. He started using meth and later went to using heroin. He overdosed several times. He was with a girl and she was using heroin as well. They both decided it was time for a change, so they went to rehab together.

She found out she was pregnant, but the rehab kicked them out

265

because they were a couple. I helped detox them in my home and they were both clean and sober. He was working construction. When they would get off work, "the guys" would go and have some beers and smoke pot.

His girlfriend was furious and told him he was not going to be around the baby if he was not 100% sober. He started using heroin and they continued to argue and fight. My son overdosed from heroin and died September 6, 2013. He was twenty-six-years-old.

His daughter was born in January. He never got to meet his little girl, Emma. If you use drugs, please stop!!!

SOMEONE OUT THERE NEEDS YOU.

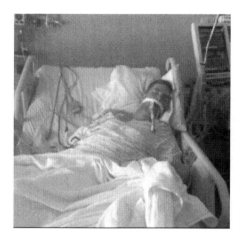

Austin's Mom,

CHRISTINA H.
Dayton, Nevada

Robbie

FOREVER 23

One pill will kill...One pill took my son away. I will never get over it. Keeping your child alive is my mission, along with making sure those that lost the battle are always remembered. This man-made epidemic is a tragedy that was simply too profitable to stop. It wasn't until the morgues were running out of room that America noticed. The shame has finally shifted. If only!

Robbie's Mom,

JENNIFER H.
Suwanee, Georgia

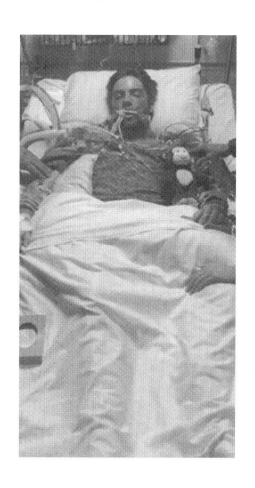

Justin

I am so thankful for the opportunity to tell my story, my son's story. If you are reading this, you probably know all too well that very few want to hear it. They seem afraid, almost like we shouldn't talk about our children, those "lowlifes," the "druggies," the "crackheads," or a multitude of other names I've heard.

Justin Andrew was born on April 29, 1990. He was my second child, but my first-born son. He had a special quality about him. He was always calm and quiet and loved to play jokes on people, just to make everyone laugh. Oh, that beautiful laugh, I miss it so much. He would light up a room the moment he walked in. People were drawn to him. I don't think he ever knew.

I first learned that Justin was dabbling with drugs when he was nineteen years old. His dad and I got the call that he had been arrested. We went through all of the motions of visiting him in jail, supporting him in court, and when the judge released him, we picked him up, brought him home, walked in the house, and right away prayed together, thankful for another chance. He started immediately turning things around. He found a recovery group that met at local churches several days a week.

We would laugh that on Monday he was Methodist, on Tuesday he was non-denominational, and on Friday he was Baptist. He was very involved with providing tech support for the groups and spent weekends volunteering to help the homeless.

That was my Justin, the guy that would do anything to help anyone in need. He loved giving gifts, family gatherings, bonfires, and holidays in particular. He loved to cook, coming up with the craziest recipes ever, and if he made you a sandwich, it was the best sandwich you ever had! Seriously! I don't know what was his magic touch. Maybe it was how much he enjoyed doing it and he would always serve it to you with that silly grin.

In 2012, he married the love of his life. He was so happy to be starting his own little family and he was great at it. He had a job that he enjoyed, and later became a dad to three little girls. He was always a big guy, a gentle giant, and gave the best hugs. I don't know where things went wrong.

The drug use was going on again, along with his wife using, and they ended up losing custody of those three precious girls. They were homeless, living a life of stealing, arrests, and whatever else it took to support their habits. I wouldn't allow him to come home because I couldn't trust them. I would stay in touch with him through Facebook Messenger.

He understood that I could not support what he was doing, but he also would get a regular text that said we loved him. I never asked very many questions. I just wanted to know that he was okay, and by okay, I mean alive. I would do searches daily and a lot of times that would bring up yet another mugshot.

It was upsetting, but then again, I knew he was alive. I didn't talk a lot about Justin to anyone and I regret that. I would talk about his older sister and her accomplishments, his younger brother and his accomplishments, but I guess I was embarrassed. I didn't want people to ask too many questions about Justin.

On the morning of January 20, 2020, I heard a knock on the door. It was our local sheriff's office asking if I was related to Justin. My heart sank. I answered, "Yes, what's happened?" He told me to call a hospital in Charleston, South Carolina.

Thankfully, it was a holiday and I went upstairs and got his dad. He made the call and within an hour, his dad and I, and his brother and sister were headed to Charleston to make what we knew would be the hardest decision of our lives. We drove seven hours from our little town in Tennessee. We all went in to see him lying there on life support and even though he was obviously in bad shape, he looked so beautiful.

I cried so hard, from what I can remember, the most blood-curdling, shrill cry ever. I don't know how the nurses do it. Seeing a mama suffer that much pain. I held his hands and they felt just like I remembered. His wife had been incarcerated in another county, so selfishly, I had him all to myself. I did let the chaplain know where she was and that she needed to be contacted. They brought her in the next day to visit and she gave me Power of Attorney. I spent the last twenty-four hours of his life hugging him, kissing him, talking to him, and my favorite, holding his hand. After the final test showed no brain activity, they declared him deceased on January 21, 2020 at 5:49 p.m.

He was an organ donor and with that, he was honored with a walk as they took him to another hospital. There were several news stories about it, and I was glad that the final memory we have of him was of the good person that he was. Now, when you search his name, that's what comes up. I don't know if the way I handled things was right or wrong. I just know I did the best with what I knew at the time. Whenever I start to question myself, I have to remind myself of that. I had always said I can't imagine the loss of a child. That seems so cliche now. I finally know what I really could not imagine.

The pain is a physical pain that I can't even begin to describe. It's an unending, first thought every morning, emotional and physical pain. There is some relief that he is not feeling that pain, fighting that demon anymore. I loved my son that much. I hope he knew.

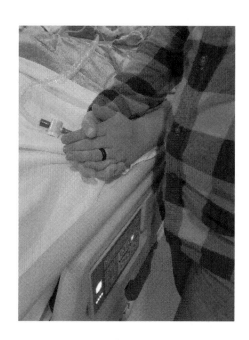

Justin's Mom,

CHRISTY H.
Clinton, Tennessee

Brett

FOREVER 31

Brett was the middle child of three boys. He was always the mischievous one. The only one to have time-outs. Brett was the artistic/musical one of the family. He was in plays, played guitar, was in many bands, and built a recording studio with his dad's help.

Brett was seventeen and a senior in high school when his dad died. His dad passed away suddenly at the early age fifty from a heart attack. He was devastated. He graduated early and went on to college for recording arts in Hollywood, CA. He was eager to get home to Illinois, and away from the drug scene in LA.

He went to school to become a paramedic (because of the series 'House') and then became a firefighter. Brett had always smoked pot and drank a bit, but the drugs became opioids after a back injury on the job. Brett also suffered from PTSD due to his job. He married his longtime girlfriend and life seemed good. Then sleep deprivation, back problems, PTSD, etc. caught up with him.

Someone on the ambulance offered him cocaine, then heroin and the addiction began. His wife left him. He started methadone treatment and moved back home. The lies and stealing started, and I kicked him out. His older brother and wife took him in. He did one rehab after another and then his brother kicked him out.

Methadone treatment stopped and then he tried Suboxone. Brett managed to keep his job and they transferred him to NYC. He did very well there the first 8 months and then started back on the "H." He was put on probation from work and sent to rehab again. Brett stayed clean for a couple of months and met a nice girl, but the drugs were too powerful for him. He started stealing from work to pay for his high. Brett and his girlfriend moved back to IL.

Life seemed to be good again. He could stay clean for almost 90 days on kratom and then he was back at it again. They lost their apartment, moved in with me and his stepfather, got a good job in physical therapy and were both saving money to move into a new place. We monitored every move he made, got him a great therapist, psychiatrist, and he attended meetings every other night and on Saturday's. Then he was back on the drugs.

He od'd. We gave him Narcan. He went to the hospital, refused rehab, but promised to get back on track. He od'd again. We gave him Narcan again. The hospital made him stay for a 72-hour suicide watch. We brought him to our house in Arizona for a 30-day watch and his doctor got him on Vivitrol. He attended meetings, got in shape, ate well, etc. He got back home to Illinois and he got busy with work, meetings, and got an apartment with his girlfriend. We sold him our car, and everything seemed great. My husband and I left for our house in Arizona for the holidays and that is when we got the call that he had broken into our home, sold some merchandise from our house for drugs, and his girlfriend found him unresponsive on our bathroom floor.

The police met us at our house, asked if they could keep his phone, etc. to try to make a case against a dealer. The autopsy showed fentanyl and heroin. After three months they said they didn't have enough evidence, even though his girlfriend (who does NOT do drugs) could

274

identify and had a picture of the guy she believes sold him the drugs. I am lost without my beautiful boy.

I had been in therapy for almost eight months before Brett died. Enabling is the hardest thing to not do with an addict. The drugs take over all their sense of reasoning and they are exceptionally good con artists.

As a mother you want to do everything you can for your child. I would have given my life to save his. He had so much potential, generous to a fault, and a smile and laugh that was contagious. I honestly believe we did everything we could to save him and had been told by numerous therapists, psychiatrists, and police officers, that it is up to the addict to do the work to get clean. They must hit rock bottom before they will do it on their own.

I blame our government for not doing enough to get these drugs and dealers off the streets. Our mental health care is awful. The amount of money we had to pay out of pocket and with insurance was ridiculous. Our rehab care was a revolving door system.

Brett and I had attended a convention for drug addiction, and he had hoped to be a speaker to young kids once he gotten himself cleaned up.

12/12/19 Brett, forever 31. Not In Vain.

Brett's Mom,

DIANE H.
Wheaton, Illinois

Derrick

FOREVER 38

My son was a heroin addict and fought the battle for twelve years. Sadly, he lost on May 22, 2020, when the Lord decided to end his struggle.

I asked my son several times, "Why do it for the first time?" He would only tell me I'd never understand.

One day he texted me and said, "I wrote you a poem and emailed it to you. Please read it."

I copied the poem he wrote that described his struggle and why he tried it the first time.

I'd Never
Lots of things I said I'd never do,
I was naive, had no clue.
Now I know I was wrong, spoke too soon,
I used that lighter and spoon

But before you judge, I was just like you,
Went to the doctor one day, and that's where my addiction made its debut.
With just one piece of paper and a pen he changed my whole life,
It would just be the beginning of years and years of strife.
Started off so innocent, I believed he knew best,
But with each new "treatment" I became more and more obsessed.
To my family and friends, I started to lie,
But all I had to do was go to the doc to resupply.
Quicker and quicker the scripts would run dry,
On the streets I found a new ally.
The dope boys I met became my new best friends.
I'd lie to myself and say it was just a means to an end. It's ok because it's still what
I'm prescribed.
I'm not doing drugs or dope; I believed my own lie.
Then one day the doc said good news you're cured, no further need for a script,
But when I woke up, I was sick, so off to my "friend's" house I skipped.
But now with no script I had to buy three times the amount,
Started looking for a way to get my medication at a discount.
Further and further down the rabbit hole I fell,
I felt like I was staring at the gates to hell.
When I can't afford what I "need" I feel like shit.
Then after saying "I'd Never" I decided to try "just one hit."
That brown liquid flowed easily into my vein,
But with it my life trickled right down the drain.
The first taste was all it took, didn't see it coming; I was already on the hook.
But I am still in control, still functioning, still doing things by the book.
How quickly things escalated, one day I'm fine: the next I'm homeless.
Never have I seen something that was so ferocious.
It was my worst enemy, yet to me my best friend.
It would be a long time coming before I could see the end.
I'm still ok I lied, I'm just on a down note.
I'll just start selling a little here and there, just to stay afloat.
The line for things "I'd never" became very blurry.
I became involved in violence and crimes in a hurry.
The only voice I could hear anymore wasn't even my own. How heroin became my
life was unknown. I'll do anything not to be sick.
When will it finally click?

For all of the addicts, the bottom is different; we find a way to go deeper.
The value of life gets cheaper and cheaper.
We watch everyone in the circle with us die,
But we become so dehydrated we can't even cry.
I don't want to live but am too scared to die.
So, I used and used just wanting to hide.
After it was all gone, I finally ended up all alone.
I looked to the sky and let out a groan.
Carry me to the finish line or kill me I begged God,
Then something happened that was very odd,
For the first time in forever, I heard a voice that was different than the drug.
It was warm and welcoming, and I once again felt loved.
I found my way broken, scarred and scared to a treatment center.
At the door I trembled scared to enter,
Now or never, it's time to decide
Which is braver? To live or to die?

Derrick's Mom,

ANITA H.
Columbus, Ohio

Connor

My beautiful son Connor passed March 14, 2020. I have not functioned very well since that day. I most definitely am not the same person I was; that one day was the worse day of my life. Then again, my change started seven years ago when Connor first came to me and told me he thought he had a problem. *Well, I can fix that,* I told myself, so ignorant of what addiction really was.

I went straight to the health food store and bought all the detox meds and everything else we thought would work to clean him up. Surprisingly, it worked! For a year and a half, he was clean and beautiful again and life was good. Connor got his dream job as a firefighter/EMT at twenty years old. I was so proud of him and he was so happy.

Then the reality that comes with the job set in. He saw way too much death. Holding people's hands, telling them they weren't going to die when he surely knew they were. He was way too sensitive and I started to worry about how he was processing all that he could not unsee. He would shrug and just say, "You just do." Truth was, he wasn't processing it and started self-medicating.

I am sorry to say I thought that was all behind us, but it was actually the beginning of what became a parent's worst nightmare. Our beautiful son was blessed with talent, athletic ability, charm, and good looks. I guess my ignorance was in thinking "not my child." He hid it well until it started wreaking havoc on the family. I noticed untruths, nodding out, his passions for surfing, rock climbing, and travel just weren't important anymore. No focus on anything. Connor made very good money but never seemed to have any. He started spiraling out of control so he went to his first rehab. That was not the place for him; I've learned about the corruption in some of the rehabs. Again, he stayed good for a while, I again did not see the signs; he was so good at hiding his pain. He was diagnosed with PTSD as well as substance abuse.

One day, Connor and I were working on a rental house of ours; well, I was working, he seemed preoccupied. I left to go get us some lunch. I came back and his Jeep was still there but the house was locked. I didn't see him in the Jeep, but I walked over to it and there he was slumped over, lips blue. I started slapping his face trying to wake him up, but no response. I couldn't get him out of the Jeep because he was too big. I screamed for help; a neighbor came over and helped me get him on the ground.

For some reason, my husband was driving by and ran up to us and started CPR until medics came. Narcan was used and he did survive. His first OD and I was there to experience the whole unimaginable thing. I just could not believe it. That's when I found his drug use had escalated to heroin. Unbelievable, not my son. He told me he had just started it at that point but it was not his last. It seemed heroin had become Connor's drug of choice. He did hate that part of himself And he kept trying to beat it. All the while, he was still working and making money. Then another spiral. This time we found a rehab that just dealt with first responders. Perfect match! For the first time, he was able to tell his story to men and women that understood his pain without judgement.

Unfortunately, his insurance did not cover that rehab so we took a loan out and paid $24,000 for a one month stay. We didn't care, it was our son and we would do anything for him. He was beautifully restored again. He had plans, and was excited about his future. His department put him on light duty, which was basically working in an office. He hated that and wanted to be back on the firetruck doing what he loved. This went on for months and I could see it was wearing him down. It seems that when you reach out for help, you then become red flagged. That is exactly why a lot of firemen and women do not ask for help. That is why substance abuse and suicide is overwhelming high. The stigma is real.

Anyway, you probably guessed it, Connor had a relapse. I'm leaving out a lot of the messy details of his addiction and how it affected our family. We were not ashamed of him and walked beside him every step of the way. Connor never walked in the shadows. He kept trying to beat it but again asked to go to rehab, this time in South Florida and again for first responders. He said, "Mom, I got this; it feels different this time." Connor was doing so well, finished his month in rehab then stayed for IOP. Three months in, and his insurance decides he no longer needs treatment. A psychiatrist that Connor had never even met said he no longer needed treatment. Understand, we were paying $1,000 a month for insurance and they cut him off. He decided to go to sober living down south as he was afraid to come back to Orlando. He did so well; we were so proud of him. He got a job at a gym, he felt good about himself and he looked better than I had seen him in years. We were so hopeful!

We went to see Connor on February 23 and had a beautiful day walking on the beach, had lunch, and visited awhile. He said he hadn't been feeling well, like he was catching something. We left earlier than normal and told him to get some rest. For the next two weeks, he continued to get even more sick. I kept telling him to go to a clinic, he sounded awful. He kept promising he would. Then on March 5, he called to ask if he could come home. There was something in his voice that sounded sad so I told him he could and we would talk about it. Connor spent six beautiful days with us. He helped his father out on some jobs. He didn't ask to go anywhere other than the gym. Then on that Friday, Connor and his dad went up to our river house to work on the dock. Chris, Connor's dad, said they had such a good day. They went to dinner and then sat on the front porch, watching the river go by.

Chris said Connor's breathing seemed not good, but they were going to come home the next day so Connor promised he would go to a clinic.

The next day never came. My husband went to bed around eleven p.m., then heard a noise around 11:45 p.m. He got up to check on it and our worst nightmare began. Chris started CPR. His phone was dead so he ran to the neighbor's to get them to call 911, all the while doing CPR. The biggest WHY I ask myself is why wasn't I there with them? I never passed up a chance to be with Connor, especially at the river. I had nothing going on that kept me at home. I am going to go with the thought that I wasn't supposed to be there and I was spared. It really hurts though. I keep thinking maybe I could have saved him but I think that was out of my hands. It's like the whole week led up to this one night that would change our lives forever. Connor was so affectionate. He told his dad at the river, "You know how much I love you and Mom, don't you?" Chris said he said that several times.

I do know 100% Connor did not want to die. He was so optimistic about his future. He did manage to take something to the river and it was laced with fentanyl. He didn't have much in his system but with an already compromised system, it was deadly. Connor was so smart, he knew "one more time" could truly be the last time. We talked about that so often. He would always say, "Mom, you just don't understand." It's the voices in my head constantly calling me. He was always wearing ear plugs listening to  music; now I think I know why, to keep the voices out. I miss Connor with everything in me and it hurts with every breath I take. Connor April 7, 1988 to March 14, 2020

Connor's Mom,

JUDY I.
Orlando, Florida

Nathan

FOREVER 23

My name is Rhonda, and I lost my only child Nathan to a drug overdose on August 29, 2019. Nathan was born on October 10, 1995 at 10:10 p.m. and was my reason for living and the light of my life. He fought his fight for over five years. I fought for him, with him, beside him until the end, having no shame, and only being proud that every time he fell...he got right back up and went back to treatment. His emotional and mental pain became too much for him to bear.

Nathan loved everyone he met so hard, wanted to make sure they felt loved, and desperately wanted to feel loved. Nathan helped anyone that needed help no matter what it was, even his last dollar or the coat off his back. Nathan wanted recovery so bad and wanted everyone around him to also find recovery. Cheering others on gave him joy. He NEVER judged anyone for anything, especially for their addiction or mental illness. He gave the best hugs and when he hugged you and said, "I love you, man," he MEANT it!

When he lost his battle in August, his friends from treatment that had he developed deep bonds with honored him by all wearing bandanas as he did almost every day. It was his signature. So many came to his funeral wearing their bandanas they called it #Bandanas4-Nate. It went viral all over Facebook.

I took it a step further and after his funeral I decided to have a fundraiser to help as many as I could get into sober living, get transportation to treatment, help with MAT, and any way else I could help folks to find and further their recovery. I continue to do this in Nathan's honor. I refuse to let his death be in vain. I will never stop telling his story.

Nathan's Mom,

RHONDA J.
Saint Charles, Missouri

Kyle Douglas

My life felt absolutely perfect after our beautiful baby boy was placed in my arms on December 21, 1995, completing our little family. I already was so blessed with a loving husband, a darling little girl, and a nice home at the base of the Rocky Mountain foothills in beautiful Colorado. My kids were my whole world. It's all I ever really wanted for as long as I could remember: to be a "Mommy." I took it all in and cherished every second of playing with them, nurturing them, teaching them, feeding them, hugging and kissing them, and snuggling with them every chance I could. I even loved kissing and trying to make their "owies better" never imagining that there would one day be an "owie" that Mommy simply could not kiss and fix.

Kyle was your typical little boy, loving Hot Wheels, Power Rangers, Legos, Bionicles, video games, those little green army men…you get the picture. Star Wars made a reappearance when Kyle was about five years old, which quickly became a fixture in his world for a long time. I would dress my little guy up in Jedi Knight outfits I concocted, and watch this delightful ball of energy bounce off of couches, roll behind tables, do somersaults, and karate kick the air, all while fighting the imaginary bad guys with his light saber. I can't tell you how many light sabers we went through, and I'm so thankful that I saved one of his broken sabers, safely tucked away in a box with some of his other favorite toys. Sometimes I would surprise Kyle and grab one of his light sabers and challenge him to a duel. We would run outside in any kind of weather, jump on boulders, hide behind trees, and just run all over the yard having our light saber battle until this mama couldn't breathe anymore. As tiring as this was, it is one of my fondest memories of playing with my boy.

Eventually, light sabers and other favorite toys took a backseat to sports. Kyle began gymnastics, quite by chance actually. He was watching his sister in her class, but could not stop doing cartwheels and handstands himself. After her class ended, he would often run out onto the floor, trying to be a gymnast too. The boys gymnastics coach took notice of him, leading to a discussion, and subsequently I enrolled Kyle in classes. Kyle was naturally skilled and in no time at all, he was on the competitive team. For years, we travelled all over the state for meets, which usually resulted in blue ribbons, medals, and trophies for Kyle. The highlight was when he took first place on the parallel bars at the state finals. I could feel his pride oozing as he stood up on that podium, raised his little arm, and proudly accepted the gold medal that was placed around his neck. Baseball, basketball, football, and wrestling all naturally became part of his world too. He evolved into a very promising pitcher, even "striking out the side" to help lead his team to a tournament victory one season. Unfortunately, an overworked shoulder by some neglectful coaching took away any hope of continuing on this path.

One day, we wandered into a music store because Kyle was so drawn to his dad's guitar. My husband Steve so loved music and had wanted to learn to play. However, he came to realize that his skills did not come naturally, so his guitar sat in his office, collecting dust. In the music store, Kyle picked up guitar after guitar; you could sense the intensity of his interest. The man who would become Kyle's guitar teacher walked over, obviously intrigued by this little boy's excitement.

This was when Kyle's true passion emerged, and the journey of his life-time love of being a musician began. Within months, it was obvious that he was a natural; he practiced diligently, despite it just coming easy to him. He was offered a spot in a student band that the teacher put together.

Hundreds of people came out to witness their debut at a concert in the music store parking lot. Despite thunder, lightning, and a downpour of rain, the crowd could not get enough of these kids who were up on stage playing AC/DC at eleven and twelve years old. Kyle amazed me with his confident stage presence. I witnessed my "little boy" up on stage transform from a typical kid to a natural and gifted entertainer. The crowd raised their rock fingers, wanting more. Kyle was hooked, and High Voltage was born; an all kid AC/DC tribute band. This band went on to travel all over the state, even getting gigs out of state. They were not some hopeful kiddie garage band—these kids were truly talented and drew crowds that they left in awe at every concert. They won numerous musical awards and appeared in dozens of newspaper and magazine articles. AC/DC themselves recognized High Voltage and they all received autographed vinyl albums from the band!

While Kyle's young music career was taking off, he was still playing sports, particularly baseball. Not surprisingly, he bonded with his team-mates, so one night we hosted a campout in our backyard. We set up our tent, and a fun, innocent night of twelve-year-olds burping, giggling, running around, and talking about gross stuff kicked off. Sadly, this fun, innocent night is also when Kyle's life path changed direction. The little league team was made up of cute boys with promising talent, and their entire lives ahead of them. You never would envision this innocence could turn into something so dark and evil. But it did that night, as one of the boys offered up some pills that he had. I don't know why a twelve-year-old had oxycontin on him. I don't know why Kyle took it. He was smart, and I surely thought we raised him to know better. This is how his journey with addiction was born. An arduous and painful journey that would last over ten years, and one that he would never return from. This is where I must try to drive home a very eye-opening point. Again, this was an innocent little league team sleepover. Think about it. This could easily be your child. There is no discretion when it comes to drugs and their availability, nor who gets hooked on them.

We were a happy, healthy, close, loving family in a nice neighborhood. My husband and I spent quality time with our children. We read to them, we played with them, took them camping at all the national parks and went to a few other nice vacation spots. We volunteered in their schools, and we welcomed them into our bed when they had nightmares. My husband even spent years coaching some of the teams Kyle played ball on. In other words, we were "hands-on" devoted, loving parents. I suppose I was of the gross misconception that drugs lived in the ghettos, the inner city, that addicts were lower classed people, that they were poor, uneducated, or kids from broken homes, neglected kids and kids from abusive parents. This wasn't supposed to happen to us, yet it did.

Drugs do not discriminate; you can be wealthy, poor, white, black or even polka-dotted. You can be a Christian, a Catholic, Jewish or an atheist. You can come from a close-knit loving family, or a broken home. You can be a thirty-year-old female, or a fifty-year-old male, or you can be an innocent twelve-year-old child. YOU CAN BE A TWELVE-YEAR-OLD CHILD. Never in a million years would I have thought that that fun, bonding night out in the tent would be the night my little boy would try drugs.

We cannot keep our children reined into our sides every minute, so I do not know the answer of how to keep them healthy and safe all the time. We can only do our absolute best to love and nurture them, and to somehow educate them on the devastating effects and often fatal results of drug addiction and alcoholism. While we want to be tender with our young ones, the sad truth is that our kids need to know the cold hard facts without any sugar coating. We must have these candid conversations with our babies.

Fast forward months later. We still did not suspect anything horrific like drugs. Yet Kyle was beginning to act different, so I transitioned from being a trusting parent to one who started snooping through his room and belongings. Then one night I came across a pot pipe hidden in a hollowed-out flashlight in my son's backpack. From that day on, the downward plunge began spiraling out of control, worsening year after year. Kyle's interest in sports disappeared. He'd throw a football in the yard with his dad and sister, but the once promising running back, pitcher, gymnast, and basketballer was gone. As far as school goes, Kyle was very smart, particularly in writing—his poetry was often complimented by his teachers. But the drugs drained him of his drive and determination at school as well, and he fell about one month short of graduating twelfth grade.

He always talked about going back and getting his GED. Skateboarding became his main source of activity. And of course, his guitar playing. Our son was massively talented with his instrument and after High Voltage parted ways, Kyle went on to form other bands. He was always in a band, up on stage, or writing music. The last concert we saw him in was actually a tribute to Kyle's closest friend growing up, who passed away due to a pill laced with fentanyl. Kyle had the natural gift of heart-felt soul when he played. He came alive on stage, and made that guitar sing. He entertained like none-other, playing on top of speakers, pool tables, falling to the floor and moving his body around in circles, even disappearing to a hidden area of the venue, making the crowd wonder where he was playing from. He mesmerized everyone that saw him perform. He wrote all the music, all the lyrics, taught many of his bandmates how to play, and he sang.

After his passing, many paid tribute to him by labeling him a legend. He was so talented and had so much potential to go far in the music industry. I tell you all this not to brag, but to demonstrate that even with talent oozing from his body, even with the whole world in front of him, even with the undying and unconditional love from his family and friends, the drugs were more powerful.

I cannot paint a picture of Kyle's life without talking about his heart. He was a very loving young man with a heart-of-gold. He blessed our little family with his goofy nature, his Mick Jagger-like lips, his innocent crooked smile, his silly laugh, his competitive ping-pong games, and just his loving nature in general. I like to feel like I had a very loving, close mother-son bond with him. As a twenty-four-year old young man, he was still my "baby," often cuddling up on the couch with me and shimmying his head onto my lap for a scalp massage. He would often sneak up behind me and initiate a tickle-fest. His little boy antics were as endearing to me at twenty-four-years-old as they were when he was three. Kyle also hugged and thanked me for every meal I prepared for him, often insisting on doing the dishes afterwards. Kyle frequently gave his last dollar to a homeless person, even with so little money himself.

Throughout his drug journey, he cried. He literally sobbed over and over and over again to us (his dad and I) about how he knew he was hurting us, hurting his sister, hurting his friends, and most importantly, hurting himself. He did not want to be this person, and he tried tirelessly and bravely to beat this disease. He was so ashamed and sad for the person he had become.

But as much as I want to show a loving, big-hearted son, I surely must confess that there was the "other" Kyle, the one who said mean things, hurt us, and took advantage of our help. Having an addict as a child is heart-wrenchingly painful and it drains you of your own health and sanity. It ages you profoundly. It causes arguments between you and your spouse. You love your child with every ounce of your soul, and desperately want to help. You don't ever want to make them feel guilty, so you either cry yourself to sleep every night or lie awake worried. Worry like that has no internal clock. The cell phone that sits on your nightstand becomes your biggest comfort yet your biggest fear. It will indeed ring at two in the morning. Your child calls, crying, crocked out of his mind, and all you can do is keep him talking on the other end so that he doesn't hang up and pass out in a ditch or something.

Perhaps you are like us, where you are hours away from where your child lives. You WILL get in your car at one a.m. and drive to him after one of these calls, with no idea what you will find when you get there. You can't call the police because you have no idea where your child is, yet you drive on into the night, not knowing where you're even going. I am surprised I was not fired from my job, as I left so many times during the day, and couldn't come in so many times because of sleepless nights, or nights spent in the ER, or entire nights just sitting up with my drugged-out child. I am very fortunate that I was not in a car accident, driving for three hours at two a.m. with tears streaming down my face. My husband went through all of this too, and then some.

Then there were the special occasions; holidays that start off beautiful get tainted with something sour. Events such as college graduations, family get-togethers, weddings; they all become a battle because alcohol is always present. The day before my daughter was to present her college thesis that she worked for years on, she found her brother face down in a pile of pills. He was taken to the hospital and then placed in a facility for a bit. The trauma my girl faced that day caused her to get very ill, and she ended up in the ER the night before her graduation, very, very sick. Psychosomatic perhaps, as we feel she was suffering the fallout from what she had gone through. With little to no sleep, she smiled through her graduation ceremony and party, but behind that smile was so much pain and worry for her brother. A brother who was in a detox center instead of watching his sister graduate.

So you can see that siblings also pay the price of addiction. They are often sadly forced into a lower priority, no matter how much you love them and recognize you are doing this. We are so blessed that our Jessica was such an understanding, loving, patient, and compassionate daughter every step of the way. This evil intruder called addiction definitely affected our daughter and I feel so pained that this was such a big part of her life. If anything possibly good comes out if it, it will be that she will have first-hand insight and awareness into the signs of drug use, and the trials, tribulations, and pain that addiction can cause. Hopefully, this will be a powerful tool for her, if she ever has children of her own.

Then there are the vacations or little weekend get-aways. Forget about planning a well-deserved trip for you and your spouse, because you are worried sick about being far away from your child. What if he needs you? What if the hospital calls? Where to go on vacation is not the struggle, as you are instead questioning if you should go.

We tried for ten-plus years to help our son, and Kyle certainly tried too. He was in and out of rehabs, therapy sessions, hospitals, a few jail cells, and probationary periods with the law. He tried to attend all the recommended classes, such as Narcanon, AA, and he was involved in community service. He wanted to do all the right things to get better and turn his life around. He wanted so desperately to pull out of this hell he was in. But it just wasn't meant to be. With sober living arrangements made, Kyle was weeks away from moving in but developed COVID-19-like symptoms, along with a female friend he had been spending a lot of time with. Presumed positive (but not tested) by the hospital, they needed to go into quarantine mode. Her parents generously offered their home as a retreat for them to quarantine in. We would have done the same in a heartbeat, but due to a removed spleen, my husband's immune system is compromised.

Kyle and his friend were a few days into their stay at her parents' home when a bottle of an opium tincture was found by either the girl, or Kyle. This tincture was used by her mother to alleviate cancer-induced pain. It remains unclear how the tincture was discovered by our kids. We recently received a letter from the girl claiming she was the one who found and took it first, and that Kyle discovered her in a bad state on her closet floor. But once "Kyle the addict" was tempted by this opium, it was too powerful to abstain.

We are not sure and probably will never know exactly how this night unfolded. While I have my theory on what happened, my heart will not let me postulate on this with any confidence, so I must simply make peace with this as is. What we do know is this: The effects of the opium contributed to Kyle drifting off to sleep while sitting outside for what was supposed to be only a few minutes, the night of March 28th.

The girl was indoors and later found him unresponsive, so she threw cold water on him, then supposedly removed his wet shirt. She went inside to charge her phone, but due to being under the influence herself, she ended up passing out and sleeping for hours, indoors. Kyle was left outside, wet, uncovered, and exposed to the elements of freezing twenty-four-degree weather for hours. Yes, the drugs were the initial instigator of his demise, but hypothermia played a big role.

She did eventually awaken and run outside in a panic, making a makeshift bed with blankets. But it was too late, as his organs and body were already shutting down. She fell asleep cuddling him, under the stars, clueless that he was dying. By the time her parents woke up and discovered our son was unresponsive, he was already gone. Such a senseless and preventable death, yet it all goes back to the one thing: drugs. And to think, we were going to drive out to pick him up and bring him to our house that very next day. ONE DAY TOO LATE, and my guilt overwhelms me.

Yes, there is that thought that even if we did bring him safely home, this could inevitably play out another time in his future. But maybe not. Maybe his last attempt at going into that sober living would have been his saving grace. We will never know, because drugs won that night. Our beloved, beautiful Kyle died the morning of March 29, 2020. Due to COVID-19 being at the height of intensity at this time, we held a ZOOM memorial service for our son. It felt so cold to me, but yet the support, love, and responses from attendees that we interacted with was overwhelming and comforting. My husband fought back tears as he bravely shared our son's journey with our online guests. He felt it was important to erase the stigma that attaches itself to so many addicts.

Addicts are not just worthless junkies and bad people. Addicts are loving and talented children and adults who for some horrific reason developed this disease. As painful as it was to talk about at Kyle's memorial, if it could reach and help just one person who was struggling, perhaps Kyle's death would not be in vain. I think in simplest forms, the words I want to shout from rooftops is that it can happen to anybody, even a young child with their whole life awaiting them. The world will never know Kyle's musical talent. He was on his way, but his route was detoured to a dead end.

My world stopped turning the way it should when Kyle left, and my heart is forever broken. I live because I have a beautiful, loving daughter whose life I want to be part of, and a loving husband that I want to grow old with. I go on because Kyle would want me to. I love that boy with every ounce of my being, and I cry at least a few times every day. The instrument that could have paved the way for my son's brilliant future in music is now his home. We had a beautiful guitar urn made for Kyle, and now our son eternally rests on our mantle. While it is a sight to behold, this is NOT how any parent should be spending time with their child. I thought one day we would display a gold record on our mantle that Kyle and his band produced. Instead, we have this.

I don't have the answers nor sound advice for anyone out there that is drowning in this abyss. I'm not an expert, although after what my husband and I have been through, we both certainly could unofficially qualify as one. My biggest regret is that we loved our child so much that we turned into enablers and couldn't pull out of that role. We constantly helped him with money for food and so he would have a roof over his head.

We knew in our hearts that this was likely detrimental, but only a parent knows the heart-breaking pain of thinking your child is cold or hungry. Most parents will give their own life to save their child's. We also helped solve too many of his problems, not teaching him the consequences of his choices. Every time he fell, we were there to help pick him back up. We desperately wanted to help him, but the love we had for Kyle filled our hearts more than it filled our heads.

My advice to any parent forced to embark on this journey is to find the resources to help your child early on, design and insist on a recovery plan, putting your foot down on it however you can, and draw that line once you realize you are becoming an enabler. It's gut-wrenchingly hard to draw that line when it's your beautiful child, but in retrospect, I think it may have saved or at least prolonged our son's life, had we taken this step earlier. Enablers or not, most of the desire to change has to come from the addict, so despite all the years of tirelessly trying to help him, and loving him unconditionally, the bottom line is that change had to come from within himself.

I intend to try and make a difference somehow, someway, some day. His death is still quite fresh, so my hope is that if and when time heals me a bit, I might try getting out there and speaking. Telling Kyle's story to a middle school, a high school, or any group of young people that will listen. It wouldn't be to glorify Kyle, but to reach that one person that sees Kyle in themselves.

Kyle would want this, and I vow I will try when and if my energy and desire to move forward kicks in. I don't know if this story will be published or not, but the more I wrote, the more I felt Kyle was inspiring me to do so. I found an oddly comforting sense of therapeutic relief writing this, even if it is destined to remain for my eyes only. As a matter-of-fact, I just realized this write-up could easily become that speech I give to those schools one day.

Not in vain my loving Kyle; senseless and painstakingly heart-breaking, but not in vain. I love you forever and ever, my beautiful son.

Kyle Douglas December 21, 1995 to March 29, 2020

Kyle's Mom,

JOANN J.
Colorado Springs, Colorado

Samual Justin

FOREVER 34

How to begin? Justin is my heart and a big part of my soul. He died July 8, 2020, alone in his apartment thirty miles from where I live. My very worst nightmare came to life. I didn't receive any texts from him the previous day, which always concerned me, even though he would lose his cell phone from time to time. He always managed to find someone who would lend him a phone long enough to call me, because he always knew how much I worried about him.

I should have jumped in my car and drove down to his apartment before going to bed. I had been up early that day with house errands. I then shopped all afternoon for an upcoming trip to Delaware to visit my sister. I was beat! The next morning, I woke at 5:50 a.m. and remembered, I received no calls during the night from Justin. I frantically drove to the town where he lived, pulled up outside, and saw lights on in all the rooms and thought, "Ok, he is getting ready for work." He had an upstairs apartment, which I always had trouble with because of the stairs (stroke in 2014), but that morning I made it up there in no time. I knocked, but there was no answer. So, I put my key in the lock and ran through his kitchen to his bedroom. Immediately, I saw him laid out face up on the floor next to his bed, knowing from one glance that he was gone. I got down on my knees and tried to put his arms around me, but he was already stiff. I began to wail and called out to him, telling him in despair that he had made my worst nightmare become real.

That was twelve days ago and the pain is unbearable. Every time my cell phone signals a message, my heart beats faster, thinking it might be him, until reality sets in. I see him in everything here at the house. He came home every weekend. He struggled a long time with drug and alcohol addiction. He went to many rehabs, work programs, etc. He really fought hard, but the devil won out. I FEEL I HAVE FAILED HIM, even though his dad and I got him into as many programs as we could, encouraged meetings, and private counseling.

Why did I have to be so tired the day before that I couldn't get to his apartment in time? How am I going to live without my only child, a grown man that never had the opportunity to have a life outside of on and off jobs, occasional female relationships, and episodes of living at home from time to time? Justin was the most hand-some, intelligent, humorous, talented person I ever had the opportunity to know, much less be the mother to. He was such a sweet, caring young man. I saved his life on several other occasions  using CPR, but I don't want to go to my grave wondering why couldn't I have made it on time this one last time? It's killing me.

Justin's Mom,

CINDY K.
Sanford, North Carolina

Christopher

My son, Christopher Lee was born on June 27, 1985, in Iselin, Pennsylvania. Christopher was a happy and very intelligent child and during his early years, he cried when he had to miss a day of school. He was prone to some serious temper tantrums. We went the usual route of child psychologists and we tried Ritalin for ADHD and nothing really helped.

As he got a little older, during a routine physical at school they noticed that one of his testicles was smaller than the other and referred us to a urologist who diagnosed a varicose vein around his testicle. He had surgery and developed more problems and eventually, they had to remove the testicle altogether. I know this worried him because he wanted children someday. Christopher's depression became more and more evident after that and since his father and I both suffered from depression, we understood some of his problems.

Our marriage fell apart when Chris was in his early teen years. Although I didn't move far away and saw the kids often, they did not live with me since I worked twenty-four hour shifts as a paramedic. I am

297

pretty sure this is when Chris started experimenting with various drugs. He had been prescribed opioids during his various surgeries, but this is when the experimenting really got serious. I didn't realize my son was using heroin until a few years later when he was arrested for selling it.

He totaled many vehicles over the years, many accidents that he really shouldn't have survived. There was always an excuse: a deer, an idiot in front of him...but I now know that he probably was nodding off from the heroin. He wasn't a big-time dealer or anything. Everything he made went into his arm. When he was released from jail, he went to rehab and seemed to be doing okay, but eventually he started stealing from me and his father to get what he needed. His excuses and his stories were very good about why he needed money. He stole more from people than I know about. He took his elderly great aunt's debit card when he was mowing for them and took over $10,000. Every time he would get into trouble, he would sign himself back into a rehab until he was kicked out of most of them in our state.

When he would flunk a piss test while on probation, they would put him in jail for a weekend and then let him out! I never understood our judicial system other than it doesn't work. At one point, Christopher had charges against him involving an armed robbery at our local gas station. He was the getaway driver. I think he got around a year for that one and more fines and probation. During that year, we had some nice visits. It was nice to talk to him when he was clear headed and moti- vated. He got on the kitchen crew in jail and he looked forward to it. He did excellent work when he was clean and was a perfectionist. Toward the end of his stay, I had to break the news to him that his best friend growing up had died from an overdose. I really hoped that this would keep him from using when he got out. He wrote me a beautiful poem. This was so hard for me too. I had known Sam's family forever and watched the boy grow up. I even took him on vacation with me and the kids when they were teenagers and what fun we had!

When I picked him up from the jail after that stint, he looked amaz- ing! He was clean, healthy, and had a spark in his eyes that I hadn't seen in a long time. I remember telling him that I would never be picking him up from jail again (sadly I was right). He started using again within probably a week. Again our journey through rehabs and halfway houses continued like revolving doors. I had quit giving him money for anything a few years before this, but he was able to talk his father into giving in quite often. By this time he had gotten disability benefits so he had an "income" which all went to drugs and his fines and restitution. He had also stolen thousands from my sister through the years.

Chris loved music and during his clean times, we would go to karaoke or just go shoot pool together. When he was in jail or rehab, I would print lyrics he requested and send them to him and we had some great outings together during one of his long stints at a rehab that gave me memories that I will always cherish. During this particular rehab, they even had him working, but when he graduated from the halfway house to the next level (a ¾ house), we didn't have the funds to continue his care so he went home to his father's where he once again started using. I was bartending at the time not far from Christopher's house when he came into the bar where I work. There weren't any customers and it was about closing time. Chris was acting kind of funny so I told him I couldn't close until he left. He finally left, still acting strangely. About half an hour after he left, he texted me, telling me to look beside my car. There in the parking lot I found a gun. It looked real. When I got home I called Chris and he said that he was there to rob me that night, but couldn't. I told him that I would have probably just told him to shoot me. I still have that gun. It was a pellet gun, by the way, and not loaded.

In early 2018, I got a call from Christopher's father telling me that Chris had overdosed and the ambulance was coming. I rushed down there to find Christopher leaning against the refrigerator saying that his legs wouldn't work right. I guess he had laid on the floor in one position after using too much and passing out. He wasn't in distress. The police showed up and wouldn't even take the heroin that was in plain sight; they said they weren't allowed. I took it home and burned it. After the ambulance came, Christopher refused treatment. He later got my sister to take him to the hospital where they later transferred him to a trauma facility. He had nerve damage in his right leg and his kidneys were shutting down. After a lot of prayers and therapy, his kidneys did start working again and he was released and my sister took him home since she doesn't work. Within a few weeks after he felt better, she found drug paraphernalia and asked him to leave. I knew at this point there wasn't much hope, but hope is all I had. I talked to Christopher and even read something to him that I had written while he was in the hospital and told him that I would probably be reading it at his funeral (I did). He said, "It won't happen, Mom, I've tried and can't die from it." Here is the poem:

I can still feel you here in this place,
I can still see the smile on your face
I can still feel the warmth of your touch
I hope that you know that I miss you so much
I can still hear funny things that you said
As thousands of memories run through my head
I can still see the spark in your eye
And I can hear you telling me to please not cry
I know that you tried to win this fight
But the demon's grip was far too tight
But your death will not have been in vain
I know you will save someone else in pain
By standing beside them and making them strong
And showing the path that was there all along
Each life you save will lift you high
And never again will we say good-bye
I can still feel you here in my heart
Knowing we won't always be apart
I won't ever say goodbye to you
I'll see you again when my time here is through.

A couple of months later, he was back in rehab. When he was released, a counselor whom Chris had gotten close to was opening her own ¾ house and the price was reasonable enough that Chris could pay for it with the disability money and still pay on his fines. Since she just opened the place, Chris was the only "client" there. He was attending meetings regularly and was getting monthly Vivitrol shots (a patient is unable to obtain a high when it is in their system). On November 10, 2018, Christopher came to my house to spend the night with me and his only nephew, Dylan. Dylan had not been around his uncle much because Chris's only sibling April held a lot of resentment towards Chris from watching what he was doing to his father and me. She had only recently started to rebuild a relationship with Chris. She originally didn't want Dylan around him for fear he would get close to Chris and then lose him. Anyway, we had a great time that weekend and Dylan (three at the time) totally wore out his "Uncle Chris." Chris sang and played his guitar and we had a great time. Chris went back to his home (the ¾ house) which was about an hour away. He was still the only "client" there although it had been a couple of months. He was due for his next Vivitrol shot but it was postponed for some reason.

The following Friday, November 16, Christopher stopped in at the shop that I work at. He was on his way to his father's house to do laundry (that is what he told me at least) and I tried to get him to come to my house for a repeat of last weekend. He came up with a couple of excuses, but I didn't think too much of it. I gave him a hug, told him I loved him and he left. If only I would have known that this would have been the last hug, the last, "I love you mudder," that I would ever get from him I would have held on much longer and never let him go. So many "if only" and "what ifs" have gone through my head.

On Sunday the 18th of November, I was having coffee with my cousin who lives nearby (it was her birthday) and we were being entertained by Dylan's antics when my phone started to ring. With the normal eye roll when I saw it was my ex calling, I answered the phone. He said something to me like, "The boy is gone," and I said, "Where is he, jail or rehab?" He said no...he is gone...dead...or something like that. My cousin made the calls to my family because the next thing I know they were there to try to comfort me through one of the most painful days a mother could have. I don't remember a whole lot more than that...I think I asked the appropriate questions but I thank God my cousin was there to take care of my only grandchild because I was "broken" and would never be the same after that call. His father and I went to meet with the funeral director within a few days and since Chris had told his father that he wanted to be cremated, that is what we planned, a two-hour viewing if possible then cremation. Luckily, Christopher's father had put money aside for Christopher's inheritance from his grandfather so it was used to cover the service and the urn and even a beautiful cross pendant with my birthstone that holds a little of his ashes. Christopher's dad told me, "If you want it, get it, it is a gift from our son."

We didn't know if we would have his body for the service at this point until they determined what drugs were in his system and what condition he was in. The day of the service, the funeral director called and said they were on the way to pick him up. It was the day before Thanksgiving and as I walked into the funeral home I was numb and terrified. When I saw my son, he looked perfect! So content and so peaceful. The funeral director did an amazing job and for that I will always be eternally grateful. I sat at Christopher's side the whole time, memorizing his beautiful face and counting his eyelashes and holding his hand. I know that I never would have accepted that he was "gone" if I had not gotten that closure. Towards the end of the service, I noticed that the makeup was starting to wear off at the bottom of his nose and you could see a tiny bit of blue. To this day I have a spot on my nose in the same place.

Even as I put these words down after almost twenty months, everything is replaying in my head like a horrible dream that I can't wake up from. My tears fall freely, but I know writing his story is something that I need to do. My hope was gone and my firstborn child was gone. I did initially want to blame someone...the people who gave the shot for postponing it...the counselor who never checked on him (they are guessing he died on the 16th but he was found on the 18th)...the dealer who sold him the drugs...myself...my ex...anyone...but it doesn't do any good. I am still getting to know the person that I have become, starting to find happiness in some things again, but it still hurts, every day, every breath that I take.

I have lost a few people in my life since then, but they were at least older and natural...the correct order of how the circle of life is supposed to work, but the ones who are younger...no matter how they die. I KNOW! I feel every mother's anguish and pain...I live it each and every second until it is my turn.

May God be with each and every one of us who walk this journey and may lives be saved by us sharing our children's journey so they didn't die in vain.

Christopher's Mom,

Ruth K.
Clarksburg, Pennsylvania

Authors note: We lost Ruth before this book could be published. We are including one of her final notes about Christopher. May you both rest in Peace, sweet Christopher and Ruth.

October 7th, 2020 at 8:03 PM (public Facebook post from Ruth)

"As you all know, I lost my son Christopher to the drug epidemic almost two years ago. To help me with the pain and anguish, I joined a group called Not in Vain. This group is for mothers only who have lost a child or in some cases more than one child to drugs. This group is very helpful since everyone shares the same soul-crushing loss and we all have the same questions and feelings of guilt, pain, and emptiness.

 This book is about a lot of our journeys and our child's journey through addiction. My story about Christopher is included in this book which will be released on October 31. Please look into it. Addiction is not discriminatory. It strikes rich, poor, black or white, and rarely releases its hostages. If you think you or your loved ones are risk free, think again. Look at these pictures and know that all of these beautiful children are gone. Read our stories to understand what our children went through. Love and prayers to all."

Richie

FOREVER 29

There is no good choice between tough love and unconditional love. They really are just two expressions of the same thing from two different perspectives. Tough love by its nature does not allow some things to be said. I'd been telling my son for a long time that my house was not his home. He lived with me, and he had his own room there. I just didn't want him getting too comfortable living with Mom.

I wanted him to take responsibility for his own life. What I really wanted was for him to be able to move back with his family and lead a sober life. I wasn't going to be around forever, and I wanted him standing on his own before anything happened to me. I worried a lot about what would happen to him when I was gone if he remained on the same path. Our last night together, I felt like I was with my boy again for the first time in forever.

I actually decided that it would be OK sharing a home if it stayed like that between us. I slept happy for the first time in a long time. I didn't tell my son, though. I didn't want to knock him off track. It's one of my biggest regrets that I never got to tell him I would love my house to be his home. Unconditional love by its nature allows you to say what needs to be said, but also seems to give permission to continue with bad decisions.

Every time I bailed him out of trouble, sent him money in jail, covered his debts or let him move back in after I had said he couldn't, it told him that I still loved him despite the addiction.

It also took away his motivation to change. It gave him a safe haven from consequences and hardship. It allowed him to not have to grow up. Tough love is the willingness to step back from one of the most important relationships in our lives for the sake of our children.

Unconditional love is the willingness to accept things which cause us great pain in order to support our children. Both include great sacrifices from the parents. Both are done to put our children in a better place. And both cause guilt when we fail to save them.

I was very fortunate that I was able to explain to Richie that tough love was still love, and in some ways harder on me than it was on him. Not that he needed me to explain that to him. He was one of the few of his "boys" that still had family support and lived in the family home, who got phone calls and visits during rehab and jail.

He knew he had support. The day before he died, I was so frustrated by Richie's refusal to isolate that I told him he couldn't stay at my house anymore. When I dropped him off at a friend's house, he realized he had left his debit card on the counter and I told him he could get it when he came home. We both knew he was coming back.

We both knew tough love did not mean rejection. So no, I didn't explain the love behind tough love to make my son understand how it worked. I told him that for me. I told him because I could feel the end coming and I wanted to make sure that I had tried everything, and that he knew I'd tried everything I could to help him.

I told him because I didn't want hindsight and guilt to make me doubt that he really understood. In the end, it doesn't matter what we tried and what we didn't. It just matters that we tried our best, and that they knew they were worth the fight.

Richie's Mom,

SUSAN K.
Detroit, Michigan

Jessica

FOREVER 35

I'm going to tell a story about a girl that became a woman, and her view, pain, love, and hate of this world and the people in it and her difficulties to cope with each. I'm writing this as her mom, but some of the content of this will be her words that came from a few journals that we found after her passing. I battled for days, weeks, and now months, whether to make her life/cause of death public, but knowing Jessica, if this could help just one person, she would do it!

In an excerpt from one of her journals, she wrote the following:

"It must almost be over. What am I going to do then? All my friends are going to go to hell. I can't handle any of this ... anymore ... life ... people ... talking ... breathing ... being a part of this thing called living. I absolutely can't deal. God please help me ... Nobody can understand, not anymore ... everything seems so useless and hopeless ... I'm so weak. I can see the future, but I don't know how to help my friends, the people that I love ... they don't know God ... just like everybody else I know ... I'm so lost ... far away ... gone.

"I love them too much...I care about everybody too much. I wish I could stop ... I want it all to go away ... everything ... to run away ... that's what I want to do. Leave the world behind ... the depression ... sadness ... loneliness ... emptiness ... the infinite sorrow of death and pain. The torture of living. I want it all ... to stop. But I don't want to die I just can't do that ... I care too much about everybody else ... to hurt me ... that damn caring thing again. God help me. I see so much beauty ... but it all comes from the pain and sorrow - it hurts- but I can see the beauty- what is wrong with me? God please help...help me please. I don't know what to do and I don't know what I'm doing anymore. There's no point. Give me someone to talk to. Why can't I just be like everybody else ... somewhat normal- but please-no one is normal, maybe I am - no I'm not. God please. I'm tired of fighting with myself and with life."

That was my daughter pretty much in a nutshell, and this was written in middle school, so she carried these feelings of hopelessness for decades! She cared so much for other people and their ups and downs, their sadness, their losses, their hopes and dreams, and she absorbed all of their misery and carried it day to day, and if she couldn't fix their problems, it ate a hole through her soul. This is a girl who found it extremely difficult to help herself and couldn't fix her own problems, but she would always be at your doorstep if you called. She had to fix people. She attracted the broken ones.

This was, I'm sure, why she chose to find ways to numb herself. First it was the doctors, anti-depressants, anxiety meds, etc. Nothing worked. I don't remember the first pain pill, but she soon realized the euphoric feeling was the answer to all her misery! Now I do realize that she dabbled in many things off and on through high school and college. It wasn't something she did every day or even every week but the different "highs" she experienced made her forget how she felt, for a little while at least. Later on in life she actually started withdrawing a lot. She ignored phone calls, messages, etc. This was partly her disease and partly because she realized trying to be everything to everybody was killing her. She did this off and on for the rest of her life. She also struggled with her appearance. She was taunted in middle school and that left a very deep scar. So, when she started losing weight it really didn't raise any red flags. Needless to say, it wasn't done without a drug. It didn't matter what drug it was, but she went through methadone treatment and NA to get off of it, and she did.

That was many years ago, so we thought she was finally on the right path. Then she started drinking, a lot. Jessica always had a smile on her face, and you would never know that she was going through anything of any magnitude. She worked forty plus hours a week, she made good money, and customers loved her. She was high functioning with her addiction. She didn't look like your "typical addict." This girl struggled with how people treated each other, how they treated animals, what the world was becoming, and the pure evil that surrounded us! This also was her pill to swallow. She hated this life. She was not of this world; she was just playing a part until it was her time to go. She came to us to teach us, and then left us to teach us something else.

Jessica was an angel on Earth and now she's returned to heaven as a heavenly Angel. Mama loves you baby and I will never get over you leaving us. Jessica died in my bathroom floor all alone. This haunts me! The ME's report says she accidentally overdosed on heroin. Yes, she had heroin in her system, but she also had an artery that was 90% blocked for almost a week prior. She was having trouble breathing, and of course, she thought it was her asthma, so we never thought much of it. Now I will never know. What if she had gone to the ER?? What if?? I have a lot of "what if" and red flags, like moodiness. But hell, that was normal sometimes! I never knew she had ever used a needle let alone heroin. This was something we talked about and she said, "No way, I'm too chicken to do that!" Pay close attention to the people in your children's lives. No matter how old your children are pay attention to their new friends or old friends that reappear in their lives. This was our first red flag!! I wish like hell now that I would have been "psycho mom!" There is always that one person that you just can't put your finger on, but something is off. Another "what if?" But the sad thing I must come to terms with is that Jessica was a grown woman and I probably couldn't have done anything that I hadn't done already or tried to do.

Burying a child is unnatural. I will never be the same, that's all I know for sure right now. Love your kids, never take them for granted. This was something that happens to other people or in the movies. Well, I'm not in the movies so I guess I'm one of the "other" people now. I did not write this for sympathy or any kind of attention. I wasn't sure if I should put Jessica's deepest thoughts or demons she fought out there for everyone to see. I'm still struggling, but addiction is killing more and more of our families and I never in my wildest dreams would've believed our family would become a statistic. I hope the details of Jessica's life and death touch someone out there and give them the strength to get up and reach out to somebody for help.

PLEASE, PLEASE, SHARE THE HELL OUT OF THIS!!!! I need it to go far and wide to reach those that need it. That person sitting on the side of their bed wondering if this is how life is supposed to be and if life is even worth this pain. Relying on a drug to get through the day; is that living? Even though my daughter didn't commit suicide it's the same result.

She knew that every time she let the devil take over and pierce her skin with that needle it could be her last. She took that chance every time. It's not worth it! Get up off the bed and tell someone, anyone that you need help! Hell, if you don't have anyone else call 911. Call the suicide hotline, check yourself into a rehab, just DO SOMETHING! Your life IS worth it!! I will always remember the morning of November 5th as the day my heart broke in two.

Jessica's Mom,

Theresa K.
Carpentersville, Illinois

Emily

FOREVER 21

Emily was the most amazing kid in the world, and I was so proud of her. She was intellectually, artistically, and athletically gifted. I always told her that with so many talents comes great responsibility to bring those gifts to the world.

Perhaps it's no surprise that since her birth was made public because of my job, in the spotlight as a TV news anchor, now her death is public. I have to embrace that. And I believe it is best that I tell our story to let people know what happened to my daughter. It can happen in anyone's family and it all starts with addiction.

In Emily's later teen years, it was evident that the drug culture was attractive to her and I was very concerned. It is very difficult to figure out how to get a rebellious teenager on the right track. I feel for anyone who has a child struggling with addiction, because you often don't know where to turn. There is also so much stigma surrounding the problem, which makes it even harder to talk with other people about it.

Everything in my instincts told me something was seriously wrong with Emily. We would see her quite a lot, even though she wasn't living with us because she was twenty-one and on her own. However, the more time I spent around her before her death, the more alarm bells went off in my head. I convinced the rest of our family to take part in an intervention to get her into treatment.

We met on a Saturday with the interventionist. We planned to confront her and get her to a treatment center the following Saturday. Emily died that Wednesday. We didn't get the chance to get her into real treatment, to get her help. The cause of her death was unbelievable to me. The fact that my daughter was using heroin and needles was shocking. My beautiful daughter, who was privileged and had every opportunity in life, had gone down this road. The police narcotics detective investigating her death told me, "Parents never know."

I consider myself a wordsmith because I write for a living every day. But there are no words to describe the devastation I now feel at the loss of my daughter. There is nothing that can even come close to describe the grief, the sorrow, and the pain. There is also the loss of what could have been had she been able to fulfill her full potential in life. Now, I have a hole in my heart that will never heal. I have other children and a husband, whom I love, but nothing and nobody can replace the loss of my oldest child. Emily was just twenty-one.

According to the autopsy report, Emily had six times what would be considered a therapeutic dose of fentanyl for the largest man. She was just a small, young woman and didn't stand a chance. The fentanyl killed her almost instantly, after she injected it. Her chair sits empty at the kitchen table and when I look across the table, I think about how I was robbed of my daughter. No matter what happens to the dealers charged in connection with her death, nothing will ever bring her back.

She was a beautiful girl, who deserved to live. She also deserved a chance to get help. While she engaged in risky behavior, that doesn't mean she deserved to die.

By telling Emily's story and my own pain and suffering, I'm opening myself up and being vulnerable to our television audience in a way I have never been before. I feel it's important I do that, because if just one person hears me, if just one person does one thing to save a life, it will have been worth it. While some may not understand and judge me and my daughter, I will still speak out. I want to stop other mothers from experiencing this kind of pain.

I've started the charity, "Emily's Hope," because I never gave up hope on my daughter. I want that hope to live on in others. The money raised is offsetting the cost of addiction treatment. We also support sober living homes. Additionally, we've set up an art scholarship in her name; Emily was a gifted painter.

I speak to audiences across the country to end the stigma surrounding addiction and to make people under-stand that it is a disease of the brain and we must do better at identifying it and treating it, as well as helping fami-lies caught in the crossfire of substance use disorder.

Emily's death has given me a new mission in life. I will dedicate my talents and my platform for raising awareness on the disease of addiction and helping others who struggle, as well as their families. I host a blog and write a podcast to help others. You can follow our efforts and my blog on our website:

https://www.paintingapathtorecovery.org/

Emily's Mom,

ANGELA K.
Sioux Falls, South Dakota

Katie Ann

FOREVER 31

Katie was my baby. She had a brother, seven years older, and sister, six years older. Katie saw her brother and sister and their friends smoking marijuana and would say she would never do that. She was not a "pot smoker." She was the kid that loved her family and friends.

She moved out to Lake Tahoe at the age of twenty-one to be with her older sister and cousin. She worked as a hostess in the summer and at a ski lodge in the winter and did really well for herself! She began working as a waitress and started drinking. One morning, she was having a hard time trying to get ready for work from a bad hangover and her sister gave her one of her prescription drugs. She soon felt better and now the drug war begins!

Katie was around twenty-six when the drugs took her over. The pharmaceutical industry became aware that this certain drug was being abused, and they fixed it so you could not get the high anymore. Now both my girls are using heroin. I started getting calls for money. I was having my own issues; my husband was abusing alcohol and cocaine and cheated on me. Katie was home for a funeral and another time, a wedding, and saw the breakdown of her parent's marriage. This hurt her so badly as she was so proud to be one of the only kids with both parents, growing up. She also witnessed her father snorting cocaine. He didn't know she was in my bed at the time. My life was a mess. I was trying to save my house and start a new life when my girls got deep in the drug life.

Katie ultimately started dating, and soon after, living with her boyfriend, the heroin addict dealer. Now her life had gone down even further. The DEA busted down the door; she had a gun pointed in her stomach, she thought she was dead. She did county jail time, got out, and kept using. Both girls continued declining. Katie's sister's boyfriend shot at the drug dealer's house multiple times, because he gave her sister heroin. Katie got out of the house, just in time. Her sister called her to let her know he was going there and had a gun. Her sister's boyfriend went to prison and then she lost everything, became homeless and on the streets, in and out of jail. Katie moved from place to place, hotels, people's couches, her boyfriend's parents. Finally, she came home, and brought her drug addict, dealer, boyfriend, claiming they were coming home to stop using. It was a living hell. My house got ransacked, my valuables got pawned, and I was trying to help them stop using.

At the time, my son was going through a divorce and living in my house; he was at his wit's end when he realized there was no helping them. I was dating a nice gentleman and he had to witness my life out of control. It was so awful, and I couldn't stop this. I could not kick my daughter out, so they went to live with her father. My other daughter was now off the streets living with her father too. (She ended up getting pregnant by a hardcore heroin addict, a whole other mess I had to deal with.) Katie's dad could not handle the boyfriend. He was very bad news, so they ended up back at his parents. Then, back to my house and finally, Katie was getting tired of hurting herself and family. I had to get him out of my house. The last straw for Katie was when he stole my diamond ring; I told him to call his parents for a plane ticket home ASAP. My boyfriend drove him to the airport, made sure he was gone from our lives, and told him never to come back!

I also fought and struggled so hard to get my oldest daughter off heroin. I got her into a program. She was finally getting help, while pregnant. She was in a methadone clinic, a whole other story; my poor, newborn, granddaughter had to stay two weeks on a pain medication to come off the methadone. It was awful; she would cry and shake uncontrollably for the first month of her life at home! The day we brought my granddaughter home, child protective services came, and we found out my daughter's placenta tested positive for heroin. This broke my heart. Now, every time the case worker came to check on the baby, Katie would hide because they didn't know she lived in the house. They lived in fear the state would take the baby because Katie was actively using again.

Another year went by; Katie was finally in a methadone clinic with her sister. Katie was waitressing, doing well again, but continued to use. She was also prescribed Xanax for her anxiety, which she also abused. Now the baby is a toddler; she is bonding with Katie, as she's now off heroin, but still abusing her prescription. One day Katie drove herself to the clinic and on the way home she kept driving because the drug dealer called her. He had heroin that she bought, not knowing the authorities were watching the dealer. The drug task force got her plate number, called it in, and she got arrested. We were in and out of court the next few months. She spent a few days in jail, so the judge dropped her case, with time served.

She was a beautiful young lady, which helped her case. She did not look like a drug addict and she had been doing better. However, she lost her job, which she loved, because of this. By this time, I nearly had a nervous breakdown. Checking on my girls and granddaughter almost daily because by now I've seen it all. I became the mother that walked in on my daughters shooting up, who picked up my grandbaby from a nap, and found a lighter under her. I had all I could do to stay sane.

Another year goes by; they are both trying hard to stay clean. It was February 17, 2018; their father bought tickets to Disney on Ice. Katie was so excited. I went with them. We took the train in. It was a good time. Katie and I went to get some food and she said "I feel like a beer. Do you want to have a beer with me, Mom?" I said "Sure." It was truly a wonderful time with my girls and granddaughter. I noticed young men looking at Katie. She was stunning when she dressed up, and on our way home I told her how good she looked, and she sat up straight and felt good about herself. It was nice!

Two days later, February 19, 2018, President's Day, I had the day off, so I went to visit my girls. Katie was having breakfast; she was in a great mood. I helped clean up. I was doing the dishes. She put a picture of herself in front of me and said, "Look how good I look." It was nice. Before I left, I went to talk to her father and be with my granddaughter. I didn't say goodbye to Katie, like I normally would. I got home and got a call from her father: "Katie is overdosing, get here!" I left my house screaming in my car. I saw the police and paramedics and almost got into an accident. I was out of my mind. I screamed at Katie's sister, "What did you do?" Then I saw a couple my daughter was with; they looked like addicts and I almost screamed, but I stopped myself. I took my granddaughter out and brought her to my house. On the way home, I received a text to call from my ex. When I called, he told me "Katie is gone!" I knew in my heart and soul she was with my dad, whom she loved dearly!

But now my nightmare begins with my other daughter. My God, how was I going to survive losing my other daughter? She went off the deep end. She was now drug-induced suicidal. Everyone knew how bad she was at her sister's service. She looked like death; she left her baby at the service luncheon and told no one. She was on the streets now; crashed her car and passed out. I tried nonstop to get her help. She was in and out of the hospital. She'd checked herself out, get picked up at 3:00 a.m. and have to work the next day! Now she was getting arrested, using her dead sister's ID to get her dead sister's prescriptions. I had to go in and out of court with her. It was finally apparent to the DA that she was out of control and her life needed to be saved. I lost one daughter; this one needs serious help. She had a toddler to live for. The judge had just started a new program: instead of prison they go into a detox program then rehab. I went to meetings and visits, I thought thank God!

However, when I got her home, after ninety days, I could see she was not in a good place. She stole her father's car that night, went to an old, drug addict, boyfriend's house. I had custody of her daughter, thank God, or the state would have taken her. Well, she got pregnant again, days out of rehab. When she realized she was pregnant, she stopped abusing drugs.

Her baby is almost a year old now and she is a good mom. She does yoga and takes her girls for walks every day! I still worry about her relapsing; I will monitor her until the day I leave this earth and join my precious daughter Katie.

God how I miss my baby! How have I survived her death? I think about how empty my life would have been if I never had her. She truly enriched my life; she brought so much good into my life, it most definitely outweighs the drug years! There are days, times of heartache, and so much  more I could say; but I have to say the worst part of this disease is how badly my girls hurt themselves, marking up their beautiful bodies with the needle. What hurts my heart and soul is how bad some family members treated them. Their brother stopped inviting them to special occasions. It was painful watching them hurting. That's truly the worst part of this disease. I'm tearing up for my Katie. I love and miss you, my baby!

Katie Ann's Mom,

DEBORAH K.
Merrimack, Massachusetts

Randall

FOREVER 27

Love You More

I am honored every moment I can speak my son's name, Randall, tell his story, and engage others that think it just will not happen to their family. It hit home for my family; it can hit yours too. Addiction is a disease; the drugs are the enemy. It lies to our children; it tells them to come closer, that the world will not understand or accept them. This is part of my memorial to my son to bring attention to the epidemic and not cover it up like a dirty secret. This is an honor, it is painful; this is truth. This is my son's story from beginning to end. A short twenty-seven years filled with a lot of life, a lot of struggle, and a whole lot of love.

My son Randall was born on November 14, 1991, in Canton, Ohio. It was a crazy pregnancy. I was twenty-one and had no idea what I was doing. I took good care of myself. I ate everything and waited patiently for the birth. I was a week and half overdue and Randy did not want to leave the womb. I was in labor for about twenty-seven hours. I was terrified and excited to meet my newborn. Finally, the day came, it was a baby boy! I instantly fell in love. Randy was my first born. When they placed him on my chest, I was in awe of the miracle that he was. After the shock and the business that surrounded us settled down, I then realized my life no longer belonged to me and my husband, it all belonged to this child, my son Randall.

On Randall's second birthday, we were bringing the next-door neighbors some cake from his party. It had just rained, and the ground was wet. As we walked my boy looked up at me and said, "Mommy, the ground is saturated!" What! He was a sponge. My boy was a genius, I tell you. He spoke so fluently, he felt VERY deeply, and he was a master-mind in every way you can imagine. He was funny as a child, and that continued throughout his whole life. At one point around age three or four, Randy became obsessed with vacuum cleaners.

When I say obsessed, it was an addiction with him, now that I look back. He would demand, cry, and beg for the Sears catalog to look at them. He examined ours at the house daily. When we would go to someone's house, the very first thing he would ask is, "Do you have a vacuum cleaner and where do you keep it?" YES, this was a fascination and a need to understand. He would then examine and focus on their vacuum for hours. In case you are wondering, yes, I sought advice from a counselor, because this was a trait that I was unaware of and wanted to understand where this fixation was coming from. He needed to know how things worked and if he could not, it would work him up to a panic and cause great anxiety. This was a first indication of his anxiety and addictive behavior. But you never think that this behavior is going to carry through their entire life, right? Well, I didn't. I was wrong. Addiction is tricky and deceptive.

I had a second child, Alexandria, and they were fast friends. Randall was the best brother. He loved her, played with her, even played Barbies with her. They were best friends, always together. Randall was a smart and intelligent child. He would encounter a problem and find a way to solve it. He was a whiz in math. He showed Alexandria the ropes and was always protective of her. I called them the wonder twins. This has stuck even through the present day. Nothing but true love and friendship.

Randy and Alex's father and I divorced in 1997. This was hard on the children, but we managed. I quickly got all of us in counseling to talk about any issues that we may have had. Needless to say, it was a change for me, as a stay at home mom, to find work and provide for my children. Randy did well in school; he excelled in all that he did. However, I think that he was bored most of the time in school. He understood and learned the material so fast that he was beyond the lessons that they were teaching. He went to a Catholic school, up until I could no longer afford it.

He was never interested in sports, however, I had him try all of them, T-Ball, soccer, football, and karate. I think karate was the longest one he stuck with, becoming a high Blue Belt (this is a belt earned after a Green Belt). He was fair in them, but never really in love with the idea of the whole competition thing. It just was not him. He had friends, mostly girls. He was sensitive, strong, and just got along better with girls. He had some male friends, but was awkward around them as they were into sports, etc., and he just didn't have that in him. He loved music, video games, outdoor adventures, and LAUGHTER. He was always laughing.

We moved to Georgia in 2005 and had a chance at new beginnings. I signed him up for baseball as soon as we got here! Yes! I wanted to infuse social situations and activities. He met a million people; they loved Randy! The name Dexter came into play his first year here in Georgia, because he was smart and attentive to detail, and the T.V. show *Dexter's Laboratory* was a thing at that time. He was handsome, funny, and the center of it all. He was finally out of his shell and had an explosion of fun, friends, and laughter sprinkled with a lot of shenanigans! He was introduced to marijuana from a few of his friends. One girl was his partner in crime. They were the closest to a brother and sister without the genealogy. They experimented with drugs. It started with marijuana and progressed.

I was called into the school numerous times for various things because my son Randall would get in trouble. Fart machines, yes, I said it, fart machines in gym class. Pretending to be a foreign exchange student with the substitute teacher, so he could hang with his BFF, and taking the clock off the cafeteria wall and hiding it in an unaware person's locker. He was a trickster and so funny, but harmless. Truly, he just wanted laughter and silliness in his world. But that was, as I would later find out, because the drugs were giving him a sense of power and invincibility, the art of getting away with it.

Randy was around thirteen or fourteen years old when he started using. I did not know what was being used until one day I found a bong, then I found Delsym bottles in his room. Damn, I found Delsym bottles in the subdivision's termite traps, hidden so I could not find them. I would find pills and weed. I became unstoppable, randomly searching his room; I flipped mattresses, and would constantly badger Randall, to the point of resentment from him. He would lie, deceive, and argue his way out of everything. Then the train started going full force and I did not know what to do. I called rehabs, I called counselors.

I admitted him to a rehab, unwilling of course, but he was still under the age of eighteen. I called 9-1-1, more than once, and had his stomach pumped. I had friends from the Forsyth County Police force and Cumming Police come to the pool to check on the kids at home while I was at work, just to help keep track of them. I used my insurance to its max. I cried, thinking I did something to cause this. Why did I move away from family? Why do I have a job that demands all of my time and allows them to be alone at the house, to take advantage of the situation? Remember, addiction is a master manipulator. It will convince you that it's ok, and give you reasons, any excuses to use and numb your feelings, instead of finding a way to deal with them.

Remember the boy that was protective of his sister? Well, he never lost his love for her and always wanted the best for her. But in the long run, he introduced her to drugs. I had two children that I would take a bullet for who were now hooked on anything that would let them feel euphoric and unstoppable. They stole from my medicine cabinet to get high, so I bought a safe to keep them in. Randy figured out how to break into the safe. I threw the safe away. I kept wondering WHY! One time I came home, and the pharmacy delivered the medicine to my home. It was Xanax for me because I felt like I was going crazy! I thought for sure that I was the only parent going through this.

Well, when I came home from work, both my children were high as could be; they took THE WHOLE bottle. I called 9-1-1 and the ambulance and police were at my house once again. They were taken to the hospital to get their stomachs pumped. I sat and watched both of my children fade in and out. I remember kneeling on the floor and begging

God to please help heal my family. To please show my children another way. I had the support of a few good friends and family but really, I was in the trenches and had to deal with this on my own. I would beg for the hospital to admit them because then I would know they were safe. But Randall figured out quickly how to manipulate the system, as he did with all the doctors and any authority.

There were many trips to the ER with accidental overdoses and overuse of pills. One of the ER visits was because my son was at a friend's and they were using. Randall took too much of something (I think it was pills) and they could not wake him up. They drove him to hospital. Thank God they didn't just leave him at the house and left him there in the ER. I received a call that, "Your son is at the hospital, it doesn't look good, please go see him!" I lived in constant fear of his death and this was too close to my nightmare coming true.

I sat with him hooked up to machines in the ER and prayed. That is all I could do, pray and cry. He made it out of that one, and said he was grateful and that he did not want to die. I asked him, "Why do you continue to use and play Russian roulette with your life, Randall?" He said he's not trying to; he didn't mean to take it that far. See, when he would get high, he would forget how much he did and then do more and more, until he was close to a fatal overdose. He escaped death several times and knew that he did. My heart, oh my God, my broken heart.

Along with the pill usage and other illegal substances came violence and stealing from Randy. I hate to think about those times, it physically makes me sick, but we are speaking truth here and this was the cycle that we lived daily. He would use; he would feel better because he was numb. Then he would start coming down and be so agitated to the point that you could not say anything without an explosion. Then after he would get clean for a day or two, the sweet Randy was back, until the cycle started up again. Once he pushed his little sister against the wall and held her there, until I came up in back of him and pulled him off as he swung at me. I called the police. They took him away. He cried, he said he was sorry.

He screamed, "I'M SORRY, PLEASE DON'T LET THEM TAKE ME MOM." When I would not bail him out (I had bailed him out a time or two before, but this particular time I did not), he would call me every name in the book, and come back, after he was clean, and apologize for anything he did and most likely didn't remember. Randy stole my jewelry, things that were given to me by my father (who has since passed, while Randall was alive). He would sell them or trade them or take to the pawn shops for money to get high. I would go to the pawn shops and retrieve my items and I never pressed charges.

Thinking back now maybe I should have, maybe that would have stopped this madness from continuing. I remember being mad, embarrassed, and frustrated. It just wasn't getting better. This was the hardest part of his addiction. To live the life of a mother, watching her son disappear into a world that would eventually eat him alive. I could not stop this, BUT I kept trying with every new day and every breath in my body. I thought because I was his mother, I carried him, I birthed him, I had the most love for this child, that I could stop this thing from happening. I would soon learn, several years later, that I did not have control over this. That the addiction would win and take my boy's life.

I was a single parent, with only the resources that I could find and create. I wasn't going to stop fighting for him.

Around seventeen to eighteen years old, Randall had already been in jail, over four rehabs, and a boarding school, all because of his drug usage. We didn't have family members that go to jail or rehab. This was not a common thing for us at all. I was in charge of trying to explain to the family about addiction and everything I was learning. I was exhausted and getting resentful of my son. Damn, I hate to say that out loud, but it is the raw emotions of anyone dealing with a loved one's addiction. It's exhausting and takes a toll on everyone.

Randy would always think that he was invincible, that he could manage his drug use and function. He had jobs, graduated from school, had friends, and had a car. Looking back, I think he was impaired more than he wasn't. He would use and get behind the wheel and find himself in a ditch or having rear ended a car, thankfully without a major injury to himself or others. Please know that I would take away the keys, no car for Randall for a while. Then things would get back to ok, he would swear that was a one time thing and it would never happen again, and then the cycle would happen all over again.

I found myself being awakened up at the latest hours with a call from police, fire departments, friends, or Randy saying please come get him, "Please come get the car, Mom; Please come pay for a tow, Mom, I am in a ditch; Please bail me out of jail, Mom, I am scared and I'm so sorry." Your heart breaks, as a mother for her children, addict or not. You never want to watch your child go down a path of destruction and pain. Drugs = Jail or Rehab and eventually Death. This was a part of my son's life for many years, until he passed on December 14, 2018.

Randall was in his twenties and moved out with a roommate, attempted college again, and worked. I thought all was going to be ok. I set him up for success, helped pay some bills, and would bring food over, like a good mom. This lasted about seven months and then the shit hit the fan. Unbeknownst to me, the drug use became worse; he was now doing meth, pills, and, I believe, heroin. I did not find this out until I got a call from the roommate one night.

He said, "I can't wake Randy up he's fading in and out." Paramedics and police came to his house and took him away. He was sent to drug rebab for a while. I prayed that this would be the time it works, that it kicks in. When he came back within three weeks time, I got a call from the Dawsonville Police that he was in a bad car wreck and they were taking him to jail after the hospital. He was cut up, but nothing major on the outside.

The inside of him was a different story. He had eaten a bottle of Ativan that he conned some doctor into giving him and blacked out. While in jail he was put on suicide watch and was coming off his overdose of pills. I did not bail him out, however I was in contact with the nicest officer in the jail. She was an angel, sent because she could see the sweet Randy that was crying out. She would give him messages for me, and she would call me to give me updates on his wellbeing. She was amazing. A glimmer of support and love from someone that sees the ugliness in this world. She treated my boy with respect and dignity.

As his mom, I loved him through all his ups and downs, but you know how outsiders look at a drug addict, right? They see them as a disease in this world. This lady gave me hope for a brighter, better day. The court sent Randall to another rehab and he had to finish the program. Randall would go back and forth with using and staying clean. He started talking about his feelings and trying to understand his addiction and why he could not stop. He explained to me that he knew the abuse takes a toll on everyone that loves him and that he was sorry for that and that he was trying to kick it. But that ugly addiction would start talking to him and convincing him that he can control it; he was smarter than most drug users and he was in control. It lied.

He was then kicked out of rehab and came to live with me again. At this time, I found out that there was a new player on the scene, and it was heroin. Now, my boy Randall was terrified of needles and the seediness of shooting up. So we both thought. He had me convinced that using heroin was a onetime thing and that he did not think that this was going to be an issue. We were wrong. He was shooting up. Let me back up a minute, for reference, of how this all comes to play in an addict's life.

In Randy's life, he started with marijuana; he said he would never be interested in pills! I believed him; I think he believed that statement as well, but it happened. He was taking pills. Once pills were an issue there was always talk about meth and hard drugs and how he would NEVER do those kinds of drugs. He began to use meth and heroin and everything in between, anything to get numb and feel that high. It was, again, a lie from the enemy, the addiction. SO, I go back and again think WHY COULDN'T I HAVE STOPPED THIS! It was not in my control to do so. I never understood this until now.

Heroin, Oh My Dear God in Heaven where does someone buy heroin? What kind of people would sell to this middle-class, white kid from Forsyth, Georgia? I came to find out quickly where and how he was doing it. He would lie and tell me he was either going to work or had to pick up a friend to go to an NA meeting, but instead, he was running to Atlanta and getting his fix. There is so much detail that I am leaving out on how this all came to fruition, on how I discovered the lies and manipulation over and over again with his using. But it became clear that he was on a path that was going to take him out and we both knew it.

One of many examples was the time I cleaned his car out when he was sleeping upstairs. I found these little baggies (Ziplock). Super small like they sell jewelry pieces in or something at the store. But they were everywhere hidden in crevices of the car and fast-food bags. I was curious. I went to my friend who is a detective with the Forsyth County police, and he said, "These are heroin or cocaine baggies." WHAT! Much different from the weed baggies I would find. And isn't that funny how I was so immune or numb regarding the weed and sometimes the pills.

As the saying goes, "Better the devil you know than the devil you don't." I think my son trained me well as to enabling and looking the other way, and making excuses. We want to believe what our children say, trust they are making good decisions, and we never want to throw them to the streets or disown them because of the disease. So, we try and find ways to keep them safe and handle the situation, even when it's out of control.

I immediately got drug tests and demanded he take one. There was always an excuse about why he could not pee, or that he took a certain medication that the doctor prescribed so it's going to turn up positive. I even offered him money to take the test! Are you kidding me? At the time I thought this was a good idea but looking back I was grasping at straws to know the truth; no mother wants to say, "Yup, my kid is a heroin addict." I was an enabler; at times I would make deals with God and beg for the answers.

In September of 2018, when Randy came back to my house for the last time to stay and really try to get his life together, it was our final battle for his life. I did not realize, at the time, how important this stay at my home would be, until he wasn't here anymore.

I made a choice to have my son move back home and my fiancé and his daughter moved out. They did not want to be part of the destruction and addiction that Randy was bringing to the table. My stepdaughter was seven at the time. She in no way was going to be subjected to the craziness and possible chaos of the situation. It was heartbreaking, because I loved my fiancé and my stepdaughter, but I understood. Not at the time, but I do now. I wanted to save my son and was prepared to go to battle for his life. This was the last time that I was really able to focus all of me on my son and have our last moments together.

Randall and I went to concerts, Six Flags, we traveled to see family back in Ohio. He got to spend some time with people he had not inter-acted with for some time. Randy and I had the best talks. I assured him that God was a loving God. That He wanted to see him succeed and just wanted Randall to see there are other ways, and to reach out to Him and let God heal him. Randy thought that God was mad at him for the drugs and the crazy lifestyle choices that he had made. I truly believe that Randall heard me and for the first time really listened and took the goodness of life in for the first time in a long time. Randall would share with me that he was tired and that he would NEVER take his own life, but if it happened, he would be ok with it. He said that the world was hard, and he wasn't good at navigating through it. He said I was his biggest cheerleader and without me in his corner he would have died a long time ago. He was always grateful and loving. He wanted to get better; he didn't want to live like this anymore.

He celebrated his twenty-seventh birthday on November 14, 2018. He had his beloved sister and two of his dear friends with him. I was blessed to be able to tell my boy his birth story, as I had for all the birthdays prior. Except this was going to be last time I could speak it to him. In between then and his passing, Randall had started reaching out to friends that he had let go because of one thing or another. People that he truly loved, but lost touch with. He made amends for all his past iniquities to family and friends. He had so much love in his heart and was feeling for the first time in a long time the blessings that life has to offer. I did not have concerns about him using during this time; he was good, no he was GREAT at this time. Smiling, dancing, talking about feelings, love and emotions. How he was looking forward to getting a job again and getting on his feet.

The morning of December 14, 2018, was like any other morning in our house. I woke up early for work and would wake him every morning and say, "Wake up boy, what are we going to do with this day today!" He would get up and have a cup of coffee with me and send me off to work. We had a heated discussion before I left this time. I asked him to please get it together, get a job, get motivated, and start the healing process. He said, "Mom, I'm trying, I really am, be patient and I'll get it together. I promise." He looked at me and said, "Have the best day at work, I love Madre." I said, "I love you more son," and left for work.

I got a call from my daughter around four p.m. and she asked if I had heard from Randy at all that day. I said, "No, my tire blew on the way to work, I had meetings and I've been very busy, why Alex?"

"I've been calling him all day Mom and he hasn't answered."

Panic raced through my body and I found that I forgot how to breathe. I asked her and her girlfriend to go to the house and see if he was ok. My commute is about forty-five minutes to an hour. I was racing home and could not get there fast enough. I was calling him, I was texting, I was praying out loud, God what is going on? As I was about a mile from my home, I saw a police car and an ambulance race in front of me and they were heading towards my subdivision. I got a call from my daughter screaming, "He's gone Mom, he's gone!" They had to break into the house because everything was locked. AJ, Alex's girlfriend at the time, ran to Randall's room and found him lying on his bed, asleep, until she turned him over and started CPR. It was too late. I ran to the stairs and tried to get past the police officer. He refused to let me see my boy.

I was in shock and didn't know what was happening. I can't remember a lot from that day, yet the pieces I do remember are vivid and etched in my memory forever as if it's happening in front of me. I had officers and detectives and then the coroner come into my house and I flipped out. My greatest fear of losing my child was happening right in front of me. This was not a movie, this wasn't someone else's child, this was mine and our life. Unreal. I still today have those moments of denial, almost like it cannot be true. It's been one and half years this July.

The coroner came down the stairs and told me that this was not an overdose. He said my boy Randall went to sleep and did not wake up. There was not any paraphernalia on the floor or anywhere that they saw. I still could not believe this was happening and these strangers were telling me that my son had passed away.

Randall's father drove from Ohio that night and showed up at my door the next morning. I had not slept. No one had. Randall and his father had not spoken for many months and now this is what brought them back together. We planned a funeral, we had to pick out pictures of our boy to display. I was angry and scared and confused. I prayed and I prayed hard. I hung onto one scene from the movie, *The Shack*, through this whole ordeal. God is standing on the side of the lake and the lake is getting black. The man in the boat was terrified and couldn't breathe and Christ said, "Keep your eyes on me, don't look around at the scary destruction in front of you, just focus on me. I love you and I promise I will not leave you, focus on me." I did exactly this and leaned on my family and loved ones.

My son Randall Robert died at the age of twenty-seven. What took his life was a pill that was fentanyl. He took it in the morning and passed around nine a.m., with his dog seated right in front of his door waiting for me to get home. I believe that God was waiting for my son, he knew how much he was hurting inside with this addiction. This disease does not discriminate, nor does it ever give up. Trust your gut, involve yourself daily with your children, and never, never give up. This enemy is after all our children and will not stop unless we can unite and bring light to this epidemic. Randy was smart, funny, and the most loving human being. He had issues, but I never allowed him or anyone to define him as just an addict or anything other than a boy, who while dealing with his demons, brought joy and love and light to all that he knew.

Bridge the gap and make your voice heard. We can't control what anyone does, but we can influence and spread love and light in this world. My son told me a week before his death that if a mother's love was enough to stop an addict, then there would not be any addicts in the world. Love hard, pray hard, and don't be silent. My last words to my son were, "I love you more." I'm grateful these were the last words that he heard from me. I'm thankful that God allowed me to be a mother to Randy and he was my gift for a short, twenty-seven, amazing years.

Randall's Mom,

SAMANTHA K.
Cumming, Georgia

Alexander

My son, Alexander "Alex," was born on February 16, 1994, at 12:06 p.m. in Fairfax, Virginia. The absolute happiest day of my life. He weighed eight pounds and thirteen ounces. The doctor joked that the Washington Redskins needed a new linebacker. Alex's dad, my mom (who flew in from Utah to be there for Alex's birth), and a firefighter in training witnessed the amazing thing of childbirth.

Alex was the best baby, my first born. He slept through the night at three weeks, walked at nine months, and I had no problem weaning him off the bottle. When Alex was about three months old, we moved back to Utah; I was from Utah; Alex's dad was from Oklahoma. We didn't have family in Virginia and thought it would be best for Alex to have family around. I am beyond happy that we made this move. My mom passed away when Alex was two-and-a-half. Potty training was easy for Alex.

A couple of funny stories during those potty-training days: One day, he went to the bathroom and said, "Hey Mom, look I pooped green, do you think I could poop blue tomorrow?" Of course, I couldn't stop laughing. During this time, Alex's dad and I were having marriage problems. He moved out of our house and I needed to get a roommate. During an interview with a potential roommate, Alex went to the bathroom and a few minutes later yelled, "Mom, come wipe my butt." Awkward moment.

I never had any issues or concerns with Alex during preschool (he would tie all the kids' shoes for them in his preschool class). By this time, I was a single mother and I tried my best to give Alex the best life he could have. I wanted much more for him than I ever had. And I can honestly say I think I achieved that goal.

Alex loved tractors. He could name almost every one and what they are used for. I remember we drove passed a teal-colored tractor and he said, "That's a fancy blue tractor."

He also loved Pokemon and could drive me a little crazy about getting the new ones. He enjoyed watching *SpongeBob*, and as he grew older, he discovered *Friends*. He loved that show. Whenever our entire family was together, there was always talk about *Friends*.

When Alex was almost four, his baby sister, Alyssa, was born. He adored her. As they grew up, they were best of friends. Yes, they had their normal brother/sister arguments, but they never lasted long.

As Alex went through elementary school, I had no trouble with him. I always volunteered to be the room mother to help with all their parties. It made me feel so proud of Alex and I could tell he was proud of me for being there. One of the last days of elementary school, I took his class all the goodies to make banana splits; those kids were beyond happy. Again, I could tell Alex was proud of me for doing that at the end of the school year.

Alex had a good childhood. We went on family vacations, Disneyland, Disney World, a cruise. We were due to go on another cruise just after he went into rehab again; it was the previous year's family Christmas present. Alex and Alyssa remained close to their dad and he taught them how to ski and took them on vacation with his current wife and kids. Well, all got along great.

Then Alex hit junior high school. It wasn't right away that I started to notice the change in Alex, but probably between eighth and ninth grades. I look back and try to figure out what changed and how. His seventh grade year was spent in a school which was not known to be a good place. After seventh grade, we moved to what we thought would be a much better environment for him. I can't tell you when he started using drugs, but my guess is between ninth and tenth grades. He was using marijuana and I went through several calls with parents about their sons getting caught and telling their parents they got it from Alex. That was hell. Alex was not selling, but using, so I never knew quite what to say to the parents, it was rough.

Alex did not finish high school. We all want our kids to walk in their cap and gown and smile knowing that's your kid. He did earn his diploma and went through a couple years of college. He stopped going to college because he told me he couldn't handle it. After that, all hell broke loose in our lives. He moved out to live with friends and every time I would visit, all I got was the smell of pot. I begged and begged him to stop. He moved several times during the next year or so, then he hit rock bottom.

I got that phone call, "Mom I need help." Before he could be admitted to a detox center, we had to go to the emergency room for evaluation. When the doctor came in to ask him what drugs he has taken, he seemed to say every drug I have ever heard of. I was sick, wanted to throw up, I cried. He said, "I'm sorry, Mom."

He was in the detox place for only a few days. Not long after he was released, I got another call. He needed more help. I called Alex's dad for help. He has a lot of connections. His dad found him a place in Southern California and within hours, Alex was on a train to a treatment center.

I thought that was the best thing for him. We had a family weekend at the center, and he looked amazing, clean, he had a California tan and told me he really liked it there. After his time was done there, he moved to a sober living center and seemed to be doing great. I would visit as often as I could.

Then one day I received a phone call that Alex was trying to offer drugs to the other guys in the home. Unfortunately, he was kicked out. He ended up moving to Las Vegas (not the best place for an addict). His life seemed to turn around in a good way. He loved making music and he met friends in Las Vegas with the same interest. He got a great job and stayed there for a while. He met a wonderful girl, and they moved in together. I was grateful. I always thought if Alex could meet a nice woman and settle down, the drugs may go away.

I was visiting him one weekend and he told me he was going to hang out with a friend. Right then I knew the drugs were back. He left his girlfriend home and was gone all night. We all tried to connect to him throughout the night with no luck. He showed up back at his house at about the time I was leaving. He looked terrible. I hugged him and asked him not to do this to himself or his girlfriend. His life was on the right track and he had a lot going for him. We both cried and he said, "I know, Mom."

Within the next five months, the addiction took over. He was in and out of two relationships and lost his job and wrecked his car. I got yet another call that he needed help. I got him into a rehab in Southern Utah and he was there for a couple months. We visited him on Thanksgiving 2019; they had a family dinner. He came home around December 1 of the same year. He was trying to get his life back together. He got a job, bought a new car, was making tons of music with his friends.

Christmas 2019 was our last Christmas together. He seemed very happy. He woke up and made breakfast with his sister and her boyfriend. We spent the entire day as a family, it was the best. After dinner, we played board games and I just watched Alex with a heart filled with love. He was with his family and having a really good time. Alex always made it home for every Christmas. One Christmas a couple years back, he was living in California (we lived in Utah) and said he could not make it home for Christmas this year. I was devastated. My first Christmas without my son home. We were texting and he was apologizing. I was crying. Then there was a knock at the door, and I went to answer it, and there he was at my front door, home for Christmas. His dad and sister made the arrangements with Alex so he could make it home for Christmas and surprise me.

Between December 1, 2019, (when he came home from sober living) and February 8, 2020, I don't know when or what went wrong. He seemed okay. He was getting up for work very early and spending a lot of time making music. He was very proud of what he was doing. He performed locally to get his name out. He released a new album on January 1, 2020. He was scheduled to perform on February 20, 2020, and was very excited about it. That performance ended up being in his honor, another proud mommy moment.

On the night of February 7, 2020, he was fighting with his stepdad. He had caught Alex using in the middle of the day. He was told to leave the house before nine p.m., or he would call the cops. Alex had nowhere to go. I finally talked his stepdad into letting him stay. I sat and spoke with Alex and let him know we will make this work. We will find a place for him to live. I asked him to just relax and take a bath; his stepdad would be gone for the weekend on a fishing trip, and we will get it together. He said, "Mom, I really want to work on my music." I said, "Then you should." He loved making music, writing and singing.

I left him in his room about ten-thirty to eleven p.m., and he was texting his cousin and friend way after midnight.

I woke up and started cleaning the house for a few hours and then had to take something upstairs to where Alex slept. His door was closed, and I thought I better check on him. I knocked lightly a few times, then started knocking louder. I heard nothing. I slowly opened the door and my most horrific nightmare happened. Alex was face down on the floor with whatever device he used for the drugs still in his hand. He was cold, stiff, and heavy. I just yelled his name over and over to please wake up and this can't be happening.

I ran downstairs for my phone to call 911. The 911 operator kept asking me if I could roll him over and try CPR. I knew it was too late for CPR and I could not move him at all. He was not a big kid, tall and skinny, his friends called him "stick." The next hour, there was so much commotion in my house. I had close family there, police officers, detectives, and the medical examiner. I asked the medical examiner if I could please see him one more time, and he said it wouldn't be a good idea because of the way he had been laying on his face; it was very black.

I did have the honor of dressing him for his funeral. I was very skeptical about doing this, but grateful I did. It was a very emotional and moving moment. My daughter and Alex's stepmom were also involved in this process. A memory to last me a lifetime.

Alex had several friends overdose and die before him. I prayed Alex would get it and know that it could happen to him. He really needed all the help he could get to stay clean.

I listen to his voice every day and

I'm grateful I have his voice forever. He met many friends through his music who have been beyond kind to me and my family since Alex passed away. His friends got tattoos in Alex's honor. They made canvas pictures and made the album Alex released on January 1, 2020, into an actual album.

I will never see Alex watch his beautiful bride walk down the aisle and have children of his own. I will never see him make his biggest goal and be at the Grammy's.

Alex passed away one week before his twenty-sixth birthday. He had his whole life ahead of him.

I love you my beautiful, beautiful boy. Until we meet again.

Alex's Mom,

LORI K.
Lehi, Utah

Tyler

FOREVER 22

Hello, I am a grieving mom. I lost my son Tyler at the young age of twenty-two. He was a huge New York Yankee's fan and pretty much loved to watch and play almost every sport. I remember the tender years of going to watch his little league games and being able to see my baby boy on the field!! He was so full of love for the game of baseball that he one day dreamed to be a star too! Little did I know that a demon aka drugs would enter the picture.

I learned of Tyler's addiction one night when I received a phone call from my ex-husband saying I better come get him before he has nowhere to live. I was shocked and pretty much like WTF is going on?? Needless to say, after much argument with the ex, Tyler confirmed what his father told me. I was devastated and angry. I was mostly angry at his father and mostly blamed him. We had a nasty divorce and I pretty much

336

blamed him for the situation at hand. I told Tyler I would help him in each and every way I could.

"I love you, Tyler, and we will get you the help you need."

Tyler wasn't so thrilled about rehab, however he did agree he needed help. After calling my insurance and many places in St Louis, I found there was little hope for recovery here. I did find an outpatient treatment center and we went for the consultation. I did not know at that point what his drug of choice was nor did I press for that information. I was proud of him for admitting he had an addiction and coming to me for help. After a few times at the clinic, I was not able to afford to send him as the first visit was $500 and I honestly didn't even have that.

Some time went by and he seemed to be doing much better. Then in December his girlfriend of about years broke it off for good. Tyler was devastated; now we're back to square one. He was using, heavily. He overdosed for the second and third time on the kitchen floor of the home he shared with his father. His dad did CPR until medics arrived and administered Narcan. They saved his life! Then came the third and fourth time. This time, it was a Friday evening and then on a Saturday morning, back to back days. The fourth time, he had a choice given by the police. Either go to jail for all the paraphernalia or to the hospital for help.

After much deliberation, Tyler decided to go the hospital. He was admitted to the psych unit for five days until I could get him into the second rehab in California. I received a call from his very good friend, Tom, who recommended I send him to rehab in California with him. At first, I wasn't sure about sending him there with his addict friend. I then realized they needed each other; Tyler went! The first few days were terrible for him, withdrawing and being afraid of what was to come. By the grace of God, he made it through and was doing amazing.

That was September, fast forward to December. Since he was doing so well and Christmas was around the corner, I gave him the gift of being with his family and flew him home for four days. He was so happy and finally back to being my boy. The loving, kind, sweet, boy I always loved and knew! I was so very proud of him!! The visit was great, no issues and all smiles! Hands down the best Christmas we have ever had.

He went back to California and things just weren't the same. Tom graduated the program and would be coming back to St Louis to tie up some loose ends, then go back to California. Tyler was not able to accept that he would be there solo and got kicked out of the house. I was told he took a Flexeril from someone he knew at work who had an on the job back injury. He came home in early January. He stayed at my house with my husband and his little sister and brother. They were so happy to have their big brother home!! That didn't last long as he had no motivation, was not working, going to school, or attending any meetings to stay sober.

My husband and I couldn't allow him to stay here for fear he was using again. The hardest conversation I have ever had was telling my own flesh and blood he had to leave our home, his safe place. He went and stayed at his buddy's house from that time on, about a month and a half. I spoke to him almost every day. He was not himself. On February 28, 2018, he overdosed again, number five. He went to the ER and when I arrived, he asked me why I was there! I was crushed, angry, and a ball of tears. I said, "You don't want me here," and I left. The worst decision I have ever made, walking away from my son who needed me more than ever (he left the ER later that night with my parents who dropped him off at his buddies). That was around eleven thirty p.m. Tyler overdosed for the final time around six a.m. on March 1, 2018. I am forever lost, heartbroken, and angry! Thank you for the opportunity to share my sons' story!

Tyler's Mom,

Michelle K.
House Springs, Mississippi

Nicholas

FOREVER 27

They say when you die, your life flashes before your eyes. I never paid much attention to this, until I lost my son, Nicholas. Then I started to obsess about it. What did he see? Was it filled with the happy, fun memories of childhood? Or did the darkness of his addiction and terrifying nights in prison creep into his final memories of his life here on Earth? What exactly DID the movie that played in his mind look like?

Rewind back to April 10,1991, a planned C-section at the hospital. I was honestly surprised when the doctor said, "It's another boy!" I swore my second child would be a girl. I always dreamed of the perfect family; one boy, one girl, and we'd all live happily ever after. Of course, I was still thrilled with my sweet little boy. I came to realize I was truly a boy-mom and loved every minute of it. Fishing, playing catch, shooting guns at the range, spitting and cussing.

We had a lot of fun together. Turns out it WAS nice to be the only girl in the house, though sometimes playing referee to wrestling matches and falling into the toilet seats left up was challenging. My sons loved their momma and were fiercely protective of me. They weren't embarrassed to say they were momma's boys, even as adults.

Nick was a happy baby and a cuddle bug, who always had to sit RIGHT NEXT to his momma. He was so loving and never fought or argued. He rarely got into trouble. Even when he did do something wrong, his big brown eyes and sweet smile always got him out of it. His big brother, Brandon, whom he IDOLIZED until the day he died, was three years and three months older. Nick tried his best to keep up with the big kids. He was fearless, swam without water wings, rode his bike without training wheels, jumped ramps, and managed to hang, just fine, with the big kids. We lived on a small, tight-knit circle, where everyone looked out for everyone else's kids, and the parents were all friends. The kids all went to school together. It was picture perfect. Looking back, I never dreamed a kid this happy as a child would later be so tormented by his own thoughts, and struggle with depression and anxiety to the point of self-medicating to numb himself emotionally and mentally.

Nick wasn't really into sports; his thing was music. He'd dance around in his underwear, playing his toy guitar or his drum set, singing his heart out to 90's rock. Later, in his teens, he developed an appreciation and love for classic rock. He attended music festivals and I always said he was born in the wrong decade. He was a "hippie" at heart and would've fit in perfectly at Woodstock. He was fun and funny and always had a smile or a word of encouragement for his friends. Several of them messaged me after he died and told me he would stay up with them and talk them through some very hard times of their own, even as he suffered himself.

Throughout Nick's life, his father struggled with alcoholism and had a pretty short fuse, combined with a mom who suffered from severe anxiety; this was a recipe for disaster for our children. I tried to tiptoe around and smooth things over, be the peacekeeper. Their father was stressed about his career and had a lot of other things brewing in his mind I knew nothing about at the time. We separated and reconciled, not once but twice. He'd get sober, make promises, and we'd all be one big happy family for a few months. He meant well and was a very hard worker who provided well for our family, but he had demons of his own he couldn't overcome. Over the next few years, my boys began to hate this man who stormed into the house, belittled them, or started fights and bullied everyone. He made it clear a few times that he never wanted kids to begin with and we were a burden. We waited for him to go to bed at night so we could laugh and watch TV together and feel free to be ourselves. I tried my best to keep the boat from rocking too much or worse yet, tipping like it did a few years later. In 2009, he finally said he didn't want to be responsible for us anymore and he left for California. Sadly, that would be the last time Nick ever saw his father, but not the last time his father saw HIM. That would be in the ICU during Nick's final days.

I try and try to pinpoint exactly when I think Nick started using drugs, but it's so vague now. I knew he smoked pot in middle school and although I wasn't happy about it, it wasn't a huge deal for me. I figured if it grew in the ground, it was harmless. Then he moved on to pills, Xanax to be specific, to deal with the anxiety he started suffering from. It seemed "okay" because after all, a doctor prescribed them (insert eye roll here). Nick would eventually take more than the doctor prescribed and soon he'd run out before it was time to refill them.

This was taking a turn for the worse, I would soon find out. I remember picking Nick up from a party at a friend's house after he'd taken something and passed out. I remember trying to find Nick once when he was walking home, lost and on several hits of acid, with him not even knowing what street he was on. His brother had to kick in his bedroom door a few times and throw him in the shower to wake him up. I remember dragging my son out to the car to take him to the ER, once while his father was passed out. I kept thinking, *He's so heavy and why do we have to own an SUV I have to lift him up into?* That particular night, he had decided to drink Captain Morgan Rum and had taken several Xanax and I couldn't wake him up. The hospital just left him on a gurney in the hallway, seemingly ignoring him. To them, he was just another stupid kid who was high.

These incidents went on for a few years. On weekends, I'd sleep with my clothes nearby and my contacts in so I could jump up and be ready for the hospital call or police station or ER run, if I needed to. His brother had moved out and his Irish temper flared up for a few years.

341

He would get into fights, but his brother never touched drugs. Their father was drinking and taking pills and had a few encounters with police and hospitals as well. I had the local police on speed dial. I knew most of the nurses at the hospital from going so frequently with my three guys. One particular night, Nick got into a fight at a party and his brother Brandon stepped in and they were both arrested. I was "relieved" because they were both at the same police station. Oh good, only one stop that night. For a few weeks in 2009, I slept in a recliner in front of the window with a shotgun in my lap after Nick told me he owed money to a guy who was going to come over and kill us. It seemed so surreal, because by day I'd go to work and smile and be productive, and NO ONE had a clue what was going on in my personal life. *Where is my Academy Award,* I wondered?

Then came the day when he was arrested for having Xanax and Valium in his pocket. I was terrified but relieved. He would be "safe," I thought, in jail for a few nights. He was crying, begging me to bail him out, swore he'd never do it again, so of course I did. Then he did it again. Arrested for possession, but this time he had to stay in jail a few months. I thought, *I've seen enough episodes of Scared Straight, THIS will do it. He will come home, and we will be like the mom and sons on Leave it to Beaver, minus Ward, of course, who was off in California somewhere drinking and unaware of what his son was doing.* When his father was sober, I'd tell him what was going on and his way of handling it would be to yell at Nick over the phone to "Get his head out of his ass." Gee, that'll help, sure. Why didn't I think of that?

Eventually pills led to heroin, introduced to him by a girl named Emily. I wondered why she slept so much when she was at our house, but then I soon realized what they were doing. One night I found out she was stealing money and clothes from me. I took the dog for our usual walk and with a switchblade I kept in my nightstand drawer, I made the tiniest slit in the soft top of her Geo Tracker. Not my proudest moment, but it sure felt good to do. I told Nick she had to leave and couldn't come back again. To this day, I chuckle when I think of the whistling sound she must have heard when she drove down the highway wearing my favorite shirt.

So, Nick would come home from jail, be on probation, then somehow mess up by not seeing his PO, or getting caught for possession again. He spent the majority of the ages between eighteen to twenty-seven in and out of prisons, jails, and rehab programs, with hopeful recovery time in between. He was a very hard worker and sometimes held two or three jobs at a time. Even after all the times in and out of jails and prisons, he never strayed from who he was at his core; he always loved his family fiercely and was a friend to everyone. I was "proud" of how my boy adapted and adjusted in there, seeing things that would make a grown man sick. The stories he told me sometimes were terrifying, yet he never got into trouble and just managed to get along with everyone. He called me every single day, sometimes two or three times. We talked about everything. He wanted to hear the boring details of my day, just to keep him going and stay connected. He would watch *Seinfeld* on the prison TV because it reminded him of "a simpler time," when he was a kid. He would read my letters to fellow inmates for encouragement and bought a photo album to show the pictures of our family to them. He'd ask me if it was ok to let a friend use his phone account, since they had no money for the phone themselves. He'd share his commissary food with others and learned to "cook" with the few ingredients they were able to buy in prison. He was the "MacGyver" of prison food. He returned to his love of music and joined a prison band, playing the drums. Music soothed his restless mind and soul. I'd give anything to have a video of him playing until his hands bled once at a prison concert. We cremated him with those beloved drumsticks.

In 2012, I realized just how bad his addiction had become, when one night as I was folding towels, his brother called and asked what he was doing and "how does he seem?" This was his way of asking me if Nick was high or not. I said, "I think he's using" and he said, "Go check on him." I said I would, and he said to do it now. He was still on the phone with me as I walked into Nick's room and saw him laying back on his bed, eyes half open, face grey, lips blue. I screamed for my husband, Nick's stepdad, to call 9-1-1. I remember screaming over and over, "I'm sorry! I'm sorry!" but I don't know what I was sorry for, maybe everything I didn't do to help him. I was frantically trying to remember the date, what was the date, as I would need it for his funeral mass card (you can't help where your mind goes when you find your child dying). His brother was screaming and crying on the phone as the paramedics raced in and administered Narcan. I asked the paramedic,

"Will he live?" and she just answered coldly, "I dunno." Like this is a daily thing for her. Another dose of Narcan and he woke up and looked right at me. They took him to the hospital, and he was released immediately. Thirty minutes later he was eating McDonald's Chicken Nuggets. It was so unreal to me that an hour before this he was dead and now, he's asking for more honey mustard sauce. This didn't seem to faze him, at all. I stayed awake all night watching him. The next day he told me he'd had several other near fatal overdoses and always woke up on his own. He said one time he passed out in the bathroom and hit his head on the sink, waking up to a bloody ear that he couldn't hear out of. I was floored. Near-death never even scared him enough to stop using. Then I realized this is truly a disease and not one that is to be taken lightly. I begged him to stop and told him more than once if he dies, they can just dig two holes because I'd die with him from a broken heart.

This went on for a few more years. Prison, recovery, the hopes and dreams once again of a happy healthy life, then a relapse. I heard him one-night (July 4, 2015, to be exact) sobbing on the phone to his sponsor that he had relapsed again. It was more powerful than he was, and he knew if he stayed on that path, he would wind up dead. My heart broke hearing my baby, my brown-eyed boy, crying his eyes out about something he felt he had no control over. He didn't want to be this way, he didn't want to hurt us or make us worry, he hated himself for his addiction. Before then, I would just get angry with him and ask him why can't he just STOP? I didn't understand. He would say, "Mom, I'm an addict, I can't." I thought that was just an excuse to keep using, to crash my car, to say his wallet was stolen or his laptop was lost, just to realize he had pawned his items for money to buy drugs with. Nick wasn't your typical addict, as defined by society though; he never stole a dime and never hurt anyone. He never yelled at me and was never hateful or mean. The only person he hurt with his addiction was himself. Sure, his brother and I were hurting because we couldn't help him, but he always knew we were in his corner and loved him more than anything. We tried tough love, we bought into the bullshit the "experts" were selling, "let them hit rock bottom" blah blah blah, but that doesn't work for everyone. It made Nick feel unloved, alone, and he'd end up using again.

I vividly remember one Easter Sunday, after I'd gotten stuck by a syringe I found in the couch cushion, kicking him out in the rain with nothing but his pillow and phone charger and a ham sandwich. I could hear him crying on the front porch begging friends to come get him. But I had to "be strong" because that's what the tough love advocates said I had to do. There is no ONE SIZE FITS ALL CURE for addiction. It just doesn't work that way.

Eventually, Nick landed in prison for a two-year sentence, followed by a six-month rehab program in Farmington, Missouri. He had a few slip ups in prison, and by slip up I mean relapses. I would later find out it was fentanyl they were using. IN PRISON. You think they are safe in prison, but actually drugs are everywhere. When he was home, I was an expert detective, stalking his every move, tracking his phone, texting and assuming if he didn't reply he must be dead. A few times along the way, I wished I'd die; I wanted to be free of the pain of watching my baby lose his fight to this demon. I'd go visit him and put on my smiling face, get the biggest hug and kiss on my check from him, play solitaire, eat vending machine food, laugh, tell stories, then cry all the way home.

He was transferred to the six-month treatment program in March of 2018 and it completely turned him around. He was journaling, he was working out daily, he was eating better, he stopped smoking, NO DRUGS, and he was focused. Ironically, the last entry in his journal says, "If I use drugs again, I will die."

September 11, 2018, was almost here, the day Nick would FINALLY come home, in the best shape of his life, mentally healthy and happy to pick up the pieces and start his next chapter. I was a nervous wreck. I had no idea how long his recovery would last or when a relapse might happen, if at all. Or what to expect this time and I was terrified. I clenched my teeth and my hands while I slept.

Nick had a wonderful six days, after he came home to us. He looked amazing! So big and muscular and healthy, he was a man now, not the boy who went away two years earlier. All grown up. We took a ton of pictures and I felt a little bit of relief. He was all set up in a room at our house and he spent the majority of his time with his best friend, his brother. I'm so happy they had those six days together and their final moment was a big hug and the words, "Love you brother." That was Saturday.

On Sunday, he went to help a friend move. I was hesitant for him to hang out with anyone besides family yet, but he insisted on helping him and I couldn't stop him. He came home and immediately went to work. Later that night, he came home and went into his room. After a few minutes, I knocked on the door to talk to him. No answer. The old panic from years ago came right back in an instant. I opened the door and he was slumped over. I couldn't wake him up. I assumed it was heroin, so I grabbed my Narcan and gave him the nasal spray. He instantly woke up and said, "Mom! Mom come on, it's not that, it's not that." I said I won't do this again and if he can't stay clean, he can't stay here. He said he had taken an oxycodone and a Xanax, and it made him sleepy. I went to bed and said, "We'll talk about this more tomorrow." He swore it wasn't what I thought it was and said, "Mom, you can drug test me."

Monday morning, September 17, 2018, I went to work as usual, but before I left, I said goodbye and told him I loved him. He said it's not what I think and don't worry. We texted a few times, the usual stuff; he needed to renew his driver's license and where was his birth certificate, etc. A few hours later he stopped texting. He didn't reply to me. I called, and no answer. I had that feeling in my gut again, I knew something was wrong. Finally, at 4:45 p.m., I told my boss I had to leave, and I drove the five minutes home as fast as I could. His brother called me on my way, and I told him what was going on. Again, he was on the phone with me. I ran in the garage door and raced up the stairs and burst into Nick's room. The bed was made, he wasn't there. THEN I SAW HIS FEET ON THE FLOOR. I screamed, "Doug call 9-1-1" and set the phone down. Nick was on his left side, somehow wedged between the bed and TV stand. He had a small scratch over his left eye. His face was blue, but his body was tan and warm, so I thought, *Ok, he's alive.* He looked like he was sleeping but his mouth was open just a little bit. I never even checked for a pulse, I just rolled him onto his back and gave him a dose of Narcan my husband had brought into the room. Nothing happened, so I immediately started chest compressions. I'll never forget the sound the air made as it came out of his mouth, a sort of whistling sound. His pupils were fixed and dilated. I knew he was gone, but kept going until the paramedics arrived, hoping for a miracle. My legs were numb, and my hands hurt, but I didn't care. His brother listened to all of this unfolding and was headed to the hospital to meet us there. I asked, "This is it, isn't it?" and Brandon replied, "Yes, Mom, it is." We knew.

Once we got to the hospital, they told us they had gotten a faint heartbeat back in the ambulance, but he coded again, then they got him back again. I stood next to him in the trauma room, hooked up to machines while his brother was outside vomiting and crying. It was the worst day of our lives. I just stood there memorizing every detail of my beautiful son's face, touched his hair, studied his tattoos. I heard a gurgling noise and then smelled the smell; he had gone to the bathroom. I knew at that exact moment he was gone. This was it. The machines kept his body going for three more days, but I knew he was already off on his next journey. I wondered if he could see us all there, the niece he adored, scared and in the hallway with her mom, his brother outside throwing up in a trash can, his stepdad, and me, speaking very business like with the staff and insanely calm.

For three days we waited with him, for some kind of sign, something, anything. A movement or a blink or a miracle that I knew in the back of my mind would never come. Even if he did somehow survive, he wouldn't be himself, he'd be blind or deaf or unable to talk or walk and I knew he didn't want that. He'd rather die. I prayed for God's will, whatever He thought best, to be done. Hundreds of friends and family paraded into and out of Nick's room, crying, praying, while I sat there, numbly holding his hand. He hadn't seen these people in over two years, and I was sad that he missed out on so much: weddings, funerals, special occasions, etc. They all said, "God performs miracles," but I knew he was gone. There would be no such miracle, but I played along with them. I had rehearsed his death for years while he was using to prepare myself, but it was nothing like I imagined. Not one bit. It was a thousand times worse and still is. The constant worry about him is replaced by a constant ache in my soul, a numbness in my heart.

They told us there were no drugs in Nick's system, no heroin, nothing except Benadryl and Benzos they said (Valium, he had taken one of mine to help him sleep). His heart condition was worse than mine, with only a 30% ejection fraction. That must have been what suppressed his respiratory system, we figured. His weak heart couldn't handle the Valium and Benadryl that put him to sleep. We were relieved that he kept his promise to me only days before, when he said he'd never use a drug again that could kill him. Three months later, we found out there was fentanyl and Benadryl in that blue and white temazepam capsule he had taken. I saw one on his TV stand the day I found him and gave it to the police. They later destroyed it without even testing it. We were floored. It made sense now. Fentanyl doesn't show up in the usual hospital bloodwork. Did he know he was taking it, or did he think he was just going to take a temazepam (benzo) and get a good night's sleep? Or did he think he could handle it because he'd taken it several months ago in prison?

Thursday, September 20, 2018, they declared my boy brain dead. I asked if he could be an organ donor and they said they would contact Mid-America Transplant. He was able to donate both kidneys and his liver, but not his heart due to a hereditary heart condition I have, my mom had, and we were unaware he had until he was in the ICU. When they checked his license, they saw he had signed up to be a donor himself, which confirmed what we already knew to be what he'd want. A few hours later, he was ready to make his exit from the hospital and go to the transplant facility. We escorted him out, down what felt like a hundred hallways, all lined with hospital staff for the Honor Walk. Some people cried, some didn't make eye contact, some reached out their hands to us, but everyone was moved that day by this touching exit my son was making, on his way to give his gifts of life.

Most moms say they are thankful it wasn't them who found their child. I think the opposite; if it had to happen, it HAD to be me who found him. I was there when he came into this world; of course, I had to be there when he left. It was the best possible scenario for the worst imaginable event in any parent's life. I feel blessed to have been there for him, instead of someone else finding him (his brother, niece, a friend who would abandon him) or getting a call or not knowing where he was or who he was with, or not knowing all of the details.

Even in death, my boy still gave hope and love to others. We are now friends with one of his recipients. It has helped to heal our pain a little bit, knowing she is alive because of him. She received a double transplant, his liver AND a kidney. She and her family honor and thank him every day. They feel like family to us. It still seems unreal to me to think she is walking, talking, and LIVING her best life now because of

348

my son. She goes camping, fishing, attends concerts, all the things he loved. Our loss truly is not in vain, as he lives on through others.

Nick's wish was always to travel. We honor that wish now with "NICK-DUST," little sprinkles of his ashes traveling the world with family and friends. He has been sprinkled in Ireland, Canada, Italy, Paris, Mexico, among many other places by people who love him. We started a Facebook page called NICKDUST to document his travels and the many random acts of kindness performed in his memory.

Some days I can barely breathe; other days I am numb. Some days his picture makes me smile and other days it sucks the wind out of my lungs and I literally gasp out loud. The pain isn't as sharp as it was the first year, but it's HEAVIER, if that makes any sense. But I'm trying. And to me, what it comes down to is when it's time to have MY life flash before my eyes, I'm going to make sure it's worth watching. I'm going to do all I can to honor my son's memory, until the day I am reunited with him.

Nicholas's Mom,

GINA K.
O'Fallon, Missouri

Wiley

FOREVER 31

Wiley was my second child, but my firstborn son. At eight, he got caught in the middle of a bitter divorce between me and his father. In the fifth grade, his teacher told me, "I have never seen a more depressed child." But Wiley was so kind and loving and kept things to himself.

When he was thirteen and in the eight grade, he broke his ankle while visiting his father. He suffered for three days before I went and got him and took him to the ER. The attending physician asked if he needed something for pain. Of course, I said yes. This child had been suffering. He had one prescription for hydrocodone and one refill. I went and got them and gave them to him as prescribed. Later he would tell me that his addiction began with the first pill that he took. I had no idea what was happening. I trusted my healthcare providers.

When Wiley was nineteen, he was injured in a boating accident and was given more opiates. Refill after refill. Months later, a friend told me that he had suspected Wiley of taking his opiates (the friend had had open heart surgery). When confronted, Wiley admitted it and at twenty years old said, "Mom, I have a problem." My ex-husband's family and I joined resources and with health insurance were able to get him in a very expensive, thirty-day program. We all went to the family group sessions and tried so hard to love and support him, but it would be a ten-year struggle. The health insurance ended when he was twenty-six and so did the support from most friends and family. With no insurance, we struggled to get help.

In 2017, he was arrested and charged with several felony thefts. I let him stay in jail about six months before the court sentenced him to drug court. More rehabs and failed attempts at sobriety, but I believe drug court gave us time we otherwise wouldn't have had.

On March 11, 2020, drug court sent him to a thirty-day rehab. The pandemic had just broken out and we were quarantining, but I put on a mask and gloves and drove the three and one half hours to bring him some things he needed and wanted. Pillows, blankets, cigarettes, and money. I left at five a.m. and by eight-thirty a.m., was back in my car headed home. Within minutes, I got a call from the rehab. It was my son. He said, "Mom, I just want to thank you for never giving up on me and for always doing everything to help me. I know it's going to be different this time Mom. I can't explain it, but I just know."

Thirty days later, on April 11, I went to pick him up and bring him home. His wife (a recovering addict herself, who is rocking recovery) and his three children, ages three, four, and five, all lived with me. We were so excited for him to come home. We had been quarantined for seven weeks; me, my daughter-in-law, and three children.

Wiley hadn't been home a week when we knew he had relapsed. Then, on May 8, Wiley took $20 from his wife's wallet and left a note that said, "I'm sorry...this is the last time, I promise." When he got back, I told him he had to leave. He cannot stay here in active addiction, and he headed out on foot. He didn't say a word, he just started walking. Within a few minutes, I regretted my hastily made demand for him to leave. What if he were to overdose? What if something happened? My heart couldn't take it, so I asked his wife to go find him. After a few minutes she called saying there was no sign of him. I opened the door and there he sat. I was so relieved. I told him I was sorry that I told him to leave and that I didn't want him to. I told him I didn't know; what was I supposed to do? He said nothing.

On Mother's Day, May 10, 2020, we had the most amazing day. Wiley grilled his amazing steaks for us, his brother, his wife, nephew, my aunt, and his mother-in-law. We visited and enjoyed each other so much. Wiley even went and got flowers for both me and his wife. He cleaned the kitchen. The "works." It was a wonderful day.

About nine that night, I took the baby girl (three) to sleep with me. My daughter-in-law was laying down with the oldest (five) and Wiley was laying down with the four-year-old. Alyson, my daughter-in-law, got up about 11:20 p.m. to go to the bathroom and noticed he was not laying down with Jaxon. She assumed he was outside smoking a cigarette and started to go back to bed. But something told her to check. When she opened the door to the carport, she saw him, slumped over on an outdoor loveseat. She tried to wake him and came screaming for me. I jumped out of bed and ran out. I too, tried to shake him. She called 911. I ran in and got the Narcan. I gave him two doses up his nose. I had her help me lay him down as she was on the phone with the dispatcher and I started CPR. I was begging God not to take him, wailing and screaming and crying "NOOOOO" over and over. I looked up and there was the baby girl and the five-year-old with looks of pure terror on their faces. We had no idea they were there.

When paramedics arrived, the looks on their faces and the lack of effort on their part to do anything let me know he was gone...and yet I prayed and prayed and said, "Please God." But he was gone. The truth is, he was gone when we found him, but I had to try. Narcan has brought many a person back. Not my son.

We found out later he had been picked up by a couple guys who brought him what he thought was heroin, but turned out to be fentanyl. He started overdosing in the car with them and instead of getting him help or ringing the doorbell and running, they drug him back under the carport. They just left him for dead. No one will come forward, so there will probably be no prosecution. I am one of more than 400 mothers who lost a child, to addiction, on Mother's Day.

I believe that God knew my son

would continue to struggle, so He brought him home to a place of peace and rest for his weary and tormented soul. I will live my life telling his story and encouraging parents to #justsaynotoopiates for their children's injuries.

Today, we know the dangers of opiates. We didn't in 2003.

Rest in Peace, my beautiful boy.

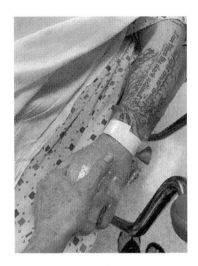

Wiley's Mom,

KELLIE K.
Greenville, South Carolina

Brittany

FOREVER 24

September 19, 2018 at 3:56 p.m., our lives changed forever. I will never forget the knock on the door telling me the horrible news that we lost our beautiful Brittany (B Lap), our free-spirited, full of life, daughter, sister, niece, granddaughter, cousin, and friend. I was in disbelief, shock that my worst fear as a mother had come like a thief in the night. On this day, she was taken from our world and lifted up to heaven and reunited with her baby Boy Ayden.

My daughter was twenty-four the last time I held her hand, in the upstairs room of a funeral home. She was twenty-four the last time I kissed her and told her I love her.

As I held her hand for almost an hour, I apologized to her; at that moment, I felt I failed her as a mother. I told her that I would miss her terribly, and that my life would never be the same. I knew at that moment I would never see her smile again, talk to her, argue, laugh, or cry with her. Even if we didn't always see eye to eye, we had love for one another.

She was my first child.

She was the child who made me a mother.

She was the one who taught me both the incredible joy, and the unbearable pain of being a mother.

She will never marry or have another child to fill the void from the loss of her only son.

As I studied her face, as I held her hand, I looked for anything that might make this all just a terrible mistake...but it wasn't.

I wondered what I could have done to have changed her outcome.

Our outcome...this intense, incredible, and indescribable pain.

Her death. And now I'm still searching for a way to be okay.

With all our love to you Britt Nicole.

Until we meet again...

Britt's Mom,

STACY L.
Chauvin, Louisianna

Jonathan

FOREVER 35

Jonathan was my youngest son and the joy of my life. He had a giving and loving heart, but struggled with depression in his teen years, leading to recreational drugs. Jon would light up the room with his big, bright eyes and beautiful smile. But after struggling with back and neck pain in his early twenties, he was prescribed Oxycontin and then went on to heroin in his later years. In his mid-thirties, his world became dark and angry with the demon drug taking over his sweet soul. Jonathan always wore his heart on his sleeve. He loved his young wife and two baby boys the best way he could during his struggles with his addiction. I somehow knew the day I found out he was doing heroin I would get "the call," and two and a half years later, I did. Unbeknownst to him, he was given pure fentanyl. He was at my brother's house in Massachusetts. He had come full circle. He was born in Massachusetts thirty-five years ago, under duress. The cord had

356

wrapped around his throat and I had to have an emergency C-section. On that fateful day, the first responders revived him after four shots of Narcan and he was taken to the hospital and put on life support for four days.

During those long heart-wrenching days, I never left his side. When the breathing tubes were removed, I held him close and whispered gently to him, it was okay to go, that we would all be alright and we would see him again. After thirteen minutes of caressing his face and telling him how much I loved him, and with my mouth on his, he took his last breath. My sadness lies not in his freedom from pain or struggling with life on this earth, but rather in the fact that his wife, boys, and I will not have him physically here to share all the milestones ahead for them. Jonathan's father was an addict and died in a car crash at the age of thirty-two when Jon was six years old. We had already been divorced for a few years. Jon never really knew him in life, but I believe they are together, now in death. This gives me a sense of comfort to know they will be waiting for me on the other side. Until then, I feel my Jon Boy with me spiritually and he is constantly sending me signs since his passing on that fateful Monday, January 23, 2017. I still celebrate his birthday every December 8, and thank my Lord for allowing me to be his Mom, for the years that he was with us. Death to me is a new beginning and a pain-free journey to eternity. There is no sadness in Heaven.

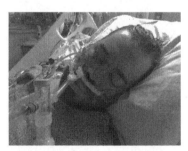

All of our children are united now and we must honor them by living our best life in our world of grief as we continue to walk this earth. I believe this is the only way to show others that their lives and early deaths were not in vain.

Jonathan's Mom,

DEBORAH L.
Fort Pierce, Florida

Danielle

I'm a recovering addict of eighteen years, from opiate pills. I have four children. One of them was actually lying next to me, once, when I OD'd. She was seven years old. All my children knew of my struggle to stay clean.

My youngest daughter, Danielle, the one who was with me when I OD'd, grew up to be a beautiful girl, full of life. She met the love of her life, at fourteen, and they had five children by the time they were twenty-six. She was the more reckless one, but I never thought she'd pick up smoking 30 mg percs one day, just to try. She didn't tell anyone, but there were rumors among her siblings about what she was doing. I approached her and she denied it. Not three months later, I got a call from her crying, she couldn't go through the withdrawal. Long story short, I went and stayed with her and her boyfriend and put them in their room with a bunch of Suboxone, while I took care of the kids (ages nine, four, three, two, and one for nine days). Needless to say, it didn't work. This was February of 2019.

They did, sort of, get clean a couple months later, by then living with a friend. But they had started selling heroin to afford rent. They were caught and arrested, and the children were placed in DCF custody. Over the next five months, my daughter Danielle did everything they asked. By the beginning of February 2020, she had a four-bedroom, section-eight house, each bedroom set up for the kids. Even a Christmas tree, set up with presents (because they were taken before Christmas that year). She had been attending classes, drug screenings, and had a full-time job. The problem was, she still hadn't admitted to anyone but me that she had gotten into that, not her dad or siblings. So, she wasn't in any drug treatment.

In February of 2020, Danielle and her boyfriend had some arguments, which resulted in him going to stay with his parents for a few days. My baby girl was depressed that week. She had inherited the family affliction of anxiety and depression and wasn't getting treated for it. On February 20, she decided to call for some heroin. Only it wasn't the regular guy they usually called. This guy brought her straight uncut fentanyl. She had not done that before, plus her tolerance was low from being clean. This was on a Thursday night around eleven p.m. She was alone. The next day when she didn't appear at work, they called her emergency contact, her boyfriend. It was two p.m., Friday the 21st by then. He went to the house. The doors were locked. He looked in a window and saw her on her knees, hunched over. Dead. My baby girl had been there for fifteen hours. I got the call around six-thirty p.m. that night. I had to inform her siblings, father, and grandmother. It was incomprehensible. One last time.

A whole life mostly spent nowhere near drugs. A life partner that loved her right back. Their five babies. I still don't understand. There are so many reasons I don't understand why she decided to do this. She berated me for most of her life because of my addiction and the follow-up treatment I still get to this day. We hadn't even spoken in months. I hadn't seen her in months. She was still angry with me. She loved her babies so much. She wanted all of them. Three of them might never remember her. We have to keep her alive through them. They are still in

DCF custody, but we (me and my other children) are working on getting them with us all.

My daughter Danielle was so outgoing, loved by so many. I collapsed when I saw her for the first time in the coffin at the wake. It's been five months now and I'm still in the stage of, "Why did this have to happen?" We need to find a way to make sure her children know her. I know everyone says this, but my daughter was absolutely beautiful, charismatic, full of life, and doted on her kids. She got into using for such a short time, and then it ended her life. All I want is to have her know how much I love her and wish that we had gotten everything together before this happened. Her father and siblings only found out the truth by seeing the medical examiner's report. I want her life remembered for so much more. As her Mother it's so hard to accept this. I wish I had done more.

Danielle's Mom,

JULIE L.
Framingham, Massachusetts

Steven

FOREVER 39

My Stevie was an unexpected blessing. He was the quietest, gentlest soul you could ever meet. He had a passion for reading, for his friends, and family. But somehow, somewhere, he started experimenting with drugs. I can remember begging him to be careful. Crying and telling him I loved him and needed him to be around to take care of me, in my old age.

He was always a sickly kid, due to severe asthma, so I kept telling him to quit smoking cigarettes and marijuana. He would always just laugh at me and say, "MOM, I am GOOD, don't WORRY." He once told me, "Mama the only time I am sad is when you're sad and the only time I cry is when you cry." So, he must be crying a lot in Heaven now.

October 28, 2016, I got a phone call from my youngest son, saying somethings going on at Stevie's house; Kevin called and said the cops are there. Of course, I thought "OH MY GOD," what did he do. I didn't know he was back to using because he had been clean. We waited and waited to hear something and finally Matthew called the police station and asked, "What's going on with my brother?" They told him he needed to get his parents to come down and talk to them.

I knew by the look on the deputy's face it wasn't good. They took me into a room with a DCI guy, who started asking me questions and I just kept asking, "Where's my son, where's my son?"

Finally, he said, "Mrs. L, I am sorry, but we found your son deceased today."

I looked at him and said, "You're a bold face, damn liar."

He said, "No, ma'am I am sorry, it's your son."

I lost it, I started to cry and demanded to see my baby. I couldn't because by the time they found him decomp had set in and they wouldn't allow me to, no matter how much I begged and pleaded. I could never kiss those handsome cheeks, hug him close, or tell him I loved him. My world came crashing down around my shoulders, all because of a bad decision my son made to take meth that night. My sweet gentle baby, gone.

I can't describe my pain or heart-break. I walked around like a zombie for weeks thinking this isn't real; I am going to wake up from this nightmare.

But now almost four years later, I am still living this nightmare. Please, please, if you're reading this and love someone who is an addict, get them help. Save them, so my child's life wasn't in vain.

Steven's Mom,

CHERYL L.
Hot Springs, South Dakota

Michael

FOREVER 31

As I open my eyes each morning and the day begins, reality hits and it is as if someone has punched me in my stomach. I gasp for air because it is at that moment, I remember my son tragically died of drug toxicity: carfentanyl and fentanyl. I am filled with deep sorrow as everything comes rushing back to me. The release of pain and sadness I receive from sleeping each night is now gone. And as I move on to making my bed, I find balled up tissues in between the sheets from last night's cry. These morning events have, sadly, become my new normal.

Michael Justin was born on January 4, 1989, in Mayfield Heights, Ohio. Michael was a colicky baby and born breach. He was so cute and charismatic, with an irresistible, sweet and loving personality. He was our second child, born four years after his older brother Anthony.

As a toddler, Michael was entertainingly peculiar, charismatic, and filled with energy. He had quirky behaviors that often entertained most everyone he was around. Michael developed quite the personality in his early years and a kindness shone through that seemed almost unearthly. Despite his temper and his strong and defiant personality, he had a heart of gold.

In middle school, Michael won the Avis Award, which was for children who went above and beyond with others. He would often stop others from bullying kids and accompany those that did not have anyone to sit with in the lunchroom or in class. I would later find out through numerous people that went to school with him that this was the case more than we even knew. Michael's personality did not change and as he grew older, he continued to focus on making others happy.

Throughout Michael's life, he was often described as funny, energetic, filled with life and a true spirit. Michael was always the goofy one and loved the idea of entertaining and making others happy. He rarely just walked into a room; he often came hopping in and hugging everyone. Michael was renowned for singing girl pop and performing for his friends. There are many videos of Michael singing at the top of his lungs: Taylor Swift, Halsey, Evanescence, and Katie Perry. He had a positive attitude and magnetic personality that I sometimes wished I could mirror. Unfortunately, the positive attitude may have been his demise, often translating into denial of his issues.

In his middle and high school years Michael was extremely passionate about football and baseball. I have never seen anyone want or work so hard at something. I say this not because he is my child, but because it is true. He was a gifted athlete and overall a gifted human. Hours and hours of practice, work outs, traveling on different teams, with multiple expectations for school and sports. He lettered in both football and baseball and was recruited by several colleges on scholarships. Popular and good looking, he kept himself humble and remained loving and kindhearted.

Unfortunately, right around that time, he was in a relationship with a young girl that turned into trouble. His dad and I had shared parenting, but his defiance got so bad with me that I had to insist he stay with his dad. Our relationship was a bit strained until he and the girlfriend broke up a few months later. Slowly we rebuilt our relationship only to find out we were much more alike than we had known. Michael was very extroverted and transparent with me. He leaned on me heavily over the years and struggled making decisions without talking to his dad and me. Over the years, I became very close with Michael, especially through his addiction.

Michael's brother began using drugs and getting into trouble around the time that Michael was also acting up with his girlfriend. Michael was very upset about his brother's situation and swore he would never use drugs or ever do what Anthony had done to me and his dad. That sentiment did not last because by the time Michael started his first year in college, we realized we had an addiction problem with him as well. It started with Adderall, alcohol, and Percocets, and then progressed to Oxycontin and finally heroin. Many times, we have tried to understand what made Michael turn to drugs. To say his father and I were devastated would be a huge understatement. How could this happen? Why would he possibly do this when he swore it from his life and despised watching what his brother had been through? Were we bad parents? But no, I knew we were not because our whole lives revolved around our children. We both blamed ourselves day after day, year after year. Both of our kids told us time and time again that we were supportive and wonderful parents. We would go on to doubt ourselves for many years. Pure torture that no parent should have to experience.

The stigma in society about weakness and choice of drug use was staggering and discouraging, to say the least. Comments that were made by unknowing bystanders about junkies and losers, comments that we should just let them die, were hurtful and painful. Not in one million years had Michael's father and I imagined this would happen to our children. I recall the DARE programs and the push to not use drugs during their childhood, but we had not imagined our children's entire adult years would be made of this hell we were in. I can only say that my son had the disease of addiction and that certain societal influences made him predisposed to begin using.

As the star running back for his football team, well respected, I watched him spiral downward when in year one of college, he was not chosen to play. It was at that time I realized his coping skills and confidence were almost nonexistent. As things progressed, he began doing poorly in college and things started to go missing as he began stealing from family members and even friends of family members. We noticed strange things such as lying, personality changes, spoons missing, and jewelry gone.

About two to three years into this hell, his dad found Michael unresponsive in his home. Thank God he was revived with Narcan. However, we were left horrified. This was new territory for us. Despite having been through years of watching our kids be arrested, in jail, in and out of numerous rehabs, homelessness and so many other things, we had no experience with overdoses. The Michael we knew was slowly disappearing.

For ten years, Michael relapsed on and off, disgusted at himself more and more each time. Michael hated his life as an addict, and he hated the stigma it brought with it. During that time, he was in numerous rehabs, had over four to five overdoses, and multiple arrests from being under the influence while driving and police finding paraphernalia. He lost great jobs, had no permanent home, lost his license numerous times, and spent years on probation. Despite the falls, Michael constantly picked himself back up and worked hard at it. He got his certification as a personal trainer, working at several gyms over the years, and went on to coach football at his old high school. There always seemed to be a cotton candy cloud over Michael's head and he continuously landed on his feet again and again.

Each time, we would see the Michael that we knew and loved return to us. Over the years despite all his trials and losses, he would land amazing jobs making great money and meeting all the right people. His charisma, kindness, desire to make others happy, and energy kept him going and everything he touched seemed to turn to gold. He would turn a gym around that was failing within no time, always touching people's lives with his magnetic personality and leaving his impression. But rarely could Michael maintain his sobriety for more than nine months at a time. During those years, Michael sadly watched two of his best friends die of overdoses. He rarely showed any emotion during that time, although I know he was hurting.

Michael liked to stay very positive and happy. He disliked talking about or dealing with the reality of things. I believe the inability of admitting his disease and owning his recovery, without shame, was a large reason for the lack of continued sobriety.

Michael was so ashamed of his problem that he rarely told anyone, and if he did, he usually called it alcoholism. Heroin carried so much stigma that he did not dare mention it to anyone. When first out of rehab, he would go full force, going to meetings and working hard at sobriety, yet always hiding it from everyone outside of AA. After a few months, it would slowly fizzle out and you could feel his discouragement surfacing again. He often told me about the internal battle he would have with himself about using, even as everything in his life was going in the right direction. When he slipped, he would beg me to help him, crying about hating his struggle. He fought so hard whenever he would have a relapse.

A few years ago, Michael began a relationship with the love of his life. They moved in together and Michael wanted nothing more than to get married and have children with her. Although I wanted to believe he was doing well back then, the reality was he was using a good majority of that time. I just could not understand why with such an amazing job, his new life with his girlfriend and everything going in the right direction, he would jeopardize things again. Eventually he hit rock bottom and overdosed. That was about two years ago.

His girlfriend had had enough and ended the relationship, not looking back. He lost his job, his home, and his brand-new dog Leo whom he loved so dearly. He was devastated and brokenhearted. Watching his pain and brokenness during the first few months was extremely rough. He stayed strong, however, and finished up rehab. Again, landing on his feet with a great new job at a local gym. Despite not having his license, he managed to Uber to and from work, at a reasonable price. All the while he stayed positive, yet kept his secret from his boss and everyone else because of his shame. He built his relationship with that owner and helped turn the gym around. I would later hear from his boss that if it were not for Michael, he would be closed.

Michael focused heavily on his career during that time and eventually moved on to a progressive gym as their sales manager and trainer. It was fall of 2019, and he had about a year of sobriety, a great job, and seemed to be doing amazing, better than I had seen him in the past. I began taking classes at the gym and it was great to build an even stronger bond with him. He was always so proud to have me there. Every morning that I would walk in he would say, "Hi Mommy, I love you," and come leaping at me for a hug. His other students loved to watch the two of us every day. So many other mothers there would comment at how special our relationship was. He would constantly tease me while I was training, yet always make sure to look out for me and what I might need.

To this day, I still hear from those moms about how much they loved him and how special he was to them. They would talk often about his energy and how he never just walked in the room, he skipped in the room singing and dancing. He continued to entertain by singing his girl pop songs and showing the new fitness friends his singing skills. One thing that I heard time and time again after Michael passed away is that he had a knack in making everybody feel special as if they were his only client. I was told by many of his clients that he made a huge impact on their lives and is missed beyond words. The fitness community was devastated. I have never met anyone that had such a knack for making every single person feel like they were the best. Anyone that knew Michael would testify to that. He truly was very special in that way.

Over the years, Michael and I spoke almost every day. Many times, far more than once a day because as his ex-girlfriend would say, "He always overshared with you anyway." He always called himself a mama's boy, and he wasn't ashamed to say it. We would tease each other, him saying, "You're over momming," and I would say, "You're over sonning." If I did not call him back, he would call me and say, "Mom, you're a bad mom! You never call me back." All in fun, of course.

By the early months of 2020, I noticed a change. He was still showing up for work every day and on time, but something was different. He seemed less responsive to me, less loving, and more distant. His dad and I found out he had started drinking, which typically led to other things. We expressed our disappointment and that is one thing he hated...us being upset with him. He promised us he would stop drinking, because he did not want to make us feel sad.

In March, COVID hit and slowly things began closing in Ohio. They enforced the quarantine and Michael and his girlfriend decided they would be staying with me. In mid-March, his gym closed down. I watched the pressure start to intensify with stress increasing for the gym to stay afloat. That included driving sales and working towards virtual classes. I could see Michael becoming more and more anxious, pacing my house and very distracted. This was not Michael and yet when I tried to get him to talk about it, he would just say he was fine.

On Sunday, March 22, in the early morning, Michael, his girlfriend, and I went to the gym to get a workout in. All three of us left and went our separate ways. Michael advised me that since his girlfriend was going to go back to her house for the night, he was also going to go back to his house to stay. I asked him to please just stay with me, that we could have some bonding time, but he said he missed his bed and would be back the next day. I assumed he needed some alone time and was not too concerned. I texted with him that night a little and went to sleep with no issue.

On March 23 at seven a.m., I woke up to missed calls and texts from his girlfriend. She advised me that she and Michael were supposed to meet at the gym for a workout at five a.m. and he was to bring her computer with him, but he never called. She had been calling him for hours and he was not answering. Michael was never late for anything, especially in the early hours of the morning because he was up by four a.m. every day. I immediately went into panic mode because this was how it had happened in the past. He would go missing. I told her to get out to his house and I would get dressed and start calling the jails and the hospitals. She told me she was already on her way.

I hung up and started to get dressed when the phone rang again. She was screaming that he was dead. I fell to my knees in the bathroom screaming at the top of my lungs. NO! Over and over with my voice almost gone. I do not recall much after that, but somehow, I got a hold of my ex-husband and son. I recall trying to dial their numbers, but my hands were shaking so bad that I could not get it right. My son and his wife picked me up to take me out to the house where Michael lived. It was from that point on that were the most traumatizing moments of my life. No one should ever have to see their child dead and blue. My mind was racing...did he suffer? Who gave him these drugs? When did he die? How did he die? How long was my poor baby dead in that room all alone?

It has been almost four months now and I am a shell of my old self. There truly is only half of me left and certainly only half of my heart. I spent most of my life helping my children through childhood and then the adult years of addiction. What was I now? My "overmomming" job had been taken away from me and left me with bare bones. My older child Anthony is married now and just had his first child Gianna Michela, one month after Michael died. Gianna will never meet her Uncle Michael.

With Michael no longer here, there was no daily communication. That is all I knew. His brother Anthony is happily introverted. Anthony is amazingly mature and independent. He has truly grown into a man that I am so proud of today. I look at my son as my hero; he has survived a life of addiction despite many barriers and gone through more than anyone should ever have to. I respect his growth and autonomy and although he needs me, as his mom, he is very self-sufficient. So, what was I now? What will this new world of not being needed look like? How can I go on without my son?

I will never see my son get married, have children, grow professionally, and live a happy sober life. I feel ripped off, as I watch other parents brag about their children. I am so grateful for my son Anthony and I love him more than life itself, but he had a brother that I also loved, and I've lost him to murder. We are all suffering and all broken. And although Anthony does not speak of it often, I understand how truly painful this is for him.

Michael's death is not a case of an overdose. The toxicology report showed only carfentanyl and fentanyl in his system. Although Michael was aware of the risks, his disease got the best of him and he relapsed. He did not get what he thought he was getting and never stood a chance. This one relapse would cost him his life, because of illegal synthetic drugs that are coming into our country every day and that our government will do nothing about. Yes, my son had the disease of addiction, but he did not deserve to die at the hands of greedy drug traffickers and the lack of governmental responsibility to our children.

Michael was loved by so many that the outpour when he died was overwhelming. There's never a good time to lose your child, but during this virus and quarantine we were unable to have a proper burial and funeral. This made it hard for so many that wanted to be with me and my family and express their condolences. (I am not sure where we'll will be in the next year, but we're hoping to have his memorial of life, sometime in the near future.) During that time and even the months after, we would receive so much feedback about Michael and his character that it is honestly hard for me to summarize all of it. I can't honestly write everyone's comments here, but some of the sentiments that came up over and over, or simply stood out are as follows:

- When he asked how you are, he truly cared and wanted to know—not just because it is the natural thing to say.
- His genuine caring, infectious smile and HUGE and sincere hugs—I think I heard these qualities echoed over and over the most.
- What I remember and loved most about Michael was his amazing sarcasm and silliness that could make any room crack up at any given moment.
- As a fitness student of his, he challenged me but at the same time, led me to believe I could do it.
- Michael had such a contagious energy and optimism. I feel like he could put anyone in a good mood. He was so warm, kind and energetic—Michael was honestly one of a kind.
- He would just hug you like he truly cared—like a mom hug.
- Michael was so kind to me from day one. There was this ease of communication with him and there was absolutely no judgment.
- I loved the way Michael would say, 'Mommy' in front of the exercise class! He didn't care what anyone thought about how much he loved you.
- No one could ever make me laugh as hard as he could.
- He made everyone feel special and always lifted your attitude and spirit.
- I've never met anyone like your son; he stole everyone's heart. He was just that precious of a soul.

And finally, from a very close person in his life, "Michael always wanted to be everybody's everything, not realizing that he already was. Just not to himself."

There was always a feeling in the back of my mind that I could lose my son. I never truly believed it would happen, but I did often think about the chance that it could. I know that I need to go on for my family, my son and my new grandchild, but I am simply a shell of what

I was at this point. I no longer fear death at all and if it is a chance that I could possibly see my son again, I welcome it. As my best friend put it so eloquently, "You are basically homeless with no walls, no bed, and no furniture. You have got to figure out how to build those walls and what this house will look like, while you sleep on the floor for who knows how long."

I know that I will never get over what happened. I will never be the person I was prior to March 23. Michael has left behind so many broken hearts and so much pain and agony. He was loved by so many and I have seen many of their hearts broken after his death. Friends, family, co-workers, and students that loved him so dearly are now trying to pick up their own pieces.

I will leave you with this special text I received from my son Michael in 2017. He always tried so hard to make sure I knew how special he thought I was and that I knew how much he loved me. I am so fortunate to have thought enough to save this.

My son Michael's text from 12/22/17:

> *I love you so much mom like I really do. You're so hard on yourself, I mean I truly believe that you are a fantastic mother and always have been. I love dad with all my heart, too. But against all odds, I watched you pull yourself thru a nasty divorce with no education, mountains of debt and minimal support minus some financial aid from grandma and grandpa. You then attempted to finish school with multiple degrees and raise two kids all while only having the income of cutting hair and taking care of mentally challenged adults. During which you never missed one of my sports games or Anthony's concerts. You were always fucking there no matter how busy you were. You did everything that a mother should do and then some, all while dealing with so much more than your average parent and you did it ALONE. Oh yeah did I mention you also had to deal with helping your two sons battle thru their drug addictions. Your story is ridiculous, and you are my fucking hero. You sacrificed so much for us and I love you more than you know. You give me strength to be the best daily and if I end up*

amounting to half the human being that you are then my life will be great.

Michael's Mom,

CATHY L.
Mayfield Heights, Ohio

Joshua

FOREVER 33

"To know Josh was to love Josh," was an often-repeated theme at his celebration of life service. Josh was remembered as a loving, caring, and authentic person with a calm demeanor and a tender heart. He loved people unconditionally and was always interested in hearing their stories and sharing their struggles. He led NA meetings and encouraged so many people with their walk in sobriety.

Josh was an avid movie buff and loved animals, wanting to save every stray he came across. He was also passionate about his sports teams, especially the Dallas Cowboys and the Lakers. He was a phenomenal pitcher, making the All-Star team every year. He also played soccer, basketball, and golf; it was during his time on the golf team that he was first introduced to drugs. He struggled with drugs throughout high school and went to several rehab programs. We moved after his senior year, two hours away and Josh enrolled into community college and received an associate degree in Criminal Justice.

Josh then moved into an apartment with his uncle and best friend and found full-time work. It was during this time that he started using pain pills and Xanax, which would eventually lead to a heroin addiction. He entered several rehabs from this time and could only stay sober for six months before he relapsed.

In 2016, he really wanted to get off drugs and went to rehab in Wilmington in April. He completed a thirty-day program and IOP and was at a sober living house. He would relapse there and go back into rehab three more times over a six-month period. Something finally stuck and he was able to get a job and stay sober for almost a year. He lived within a mile of a local car wash and rode his bike to work. It was not his ideal job, but he was sober and being responsible. He met someone and told me he was in love for the first time in his life. This worried me a bit because I was afraid he would relapse if she broke up with him, which is what happened. Luckily, after about three months, he was able to get a scholarship into treatment on his own and went back in. He was able to get his job back and continued working and he got back into meetings.

Family was very important to Josh and he often apologized for his drug use and the effect it had on his siblings and other family members. Though Josh tried many times to overcome his substance use, he got more motivated when he started working the steps with his sponsor, Matt. After a year of sobriety, Matt helped him get a job with Ashley Furniture and he was consistently a top salesperson and very proud of his accomplishments. Josh was able to maintain his sobriety for almost two years, largely because of his strong relationships with his "fam bam," a group of guys in recovery who met each week. He was doing so good, had his own place, and was making good money.

Even with all of his success, Josh was feeling overwhelmed with anxiety. He felt confident he could manage a low dose of anti-anxiety medication, but within a month Josh relapsed and checked himself into rehab yet again. He checked himself into to rehab on Super Bowl Sunday. He was a huge sports fan and for him to miss that spoke volumes. He hated his addiction. He told me "I need to get to the point where I don't think about drugs. I want a family, I want kids." He told me and his manager that he had stopped thinking about drugs at this time. We believed him and felt that he really had. He left rehab before he could get a Vivitrol shot because he needed to get back to work. He was unable to get that shot because the place he went didn't honor his private insurance.

He had made plans to stay with my brother in another town until he could get the shot on a Friday. He wanted to leave so he wouldn't use. He was supposed to leave that Sunday, but never did. His car was gassed up and ready to leave on Sunday. He called me Saturday night telling me he was going to beat this, and I could hear optimism and hope in his voice yet again. I called him Sunday morning and his phone went straight to voicemail. I somehow knew he was gone. I called his roommate and a friend to check on him and he was gone. I know Josh and I know in his mind he thought this would be the "last time." Toxicology report revealed fentanyl.

Josh tried so very hard, because no one worked harder to be sober than he did. He hated being addicted and even described what it was like. I would explain it as being trapped in hell. Watching him spiral out of control was the hardest thing I have experienced. I was in a constant state of fear even when he was sober, because I knew a relapse could happen any time. If Josh was using, that little green dot on Facebook, showing he was online, was sometimes the only way I knew he was alive. It may not seem significant to many, but it meant there was still hope. It was hard for me to block him, which I had to do at times. I had a friend who was a substance abuse counselor tell me to make sure to treat every conversation that I had with him as if it were our last. That was very hard to hear, but so true. I am thankful that Josh was not the type of person that belittled me or stole from me. He didn't have a criminal record, with the exception of some speeding and seatbelt tickets. He had a gentle soul that was loved by many!

I am at peace with the fact that there was nothing more I could have done for him. I loved Josh more than life itself. My heart is heavy from the crushing reality that I can never see, hear, or hug my first-born son again. But I know, without a doubt, that Josh would want me to live my life to the fullest and that's how I choose to honor him.

If I know now what I didn't know then, it's this: No one can change an addict, until they want to change. No matter how much you want it, it doesn't matter. They need to be the one to get themselves into programs and find their way. In the beginning of his addiction, I had no way to know how to navigate. Everyone else is quick to give their opinion for sure. It is so hard to watch someone self-destruct. Josh later told me thank you for not always catching him while he was falling. It wasn't until he started the recovery himself that he succeeded. We had almost three years of sobriety with Josh and I am so grateful. He had his own place, car, and great job and money in the bank. Even with all that, the addiction would never go away. I will always wonder if this last relapse would have led to a lifetime of recovery. Many people told me that when you experience that much progress/success in a short period of time, a relapse would be inevitable, and his true recovery would begin after that. I will never know, but I am so grateful that I was able to have my son back the last few years of his life.

I always told Josh I loved him and would be there for him when he was bettering himself. When he was using, I would take his calls and even call him. I always let him know I loved him and that he had a purpose in life. I know now what the purpose was. During the last three years of his life, he developed so many friendships in the recovery community where he lived. He inspired many people to get clean and was always there to listen to people's stories. He was many people's sobriety cheerleader. Upon his death, I received hundreds of messages about how Josh impacted their life.

Here are a few of those messages:

Cecily: Josh was always willing to do anything that he could to help another person, he didn't know a stranger. It would be impossible to pick just one incident. Josh was constantly bringing home strays...some were animals, some were human. He had a knack for finding those in need and a heart that was so big that he couldn't resist giving them a helping hand. Whether he was offering food, a warm bed, or a ride; Josh was always willing to give, whatever he had to offer to help a human or animal in need.

Karen: I loved that he always believed in me and made me laugh, even on my worst days. He always was so interested in what I had going on and was so caring and considerate of how I was doing, no matter what was going on with him. You never meet people like that. Most people are only concerned with themselves and how you can help them, but not Josh. Josh would always make me feel better and help me get into a solution. He would tell me multiple ways in which I could get through my problems, reassure me that I would be okay and tell me how awesome I was. He was ALWAYS my biggest cheerleader. He was so loving and would do anything in the world for the people he loved.

Chad and I first met Josh in 2016 and stayed close when we all lived in Wilmington. We had the privilege of all being together again this last time around. I was in detox on Super Bowl Sunday and had just been separated from my husband, so my heart breathed a sigh of relief when I saw Josh walk in. My first thought was "I'm so surprised Josh chose THIS night to check in, because I just know he has money riding on the football game". He wrapped me in one of his famous hugs and I felt so grateful I got to share the path to recovery with him  once again. "To know Josh, was to love Josh." I know every single person would agree with me on that. I am sure you are realizing what an impact Josh had on those around him. Josh, Age 33; Lived with addiction for fifteen years.

Joshua's Mom,

WENDY L.
Wilmington, North Carolina

Alexa

FOREVER 28

Alexa is my beautiful daughter. I use the word "beautiful" often when I describe her because not only was Alexa stunningly beautiful, physically, but she was so very beautiful on the inside. So kind to others, compassionate, as well as empathetic. It truly bothered her when she'd hear of someone, somewhere suffering.

Alexa was two and a half years old when Jeremy was born. She couldn't wait to have a baby brother of her own. She wasn't jealous of him when he came home from the hospital, not once. Lexi, as we called her, was so loving and always wanted to play with him and make him laugh. They remained so close over the years.

Starting at two years old, we would visit her grandparent's farm. She "helped" when the ducks and chicks were hatching and were ready to come out of the incubator, and she was so gentle when she touched them. The horses, when Alexa first saw those horses, she fell in love. Alexa had her own little grain bucket and muck boots, so she could help feed the horses. I watched my little girl from the deck above as she walked around the pasture and between the horses to dump a bit of grain into their buckets. I could hear her firmly tell them, "BACK" as she put her free hand out to warn them to get away so she could feed them. All seven of those horses listened to her and moved away and waited for their grain.

From kindergarten through second grade, Alexa insisted on wearing dresses, tights, and nice little patten leather shoes; always a "girlie girl." At five years old, she was in dance class and all the little girls were lady-bugs for the recital. By the middle of their song and dance, all the little ladybugs watched Alexa and followed her lead. Everything she attempted, she excelled at. She loved school, loved writing stories, and was proud of herself for her grades. She truly was a delight to be around. And I was so proud of her, because she always did her best at everything. And she was kind, she made friends easily. Teachers would tell me at conferences how sweet and caring she was to all the kids.

When she learned about children not having enough to eat and about their poor living conditions, she was so bothered. She thought how sad it was that there could be children in other places without enough to eat, or a warm comfortable bed to sleep in. As she learned more about the world, she wrote papers and passionately spoke about injustices and how she wanted to help to figure them out, so that no one suffered. She was deeply passionate about reading about the Holocaust and how there could be such cruelty of humanity.

Throughout the years, horses were her love. In middle school, she took horseback riding lessons, then decided she wanted to be in shows with her horse. Her very first show, she won a red ribbon and she was so excited. She continued to show horses and received mostly red and blue ribbons. She was in her glory.

Alexa thrived in school until she was a sophomore in high school. A new boy from California had moved into our small town in Maine. Before long, this boy was calling Alexa. They would stay on the phone for hours. I watched her talk to him with sparkles in her eyes and the biggest smile on her face. To her, he was Prince Charming, her first boyfriend. I wish I had known earlier that it was all an act. He knew how to "work" a girl. He told her how beautiful she was and how lucky he was to be talking to her on the phone. This went on for several weeks, maybe months. He bought her cards and wrote about his undying love for her. Lexi was clearly infatuated. She went out on several dates with this boy and was falling in love with him. She told me how good he made her feel, told her she's so beautiful, and how much he liked her.

A month into their relationship, Lexi was found to be drunk at a school dance. She was with her boyfriend and some girlfriends and their parents were called to pick up their children just as I was. I talked to the other parents and the consensus was that this sort of thing happens around this age and it's "no big deal." Myself, growing up in an alcoholic home and understanding the genetic factors involved, I thought it was a very big deal. I talked to Alexa, explained that it was not ok for her to continue to drink. She cried. She appeared remorseful. I thought everything would be fine. Alexa was grounded for two weeks for the incident.

One time, Lexi came down to the kitchen in her robe while I was cooking dinner. She said she needed to get something from the garage. After a few seconds, I looked out the front window. Lexi had worn her clothes under her robe, took her robe off, got into a car in our driveway, and the driver took off. Things like this were happening more frequently. The lying was a constant. But still, you want to believe your children. Believe that they wouldn't lie to you. Even though you know it's not true. Lexi was staying after school to try out for tennis. I later found out that she didn't stay at the school for tennis. She left the school with her boyfriend and his buddy. The lies had started. Lexi's boyfriend was telling lies. She was telling lies. I'd forbid Alexa to see him, then find them together. It was one thing after another. Time and time again, the boyfriend told her to be ready for him to pick her up at seven. She spent hours putting on her make-up, doing her hair, picking her outfit. The boyfriend doesn't show up at seven. She waits and waits, becoming more upset, as the time ticks away. She cries. Then a call, the boyfriend is on his way. Get ready. She'd dry her eyes, become giddy, then wait. Sometimes he eventually showed up, sometimes not. Sometimes cheats. Sometimes doesn't.

Alexa swore there was no drinking or marijuana with her boyfriend. I had explained my worries many times about alcoholism and drug abuse. I trusted her, even though she had begun lying so very easily to me. I have only ever found heroin cotton once. I found several needle caps. I noticed my spoons kept disappearing. I found cigarettes many times. But never found any pills, marijuana, powder, nothing. She hid it very well. Believe me, if there is a reason to be suspicious of drugs, it's ALWAYS the right thing to go through their things, that's just my opinion.

What I found out, much later, was that Alexa's boyfriend brought her to places where there was not only marijuana and alcohol, there was every other drug, except for heroin and crystal meth. Once the cheating started, and he was continually late picking her up, as soon as she got to the party or to wherever they went, Lexi would head for the alcohol and drugs. She didn't want to feel that heartache, the longing for the boy she loves who is abusing her. We talked about why her addictions all started. There was an incident when she was fourteen that hurt Alexa terribly and it was her cheating boyfriend "messing" with her head that introduced her to drinking and drugs. She learned that getting "messed up" is better than your heart hurting, in that moment.

I brought Alexa to counselors and doctors in attempts to help her to resolve her issues of heartache from her boyfriend and anything else that may have been going on. She never wanted to talk to counselors. She minimized her emotional issues and her taste for drugs and alcohol. She refused honesty. After a year and a half, the boyfriend moved away. I thought Alexa's problems were all over.

Was I wrong! The summer after her junior year in high school, she worked at a restaurant. She was getting into minor fender benders, getting pulled over by the police, sneaking out of the house while we were all sleeping, and I suspected using drugs and alcohol. But she was such a good liar. God, I hate to say that about my daughter. But it's true; addicts tell the best lies. She convinced me that there was no way she would ever try any other drugs. Of course, she did. Her addiction was already in control.

I found a treatment facility for teens in Utah with an equestrian program. Five weeks later, I brought her home, because Lexi had been given a tour of the horse barn once and she wasn't able to spend time with them. Her passion was still horses and I felt she would benefit from their program. I brought her home.

Two days later, a week before Christmas, I brought Lexi to a program for teens, in our state, where she begged, cried to me, and swore she didn't need to be there. After an hour and a half of telling her she needs help, I said, "I love you and you need to stay here." She looked at me in disbelief. As desperately as I wanted to bring her home with me, I just knew I couldn't. Again, my heart broke...and hers did too.

Lexi stayed for six months. She spent Christmas there and we couldn't bring her gifts or visit. Every Saturday there was family group therapy from nine a.m. to one p.m. All the parents attended, their children as well. We learned about addiction and what we could all do to help our addict children. We learned about the seriousness and urgency, that the kids there all needed to stop the drugs and how their lives could be successful, and they could feel happiness.

That summer she lived and worked with her aunt two hours away from us. Things were looking up for Lexi. She waitressed and spent time with her aunt and met a boy, three years older than she, who was a deep-sea fisherman. She went to community college and spent time with her new boyfriend. Things seemed great for her. She went through that school year seemingly "fine."

The next summer, while visiting before moving into the college dorms for her sophomore year, she told me she had something to tell me. She made me promise not to get mad at her. I was thinking to myself, "How bad could this be?" And then, "I tried heroin." Immediately I became upset. I had no idea that heroin was even around anymore and the only thing I did know about heroin was that it was around in the seventies and it killed people. I cried, begged, yelled, "Don't ever touch that ever, ever again. It can kill you." To Alexa, I was overreacting.

Lexi moved to the dorms, made the greatest friend she had ever had, and enjoyed the college life. She made the Dean's List. But when she came home for the summer, something was clearly wrong. I didn't know what. But something was wrong. Alexa told me she was sick. She explained that she had been using heroin. She said she had met a "friend" while at school. She had him inject her with heroin for the first time. And now she felt that she needed help because she was getting so sick when she stayed away from using. She felt so ashamed. I felt the pain in her eyes. Still, I didn't understand the pull of heroin, the physical addiction. The mental torture. The addiction was clearly in control at this point.

We brought Alexa to outpatient rehab. Her birthday was during her second week there. For her birthday, after she came home, we had dinner and cake and presents. Lexi's eyes looked different to me. I asked her about it. She told me she was taking Suboxone to help her with her heroin "thing." I believed her. For the next several hours, Lexi and I sat out on the deck and talked. She increasingly sounded more "different" and when I asked, she said, "Mom, I just feel normal. That's all Suboxone does." I remained suspicious but didn't say anything further. We all went to bed. I awoke at two a.m. with a feeling that I needed to check on Lexi. I brushed it off, but the feeling kept at me. I went in to check on her and she was on her bed slouched over, her sketch pad on her lap and her pen in hand. I asked her what she was doing. She didn't answer. I went to her, shook her. She didn't respond. I ran to the phone, screamed for my husband, and started CPR.

As the paramedics walked into Lexi's room, I looked up. Walking in behind them was Jeremy, a junior in high school, watching me desperately pumping on his sister's chest. Alexa was whisked away to the hospital. Once we arrived, the doctor told us that had I not gone in to check Alexa, five minutes later she would have died. She was crying, apologizing, clearly in shock herself. She remained in the hospital for five days so that tests could be done on her heart. It was then that we learned Alexa had damaged her heart using so much cocaine. I read in Alexa's sketchbook, after she passed, that she overdosed on methadone and it was given to her by a fellow rehab patient.

Alexa's next two years were horrible for her and for our family. She used heroin regularly, then felt the guilt and shame, felt sick, and wanted to quit again. Her dad and I had brought her to several hospital site rehabs, halfway houses, outpatient rehabs, counseling, continuously over the next couple of years. It was during that time that she had written in her journal, "I'm addicted. And it's disgusting." I didn't read that until after she passed.

A friend of hers talked her into trying methadone to get off of heroin. He had been a heavy user and was doing well on methadone. She went to the methadone clinic and that was the first time that she felt she had a chance at getting clean. For the next roughly four years, every day Lexi would be waiting at the methadone clinic door for it to open. She awakened each morning filled with self-hatred, remembering her behaviors while using, remorse for hurting her family, and then she would start to have withdrawal symptoms.

For four years, Lexi was responsible, held down jobs, and started school again.

On her last Christmas, 2017, she totaled her brother's car driving to the methadone clinic. She should have died. She went for seven miles on the highway, hit the guardrails then veered almost off the right side of the highway, then back to the left hitting the guardrail. There were several calls to 9-1-1. Finally, she went off the highway, through trees and smashed into a stone wall. She had to go to jail, because she was clearly under the influence. Her dad wasn't allowed to pick her up from jail until the evening, it was Christmas. She was arrested for driving under the influence. That's when we found out she was using cocaine every day and Xanax and alcohol on top of the methadone.

We all talked to her about the need to stop drugs. She agreed but wasn't going to rehab. She refused. I had no idea what to do. One thing I did know for sure was that she was going to die if something wasn't done for her. So, in February I went to the court and petitioned the judge to put Alexa into a locked rehab. She had been arrested and brought in front of the judge. I explained her drug use and my fear that without a locked rehab she would die. Lexi was so angry. She said she wasn't doing any drugs except methadone from the clinic. Then I told the judge that she was doing other drugs too. The Judge told her he would get all her drug screens from the methadone clinic and if she had ever tested positive for drugs, he would send her. She refused to release the methadone records. So, the judge said that she either give her permission to get her drug screens or she would go to rehab. What's it going to be? She screamed at me, said she hated me, I was dead to her, how could I do this to her? It broke my heart, yet again.

Lexi was brought to the rehab, and on her own decided she wanted to get off methadone. Two months later her dad brought her home. The first thing she did when she walked in the door and saw me was break down and cry. We hugged and cried, and she thanked me for making her go to rehab. She came home with one medication, mirtazapine, to help her sleep. We spent the next month gardening, cooking, shopping at our favorite stores: TJ Maxx and the Salvation Army. Then she drove down to Virginia to live with her boyfriend, the merchant marine. They were so perfect together. She loved him so much. Lexi came home to visit, twice, that summer and was so healthy. She brought her Yorkies each time and walked them every day, talked to her brothers about the importance of believing in themselves and that they can do anything they set their minds to.

Alexa came home one more time in early September. She was due in court on September 21 for the Christmas accident; she was so scared. She had been arrested many times throughout her years of using. She was afraid she wasn't going to get off this time and she'd have to go to jail. On Saturday, we spent the day shopping. Then home to make fruit salad. Once I pulled into our driveway, Lexi said she was going on a quick bike ride. Her dad made her wait so he could put air in the tires. She kept saying, "Dad hurry up, it's not a big deal, you don't have to put air in the tires," but he made her wait. Then she took off on my bike. Lexi was back home in less than ten minutes and said she had forgotten her phone and didn't feel like going after all. Her eyes looked funny...and for a second, I thought heroin and said, "Are you ok? Your eyes are kind of funny." Alexa rolled her eyes, annoyed like she always was whenever I questioned her...and she said, "Mom, stop. I'm not doing anything bad." I felt bad for questioning her. Together, we washed our faces, then kissed and said good night. I received a text from her a few minutes later, with a picture of a pair of socks saying, Do you want these?" That was my last text from Alexa. EVER.

Lexi's dad went to wake her at ten thirty a.m. A few seconds later: "CALL 9-1-1, CALL 9-1-1!" I ran to her room...my daughter was laying on the floor in her shorts and t-shirt. She looked like she was sleeping. I felt her wrist...she had no pulse. She was warm. Chris immediately put his hands on her chest. Pump, pump, pump continuously. I looked up and there at the door was Jacob, sixteen years old, watching his sister in horror. Just as the paramedics took over, I felt Lexi's pulse beat.

The next morning, the doctor came to see us. He wheeled a table with a computer on it and showed us Lexi's brain scan. He pointed out all the white. Her brain was almost all white, except for her brainstem. He told us that the white meant there was no brain activity; there was no hope for any recovery. He said if she were to pull out of this, she wouldn't be able to see, talk, eat or move her arms and legs. I kept asking why, what if, are you sure? Then he said, "Out of 700 scans, I've seen...Lexi's is the worst."

NO HOPE AT ALL. NONE. OUR LEXI WAS NOT GOING TO BE OK. EVER AGAIN. NEVER.

I stayed in the hospital for three nights with Lexi after our family left. She was hooked up to life support. It was beyond heartbreak; beyond devastation for me to know she was going to die. I talked to Lexi and I massaged her amazingly soft skin; I counted her freckles; traced her nose with my fingers, and her ears; taking it all in and etching it in my mind, so I would never forget. I rubbed lotion on her feet and legs, amazed at how beautiful she was. I talked to Lexi and I put Chapstick on her lips. And I hung pictures of Alexa up on the walls and I told Lexi stories. I wanted everyone to know that my daughter is dying and yes, she is an addict. And she is the most amazing daughter I could have ever asked for. And I am proud of her kindness and compassion.

On Lexi's last night, I helped the nurse wash Lexi's hair and then she put it in the most beautiful braids. Then the nurse asked me, "Would you like to get in bed with your daughter?" I hadn't even thought about that, but "Yes, I would love to." Two nurses together moved Alexa over in her bed and they helped me to crawl in beside her. It was almost three a.m. I had been counting down the hours until I had to say goodbye to my girl. I snuggled into Lexi's neck and I cried and cried. I told her I was so sorry I couldn't help her with this heroin addiction. Those last hours, I was so grateful to be able to spend time with my child, thinking of the many parents who don't get to see their child at all before they pass. Some parents find their children already gone. And I got to see my child sleeping, warm, alive. I had her to myself for three whole nights.

At eleven a.m., family started arriving at Lexi's hospital bed. I stayed in bed with Lexi until it was time to move her bed. They prepped all the cords and tubes and plugs; they worked to prepare to move Lexi's bed. At 11:40 a.m., it was time to go. Lexi's aunts, uncles, grandparents, brothers, her boyfriend, and her dad and I surrounded Lexi's bed. I leaned down and buried my face in her neck. I stayed there as we walked Lexi down the hall and to the elevator. I told her I was so proud of her; I love her, and I was sorry. Our family recited together, "The Prayer for Protection," as they walked beside Lexi to the elevator doors.

I felt an arm on my back and I knew I had to say "goodbye." How do I say goodbye to my daughter? I kissed her one last time and told her I loved her. She was wheeled into the elevator. As the door closed to the elevator, my heart shattered into a million pieces.

Five hours later, I received a call. It was Lexi's nurse. She said, "I want you to know that Lexi is a hero. Both surgeries have gone very well. Your daughter saved two women by giving them her liver and her lungs."

Lexi loved us so much and she tried to shield us from the pain of seeing her addicted. Her journals are heartbreaking. She expressed her pain with poetry and sketches and after reading them, I feel like I know exactly what it feels like to be her. She was so full of self-loathing and so critical of herself. She was in so much pain. All because heroin destroyed everything good in her life. And then it killed her.

As I sit here and write, almost three years later, the pain is just as strong. I long just to see her one more time. To hear her voice. To touch her beautiful skin. The pain from her loss will be with me until the day I die. I've spent most of this time existing. I'm not sure how to live yet. I do, however, know that I will continue to share my  Lexi's story in hopes that kids and parents both will believe me when I say: "If it could happen to our children, it can happen to yours too." Please believe that it's not "just" heroin anymore. There are pills being sold as Xanax and Percocet that have fentanyl in them. All it takes is a tiny sprinkle of fentanyl into a pill or into cocaine and other drugs to kill your child. Please take it from all of us, please. It breaks my heart over and over again, whenever I hear of another child dying from fentanyl and/or heroin and the unimaginable pain that comes with it.

Alexa's Mom,

Susan L.
Brunswick, Main

Dustin

FOREVER 29

I always said that my nightmare was one phone call away. This is my story about how I know that to be true.

Parents shouldn't think about the possibility of their children dying at any moment, but they do...

Parents shouldn't dream about their children overdosing alone in an abandoned house, but they do...

Parents shouldn't fear getting a midnight call saying their nightmare has come true, but they do...

I know they do because I am that parent who lived daily with that fear for the past eleven years.

I am a mother of three young men. I have lived a cyclical fear that went up and down over the past eleven years, often requiring my own counseling for uncontrollable anxiety stemming from self-guilt.

I would ask if I was simply not good enough. I worried that my failures started my child's path.

This American health crisis takes lives every day. I have witnessed the life it stole before it took my son.

My son grew up in the Pacific Northwest and never wanted to leave.

His wild youth and his quest for adventure brought him closer to addiction and that battle led him to the respected rehabilitation facilities in Del Ray Beach, Florida.

My son saw how the promise of sobriety was often nothing more than an insurance scheme that did more harm than good. My son fought through the dirty process and proved to be a success story.

My son won his fight. He got a job, a girlfriend, and he fell in love. He lived in the Florida sun, got a dog, earned a driver's license, joined a boat club, and amazed all of us with his Snapchats on boats and jet skis.

Dusty finally moved into a one-bedroom apartment and started to accumulate the essentials to live on his own in Boynton Beach.

That was seventy days ago...

On Feb 5, 2020 at 1:05 a.m., my son lost his battle with addiction and the phone call that I had been fearing became my reality. It proved that my nightmare was really one call away.

Dustin's Mom,

DARLENE L.
Bethlehem, Pennsylvania

Brandon

Brandon made his grand entrance into this world on June 8, 1993. He was born with a full head of black hair that stuck up everywhere. I nicknamed him "Bug" because he reminded me of a fuzzy caterpillar. That nickname would follow him his entire life, much to his displeasure as he grew older. He was your typical happy child growing up. He started playing hockey when he was four-years-old and was a gifted athlete.

Middle school came and he was that guy all the girls wanted to date and that guy everyone wanted on their team. Around eighth grade, he started skateboarding. He went from wearing nice American Eagle clothing to more skateboard style clothing. His friends started to change. It was around this time we caught him with cigarettes and later a bag of weed. We did the typical parent lecture and he assured us that he wouldn't do it anymore. We noticed he'd come back from skateboarding with glassy red eyes, obviously high. He lost interest in his beloved hockey. He avoided spending time with the family and when he did, he would have headphones on.

In high school, things really started to change. We got a call one night from one of Brandon's friends stating Brandon had a seizure and they called an ambulance. We went to the hospital and he seemed fine other than being tired. The CT scan was negative. These random seizures would continue. A neurologist placed him on Keppra to prevent the seizures. Little did we know the seizures were from benzo with-drawals. He had started snorting Xanax and taking Klonopin. We have no idea where he was getting them. I felt so helpless when he had a seizure. Watching him convulse and foam at the mouth was horrible. After he recovered from one of the seizures, he was so disoriented that he started swinging at me and our other son had to restrain him.

During Brandon's high school days, he managed to get two minor possession charges. Of course, as parents we chalked it up to teenage behavior. As parents, we hired an attorney both times. So, we incurred those costs, trusting that it was just teenage drinking. He graduated, but barely, with us helping him do most of his work—always thinking we were showing love and support. He always seemed to have a hard time holding a job. He was fired from several jobs, for poor performance. He, of course, always had some excuse as to why.

Brandon got arrested for a DUI. Apologizing and promising that it wouldn't happen again, we paid the attorney fees, court costs, and all the fees for the classes that he was required to take. Our attorney warned him that usually people get a second DUI right after the first one. Brandon assured us he never wanted to go back to jail. Well, we hadn't even finished with court for the first one and he gets a second. More jail time and our car was impounded. More court fees, attorney fees, rehab, AA classes, extended probation, and a home alcohol moni-toring system. We noticed he had strange sleeping patterns. He would be up all night and slept all day. He started eating nothing but junk food and constantly wanted candy bars. I would always check on him before I left for work to be sure he was okay. We noticed burn holes in his clothing and he wore hoodies all the time. Several times, we found him slumped over sleeping on the toilet or holding a plate of food. He said he was just tired. We noticed that all of his friends, since elementary school, disappeared and there seemed to be new friends that appeared.

We heard from Brandon's friends that he would get drunk, start fights, and cause a scene. Brandon started to have bouts of asthma attacks. Mind you, he never had lung issues growing up. One incident had him in ICU for a week for pulmonary failure. Pulmonary failure at twenty-two years old? We noticed scabs all over his arms, neck, back, and chest, and he explained them away, that he had popped some zits. We left the hospital that night knowing our suspicions were correct. We tore his room apart and only found folded up keno tickets. No drugs. I googled what that might be—heroin, no, not Brandon. He may be using drugs, but never heroin. He's terrified of needles. Of course, he denied using anything.

Christmas time rolls around and he wants to go hang out with a friend and says he will be back in a bit. I tell him, "Brandon, don't do anything stupid. You have missed the past two Thanksgivings and Christmases from being in jail or rehab." He laughs and leaves. Not two hours later, I get a collect call from jail. He is drunk. Mind you, it's only been two hours since he left. He is yelling, wanting to be bailed out. I hang up on him, as I am heartbroken and pissed. Another Christmas ruined. Now he has a third DUI, a felony in Michigan, and he was caught with drugs and drug paraphernalia. The car that we bought him to replace the one that he flipped upside down in a creek bed while drunk was impounded, and it was damaged. Apparently, he was seen swerving all over the road, hitting curbs and driving on flat tires.

We avoid Brandon's phone calls for a few days, until he sobers up and is halfway logical. I remind him that he is now going to be a felon and will never get his license back. I let him know that after rolling his previous car, he was lucky he caught a break, because we arrived before the police. (They tried to give him a break by not arresting him that night because he was already in our car.) Did I mention what fools we have been? The night he rolled his car, we climbed into the creek bed to hide the beer cans before the police came. Brandon was pissed because we wouldn't go back in and look for his phone and punched my husband in the face. This is the thank you we got.

We get the usual, "I'm sorry, I know I f***ed up again." Once he is released, he goes back to rehab. By this time, he knows how to work the system. He knows that's what the judge will want to see. We would find out, later, he would always shoot up before going to rehab and

393

then on the day he got out. Court day comes and I'm hit with watching them take our son away, in handcuffs, after being sentenced to five years in prison. No, not jail but prison. Again, we get the collect calls, blaming us and that we knew he would go to prison. After a week, he settles down and now begins the manipulation for ordering supplies and food from the commissary. (Which they trade for drugs or whatever else they want.) By now, we are over $20,000 in debt due to court costs, attorney fees, hospital stays, classes, and two wrecked cars. I hate to say it, but I was always able to sleep better when he was in jail. By this time, I have spent four years of sleeping with my phone, driving around at night trying to find him, and constantly getting up at all hours to be sure he is breathing. My husband would check on him before he left for work, I would check on him before I left for work, I would text him randomly during the day and check Facebook to see if he had been active.

Brandon would always say I liked to have him locked up; I would say I liked to have him alive. He goes to prison and qualified for boot camp, which was like being in the military. If he graduated, he would be out in six months. He graduated boot camp top of his class. He is now a felon at twenty-four and on parole. He has no driver's license. We have to drive him to meetings, drug testing, parole report, and seven days a week to the methadone clinic. Word to the wise: the methadone clinic is a joke. Dealers wait in the parking lot and they just make more drug connections. My husband, Rick, comes home from work one day and is talking to me on the phone, and I ask him if he has checked on Brandon. He checked while I was on the phone.

Rick said, "He's fine, hun," and then said, "Oh my God, no, he's passed out with a needle in his arm." I said, "That's it, he's got to go." Rick was able to wake him and told him to get dressed. Brandon gets in the car and they are headed to the rehab. They are almost there and Rick notices Brandon is now slumped forward, drooling, and not breathing. He runs into the rehab for help. They give him two shots of Narcan and nothing. They pull him out of the car and give him two more shots and he starts to come around. Meanwhile, I am on the phone and Rick tells me he stopped breathing in the car and is on the ground in a parking lot and EMS has just gotten there. I leave work and head to the hospital. Brandon tells us that when Rick went upstairs, he snorted the rest of the heroin so we wouldn't find it. He violated his parole and I am hoping for jail again. Nope, back to rehab.

He comes home from rehab and we can tell he, again, went because he had to, not because he wanted to. He's home for a month and seems to be doing well. He got his job back, washing dishes. (His boss was always so supportive and never lost faith in him.) My bedroom is across from his and one night we both said goodnight. Not five minutes later, I hear him fall. I run into his room expecting to find him having a seizure. Instead, I find him lying on the floor with a needle in his arm. He is blue, foaming at the mouth, and is making the death snore. If you have never heard this sound, I pray you never do. I yell for my husband to call 9-1-1. I am shaking him, giving him a sternal rub, turning him on his side to get the saliva out of his mouth, all the time yelling, "Brandon, please don't leave me." I begin to give him rescue breathing and CPR. By the grace of God, he opens his eyes. In what seemed like forever, EMS shows up, as well as the police.

I begin trying to find any drugs in his room to give to the officer. He instantly stops me and tells me not to touch any of the little envelopes, as fentanyl can go right through the paper and kill me. I ask him if they can bring a drug detection dog into the house to search for any drugs. He states that they do not do that, as the drugs are killing the dogs when they sniff it. After they leave, we begin tearing his room and our house apart. Part of the conditions for Brandon to return home was that no drugs were to be brought into our house. We find pills, liquor bottles, needles, and more heroin hidden in the basement ceiling tiles and in CD and DVD cases. We pulled all his dresser drawers out and under that little space between the floor and the drawers is something out of movie. Spoons, needles, keno tickets, plastic baggies, more pills, more liquor bottles, my chore boy pads, his asthma inhaler (which had been turned into a device for smoking heroin and crack). We are even more heartbroken; I am numb and in shock from finding my son's para-phernalia. To this day, I will never get those sights out of my head. Brandon goes to live with my ninety-one-year-old mother, as after what I witnessed and found, I cannot have him at home any longer. It was the toughest thing we ever did. We had convinced ourselves that we could keep him safe being at home with us and found out differently very quickly.

Brandon eventually gets an apartment. Things go great moving him in; a friend of his from high school came out and handed us an extra key as the apartment used to be his girlfriend's. That key was my comfort. I could sneak over when he was at work and nose through stuff. We were so proud of him that we even paid his first month's rent to show him that we supported his sobriety. Our sneaking over would only turn up beer or alcohol, at least for a while. He gets his income tax return and this is where the downward spiral really begins. We notice that the sores all over his face and neck are all returning. He's missing work and nodding off at work. He calls off work one night and we decide to go over. We peek in his apartment window and it looks like a drug house. We call the police and they cannot do anything. We let ourselves in and a shit storm ensues.

Needless to say, he loses the apartment and my mother takes him back in because she is not going to let her grandson be homeless. She has no idea the seriousness of what we are dealing with. She falls and ends up in a nursing home for two months and he is alone there in her home. We stop over to check on things and find him and his girlfriend passed out on the couch, needle and straw on the table. Disgusted, we leave. A few hours later, we decide to go back over because now we are pissed. We get there and he isn't home. Remember, he has no driver's license. He never gave me a key to the house either. He shows up to find us inside with the doors locked. He bangs on the door and then calls to say he's outside. We tell him he is not allowed back into the house. We notice that he is high, but this is a different high, not a heroin high. We call the police and explain the situation and they try so hard to arrest him to help us out, but he's compliant and has lived there for more than three months. We are told we have to legally evict him. We decide that it is time for an intervention. It goes well but he does not want to go into treatment until the next morning. Out of fear, we convince him to stay at a local treatment center just for the night. Reluctantly he agrees. We get him to treatment and things are different this time. He is threat-ening to beat a guy's ass for stealing his food and his attitude is different. We inform him that he can't go back to my mom's when he is released. He, of course, finds a buddy at rehab and they leave treatment early.

Before, Brandon would always follow through with treatment. He apparently is staying with this guy for a week or so and calls and says he was jumped and beaten up while walking into rehab and has no ID or anything. Somehow, he finds a friend here in town to move in with. The kid's mother will let him live there and pay rent, so he goes back to work and the same thing starts all over again.

I would text him several times a day to be sure he was okay and check Facebook to see if he was active so I knew he was alive. One day after texting all day and calling with no answer, we go over to the house where he is staying. The lady lets us in and we head for Brandon's room in the basement. He is sleeping. I can tell by his skin he is back using and he denies it. I grab his pants on the floor and go through the pockets to find needles; an argument, of course, ensues. I go upstairs and tell the lady as I shove the needles in her face, "This is what is going on in your home. You need to throw him out or he will die in your home." She stated she knew he had addiction problems, but was trying to guide him through it and she couldn't throw anyone out on the street.

The pandemic hits and everything comes to a standstill. He's not working, so no money is coming in; we should be good, I think. We see him as often as we can, asking him to come over or just to take a drive with us. We text every day like we have for years and he keeps telling me he isn't using, but we know better because he avoids doing anything with us. His skin was a dead giveaway.

April 16, 2020, at 10:18 a.m., there is the knock on the door that I have been dreading for years. Three officers are standing there and want to speak with me. All I can say, "Is he gone?" They said yes. I want to see my boy and am told that I can't as he has been taken to the medical examiner's office and due to COVID, we can't see him. We are told that the lady in the house heard him yelling for help at seven a.m. and told them to call 9-1-1, as he couldn't breathe, and then he collapsed. EMS was unable to revive my boy. What if he was here at home? I bet I could have saved him. I saved him before. All the "what ifs."

I call the funeral home to make arrangements for his cremation, after the autopsy is completed. Am I dreaming? What am I doing? I ask if we can please see him and we are allowed one hour. I am told he would be dressed in just a long t-shirt and covered with a blanket. I ask if I can please bring him some clothes and if I can help dress him. I put his first set of clothes on him; I want to put on his last. I was able to put a hoodie and one of his favorite hats on him. When that door opened and I saw my beautiful son laying there, all I could do was run to him and put my head on his chest and cry. I stroked his hair, held his hand, and kept asking "Why? Why didn't you call me? You always called me when you were having trouble breathing and we always took you to the hospital. Why? Why wasn't my love enough?" I watched his brother fall to pieces, I watched his father breakdown, I watched his grandparents cry, I watched my strong marine, protector husband crumble. I was able to bring his ashes home and slept with them next to me for two days. April 24, 2020, we buried his ashes in the most beautiful cemetery. We had a small beautiful service.

Just like that Brandon was gone and I am left broken. What do I do? I keep checking my phone waiting for him to text and he never does. I no longer have to sleep with my phone by my side, as I did for years, fearing that call. Our lives were so consumed by his addiction; I spent all my spare time checking on him to be sure he was okay and now he is gone.

My husband and son have to deal with this empty shell of my former self. I know they say time will heal, but right now I don't see that. It's too fresh. My husband said to me, "Heroin is going to kill you too and then it will win again." I mostly wanted to crawl into that ground with my son, but I know I have to take that love and pour it into my husband and other son. All I can do now is be Brandon's voice and continue his fight by helping others.
Hopefully along the way I will be able to truly smile behind the mask I wear.

Brandon's Mom,

Lisa L.
Swartz Creek, Michigan

Andrew

FOREVER 34

I made it through high school never knowing about drugs. I didn't even know what marijuana was. It wasn't until I was at a party and I walked into a bedroom to get my coat that I saw people "shooting up." Fast forward many years. My son, Andrew, was twenty-two and I caught him shooting up. He admitted he had been doing it since high school and wanted to stop. Andy's dad arranged for him to detox at a local hospital that had a program. We dropped him off that night. It was rough on Andy, but he made it through. He admitted that he had been stealing from us for years. Andy also admitted to stealing from his sister and his great aunt who was living with us. It wasn't only money, but jewelry as well. Suddenly things started making sense. Andy worked the 12-Step program like a pro. He attended all his required meetings and extra ones, when he felt the need. He stayed clean for twelve years. He was very proud of that. But Andy was a lost soul. He decided he wanted to be a police officer. He applied to the police academy and passed all the steps except the physical. He was preparing for that when he twisted and hurt his back. We went to his primary care physician who recommended an orthopedic surgeon. The surgeon recommended a rheumatologist. The rheumatologist thought he had fibromyalgia and ordered tests. No one offered medication to take care of the pain. Andy must have been in so much pain that he turned to the street. On May 19, 2020, sometime between seven-thirty a.m. and ten a.m., Andy shot up high-potency fentanyl mixed with other drugs and died. I found him at ten a.m. draped over his garbage can. I called his dad and told him Andy was dead and to get home. Then I called 9-1-1. I am a nurse and I could tell, based on my assessment, he was gone. I had Narcan in the house so I gave him that. I could not move him, so I kicked the garbage can out from underneath him. He fell to the floor and that is when I saw the syringe. When he fell to the floor, he did so in such a way that I could not turn him to do CPR. It took ten minutes for the ambulance to arrive. He was in asystole, which means his heart was flatlined, so they could not use the defibrillator on him. They did CPR and took him to the hospital. Once we arrived at the hospital, we were placed in a private room, where the doctor came in and told us they worked on him for one hour, but he remained in asystole and pronounced him dead.

They let us see him with the chaplain. Then the police greeted us. They followed us back to our house and we were not allowed in Andy's room. A forensics truck came and they tore his room apart. They found the baggie of drugs he was using. That's how I know it was high-potency fentanyl. The toxicology screen has not come back yet. It takes three to four months to get that back which also delays the complete death certificate. If you have life insurance you have to wait for that copy. Because of COVID-19, we cannot have a funeral or a celebration of life for Andy. So, we wait.

Andrew's Mom,

PATTY L.
Wesley Chapel, Florida

Michael

FOREVER 38

I'm sorry if this is too long, but I don't often get to talk about my son.

Mike was born on March 11, 1980, in Skokie, Illinois, a suburb of Chicago where I grew up. I was a newly married housewife and dad was a police officer in another suburb. At eighteen months, we moved into a townhouse with my dad. While Daddy worked, we spent many happy days going for walks and to the park with Grandpa and to the pool in the summer.

When Mike was a baby, he developed an allergy to milk and eggs and had his first asthma attack before his second birthday. We began spending a lot of time at the doctor's office. It was then, I believe, that his lifelong dependence on drugs and steroids began.

Mike's childhood was average, other than his health problems. He played and was a happy boy. When he was six, his sister was born. Needing more room, we then moved into a house in another suburb and Grandpa came with us because he became blind in one eye and retired. Mike was a little shy and slow to make friends, but enjoyed the freedom offered by our new house's hilly area. He began learning t-ball and spent many days practicing and playing. Then came little league and Mike was in heaven!

Mike was never a great student but tried his best to keep up. He did love to read and when Nintendo came out, he soon found another passion! What Mike excelled at was sports statistics! He would scan the sports section each day, compiling lists of each team and the players and committing most of them to memory. He filled many spiral notebooks with these lists and when we finally got our computer, he created files and entered them in order to keep more accurate records.

The years of asthma drugs and steroids wrecked Mike's physical appearance, along with his insatiable appetite for Grandpa's spaghetti dinners, Chicago-style pizza, and Dr Pepper! He couldn't get enough of that soda and developed a lifelong love of it! Mike developed gyneco-mastia, man boobs, and became embarrassed and ashamed of his body. When we went to the pool, he always kept his shirt on, telling the life-guard it was because he sunburned easily.

By the time Mike was a freshman in high school, he was bullied by other kids and began asking if he could change schools. I began working at our local police department as a clerk to pay for a private Catholic school. It was pretty far from our house but luckily, Grandpa was able to drive him there, until Mike was old enough to get his license and use Grandpa's car. It was at this school that Mike met his lifelong three friends, who became his roommates for twenty-two years.

Mike began his teen years, like many others, moody, sleeping a lot, and except for baseball and sports, not having much interest in anything else. At about this time, he began using Grandpa's car on the weekends, telling us he was going camping with friends or to a concert and would stay out overnight. We never questioned him, as he was a "good boy" and we were happy that he had met friends. They were nice boys from a good school, although we never met any of their families.

After graduation, Mike attended a community college and worked at FedEx part-time. Once he began earning money, he decided that he didn't really want to go to school and got a job as a security guard, on campus. He also applied at his dad's department as a 9-1-1 dispatcher. He was hired and we were happy and proud of his work.

It was about this time that Mike told us his plans of moving out and in with his friends. I didn't want him to leave, but realized that he was almost twenty-one, and it was time to let him go. So, we helped him, with our blessings and some of our furniture! The boys were all working and so happy living together.

It was about this time when 9/11 happened and that day affected our whole family. I began to have nightmares of losing my husband while responding to calls at office buildings around O'Hare Airport, which then would collapse on him, in my nightmares, as I watched! So, the decision was made for him to retire from the police department, and we made plans to move to Las Vegas. Mike told us that he wanted to stay in the Chicago area and would visit us, each year, on vacation.

I realized that this was no way to maintain our closeness with just phone calls and one yearly visit. Soon, the calls were only on holidays and there was no contact in between. I should have made more of an effort. I am so sorry that I did not listen to my gut feelings. I kick myself, in hindsight, for letting this distance grow between us. But, please believe me, I walked the fine line of wanting to give him his space and not being an Italian mother! I, in my mother's role, never thought for a moment that my son was in trouble! I was naive and selfish!

My dad, Grandpa, died in 2014. It was sudden and Mike never had the chance to say goodbye. I have always had a shopping problem, but it got out of control, and I spent just about every dollar my husband made. We had no savings, having always depended on my dad if we needed it.

Mike was supposed to make his visit in early December of 2017, but I had to tell him in November that I couldn't afford his trip because of my spending. I will never forget his voice when I told him that, it haunts me to this day...

For Christmas, I sent him one of those DNA kits, and joked that I wanted to know what this crazy family was made up of. Mike made excuses for why he never completed the test each time I talked to him. And the calls stopped for a few months. We had our usual chat on the holidays, but there wasn't much to say; I was just happy to hear his voice.

Then one beautiful, sunny, hot, August, Sunday afternoon, the phone rang. The caller was a doctor, from the ER at Mercy Hospital in Chicago. He asked if my son was Michael and if he had any medical conditions. He then advised me that my son had a massive heart attack and was in very critical condition. He said he would call back when he knew more. I was in shock and waited by the phone for further word. The doctor called and asked what medications my son took, and I told him of his asthma. Again, he said he would get back to me. Well, he did and what he told me next was unbelievable.

He told me that Mike had overdosed on cocaine and that his heart had exploded. His condition was grave, and that I should come as soon as possible! "You're wrong! My son has never used drugs!" As I thanked him and hung up, a million thoughts were running through my head! How am I going to get to Chicago? We don't have any money and Gerry doesn't get paid for another two weeks!

I called my good friend, or so I thought, asking to borrow the money for the plane ticket until payday. She hemmed and hawed, telling me that she had her vacation planned and her money was put aside for souvenirs and whatnot. She would let me know.

I went on Facebook, posting on former co-workers' pages that I was in dire need to get to my son and I needed their help. The jail crew always had each other's back and I had donated on many occasions, but I hadn't worked there for a few years. Would they even remember me? I never heard a word from anyone.

I then went on my Weight Watcher's page. I made a mother's plea for help getting to the bedside of my dying son. These are women that I had never met, just posted with encouragement and the trials of dieting. I must have struck a nerve because within twelve hours, those wonderful women had raised the $500 I needed to purchase my ticket! I flew out that Monday night and went directly to the hospital.

When I walked into Mike's room, I saw him lying on that bed with tubes and machines everywhere and he was still. Except for the clacking of the ventilator, you could have heard a pin drop and I almost did! I suddenly knew that my son, my giant boy, was gone and only his body remained. I hugged and kissed him and held onto his right foot that was sticking out of the sheet. How did it come to this, Mike? What happened to put you here?

I settled into the chair and began talking to him, playing music and waiting to talk to his doctor. In a few hours, the doctor arrived, and we had a long talk. He leveled with me, Mike was in a coma and most likely would not survive. If by some miracle he did, he would probably be no more than twenty percent of his self. I made the decision, right then, that Mike would become an organ donor. The doctor told me to keep talking to Mike and playing music, as hearing was the last sense to go.

I spent the time I had left with Mike at his bedside, singing, talking, reading to him, and playing music... I could not, would not, leave his side. Mike's friends, those same guys/roommates, came to visit after work. They brought me food and a duffle bag with his clothes, some books for him, and his shaving gear. I sadly told them that Mike would not be coming home to them and they cried.

It took some time to coordinate the transplant team and it was set for Thursday night. It gave me about forty-eight hours to spend with my big, beautiful boy...There weren't many tears as shock had set in. I talked to many people, from the organ donor organization, nurses, other doctors, pastoral staff...and many of Mike's friends and co-workers came by to give me support and see Mike. I didn't have the heart to tell them that a drug overdose had put him in that bed. I didn't want to tarnish him. In my eyes, he was perfect and would always be.

On Thursday, many of the same people came back to say their final farewells and give Mike a sendoff into the afterlife. There were more than twenty people crowded into that little room and many funny stories and tears were shed. When the time came, we all took that long, silent walk through the hallways, down the elevators, and into the surgery suite.

It was surreal. I walked as if I were on a cloud. I was Mary following Jesus as he carried his cross... knowing that his crucifixion awaited. "Please God, help me, help my son," I prayed. I led the group in saying , "The Lord's Prayer" and played my favorite song, "Somewhere Over the Rainbow" by IZ, which seemed so appropriate, and fought back my tears. I put Mike's favorite baseball hat on his head, his Sox hat...and each person came up to touch him one last time and say their goodbyes.

They turned off the ventilator, and we all watched the clock tick in silence, praying for the miracle that Mike would begin breathing on his own. Mike's body became oxygen depleted and began to turn blue, even more lifeless than before, if possible. The doctor called the official time of death and they began to rush him into surgery. I was being led away and looked over my shoulder just before the doors swallowed him up. I called out, "I love you Schmikey," our favorite nickname for Mike, and he was gone...forever.

I don't know how I left the hospital, but the next day I called a funeral home from the yellow pages. I had to have Mike cremated and shipped to me. I flew home that night, and the HELL was just beginning.

How had this happened? If only we had not blindly trusted that our son was a "good boy" and hung with others that were the same. We had no idea that they might have been trying or using drugs...though his friends swore to my face they had only smoked some marijuana. Where was he all those nights we thought were so innocent? But he worked full time, never lost a job...How could he be using drugs? Wouldn't his friends or employers know?

Mike's dad was a police officer and I worked in the police department...Grandpa lived with us...we're a normal family! We don't drink or party...NOT MY SON! He's a good boy!

How has Mike's death affected our family? His dad and I are still married, but we fight like cats and dogs (sorry pets). I began shopping again, and isolate at home, not able to associate with anyone most of the time. His dad has developed a gambling habit to hide his grief, losing thousands of dollars that we don't have. We have filed for bankruptcy and with this pandemic are forced to live at home with nowhere to go and no money to go with. There are many times when I wish I was dead, as there is no more hope for our future...nobody to take care of us in our older years (we are already old)...there will be no grandchildren, no more holidays, no more family vacations. Life as we knew it is over.

If I could shout from the rooftops, I would beg our youth to take heed and our parents to pay attention to the warning signs! I would beg for help from their schools, their doctors, the police department, employers, elected officials...Anyone!

Somehow, we are failing our children. The lure of drugs to forget and not feel anything but pleasure...awareness of this epidemic and how it's exterminating a great portion of our younger generation... somehow that has got to change, or else the future of our world is doomed!

It's happening to all families in some way, everywhere! The rich, the poor, black, white, brown, yellow... Drugs don't care! No one is immune to these drugs!

NOT MY SON!

Michael's Mom,

Julianne L.
Las Vegas, Nevada

Christopher

FOREVER 28

When I found out, after years of praying for another baby, I was finally pregnant, I fell on my knees and from the depth of my heart cried out in praise to God for answering my prayers. I was so thrilled when I was able to hear his tiny heartbeat at my doctor's office when I went in for my prenatal exam. I remember the doctor saying he hoped it beat for 100 years. I did, too.

A little over twenty-eight years later, my heart completely shattered and I fell to my knees wailing from the depths of my heart as a different doctor informed me that despite all they tried to do to save my precious son's life, his heart no longer beat. How did this happen? It's a question I ask myself every day...

I asked Christopher that question one week before he died. He had come home that Sunday afternoon after work, and we had a conversation about his life and his future. I asked if anything happened in his childhood or teen years or what I may have done wrong to start him on this path of drug use.

At that time, I truly had no idea how extensive his drug use actually was. The little use I did know about had been a problem in our lives for about ten to fourteen years. It had caused so much strife, tension, chaos and drama for him, me, and his sisters.

This time, I was trying to harder to understand and get him the help I thought he needed. He calmly told me that he tried drinking and smoking weed when he was in his early teens because "he was just a dumb kid" and went on to reassure me it was "all in his past" and I didn't need to worry about it being a problem anymore. He had lost a music acquaintance a couple of weeks earlier who took Xanax laced with fentanyl.

Christopher told me this was an "eye-opener" for him because he abused Xanax due to issues he had with severe anxiety. I told him I was so scared and wanted him to see a doctor to help him manage his anxiety and to promise me he wouldn't take anything from off the street.

For once, we were able to discuss my concerns about his substance abuse without him getting upset. I had hope that his substance abuse may actually be something "all in his past." I was so naive.

When we had that conversation on his last Sunday afternoon, he said he was a "dumb kid" when he first tried drinking and smoking weed. Now that I know a little more about addiction, I think he may have been right. I believe there are people who have a genetic predisposition for substance abuse.

My ex-husband was a workaholic who became an alcoholic. (His absence from Christopher's life may also have played a big part in Christopher's issues.) Our grandfathers were alcoholics. I think Christopher's first drink or the first time he smoked pot woke that addiction gene in him. Like most teenagers, I think he struggled with self-esteem. Because of his severe anxiety, I think he used to self-medicate.

That led to years of abuse. Just as I thought he was doing well, for some inexplicable reason, Christopher and his girlfriend (whom I later found out was a heroin addict) ordered fentanyl from the dark web and researched how to "safely" get high using it. He died

that night on December 3, 2017, when he and his girlfriend attempted to smoke it. She is currently in recovery.

Christopher's Mom,

ROXANNE M.
Missouri

> *"Loosing my child has made me acutely aware of how much I had been given.*
> *Some people never have that much to loose."*
> ~ *Terri Z.*

Amber

FOREVER 23

Amber was the light of my life, my best friend, my only daughter. Always a sweet child, she had many friends growing up. Amber was very compassionate and cared about others to the extent that it lured her into addiction. Her story starts as a typical child, loved and a little stubborn, but typical. Amber loved to play sports and exceeded expectations in most athletic events.

When she was in grade school, she started having issues with her body, the most embarrassing to her would be excessive sweating. Amber was so self-conscious about the sweating. She would wear a sweater no matter what season it was. She then developed migraines. We took her to see a medical professional and she was prescribed medication and we dealt with the issue the best we could. She knew something was wrong with her and felt she wasn't taken seriously, so she asked if she could see a psychiatrist.

The psychiatrist was not helpful to Amber, the way she needed her to be. Amber was prescribed more medication, not what Amber needed. Around three weeks of taking the new antidepressant, she tried to take her own life; her psychiatrist's answer was a higher dose. Every three weeks there was another attempt and a higher dose was prescribed. Amber was not feeling better and continued to spiral. She asked if she could move to her dad's home for a fresh start. She was thriving at her new school in Idaho. She had new friends and was off her medication, but she still didn't feel like herself.

A friend introduced her to "skittles," dextromethorphan, an active ingredient in cough medication; in large doses it can make you feel euphoric. This was the start of Amber's self-medicating. After a year, she moved home and started the eighth grade. She had a boyfriend and was feeling better. She would still take the skittles and was falling into a pattern of self-destructive behavior.

Around tenth grade, Amber started using heroin. I had no idea that any of her self-medicating would end up with a drug like this. My husband had a heart attack while scuba diving and was flown into Los Angeles for treatment. I was traveling back and forth to help him, and she was using heroin. I was in her room one day cleaning and I found at least 200 foils stashed around her room. I was devastated, and we started her first time in rehab.

Rehab would help, but still she was self-medicating when she got out. She would do well for a while, then fall back into the same routine and would go back to rehab. We finally found a doctor that listened, and Amber at seventeen was diagnosed with a tumor on her pituitary gland. She was so happy to finally get a diagnosis and show everyone that she had a real issue and was not making it up. The tumor came out, but caused her to become adrenal deficient, steroids for life. The steroids caused her to gain weight and changed her appearance. Amber, once again, went back to drugs.

At some point, she was introduced to needles, which she realized intensified the high. She was getting high and not taking her steroids, which caused her another hospital visit. If we weren't at the hospital for drugs, it was for her not taking her medication. Amber was getting further into her addiction and met a guy that helped her get high. One day she didn't come home. I called her and she told me she was happy with this guy.

She was over eighteen, so I could not make her stay and she was communicating with me, so I could not report her missing. What I did not know was this man was having Amber sell her body and he would give her drugs. She was made to say she was fine and not to worry, while this man held her a prisoner and kept her stoned. She called me after a few weeks, scared he was taking her to Mexico. I called the authorities and they had no proof, so her friends went after her. We got her back, safely, but she was not the same afterwards.

We got her on methadone, which seemed to help her. She met a few people at the clinic and being the kind of person she was, would sneak them into the house to sleep, as they were homeless. She fell in love with a guy named Daniel, and at some point, became pregnant, not his child. Amber knew she could not stop the methadone because the withdrawals would cause her body to miscarry. Daniel was her savior. He stayed with her through the whole pregnancy. Amber had a beautiful little girl in November of 2016.

She tried to be a good mom, but CPS got involved and took the baby from her. The baby was given to me and Amber was ok with that, to an extent. She knew she could not care for herself, let alone a baby, so she accepted that. Daniel went to jail and Amber was upset. I did not know he got out early, I put the baby to bed and laid down to go to sleep. At ten p.m., Amber ran into my room saying, "He is dead, Mom, please help." The love of her life had overdosed in my home and she had nodded off. He had been dead about three hours. This devastated Amber and the spiral was going down further.

After Daniel died, CPS told me I could not have Amber and the baby in the same house. I was worried about Amber's stability and my mom took in the baby. Amber was not going to make it without me. The drugs were back, and she was using meth at this point too.

Amber met a new type of guy next, one that was pleasant when we were around and then would beat her up when we weren't. I feel like after Daniel died, she felt she didn't deserve anyone being nice to her. She moved in with a few friends and this new guy named Ben. Ben would beat her, ran into her with her own car, hit her so hard she blacked out, and held a knife to her, but she would not leave him. I tried talking to her and this guy would be back within hours. I got her into a new rehab, moved out of my home due to a separation, and asked her to live with me after rehab. When I was at work, she would let him in.

The spiral was now going faster. Ben was put in jail and Amber was alone. My daughter hated being alone and to her anyone was better than being alone. Ben was in jail, so Amber started meeting men online. She told me she found a really nice guy that treated her well and she was really happy. Anytime your child is happy you feel ok.

On November 25, 2019, I came home from a Halloween party and was thankful she was home. I knocked on the bathroom door and she was annoyed I was bothering her, so I went to bed. I woke up the next day and she wasn't home, not an uncommon thing for her.

I texted and called her, no answer, also not uncommon. Around six p.m. on the twenty-sixth, I got a call from the chaplin of the hospital telling me she was there and I needed to come down. I called my family and they joined me. Amber had been in the hospital in the past so many times I was shook, but she always pulled through.

The night is a blur, but she had 9-1-1 called by someone and she was unresponsive when they arrived. They brought her back, but she coded at least six more times that night. The doctor asked me if we should continue resuscitation and I said yes. Amber's dad came out and Amber hung on for two more days. She passed, surrounded by her family and friends, October 29, 2019 at twenty-three years old.

She was the most amazing person. I miss her every day. I can't help but think what I could have done differently. It doesn't make it easier. I see her in her daughter, and I know she would be proud of the little girl that she has become. She does not know Amber as her mother, but she will when she is older and can understand. Her daughter asks where Amber is often.

The week before she died, the family, including Amber, had gone to the pumpkin patch. For anyone going through this horrible disease, please know that the people around you love you so much. Amber was more than an addict, she was my daughter, a mother, my best friend and very, very loved.

Amber's Mom,

ROBIN M.
Roseville, California

> *I loved greatly, and so I grieve deeply.*
> *It is okay to grieve.*
> *~ Julianne L.*

Nick

FOREVER 19

Yes, my son was a beauty on the outside, but inside is where his true beauty was. He was sweet, kind, funny, warm, respectful, laid back, and a good, loyal friend who loved his family deeply. His passion was playing sports. He started in Soccer at age 4. He had a competitive streak in him and grew to love all sports, playing Soccer and Basketball on local, travel and school teams. He spent many years goal-keeping and spent his high school years as Varsity keeper.

He also loved football and was an avid NE Patriots fan from an early age (since he was born in MA). He was a smart, popular, good looking kid with a very active social life. He enjoyed fishing and skate-boarding with his friends. He loved to have a good time and laugh, I always laughed when he laughed! He loved his dogs and they were such loyal companions to him. He enjoyed good food and was always there to polish off the leftovers and would thank you over and over for a good meal. He enjoyed chillin', watching movies, listening to music and dancing. He was fresh, stylish, loved shoes, and had the best hair ever! He and I were so very close. We did everything together, from soccer games and practices to watching TV to shopping. His brother is 7 yrs. older than him, so Nick was always truly, my baby.

I became a single parent when Nick was 5 yrs. old when his father passed away from cancer. Our life was not perfect, but it was a good life. We had a nice home in a very family-oriented neighborhood. I always worked hard, paid my bills, lived an honest and decent life and set good examples for my kids. I never did drugs and only occasionally drank alcohol. I provided everything my kids needed and much of what they wanted. I lived for my children. Life was good. But, as Nick approached middle school age, I became concerned about the peer pressure he would face, specifically regarding drugs.

His paternal side of the family had a strong history of addiction, including his father, who at different times, struggled with addiction. I firmly believe that genetics play a very prominent role in addiction. So, I started talking to Nick in middle school about the dangers of drugs, how addiction develops and tried to prepare him to deal with peer pressure. We talked about his family members who had succumbed to addiction. It was important for my son to understand the role genetics play in addiction and I hoped his understanding of that would be a further deterrent to drugs. He understood how dangerous they were. Sometimes, he would tell me about this kid or that kid who smokes pot and he was upset about it. He made it clear he had no intention of doing drugs.

From that point, life continued as usual for the next 2 years, he was loving life, and doing well in school. He was happy, healthy and active. I was at ease that he was on the right path. I was so proud of both my boys. We were so very close and still did so much together. We had open conversations about life and he sought and respected my opinion. I was always very affectionate with my boys. Nick never outgrew it. He always allowed me to hug and kiss him no matter who was around. He was definitely a mama's boy and in the sweetest way.

Then he reached high school. One morning, I was leaving to go to work and as I left, I heard a noise in the shed outside of our house. I approached the shed and opened the door, there stood my boy, alone, in the shed, smoking weed before school. I was stunned. I couldn't believe

417

what I was seeing. Nick tried to minimize the situation, he said, 'it's just weed Mom' Many people smoke weed and go no further, but for others, this is how addiction begins. I talked to him about how disappointed I was and why and when did he decide to make this choice? He acted like it wasn't a big deal.

We needed help communicating so I took my son to a therapist who specializes in adolescent drug use. We counseled together with her and he was drug tested each week. He would say what I wanted to hear while we were there, and he was passing the drug tests, but I had an uneasy feeling that he wasn't drug free. About 6 weeks into the counseling, we arrived for an appointment and I noticed before we went inside that my son's pants were wet. It turns out he had been smuggling in a friend's urine and using it to pass the drug tests. We stopped the therapy after that since he was not being truthful.

Over the next 2-3 yrs through high school, Nick never stopped smoking weed and he experimented with a few other drugs, acid, Xanax, mushrooms are the ones I know of. One night, he had taken so much Xanax, I thought he might die. I sat up with him all night to make sure he was breathing. By this point, I feared he might develop an addiction, but there was still a measure of denial in me. Even knowing all I knew about addiction; I couldn't absorb the possibility that my son might become an addict. I rationalized by telling myself most kids do experiment with drugs and turn out fine. But, at the same time I was panicked because of his familial history of addiction.

Things got progressively worse. At one point, I had him involuntarily committed for psych holds on 2 different occasions because he stole money and medication out of my purse and was being very rebellious, sneaking out of the house at night, etc. I was hoping that doctors could help us but each time, they sent him home after a week of inpatient therapy and assigned intensive home therapy 3 x per week, which was useless. All through high school, he maintained his grades, continued playing sports and remained popular and very social while still intermittently using drugs.

I kept hoping he would grow out of using drugs (like many do) but once he graduated, it got progressively worse. He felt lost after graduation. He wasn't sure what he wanted to do with his life. Several of his friends went off to college, others got full time jobs (as did Nick) and others just simply grew apart and so life was very different for him. He started to feel depressed and lonely. He was working, but the social life had all but disappeared due to everyone going their own way. He had no plan for his future and he was worried. We talked about it a lot and I assured him what he was feeling was normal and he would find his way in life. I could see he was struggling with depression and loneliness. I suggested going to the doctor to get some help with the depression, but he refused. His life went quickly from being on top of the world to being depressed and isolated. I was worried about him, but I also knew in my heart, that he'd get through this phase. He was only 18 yrs old and I knew with a little time, he'd get a plan for his life.

He started to hang out with a kid I didn't know. Within a couple of months, I was with Nick one day and we had stopped to clean his car. I walked to the driver's side of the car while he was vacuuming the passenger side and in the console in the door, I saw a needle. I stood frozen, just looking at it, trying to comprehend what I was seeing. Words cannot describe the panic and fear that overtook me. I picked the needle up and said, 'what's this'? He looked up, saw what I was holding, and got very upset and angry. He came over to me, grabbed it out of my hand and threw it. He swore that it belonged to that particular 'friend' that he had started to hang out with. He told me that his friend had a problem and that he had left it in the car. I questioned why it was on the driver's side, but I don't remember his answer. My eyes were pleading with him to convince me it wasn't his. And he did. Whatever he said, convinced me that he would never use a needle. I believed my son that day. Looking back, I wanted to believe him. There was no way I could fathom that my beautiful, smart, popular kid would use a needle or try heroin. Even with all we had been through, even seeing evidence right in front of me, I chose to believe him. For me, the other option was not an option.

Two weeks later, my son overdosed on a combination of Heroin and Xanax. The same person who he said the needle belonged to had been with him and drove Nick to the hospital. When I arrived at the ER, the doctor told me that my son was DOA. When hospital staff pulled him out of the car he was blue and unresponsive. They immediately started CPR and administered Narcan. It took 3 injections to bring my son back from death. That night, our descent into hell began. The hospital sent us home and for 24 hours he asked me the same 2 questions over and over. Surely, he had brain damage. I was terrified, but he returned to normal after about 24 hours. At this time, I convinced myself that we could handle the situation. I was in shock but also knew that my son had a serious drug problem, but thought we could keep it in the house, seek treatment, get past it and no one would be the wiser. No one, outside of 3 family members knew this had happened and I really wanted to protect my son from any judgement. Although he had no memory of the overdose, it really scared him to know it happened. He cried and said he didn't want to die.

He was willing to do anything I asked, such as go to NA meetings and swore he would never do heroin again. Things were calm for a few months (or so it seemed) but then I began to see small signs that he was using again. Soon it became obvious he was. We would argue and fight about it, I begged, pleaded and even tried to bribe him to stop. I thought he could stop if he wanted to, especially since he was not an everyday user. I lived in fear and worried constantly. I couldn't sleep if he was home or out of the house. We still went to NA meetings when he was willing, but the willingness was fading. He would go quite some time without being high and each time he went a stretch being clean, I thought, this time he has a handle on it.

In April 2018, I received a call while at work that my son, again, had OD'd and was again at the ER. I was so angry when I arrived at the hospital. I could not believe that he had done this again. I'm ashamed to say that I was angry, but I was. I was so exhausted from living in fear. I was defeated and helpless. I finally began to accept that my son was an addict. After this second OD, every aspect of my life was impacted by my son's addiction. My family became tired of 'dealing' with it, they started to resent him because of what it was doing to me. My relationship with my fiancé, my other son, my family, my friends, my job, all suffered severely. Very few people outside of the few family members knew of my son's addiction. No one could tell he was doing drugs, not by his appearance, nor demeanor. I thought by keeping it private, I was protecting my son. I regret that. I wish I had reached out to anyone who would listen because someone might have been able to help us.

I became obsessed with my son and his addiction and everything else was secondary. I started to develop health problems and I knew it was due to all the stress. I became very isolated. It was torture to have him in my house high, but no less torture to have him out of the house. I lived in such fear of another overdose. I never slept. I did things like take his paycheck to keep him from buying drugs. He stole from neighbors and strangers and eventually me. He blamed me that he had to steal because I took his money. I realized then that taking his money helped nothing, that an addict will do whatever they need to do to get high. I dragged him everywhere trying to get him help. Because he had no insurance, the only option available was a 14-day State run detox but he refused to go. I just could not get strong enough to not enable him. It became a predictable pattern that he quickly learned to manipulate. I never knew what to do, it seemed there was no right or wrong answer. I knew I needed support, so I joined a support group for parents of addicts. It helped me to know I was not alone and wished I had joined earlier. I needed much help to gain strength to implement strategies to stop enabling my son.

One night in September 2018, Nick and I had a small argument and he went to his bedroom. After about 10 minutes, I noticed I didn't hear his TV on, so I went and opened his bedroom door. He was sitting in a chair, eyes closed, lips blue and a needle was on his dresser. The moment I saw him, I knew he had overdosed. Again, and this time inside my house. I ran to get the Narcan I had but didn't know how to use it, so while frantically trying to open the package, I accidentally set it off. I still administered the Narcan, hoping there was some left. I was shaking so badly; I could barely dial 911 and it took several attempts. While I was on the phone screaming for them to hurry, I could hear my son becoming responsive in his room. Thank God! He heard me screaming into the phone and came out of his room. He was angry that I had called 911. EMS came and ensured he was ok and they told me there was enough Narcan left and that it likely saved his life. The police also came. I was so terrified that he might OD in my house again that I made my son leave when the police left. This was the first time I did not allow him to sleep in the house. I did not let my son back in my house for 2 weeks. I actually took out a restraining order on him because I knew without such a measure, I would let him come back home. He stayed with his brother some nights and in his car others. As usual, I didn't sleep for fear he would OD wherever he was. I constantly prayed for God to heal my son or for me to know how to help him. I felt so helpless.

He finally called and said he was ready to go to the detox. I knew in my heart a 14-day detox was not enough, but it was better than nothing. The very night he got out of detox, he used heroin. I knew death was chasing my son. But somehow, I still thought we could get his addiction under control. Once again, made him leave the house, but eventually let him come home. He stayed clean for a while but began using again.

On Christmas day, he was high. He and his brother had a terrible fight over that fact and I made Nick leave. I don't know where he spent most of Christmas day or that night. It hurt me so badly to throw my son out on Christmas day, of all days, but I also hurt so badly for us having to deal with his addiction. I allowed him to come home the next day, but he continued the same pattern, high one day, not the next. I was finally able to get him health insurance effective 01/01/19. He had an appointment for rehab on 01/26/19 (the soonest they could take him). I kept thinking, if we can both just hang on until then, he actually has a chance to get clean. He was ready and willing to go to rehab.

The week of January 14, things took a turn for the worse. Nick and I had an argument over $20 and for the first time in my life, my son scared me. He punched holes in my bedroom door while screaming for me to let him in. I had never felt afraid of my son, ever. I called the police, but he left before they came. My son never had been violent toward anyone, he was a very laid-back, gentle kid, but heroin changed him.

On Friday, Jan 18th, I let him come back home. He swore he would not do any drugs and I could see he was truly broken down. He had no one. Friends wouldn't even respond to his texts. He seemed ready to get the help coming to him in another week or so. I made it clear he had to stay clean until rehab or he would be out for good. We had a great weekend together. He was clean and seemed much like himself again. He was grateful and relieved to be home safe with the person who loved him most. I loved having him home because he was more like 'my' Nick. We went out to eat, watched the big football game on TV that weekend and watched Redbox movies and talked a lot. He had no money and he wasn't trying to leave the house. He was more at peace than I had seen in a long time. I too felt some peace knowing that as each day passed we were one day closer to rehab. My one and only hope was fast approaching.

That Monday, January 21, was a holiday, so I was off work. I had been out running errands and when I came home about 3pm he was just leaving to take a Redbox back. I got nervous because he was leaving the house for the first time since the weekend and I questioned him. He assured me he would be right back. As always, we hugged and said I love you before he left. He never came back and wouldn't answer my texts. I grew anxious and scared to death that he was getting drugs. He finally answered my texts about 7:30pm but lied about where he was. I was at my Fiancé's house at the time and Nick told me he'd be home soon. He called me at 8 04pm to tell me he was home. I arrived home at 8 37pm. I found him face down in our laundry room, not breathing and I saw that his fingernails were blue. I administered Narcan and called 911. They instructed me to do CPR, but I could not turn my son over because I didn't have the physical strength. Panic and shock overwhelmed me. They told me to run to a neighbor for help, but I couldn't leave him. I couldn't move. I'll never understand why, and I'll never be able to forgive myself. I just kept screaming for 911 to hurry. A volunteer fireman and my fiancé were the first to arrive. As they started working on my son, I sat in disbelief, praying to God to save my son. The police and ambulance arrived. They worked on him for about 20 minutes and got a heartbeat. At that moment, I was hopeful.

They transported him to the hospital where he was put on a ventilator. The doctor met with us and told us that he likely would not survive beyond 48 hours. Shock would still not allow me to believe he would die. I got in the hospital bed with my son and held him. He looked so healthy, like he was going to open his eyes any moment. His beautiful, flawless skin had the glow of youth, his full perfect lips were as pink as they always were, every beautiful hair was in place. The warmth of his body and the familiar scent of his hair let me know I was not dreaming. I told him how much I loved him. I held him and comforted him as only his mama could. I felt he knew I was there. He passed in my arms at 4:10am on January 22. 2019. I thought it, but never fully believed addiction would actually take my son from me. I can't understand how I stayed in denial about the power of his addiction for so long. Nature would not allow me to believe my child would die, even though I thought it, because it is too painful. The cause of death was accidental overdose of Fentanyl. I'm certain that Nick did not know he was buying Fentanyl and I know he didn't want to leave me.

As I look back over our journey with addiction, it was short. Drugs stole my son's life, and mine, in 15 short months. Part of my soul left with him and I will never recover from his loss. I loved my son more than my next breath. I have no idea who I am anymore, and many days feel as if I'm just waiting to die. I still and will always have moments where I can't believe any of this happened to us. This is a very condensed version of our experience with addiction. I could have easily written a book on everything we went through and how addiction is so misunderstood and stigmatized, how society needs to be educated on it and how treatment should be available to all regardless of cost or lack of insurance.

A 'stereotypical' addict does not exist. Addiction does not discriminate and my 'all American boy' is proof of that. He was so sweet, had the kindest heart, had a loving, respectable family, a wonderful life and the world at his feet. No one saw this coming. There are many people who sit in judgement of addicts they think this won't happen to their kid. They might be right, but they might also be wrong. It might not happen to their kid, but it could happen to their grandchild, niece, nephew, best friend, anyone they dearly love. I think the fact that we all know someone, near or far, struggling with addiction (drugs or alcohol) shows that it doesn't discriminate, and no family is guaranteed immunity from its destruction.

Human life is fragile. If someone you love becomes addicted to drugs, fight hard against denial and treat it as life or death, because it is. Drugs are not 'recreational' they are killers.

Nick's forever heartbroken Mom,

JILL M.
Willow Spring, North Carolina

Zoie

FOREVER 22

An ominous winter storm pounded the majestic peaks enveloping the small town of Glenwood Springs near Aspen. I cautiously navigated the harrowing blizzard through dark, winding mountain roads while Zoie texted relentlessly. Unfamiliarity with my brand new car necessitated our pulling over to free the windshield wipers. Together we confronted prickly ice particles hurling sideways. Inconceivably, the whiteout shut down the internet so we couldn't check into a motel. Hyper vigilant of Zoie's communicating with thugs, I fretted my ineptitude to deter the frantic texting. After finally posting her bail after five plus months incarcerated, I was so happy to have her by my side, like old times. I naively believed if given sufficient time to earnestly examine her life, she'd redeem herself. My expectation of guiding my daughter was immediately crushed by phone calls to intricately complex associates.

In four short days following her release, my girl encountered the unimaginable. Her first day home was Veteran's Day thereby courts were closed. I gave her money to get a haircut nearby at downtown Denver's 16th Street Mall. Thursday, as arranged by her bail bondsman, I promptly delivered her to court where she encountered "homies" who offered a rack ($1,000 made from selling drugs). Friday the 13th no less, Zoie was harassed to the point of jumping out of a moving older model, red suburban. Her cell phone destroyed by its driver, she returned home shaken but concealing the perplexity of her situation. Asking if I'd replace her phone, we spent Saturday like old times, clothes, shoes, and cellphone shopping. That evening, I pleaded for her not to go out. My biggest regret is not having kissed her goodbye.

Zoie took her time getting ready, so I busied myself to stop agonizing. Around two a.m., I shot up in bed, ran downstairs and found my iPad open on the coffee table. There lay my daughter's last exchanges. I proceeded to contact each one. I'd never done this before so as to not embarrass her, but I knew instinctively she was murdered. A few hours later, I asked my husband, Michael, to accompany me to our Metaphysical Church but he cruelly declined. I spent the day alone buying dog food from Costco to donate to the charities where Zoie and I volunteered.

By evening, Michael suggested filing a missing person report. I'd doubted he or the cops cared. Truth being, the enormity of the strain of years of abuse drastically embittered me, while Michael grew increasingly emotionally distant. I was devastated. Mercifully, Zoie Alexa's body was found frozen in the garbage in a Mexican ghetto early Monday morning. I don't believe I'd have survived a cold case situation. The colors red, green, and white splashed across her body with a "caustic liquid" according to television coverage I arranged. News won't usually cover gang-related murders so as not to glorify gangs and criminals who wear these crimes as a badge of honor.

When a detective asked me to describe any identifying marks, I named her Mickey Mouse tattoo, as her fingerprints were erased. We went to Disneyland monthly throughout her childhood. My sheltered girl from Beverly Hills couldn't survive the high stakes of major drug trafficking. The DOJ had written a few months prior informing me of tapped phone lines. The detective initially admitted, "For a twenty-one-year-old, your daughter is connected on such an extensive level. There are so many moving parts to this investigation, I've spent overnights at my desk." I met with her OG, Monster Mike, who told me there were men in prison crying over her death.

Zoie had spiraled out of control by fourteen, starting to drink alcohol and smoke pot upon moving to Denver. I left her father, Denny, for terrorizing me over finances. He was an abusive, alcoholic, award-winning news photographer/TV sitcom cameraman whose other daughter from his first marriage died a drug-related death by age thirty. Michael was my bridge to leave fifteen years of physical and emotional domestic violence. But he was so intimidated by Zoie's spitefulness, he didn't dare interfere. Due to my horrendously abusive childhood, I mistakenly vowed not to spank or take Zoie's freedom away. I'd been made to play with neighborhood kids through a fence. My harsh Cuban upbringing was so insane, I ran away to New York City from a prestigious college prep school by the age of seventeen. I placed two children in private adoptions because I was so broken.

Zoie's anger made her quite abusive toward me; she was cutting herself within weeks of our move to Denver. I was about to slap her face in my car for repeatedly cursing at me on the way to school, when she vehemently pushed my hand away. I left a slight scratch on her clavicle for which I was charged with child abuse because my ring finger nail had caught her necklace which I promptly replaced as soon as the store opened on my way to work.

The authorities offered zero solutions for her increasingly dangerous lifestyle. I believe the police have no business interfering with parenting and I would launch a campaign against it if I could or reasonably believed I could make a difference. Due to my background in entertainment publicity, I immediately contacted the local newspaper in Broomfield, Colorado. They did a four-page story on my having slapped my fifteen-year-old and how I was subsequently charged with child abuse. Here's the thing: If you want to meddle in my life then make sure you are of some value.

Zoie and I were alone in a new tacky town and had left the glamour and splendor of Beverly Hills. Surrounded by people far different from us, I languished in loneliness later resulting in despair. I believe it may have been Albert Einstein who said apathy is worse than anything. I started to write a documentary which I called *Ignorant Indifference* because that is how I characterized my husband's family and many people I had now encountered. They tolerated me as I suffered their banality.

When Zoie was killed, I lost my world. All of the abuse caught up with me. I let everything material go. My home, cars, small business, and two dogs I adore and miss terribly. I couldn't trust anyone for a long time. Zoie's murder did me in. I have to admit one of the most damaging aspects of child loss is the loss of connection to our former selves and lifestyle prior to the tragedy.

In my case, my own husband's family never gave me their condolences and while I did not know a single mother who had lost a child, my mother-in-law had. In reaching out to her, I thought she would be able to tell me that I'd survive this but instead she never responded or bothered to send so much as a sympathy card. I don't know what happened after that, but something broke inside me that completely shattered my faith in humanity. It's not as though we were close previously, of course we had been at one time but her lack of interest when Zoie was at a children's hospital psych ward a few years prior caused me to end our relationship in not the most gracious manner—you do not want to get an email from me if you have hurt me.

Friends of thirty years disappeared. It is as though we have the plague—any family experiencing the horror of dealing with an addict can most likely attest to this fact. Zoie's tragic story is not unique in that there are countless mothers losing their children daily. However, Zoie's particular circumstances as in not having siblings, family, or good friends other than one or two gals resulted in a prescription for disaster. In closing, all I can say is community is entirely essential as well as the support of a loving group of like-minded people.

I wish I'd never moved to Denver because we had our pack of interesting and eclectic friends who got me and loved my daughter. They are all reasonably successful as well as well-known artists who would never judge an addict the way many people do. The stigma of addiction is probably the worst aspect for us who love an addict. The cruelty accompanying this mentality is entirely unsophisticated and cliche. Mental illness and addiction go hand-in-hand and personally, I don't know anyone who isn't crazy to one extent or another.

So I'd like to urge everyone who has known someone who is either an addict or the family member of one to educate themselves and realize addicts need compassion, understanding, and love most of all. Hell, all I needed was a little love thrown my way by my husband's relatives and perhaps I may not have lost everything I owned.

I may have been able to navigate the horror of losing my precious only child with more grace and wisdom. But that wasn't the case and I ask God to protect you if you are facing the eminent danger of the loss of your loved one. Dangerous because you will never be the same but healing is absolutely possible and available to anyone who wishes to move forward, be of service to others, and integrate the trauma into their lives in a fashion that renders the loss #not in vain!

Zoie's Mom,

OLGA M.
Denver, Colorado

Megan

Megan was my problem child. Pins petition (person in need of supervision), smoking, pot, boys, quit school. In spite of it all, she did get her **GED**, completed cosmetology school, and got her license. She got a job in a very busy mall salon, moved into an apartment with a friend, had a new car, and got her motorcycle license and a bike. That was 2004-2005.

Megan worked at this salon until 2009 when suddenly she wanted to move home. She was $16,000 in credit card debt. Mom paid that. She wrecked her car and got another one with mom's help. She found another job but was not very busy and money didn't flow. I started finding tin foil with burnt spots on it. She was doctor shopping for hydrocodone, selling two-thirds of the ninety she had to pay for the car and bike and foiling the others. Then electronic prescriptions came into effect and she couldn't get the pills, but by this time she was addicted. We tried Suboxone but she sold most of

430

them to buy pills or heroin. Heroin was cheap, and you can get needles in any pharmacy. In New York, Suboxone is regulated and "cash" only. Corrupt MDs would charge you $125 cash, send you to the pharmacy to fill the prescription, and give him five.

I discovered the IV heroin in 2014. I staged an intervention and sent her to Florida for a year and hemorrhaged money. I brought her home in December of 2015. She had a class B felony for sale pending and the judge gave her five years probation. She walked through that in about four months. A warrant was issued and she went to county to await trail. The judge offered her rehab but she refused and he gave her eighteen months in state prison. While in county, she kept complaining about headaches.

She was transferred to prison the week of Columbus Day 2016. I didn't hear from her the week she was transferred but didn't think too much about it because I figured they were not allowed phone privileges yet. At midnight on Saturday, I received a phone call telling me she was admitted to a hospital but they would not tell me why. She did get a call out to me saying her eyes were messed up and she couldn't see. Of course, being a holiday weekend, I could not get a hold of anyone to clear me to visit her.

I was finally allowed to visit on Monday, Columbus Day. When I walked into her room, I knew she was blind. They worked her up for MS, neuromyelitis optica, tumor, etc. High-dose steroids did nothing to reduce the optic nerve swelling. They finally did plasma pheresis and she started to see shadows. She was sent back to prison where she slowly regained some vision but no color and her pupils did not react to light. She also had hepatitis C ,and her viral load was off the charts. They treated her with Harvoni.

She spent fourteen months in a closed long-term care unit with seventeen other women. She came home completely clean and sober. She would never drive a car again, never see color again. Her vision was 20/400. She got disability. She found a job in a small seafood restaurant with very supportive people and loved her job. BUT...she was dabbling in cocaine, got involved with a person dealing. She felt if she wasn't using "dope" she was ok.

In July of 2019 she was diagnosed with cervical cancer. Biopsy and hysterectomy were the treatments of choice. At thirty-two, she would never have children. All in all, Meggie smiled, continued to work and "dabble." On October 24, 2019, she underwent a complete hysterectomy. She did well and on November 6, she was told the pathology was clear and she would not need further treatment.

On November 7, I came home to find her dead. Her toxicology showed a very small amount of cocaine and fentanyl. I question the quantity in her system and the pathologist stated because she wasn't using opiates, she had no tolerance and that small amount was enough.

My Meggie never got to show the doubters (her father and brother) that she could redeem herself. When it is all said and done, I was the only one that had her back. In spite of it all, I would never turn my back on her...ever. Such a sad ending to this story. I had such high hopes for her to succeed. I wanted her to taste success after all she had been through. If love could have saved her, she would still be here. She will be buried in my family cemetery in PA and I have commissioned a double stone as I will be buried right next to "My Meggie."

Megan's Mom,

SUSAN M.
Saratoga Springs, New York

Kevin

FOREVER 24

Kevin gave every part of his soul to life. He enjoyed life and all it brought to him. He was smart, especially with numbers. He was my tape measure, my VCR expert (LOL), then my internet consultant. He was hilarious. He loved sports. He would do anything for anybody. When Kevin was in high school, it would be no surprise for him to bring someone home who was hurting or had nowhere to go. I was glad to open my home up, so their parents knew they were safe. Kevin loved with his entire being. I had no idea how bad his addiction was, until it was too late. He was too far gone; the addiction had taken over and ruled his life. I turned away in denial. Now that I know more, the signs were right in front of me. I drank until I passed out, to numb the pain, the guilt, and the shame that I had myself for not being the mother I should have been. Then the day came, I got the phone call while I was at work. My son died alone in a motel room in Cincinnati. My only son was gone, just like that. At that instant, NOTHING looked the same ever again. I felt like wallpaper. Just there, stuck to the wall. People were talking to me and I couldn't hear anything they were saying. Two weeks later my son would have turned twenty-five.

I had been drinking for two weeks straight. Then, one night, I tried to end the pain by taking an entire bottle of Klonopin, with tons of alcohol. God saved me that night. I woke up in the hospital. My best friend found me. A couple of months later I made a decision: either I was going to wake up with this deep pain every day or I was going to find a way to survive in this world, not feeling the pain. So, I just started walking forward. I got help, I went to therapy (trauma therapy). I turned to God. I prayed, I developed HOPE...I stayed busy. I even took a long "vacation." I moved to Northern California for about a year. I knew no one. I had never been there before. I learned how to live a new life. I learned about diversity, finding my way around the area. I made new friends. I conquered life when it got rough. I found a thirteen-week Grief Share. The best thing I did was a grief group. Now I'm back home, helping people who struggle with addiction and studying to be a public speaker/life coach. I bought a fixer upper.

I enjoy life now. It's a different life. It's one I can laugh in and feel good in. The shades of color still shine, just in a different light. Although I miss my son like crazy, and I still cry at times, I've accepted what happened to Kevin. He is not suffering anymore or in pain. I talk to him sometimes as if he came by to visit. I don't care what people think; it makes me feel like he is close to me. My advice to you is...You have to go through the pain in order to get through the pain. Always have Hope. Never give up on yourself. It does get better!

Kevin's Mom,

RHENEA M.
Lubbock, Texas

Chase

Devastation. Grief. Aftermath. Where do we go from here?

I was so angry at Chase when he died. I mean really fkn angry at him! He wasn't an addict but he could have been headed there; I'll never know. I couldn't shake the anger and I was also so overwhelmed with the sadness that he was alone, scared, and he needed me and there was nothing I could do. What the hell happened and why?

This emotional state lasted for quite some time...many months until one day I met a new acquaintance while working on the **POSITIVEVIBES (PV)** mission. This person as a holistic energy healer that operated an alternative pain, health, and wellness service business. I met with her to discuss participating as a vendor in an upcoming PV event. I had never met her before, and she did not know me. During the meeting, she stopped short and told me that Chase wanted to tell me something. She was bringing through an energy and she needed me to listen. She told me that Chase wanted me to know that he made a mistake. That he was so upset with himself because he knew better.

My first reaction was "mistake!" You're honestly going to tell me this was an fkn mistake? I was DONE! I could barely breathe through the sobbing because this sounded exactly like something he would say!!! OMFG! Now what am I supposed to do with that? A mistake and he's mad at himself? Of course you are! I was so torn up and I realized I was talking to him in front of a complete stranger. At that point to save my sanity because I had no clue what had just happened, I asked her to stop!!! But before she would let me off the hook, she told me that he needed me to know this so that I would forgive him so that we could both move on in peace.

It wasn't long after that encounter that I attended a local county Hospice Butterfly Release event in memorial of lost loved ones. On that day, I forgave my son and let my anger go. I sent the butterfly off to let Chase know I forgave him and that I would always love and miss him from the bottom of my heart! I promised him I would keep up the fight so others wouldn't fall, and he promised me he would be right by my side!

Somewhere, I've heard we are all born with a purpose and when that purpose has been fulfilled, we leave this life and move on to another. My father, my mother, and now my son have completed their purpose and we must complete ours no matter how long it takes. I have always believed there is a spiritual world out there. I raised Chase to be kind and strong. We do the best we can. I love talking about him and seeing the signs he sends me. An example of this is six months after I lost Chase, a sunflower bloomed from the seeds I brought home and planted from our local Tri-County Memory Walk. Only one flower came up out of the ground and bloomed. It was beautiful! I was so delighted to see one of the seeds made it and I knew he was trying to tell me something. The very next morning, Chase's car was no longer in the driveway. It had finally been repossessed by the lender. I had been dreading the day I would look out the kitchen window in the early morning hours and his car would be gone! I realized something as simple as a sunflower blooming the day before was his message that he was right there to make that dreaded moment a little less painful. And it certainly did!

Missing and loving my baby boy will never end. A piece of my entire being is gone. Find your purpose. Your babies are counting on you to find peace so they can find peace. All my love to you, Chase. I will fight in your honor and memory so that your death will never be in vain! To all you beautiful Momma's: May you find your Peace.

Chase's Mom,

SANDY M.
Chesapeake Beach, Maryland

Justin Kyle

FOREVER 31

My son, who we called Kyle (born February 17, 1986) passed away August 18, 2017, from fentanyl poisoning. Kyle struggled with drug addiction for fifteen years. He had been in prison twice, been through rehab a few times, and successfully completed drug court.

Kyle's struggles began in his early teens. He and I battled this demon together for the most part. My son went to prison in April of 2017 for a 120-day treatment program. He came home August 17, 2017. I was skeptical to say the least. We had been through so much together.

I got up the morning of the seventeenth, went to work as usual. At 11:10 a.m., I got a call from his girlfriend (mother of his two little girls, my granddaughters) that he had been dumped at the emergency room and was unresponsive. By the time I got back to the office to get my car, I was pulled into the administration's office and told that my son has passed away. He had not even been out of prison for twenty-four hours yet. My world collapsed at that very moment.

I was taken to the hospital, and saw my son, who had been DUMPED there by people I'm sure he assumed were friends! He was less than a mile from a fire station, come to find out later, and these friends chose to throw him in a shower to try and revive him, losing precious time, and then drive him to the ER and dump him!! Any charges? Nope!!

Lots of "what if" since that day. Life has not and will never be the same. His babies miss him, and for all his faults, he was the best daddy!! Not real sure how to end this, other than Kyle is my first thought in the morning and my last thought at night...Almost three years later.

Justin "Kyle's" Mom,

CHRISTIE M.
Harrisburg, Missouri

Nik

FOREVER 23

After two failed local inpatient stays, I was determined to help my twenty-three-year-old son with his newfound addiction to Xanax and alcohol. Nik was twenty-two when he was discharged to outpatient after the second stay.

We arrived for outpatient at eight a.m. only to find out that this facility stopped taking our insurance about four years prior, even though that was part of the discharge instructions from the inpatient facility who had set up the appointment. It was also a facility that I worked for.

Apparently, they called my son to let him know prior to the appointment but he had no working phone and they didn't call my cell, even though my number was the contact number because of **HIPAA**.

Reeling from the news that he was not going to be able to do outpatient and having no back up plan, I spent the whole day calling every local resource I could think of to get my son continued help. I even called the crisis hotline. Nothing was available. It would be weeks before anyone could see him. We had no other dual diagnosis center around here.

One of my friends that I worked with in the ER mentioned a place in Port St. Lucie, Florida. I called and I was able to get him a flight there the next day. This place worked well for Nik, he had over 100 days of sobriety in and he was serious about making a change. Unfortunately, his heart had other plans. He met a girl in recovery there, they transitioned to a sober living house together and they decided they were good, so moved out on their own into a small trailer in Delray Beach, Florida.

That was the beginning of the end. From June 2018 to December 22, 2018, Nik and his girlfriend relapsed, recovered, and repeated. They were shuffled from one rehab to another, from one location to another. One rehab even had its own pharmacy on site. They were homeless at one point and found one of their last detoxes. While there they were both offered a job at a local telemarketing company that exclusively hired addicts and/or people in recovery.

They both took a job there, found a doctor close by who would give both of them unlimited quantities of Klonopin and for extra cash, he would give them each another blue bottle of Klonopin. Apparently, this doctor has been "on the radar" for more than six years by the DEA, but they just don't have enough evidence to nail his door shut.

After working at the telemarketing company, they found a room for rent in a "sober living home" which was unsupervised and unregulated which happens to also be owned by the owners of the telemarketing company. How convenient.

They have a room; they can lock their door and do as they please and no one will bother them. There are four other couples in this house that also rent rooms. The week of December 18, Nik and his girlfriend make another trip to a different doctor, who also gives them unlimited quantities of Klonopin.

The day before, in Nik's last Snapchat, Nik is shown emptying one of the bottles of Klonopin onto a dresser. Later that day, Nik decides to smoke crack cocaine and goes into work with his girlfriend. They are both high and unintelligible and they are both sent home by a supervisor that also happens to live at the same house.

The same day, Nik buys four heroin capsules and they decide to try heroin, on top of the Klonopin and crack cocaine, and that night, they both overdose in their rented room. Apparently, one of the other tenants heard weird noises coming from their room and someone decided to break the door in as it was locked.

Nik and his girlfriend are both found on the floor, both having overdosed. Unfortunately, also in this "sober living home" there is not ONE dose of Narcan present in the house. One person starts CPR on Nik and his girlfriend, another person runs to a nearby house to retrieve Narcan and 911 is finally called.

The Narcan was administered to Nik's girlfriend and after two doses, she is revived. Nik is not responsive to the Narcan and as EMS arrives, they also administer Narcan and he is still unresponsive, although he has a pulse. They arrive at the ER and after two hours of end of life measures, including intubation, Narcan, the Lucas machine performing CPR and an IO line, they pronounce Nik's death at 2:14 am on December 22, 2018.

Nik was twenty-three-years old, had traveled around the world, and had goals and aspirations, just as any other twenty-three-year-old. Unfortunately, the heroin he snorted was pure fentanyl, according to the coroner report, not even a trace of morphine or hydromorphone was found in Nik's blood or urine. Nik never stood a chance.

Nik's girlfriend did live, and currently resides in her home state. The police investigation was closed February 14, 2019, due to lack of evidence, even though the captain of the sheriff's department admits that one, an inexperienced detective was assigned to Nik's case in the beginning and even though they had his phone, it wasn't accessed for months after his death, leaving the murdering drug dealer to get far away from the area by then.

Two, the captain also admits that the ball was dropped on more than one occasion.

Days after Nik's death, I went to Florida and conducted my own investigation and gave the sheriff's department an eleven-page report as to what happened, names and details. I gave them everything, except for the dealer. Too little, too late. Today it is July 26, 2020, and I have just passed the nineteenth-month mark of losing my only son.

Nikolas' Mom,

BROOKE M.
Beloit, Wisconsin

Jason

FOREVER 38

Where do I begin? My son Jason started smoking marijuana at the age of thirteen, stole money from his step brother to buy drugs, and robbed stores to get what he wanted. He had a tremendous heart. As a dog trainer, he took in dogs no one wanted to rehabilitate them. Those who knew Jason, the real Jason, loved him. But those drugs were stronger than him and he was strong.

Things spiraled downhill as he got older, in and out of juvenile court. At the age of fifteen, he moved out of the house and moved in with his sister who was eighteen. At age eighteen, he started his own dog behavioral business, which was very successful, but with success there were now different kinds of drugs: crack, coke, pills, you name it. Now jail time and rehabs were in his future. Fortunately, he always landed on his feet.

In 2015, he got married, which only lasted two years because of the drugs. When I think about how hard he struggled only to wind up dead, it still baffles me. He tried so hard; when he had to check in when he was on probation or parole, he went. Last time he was in prison, he said that he would never go back there. Who would have thought that God wanted him, so he wouldn't suffer any longer?

The road was long and hard for both of us. I never gave up on him and he knew that. I never put him down and he knew I would always be there for him.

Our song was *I Turn to You* by Christina Aguilera. Jason had a good heart. Unfortunately, I didn't know how bad and how hard he struggled, because he was mostly on his own.

If I was given one wish, I think it would be that God would have saved him to live his life clean and sober and strong. He gave him a heart of gold, which he shared when he was clean.

I'm grateful to have been given the time I had with him and would gladly do it all over again if I had the chance. Love MOM.

Jason's Mom,

Jean M.
Great Neck, New York

Aaron

FOREVER 34

I had two children so that they could depend on each other and grow old with each other. That ended on May 20, 2020, at 1:30 p.m.

The week before, Aaron, my youngest son, shot up heroin in our hall bathroom. I knocked on his door at eight a.m., the thirteenth, and asked if he was awake and he answered, "Yes, Mom."

He was supposed to help me with yard work that morning. I tapped on his door again and he acknowledged he was getting up. I went outside for about ten minutes and came in to eat a little. I didn't finish what I was eating because something made me call his name. He didn't answer. I jumped up and opened his bedroom, not there, and turned to the bathroom behind me. The door was closed. I felt myself panic, but then a little relief because the door was opening...but then it hit something. Aaron was on the floor... flat on his back with his arms to his side and his legs stretched out but bent slightly.

I had never found him like that. He was usually all crumbled up with his arms bent up, and jammed against the door so that I could not open it. I pushed on his chest, saying, "Aaron," and heard the whoosh of air come out. I paused and knew something was wrong.

OMG, I never thought he would die, I thought he would get clean and have the life he so wanted! No breathing, no pulse, they asked how long, I didn't know...ten to fifteen minutes???? I did chest compressions until they got there...I couldn't do anymore. Aaron died then. It took his breath away as it usually did but he didn't realize, or remember, he was sick, and his breath didn't return. When they brought him out they said he had a faint heart beat but was not breathing on his own.

A week later, they let us come see him and told us the bad news. Aaron had severe brain damage and what wasn't damaged was what was keeping him breathing, but he was slowly dying. So May 20, 2020 at 1:20, we had everything removed. For five minutes, Aaron kept breathing and then he stopped. Aaron's heart kept beating for five more minutes and then it stopped. I was the first to cut this little boy's hair and I was the last one to cut his hair as a young man.

Aaron Freed was born November 29, 1985, at 7:19 a.m. in Baton Rouge, Louisiana. He is our second of two sons. Such a happy boy. He was that little skinny boy that took the sun and how it browned his skin...he had a Japanese grandmother. Aaron was so smart. If he read it, he remembered it. I think as he got older he was embarrassed to always know the answer...and being shy, he turned to drugs...pain pills. I was told that it made you feel very good, basically taking all those worries and aches away.

He said he started taking them in junior high. Around that time his soon-to-be best friend, Matt, moved into our neighborhood. They were just alike, both very smart, and on the quiet shy side. They both also shared something else...an alcoholic parent. Aaron graduated, addicted to pain pills, with a 3.8 GPA. He was in TOPS so he received three years of college free of charge as long as he kept his grades up. After the first year of college, he confessed he had a problem but was dealing with it.

Start of second year, we knew he wasn't dealing with it as he pawned his laptop twice. He dropped out, lost TOPS, and we paid for the one-and-one-half years of college which he basically failed. Right after that his best friend, Matt, had been diagnosed with terminal

447

cancer. Approximately two years later, he passed away. I know it affected Aaron a lot. Both were twenty-four years old...one is dead and the other is an opiate addict.

Aaron stole basically anything he could sell fast and easy. Over eighteen years, he took a lot...probably $20,000 plus from us. We bought him cars, phone, etc. to help him get back to work. We didn't give up...though he put us into a position of hating him...trust was gone. He could lie with the best and then beg forgiveness, because he knew he was wrong. But he got away with it and some say we enabled him...it was us or someone else. And I felt he was our responsibility. He was our son. Our flesh and blood and we loved him beyond words. And he knew that.

Aaron went to numerous detox clinics, mostly state funded until he couldn't because he had been thrown out of one and none of them would take him until a year passed. We paid one place locally for treatment up to six months. He detoxed and wanted out , didn't believe in their methods, took me four months to get the rest of my money back. So I wasn't a fan of that place. But Aaron did play us to get thrown out of detox. Within a few days of detox and back home, he started taking pain pills again. The last ten years were rough. But the last five years were the worst. Pain pills, OMG, they finally say how addictive they are...well too damn late for our son and millions of others.

Aaron said he thought he would never shoot up but when the oxys and such dried up, he said the person he bought the heroin from shot him up. And that began the damage he slowly started. Ten days before I found him basically dead, Aaron was admitted to the hospital via ambulance which he told us was because he was having trouble breathing. I was so frustrated with him because this happened every time he shot up. He would have an ailment and I would tell him, "Well, you just shot up...do you think that had something to do with it????"

The hospital this time actually did check him out. I brought him home two days later and he seemed in good spirits. That last week was quiet but good between us. If I had only called the doctor at the hospital and spoke with him, after telling Aaron to relay that they could talk to me, but Aaron became agitated while there and just bad-mouthed me. I wasn't bringing him food, they were starving him, I could bring him food but I just wouldn't...and on and on. I think he forgot we were in a pandemic with COVID. So I never called to speak with the hospital, just told Aaron to call me when he was released.

After we let Aaron go, I found his discharge papers/folder. Aaron was diagnosed with pneumonia, 60% oxygen level, and given antibiotics for it. He was also told he had suffered some brain damage, which Aaron realized during that last week; it must have been true because he was having problems remembers things and people. Aaron had a very good memory! I asked why he had antibiotics and he said his ear must be infected; it had been bothering him. He never mentioned the pneumonia, and only mentioned the low oxygen to explain why he could not breathe and they said if he had gone to sleep, he could have died.

Something else he ask me during that week, "How long did I lay on the floor [after shooting up]?" He would be out for one to one-and-a-half hours. I would keep checking on him and shaking him. I thought it was normal. Aaron looked at me puzzled and walked away. Asked me again that day or next the same question with the same expression. I should have stopped what I was doing and questioned him. I could have pieced this all together because he was not remembering things. My baby didn't remember and he was trying to.

The last few months, things were happening and Aaron didn't know why because he was forgetting before he could connect it. I lost my baby because I tried to mind my own business and let him take care of it. But he needed me then and I failed him to a degree. Yes, he continued because it was his crutch and he was scared to lose it. It had comforted him all those years even though he knew his mother wasn't letting go...I wanted Aaron to be normal again just like he wanted but he was too scared to let it go. As soon as stress came on, he didn't know how to deal with it. He couldn't deal with everyday chores or responsibilities, and being told he needed to stay close so we could help him. He would turn to alcohol (which he had always hated) to ease the stress. But it just didn't do it and then he would get out and chase that dragon.

Aaron was a wonderful son. I know he loved me and hated it when he hurt me. But between the lying, hallucinations (men in black, dark cars, people in the house, shadow people), stealing, ranting, etc...I was so tired and scared. I always had the thought that when people killed themselves, they just didn't even know they were doing it. Like mentally they just were gone. And I got scared because I thought it would happen to me. I couldn't leave Aaron...I was just beat down. My husband usually works out of state so had been in Texas the last two years plus.

My oldest son lived five miles away. We were all close and spoke regularly. Aaron had taken a toll on all of us. His brother hardly talked to him and the last few months he only came over because I needed him to help me deal with Aaron. His dad would call him but then bring up stuff that was done and gone and scream at him about it, and that it better not be happening again. I told him not to talk to him if that's all he could do.

The last three years, Aaron had been mainly here with me. The last year, he was clean for three months and said how good he felt and didn't want to go back to be addicted. I got him an auto and new phone, so he could get back to work. Asked him to please try to take a job that he could come home from every day, but he said he would be alright working out of town. The last two years, he had barely worked a month or two per year. He couldn't stop using and would lose his job. So it was so good to see him happy. He sent a selfie to his brother...it was such a beautiful picture of him smiling. You could see how happy and proud he was of himself.

Probably a month and half, and he came home for Thanksgiving. I noticed a hint but thought it was me. By Christmas, he couldn't make up his mind whether he was coming home or not. Said he was staying there; the place was sixty-five miles away, but suddenly he calls me because he couldn't remember the alarm code. Then suddenly texted back, he remembered it. That should have told me then about his memory loss. Even under the influence, Aaron remembered things. By the end of a chaotic January on his part, he had called 911 on his way to work because he thought he was having a heart attack or blood clot. He lost his job a few days later.

I never thought he would die. Aaron was still thinking of what he could accomplish if he stayed clean. He always thanked me or said, "I love you, Mom," when I did something for him or got him something he liked or wanted. He loved to read...books, internet, about history, theory, loved fruit and took care of my muscadines, figs, and Asian pear. "I already fertilized them, Mom." Aaron was a wonderful son and person. He was so kind-hearted and would help out anyone. Even after his ranting at me, it would be like he woke up realizing what he had done and say, "I am sorry, Mom." Yes, he was horrible to us at times. But when he apologized he meant it. No one could believe he had suffered all these years. I just wanted him to have his life back like he wanted to.

I know now that it probably was going to end like this. Aaron was scared to let go. It had him and he knew it. He hated what it had done to him. He always thanked me and said I must have loved him for still being there for him. I had always said no matter what I would stand by my sons because I was their mother. And I may have been the only one there for them. I have thoughts of everything we went through, the bad and the good. It almost destroyed me. But instead, it destroyed Aaron.

The sweet young man that couldn't talk to me because he was a private person even when he knew I would help him. And when he did, it had already got him. Aaron was so well read that he kept up with drug info... when it was finally coming out that pain pills were addictive, he was already depending on it. So just one moment, a few seconds, to just hold his hand and look into his eyes so he could see I didn't want to let him go.

He was and still is a wonderful son, brother, and person. He had so much potential to become whatever he wanted. (I knew this would be hard, and have cried so hard...I do keep a journal to remind me of him, the good and the bad. Aaron was so loved. And he knew that and loved us).

Thank you.

Aaron's Mom,

SANDRA M.
Walker, Louisiana

Cory

My son Cory started experimenting with drugs at the age of sixteen. He never did heroin or meth until he met the girl who would become his wife. She was addicted to both. He couldn't understand why she couldn't just stop using those drugs. So, he wanted to prove to her that he could do them and not be addicted. Boy was he wrong. First time using haunted him for the rest of his life.

They went on to have three beautiful children. He loved being a dad. He did everything with them. Got himself clean on his own. Life was going good for him. He landed a good job. Was divorcing. Found himself in a good position to possibly get his kids back. But after a year he relapsed. He died at the age of twenty-eight.

He has four kids who miss their daddy so much. I tried getting him put in jail to save him but that of course didn't work. Bought their food rather than give them money. But they always found a way to get what

452

their body craved. He cried to me about who/what he had become. But the drugs won. They almost always do.

Now I live a life without my only son. And it's miserable and lonely and sad. My heart is forever broken and lost.

Cory's Mom,

Jackie M.
Neenah, Wisconsin

Jacob

FOREVER 24

My amazing son, Jacob "Jake" was born in Hazelcrest, Illinois, on January 7, 1996. I now had a perfect little family, a girl and a boy. My heart was full. As a child, Jake loved playing out in the woods, riding his bike, and fixing things on the little workbench that he had. As he got older, he played baseball and wrestled, but his most favorite thing to do was fish. He had dreams of becoming a marine biologist. Jake and I always had a special bond. When he was a baby, I had to rock him to sleep every night. As he grew older, he was always so protective of me, maybe because I was mostly a single mom. We had a strong mother/son connection.

The beginning of the drug use was when Jacob was fifteen and I caught him with marijuana. I was somewhat lenient with him smoking; the rule was, not in the house. The first time he got in trouble with the law he was out riding his bike. The police said he was trespassing at the gate entrance of a factory no longer in business. They arrested him, actually towed his bicycle, and brought him to the station. I had to leave

454

work to pick him up. I found out he had a small amount of marijuana on him. After that court date he was ordered to go to drug classes. This was his first "offense." At sixteen, I came home from work one night and he was sitting in the garage. This was not unusual because he had made a little space in there for him to hangout. I got out of the car and he looked at me and said, "I am making my last phone calls."

He had called a friend and my mother to say his "goodbyes." I immediately called 9-1-1. I saw no signs of this coming. He eventually agreed to be taken to the hospital. After they did a drug test and I found out it was positive for cocaine, I was in shock. He then was transferred to a mental health facility, after my demands that he not be sent home, because he told me, "I'm just going to do the same thing." At eighteen, Jacob was diagnosed with Crohn's disease. This really took his life for a spin. New diet, new medications, new lifestyle. It was a lot for a teen to handle.

In October of 2015, Jacob came into my room and said, "Mom, I need to tell you something." I sat down and asked what it was. He told me that he had done heroin. I had begged him that if he was ever in that scenario, to please call me and not do it. This was my worst fear. My first reaction was, "Ok, we need to get you to a rehab. We can fix this. I am here for you." I was so naive at that time. I knew nothing about addiction. He agreed to go. I drove him an hour away, late at night. We arrived and he then refused to stay because he didn't like the way the treatment program was run. Frightened, I drove us back home while he was detoxing. He was sweating, then freezing, and trying to open the car door while I drove 65 mph down the highway. I slept on my bedroom floor with him that night. We tried another rehab the next morning. That lasted for almost a week and he left.

June of 2016, I received a phone call from an unknown number. It was Jacob, calling from a hospital. He had overdosed in his car and a passerby called 9-1-1. The police cut his seatbelt off, administered Narcan again, and towed his car. December 4, 2016, I found him barely breathing wedged between the toilet and the shower in his bathroom with a needle and spoon on the bathroom sink. My hands were shaking so bad it took me three tries to dial 9-1-1. They finally arrived and revived him with several doses of Narcan. He stayed in the hospital for a week after that overdose.

During the course of the next year, Jacob was in and out of several California rehabs. October 25, 2017, Jacob slipped down a hill of wet grass and broke his ankle in three different places. Fear sets in again, because how was he going to get through surgery and recovery without narcotics? He had been clean for almost a year. December 6, 2017, Jacob and I were talking about how he was going to sign up for college classes again. I then went to work and six hours later received a phone call from a police officer that Jacob had been in an accident.

He had crossed several lanes of traffic and hit landscaping blocks surrounding a large gas station sign and flipped his car. He had to be cut out of the vehicle and walked away with only a fat lip and the boot on his previously broken ankle. At the time, we did not know that he had a warrant out for his arrest, so he was taken to jail from the hospital. I refused to bail him out this time, fearing that he would die if able to do drugs again. He stayed in jail for four months after completing a thirty-day rehab program while there.

In December 2019, on Christmas Eve, Jacob said to me that he was in so much pain and he couldn't take it anymore and that he had to "go get something."

Fast forward to the morning of March 7, 2020. Jacob had been holding down a job at the local gas station across the street from our house. He got home from work at one a.m. and woke me up excited because he had just gotten a $3 an hour raise! I fell back asleep, woke up around eight a.m., and started to cook breakfast. Jacob walked out of his room and I asked him, "Did you even sleep?" He told me no, not really. He would stay up and play video games sometimes. He asked me to make him breakfast, which I did. It was now about ten a.m. and he said he was going to try and get some sleep, and could I wake him up around three p.m. so he could go to work? At three p.m., I opened the door to his room to wake him up, but the light was on. He was lying on his side, facing the wall, with his feet on the ground. I yelled his name and see that he is lying in a pile of vomit and his lips are blue. I roll him over and start CPR. I run to my room to get the Narcan I kept in case of an overdose. I fumble through administering that, then resume CPR.

My friend calls 9-1-1. Paramedics and police arrive and work on him for what seems like forever. Being a nurse, I knew that it was too late to save him. I ask the medics to stop. They tell me they can't stop, unless he has a DNR, which he doesn't. This can't be happening. It's all surreal. Am I really seeing this machine trying to pump life into my son? They take him to the hospital, and I follow. As soon as I arrive, I am placed into a separate room. I already knew my son is gone. A parent's worst fear. My life is forever changed. I do not know if he was actively using since December or not. If he was, I couldn't tell.

There are so many "what ifs" that go through my mind on a daily basis, but I know I tried everything I could to love and protect my son from the demons of addiction and mental illness. If you love an active user or someone in recovery, let them know! They need to know they are loved. Their self-esteem is sometimes zero. Addiction is a disease and it doesn't make the user a bad person. If you think your child would never use drugs, guess again. Addiction does not discriminate based on age, sex, or race. Listen to what they tell you when they do talk to you. Pay attention to those little signs. It can be their way of reaching out, without directly asking for help.

Finally, if I could scream from the rooftops on the reality of addiction, I would say that reality can be hard to face. But if you don't face it head on, addiction will devour and control, not only your loved one, but your entire family and you may never get them back mentally or physically. Be an advocate. Don't be afraid to talk about it, you just might save someone's life.

Jacob's Mom,

Lisa M.
Lowell, Indiana

Bryant

Bryant Adam was born on November 4,1989, to his loving parents Kevin and Sue, and joining a brother, Jeremy. Bryant was a really good baby, hardly ever cried. He was a fun-loving child, always so silly. You could be having a really bad day and he would flash those baby blue eyes and big smile and your heart would melt. Bryant had an infectious laugh everyone loved. He enjoyed trips to the shore and visiting his cousins and grandmother. He enjoyed skateboarding, snowboarding, rollerblading, and video games.

At the age of seven, Bryant began having seizures in his sleep until the age of twelve and a half. He was on Depakote to control the seizures. Bryant was diagnosed with ADD. He also struggled with reading. He was placed on Adderall for a few years. I will always question myself as to whether that led to his drug abuse later. He didn't like school at all. Bryant was a hands-on learner. He was excellent at drawing. Now where did this all go wrong for him? I would say when he thirteen years old.

Bryant was drawing people with nooses around their necks and weapons. Bryant became obsessed with weapons. I took him to see a psychologist. Bryant saw him for many years. He was referred to a psychiatrist, who did not make a diagnosis. He only said to let the boy have a pocketknife, what a quack. Bryant went to a technical school in the ninth grade. He took up precision machinery. It was a hard struggle to get Bryant through school. He was cutting classes in his senior year. He had mingled with other boys that were not good influences. I later learned he had been smoking marijuana.

After Bryant graduated, he got a job working in a factory. He also met a girl, online, that he went to stay with for three weeks in another state. When Bryant came back, he was a different person. He seemed angry at most everything. He decided to move out, into his own apartment. He was throwing wild parties and selling marijuana. When he sold to an uncover police officer and spent three weeks in jail, he lost his apartment and moved back home with us. He also went on spending sprees racking up over $5,000 in debt. He was placed on probation for two years. Bryant found a girlfriend and seemed to be doing well for a few years. He slipped once with cocaine. He got back on track from the ages of twenty-three to twenty-seven.

He broke up with his girlfriend of five years. His grandmother passed away a few weeks later. Bryant fell back into drugs, doing meth, cocaine, speed balling, heroin, and marijuana. He got meth laced with bath salts and he was in a paranoid, delusional state of mind. He thought others were out to get him. He didn't recognize his own father. He saw things that weren't there. He took his bow and arrow outside to wait for the people he said were out to get him. I had to go to the hospital and get a 302 order for the police to pick him up. The police officers came to the house and picked him up and he spent two days in the hospital. Once he got out, he began using again. I found the drugs in his room. I called the police. They filled out a report. Bryant had to spend four months in jail and was placed on probation for two years.

Bryant seemed to be doing better, or so I thought, until he was pulled over by the police. They found needles in his car. He got added time to probation. I found drugs in his room again. I called the police.

He spent another four months in jail. I begged him to go to rehab. The DA gave him a choice to go to rehab or jail. He chose rehab, only staying a week. They said he would be picked up and placed in jail. That didn't happen for another few months. He spent yet another four months in jail. Once he got out, he began using again. I called his probation officer and it took her three days to call me back. She came out to test him only once. They found marijuana, but only a small amount. The police officer told me I was only buying him time and that he needed to go to a rehab away from here. I told him I would rather visit him in jail than his grave.

The laws need to change. If you're over eighteen, you should be forced into rehab instead of jail. They can force you into jail, why not rehab? Bryant was to go back to jail for two months, before he passed away. They only added another six months to his probation. If Bryant had gone back to jail, maybe he would still be with us, at least a little longer. He had his probation meeting on December 17, 2019. He didn't come home for hours. I immediately thought he was buying drugs. I called him to see when he would be home. Once he got home, he threw the paper in my face and said, "See, I told you I was clean." I never said he wasn't. It was this feeling that he was buying because he knew he didn't have to go back until April for his probation meeting. That was a Tuesday.

Bryant worked third shift. He worked with his brother. They carpooled together most of the time. Wednesday morning, they came home. Jeremy, his brother, said Bryant had been throwing up. I thought, "Oh God, please no, not drugs." Bryant had been clean for five months. He said it was McDonald's food that made him sick. He went to work Wednesday evening. I checked around his room and found nothing. After he got off in the morning on Thursday, December 19, he stopped at a grocery store. He called me several times and texted me about what I would need to make him candy and fudge for his Christmas party. He seemed in pretty good spirits. Bryant had posted on his Facebook page, the day before he passed away, how much he liked his job; how he was feeling blessed this holiday season. I told him, before I left to go to work, not to forget the candy. Those were my last words spoken to him. How I wish my last words to him were how much I love him. I often told him that. I just wish they would have been my last words.

After my shift was finished at eleven p.m., I headed home. I pulled to the end of the road across from my driveway. I saw two police officers standing there. I thought someone had been pulled over. As I pulled into my driveway and got out of my car, I saw them heading towards my driveway. I knew it was bad. I went into the house. I saw my husband standing there looking very shaken. He said, "I tried, I really tried to save him, but it was too late." I screamed, "Oh no! Please don't tell me Bryant's gone." I ran downstairs to be with him. The coroner wouldn't allow me to see him. I was frantically saying for hours, "No God, please no God, please." Bryant was thirty years old. He had told me several weeks earlier, on his 30th birthday, he was surprised he made it to see thirty. Bryant was way more than his addiction. He was the guy with a huge heart. He would help people out working on their cars, helping them move, without asking anything in return. He bought a guy groceries, twice, when he had none. Bryant would always take things out of my hands and carry them for me, even the light things. He did a toy drive, because he said every child should have a toy at Christmas. That is how I want him to be remembered.

Christmas Eve, we were at the funeral home and the cemetery making arrangements for his memorial service. He was laid to rest on December 27, 2019. Bryant had told me two years before he passed away that he was molested when he was younger. I told him it wasn't his fault. I wish so badly he had told me when it happened. I am so heartbroken that some monster could do that to a child. He told me that when he was twenty years old, he witnessed a person get their hand cut off for snitching on a drug dealer. He also said he witnessed a person getting their head chopped off for snitching. I honestly don't know if that was true or if he was under the influence of drugs. Either way it was real to him and he said that haunted him.

As a parent, I can tell you what it was like before my precious son Bryant passed away and what it is like now. Before he passed away, I was constantly checking his room. I would call or text him when he was out for a while. When he didn't get back to me, fear would flood my body. Our biggest fear was finding him in his room passed away from drugs. I never lost my temper or patience with him because I knew he had an illness which he couldn't control. I had people tell me you need to kick him out. A one-size-fits-all approach doesn't work. I knew my precious son better than anyone. I knew he would die sooner, if I had kicked him out. I told my son he was playing Russian roulette with his life. There is no middle ground. You either get sober or you will die. Bryant said he always knew what he was getting and the people who sold it to him. I know he thought he was getting heroin, not that he should be buying that. He sadly got pure fentanyl.

It has been pure Hell since Bryant passed away. Not a day has gone by that I don't break down and cry. I am forever changed. I feel like I stepped out of myself and I am living in another person's shoes. I am severely depressed. I don't know how to live without him. By the grace of God, lots of praying and taking everyday minute by minute, that is how I am still breathing. There is absolutely nothing worse than the loss of your precious child.

The siblings that are left behind don't know how to deal with the loss either. It is extremely hard on all those that love and care about Bryant. I really don't know what advice to give to other parents who have a child with addiction other than: let them know how much you love them and how valuable they are. Let them know you are there for them. Let them know your love is unconditional, there is nothing they could do to take your love away.

All my love and prayers go out to all who are struggling with addiction and those who are affected by watching their loved one slowly slipping away. To those who have lost a loved one, know you're not alone. Your loved one will always live in your heart. They will continue to be as much a part of your life as they were before they passed away.

Bryant's Mom,

SUE M.
Dover, Pennsylvania

Mark

FOREVER 29

I was driving today and saw a man who looked like Mark. That's all it takes for grief to overcome me. But as I drove, tears streaming down my face, I realized something special. Every memory that flashes through me is always a good one involving Mark.

Before I go on, let me stress the fact that life with Mark wasn't always perfect, to say the least. Mark hit the ground running from the moment he was born. As a baby he never slept. As a teenager he never stopped skateboarding, even after many trips to the ER. As he grew older, it was always apparent Mark was around, whenever you heard his loud, raucous laughter or were awakened by his size thirteen feet walking through the house.

After his passing, I relived his childhood over and over in my head. I also relived the times in his life that may have led him down the wrong path, but then a strange thing would happen. If my mind wandered to an unpleasant memory, it would suddenly switch gears and a nice memory would suddenly be center stage in my brain.

So, as I drove today, I had this thought. Is a mother's brain protected in some way by God's hand to only be able to remember the goodness of the child she lost? Does it shield us from the anxiety of remembering times when we were angry and frustrated with each other? Do grieving parents need this cushion to help us move on?

As I continue through life, I know memories are all I have of my son. Tonight, I will thank God for preserving these precious thoughts and disposing of the negative ones, because now I realize there is no space in my brain for them...there's only room for good thoughts.

Mark's Mom,

KATHLEEN M.
Finleyville, Pennsylvania

Joseph, Timothy, Lauren, Stephen & Andrew

FOREVER 32, 22, 28, 30 & 32

My life for over the past twenty years has been filled with the horrors of addiction. Five of my twelve children have lost their lives to the struggle of addiction!

My first born, Joseph, was an accomplished left-handed bass guitarist. His struggle started at sixteen, but he knew how to hide it. And at the time of his death on November 21, 2000, addiction was not talked about much.

Once he turned eighteen, he just left and would only call me every once in a while to let me know he was ok. Joey worked on a cruise ship as a master chef, played guitar, and started a recording studio. Still, he stayed away. Finally, one day another of my children told me Joey was a heroin addict and that's why he stayed away. The day he died he was found in a stairway by an unknown person. My phone rang, and because I wasn't home, the detective left me a message to call him ASAP. Once I told his brother, he took the reins and made the call. It was confirmed his brother had died. I can hardly remember getting through the next week with the funeral.

465

Next, my children's father's cancer returned. Even though we had divorced ten years earlier, my heart broke some more. After all, he was the father of my twelve children. The depression, loneliness, and heartache intensified. I no longer understood why death was so cruel.

One year later, my son Timothy died of an overdose. He was speed balling, mixing heroin and cocaine. I never even knew Timmy did any drugs. He was a carpenter living on his own, had a girlfriend and life plans. I later learned he was at a friend's house, there were three of them together doing the speed balling thing. Timmy had a seizure and his friends just put him in another room to sleep it off. In the morning when they found him, rigor mortis had set in. He had died hours earlier and his friends just kept on partying.

Three years later, my daughter Lauren, who struggled with depression and mental illness, entered a hospital psychiatric unit for a suicide intervention. While there, she was introduced to fentanyl by another patient. She had suffered for years with anxiety, depression, and whatever else you can imagine. Her one time of staying in recovery was while she was having her son. I was overjoyed with this recovery. But it was short lived. Drugs were what relieved her, but she couldn't do it the right way. She had to self-medicate. She left the hospital on February 28, and two days later she was found deceased at a friend's house.

My son Stephen struggled for years with heroin addiction and overdosed in an apartment complex hallway.

My son Andrew, who we called Doug, lived with me. His struggle was the worst thing I ever saw in my life. Narcan was always in my home just in case. Doug overdosed many times and we were always able to save him. Finally, he went into the methadone clinic and did well. He stayed in it for about two years. Then he decided he was ready to phase off it. I didn't think he was ready and begged him to stay in the clinic. He didn't stay and phased off by the end of May. I was on my guard because I have lived through recovery and relapses with him many times. Two months later, I saw the look in his eyes that told me he was probably using again.

It was Thursday, August 8, 2019, when I confronted Doug about my feelings he was using again. Of course, he told me, "No, I'm not." I looked him in the eye and told him, "You need to go back to the methadone clinic, because I don't want to find you dead." He gave me a hug, told me he loved me, and walked into his room. I walked downstairs to my room. Ten minutes later, I heard my daughter running across the hall upstairs. When I got up there five seconds later, she had given him Narcan, was doing CPR, and she looked up at me and told me there wasn't a heartbeat.

That's how my five children died. Now, some would ask what kind of life their childhood was. All my children were born to a loving family. We did all the things a family does. They were no different from anyone else. I cherish the memories we had. I remember every detail of their life before drugs.

My story is repeated hundreds of times a day to families all over the world. Our internal grief is like a fire inside us that never goes away. We lose friends, family, and sometimes our other children because, we have lost a child and they just can't understand. Will we always grieve? Yes, we will. Will our life ever be the same? No it won't. After the funeral, we suffer from the loss of family and friends who just don't understand we are no longer the same person. We watch as our children's friends get married, have children, graduate college, and make major accomplishments in life. We hear their parents bragging about them. But what we don't hear from our family and friends is the name of our children. They act like they never existed. We also hear, it's time to move on and get over it. A very insensitive thing to say, we will never get over it. And of course, there is the person who says stupid things like he/she is in a better place. This stupidity makes me cry every time.

I haven't really talked much about my children in detail. I think for the most part, all our children were a blessing and as a child were for the most part a normal child. As they struggle through addiction, they do their best to hide it from us. And honestly, they do, until they can no longer control the number of drugs they need to stay stable. This is when the signs start. Stealing, name calling, and abuse. My children did it all. The lies to get money. And all the other things they do. These signals say the addiction is stronger than the person. When this happens, we go into overdrive. We take them to detox, we support them in recovery. We watch them at every turn. We become the advocate to get all the help they need: clinics, meetings, and mental health care. We regulate their life like they were two years old in an effort to save them. But then relapse happens. We do this over and over because we are fighting for their life. For some it works, but the sad truth is eight out of ten of the clients in detox relapse as soon as they leave it.

For the people out there who haven't reached the plateau of losing someone to addiction, don't ever thing it can't or won't happen. Addicts have a stigma attached to them, but it's so wrong. They are hurting and have an illness that needs to be addressed just like any other illness is addressed. I truly hope this book reaches the people who haven't lived through addiction and the loss of a loved one. We need to bring it to a halt. We need more prosecuting of drug dealers. We need love and support. And above all,

we need for everyone to understand that substance use addiction is real and can happen to anyone. Addiction doesn't care about gender, race, or financial standing.

Joseph, Timothy, Lauren, Stephen and Andrew's Mom,

CAROL M.
Shirley, Massachusetts

Nikki

FOREVER 23

Brandy Nichole "Nikki" was a beautiful twenty-three-year-old girl, who battled addiction for about eight years! Starting with tramadol and ending with drug toxicity.

She left behind a family who adore and miss her and a beautiful son who was only three when she passed! Nikki fought hard but just couldn't beat this demon.

Nikki's Mom,
KAREN M.
Austin, Arkansa

Shane & Joshua

FOREVER 24 & 41

I have five children, two girls and three boys. My youngest two sons are in heaven. They died from drug addiction.

My first son Joshua began with pain killers and then meth, due to a back injury. He was twenty-four, married with two kids, a two-and-a-half-year-old son and eight-month-old daughter. His wife was also on meth. They asked if I could take the kids, since they lost everything and had to move. I agreed because I knew they were using.

I got the phone call on May 13, 2006, that he was gone. They were without utilities and were warming up in the car. It was in the garage, with the car running to stay warm, not in their right minds from being up for two weeks on meth.

She went into the house and Josh fell asleep in his garage. He died from carbon monoxide poisoning. She fell asleep and found him the next day. I had the kids for nine and a half years until their mom got clean.

They were only on meth for five months.

My second son Shane had spinal bifida when he was born. It wasn't full blown, but back then they did not do ultrasounds. As he got older, he was in severe pain, so he also got pain killers. He also drank. He received a severe head injury at sixteen, when he was jumped by a gang. I had both boys in football, both very well-known. Quarterback Shane got second All City.

Shane finally got on methadone. He did good for fourteen years. He relapsed several times. He had four kids. He got arrested and was in jail and on probation. He relapsed again and went back to jail. He stayed there until they got him a bed at a recovery center. He was there about three months. He got out and stayed at my house for a couple of months. He was sober for eleven months and attended meetings. He told his testimony everywhere and was very faithful to God. I'm pretty sure he had brain damage from his head injury. He was also mixing heroin and meth before he went to jail. He was not the same, ever.

I was at my mom's taking care of her; she had dementia. I got the phone call on August 21. I told his fiancé I hadn't heard back from Shane. He had gotten his own apartment and I didn't know where. Nobody had the address. This was on the nineteenth. I knew he was gone; everyone was looking for him. My oldest son was the one who called me. Shane died with another person in his apartment. They both died from pure carfentanyl, an elephant tranquilizer that comes from China. He had been dead since the nineteenth and no-one found him until the 21st of August. He was 41.

My mom died a week after I buried my second son. I'm not going into great detail since my story is about two. I couldn't begin to tell you that I screamed so loud about both my boys and that I thought I was not going to stop. There is no greater loss than your babies. There aren't even words that could describe how it tears your heart out. I'm here to be their voice and keep their memories alive. I'm currently dealing with my second son's fiancé, she's on meth. I pray that God can intervene in this horrible epidemic. Gone too soon. Addicts aren't bad people; my boys were very kind and loved by many. Addiction is a disease.

Shane and Joshua's Mom,

KATHRYN M.
Akron, Ohio

Lincoln

FOREVER 32

Lincoln was born on November 8, 1985, in Summersville, West Virginia, the same day as devastating flooding hit in a part of the state not known for flooding. Perhaps this was a foreshadowing of the larger than life personality he would develop at an early age. Even as young as three years old, Lincoln had a restless spirit when he was alone and tried to run away from home. He was very intuitive of the tension in our nuclear family caused by his father's verbal and emotional abuse of me and the physical abuse he and his older sister would endure.

Lincoln had the innate ability to draw others to him and lead them into fun activities. I have often used Tom Sawyer's chore of white washing the fence turned into a neighborhood party as similar to the ability Lincoln had to attract others to him and then convince them that whatever they were doing together was enjoyable. Lincoln was involved in many activities while growing up. He also attended church with me and his sister every week and attended vacation Bible school every summer. He loved day care and pre-school where he could entertain other kids his age and older. He frequently memorized the dialogue from children's movies and would recite selections when he saw the occasion to share. It seemed that he could behave himself at most of the places where he was active, but not all. If he behaved acceptably at church and school, he would misbehave at Cub Scouts. If he behaved himself at football, base-ball, wrestling, or taekwondo, then he would misbehave at home or church.

When Lincoln started to misbehave at public school, he would do well if the teacher could find a way to let him lead or help. But if the teacher was a strict disciplinarian, he would not do his schoolwork and find ways to disrupt. When he was in middle school, his older sister went through a stage where she frequently colored her blond hair unusual colors without any backlash. But when Lincoln colored his blond hair blue, he had to spend the whole day in the principal's office without lunch or instruction, and because he got into trouble, I was required to attend his seventh-grade prom with him. He got involved in community theater during the summers, which he loved, but he found a way to get into trouble while staying overnight at an interpretive trail event. He devoted himself to football in the ninth grade, playing every play on both offense and defense, even scoring a touchdown on defense, but his efforts were not rewarded with the six players who were honored, including the backup quarterback. This lack of recognition was a pivotal event for him, and he requested a change of school for high school.

The summer between tenth and eleventh grade, Lincoln attended church camp for the third or fourth time. He loved church camp because he could entertain people, share his empathy and love of God with others, and be in a leadership role. Before this particular church camp, our pastor, who was also director of the camp, prayed that some pastors would be called during that camp. There were three young men who were called by God to be pastors at that church camp, including Lincoln. His first year of high school in tenth grade seemed to be a good change for him, but when he was forced to go back to his old high school and his sister went away to college, things went from bad to

474

worse. He later told me that he was jealous because his sister got to be independent. After preaching at our church about how important it was to choose your friends wisely because they could help build you up or drag you down, he did the exact opposite. His old football friends, who were a better influence on him, were no longer in his inner circle. His new friends included boys from another town and some high school dropouts.

One Sunday, after Lincoln had refused to go to church, he told me that he was going to hang out at the park with one of these new friends. When I told him, "No, you can't go because you didn't go to church," he pushed me out of the way and went anyway. Later that same week, when his high school dropout friend wanted to spend the night before he moved away, I told Lincoln, "No, because you can't have friends stay over on a school night." That boy showed up at our house at ten p.m. anyway, and I did not have the heart to turn him away at that late hour with no place to go. The next day, Lincoln ran away from home with that boy and his mother, whose name I didn't even know, to another town. Lincoln was gone for two months without contacting me. I didn't even know how to search for him because the boy's last name was the most common name in that town where they had moved. What was I going to tell the police if I asked them to help? He left during the day when I was at work, so I had no idea what he was wearing, only the name of the boy who he was last seen with and the name of the town where they moved in the next county. When I cleaned Lincoln's room, I discovered empty bottles of alcohol under his bed. I had no idea that he had been drinking or using any drugs, but that did explain the mood changes from fun-loving and caring to hostile and angry.

After two months of worrying and wondering where he was, and when, or if, he would come home, Lincoln showed up at home, close to Christmas. He stayed during the whole school break, but when January 2 rolled around and I got him up to go back to school, he mumbled something as I went out the door to go to work at my own school. At the end of the school day he called me, at my school, and told me that he was leaving again, because he was not going back to school. When I asked my teacher colleagues what I should do, they advised me to stop by the courthouse and file an incorrigible petition against him, because if he didn't go to school, I could get into trouble for his truancy. After I followed their advice, I got a call from the state police saying that they had taken him into custody and he was placed temporarily with child services. I was not aware, but when I filed that incorrigible petition, I had signed away my rights as a parent to make any decisions about his care. Later, when a hearing was held, he was given the choice to go to his father's house, go home with me, or go into foster care. He chose foster care. Why would a sixteen-year-old be able to make such a life-altering decision?

After spending the rest of his eleventh-grade year in several group homes and attending four different schools in one academic year, he chose to spend his senior year living with his father, his abuser. He never came home to live with me again. I was devastated that he no longer wanted anything to do with me. I had lost both my children in two months, his sister to college and Lincoln to foster care. Lincoln did grad-uate, but he had gotten into trouble at that school when some other boy jumped him in the hall, and with the no tolerance policy, he finished with out-of-school suspension lessons sent to him in the mail. At his dad's insistence, he had taken the physical to join the armed service, but deliberately failed the drug test by smoking marijuana before he went. This was the first time I knew for sure that not only was alcohol a prob-lem, but so were drugs.

Lincoln and his girlfriend got married at the end of that summer and had my grandson in February of the next year. They struggled financially since neither of them had any trade skills or advanced educa-tion. At one point, they both decided to apply for the military. He was told that he would never be accepted because he had failed that initial drug test. She was accepted into the navy but not the air force because she had spent so much time in foster care herself. While she was at boot camp, he was a stay at home dad and seemed to love it when I visited, keeping the house and his son clean and fed. When she got back, he got employment with a local pizzeria and was loving the work. He learned to manage the business, but then he discovered that his wife was having an affair. Then, he hurt his back at work and did not have health insur-ance, so he couldn't go to a chiropractor as I suggested, but he could get all the pain killers he wanted by going to urgent care or the emergency room. His marriage fell apart, his wife moved away with his son, and his drug addiction got worse.

Lincoln moved back and forth between Kentucky and North Carolina. He was in and out of jail for a number of drug-related offenses, most of which I knew nothing about because he was now living with his father again. Once, he was even arrested in Myrtle Beach for public intoxication when he had been drinking with his father, after he stopped to help a couple change a flat tire. His dad spent money on court costs and lawyers to try to keep him out of more trouble. At one point, he lost his driver's license because he had speeding tickets in four states. Lincoln spent the next several years in and out of trouble with the law for DUI's and driving with a suspended license.

He stole leftover pain killers from each family member he visited back in West Virginia. He volunteered to go to rehab to get out of jail early and worked for the rehab center, typing notes for the counselors there, and it was in that lucid time that I got to spend my last week with him in 2015. By 2016, out of the past sixteen years, I had seen Lincoln at his own house twice and he had spent two separate weeks with me, when he had his son, in all those summers.

Finally, there was a party at his father's house, after his father had passed away a month earlier. Lincoln had seemed lucid, focused, and determined to finally answer his call into ministry at his dad's funeral, telling family members he was planning to enroll in college that fall. He had been running away from me, school, and God for sixteen years by this point. During this party, his girlfriend who was also his supplier, called 911 after she and another guy drug his body out of the house on a tarp to the driveway. Everyone else at the party left in a hurry to beat the ambulance, even driving through the neighbors' yards. The EMTs administered Narcan, but Lincoln lived twenty minutes from the nearest town, so it was too late to save him. He was transported to the local hospital.

Lincoln died on June 26, 2018 at about two a.m. outside of Louisa, Kentucky. The coroner did a toxicology test, which said he died of seventeen times the lethal dose of fentanyl. His girlfriend waited twenty-four hours before telling anyone in the family that he had passed. We only found out because a high school friend of Lincoln's and his wife's, who worked at the hospital, called her to tell her. The girlfriend used the time to back up a truck to the sliding glass doors of the house and steal everything of any value from the house and the vehicle, as well. When I

477

arrived at the house the next day, I could still see the tarp they drug him out of the house on, the EMT's gloves, a clear plastic sleeve with the remnants of a white powder, and a bloody towel. The sheriff refused to come to the house to investigate or to send a deputy with me to the house. Even after we had set up trap cameras to catch the girlfriend coming back to steal more things from the house, the sheriff refused to send anyone out.

The girlfriend had his body transported to West Virginia and claimed to be his wife to the funeral home director. She had asked that his body be immediately cremated and to have no service. The funeral director knew both Lincoln and I, so he was suspicious. When she couldn't produce a marriage certificate four days later, my daughter-in-law and I finally got to make decisions about his body. We were advised not to look at his body or let my grandson look at his body, because even though he had been refrigerated, the condition of an unprepared body was not something we should remember. The girlfriend's actions threw up all kinds of red flags to all of us, but I later learned that anyone could claim a body in West Virginia; you don't have to show any proof of relationship. The state of Kentucky would not do an autopsy, so, consequently, I paid for a private autopsy, but I had to tell the doctor what to look for. When he asked me, I thought to myself, "Really, you're the doctor!" I suggested he look for needle marks in his right arm because Lincoln was right-handed and could not have given himself a shot there. I also had to call multiple times over weeks and weeks to get the results, for which I had already paid $5,000 for.

After investigating through Facebook, pawn shops, court records, bank records, talking to neighbors, and Lincoln's break-up letter with his girlfriend, I took the information that my daughter, my daughter-in-law, and I had gathered to a private investigator. After looking over the information, he determined that we just didn't have enough proof that the girlfriend had deliberately killed Lincoln or that she alone had taken over $4,000 of Lincoln's dad's money. Because the things were stolen in Kentucky and the girlfriend took them to West Virginia to pawn, we could not get Kentucky or West Virginia State Police or county law enforcement in either state to do anything. Even though we tracked down one of the pawn shops where she pawned some of the items, we were not allowed to know which items were pawned because we did not have an order from the police department to find out. The only bright spots in locating the stolen items were that we got to purchase Lincoln's kayak for my grandson and the bank did refund some of the ATM withdrawals made after both deaths.

I guess I will never know why Lincoln was the only one who died at that party or how he ingested the fentanyl. I can only imagine that he was having one last party before he kicked out his drug-addicted friends, and led the way to try this new batch himself. One of the most ironic things about this whole tragic story is that Lincoln grew up in Huntington, West Virginia, and even though I had thought I had taken him out of that environment early enough in middle school, it still did not keep him away from the available drugs. He actually started his addiction to pain killers in North Carolina, but Huntington is known as the epicenter of the opioid epidemic in West Virginia. That sad fact was played out in the lives of the kids who grew up in our middle-class neighborhood in Huntington. Out of the six children who spent almost every day at our house in the summers, growing up together, four of them are now dead from overdoses or suicide because of addiction. Only my daughter and the son of a policeman survive today. Among that small group of close friends, two young men and two young women were victims of this dreaded disease. These were good kids from good families. My children were the children of a schoolteacher and a home improvement store manager. Two families had divorced parents, but two did not. One of these kids was the son of a nurse and a coach. We all were involved in our children's lives growing up and took them to church (different denominations), teaching them morals as well as how to show love to others.

My heart is broken because God did not help save my son from his addiction in the way I had envisioned! Instead of helping Lincoln live out his call into ministry, God chose me instead. I am still healing and hope to help others in their own journeys through grief and maybe help some other families avoid the pain I have experienced. I don't know what advice I would give other parents except to love your children the best you can and pray that they never feel the need to run away from you or their lives. Perhaps I should have insisted that Lincoln get counseling when he was sixteen, but what I chose to do in an effort to help him actually took that choice out of my hands. Do all that you can to help your children, but there will probably come a time when no matter what you choose to do, it will not change the reality of the strong attraction of these powerful drugs. Everyone makes mistakes, but the mistakes our children made had such dire consequences that they never got another chance to do better. Many people in my generation have tried drugs, but they had the chance to grow up and learn to make better choices. The children of this generation can become addicted from doing what is medically necessary or taking illicit drugs; opioids don't make that distinction, and neither should we in judging whether someone deserves to get the help they need. Opioids actually change the function of the brain to the point where the capacity to reason is gone and those centers of the brain must slowly be rebuilt.

Substance use disorder is not a character flaw, but a chemical attack that destroys brain function. Long-term rehab with a transitional living situation afterward is probably the only solution to help those addicted. There can be life after addiction because I have seen it. A friend of mine was talking to someone about the hopelessness of the addiction problem, doubting that anything could work, when that person said, "Well, I was a heroin addict, and now I am a neurosurgeon." I just pray that your children

get a chance to get that help and remember that God loves us all. Sometimes ultimate healing only comes when God calls us home.

Lincoln's Mom,

REV. PAULA N.
New Haven, West Virgina

Ian

FOREVER 30

No one wants to have to write that their child has passed on due to a drug overdose. First, I have to say my husband fought with alcoholism his whole life. My kids grew up seeing this. He took his own life eight years ago.

Both my youngest and oldest child struggled with drugs. My youngest tried hard not to do drugs. It's such a long story and journey I have had with both boys.

Ian moved back home with me because he had no job and no money, and was doing good. I would not give him any money. He finally got a job. With his first pay check, he went and bought heroin. I found him dead in his room one night.

Words cannot describe the horror of that night. I lost another part of me. I know I could write so much more. I am still fighting to help my oldest son and his wife to stay clean.

They had their kids taken away from them for a year. They lived with me while I helped them get clean. So far, they are doing well. I don't judge anyone who does drugs. I just would be there to help them.

Ian's Mom,

DIANE N.
Newark, Ohio

Alecia

FOREVER 24

My Daughter Alecia, our lil "Lee" and babygirl, battled addiction. Alecia was the girl that if you met her, you wouldn't forget her. I smile as I describe her as she had a way of making everyone feel like family. She also carried with her a deep faith all of her 24 years and believed that she would recover. Unfortunately as strong as our little girl was, she fought a war with a demon that ultimately won. Throughout this fight however she always had with her journals which tell the story of her life, setting the timelines through her battle including the turn of events and eventual tragedy.

A man, a well-known man, in the recovery community came to our home and sold us on the quality of treatment our sweet Alicia would be provided as well as the steps that would be taken to prevent a patient from leaving the facility. He then arranged for Alecia's flight to a S.

Florida addiction rehabilitation center. She left on May 23rd, 2015 and returned four months later lifeless, in a cold wooden box several days after her Sept 23rd, 2015 death.

That man also attended Alecia's funeral services and he brought with him a "crew" of other people. For what you may ask? Later we found out it was to recruit others struggling with addiction who were at the funeral to do the same in leaving our state for treatment. There were 350 people in attendance, surely there had to be a few more suffering from addiction. He was right. You see, having PPO insurance, especially from out of state, was a "Golden Ticket" for what they call "body brokers" that could amount to $500-$3000 or more per person they sent to treatment. For the facilities receiving the patient, it amounts to multiple thousands of dollars a day per patient.

Looking back I now understand that Alecia enduring multiple surgeries, her ongoing medical conditions and mental health challenges would be on the top of the list for setting her up for relapse. A medical condition would arise while she was in that S. Florida treatment center . As a result, a decision was made between Alecia, her therapist and myself to transfer her to a facility better able to accommodate treating her addiction in the setting of other medical issues. When we made these arrangements with the facility, they said they would escort Alecia to the airport at 5:30 am to board her flight.

A plane ticket was purchased for Sept 23rd,2015 at 7:30 am for a flight to Jacksonville, FL. On Sept 22,2015, Alecia was taken by a center treatment tech to the doctor and then to a local hospital ER. She would have many tests, was given morphine for kidney stones and then discharged though she was still in extreme pain from multiple health conditions. She called me several times that day with her final call that evening.

"They didn't take me back to the facility. They took me to the airport about 12 hours early", Alecia said.

My husband and I would call 20+ times pushing every number on the phone for extensions, but couldn't get a hold of anyone at the treatment facility.

Alecia found an elderly gentleman at the airport who allowed her to charge her phone, however she was in pain suffering. Her last FB post said "Dear God please guide me & help me find the strength to save myself from myself." Her earthly saving would not come to happen, she did not survive the night. She left the airport, became a victim of foul play and died of an overdose.

There needs to be a complete and total overhaul of treatment for addiction in this country. We need qualified, educated, degreed, licensed healthcare providers and physicians to provide "substance abuse disorder care". This is a disease, not a moral failure of the person nor the family. We are losing nearly 200 people a day from this horrific opioid epidemic. Please research and choose care providers carefully making sure it fits best with your family member's personal situation.

I am so thankful for this opportunity to bring awareness. I feel blessed to know Bobbie Ziemer (Madison's mom and Author of this book) as well as PJ Champion Sallie (Christina's mom and Founder of #NotInVain). I will personally be eternally grateful for #NotInVain and all of the angel mamas I've met through this unfortunate "sisterhood". Through our tragedies we have united, lifted, supported and picked each other up. For as one we can do so little but together we can do SOOO much.

Love, hugs and prayers to every parent that has a piece of their heart in heaven.

Alecia's Mom,

KIM N.
Orland Park, Illinois

Kevin

FOREVER 27

I was shivering uncontrollably. I was scared. My baby needed to be delivered by emergency C-section. The cord was wrapped around his neck. Doctors and nurses dashing for supplies, hooking me up to monitors, raising a screen so I couldn't see the cut they would make in my abdomen. Pressure and pulling, a warm tear sliding down the side of my face, hoping that my baby would be okay, and then he was born. He was perfect, he was crying, he was healthy, and I fell in love with my second son Kevin.

I didn't know then that this beautiful child of mine would bring me so much love and laughter and so much heartbreak and tears. Kevin had a cherubic face and long, dark eyelashes that framed his big brown eyes. His smile and laugh were infectious. But no matter how sweet and bubbly his personality seemed from the outside, Kevin was always dealing with turmoil inside. He could be happy, laughing, and content and then become frustrated, angry, and controlling in an instant. I often wondered if something happened to him when that cord was wrapped around his neck. Or was it simply the circumstances of his life that made him feel this way?

Kevin always felt like he was competing against his older brother, Bryan. Competing for attention, competing for love, competing for recognition. I tried to give Kevin all the attention, all the love, and all the recognition he needed, but he didn't need it from me. I divorced the boys' father when they were very young. Kevin was not even a year old when we separated, and he and his father never built a relationship. When the boys saw their father, Kevin felt left out and as if he were a burden. He never had the support he needed from his father.

Kevin had difficulty making friends as a child. He was bossy and controlling and because of this, other kids didn't want to play with him. He never had the support he needed from friends. In school, Kevin was a bright student, but his behavior was immature, and he was placed in a pre-first grade classroom to give him time to mature before moving on to first grade. You wouldn't think that a six-year-old would comprehend that he was being held back a year from his peers, but Kevin knew what had happened and resented me for taking him away from the kids he had made connections with. Teachers constantly compared Kevin to his older brother and mentioned how they loved having Bryan as a student. He never had the support he needed to feel comfortable in school. I gave Kevin everything I could: love, toys, safety, home, care, but I could never give him the things he felt were missing. I couldn't give him what Bryan had; a relationship with his father, teachers that adored him, and friends that he could count on.

Then as Kevin grew older, his body stopped growing with him. As a ten-year-old child, he had the stature of a six-year-old. Instead of growing taller, he began to develop a chubby stomach and stocky legs. His physical features were not ideal for a boy that was starting middle school and Kevin grew tired of the negative attention and bullying that he endured due to his size. A year of medical tests revealed that he was lacking human growth hormone and he began taking a replacement. Kevin learned to inject the replacement himself, into his stomach muscle every morning for two years, until he grew to an average height and lost the weight he carried in his mid-section. The physical growth Kevin went through changed him into a handsome young man with a thin frame, an angelic face, and the same beautiful eyes he had as a baby. The physical acceptance made him more outgoing and popular among his peers.

In school, Kevin became defiant and uncaring about his grades. He skipped school, hung out with a new group of friends, and took physical risks when skateboarding and doing tricks on BMX bikes. Kevin finally received the recognition, had the friends, and had the attention that he had been craving. I didn't know it at the time, but his newfound acceptance was developed through the use of alcohol and drugs.

I clearly remember the night that I discovered that Kevin was experimenting with drugs. I caught him and his friends behind the shed in our backyard smoking pot. I smelled the smoky, sweet scent in the night air, long before I saw them. They were sitting in a cloud of smoke and laughing at things that would only be funny when under the influence. I was angry that all the conversations Kevin and I had about the danger of drugs meant nothing. I was disappointed that Kevin could so easily be swayed by peer pressure and friends. I thought that our special bond and the way I had always protected Kevin would keep him from such dangers. I was wrong, so very wrong.

I learned in the next few months that it didn't matter what I said, what I did, or how much love I had for him, alcohol and drugs controlled Kevin more than I ever could as a parent. I don't know when a few beers and some weed turned into more, but it happened fast. I started getting calls from school that they believed Kevin was under the influence. Drug testing became routine and Kevin became more defiant and withdrawn. In the summer, he would be out all day and then come home with wide pupils and a nasty attitude. My sweet boy that once hugged me and told me that he loved me now spewed obscenities and hate when I asked about his well-being.

My days turned into worry and my nights turned into restlessness and sobbing at the way he had changed. Money, prescription drugs, and possessions began to disappear, and I desperately tried to find help for my son. We were living in New Jersey, a state that did not consider addiction a disease, and there were few resources available. I would spend hours searching the web for treatment facilities and call them to find out that they didn't take insurance, they didn't take adolescents, the program would cost $35,000 at minimum, and that they could help me take out a second mortgage on my home to pay for their services, which were not guaranteed to work. I finally found a rehab in Pennsylvania that would take him. On the intake call, I found out that Kevin was addicted to alcohol, marijuana, benzos, and opioids.

That evening, I tried to help Kevin pack his belongings, but he didn't want my help. He didn't want to go to rehab but said that he would "rather go there than spend one more day in this house with this bitch," which was me, of course. The four-hour car ride to the facility was quiet and stressful. What do you say to someone going to rehab? I wanted to tell Kevin everything I had in my heart; that I hoped the recovery would help him; that I loved him no matter his struggles; that I would always be there for him, but Kevin had no intention of talking to me, the bitch that wouldn't leave him alone to live his best life.

Checking into the facility was a long process of waiting and completing paperwork, but after a few hours, they finally called him into the room for intake. I followed and was stopped at the door. I was told to leave, to say goodbye, and to go home. As a fourteen-year-old, Kevin was old enough to have medical consent for his own mental health treatment. It didn't matter that they were taking my insurance, my payment, my child, it was now none of my business and I was floored. I left not knowing if Kevin would give the facility his permission to share any information with me at all. I was told if he did not give his consent then they would deny knowing who he was if I called. I felt like I had just lost my child.

Fortunately, Kevin gave consent for me to receive information regarding his care and after two weeks I was given the opportunity to attend a family session and to see Kevin. I drove up the night before and stayed at the hotel where a shuttle would pick up the families in the morning. As the shuttle bus drove up to and through the grounds of the facility, family members vied for a glimpse of their child, and we were ushered into a meeting room. Introductions were made and I was the only single mom attending and I had the youngest child at the facility. I just knew the other parents were staring at me, judging me, and deciding that I was certainly an unfit mother. I felt like a failure. But I listened and learned as the counselor explained enabling, as she walked in a circle and kicked obstacles out of her way.

A kick to the tissue box on the floor and she exclaimed, "Mom gave me money for my bills, but I will use the money to buy drugs." A kick to a book on the floor and she stated, "Dad lets me stay in the house. I don't need a job and I can spend my day getting high." I related to some of the examples, but not most. My child was fourteen. I was responsible for the health and welfare of my child. I couldn't throw him out on the streets. I learned about Al-Anon and tough love. I saw Kevin and told him I was proud of his success with sobriety. We talked and hugged like old times. I left feeling like all would be good in the world again.

> *Kevin: got oxy???????*
> *GT: dude u outta rehab u clean??*
> *Kevin: bin waitin 30 days 2 get hi tunnel in 10*

Yes, I set up an app on his phone to spy on him. I felt bad betraying his privacy, but this is why. Kevin had been home from rehab for less than thirty minutes and he already wanted to get high!

The outpatient counselor that came to our home had not been able to get through to him. He's high again every day. He's been kicked out of high school for truancy and drug use. He's had his nose broken in a fight. He's on prescription medications for anxiety, but he says they don't help. I had him arrested for punching a hole in my wall. He's been to court and released back to me because of his age. He threatens to kill himself. He threatens to kill me. I have had him committed for mental health. He gets released after a few days and it all starts again. I have to hide my purse when I come home. He took they key and stole hundreds of dollars out of the safe. Where is my camera, the leaf blower, the TV in his room? Probably pawned or sold for drug money.

My brother tried to let him move in with him, but he was arrested for drugs on the third day he was there. He becomes unresponsive after using and I am worried that I should call an ambulance, but I don't because he gets mad when I try to intervene. I go away for the day on my birthday and my backyard turns into a drunken party with twenty teens, a keg, and all the meat I had in the freezer, now on the grill. It is not unusual for the police to be at my door. I watch the monitor in his hospital room and hope that his blood pressure comes up to normal and then I cry as he calls me a "f-ing bitch" for taking him there. One more rehab stay. He is kicked out after two weeks and he calls me at two a.m.

to say that he is wandering the streets in Phoenix with no money and no place to go. I fly him home. I love Kevin. He is my son and I am his mom, but I am tired, I am devastated, and I don't know what to do anymore. I love him and I support him, but I can't change him.

Somehow through everything going on with Kevin, I have met someone, and we are getting married in Aruba. We fly all of our kids to the Caribbean and our closest family members join us there. We are enjoying our trip, until Kevin begins to withdraw the night before the ceremony. He disappears from the hotel property, comes back high, and becomes confrontational with my brother. Hotel security is called to break up the fight. Sometimes I feel like Kevin causes issues to destroy my happiness. In the past three years I haven't been able to celebrate a birthday, go out on a date, or take a day trip without Kevin causing a problem. Now it seems that he is trying to ruin my wedding. It is the night before my happy day, and I am far from happy. The next day Kevin, age seventeen, walks me down the aisle while Bryan, age twenty, plays guitar. I marry the man I love, and all is right for a while.

The addict needs to remove themselves from the people and places that trigger their use in order to recover. We move 600 miles away to South Carolina and within a few days he has met new "friends" that are dealers and we are a family in crisis again. Arrests, court appearances, panicked phone calls, missing money, missing prescriptions, fights, and more drama than ever. He overdosed in a public restroom and I rushed to the hospital. The doctor told me that he would die if he kept using. Heroin was his go-to now. I took him home knowing that nothing that was said or done had changed him. I continued to pick him up from neighborhoods that scared me, and I watched him deteriorate physically and mentally.

Then dealers started coming into our neighborhood, across the street, and then right up to our house. Again, he agreed to go to rehab. But before we could go, he needed $50 to pay off a dealer, so they wouldn't come to our house. He frightened me, and I gave him money and a ride to the house to take care of his debt. An hour into our trip to the rehab in Georgia, Kevin asked to stop at a rest area. I spent a panicked thirty minutes realizing how stupid I had been to give him money for the drugs he was now using in that restroom. I feared he wouldn't come out. I feared I had just bought him his fatal dose. I was about to ask a gentleman to check on him when he came out like nothing had happened and we continued on to the facility where he would spend the next eight weeks.

I wish I could tell you that this time the rehab was successful, but it was not. Every spoon we once had was now burnt and bent in his room. His nightstand was littered with food containers, blackened spoons, tin foil, and black residue everywhere. The siding outside his bedroom window was covered in black soot. The carpet was ruined, and the walls were dingy. He used, he slept, and he went out to get more. That was his life. Kevin was nineteen now and I had no legal requirement to keep him in my house. I couldn't live this way anymore: in fear of his dealers, in fear of his dying, in constant turmoil.

I drove him to the homeless shelter downtown and said, "Get out." He begged, "Please mom, don't throw me away. I know I have a problem. I'm trying to get better. I need you. I love you. Please don't do this to me." I cried and I took him home, again. I drove him to the mental health facility, and I said, "Get out and get help." He called me two hours later and said, "Please mom, I can't go there. I know I need help, but I can't be locked away again. I want to get better, but I need you. I love you." I picked him up and took him home, again. I wanted so desperately to help him, but I couldn't leave him on the streets. I knew I should, but I couldn't. I thought I loved him too much to see him suffer, but I watched him suffer every day, as a heroin addict.

I made him promise that if he wanted to stay in the house, he would not use in the house. He couldn't keep his promise. When he was confronted, he took a knife and threatened to kill himself. I made him leave and called the police. I begged them not to shoot him. When the police came, he bolted into the house and up to his room where he locked himself in. The officers tried to reason with him through the door, but he wouldn't answer. They asked permission to break the door down and I gave it. He was shooting heroin, getting his last fix, and then left with the officers peacefully.

They asked, "Where do you want him to go when he is released?" and I said, "I don't know, but he can't come back here." The next day he called and asked if he could come home. No was my answer. He begged me to get him help. I told him no, that he had already been to numerous rehabs and facilities for inpatient and outpatient and that he obviously wasn't willing to change. I told him that I loved him and that I would always love him, but that I could no longer support his drug use. I was holding strong and it was breaking my heart.

Again, he called and begged me to send him to rehab one more time. He said, "Please, I love you and I don't want to leave this way. Please help me one more time and if I can't get clean, I promise I will not come back." I arranged for him to go to Florida, one last time, two days before Christmas in 2012. I drove him to the airport in silence. I couldn't look at him, I couldn't talk to him. I thought I would never see him again, but I needed him to go. When we arrived at the airport I said, "I hope I see you again one day. Good luck." No hugs, no goodbye, no "I love you." I pulled away and drove home with tears streaming down my face.

About a month later I was asked to write an impact letter to Kevin. The counselor said I should be honest about how I felt his drug use over the past eight years had impacted our relationship. This is what I wrote:

January 2013
Dear Kevin,

I wanted to write you and let you know how your drug abuse has impacted my life:

1. I lost my son, for too many years, and it has hurt me very badly.

The last time I remember really knowing Kevin, I think he was about twelve or thirteen years old. But since then I have only known him as an angry teenager and a sad, young adult with so many drugs in his body that even he doesn't know who he is anymore. I have become depressed knowing that I can't help my own child, even though I desperately want to more than anything in the world.

2. I have jeopardized relationships with my husband, my son (your brother Bryan), and my family by enabling you.

Why did I put the needs of a drug addict before the needs of my other family members? Because you manipulated me and lied to me.

493

You made me feel sorry for you and scared for you. You used me. Others saw through your lies, but my love for you prevented me from doing so. This caused a lot of strain in my relationships with others that cared for me. They saw the pain that you caused me, but I didn't listen. I wanted to help you and you kept using me. The more you hurt me, the more you hurt my relationships.

3. I have worried about my job too many times.

I have told you MANY times that what you do in my house can jeopardize my job as a professional, and you did not seem to care. But this worried me greatly. I have worked very hard for the job, home, and nice things that we do have. I don't want to lose it because of your selfish need to deal drugs on my property and to take and shoot up illegal drugs in my home.

4. I don't trust you.

I know drug addicts are desperate, but to steal from your own family is low. The money, the electronics, the medicine, gifts, everything! And then to lie about it instead of apologizing just hurt more.

You don't listen. I asked you to respect my home and you didn't. I had to pull out the rug from your bedroom and repaint all the walls because it reeked from smoke. Why? Because you couldn't follow a simple rule not to smoke in the house.

I am afraid to go away. Why? You cause a problem anytime I go away. Think about it. It is like you don't want me to enjoy myself so you seek to destroy any fun I might have. What happened when I went to Montana? San Diego? You called me each time with a major emergency. Why do you do this to me?

Is it a lie? Is it the truth? Nobody knows anymore.

5. I am broke!!

How many cars did you ruin because you drove them under the influence of drugs? Three? You are lucky you didn't kill anyone! I can't even begin to tell you how much money I have spent on cars, gas, and insurance for you, so that you could enjoy the freedom to hang out with your druggie friends and dealers.

Lawyers, bailouts, police tickets, treatment centers, flights, emergency money (so you don't get killed), money that gets stolen from me, money that gets stolen from your brother, cigarettes, prescriptions, money to buy back the prescriptions that got "stolen", etc. Do you have any idea how much money you have cost me?

6. I am stressed.

When you are around there is always some kind of drama! Somebody wants to kill you. Somebody put a gun to your head. You were arrested. You need some Xanax NOW! You are going to kill someone NOW! Someone stole your prescription AGAIN. You aren't home AGAIN. You are smoking in your room AGAIN. The police are at our door AGAIN. Another drug dealer just pulled up in front of our house after I asked you not to ever have anyone pull up in front of our house. The drug dealer needs money NOW or they are going to kill you. I am in bed at 10:00 p.m. and you need a ride home. How much more of this can I take??

7. I am thinking about giving up on you.

You tell me you are doing well, but I have heard it before. I really want you to mean it this time. I can't take any more heartache of hoping you were going to get better just to see you again with a needle sticking out of your arm.

I can't keep being brought down by your drug abuse. Do I need to give up on you or are you really, ready to make a change?

Why am I even writing you this, Kevin? Because I really do want you to make a change. You have impacted my life in some very negative ways, but I will always love you.

Maybe in the near future I will be able to write you a letter on how your sober living has impacted my life for good. Can you imagine some of the things that could be in that letter? Some of the reparations you could make to me when you get your life going without drugs? I am looking forward to that. Please continue to work on making it happen.

Love,
Mom

Kevin lived in Florida for a little over two years. He completed his time in rehab, then moved to a halfway house, and eventually moved in with roommates. He met many people that became good friends and together they learned that life can be good without drugs. I even think that for the first time, Kevin fell in love and experienced real emotions, without being under the influence. I think most importantly, he was accepted for who he was, as clean and sober Kevin. It took some time for us to become close again, but through visits and phone calls we built a new relationship. I got my beautiful boy back again.

In 2015, Kevin came back to South Carolina and lived with me for about a year while he got his life in order. He began taking college courses, in Florida, and he wanted to continue his education in hospitality and tourism, at the University of South Carolina. He got a job at a local restaurant where he worked as a busboy, then server, then bar-back, then bartender. Just like when he was little, Kevin thrived on attention, personal connections, and recognition for doing a good job. He interned there for his college experience and planned to continue with the company in the future. Kevin was healthy, happy, and independent. I was starting to focus on self-care, and I was happy, but it took some time to stop feeling anxious about Kevin's drug use. I knew that Kevin did drink, but drugs were out of his life.

It was four-thirty a.m. on November 30, 2019, that the officer came to my door. She asked if I knew Kevin, to which, I replied yes and that I was his mom. I thought that Kevin was done having trouble with the law. She asked if we could sit and then her words barely registered. Kevin had passed away. I asked, "Did you say that he had died? Did you say that he was gone?" She said yes. She was from the coroner's office and was investigating his death. There had been needles and drug paraphernalia found near his body and he had been discovered by his roommate when he hadn't shown up for work. My mind swirled with disbelief, sadness, and anger. My baby was gone. After being clean for so many years, why now? I would have expected this news years ago, but not now.

Kevin had been fired from the job and company he loved a few months back because of a personal disagreement. Although he had another job, I believe this setback caused a depression and anxiety that led him back to drug use. I didn't see it coming. Did I miss the signs? Did I drop my guard because he had been clean for so long? I saw him on Thanksgiving, the day before he died. He looked strong, alert, and healthy. We laughed and had a great day. Kevin's smile, laughter, and quick wit always brought us joy. When he left, we hugged and told each other, "I love you." It was the last time I would ever see my beautiful son alive again.

Kevin died on November 29, 2019, from an overdose of heroin and Xanax, at age twenty-seven. His pancreas had also hemorrhaged from alcohol abuse. I can't explain, in words, how deeply I grieve for the loss of my son. He will forever be missed and forever loved. I will never under-

stand why drugs had to take my child. I will never be the same.

Kevin's Mom,

KAREN O.
Irmo, South Carolina

Justin

FOREVER 26

I am the mother of a beautiful, handsome angel named Justin. My story is as follows...I knew his father for years, and I knew Justin from a distance as well. Justin's dad and I finally sowed our oats and ended up dating eleven years ago, and have been married almost four years. Justin was a junior in high school. Justin was a typical pretty boy. Yes, he was (is) very handsome. He had (has) the most mesmerizing crystal blue eyes. Eyes as clear as the water of Barbados. This boy was (is) average built, very slim with strawberry blonde hair. Straight good looking. But there was something just not right inside his soul, something deep down, that no one knew. He could be so joyful and funny to boot. Then other days he was down and out. I spoke to his dad and mentioned that maybe he and Justin's biological mom should take him to a doctor, which they did. Justin was depressed, but over what, again, no one knew. Yes, he didn't have a "mom with dad" childhood, but his dad was ALWAYS involved, when he was allowed to be, meaning there was some "baby mama" drama. Justin's mom wasn't the nicest, or in her right mind, most of Justin's childhood. My husband was able to get custody of Justin, later in life. I believe, around the age of ten, is when Justin came to live with his dad and first wife, which again, was just not the best mom to have, but that's neither here nor there. Just some insight of the demons my boy had danced with. So, Justin started on some antidepressants and he began to thrive. He had a purpose, and was setting goals, and crushing them. He enrolled in a vocational school. He loved (loves) to cook, so he took culinary classes and nailed them. I would be cooking and that boy would pick me apart, and giggle the whole time, and that's what I miss the most, I think. As his junior year came to an end, I started to notice that he seemed restless, a bit withdrawn. I asked him what was going on, and he stated, "I stopped taking my medication." I informed his dad, and not much was thought of it. If his dad was okay with it, who was I to say anything? He was not my kid; I was "just" the girlfriend.

The summer between his junior and senior years were rocky, to say the least. Things ended up missing, anything from bank cards, to medication—not narcotics, over the counter ones like Tylenol and Advil. Then one night, he didn't come home. He came home super late the next night, with a story that seemed farfetched. I have worked in the medical field my entire life. I felt something in the pit of my gut. Well, I was right. As I was cleaning, I found the discharge papers from the local hospital that he left on the counter. I read them, and there it was, his first OD, right in front of me. What do I do or say? He was eighteen, and again I was "just" the girlfriend. I showed the papers to his dad, but Justin swore he didn't OD, swore they had it wrong. He tried a few pills but that's it. He said he ended up in a fight and hurt his arm and swore that was the truth, and I knew it was a bunch of BS, but it was not my place. As his senior year went on, there were some issues. Again, no one seemed to see what was going on, and when I brought it up, I would be told his mom had things under control. His dad was just that, Dad, semi-clueless, but in a good way, a typical Dad. Justin GRADUATED and it was the happiest day. He made it. I could breathe a bit, but not for long. It was his ticket to come and go and do as he please, and boy did he ever. That's when he met his little girl's mom, and that's when life as we knew it was no longer. It was also the happiest of mine because I became a mom myself when I gave birth to my only child, at 35. So, in one year I became a mom AND a grandmother. That's a whole other story with baby mama drama, but to sum it up they lived on and off with us for the first five years of our granddaughter's life. They were kicked out of so many places it was unreal. No one kept a job. They wrecked cars, they stole, they lied, and all the BS that came with being an addict, times two. Here I was raising one and trying to save another one. The fighting became more and more, words and hate flew. It was catching up with him, his baby's mama left for Florida, thank God, but the damage was already done. We were left with an addict. His father and I dealt with it daily, but not one person other than us saw it. Justin's whole, entire family refused to see what Justin was. He played, "poor me, dad has a new family," and acted like I didn't want him here. He was right, because I didn't want it around my only child. He didn't ask for an addict as a brother and I was afraid Justin was going to do something and they would take my baby. I wanted to save Justin, but I was "just" the girlfriend, and no one helped us. They fed his demons. Do you know how hard that was? I had no voice.

The stories go on and on, in and out of jail, and halfway houses. It came to a point that I said after several years, he can't come back. That was one of the roughest things I had to do. I never wanted my now husband to choose one child over the other, but Justin was twenty-five. It was time for the tough love. So, when he got out of jail he went to stay with his aunt. It wasn't long before Justin's demons began to show themselves and the family opened their eyes. But I am talking years. I had no voice, so there was a lot of work to do. Well, Justin OD'd and ended back in jail. His aunt was like "no way,"and no one else would let him in, not even his own mom, so again I was there to try. I would never, ever leave him to the streets, EVER! He was mine. I didn't like his choices, nor did I play his "poor me" games. I was blunt, I had rules, and I had expectations. I was raising mine like I was raised, so he better buckle-up. Sure enough, within a three-month period, his demons rose again, but this time more powerful, more than any other time. I was scared. He had done horrible things to his dad's parents and that stopped it for the family. He was out again. He couldn't stay with us and that was his dad's choice. He shacked up with another girl, and it was the same drama as with his baby mama. She was up to no good and I mean no good. Things calmed down for a while again, but June 27, 2018 at 10:37 p.m., my entire life changed. I couldn't believe what had happened, I just stared at his dad, and there was no life in the eyes of a man I love. He died that very night too. I was here, picking up the pieces again, but I knew they would never fit the same. How could, they cause this time, I broke too. I broke into so many pieces. I felt the pain, I felt the guilt, I felt it ALL! It was all over. Our boy was gone. It took me a long time to forgive myself. I haven't fully, but for the most part I do. The "what ifs" ate me up. Every time I touched my husband, I felt like I was being sucked into a cold, dark hole, and that scared the hell out of me. I was losing him too. I was walking around on egg shells, thinking I pushed Justin to this, like I drove him to OD. I felt it was all my fault, because I was outspoken. I didn't let too much BS fly and so forth. The only thing I wanted was a family for both our boys, that's it, honest.

Then one day I was sitting on our deck, and a dragonfly landed in the seat next to me. It was blue. Blue was (is) Justin's favorite color. It just sat there not moving looking right at me. For some reason, like I knew what I was to do, I began to talk, as if it was Justin. I split my beans, I danced with my demons, and I cried the hardest I ever have cried. This lasted awhile, and when I caught my breath, a gust of wind carried the dragonfly away. And it was at that point, I knew I needed to start making those pieces fit, even if I had to shave some edges. I have heard Justin tell me he loved my tough love, because he knew I truly cared. He wasn't mine by blood, but you will never convince my heart of that. It has been two years and one month today that my life forever changed. Changed in ways that most people take for granted, but here we don't. It changed my purpose. It changed my tone. It made a hole in my soul that I will forever have. I hold the love of my boy in there, no one else, just him. He is tucked in there pushing me to somehow put his dad back together. That's my whole purpose; I will never stop. For the love of my son, I will pick up every piece.

Justin's Mom,

MELISSA O.
Utica, Ohio

Michael

This is my son's story and mine because to tell one without the other isn't the real story…

My son's story and mine…March 5, 1993, 4:39 p.m., was the best day of my life. My son, Michael Anthony was born, weighing in at eight pounds five ounces. Healthy and happy and I am the happiest Mom on the Earth! There is an automatic sense of protection when you become a Mother. The ride home was so stressful. I was fearful of every bump, turn, red light, yellow light, and even the green ones. Finally getting him home safe and sound was such a relief.

My early days as a Mom were all so brand new to me yet I somehow knew exactly what needed to be done. Nurse him, change his diapers, take care of his circumcision, bathe, clothe, love, and protect him for all his days. All his days, now that's a concept. What a surreal feeling it is to be a brand-new Mom. Oh, the many photos I took of him doing everything and anything. I was so scared of not being by his side every moment that when I showered, I placed his bassinet in the bathroom with me so I would hear him if he woke up and cried. My son, my baby boy was such a happy baby boy. He made the most adorable facial expressions. I can still feel the feelings of such admiration and love I felt while nursing him. I felt such a deep connection with him each time I nursed him. I used to talk to him, sing to him, and promise to protect and love him always. He loved nursing and refused the bottle and pacifier and wanted nothing to do with any of it if it wasn't my breast. The only distraction he would stop nursing for was the smell of popcorn cooking in the microwave. He loved popcorn as a little boy and for all his days. He brought us so much joy just watching him grow. He walked at seven months and his independence came once he bit my breast for the first time and I vowed no more breast feeding. That hurt! And while it was an adjustment for us both, he slowly adjusted and before we knew it, he was on whole milk, then a sippy cup, and then one day he had no interest in the sippy cup anymore. He was a big boy. Grew out of Pampers and learned to potty in the toilet. What memories and what milestones!

When the teenage years hit, we were in for a rough ride. Michael's interest in girls began as did the experimenting with marijuana. I remember the first time I discovered he was smoking marijuana; I was so mad at him. I scolded him, grounded him, you know the usual "Don't do that again" spiel. And for the most part he was a good kid, aside from a few rebellious stages. When I discovered he was still smoking marijuana, I decided to move us to a better area, not that the area we were living in then was bad. It wasn't, we lived on the East side, in a good neighborhood; however I blamed it on his being friends with well-to-do kids, you know the rich kids whose parents gave them money all the time to buy what they pleased. We didn't have much money; we weren't without anything, but I never gave my son extra money. I only gave him enough for lunch. Well, we moved to the opposite side of town, still East side, only we were now living on the Southeast side of town, in a good neighborhood and better school district and we were away from all of the friends that he grew up with.

I was adamant I was going to get Michael far away from those bad influence friends of his. We were hitting the reset button, and everything was going to be okay. This was just a phase and one day we would look back and laugh about how I had gotten so overly upset over such a minor thing. The first year went as I had hoped or at least thought. When he started high school, he played on the football team and he was good! He talked about becoming a professional football player and his coach stated many times that if he continued there was no doubt he could make it to the NFL. He swore he would buy me a fancy house when he made it to the NFL. I was so proud and excited watching him play. He was really good. He was fast and because he had started working out early, he had the strength. Girls were everywhere, he was such a good-looking kid, charming, smart, on the football team, my son was the All-American high school student every guy wanted to be. He was popular, a little too popular. The high school principal and assistant principal knew him better than I preferred. He got suspended from school for showing up high on marijuana with his friends. That was the start to what would later become a nightmare spiraling out of control. Grounding him became more and more difficult as I had to work. I was a single Mom, got no support from his dad, financial or otherwise. Instead, his dad's idea of fixing things was for my son to go live with him. That was the last thing I was interested in doing. His dad wasn't the Father figure he should have been so instead I did the best I could by myself.

After yet another incident, Michael wound up in the juvenile system. Probation, house arrest, and that, in itself, was a job. As soon as I left for work, he'd invite his friends over and I later learned they would party at my house. This incident may have been the beginning to the big problem that lie ahead.

My youngest daughter who is disabled was not feeling good one morning, had a fever and I couldn't miss any more work. My son was supposed to watch her while she slept until the babysitter was to arrive less than an hour after I had to leave for work. I received a call from the supervisor of the babysitter, stating that when our babysitter arrived, my disabled daughter was alone in the house. That was just one of the instances where my son, who was normally very responsible when it came to helping me with his younger sister, failed me and messed up in a big way.

Needless to say, Child Protective Services was called, I was interviewed, told them my story and thankfully there were no substantiated findings of neglect on my part. I was so disappointed in my son for

504

being so selfish and irresponsible and mostly for fear of what could have happened if something bad had happened while my daughter was left alone. For a while after this incident, my son seemed to have really took to heart what could have happened and what he did wrong. It wasn't long after that I came home early only to find a group of kids in my backyard, all visibly under the influence of something. I reacted, better yet, I over reacted, chased everyone away, yelled at my son which did absolutely no good as he was too high to care. He listened, don't get me wrong, but being under the influence, my words went in one ear and out the other.

Michael started sneaking out of the house and I had had enough. I felt like I was losing complete control, I called his probation officer to notify her of his doings and he was placed on house arrest. It was summertime and my youngest daughter's babysitter was home all day with her so he couldn't invite his friends over while I was at work. I discovered he was smoking marijuana in my garage while I was at work. The same garage my gas hot water heater was located in. Great, he was going to get us all blown up one day. Nothing I said to my son changed anything, instead things got worse.

I discovered one morning while getting ready for work that Michael was gone, he had snuck out of the house. I decided then and there that enough was enough. I locked him out. Called his probation officer and because I wouldn't let him in the house, he became very angry. I distinctively remember this moment because it was a very scary time and I saw a different person when I looked at my son. He became more and more angry at the fact I wasn't going to let him in like I had all the other times he had snuck out. Nope, this time was different, I had had enough of his not following or respecting my rules. He threw one of his weights at my sliding glass door, it shattered, and the weight missed my youngest daughter's head by maybe a centimeter or two.

My heart was racing; I was livid, unable to believe he had done that and the fact that had the weight been one to two centimeters to the left it could have very well hit my daughter and quite possibly killed her or severely injured her. I was so upset; he and I exchanged some very harsh words and wound up in a physical altercation. He body slammed me on the floor. Who was this person? This was not my son. He had never

505

once laid a hand on me nor ever given me any indication he would ever do so. Things heated quickly; I felt like I was watching an action movie.

Next thing I knew, I went for the phone to call the police, Michael went after me, grabbed the phone, and the wrestling began again. I was finally able to break free, told him to get the hell out of my house and he left! I called 911 and that moment was the last time I saw my son, the son I knew and had raised. That was 2010. The roller coaster ride of in and out of juvie, drug treatment facilities, and counseling soon became a repetitive event in our lives. CPS was once again involved because I refused to allow my son to come back into our home. I was threatened with being found negligent even after explaining he almost very badly injured my youngest daughter. I didn't care what the system said or thought. He could have killed my daughter. Her disability placed her in a very vulnerable situation and I had a duty to protect her. I also had a duty to my son. I was torn, and my heart was being twisted into shreds between my responsibility to my daughter and to him. I couldn't bend, I had to teach him a lesson. It was time. If not then, his life would be doomed. He would learn the hard way. I had to give him tough love. I had to. Not only for him, but for myself. I felt like I was losing complete control of everything. I was devastated, I felt like a horrible person and Mother. How could I kick him out and turn my back on him? Why was this happening? What happened to my sweet, cute, loving little boy?

I received the call; Michael had run away from the drug treatment facility with some other kids. I was in a panic, where was he? Was he ok? Who was he with? What was he doing? He contacted my sister asking for money, telling her he was hungry and needed money for food. I decided to "arrange" a set up, I contacted his probation officer and arranged to have him picked up at the location he was to meet my sister. Thinking of it now, it looked like a real live *Cops* television series. Under-cover cops everywhere, a helicopter, the situation went from having him arrested so I knew he was safe in jail and not on the streets to him being pepper sprayed, thrown on the ground not by one but multiple police officers because my son refused to go down. He put up a fight and before anyone knew it, the apartment community was surrounded by police officers and not one but two helicopters. How in God's name did this happen and get out of hand so quickly? Was this really happening? This is my son, not some hardened criminal. That was the start to what would follow and become as I know it now, the roller coaster of my worst memories as a Mother and human being.

I fell into a deep depression. How could I set my own son up like that? Wasn't I trying to help him? Is that what really happened? What parent does what I did? I hated myself. I was to blame for all of this. Had I just sat down and talked to him rationally, surely, he would understand what he was doing was wrong and he would change. He would go back to being a good kid again, right? That's what I thought and had hoped. That is not at all what happened. I had tried the tough love people told me to do and that made things worse. I decided then and there I would never turn my back against my son again. He was my baby and he just needed a little redirection and he would be good again.

I didn't see my son for what felt like years; rumor had it he was living with his dad in a trailer somewhere. He never called me, never attempted to contact me until I discovered he was in jail. Checking the jail inmate roster became a daily habit. I scheduled a visit and my heart shattered seeing my son through a monitor with no way to hug him or display any sort of affection towards him. I cried, he cried, I apologized for setting him up. He loved me so much he refused to believe I had set him up, He blamed someone else. I finally made it very clear to him that it was me that set him up thinking I was helping him. I begged him to forgive me for my actions. I have never cried so much in all my life. I felt like such a horrible person.

I went through a very dark, deep depression. This was a very dark time for me and the only thing that got me through it was learning to mask my pain. I did that with alcohol. I drank more than I ever did. Not every day surprisingly but the weekends...oh what a blur they are to me now. I eventually learned to mask my depression, sadness, and all around feeling of being a disappointment as a parent and individual entirely. My son was in and out of prison/jail, staying with his dad, friends, homeless, cold and hungry, and on his own for years. My heart during these times somehow managed to keep beating. Why, I'll never know. I blamed myself for the path my son was on. When he let me back in his life, I catered to him, I bought him clothes, gave him money, but never allowed him back in my house for fear he would put my youngest daughter in harm's way again. I never got over that incident. I still carried that fear with me, the "What if he had killed her with that weight?" The memory of it makes my stomach cringe.

I gave in finally one day after my son very calmly told me all the things I wanted to hear. He was better, he was twenty-one years young. My oldest daughter and I drove to Winslow to pick up from prison. We talked on the way back about how things were going to be different. He had a job and wanted to work on getting his GED and I believed him. I let him back into my house. I even took him to a local Mexican Carne Asada spot one day for lunch and he had a Michelada since he was now twenty-one and of legal age to drink. Not that it had stopped him before. That day was such a great day; we had lunch, ONE Michelada (we weren't there to get drunk nor was I about to start "drinking" with my son), and spent the rest of the day at my sister's house spending time with family, taking photos, and having a great time. Things were so nice. I loved having my son back at home with me. My heart was happy, I was no longer worried about where he was, if he had eaten, showered, if he had somewhere to stay…my baby was home.

Michael woke up one morning, shortly after saying he had a bad stomachache and he wasn't going to go to work that day. Something in my stomach felt uneasy about it but I wanted to give him the benefit of the doubt. I had already told him prior that he could stay with me, but I would not let him in my house alone. I couldn't force him to leave with an upset stomach and I wasn't about to give him a house key. I told him, if he did feel better and decided to go to work for him to make sure the house was locked up and to go out through the garage. I attempted to check on him throughout the morning with some concern as he wouldn't reply right away (via messenger); he didn't have actual phone service and he couldn't make/receive calls on the phone he had. He had some data to get on social media and make WiFi calls but that was it, no actual phone service. He finally replied stating he was feeling better and was going to work.

I asked if he wanted me to pick him up from work as it was right up the street from my work, and he said, "Yes, please." I stopped to pick him up on my way home, no luck, he wasn't answering my messages and finally the bomb I was afraid of, I called the place he worked at and was told, "No one by that name works here ma'am." What? That can't be, he just started, maybe you know him by a different name, a nickname maybe, and again, no luck, he did not work there nor had he ever. That moment my mind spun out of control. What in the world was going on? He did it again, he lied to me and I fell for it. I was pissed; how could I have been so blind to fall for his crap once again? I should have known better. I pulled into my garage, discovered his bag was gone, I walked into my house, it was calm and quiet. He was definitely not there. I walked past my living room into the kitchen and something hit me, something looked off in my living room, but what? My 50 inch flat screen TV I had just bought just a few weeks prior was gone. How could he do that to me? He knows I have to save money for things like this. I didn't have any credit cards at the time. I was barely making ends meet. And worse, how could he do this to his little sister who watches her cartoons on that TV?

I was a basket case! I was furious, profoundly hurt that my own son would steal from me. I began messaging him repeatedly asking him where he and my TV were and to get his ass home! He responded with "Mom, really? I am at work; I don't have your TV." I responded with, "You're such a liar, I called your work, you never worked there, why did you lie to me?" He never responded until I told him if he didn't return the TV immediately, I was going to report it stolen and I was absolutely going to let the police know he was the last person in my house. He finally replied with "Mom, I'm sorry, I needed some money, I'll get it back to you just give me time." There it was, the evidence I needed to charge him with the theft of my television. But that isn't what I wanted, I wanted my TV and son back and I wanted to know why he lied to me. We exchanged a couple more messages with no results.

I finally accepted the fact that Michael was full of it, he had no intention of getting my TV back, and he was definitely not going to come back to my house. He knew I called the police. My daughter was going to be coming home in a couple of days, what was I going to do? She loved watching her cartoons, what was I going to do? I couldn't just go out and buy another TV. I remembered a friend of mine mentioned her husband had just bought her a brand-new TV. It was a long shot, but I reached out to her, asked if there was any way I could borrow her old TV until I got mine back. Her and her husband showed up at my house less than two hours later with her old 50 inch flat-screen TV. She was heartbroken at what my son did to me. She knew my daughter

509

would be so sad if she was unable to watch her cartoons. I was so appreciative of my friend for helping in my time of need.

I didn't hear from my son again and after some quiet time and thought, I accepted the fact that my TV was gone forever and my son too as far as I knew him. "MY" son would never have stolen from me. I discovered around the same time he had also stolen from his paternal grandmother, the wedding ring her deceased husband had given her when they married. That did it for me; the TV was bad but stealing his grandmother's wedding ring was the ultimate wrong! When was this nightmare going to end? What had I done that was so bad for my son to turn into this "person?" What did I do wrong? What should I have done? What didn't I do?

It was my fault, had I been a better Mother none of this would be happening. Had I not put Michael in juvie, had I not insisted tough love was the way to go, he wouldn't be doing these awful things. My heart hurt day and night. And as mad as I was at him for stealing my TV, I was also very worried about him. What if he was lying dead in some ditch somewhere? He was arrested shortly after for providing false information to law enforcement. And much to my amazement, the detective assigned to my TV theft case never stopped looking for my TV. He knew I was on a tight budget and I think genuinely felt bad for me that my own son stole it from me. I received a call from the detective confirming he found a TV at a pawn store that matched the description exactly. I met him at the pawn store and got my TV back for free! I did not have to buy back my TV, instead the cost was added to my son's theft case and he was ordered to pay it in restitution fees.

Over the years, the same things kept happening over and over. My son would get arrested for this or that and wind up back in jail or prison and as harsh as it is to say, I was relieved when he was incarcerated because at least I knew he was ok, had a roof over his head and food in his stomach. Many times, I would continue to give him money because he would give me a good story about how he needed to get a photo ID, and how he needed to buy phone time so he could call places for a job.

It finally hit me one that day that I was doing more harm than good by giving Michael money. I was enabling him to buy drugs. I was contributing to his drug use, so I stopped giving him money. Instead I would buy him clothes; I can't tell you how horrible it is to buy clothes for your son repeatedly because his were stolen or lost from being home-less. Watching him carry his bags of clothes around everywhere. Seeing him in desperate need of a haircut and more importantly, a shower.

I remember taking Michael to eat once for his birthday. He wanted to go to a buffet restaurant because he was so hungry. When I picked him up, he smelled so bad, I almost threw up. I couldn't believe my baby was a homeless person. He was in his twenties; how is it that he is a homeless person? I watched him fill his plate with food and it took everything in me not to cry. My heart was hurting so bad thinking, how did this happen? How did my son turn into this person? This person I hardly recognize. I caught him dozing off after he ate several plates of food and it was then I realized he was on something. I didn't say anything, there was no need. What could I do? I hadn't been able to save him thus far, what difference was it going to make now? He was going to do what he wanted to do. I didn't allow him into my home so what business was it of mine what and how he lived? He could change if he really wanted to and he hadn't changed so clearly, he wasn't ready to change his life.

Over the years, people would tell me if Michael wanted to change, he would. If he didn't like being all drugged out, he would get help. I started believing those statements until recently and thank God I did. Instead of scolding my son and telling him to get his act together, I started talking to him like a grown up, encouraging him to do better, reminding him that he is important and loved and not alone and that things can and will get better. I constantly told him I loved him and that I'm always thinking of and praying for him.

I remember a time at a family night at a residential drug treatment facility Michael was at, just looking around at the other young adults and their families there that this drug addiction is real, it's a very harsh reality, it exists, and it affects so many people. I hugged him so tight that day repeatedly, I just didn't want to let go. I wanted to grab him and take him home with me and lock him up in my extra bedroom until he was sober and could think straight and he was all better. This facility was coed, so there were both males and females there which I think is a huge mistake. The situation creates vulnerability and for someone like my son, having females present was a huge distraction to his treatment. He was always interested in females. That's just who he always was. He

511

was handsome and charming and there were never any issues with females not being interested in him. I specifically told him not to get involved with anyone, especially from a rehab.

I told Michael he needed to work on bettering himself, that he had nothing to offer anyone nor they to him. I was hoping he would focus on HIM and no one else. My heart cared too much; if he did without, that was one thing, but he would never intentionally leave anyone behind to fend for themselves and I just didn't want that kind of pressure on him. He never listened and wound up getting kicked out of the program for being with a female. What they were thinking is completely unknown to me. Perhaps they figured they were going through the same thing hence they had "lot" in common and would make it together. I couldn't believe the conditions they were living in. No plumbing, no heat, no cooling, and I don't recall seeing any unbroken windows at this house. There were holes in the roof so when it rained, their lack of buckets caused the rain to pour into the home. I'm surprised they had active electricity in the home. I swear that home should have been condemned. And there I was once again finding myself wanting to "FIX" everything, him, the situation, everything.

Michael once again talked me into getting him a phone so it would be easier for him to call around for jobs (don't get me wrong, I selfishly wanted him to have one so I could get and keep in contact with him) and if any employers were interested in hiring him, they could call him. I bought him a phone, took him grocery shopping so he and this female could have food to eat. I can't tell you how much I just wanted to grab him and bring him home with me. I hated seeing my son live in the conditions he was living in. It broke my heart to the core. I cried, prayed, got angry and then in an attempt to calm myself, told myself this would be the time he would turn things around. The two of them came over once for dinner. I secretly didn't want her over, but this situation turned into a package deal, even when talking about going to church together, he always wanted her to come too.

I just wanted someone, one time with my son, to sit, talk, pray, and just try to find out what was going through his mind so I could help him. The time here was not what I had expected or hoped for, he was on methadone so he was very quiet, nodding off, and once he went outside to the back patio and just looked at everything, the trees, the sky, and was so mesmerized by my frequent hummingbird visitors. I loved that image of him, just taking it all in. I wanted so badly to go out there with him to talk but I knew his mind was hazy from the methadone and to be perfectly honest, I hated seeing him like that. I hated knowing he was under the influence even if it was a "legal" substance. I just wanted my son to be clear minded, sober, and understanding of what I wanted to share with him. I was so heartbroken and silently disappointed that he opted for methadone and not the Vivitrol shot. I knew from other people battling drug addiction that Vivitrol was the best and safest way to treat the cravings. I wanted my son to get the shot but as I later learned, an addict will most likely prefer a "high" feeling, not a sober feeling.

The high sensation becomes second nature to addicts and I truly believe that after being on illicit drugs for so long, an addict's mind and body naturally prefer that feeling. They feel like if they feel high, they are high. I remember that time specifically because I knew that as long as he was dosing on methadone he would be "high" and that isn't what I wanted. He would never be "sober" again as I knew him if he was on methadone. Driving back home from dropping them off at that shack of a home, I cried; my stomach felt so nauseated. Why was my son living this way and why was he comfortable living that way? We never lived in such conditions. I eventually told myself, he would wake up one day and see that he wanted to live a better life, that he wanted a decent home to live in and I swore to myself that I would not interfere no matter how badly I wanted to. He was a man; he had to figure things out for himself because then he would appreciate the hard work and what that allowed him.

Several weeks went on, I noticed there were times I could not get a hold of Michael; I would call him, text him and get no response. I would call and text his female friend and often she wouldn't answer either. She finally called me, saying he had left with a friend of his and had not returned home nor was he answering her calls or texts. I called the jail to see if he was there and what do you know, he was. They didn't tell me much aside from he had a hearing coming up on Monday since it was a Saturday and there weren't any judges available until Monday morning. I was so upset. What the hell did he do now and why? When I was finally able to schedule a visit with him, he told me one of his friends needed help, so he went with him and got arrested because his "friend" was in a stolen vehicle.

Something didn't sit right with me; he always got in trouble because of someone else; it was always someone else who was doing wrong, and he just so happened to be with them. I remember scolding him and telling him "Mojito, why do you keep doing this? When are you going to learn that these so-called friends of yours could care less about you? They use you and they know if they say they need help with something that you're going to be there. Where are your friends now? Do they come and visit you? Do they help you when you need help? No, I'm here, I'm always here and I am so tired of this broken record with you. Over and over you get yourself in trouble and wind up in jail over and over."

My son was in jail for nine months, nine months of wait and wait some more. They were collecting evidence or so they said. They were investigating this or that. His lawyer wasn't coming through, his public defender hadn't been to visit him. There was always some reason for one delay after another. I finally heard from his drug court public defender who seemed genuinely interested in trying to help him. I explained his history to her although I didn't need to as all she needed to do was pull up his history and she would know he battled drug addiction for at least ten years. She asked if he was released if he would be able to stay with me and once again my heart broke because yet again, I had to say I was not comfortable with him staying with me again as he had yet to earn back my trust from the time he stole my TV.

With no address to provide to the court, the delays in releasing him continued and then his female friend apparently provided her address to the public defender but because she was also a drug addict, the judge refused to let my son go to her address. I pushed and pushed for them to send my son to a rehab in our city. I worked my rear off to become his representative so I could renew his insurance coverage and make sure he was on the plan they accepted. I wrote a letter on behalf of my son and pleaded with the judge in that letter to help him and send him to recovery.

A few weeks later, his public defender sent me an email with an "edited" version of my letter. She had removed my mention of a rehab and instead inserted the name of a smaller residential drug treatment facility the courts apparently preferred to work with. I wasn't happy about the changes and reluctantly agreed to the change because she said they were accepting new clients and he could be released to them sooner. That never happened; his release date was postponed yet again and apparently this time it was because his probation officer had failed to find him placement in a timely manner as the rehab facility was no longer accepting clients due to the COVID-19 pandemic upon us. I was furious! What the hell do these people do? Do they not get paid to help their clients? Did they not get in this field to help people? Why was he taking his sweet time? My son sat in jail for nine months because everyone was fiddling their thumbs; they had lives they were living while my son grew more and more impatient.

I could hear the change in his voice. He was losing hope once again, his light at the end of the tunnel was dimming once again, I tried my best to encourage him, to keep him focused on brighter days. I felt like I was losing. His attitude changed again; he was depressed, felt hopeless, and was wishing he had gone to prison instead of agreeing to this continuance or that continuance. They had promised him different scenarios always to get him to continue to sit in jail and to some extent it was a good thing; at least in jail he was sober, had a roof over his head and food in his stomach. The time finally came for him to be released and he needed clothes, shoes, and hygiene necessities. Having not been inside any stores because of COVID, I wasn't prepared. I made a quick trip to Target to buy him some clothes. My boyfriend went shopping during his lunch break and took what I had purchased along with his purchases to the facility my son had been moved to. I knew my son wasn't going to be too thrilled with the items I purchased; I basically grabbed what shorts they had, not the basketball shorts he preferred. Next best thing to Nike tennis shoes in his size were black Skechers but at least he had clothes and a pair of new shoes. My son always, no matter what, had worn nice Nike shoes. Even as a baby he wore Nike Air Jordan's, Ralph Lauren pants, and polo shirts. Not because we were materialistic but because as my first born, I wanted to buy him nice things.

Michael seemed to do well at the residential drug treatment center. His clarity came back, he was focused, and enjoyed the groups at this facility. He was still upset that they didn't place him at the facility he wanted to go to, but all in all he felt in time they would move him there. It was Friday, May 29, 2020, almost five p.m. My son called me to tell me his insurance was refusing to keep paying for him to stay at this residential drug treatment facility and he wanted to know if I would let him stay the weekend with me until his caseworker and/or probation office found him another place to go. I was furious! He had only been there five days and his insurance was already kicking him to the curb! What the hell kind of successful treatment do the insurance companies expect to take place if they're going to stop coverage in five days?!

I reluctantly agreed to allow him to stay at my house for the weekend. I thought, it will be okay, he's been sober for a little over nine months, isn't on any legal or illegal substance, it will be fine, we'll have a nice family weekend. Just before we hung up, he said, "Mom, I need to tell you something." I said "What?" He said, "I started dosing this morning." That was it, my mind was spinning, what do you mean you started dosing again, on what? Why? He responded with, "I started having cravings again." My heart literally shattered. So much for our nice family weekend; there was no way he could spend the weekend with us. I don't want to see him on that stuff. He's not my Michael when he's on that stuff. I paced back and forth, my heart was racing, a million thoughts came to mind, I was afraid, I was sad, I was confused all at the same time. Would it be ok? Is he going to try and steal something while he's here? Is he going to be nodding off the entire time he's here?

I called his caseworker back and told her I'm sorry, but he can't come to my house while he's on that stuff. I just can't handle it. She said that she understood, and they would figure something out. My son got back on the phone and I had to break the news to him. The disappointment in his voice just about killed me. The whole situation was killing me. He called me back a few minutes after and said, "I love you, Madre." I am so grateful for those last words from my son, those words have held me together the past six plus weeks. I told him, "I love you very much also, Mojito, and I really wish you hadn't gotten back on that stuff." I told him to be sure he took care of all of the clothes and stuff we had just bought for him and he said he had everything packed in the duffle bag we had also given him to store his clothes and stuff in. I told him to call me when he could. We hung up and something inside me felt very uneasy. I couldn't figure out what it was, but I didn't feel good about what was happening. We went from he was going to spend the weekend with us to he was going somewhere, and he was dosing again. All the progress he had made the nine plus months he was in jail and sober, all down the drain. I called the caseworker back and asked where they were sending him to; she asked him if it was ok to tell me and he agreed.

Five days later at 10:19 a.m., I received the call. I was at work, my babysitter told me there were two police officers at my house and they wanted to talk to me. I immediately thought, "Hmm, well I haven't done anything wrong." Not once did I think it had anything to do with my son. He was doing good now. The officer got on the phone and identified himself to me and asked how soon I could get home. I told him, "I'm at work, what's this about?" He said, "We can come to you, where do you work?" I told him, "I don't want you coming to my work, what's this about?" He said, "Ma'am, I really need to talk to you in person about this," and I then asked after my heart dropped into my stomach, "Is this about my son Michael Amado?" He said, "Yes ma'am, it is, how soon can you get home?" I asked, "Is he ok? He said, "Ma'am, how fast can you get here?" I told him, "Twenty-five to thirty minutes," and he said, "Be careful ma'am, we'll see you soon." My mind was spinning, my stomach was in knots, why couldn't the officer just tell me what the issue was? I never once thought my worst fear had come true that morning. I don't know how I got home without having an accident. I sped, prayed, and pleaded with God to let my son be ok, I repeated my pleas over and over.

I remember pulling into my garage and seeing the two police cars parked on my street and at that very moment I think I knew. I just didn't want to believe it. The officer I had talked to on the phone approached me and said what I feared most. "Ma'am, there's no easy way to say this, he's gone." The words I had always feared hearing the most. I wasn't hearing this, this was not happening, not my son, he had been doing so good, he had been sober long enough, there was no way. I asked what happened. I had no idea where he had been because I had not spoken to Michael since that last time with him and his caseworker. I hadn't thought anything of it except that maybe he wasn't allowed to make contact with anyone so early into the program. I didn't know they moved him to a halfway house. Had I known, I would have said, "Absolutely not!" He was not ready for that kind of freedom. Why did the caseworker see it as appropriate that he go to a halfway house? He had only been out of jail a very short time. I knew it was too soon; why didn't his caseworker see it that way as well? Someone was going to pay for this! The system failed my son and they were not going to get away with this!

The rest of that day was a blur to me; I felt like I was in a daze, it didn't really hit me, and why? Didn't I love my son? I should be devastated; I should be on the ground losing my mind and instead I felt numb. I cried, I broke down a couple of times when making phone calls to family and friends. I felt like I was trapped inside a bad nightmare and no one knew I was stuck inside. There was absolutely no way this was happening. Never once did I imagine my son dying from an overdose, no way, Michael was smarter than that. He had plans, we talked about his plans. He wanted to complete his GED, he started to while in jail; he wanted to get back into the gym and one day be the fitness trainer he dreamt of becoming for years. He wanted to prove stability to his daughter's mother so he could have a relationship with his baby girl. Oh my God, his daughter! Her daddy is gone! She's never going to know him, she's never going to make memories with him, oh my God this was not happening! Why? Why? Why? I became angry; I looked at everything and everyone; I wanted to blame someone, and no one was exempt from my rage. We were going to begin making new memories, we were going to spend birthdays and holidays together and everything was going to be okay. Why hadn't I known? How could I have not known the exact time my son took his last breath. Wasn't I as his mother supposed to feel something? What was wrong with me? Was I so disconnected from him that I didn't know? Maybe if I had let him spend the weekend with us, he would still be here. Why didn't I just let him spend the weekend? Why was I so selfish? He's my son, I should have just let him come over. Maybe had I said something, done something, anything, my son would still be here. Where were his things? I want his things! What do you mean his "cousin" picked his things up, he is not his cousin! Why didn't you call me? I'm his mother! "Ma'am, we didn't have your number. Michael and I were friends, we spent time together, I got a hold of his cousin through Facebook." Facebook? Why did you post anything about my son's death on Facebook before I knew anything about my son?! How dare you! Half the clothes we bought were gone, and only one flipping shoe was in his duffle bag! Where is his other shoe? Why would you keep one shoe? What else is missing that I am not aware of? Where are the other nine boxers I bought him? Only one pair was found in his bag.

In between my anger with the halfway house manager and his lack of knowledge or common sense, my mind started wandering. Did my son have a heart condition I knew nothing about? He couldn't have overdosed; he was clean, he wouldn't intentionally use again. He was on methadone, that's supposed to keep you from using, right? Why didn't anyone at the halfway house find him sooner than 8:30 a.m.? Why didn't they try to save him? Revive him? Where is he? Can I see him? Why didn't his probation officer notify me? Who was responsible for this cruel joke? Why didn't the insurance company let him complete the thirty-day program? Why say you'll cover him for thirty days and then not do that? What am I supposed to do now?

My mind traveled back to the time my father passed, almost two years before, when my brother and I were making arrangements. "Arrangements" is such an interesting choice of a word to use, don't you think? This time was so different. We somehow know that at some point we will bury our parents, but never in a million years do we visualize burying our child. Whatever it costs, I didn't care I was going to make it a beautiful service. Wait, why am I thinking about this? He is not gone! My baby boy is not gone! God please bring my son back to me! My mind knew what was happening, but my heart did not want to accept it. It still doesn't.

I began going through old photos, traveling back through time, earlier times. Oh, how I wish I could go back in time for real. I would have changed it all to avoid this road we are traveling now. I began thinking of what photos would be included in the slide show. Thinking of songs to go along with the slideshow. Hearing each song differently than before. Conversations with my son's dad were annoying me to no end! Why was he here? This was his fault! He should have had a real father/son relationship instead of becoming my son's "friend," partying with him instead of telling our son it was wrong. The nerve of him to be here! Did he honestly think my son didn't tell me? I wanted to tell him off so bad! I visualized it in my mind, but this wasn't the time for that, he's hurting too right? He should be hurting! This is absolutely his fault! I called the medical examiner's office, unable to grasp the fact that I was calling the examiner's office about my son. MY son. My son shouldn't be there. I wasn't supposed to be making this call. He should have been making this call for me when I passed. This was all wrong. I pictured my son inside a black body bag, and it broke me to the core. I imagined him trying to breathe and not being able to, he was being suffocated. He did not die of an overdose. Wait, I want an autopsy and toxicology report done. My son did NOT die of an overdose, they are wrong! Something else happened to him, I was determined, my son was not another victim of drug overdose.

Not MY son! I don't know how I managed to maintain my composure. I just knew I had to be the strong one, I had to be strong for my twenty-four-year-old daughter. I couldn't break down in front of her. I was so worried about her. I knew she was taking her brother's death hard. They were so close growing up. I had to get us through making the arrangements. I was proud of myself; I had managed to get out of bed every morning and focus on what needed to be done until his dad started trying to make it about him and talking about "decorating" our son's urn with a red covering. Absolutely not! You are not going to "decorate' our son's urn with gang-affiliated crap! My son was not a gang member! That was YOUR life! My son's favorite color growing up was blue, not red! You did this! His death is your fault! YOU pushed that lifestyle on our son. Had you been a real father figure our son, he would have never gone down the path he went down. He would still be alive! If I had moved us out of Tucson, my son would still be here. Why didn't I move us when we had the opportunity? A million thoughts were going through my mind. My mind would not rest. All the could-haves, should-haves were driving me crazy every second of the day.

I remember walking into the room where my son's lifeless body lay on a stretcher the day prior to Michael's cremation. The lady in the office warned me that because of the autopsy, we would only be able to see his face; every other part of his body would be covered. At the time, I didn't' think anything of it. I do recall as I caught the first glimpse of his body on the stretcher finally being hit with reality. Oh my God, that's my son, he's dead, gone, no, no, no. I couldn't breathe, my heart was racing, I couldn't believe this was my son. It was no longer my son but a shell of my son. I touched his face multiple times, played with his hair just above his forehead, cried on his chest, prayed and forgot the words so I started over again and thought, "How do you forget the words?" I was such a mess. This was really happening. My daughter and her dad arrived, she broke down and we both sat down and just held each other and cried. All the while, my anger and rage were building inside of me. I wanted to kill his dad. This was absolutely his fault! And here he was crying? Why? Did he not think this would happen as a result of all the horrible things he did with my son and had the nerve to brag about? My son looked up to his dad, why? All my son ever wanted was his dad's approval, why didn't his dad accept him for who he was and be satisfied with that and be grateful our son wasn't on the wrong path? Why didn't he redirect our son like a father is supposed to do? Why? Why? Why? I will never understand why my son tried drugs the first time. I will never understand why he continued and because I am not an addict, I never will. I will never understand the strong hold addiction has on one. I will never understand why addicts can't just "stop" using. I am not an addict; I will never understand. I will never know the struggle my son felt. I can't even begin to imagine. Nothing I did or didn't do caused my son's death.

As a parent, it's our natural duty to love and protect our babies. I loved my son with all of my heart, and I protected him for as long as I could. He was an adult; he made his choices. My son will not be remembered as the "ADDICT" he will be remembered for his loving, caring, and thoughtful nature. He will be remembered as having such a beautiful smile, being silly, always being there for his family and friends. He will be remembered as my happy little boy who brought so much joy, love, and laughter to my life as well as others.

My son IS Michael Anthony born March 5, 1993. My son passed away from an accidental drug overdose on June 3, 2020. My son, lived, loved, and in the end lost his battle to drug addiction; my son could be your son or daughter, addiction does not discriminate. It is not our fault that our child/children choose the paths they choose. We did the best we could at the time. We are not experts on drug addiction; we do what we think we should and if what we're doing doesn't work, we try something else because that's what parents do, we try and try again. We can't control other people's actions; we can however choose how we react, and I choose to educate others, support others, and to share OUR story.

You are not alone, I am not alone, and until the drug epidemic no longer exists, we will stand together, honoring, remembering, and cherishing all of our wonderful and even those not so wonderful memories of our babies because they existed, they matter, and they will forever be loved. My prayers may not have been answered the way I had hoped, but they were answered in God's way. He called my son home. He is safe, happy, and whole again, no longer lost and alone. Until we meet again, my son is in God's arms and forever in my heart. Sending you love, hugs, and prayers.

This journey is not one any of us ever wish to walk and it's most certainly never meant to walk through alone. I am here with you, praying for you, supporting you, and reminding you that you are not to blame, you did the best you could. Addiction is a disease NOT a choice. Our fight and enemy are with the drug. The bully that stole my son from me is forever my enemy and his name is fentanyl. I will fight to eliminate this horrible  beast and others like him. I am a mother scorned and I will not go down easy. I AM Michael Anthony's Madre. Heartbroken and devastated; blessed with twenty-seven years good and bad.

Michael's Mom,

ROXANNE O.
Tucson, Arizona

Isabella

FOREVER 23

I believe in angels. In memory of my beautiful daughter, Isabella "Izzy" Ashleigh. God needed another angel, so he chose you.

I made it through the last seven days, but I feel like I'm drowning. My week from hell, as I call it. It has been three years since my daughter, Isabella "Izzy" was poisoned with fentanyl, and passed on to the afterlife. It's supposed to be easier. That's what everyone said. You will get over it. That's what they said. Put one foot in front of the other and move on. How can I, when there are days I can barely walk, let alone get out of bed? It's not easier, nothing is easier. The pain of losing a child never goes away. You learn to smile on the outside when your heart is breaking on the inside. Everything is different now.

The grief from child loss is unfathomable. It leaves a hollow emptiness in my heart, which aches for my beautiful daughter every day.

Some days I can handle it better than other days, but then there are the "other" days. The reminder days, the triggers, that my daughter is not here. The birthdays, the holidays, the Angel Anniversaries, the Awareness Days, Black Balloon Day, and Bereaved Mother's Day. On these days, grief comes in waves crashing at me from every direction. These are the hardest days to get through, because you are not here. Maybe it is the unsettling times in the world and the COVID pandemic that has made this Angel Anniversary so much more difficult for me, or maybe I am not numb anymore. Maybe I am starting to realize that you are not away for a little while. You are not at school; you are not coming home. I cannot fool myself anymore. Maybe I am beginning to believe the reality of never seeing my daughter ever again in this life.

Day 1 ~ July 23, 2017, I found my beautiful daughter unresponsive on July 23, 2017. I brought life back into her young lifeless body, but she didn't wake up. She didn't wake up. Izzy, why aren't you waking up? You are in the hospital; you are supposed to be better. You are supposed to wake up. Why are you not waking up? I begged her to wake up. I pleaded with God to take me instead. For days, I prayed and prayed and prayed. God, are you listening? Do you hear me? For the next several days, I played all your favorite music. I played classical music, because it stimulates the brain, music I played for you when you were a baby. I played Harry Potter movies. I played voice messages from your Oma. I let you hear your kitty purring. I reminded you of happy times. I showed you pictures. I never stopped talking to you. I held your hand. I prayed. I begged for you to wake up. You didn't wake up.

Day 2 ~ July 24th, 2017, I had been awake for almost forty hours. It was almost midnight, the nurse came into your room and told me that I should get some rest. You were still breathing above the ventilator and you were stable. I laid down and kept my eyes on you until I drifted off to sleep. As soon as I closed my eyes you came to me. It was in a dream or a vision. I saw you. My beautiful girl, you were healthy, smiling, happy, and carefree. You were swaying to music that I could not hear. You were wearing a beautiful long airy white flowing gown. You were standing in the middle of a most beautiful meadow, a green so vibrant, I cannot describe. A color so beautiful that it's not of this earth. You looked so free, so happy, and peaceful. You kept smiling at me, a big beautiful smile. Your eyes sparkled. Like before. It was so very peaceful and comforting. I woke up shortly after midnight, and I looked over at your bed to see if you were still there. Sadly, it was a dream, but there was a luminous glow around you that lasted for a few minutes. It was truly beautiful.

Day 3 ~ July 25th, 2017 at 3:00 a.m., a Nigerian Catholic Priest came into your room and he prayed with me. The Father was on one side of your bed and I was on the other. He held your right hand and I held your left hand. There was an ominous presence in the room, I cannot describe it, but it had not been there in the previous days. It was a very powerful presence. After several prayers, the Father told you that you could leave if you see the light, or you could turn around and come back to me, your mother, your family, and your friends. I begged you Izzy, to come back. At that moment there was an energy that shot through your hand into mine, through my body, and out through my other hand which was placed on your shoulder. I have never experienced anything so powerful or spiritual in my life. I truly believe it was you. I truly believe you were wrapping your love around me one last time. Maybe to prepare me for what was to come.

Day 4 ~ July 26th, 2017, in the afternoon, you began to struggle to breathe above the ventilator. The doctor came in and said you could be an organ donor. Everything that was going well, had changed. I was not ready for change. I wanted you back. I continued to be vigilant. I did not give up, I prayed by your bedside throughout the night. You didn't wake up.

Day 5 ~ July 27, 2017, this morning, you had a new nurse that came into the room. She had been on vacation and you were her first patient. She was a familiar face. I could not believe my eyes when I saw her, it was Hanna's mom. Precious Hanna had passed away from a brain aneurysm during her freshmen year of high school. Hanna was such a beautiful, sweet child and a joy to be around. I know you struggled with Hanna's death, because you were not with her that fateful day that she collapsed. You were at cheerleading practice. Hanna's mom told me that Hanna passed away at the same hospital and on the same floor. At that moment, I knew that you were leaving. I knew that Hanna was there to help you cross over. At 4:02 p.m., on July 27, 2017, Isabella "Izzy" Ashleigh, at twenty-three years of age, pregnant with her first child, was declared brain dead. I found out that you were pregnant while you were unresponsive. I lost you and a grandbaby. It would have been my first. I was devastated. This must be a mistake, they are wrong. She has a bright future in the medical field; she was pursuing her master's degree to save lives. This can't be true. I cried and I screamed for the medical staff to give me a different outcome, but it was not meant to be. Please God, stop this nightmare, but there were no do overs. My heart was broken, it shattered in a million pieces. Your big sister, Brittany, she was now left alone without a sibling. Her world collapsed around her. Your Oma, at 96 years of age, lost a granddaughter, her ray of sunshine. This just cannot be happening. Wake up Izzy! Please wake up! Family and friends gathered together beside your bed to say goodbyes, to share a memory. It was bittersweet in days to come to know how many lives you touched, how many lives you saved from their demons. That evening, everyone left the hospital, they went on to continue living. I could not. I stayed; my baby still had a heartbeat. A heartbeat. I would not leave while her heart kept beating. I prayed for her to come back to me. You didn't wake up.

Day 6 ~ July 28th, 2017, while Izzy was being prepared to be an organ donor, I selfishly kept praying for a miracle that was not meant to be for her or for me. God had other plans for her future. I remained with Izzy in her hospital room for two more days, in a grief state fog. A few friends stayed with me. I talked to her. I held her hand, I brushed her hair, I held her. I cried and I cried. A thousand times I cried. My beautiful daughter, a remarkable young lady with green eyes that sparkled and a smile that would light up a room. A friend to everyone. A girl with an infectious laugh. A girl who always helped those in need. A girl whose heart was so big, always helping others. A free spirit, full of love, full of life. A caring, vibrant, athletic, talented, academically gifted, lover of animals and humankind, my sweet girl was no longer here. Twenty-three years, your life was just beginning, but it would be no more. Everything changed in an instance, everything ended at the hands of another. Why would someone give you fentanyl? What was the motive? So many questions. We will never have new memories, no birthdays, no phone calls, no secrets to tell, no shopping trips, no more "I love you, Mom." No future, no family. No more would I be able to see you or hold you. My beautiful child was gone. You didn't wake up.

Day 7 ~ July 29, 2017, Izzy is prepared for surgery. She was a match; she saved a young woman with the gift of her lungs. Her legacy lives on in this life. Her last selfless act on Earth was to give to another human being a better life. The young woman loves the outdoors, hiking, running, and she loves animals. She has a dog. She now can breathe, because of my beautiful child.

Izzy, I know you did not intend on leaving, you love life too much. You love your family, and you put Oma on a pedestal. You love your sister, and you always looked up to her. You love your friends; you love everyone. You are a ray of sunshine on a cloudy day. My mini-me. My baby girl, my Isabella Cinderella. I love you to the moon and back. I miss you so much. How do I live without you? The battle you struggled with from prescribed opiates, which led to your addiction, was too much for your precious body. I wish I could have saved you from your demons. That's what moms are supposed to do. I saved you from many monsters growing up, but I couldn't save you from your demons. God knows I tried. God knows you tried, but they were relentless demons. I am forever grateful for the twenty-three years I had with you. You are the best daughter in the world. I am proud to say you are mine. I'm grateful for all the signs you give me. You know when I need them the most. The days that I struggle with, the signs are plentiful. I always know it's you, Izzy. I love you so much, always and forever baby girl. Don't ever forget, I love you to the moon and back. I love you more than all the stars in the sky, I love you more than all the fishes in the ocean.

At 10:44 p.m., on July 29, 2017, Isabella's young heart had taken its last beat. The ventilator was disconnected. You were gone from this life. I left the hospital walking aimlessly, no direction. What do I do now? I do not even know how I left the hospital. I drove to the beach, to our special place. I broke down and cried. It was raining, the sky was crying. It was all surreal. It was the beginning of a living nightmare. Our lives are forever shattered without you here. We are those who are left behind to pick up the pieces of our shattered hearts. To try to move forward when we are struggling just to put one foot in front of the other. How can I live without you? I'm not ok, I'm broken. I cannot breathe. As I muddle through this new journey of grief, the signs that I receive give me solace. I mostly receive feathers, because the feather has a significant meaning to us. We would put feathers in our hair as a ritual at the start of summer. It was a fun thing to do. I receive signs from animals. Cardinals have been coming to me since she passed. The signs that I have received and that I continue to receive almost daily, from Isabella, these signs, are my lifeline. The Angel signs give me peace. They comfort me. They are very powerful; they give me purpose. They are messages from her in her new world. It is but a thin veil between us and our Angels. She has come to me several times, and she has brought others with her.

I will continue to be her voice for justice and accountability for her homicide, and the homicide of her child. My daughter did not die in vain. She may be gone, but with my last breath I will continue to say her name. I will have justice. Our children are with us, and I know they never wanted to leave. If you clear your head you can see the signs that they leave for us. They have connected with each other in Heaven; they have connected us. Our children are too beautiful for the world we are living in. God rescued them before the demons devoured them. I truly believe this. I know one day, we will all be together again, just as the sun rises and the sun sets. I love you and I miss you Isabella Cinderella. I believe in Angels.

Isabella's Mom,

KAT O.
Isle of Palms, South Carolina

Justin

FOREVER 37

Our stories are all pretty much similar, but with each one there is a unique-ness that each one of our children brings to the devastating opioid epidemic. We have dealt with Subox-one, methadone, and Vivitrol. We have been schooled on inpatient and outpa-tient, drug detoxes, dual diagnosis and I'm sure I've forgotten some others at this point! Let's be honest, we all have done things we never imagined we could ever do, ALL in the name of trying to save our child (children)!! I, for one, had to, twice, buy illegal drugs, once from a dealer on the street and once from an acquaintance of my child's, so he wouldn't be sick!

My story begins with a beautiful boy. Justin was my someone; he was my twin in every aspect, my first love. Justin was beautiful, extremely intelligent, charismatic, witty and loving, but fought demons from a very young age. His addiction began when he was twenty (2001). He got into a fight and broke both the tibia and fibula in his forearm, and had to have surgery and plates put in to hold his arm together. He was prescribed opioids, and the story begins. At the age of twenty-nine, after struggling for nine years, losing his job, his apartment and his truck, he decided he was going to pick up and move to New York City (2010), where he researched a rehab that was part of the Salvation Army. He said if he didn't move away that he would never get better and he would die, which is exactly what happened eight years later. My son died on a subway train in Manhattan, New York, on his way back to his sober house, ALONE!

During his eight years in New York City, Justin relapsed a few times needing more rehab, losing jobs and apartments. The whole time he was there, we (his family), which basically consisted of my mom (his Auggie) his sister Kailan, his brother Seth, and my sister Jodi, always visited, sent money, kept his phone on, and made sure we paid for him to come home every holiday and in the summer. It wasn't perfect, but it was what he wanted. He wanted to stay in New York City. As much as my mother and I would beg him to come back home, where he always had a clean bed, food, and his family, he refused. On one occasion, we had to rush to New York to find Justin, because he had threatened to kill himself. My mom, my daughter, and my sister drove up there to find my son, incoherent, walking the streets of Manhattan with a fifty-pound bag of dirty, half-washed clothes (everything he owned) in 90° weather, while he was dropping half of them out of the bag onto the dirty side-walk. He had taken enough drugs to kill himself, but was a walking zombie. Justin was admitted into the hospital, where he was taken to a psych ward and admitted for a week, then transferred to a drug program. That was in 2014, and that began his journey with the methadone clinic, after relapsing on Suboxone and Vivitrol.

Three years of the chain and ball of traveling twelve New York City blocks every day, in the heat, in the cold, and in the rain, while being "dope sick" every morning to get to the clinic before it closed at noon! This is the real-life struggle of a "recovering" addict! A "normal" person can't even fathom the obstacles that face our children every day, just trying to be "normal" like every other person! From there, they have to get to work and maintain the normalcy. My heart just breaks reliving their everyday journey!

In July 2017, Justin came home on a Friday. I picked him up at the bus stop at eleven thirty p.m., after his day began at five a.m., getting to the clinic, working his eight-hour day, and traveling four hours on a bus. I was so happy to see his face, he just wanted to go HOME and get something to eat and collapse in his clean bed. He was too tired to shower. The next day he said, "Mummy, I don't want to do this anymore, I need you to help me find a detox that will get me off methadone! I can't do this anymore, please, please HELP me!" So, I enlisted my sister and my daughter to help me find such a detox in New York. After five days, I finally found a detox that had availability and would accept my son, but by now he was so sick because he didn't have his methadone. I had to find a person who was selling methadone to get him through the next couple of days, until I could, once again, put my child on a bus and send him to New York. That was the last time I would see my son, hug my son, kiss my son.

Justin entered the program the first week of August, completed their program, and was set up in a sober house. He got a job. He was happy, thriving, looked amazing. My BOY was back! Justin was in the program a little over eleven months. We knew he had turned the corner and maybe, by the grace of God, my son was one of the success stories. We face-timed every week. He was so proud of what he was accomplishing and so was his family. In those eleven months, we didn't have to send him money. Not once! He paid his own cell phone bill, purchased his own clothes, he was going out to dinner with friends, and was dating a young lady. Oh my God, can this be? Justin called around the 4th of July, 2018, and said, "Mom, can I come home and stay for a month in August? I need to work on my OSH-10 certification to get a better job." "Yes, of course you can, I'm so PROUD of you JUSTIN!" He said, "Thanks, Mom, but I will always be an addict. It's a struggle every day to stay clean."

Then, the phone call came at 11:45 a.m. on July 20, 2018. The voice on the other end of the phone said, "Is this Justin's mother? I'm sorry to inform you that your son passed away at 11:40 p.m." "NO! You made a mistake! Please, please check again, that's not my son!" And they went on to say, "We're sorry, but he was identified by his ID in his wallet." "NO, you don't understand, he loses his wallet at least once a month, someone must've found it and it's NOT MY SON!! Please check again, I can describe every tattoo and scar he has, please just check again! PLEASE I'M BEGGING YOU." And they replied, "Sorry, Mrs. S, it is your son, Justin." I immediately hung up and called the sober house, thinking he would be sleeping in his bed. I spoke to the person in charge, and he said Justin wasn't there and that he was just writing him up for missing curfew! My world was obliterated, everything was moving in slow motion, I couldn't hear anything.

My son was found with one and one half pills in his pocket of what was basically fentanyl masqueraded as Percocet. One-half of a pill took my son's life. My son died on a dirty New York City subway train ALONE. A stranger flagged down transit police because he looked like he was sleeping, and his phone wouldn't stop ringing. In a blink of an eye my dreams, my hopes and any expectations of a happy, normal life for my son and for myself were GONE.

Justin's Mom,

Kim S.
Fairhaven, Massachussettes

Kim also lost a daughter, Kailan, to drugs. Due to a current lawsuit, her story can't be shared.

September 5, 1986 to August 18, 2019. Forever 33

Ian

FOREVER 38

Let me tell you about my Ian.

Ian Paul was born on March 4, 1979, a day after my first year anniversary and the day after his grandmother's birthday. She was already his angel. Ian was my middle child; he has an older brother, Chris, and a younger sister, Crystal. Ian was born in Springfield, Vermont. When he was born, he was given twenty-four hours to live. He was born a month early, and had to be transferred to a medical facility in New Hampshire. They had the best NICU. I couldn't go at the same time as Ian, but I was there the very next morning!

Fast forward to the toddler years, he was full of life! Always playing and wanting to be in my lap, even when he was a teenager and young adult he wanted to sit in my lap!! Ian was very smart! He loved to take things apart and put them back together. He loved skateboarding and always wanted to be a professional skateboarder! He was good at it!! He gave his great-grandmother a heart attack by skateboarding down the Claremont/Newport dump hill. It is very steep and she was driving up the hill while he was skateboarding down the hill!! Needless to say, she was terrified!

During Ian's teen years, I knew he smoked marijuana; peer pressure was the cause of that. Fast forward to his adult years. Ian found and fell in love with Monica; they had a child together, Darren. About seven years later, he loses her to an accidental overdose. Here is when I think he started to use other drugs. He was a single dad and moved back home with us. The effects of his drug use took a big toll on us. He stole from us, including about $5000 in jewelry. He overdosed many times. His sister always found him and always saved him. He did rehabs, 12-Steps, always said he was clean, but always relapsed. Sometimes, I believed he didn't want to be clean, but I know he didn't want to die!

"Not my child" is an understatement! Drugs do not discriminate! The drug dealers do not care about you! They are not your friends! They are murderers! My Ian passed away July 1, 2017, due to carfentanyl. He thought he was getting heroin, but it wasn't. My heart is shattered beyond belief! I will never be able to hug him, kiss him! I will never be able to hear him say to me, "Hey there Momma! Has anyone today told you how beautiful you are? And that I love you!" I miss hearing that so very much! I love you Ian, and I will miss you forever. Until we meet again! Love Forever ~ Mom.

Ian's Mom,

BRENDA P.
Ruskin, Florida

Thomas

FOREVER 40

Tommy was a loving person and kind to everyone. He was always joking and making people laugh. His laugh was contagious.

At the age of sixteen, he was the quarterback for his high school football team and injured his knee. Back then, the doctors prescribed him Percocet for his injury. This was before the opioid crisis, as he was forty when he was poisoned by fentanyl. Tommy met his ex-wife when he was in sales. She lived in New York and we live in Maryland. They got married and had three children, one daughter and then six years later they had a set of twins.

Tommy's life as a salesperson was a high-pressure job and he traveled all the time. He began using uppers to sell land and then downers to be able to sleep. Eventually, he turned to heroin. I will never forget the day he told me. I was so naive to heroin. The only words that came out of my mouth were, "We don't do heroin in this family." I had to quickly learn about heroin, as he entered into a divorce. The heroin was his vice going through a bad divorce.

Finally, he got clean as he was invited to church. He got saved and was clean for four years and was very involved with the church. His job changed his shift so he couldn't make it to church often. November of 2018, Tommy went to a Christian book store and bought his three children teddy bears with my mom. He was planning to get ahead of his shopping that year. Then, he got sick with a sinus infection and went to the ER and got an antibiotic. After being sick for a week, he told me his neck and back hurt. I thought it was because he was laying down too much from the sinus infection. I told him to get some deep heat rub. We decided since everyone was sick, we would not celebrate Thanksgiving that year, as a family. So, on Wednesday, the day before Thanksgiving, he reached out to his doctor for pain medication. The office was closed due to the holiday. He called a man and asked for heroin to ease his pain. Little did he know that the man who drove to Baltimore brought back straight fentanyl. Tommy did research on Google, because the dealer said they were capsules and he must not have done that before. Google did say heroin can come in a capsule form.

The day after Thanksgiving was the day my heart stopped, when my youngest son called me to let me know that Tommy was gone. There is a case, and they have traced who sold it to  him. We are still waiting to go to court as Tommy's advocates. I had never even heard of fentanyl until November 23, 2018, when my son was poisoned.

Tommy's Mom,

TRACI P.
Hagerstown, Maryland

Kirsten

This is a story of a beautiful, loving, and smart young lady. She is my precious daughter, Kirsten, who was taken from me by heroin and addiction.

Kirsten was my first child and I had the privilege of staying home with her when she was born. I loved her the minute I knew I was pregnant. She was the most adorable baby with thick, dark hair and blue eyes. Kirsten was a mommy's girl from the start. We were two peas in a pod. When Kirsten was younger and started school, she wanted to be a janitor or a waitress. There may have also been some talk about being a doctor.

Before Kirsten's death, she was working at UPS, where she was a model employee. Her supervisors spoke highly of her. It was tough work, but she overcame any obstacles. Kirsten enjoyed reading, working out, eating healthy, dancing, laughing, singing, and playing volleyball.

She loved spending time with her family, especially her brother, J.W. They played video games, watched movies, wrestled, texted, and loved one another intensely. He called her "Sis" and she called him Bubba. Kirsten and her dad had a special relationship. They were best friends. Kirsten was also close to her Aunt Nicole. They "got" each other. Kirsten's middle name is Nicole after her Aunt Nicole. February 29, 1996, is her birthdate and she joined the special few who were "Leap Year" babies. She also had a "Spock" ear, which other family members also had. One of my favorite memories of Kirsten is when her brother brought personalized M&M's from New York. On some there was a recovery message and the others her name. Kirsten cried and was so grateful for his gift.

I started noticing changes when Kirsten went to middle school. Her "friends" were involved in some questionable activities. Drinking, drugs, smoking, and sex were a few. Kirsten was engulfed in the attention and it was a release from her everyday challenging life. She started skipping school, getting low grades, sleeping a lot, not participating with the family, and her attitude was harsh. I spoke to teachers and counselors; they gave suggestions. I spoke with police and they listened. I got Kirsten a counselor and she was a sounding board for Kirsten. Kirsten had started to sneak out and stay out all night, so I got an alarm system to keep her in the house. Her friends, except for two, were all older than she was. She was introduced to an adult world that she had wanted to partake in for a few years. This is when I reached out to anyone who would, or could, help us both.

Kirsten quit high school in her sophomore year and attempted online schooling. This, unfortunately, did not happen. Eventually, Kirsten obtained her GED and we were very proud she completed her schooling. Kirsten was in treatment or a program at least five times during her struggle with addiction. She completed one program, graduated drug court, and had six months of sobriety before she overdosed. She also had many on and off periods of sobriety, where we could witness the "real" Kirsten.

What do I wish could have been different about this brutal experience? Earlier support and knowledge about how to handle someone who is active in their addiction. Fortunately, about two years before her death, I was introduced to a parents and grandparents Al-Anon group.

They knew what it was like to live with addiction and they had wonderful suggestions to keep me sane. I found out I didn't cause her addiction; I couldn't cure Kirsten's addiction and I couldn't control it. The message that I received was love the child, not the disease, and that my family can be at some peace, whether she was using or not.

All of Kirsten's relationships were altered due to her addiction. This was hard to watch and difficult to explain to others. Heroin stole Kirsten's soul and made it impossible for her to be a productive member of any relationship. The last days of Kirsten's life left a lot of unknowns and pain. She was missing for five days and we frantically searched for her. Previously, she had gone missing when she was using, but inevitably, she would send a text or message and we knew she was alive.

That's what was different this time. No word from her. No text, no message of, "Mom I'm ok," and that's how I knew, deep in my heart, that she was no longer alive. She was found at Idlewild Park in her car, dead in the backseat of an apparent overdose of heroin. It was her twenty-first birthday.

Our lives were forever shattered and those who had any connection with Kirsten were devastated. Losing my girl is the most difficult time I have ever been through. I am forever grateful for the support of my family and friends. Mourning Kirsten has been softened by love, kind words, memories, and gestures. However, this will be a lifetime of ache and I am a different person. Kirsten, you will always be loved and never forgotten.

Kirsten's Mom,

DARCY P.
Reno, Nevada

Ashlyn

FOREVER 18

Ashlyn Marie, eighteen, was a vibrant teenage girl. She was so excited to start her senior year of high school. She had big plans to enjoy all the senior activities and for college.

During her senior year, she had her wisdom teeth pulled. I have so many funny videos from that day, all similar to the ones you would see on YouTube or Facebook. When we got home, I gave her some ice cream and put her to bed. A friend of hers wanted to come see her. This friend had a history of bad behavior that Ashlyn was always overly concerned with. I remember Ashlyn sitting on the counter while I cooked dinner expressing worry for her friend in the weeks before. I gave her the advice to love from a distance but show support, and when she was doing good to spend time with her.

Her friend was doing well at the time and we thought she could use the good influence of Ashlyn. I allowed her to come over for a couple hours. I later found out this was a fatal mistake.

You see, while Ashlyn was still coming off of anesthesia and very loopy, this friend cut out lines of heroin, and Ashlyn, not in the right frame of mind, partook.

I knew something was wrong with my girl—for a couple months, things didn't feel right. I kept worrying something was wrong. She continued to come home by curfew, which was ten p.m. She continued doing her chores. She continued participating in family activities, but something was different. Her grades began to drop, she always had the sniffles, and on occasion she was still asleep when I woke up (this was very odd because she always set her alarm to get up extra early for hair and makeup). I noticed she was going to school with her hair in a bun and sweatshirts very out of the norm for my princess.

We were paying attention. I asked her multiple times what was going on. I knew where she was at all times and who she was with. It didn't prepare us for what was to come.

On March 17, 2016, I got a phone call while I was at work. It was a friend of Ashlyn's whom she had known since birth. She was mad at Ashlyn for some teenage drama and wanted to get her in trouble, so she called to tell me that she was on drugs. Heroin. You see, unbeknownst to me, heroin had become as relevant in these kids' lives as marijuana was to kids in my high school days.

Ashlyn and I had a very long talk about what was going on. She was honest with me. She told me after that first try with heroin she woke up with a hole in her that she felt could only be filled with this drug. She knew where the kids that sold it hung out at her high school and she began approaching them. She told me heroin was done in the bathrooms, sold in class, and shared in the parking lot. Her father and I immediately withdrew her from school and put her in a rehab located in Louisiana, fifteen hours from our hometown of Murrells Inlet, South Carolina. I remember the fear in her face as I left her there. I also remember pulling over to vomit as I left my little girl. I slept in her bed thinking the worst had come but thankfully Ashlyn was on the mend.

Ashlyn was released from rehab the beginning of summer 2016. She was positive about the future so were we as her family. Ashlyn got a job with the help of her stepmother and began to have high hopes about the future again. Unfortunately, heroin had other plans.

She relapsed quite a few times over the next year. And as her mother, each time was devastating. You believe each time is going to be the time they get it together and overcome this demon. Each time you are wrong. I had a tracker on Ashlyn's phone for a while. When she left, I would follow her. Our county, which encompasses Myrtle Beach, South Carolina, has multiple hotels along a boulevard. I remember walking up and down the boulevard searching for her night after night. On lucky nights, I would find her and try to talk to her. I would tell her she is so loved and she is better than any addiction. She would listen and cry.

Heroin was always stronger than my love. She would tell me songs she listened to that reminded her of me and she would cry as well— longing for what was. She was different now, we both knew it. I began to grieve the loss of my daughter who was still alive. I started a Facebook page, "Stop the Heroin Epidemic, Horry and Georgetown County SC." My hopes were to find help to stop the epidemic, and support and help parents and loved ones like myself deal with the situation. I filed a judicial pick up order through a mental health facility. We had court the end of July 2017. I was trying to get her involuntarily committed into a ninety-day rehab. Ashlyn wasn't mad at me for filing the order. I actually drove her there. She said she understood why I was doing it and that she loved me for it. That didn't change the fact that she didn't want to go to rehab again.

Once at the courthouse, two people talked with her and evaluated her. When we arrived in court the judge recommended outpatient treatment. She stated if Ashlyn didn't comply, she would be brought back and put into inpatient therapy. I told the judge I didn't want to bury my daughter, but her decision had been made. Ashlyn would die just over two months later. She would have still been in rehab had the courts listened to my cries.

There were many times when Ashlyn came home and wanted to get better. She cried to me multiple times about who she had become. She began hating herself. This ate me alive. We want our children to know their worth and know what they have to offer the world. I know first-hand Ashlyn had so much to offer. She was a beautiful person, a beau-

542

tiful artist, a beautiful writer, a beautiful daughter, and a beautiful friend.

After a year and a half of on again, off again recovery, she called me and said she needed help. This is something she had never said before. She said she wanted to come home. She said she hated her life. She said she didn't want to live like this. She was home within two hours. She told me she wanted to move. She wanted different people, places, and things. I agreed. We began to plan our transition to Ohio. My husband at the time was from Ohio and we had visited a few times. She wanted to go to a school of art, and she began making a portfolio. For the first time in a long time I saw her spark. We began packing, put in notices, found jobs, etc.

Ashlyn decided to go out with friends one night. That night turned into eight days. We video chatted daily and she messaged me often. On October 4, 2017, she messaged me not to worry. She wasn't doing drugs and she would be home in the morning.

I don't know why but for some reason I cried throughout the night. I woke up multiple times hysterically crying. My ex-husband tried to comfort me. I remember telling him something was wrong and that my world had shifted. I finally lay down again that night around 3:00 a.m. only to be woken by my doorbell at 3:44 a.m. I remember walking to the door and seeing a woman standing at the window. I thought it was Ashlyn. As I got closer, I realized it was a woman and a man both in suits with badges. They were there to tell me my baby had died.

I will never know the details of that day, but what I do know is this: Ashlyn bought heroin and overdosed around 2:30 p.m., only a couple hours after we talked. My sweet girl went to the hospital as a Jane Doe. She was with two adults in their mid to late thirties. They waited nine hours to call 911. Instead of calling for help they put her in a cold tub to try and bring her back. I later found out as they were slapping her face and telling her to wake up that only when they would say "Your mom is here," would her eyes flutter and try to open. While she was unconscious, they injected her with meth in an attempt to restart her heart. When this didn't work, they put my baby on a luggage rack and wheeled her behind a hotel, left her near a dumpster, stole her belongings, and left her alone. On the way to the hospital and at the hospital they worked on her and got her pulse back. She took her last breath at 12:08 a.m. on October 5, 2017.

Her cause of death was drug-induced cardiac arrhythmia caused by the meth. Her case was closed and neither of the two were charged with her murder. The Horry County detective told me that's just what addicts do to revive someone who has overdosed. I was told the reason they didn't call 911 was because they were scared; yeah well so was my little girl as she lay dying.

As her mom, I am forever stuck in that day. It is still October in my heart. I obsess about what her last moments were like—if she was in pain, scared, cold, if she wanted her mommy. I find myself constantly longing to hear her voice and look for her in crowds often. The thought of living life without Ashlyn is unbearable at times. She wanted to be a mother one day. She dreamed about a wedding. She wanted to share her art and love for interior design with everyone.

Ashlyn's funeral was on her nine-teenth birthday.

Ashlyn was loved, so beautiful, and she was mine. Until the day I'm lucky enough to be with her again, I will grieve and hold an unfathomable amount of pain in my soul. She was mine and I was hers and nothing can ever take that away.

Ashlyn's Mom,

ANGEE P.
Murrells Inlet, South Carolina

Ashley & Justin

FOREVER 30 & 31

I lost two due to fentanyl, heroin, and cocaine overdoses. Seven weeks apart.

Ashley, my only daughter, was a kind, loving person, who was loved by many. She had a son, twelve, and a daughter, two at the time. She had it all, a great job, a house, a car. Her son's father was an active user of heroin, which Ashley never used, although they were together for twenty years.

He went to jail and brought a friend home with him. Ashley got together with the friend. They had a daughter and he introduced her to heroin. Then she lost everything, even her children. She cashed in her 401K. They went through $25,000. He went to rehab first, then Ashley went.

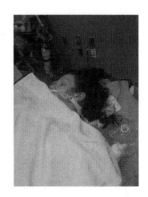

She was seven months clean, met a guy and moved in with him, even after I explained to her why they shouldn't move in together. He relapsed and so did she. She overdosed on August 6, 2019, in their townhome, in bed next to him. She died during the night. They were using together. He went to sleep. She must have gotten up, used more, and overdosed. I was supposed to go visit her on the day of her death. Three days before, she said the new boyfriend was abusive, but everything was going to be OK, because she was leaving him. I think she was using heroin for two or three years.

Justin was my middle child he had three children, ages 11, 4, and 3. He lived his children and was a great father. He was with his girlfriend for fifteen years. I really don't know how long he was using heroin. He was in a dirt bike accident and hit by a car. He had a metal plate put in his hip and leg in 2005. He was stealing from his family. They lost everything and were homeless, living in hotels.

She made him leave and he was homeless the last two or three years before his death. Living on the streets of Baltimore, I still took his kids to see him and we would have lunch with daddy. He got caught shoplifting and went to jail for four months. He was out of jail for one day and overdosed. He promised me when I dropped him off, he would not use. Seven weeks after Ashley.

I discussed with them both how that one last time could kill you. I did the best I could. Tough love. No tough love. Rock bottom meant nothing. They both lost everything. They both were severely depressed.

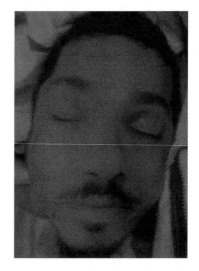

I divorced their father fifteen years ago. I'm not blaming him, but they both missed him not being in their life. They tried so hard to have a relationship with him.

My oldest is now 40 and is a recovering addict. He's been clean for seven years. I thought since they grew up in the chaos of his addiction, they would never try heroin. It's been almost

546

a year. I have my good days and bad days. I will never stop grieving for them. My faith is what gets me through each day, knowing they are with God.

Ashley and Justin's Mom,

DENISE P.
Baltimore, Maryland

Grief leaves you essentially homeless. You have no walls, no floor, and no foundation. You must define what all of that will look like and rebuild from the ground up.
~ Suzii B.

Michael

FOREVER 38

My name is Mary. I am the mother of Michael, who died on August 24, 2014, at the age of 38, the result of a heroin overdose. He was my first-born child. He was the pride of my life.

He was perfect when he was born. He had ten fingers and ten toes and the most beautiful face. And not one scratch or bruise or needle mark. His smile was engaging and as he grew, he was friendly and smart, and loved people. He wanted life to be simple and fun. But he had a disease. It was hidden for a long time, but his father and other members of our families struggled with addictions as well. And his tendency to use alcohol and drugs grew with him.

When Michael was twenty-three, he was in a car accident that caused serious injuries. He was in a lot of pain, and in order for him to function at work, the doctors prescribed oxycodone. For the next ten years. During this time, Michael was married, had a son, Liam, and steadily built his career as a chef. He attended culinary classes at Waukesha Community College. He worked as a chef at a five-star restaurant. He was considered by many to be one of the best chefs in Milwaukee. Michael loved Liam with all of his heart and was a great dad. He and his wife separated when Liam was eighteen months old, and they shared custody. Liam remained with Michael, and Michael was his primary physical custodian until he was eight. At that time, Michael went into a treatment program for his addiction for six months at the Salvation Army. When he finished the program, Michael had a job as a chef at a local restaurant in Wauwatosa. Liam immediately resumed living with him. They had a very strong father/son bond, and Liam is still very affected by Michael's death.

Like many addicts before him, and those yet to come, Michael had become addicted to opioids after being on prescription drugs for pain for many years. As his addiction grew, he headed down the slippery slope of manipulation and lies that accompany the need for more and more drugs. While I always had hope that Michael could beat the monster (addiction), it was heartbreaking to watch him struggle. He continued to work, and continued to be a good father to Liam, but he couldn't resist the overwhelming demands of the disease. Especially when his dealer continually sent him texts offering him "deals" that were just within his reach to satisfy his body's craving. My son went through the paranoia, the cravings, the lying and stealing, the seeking of treatment, and the hope that he could recover. But along with the support and love and encouragement from family and friends, he would be lured by his dealer, offered deals that because of his affliction he could not refuse. In spite of his love for his family, and his love for his son, and his passion for living, he could not say no. He died.

I lost my first-born son, my hope, and my belief in god because a predator, his addiction, "won." How has Michael's death affected me? He was my confidant. We talked almost every day. I never stop aching. I never stop feeling guilty. I never stop worrying about Liam or my other son, Sean, or my grandchildren. I retired because I couldn't do my job anymore. I worked for forty-five years with mentally ill, emotionally disturbed, and drug-addicted adults and adolescents. I feel like the shoe-maker who has no shoes. I have a broken heart. I have a hole in my life bigger than the Grand Canyon. I love music but can't listen to it anymore without crying. I can't believe in god anymore. He didn't listen. I can't hope anymore that Michael will overcome the horrible disease of addiction. I can't hope he will be happy and give his son a good childhood.

Now I have no hope for that. None. He is gone forever. I am a shell of my former self. My relationship with my significant other has suffered greatly because of my loss. I can neither give nor receive consolation or intimacy. And I am afraid she will go away too. I am taking an antidepressant and can't sleep without medication. I can't work or remember details. I used to exercise regularly, work out, ride my bike, run a half-marathon every six months, but I can't motivate myself anymore. I am seeing a therapist to work through these issues, but at the moment it seems as though there is no light at the end of the tunnel. I want to move on, to enjoy the pleasures of life that my grandchildren and the love of my family offer me. But losing a son is a very difficult challenge. Right now, I have no confidence that I will ever get over this. "Forever" has transformed from a promise of lasting joy to a threat of never-ending grief.

Michael's dealer had a long history of ignoring and breaking the law. He spent years of his life preying on vulnerable disabled people. He didn't "just" sell drugs, he sought out addicts and lured them into his trap by offering them a poison they could not refuse. And then he offered them more and more of it, because the more they used, the more he sold, and the more money he made. He has no regard for the law, or for the lives of others. We tried to stop him. In the last year of Michael's life, three different members of Michael's family notified the police that the dealer was contacting Michael trying to sell him heroin. He even texted Michael while he was in treatment. The police were called, but they didn't respond to our pleas. We gave them his first name and phone number. They did nothing until Michael was dead.

If you give the dealer fifty years in prison, or if you give him ninety days of probation, my son is gone forever. Maybe you could give him a month in prison for every bag of heroin he's sold or for every one of his victims. We know he killed Michael because he admitted it. How many others died that he didn't admit to or kept moving further towards a horrible end because of his "deals?" I do not want him back on the streets where my grandchildren could be lured by his poison.

Nothing will fix all that I have lost. Nothing will bring Michael back. It is useless to hate his dealer, but I do hold him responsible for feeding

Michael's addiction, relentlessly, until he fed him enough to kill him. I only hope that someday I can turn my pain into a purpose. That I can reach out to others who share my grief and give them comfort and compassion.

Michael's Mom,

MARY P.
Milwaukee, Wisconsin

Joseph

FOREVER 28

This is my youngest son, Joe. Yes, he bought a drug, but it did not warrant a death sentence. No, he was not an addict. He had not had drugs in a long time. He turned to drugs when his dad died in 2018 but he quit on his own. Let me tell you about him. He played hockey at the Y. He was in band in high school. His father and I were hands-on parents. We never missed a game or meeting. He was going to college for automotive technologies, was a state certified inspector, and had 2 ASEs under his belt. He would have taken an exam for a third by the end of December. He was never mean to anyone. He took me everywhere I needed to go so I didn't have to walk so far. I have bone on bone knees. He loved to help people and didn't dislike anyone. Even in a game if he destroyed someone, he would feel bad and help them rebuild.

I had never heard of Black Balloon day. Unfortunately, I have now. Unscrupulous drug dealers are killing our children for an extra buck by cutting drugs with fentanyl. Problem is they don't know what they are doing. The saddest part is Joe was getting ready to go to bed and this guy called him for a ride and sold him the heroin, assuring Joe it had no fentanyl. Joe got up and got dressed, went out, and took the guy to his girlfriend's house. Joe died that night of drug-induced homicide. There was fentanyl in the toxicology report. Do you see him now? Please share and help us spread the word.

Joe's Mom,

THERESA P.
Rural Hall, North Carolina

Sammy

FOREVER 38

My son died from an accidental drug overdose on 11/11/18. He was 38 years old. Sammy was in and out of Rehab's. He was only clean for 2 year which is so sad. He tried to stay clean but could never make it to that point.

I mourn his death every day. His death has left a whole in my heart which nothing can fill. I pray every day for those afflicted by this disease so no families should have to go through what we've been through.

It's not normal to bury your child, they should bury us.

Sammy's Mom,

NANCY P.
Philadelphia, Pennsylvania

Jack

FOREVER 22

I lost Jack to a lethal combination of cocaine and fentanyl on September 30, 2019. I think my son's addiction may have started in his senior year of high school, but I don't know for sure. His drug of choice was Xanax and used it to self-medicate.

When he attended East Carolina University in the fall of 2015, I noticed that he seemed more anxious and at times depressed. Knowing that college can be a big adjustment, I wasn't alarmed but I did encourage him to speak with a therapist. He didn't feel the need.

Jack ended up transferring to West Virginia University for the spring of 2016 semester. While there, he joined a fraternity, which I wasn't happy about. It was while in this fraternity that his addiction grew due to the prevalence of drugs available.

After unsuccessful semesters, he had to leave that college and take classes at a local community college. It was during this time that his behavior really changed. He was erratic, manipulative, angry, and verbally abusive.

I repeatedly tried to get him help. He was resistant, but finally agreed to see a psychiatrist. We went through three different providers and several therapists. Due to privacy issues, I was left in the dark on truly what the issue was. He shut me out.

It was such a feeling of frustration and helplessness for me.

In December of 2018, I finally had my chance to get him help. He was threatening to kill himself and was uncontrollable. His stepfather called 911 and after evaluation, we were able to have him held against his will. He went into rehab at this time.

When he came back home, I felt like I was getting my son back. He felt so encouraged to move forward with his life now that drugs were out of his system. He was motivated. I wish that I hadn't been so naive in thinking that he would beat the odds with only one round of rehab.

On September 29, he went out seeking Xanax but settled for something else when he couldn't find it. He didn't want to die.

Jack made friends so easily and I attribute this to his kindness, caring, and just the fact that he was fun to be around.

In his short life, he was very athletic and participated in all types of sports, but soccer was probably his favorite.

During his teens, he was very involved with scouting. He achieved Eagle Scout and his project reflected his compassion towards others less fortunate. He built shelving under a stairwell of a homeless shelter to provide additional storage for supplies that freed up room to bring in additional families.

In his honor, I am doing everything to bring awareness to the mental health/addiction crisis in this country. I've volunteered to speak with middle and high school students locally to discuss the dangers and to put a face on addiction. I pledge to also appeal to our law makers in hopes to bring about legislation to provide better access to mental health and addiction treatment. Drugs are almost impossible to stop from flooding into our communities. We need to treat the disease.

I miss my son every single day.

I will continue to tell my story in hopes of saving someone else and so my son did not have to die in vain.

Jack's Mom,

MEGAN P.
Fairfax, Virginia

> *I miss you past the moon and beyond the stars.*
> *~ Mary W.*

Chris

FOREVER 34

My first-born son Chris: who gave me purpose, confidence, pure happiness in becoming a momma.

Chris was born January 27; five pounds, twenty-one inches. I was just eighteen, married and living in Monroe, Michigan. He was the best baby ever, I always said, the most easy-going young babe. As a child, Chris always shared and cared for others and loved to draw. As he grew, he loved sports too, football and basketball well into his teens, and even taught himself to play the drums and eventually was in a few bands with a few shows. He always seemed to have a lot of friends and was well liked. He was a gentle kind of kid.

When he started experimenting with alcohol, pot later, I found out about pills etc. I really thought it was a phase. Lots of talks and grounding went on. Around the age of eighteen, Chris had major nerve surgery on his arm and started taking pain pills even more. Still, at this point in no way did I ever think addiction or addict. I figured he would grow out of the partying stage as he got older and started working. As life went on, he held jobs, was a high functioning adult, and a father to two amazing children, one boy named Maze and a daughter two years later named Kendell. His relationship with their mother wasn't the best; she also was doing pills, etc. As his life progressed with our love and support to better himself, he left that relationship for another and at the time seemed better. But behind our back, his wife was a heroin addict and kept our son, Chris, away from his children and our family. As much as we could, we tried to get Chris alone and talk about leaving her and going to rehab.

At the end of 2017, Chris finally started coming around; he wanted a change. His stepdad, one brother, and I were making an escape plan for Chris. Conversations were many, but not known to all, as we were afraid of what his wife would do if she found out. In June of 2018, we saw Chris when we came down to Tennessee from Michigan to visit; we were in the process of moving back to Tennessee soon. Chris told us he overdosed in April, and was scared, so he was only self-medicating, a patient dose every three days. We tried talking him into rehab and getting him a medical script for something instead of off the street. Never ever thought that was our last visit, touch, hug, and kiss. We had plans in motion.

On August 18, 2018, I got a call from Chris around noon, telling me his grandmother's Facebook page was hacked. Very strange but true. Strange cause Chris didn't use Facebook that much. We were at one of our granddaughters' second birthday party, so I said, "Love you, stay away from it all, and call me later."

Later that night his name popped up in my phone. I answered it like I was going to talk to Chris, but instead it was his wife telling me this long drugged-out story about how she woke up and saw Chris drunk and high on heroin stumbling into the house to the couch. She went back to bed and woke up later to find him dead. According to the corner's report, NO ALCOHOL OR HEROIN was found in his body, just gabapentin (nerve pain pill) and a fatal dose of fentanyl.

ONE PILL ONE KILL...HIS life was taken...I call it RUSSIAN ROULETTE...Took one more pill and someone laced it.

My whole world shattered that day. My stomach was empty; my

560

heart was broken in so many pieces. I couldn't breathe, talk, or even process this...(#forever 34). We have two children in active recovery, before Chris' death and after. Sadly, we have one son fighting and hiding his addiction to meth. We can see clearly now how addiction works and what it looks like.

My best advice is to always support with your love and action and influence, not judgement. They literally have to come to terms and want that help and change. They can make that step when they don't feel so bad about themselves. Awareness is key, experimenting is no longer just experimenting; the drugs, alcohol, cigarettes, are all too lethal with poison. Never, ever thought this was happening to this kid...HE HAD PLANS...TO LIVE.

Forever Chris will be missed, loved, and remembered. Forever will we take care of his two children. Forever I will keep AWARENESS for my family and others. The #NotInVain support group saved my heartbreak and made me realize I'm never alone and there are other people who understand my heartache without judging me in my darkest hour. It has given me a sense of purpose, hope, and strength to go on.

Sadly, forever missed and loved by Chris' 2 children Maze and Kendall, 6 brothers and 1 sister, sister- in- law's, brother-in-law, fifteen nieces and nephews and lots of family and friends, stepdad (pops) Elzie, but mostly me, Chris' Momma.

See you on the other side of the stars my son.

Chris' Mom,

JENNA P.
Knoxville, Tennessee

Brandon

FOREVER 31

Brandon was born in 1987 in Zanesville, Ohio, to a young couple that were high school sweethearts never meant to be. Before Brandon's first birthday, his father and I were separated, and Brandon lived with me. Both his father and I remarried prior to Brandon turning three years old.

Brandon moved with me and his stepfather Mark from Zanesville to a suburb of Dayton, Ohio, due to Mark's job change. Brandon visited his father and stepmother regularly. Many times, he would come home with stories that worried his mother. Tales of his father drinking, loud noises, arguing behind closed doors, and his stepmother crying.

But all in all, Brandon was a happy child when he was with his family members, his grandparents, and me. He participated in football and basketball, and had several friends.

Soon there were stories of gangs at the local junior high school Brandon would be attending. His stepfather and I decided it was time for a change, so we built a home in a new and upcoming community south of Dayton, Springboro, Ohio.

Later, Brandon told me, "You moved me from an area where there were gangs selling drugs to an area where drugs were easily accessible because the kids' parents had money, so they wanted to buy drugs!"

He began hanging out with boys that always got in trouble and the police were always at our door. I began to find spoons hidden under his bed, needles (rigs) under the cushions of a chair in his room, and noticed a belt that he never wore, but always took with him. Things began to disappear from the house that he would cleverly disguise so we wouldn't recognize the loss until long after the item was gone…too late to be retrieved from the pawn shop.

We offered him help and re-financed our home twice for close to $60,000 to send him to different rehabs in hopes of helping him. One rehab in Oklahoma seemed to work. He came back looking like his old self. But he went out one night and got caught drinking and was kicked out of there too.

After Mark kicked him out of our home for stealing, Brandon lived on the streets for years. Never had any offer of help from his father. So, I helped him with hotel rooms, food, and clothing. I took him to different rehabs when I found them. I picked him up when he called crying and took him to the hospital when he needed help. Until one day he called and said he was in jail, and I told him that is where he would stay until he sobered up. I tried tough love this time. He was there for four months. When he got out of jail, he was clean! Yay! A new beginning!

He came to stay where I worked in Richmond, Indiana, so I could see him every day and support him. I paid monthly for a hotel room that was less than a block from my job. He was thirty-one years old. He would come to see me every day, and things were looking up. We would have lunch together. He was completing job applications. Looking healthy, gaining weight, just overall back to his normal self.

We met for Valentine's Day 2019 for lunch, on Thursday. That Friday, he came to see me before I left work. We had plans to have lunch that Saturday after I had my hair cut. I texted him and told him that my hair appointment had changed and wanted to know if he still wanted to do lunch but didn't get a response. So, I thought maybe he was still sleeping or was out somewhere.

But that night at 2:32 a.m., I got a call from the Wayne County Coroner's Office asking, "Is this Denise? This is the Wayne County Coroner, and I am sorry to inform you, but we have found your son Brandon deceased." I don't remember anything after that. Mark took the phone. I just started crying. That's when my life ended.

Brandon was a beautiful soul. He didn't deserve any of this! He told me Friday he was bored. The coroner said that they had found pure fentanyl beside him.

No one deserves to hear they have lost a child. Addiction can affect anyone, rich, poor, young, old, mother, father, son, daughter. ANYONE. I beg each and every person to stop and look past their idealistic vision of what a perfect life is or should be, because that is NOT how real life is. These are people who deserve to be loved, and we can't give up on them.

I wish every day that it was me. And you bet every day when I see someone standing on a corner in ragged clothes begging for change or a meal, I feed them. I help them. Because I see past their clothing, their sign, and their unkept appearance. I see the person. I see my son begging for help.

Brandon's Mom,

DENISE P.
Greenville, Ohio

Grant

FOREVER 19

My son Grant was a beautiful and talented athlete all of his young life. In ninth grade, he tore his ACL twice. This led to him being unable to participate in all of the sports he loved. Sports were his life. He was lost.

He started using marijuana, dabs as he called it. It was a synthetic marijuana that he would use a blow torch to smoke. His marijuana use caused an illness called cannabis hyperemesis syndrome (CHS), which caused him to vomit about twenty times a day, causing his kidneys to fail, and his heart to go into tachycardia. This happened about every three months and would land him a three-day stay in the hospital. These bouts would last anywhere from five to fifteen days. Grant hated that he couldn't smoke pot. He started drinking and taking pills to get that feeling of being high. I had to stand by him and watch him wither away, begging him to get into treatment. He had scars all over his body. There were holes in the walls all over in his room. I later found out that the scars and holes were from him crashing into the walls.

I knew he had messed with pills here and there, but I had NO IDEA the extent of it. On April 7 of 2020, I realized I hadn't heard Grant downstairs for quite a while. Usually, he would have been upstairs grabbing snacks and I would hear his video games. I went downstairs and I saw him from down the hall. He was slumped over and grey with foam coming out of his mouth. My thirteen year old daughter followed me down and called 911. I performed CPR on his cold body. I knew he was gone the second I saw him, though. When the police arrived to take over, I kept screaming, "My baby is dead!" He was pronounced dead the early morning of April 8. The toxicology report said that Grant had died immediately due to a PURE fentanyl pill. Grant's friend told me that he had Facetimed with Grant right before he had taken the pill. Grant thought he was taking a Percocet but instead the pill that he took had sixteen milligrams of fentanyl; three milligrams is enough to kill a person.

My life will never be the same. I always wish I had went down to his room earlier; maybe I could have saved him. The first thing I think of each morning is my boy, and the last thing I think of at night is my boy. I know that Grant's story will help save lives, if even just one. He was a sweet, kind, loving soul. I know he is proud of me for the work I am doing to educate others. I'm not alone though; he is with me every step of the way.

Grant, I'll love you forever. I'll like you for always. As long as I'm living, my baby, you'll be.

Grant's Mom,

Christina P.
Maple Grove, Minnesota

Mike

FOREVER 38

I had just turned sixteen, gotten married, and three months later became pregnant with my son, Miki. I had no inkling of how to run a home, be a wife, let alone be a mother. It was hard.

Miki was full of life, a wanderlust, an adventurer, and astonishingly bright, which is why the school recommended he skip grades and advance. Miki and I went through hardships together; my spouse traveled throughout the country for work. Throughout marital hardships, Miki was always with me, and often reminded me, "Mom, you and I went through a lot together." I still hear those words.

I had tons of separations with hopes of keeping the family united for the sake of the children. I gave birth to my second child, a daughter. Miki loved her so much and was so excited! For a long while, we were okay, but that changed after I had serious health issues in 2003. My husband's business picked up and he made a good income. He also made new and strange friends and that wasn't a good thing. My children were beside me, and watched things unfold. It was hard. Miki was especially vulnerable.

Needless to say, I had no idea how to manage this. I struggled to keep the children in school, educated at a higher level, and luckily, I accomplished that. I saw no future for myself. Throughout that entire struggle, I didn't know, or realize, that my boy, Miki, was stealing things from me, and from the home, until I noticed my cappuccino maker outside by the side of the house, and wondered why it was there.

Miki was fighting his own battles, and I was oblivious to that. I was told he had planned to pawn that and use the money for video games. Little did I know. Later, I was informed he used it for alcohol and marijuana. I had zero knowledge of anything worse than that. I only found out later (to my embarrassment) that he was using cocaine and for a long time. I didn't know. I was, and am still dumbfounded. He fooled me with immense success.

Miki was, by nature, an optimist and always had grandiose ideas of business ventures, and he wholeheartedly invested time into his ideas, making drawings, schedules and all. He would show his work to me with pride and wait for my approval and praise, which of course, I gave. He was amazing with all his ideas! His friend would tell me, "I rely on Miki for obtaining work, because he walks into a restaurant to buy a hamburger and walks out of there with a new client and job!" Miki created and installed signage, he was an exceptional designer, construction manager and worker, and he was a brilliant entrepreneur. But destiny had other things in mind.

I wrote a book in 2004 and it was published in 2005. Miki kissed the envelope before we mailed it to the publisher. Somehow, that kiss made my wish come true, and it was accepted and published. Recently, last year in fact, a couple of months after losing my boy, I received a rejection letter for my latest book, but the rejection was so heartfelt and so inspiring that I couldn't believe my eyes. After what we went through, and our loss, this rejection seemed more like a heaven-sent letter filled with kind remarks of my latest venture. I thanked them, as I had never received such an inspiring and motivational rejection letter, one filled with praise. I thanked them and explained how it touched me, especially now after losing my son not long ago. I had an idea at that moment. I will write about Miki's life, all he did, the ways he was misunderstood, and I asked the agent whether they would consider it. Immediately the response was positive, and they said they'd welcome the opportunity and applauded me for even contemplating it, for the purpose of helping other parents and families.

Miki had a lifelong struggle with ADHD, and slipped through the cracks, as nobody told me and I had very little knowledge of that back in the 80's, and in my teen years. A summary or at least an attempt to amalgamate Miki's true identity would take a book, but for now it is without doubt, my family and I can state that Miki was the most loving, caring, and selfless person. There is a myriad of examples, all of which I noticed that many of the moms in our loving group "Not In Vain" have in common and often declare. Miki: the peacemaker and keeper; the beloved grandchild who spent most of his life with his grandparents and me; a nephew to an aunt that still cries daily; a brother who loved his sister beyond imagination; a son who always showed his love by deeds, words, and thoughtfulness; a father who loved his son so much, beyond from what I've ever seen.

I lost my angel because of my stubborn and old school "tough love," to which my entire family believed in without question. Needless to say, we now suffer to such an extent that we can't get over what happened to our loving Miki, all because we didn't help him get off the streets when he asked, as we held firm to tough love. That is exactly what I'll be writing about to forewarn parents: it can backfire and in such a way that brutally changes your life forever more. I pray for forgiveness from our Father in Heaven, and from my beloved angel, Miki. My love is eternal as our bonds never did break and never will.

We all thought Miki was crying wolf, again. We held firm in our resolution, but it kept us up at night in tears when we denied him. He ended up with bad people, and we had no idea of that. He lost his life to the deadly elephant euthanizer carfentanyl, and not just one lethal dose, but five times the lethal dose. I had never heard of carfentanyl until the detective explained it to me. I am now educated in this, ever since it took my boy's life. The investigation is exhaustingly still ongoing, and looms over our heads as a virtual reminder of our mistake, our tough love idiocy, and how maybe we could've saved him. That we will never know, as only our Father in Heaven knows that. Nonetheless, we suffer. The least I can do is write about my son, have his story heard, his life and struggles (which he didn't deserve) told, and while doing so…with gargantuan hopes that other parents will thoroughly examine all aspects and outcomes of the "tough love" approach, and perhaps help to save a life.

In Miki's honor, I will do that. He made efforts to get help and I attended with him. I also observed the lack of help there is, unless you have thousands and thousands of dollars to send your child for rehabilitation, according to the brochure given to us at the hospital where we waited for more than three hours and where he wasn't even seen or spoken to by a doctor. The system failed him, his family failed him, and I must do something for him, in his honor. It seems the investigation is failing too, and I am struggling with that.

With God's grace and blessing, it shall be done, at least I will try with all my might. For all the beautiful and loving children and for my Miki that we lost, I dedicate my future book. Their lives, Miki's life was not, is not in vain.

Miki's Mom,

Marina R.
Toronto, Ontario, Canada

Alysha

FOREVER 23

My beautiful baby, my sick girl, the softest cheeks, the best smile, my first love, Lysha Bug, artist, free spirit, depression, firecracker, greatest laugh, baby girl, mommy, friend, so funny, so sad, sister, lost, bold, daughter, fierce, scared, hard worker, anxiety, loveable, beautiful soul, strong, biggest heart, lowest self-esteem, high hopes, fighter, my heart...

At four-years-old, Alysha was molested, and at twelve-years-old, she was raped by a sixteen-year-old boy. Those events changed her life. Alysha struggled with depression and anxiety that would leave her in bed for days and keep her up all night. She even started self harming in middle school. She saw many counselors and tried many medications. But those sexual assaults haunted her and she was unable to find peace and healing. She became promiscuous. It's not abnormal for victims of sexual assault and rape to act out in this way. At fifteen-years-old, she gave birth to a beautiful baby girl. For the first year, she was attentive and loving, a perfect little momma despite her young age.

When Alysha was about sixteen-years-old, I found drugs in her purse. It was a large baggie of marijuana. My husband flushed it down the toilet and we had a long talk with her. I let her know that we would not tolerate her using drugs and that Elayna needed her mother. She was very angry at us. As time went on, I would find empty liquor bottles stashed in her room, more marijuana, and we would ground her and lecture her. I did not think at the time that she needed help. I just thought she was being rebellious. She started sneaking out at night and as time went on, I was taking care of Elayna more than she was.

Getting her through the high school years was a complete nightmare, but Alysha did it. She graduated high school in 2014. And things got worse. At that point, she was using more than just marijuana and alcohol. I came home from work one day and found her passed out on the couch. Elayna, only three-years-old at the time, was running around playing by herself and there was a straw and some white powder residue on the table. I woke Alysha and asked her what was going on. She denied using drugs and acted like I was crazy despite what was right in front of both of our faces. I told her I was filing for custody of Elayna and that she would need to find somewhere to stay. I woke up the next day and headed to the courthouse and filed for emergency custody of my granddaughter. I have two sisters who are addicts and I was NOT going to enable her like my mother did with them. But I did. I let Alysha stay. I could not kick her out.

So we lived like that for a little while. Finding more drugs, explosive arguments, denial. And then in October of that year, my little sister was attacked by her husband, stabbed 28 times. She died of her injuries on November 9. Our whole family was devastated. My sister had five children and I ended up with custody of her only daughter. And Alysha spiraled out of control.

The drug use got worse. She was pretty much high all the time for the next six months or so. I was blinded though with the grief of losing my little sister and had no energy to fight her addiction right then. But one day, I decided to look in her phone to see if I could find out what she was using. And right there in black and white was a text from her "friend" giving her step-by-step instructions on how to shoot heroin into, her veins. I was in disbelief! Heroin?! I immediately confronted her. She denied it and yelled "How could you think I would do something like that? What are you talking about?" I asked to see her arms. I wanted her to show me that she had no needle marks. She refused and I grabbed her arm and we ended up on the floor and there it was. Two fresh needle marks on her arm. I was devastated. I told her to get help or leave. She packed a bag and left that night. She stayed with her "friend" for a few weeks and she called and said she was done using and wanted to come home. I told her no. I was not ready to welcome her back if she was not getting help so she moved in with her grandmother on her estranged dad's side. I believed she used the entire time she lived there although she was working and trying to be a better mother to Elayna from a distance.

August of 2015, I was back to school shopping with my youngest son when we got a call saying that Alysha had overdosed at work but they were able to revive her and she was being taken by ambulance to the hospital. I called my husband and we met at the hospital. I walked in her hospital room and instead of hugging her and thanking God that she was alive I just yelled at her. I was at the end of my rope with this addiction! She just stared at the ceiling probably ashamed, mad, sad. I softened up and hugged her and told her we would get through this. Once she was released from the hospital, she was placed under arrest for heroin possession due to the needle and heroin found in her work apron. They took her off to jail. I couldn't take it. How was my beautiful Lysha Bug being put in jail? How did we get here?

But something good came out of this. She was court ordered to drug rehab in lieu of conviction. Yes!! My daughter was going to get well. I was feeling so blessed and just ready for this all to be over. She spent four months in rehab. We got to visit her weekly. She asked to come home and I agreed. She was determined to stay clean and get her life back on track. She was still in drug court so she had to go to outpatient classes several days per week, and she was doing great.

Throughout the two years in drug court, she relapsed a couple of times and had to stay in jail for a week. But I was learning through this journey that relapse was a part of recovery so I continued to support her. And then she was approved for the Vivitrol shot and she excelled at recovery. It took away her cravings and she was on top of the world with how she was feeling. She eventually graduated the drug court program and the charges were dropped. She was working as a server and bought her first car and was so proud of herself! Life was going good!

In 2017, she met Brandon. He was a really nice guy. They started dating pretty seriously and in March of 2018, she became pregnant. Alysha and Brandon decided to move in together. In September of that year, they rented a condo and Elayna wanted to live with Mommy. I agreed with the condition that I would keep custody until she had a couple more years of sobriety under her belt. She agreed.

Life was great! My oldest son was out on his own, my youngest son was in college, and my youngest daughter and my niece were in their last years of high school. Alysha, Elayna, and Brandon were settled in their new place with a baby boy on the way. December 2018, Alysha gave birth to Rayden James on my birthday! He was perfect! I was blessed!

Alysha did really well...until March of 2020. I was visiting Alysha and the kids and I swear Alysha's eyes were glossy and her pupils were very small. I denied what I saw and left later that evening. Then things started happening. Alysha lost her job. She was live on Facebook doing a makeup tutorial and as I was watching she starts nodding off. Oh my God! Not again. She was using and I knew it and I confronted her. She denied it of course. She said she was just tired but I knew, and again I denied it.

On Memorial Day, she admitted to me that she had relapsed and told Brandon. She asked if she and the kids could come home because Brandon was angry. I agreed. She detoxed on the couch in the family room for five days...extremely sick. She refused to go inpatient but found an outpatient clinic and went for the intake meeting a week later. They prescribed her Suboxone and evaluated her mental health and started her on an antidepressant. Alysha was doing good and she and Rayden moved back in with Brandon. Elayna stayed with me.

On June 30, I woke up to a text from Brandon saying that he came home and found Alysha passed out in the bathroom and Rayden was alone on the couch crying. I called Alysha and she started crying and telling me that she took two Suboxone and drank some whiskey. She knew she had messed up but she was sorry. She went on to tell me that she and Brandon had a huge fight and she didn't want to stay there anymore. She asked if she and Rayden could please come stay with us. I agreed on the condition that she get back on track and continue her outpatient recovery program. And she did.

Alysha found a job as a collection agent and started working. She was proud of herself, liked the job, and was going to be making a decent salary. And she and Brandon decided to start working on their relationship. But after about three weeks of working, she started coming home later and later and I could see those glossy eyes and small pupils and I confronted her. She promised me that it was just the Suboxone and I believed her. I really did, but was also doubtful. I didn't fully trust her but decided to give her the benefit of the doubt.

Then the car accident happened. I received a call from Alysha about seven p.m. on a Wednesday evening saying that she ran into a telephone pole and her car was totaled. I immediately went to the scene. When I got there, Alysha was talking to the police, all kinds of people were standing in their yards watching, and a random stranger was holding Rayden. And there sat Alysha's car almost split in half by the telephone pole and I was just in shock. How did they even survive this?! Was she high? How did this happen?

I ran to Rayden. The ambulance checked them both out, a tow truck took her car, and they were released. On the ride home, she said she dropped her sunglasses, reached for them, and the next thing that she knew, the telephone pole was on top of her car. I was skeptical and kept looking over at her to see if she was high, and then she started nodding off. I smacked her arm and said, "Alysha, wake up! You were nodding off! Are you high? Is that how this happened?" She had the normal response. "I am not high. Why would I do that with my son in the car? What are you even talking about?" We argued back and forth the rest of the ride home. I was not letting up. I KNEW she was high and she almost killed herself and her son, my grandson.

I walked in the house and my youngest, Natasha, asked what happened. I told her. She then started crying and confessed to me that she knew for a fact that Alysha was using again because she let her try heroin a couple days earlier and she was really scared and felt really sick. I was livid!!! She let her sister try heroin? What the hell was wrong with my child? I was beyond angry. There was an explosive argument between Alysha and me and my husband. We demanded that she call

Brandon to let him know what happened to their son and made her go back to the outpatient clinic in the morning.

I was so mad at myself that night. I kept thinking, why didn't I tell the cops I thought she was high? They could have tested her, she would have been arrested for driving under the influence and child endangerment, and she would have went to jail where I knew she was safe with possibly another court ordered-inpatient rehab. But I did nothing. I was scared of what would happen to my grandson and my daughter.

The next morning, she went back to the outpatient clinic to get back on track. I was still mad but knew that as long as she was trying to get better, I needed to support her. I took Natasha to our family doctor because I was worried about her and the fact that she had tried heroin.

Things in our home became very tense. Bryan and I were mad at Alysha, Alysha was mad at Natasha for telling on her, and Natasha was mad at Alysha for being a drug addict. About two weeks later, everything boiled over.

Alysha was going to her outpatient program daily and she was trying to make amends with her sister but Natasha was not having it. They had an explosive argument that turned physical and I had had enough! I told Alysha to call her grandparents to see if she could stay with them. Her grandma was retired and she would help her with Rayden while she continued outpatient treatment. I had to keep Natasha and Alysha apart. Despite their recent argument and physical altercation, Natasha looked up to her big sister and was easily influenced. I felt I needed to make sure she was safe and Alysha was safe. So Alysha and Rayden left that night to stay with her grandma.

Alysha stayed there and worked on her outpatient treatment while trying to find a new job. She found a temp job at a factory. She got her first paycheck and relapsed again. I received a call at work from our family doctor stating that Alysha had an appointment at their office and they found her passed out in the parking lot. They brought her in and she was nodding off and showing signs of being high.

A couple of days later, the doctor called to say that they did a drug test and that she was positive for heroin and fentanyl. This was our family doctor. She had seen all my children since they were very young. Dr. Neal apologized, but she said that she was going to call child protective services because she knew Alysha had custody of Rayden and she had an obligation to make sure he was living in a safe environment. I was happy actually. I thought this would wake her up and get her moving on the right track if she was held accountable by the state.

A couple of days later, the social worker came to do their investigation, saw that Rayden was in a safe environment with Alysha's grandparents, and they said they would be in touch about setting up some parenting classes They were also going to refer Alysha to a counselor. That never happened. She called several times to follow up with the caseworker but never received a call back. She continued to go to the outpatient clinic and was eventually approved for the Vivitrol shot again which had been her saving grace the last time she was clean for an extended period of time.

In the meantime, Alysha was preparing to be a bridesmaid for her cousin's wedding coming up that fall. I kept praying she would stay sober, alive, and not let her cousin down. She was so excited about this wedding. And she did! She was beautiful that day. Just beaming! She was so proud; she had Brandon, her baby boy, and little girl there and it was just a fantastic day!

A couple of weeks later, Alysha interviewed for an assistant manager job at a tanning salon and got the job. We met for dinner to celebrate and she asked if she could come back home. I told her that I thought it was best for her to stay where she was, continue working on her sobriety, and try to get back into her own place. Deep down, I was just scared about Alysha and Natasha living in the same house, and my husband and other kids thinking that I was enabling her. She looked so sad when I told her "no" but she just said "ok." She did not put up a fight or start an argument.

A couple of days later, she asked if I would watch Rayden. Her childhood best friend was going to pick her up from her outpatient class and they were going to have dinner. I was great with that! Steph was a great friend and not a drug user. She called around seven that evening and said that Brandon was going to pick Rayden up because she was going to stay out with Steph a bit longer. A little while after, Brandon called to say that Alysha went to a bar with Steph so he had his mom keep an eye on Rayden while he checked on her. When he got to the bar, Steph informed him that Alysha had left with Damian (her dealer). Brandon and Steph were so worried. We all tried to call her, but she wouldn't answer. A couple of hours later, she showed up at Brandon's condo high. He would not let her in and his mom begged her to let her drive her home, but Alysha was angry and cussing and left. She ended up at Damian's house for the night.

The next morning, Alysha called me frantic, begging me to please call Brandon and tell him that she didn't do anything wrong. He was mad at her and was done trying to work on things. I refused. It was between her and Brandon. She got mad and by nine a.m. that morning, she was posting pics on Facebook. She was pissed and drinking wine. She stayed at Damian's for most of the day and ended up back at her grandparent's house that evening. Her grandma called and said that Alysha was there but she was high. Of course Alysha denied it. Kathy cared for Rayden and Alysha ended up passing out.

Two days later, I got a call from her grandma in the middle of the night saying that she found Alysha passed out on her bedroom floor with Rayden crying alone on the bed. She said they were having a hard time waking Alysha and they believed she had taken a bunch of her antidepressants. An ambulance was called and we met them at the emergency room. She was in ICU because she was having seizures. By mid-day, she was stable and she was moved to a regular room to be monitored. I was so scared, but was at this point just wanting all this madness to end somehow! I just wanted her better. I stayed with her most of the day. She was really out of it but she asked me to brush her hair so I did.

Alysha kept asking for Brandon and I tried to explain to her that he probably wasn't coming. I reminded her of what happened a couple of days earlier, but she had no memory of being with Damian or using. I hated seeing her like that. It broke my heart. I talked to Brandon about what happened and he said that he did not want to see her like that. I understood but told him that we needed to discuss Rayden. I told him he needed to file for emergency custody or I was going to. Of course, child protective services was called because Alysha tried to commit suicide with her baby in the room with her. Brandon said he would take care of it first thing Monday morning, and he did.

Alysha was moved to the psych floor the next day for a seventy-two-hour hold. She called me begging to tell the doctors to let her come home. I kept telling her that it was not my choice and that she needed help. She cussed me and was furious. The second day in the psych unit, her psychiatrist called and wanted to talk about Alysha and what happened. He asked if I thought she would be safe to come home the next day and I told him absolutely not. Once she learned that Brandon was done and he filed for emergency custody, she was going to flip out and do something to herself. He said that they could get a court order to force her to stay if she would not stay voluntarily after the hold. I was in agreement with that.

The next day, I got a call from Alysha saying that she was released and her grandparents were on their way to pick her up. I was furious! How could they just let her go home like this?? Not even an hour after being released, she was calling Brandon threatening to kill herself again. He stopped answering her calls and she left her grandparent's house and went with Damian's girlfriend back to their place. She used that night and did not show up for the custody hearing the following day. I could not believe it! She loved Rayden. That was her baby! How could she just not show up?

Alysha ended up back at her grandparents later that day. Her grandma watched Rayden and Elayna the next day while Brandon and I worked. She knew Alysha could not be left alone with the kids. After work, I picked the kids up from her grandma. Elayna had a doctor's appointment and I was keeping both of the kids that night. When I got there, Alysha was sitting on the bathroom sink picking her face, something she did often when using. I just looked at her and walked out. I was so angry that she didn't go to court for her son. I mean, I knew she was in no position to have custody at the time but I thought she would have at least shown up to let the judge know she wanted her baby and that she was going to do whatever it took to get him back. Something. I didn't speak to her. Just took the kids and left. She died the next day of an overdose.

Alysha died on a Saturday. It was a beautiful October day. I got up that morning and took her children, Elayna and Rayden, to the Pumpkin Festival. I did not invite Alysha. I always invited her everywhere whether she was in active addiction or recovery. I was just so mad at her because she had relapsed and was losing custody of her son. After we got home from the festival, Elayna went to a Halloween party with her dad and Rayden's dad picked him up. I was exhausted and hungry

579

from a long day of fun with my grandkids. I ordered pizza and turned on a movie and kicked my feet up. I texted Alysha a pic of the kids. She responded, "No invite?" I told her I loved her but I was just mad. She responded, "Yeah because everyone being mad at me right now is really helping how I feel. It's cool." I told her I was sad about the choices she was making. We texted back and forth a little more and her last text at 6:04 p.m. said, "I made a stupid decision because I'm sick in the head and now I don't deserve to have my son." My phone started dying so I put it on the charger. At 7:27 p.m. I texted her, "You just have to get well so you don't make unsafe decisions." She didn't respond which was not unusual when she was angry. I was getting tired and wasn't feeling great so I took some sinus medication and went to bed.

At 10:30 p.m., my husband came in our room and tapped me on my leg and said, "Come on. You got to get up. The police are at the door. It's about Alysha." My first thought, "Oh no...what did she do now?" I went to the door. The police officer said, "Are you Alysha's mother?" I said, "Yes." He said, "I'm sorry to inform you that she passed away tonight." I hear my husband scream, "No"! I put my hand up to my husband and looked at the officer and said, "What happened? Are you sure it's her?" He went on to tell me that she overdosed and a friend that was with her positively identified her, handed me a card with the number of the coroner, and all I could say was, "Okay," and shut the door. I was in complete shock.

The next week was a complete blur. I know we planned the funeral; someone took me to get a dress to wear and we had the funeral. That's it. But the day after the funeral, everything hit me like a ton of bricks...I was hysterical. I felt like I couldn't breathe. I just remember telling my husband, "I can't do this. I cannot do this." He held me until I fell asleep. I spent the next several months crying. I went to work and cried as soon as I left. The weekends were spent crying. Here we are, almost nine months later and my heart is torn to shreds. So many things I would have done differently. The guilt is unbearable some days. And I miss her like crazy!

My whole focus was not to enable Alysha, tough love. I was not going to tolerate my daughter's addiction. But Alysha was sensitive. She needed me. She was sick and I wish I would have looked at it that way instead getting so frustrated with her.

My goal now is to help others who are struggling with mental sickness and addiction. I am not sure what I am going to do or how to accomplish all the things in my head that I want to do but I do ask God regularly to show me what to do with this pain. I know He will when He knows I'm ready.

Alysha's Mom,

HEATHER R.
Cincinnati, Ohio

Derek

FOREVER 24

I was blessed to be chosen as Derek's mom for 24 years. He was handsome, funny and loved girls almost as much as he loved football. But on March 17, 2013, everything changed. I received a call from the Dean of Students at the college where my son played quarterback. He said that my son was being kicked out of college for drugs. I told him that he must have the wrong number. That is the day that things went from good to bad very quickly. Looking back, there were signs that I missed. We had many conversations about drugs and sex, and there were no secrets. But then the mood swings were suddenly crazy, and his blue eyes were really bright blue! I eventually learned that opiates make your pupils really small, and the mood swings were withdrawals. Derek also had a habit of chewing on plastic straws since he was a kid. I started to find chewed up little orange "straws" everywhere.

I later learned that they were needle caps. One day I took him to the store to get school supplies. I picked up a nice pen with a clicker on top. He said he just wanted the pack of cheap black & white pens with caps.

I know now that those can be taken apart and used as a straw to snort drugs. I never missed one of his games, but one day, there was a bruise on the inside of his arm. Strange place for a bruise, but I thought it was a football injury. He said a bookcase fell on him. Ok. I had no reason to think that would be his favorite injection site. I even received a phone call, where I was told that they saw Derek in a video using drugs.

Of course, I asked him about it and he said it wasn't him. Whew, what a relief! The three years that followed that phone call from the Dean were a roller coaster of ups and downs. Right away, I took Derek to the County Behavioral Clinic. She said that Derek was a drug abuser, but not an addict. Whew again! But things kept getting worse. Lies, defiance, missing money, and stolen debit cards. I was hospitalized for what could have been a stroke. I suddenly could not stand up or walk and had severe vertigo. It wasn't a stroke, but the doctors assumed it was stress related. I soon realized that my son was an addict.

Instinct kicked in to do whatever I had to do to save my son. I chased him in the rain down the highway in high heels begging him to get back in the car so that I could take him back to the outpatient rehab program. And when that didn't help, my sister and I kidnapped him and drove eight hours to drop him off at an inpatient rehab. That helped for a while. Then he was arrested for stealing lawnmowers and selling them at pawn shops for drug money. For six months, I would go through the pat-down and humiliation of visiting an inmate every week just to see my son through a glass window. I visited him on his birthday and could not bring any gifts, or his favorite cookies. When we had spent our last dime on lawyers, Derek finally came home, and after another thirteen months, he graduated from drug court.

Our last Christmas with Derek was in 2015. At that time, he was sober, happy and looking forward to returning to college. He was given the opportunity by a former coach to finish his last year of college, and not only play football again, but also the chance at being a coach, his lifelong goal. How could anyone possibly relapse when you have lost everything and worked so hard to get it back? Things were going well again.

But now, I'm going to tell you how things went from bad to worse. Not for sympathy or sorrow, but to make you aware of the effects of addiction. On February 21, 2016, as I was getting ready for church, I received a frantic call telling me that Derek was found dead in his dorm room. My husband drove me the three hours to his college and I was in total denial. Halfway there I spoke to a police officer on the phone, who told me that it was true and he was found with syringes and a white powder. We later learned it was heroin and fentanyl.

When I arrived at the college campus, there were police cars and yellow tape around Derek's dorm room. I was still not convinced that he died and I was not allowed to enter his dorm room, so it couldn't possibly be him. I remember a police officer blocking the stairs to his room. We locked eyes because he knew I was about to run past him. The next thing I knew, they brought a large 6-foot long blue bag down the stairs. I screamed and told them it couldn't possibly be him.

The police officer asked me "Does your son have a tattoo of 'Debbie' on his arm"? They eventually let me touch what I think were his feet from the back of an SUV. It was hard and felt like his shoes were wrapped in a bandage inside that bag, like a mummy. Then I watched them drive away with that blue bag. The next couple of days were another blur of making funeral plans, visitors, tears and screaming, but then the day comes for the viewing where I would finally get to see him. The doors were opened to the funeral parlor and I was told that I could enter.

After a few steps, I saw Derek laying in a casket. I knew it was him. But I was sure he was still alive. I began yelling from the aisle over and over, "Derek wake up! Derek wake up!!" I was convinced he was playing a joke and laying in that casket. That night, hundreds and hundreds of friends, visitors and teammates walked past me, and it's still such a blur. I was told that people waited for two hours in line just to pay their respects. The next day was the funeral. I've also been told that it was the most touching funeral with some of the best messages about faith, love and addiction. At the end, I walked up to the casket to touch my baby one last time, and I passed out. I barely remember my own son's funeral.

The days that followed were full of tears and screaming, but unfortunately the worst was still yet to come. Several months later I received the autopsy results in the mail. I was advised not to read them but felt compelled to do so. My baby's brain weighed three pounds! His heart weighed eleven ounces! That was the day I knew he was dead.

That was THE WORST DAY of my life. I screamed and screamed all night long and couldn't believe they took my babies heart out of his body to weigh it! Or his brain! Did they at least put it back before we buried him? To this day, anything that resembles a body bag or a heart or brain brings me back to that terrible night. I've since learned to live without Derek, but life will never be the same. I suffer from PTSD, anxiety and depression. So

many times, I have wanted to just go lay by his grave site and never wake up again. I prefer not to think about those years of the lying, stealing, rehab and jail. That was not MY Derek. I prefer to remember my little boy that loved his Momma so much that he would never hurt her the way that I hurt now. It is a pain that you just try to live with. A life sentence of heart ache. Addiction does not just affect the addict. It affects us all.

Derek's Mom,

Debbie R.
Middleburg, Florida

Gabrielle

Gabrielle was my only child until she was eight-years-old, so she was always around adults. She was very quiet but always so loving. She was like an old soul. She was a genuine caregiver by nature. I remember during the funeral of her stepsister Christina, when Gabrielle was just a little girl, she covered her own emotions to try to be the adult taking care of her father, watching over him in his grief. If she loved you, she was your true "ride or die."

Gabrielle fought depression most of her life. I started seeing signs of depression when she was fourteen. When she was seventeen, she attempted suicide. She found a doctor who prescribed Xanax, an anti-depressant. It helped, and it didn't. When she was taking it, she complained that she couldn't feel anything; she was just numb, the most horrible feeling. She would be off it for periods of time, but Xanax was always her drug of choice.

Gabrielle was aiming for a career in health care. When she was in the hospital after her suicide attempt, she said, "Ma, I think I should be a nurse." She had fallen behind in high school, but she went to classes during the day, at night, and on Saturdays to catch up and she graduated with her class. She trained and became a certified nursing assistant. Then she worked two jobs in nursing while she went to college. She did have a lot of stress and anxiety, but she seemed to thrive when she had a lot to do. She was on the dean's list and in the honor society. She was studying to be a psychologist, just to help those that struggled with depression, those like her.

Gabrielle loved beach vacations. When she was young, every year we went to Saugatuck, a little vacation town on Lake Michigan. She just loved going there, even a couple years before she passed away. I have a photo of us waiting to go on the dune buggy rides. She loved shopping in the little stores. That was a highlight of her summers.

When she was twenty-one, she met a guy she fell deeply in love with. I knew there was something off, mother's instinct. He was a heroin addict. I confronted Gabrielle, and she said, "I'm going to help him get off it." I told her that nobody could help unless *he* wanted to get off drugs, but she was bound and determined to help him get clean. Our relationship then changed. We fought over her boyfriend, a lot. I told her I didn't agree with his lifestyle; I didn't want him in my house. I regret that now. It is so important to provide support to someone with addiction. I think she felt so alone. They felt so alone. They felt like the world was against them, and at that time, I *was* against them. I feel so bad now. I should have been more there for her and him.

I was so scared Gabrielle would try heroin. She insisted she wouldn't, but her depression had her in a downward spiral. Eventually, she gave in to the temptation. She wanted to see why he loved heroin more than her. He didn't love heroin more, it just had control of his life. Soon, it controlled her life, too.

She tried heroin for the first time on December 19, 2017. How do I know? She told me. She told me everything. She used for the first time on December 19, 2017, and she passed away from fentanyl poisoning on February 8, 2018. Forty-four days, that is all it took.

The day she passed away, she sent me a text out of nowhere at four p.m., saying, "I love you." I tried to call her at five p.m., and she didn't answer. I just knew in my heart.

Gabrielle would want to be remembered for being one "badass" who never gave up or gave in. She loved who she loved. She lived and loved life. If I could say one thing to Gabrielle, it would be, I would give my life to have you back. I love you, Gabrielle. Until we meet in heaven.

Gabrielle's Mom,

JULIE R.
Roseville, Michigan

Clay

"I need help, Mom. I can't pay my mortgage."

That was how the conversation started that forever and dramatically changed our family's lives.

It was early 2012. My son, my smart, handsome, athletic, successful, loving son, Clay, broke down and confessed that he was addicted to pain pills. Our six-year struggle that ended in the most unfathomable tragedy had just begun.

Clayton (Clay) was truly the All-American boy. He was raised in a close-knit, Christian, middle-class family in small town Waynesville, North Carolina. Although his father and I divorced when Clay was in second grade, we co-parented well and he had very loving step-parents. He was the oldest of our two boys and was very close with his younger brother, Bradley. Clay excelled both academically and athletically and was a standout baseball player. He was an avid outdoorsman and his favorite hobbies were fly-fishing, hunt-

589

ing, hiking, and playing disc golf. He also loved to read and was a beautiful writer.

He had a servant's calling and loved volunteering, especially with special-needs kids at school. Clay had a tender heart. He loved big, spread happiness with grace, and had a laugh that was so contagious, you couldn't help but laugh, too. To know Clay was to love Clay. He made friends with ease, was respected by his peers, and appreciated by his teachers. "His smile is unforgettable," one of his teachers told me.

After graduating from high school in 2007, Clay attended Haywood Community College where he continued to excel academically, then transferred to Western Carolina University where he chose business and entrepreneurship as his major. He dreamed of owning a fly-fishing shop and being a fly-fishing guide. Even while he was a full-time student, Clay worked hard to establish excellent credit and he purchased a home when he was only twenty-two-years-old.

All through his teen years, Clay suffered from chronic sinus infections. He also had a deviated septum from an injury. In 2011, he had a routine, outpatient sinus surgery. He was prescribed Percocet. When he ran out, he called for a refill. The doctor wrote him another prescription. Then another. Unbeknownst to us, Clay became dependent on and addicted to opioids. For about a year, he was what I now refer to as a "functioning addict." He was buying pills on the street, secretly, yet able to maintain a pretty outwardly normal appearing life…steady girlfriend, good job, nice house. Then life started unraveling for Clay. The further into his addiction he spiraled, the more money it took. That's when he asked for help for the first time. I remember the conversation like yesterday. We were sitting in my car and Clay told me he couldn't pay his mortgage because he had spent all his money on pills. He told me he had a drug addiction and needed rehab. And that's when the dreadful, chaotic cycle of addiction and rehabilitation that became Clay's life for the next six years began.

I painfully watched my son go to rehab, get clean, get sick, relapse, go back to rehab, get clean, get sick, and relapse again. Every time he relapsed it got worse. I watched with a broken heart as he fought and failed and his life was no longer his to control. Clay lost his girlfriend, he lost jobs, he sold most of what he had to feed his habit. We had to turn his house into a rental so he wouldn't lose it. Still, Clay's father and I never gave up on him. We helped him get to rehab after rehab from city to city, state to state. Each time hopeful that it would be the last. Somewhere around 2015 or 2016 after a relapse, Clay was introduced to heroin...by a drug dealer...because it was quicker, easier to get, and much cheaper. We couldn't believe it. Our sweet son who had the world at his fingertips and who, by the way, was terrified of needles, had become an intravenous heroin user. We were crushed. He was crushed. He fought so hard to free himself from the strongholds of addiction. I remember him crying on the phone one day, "Why me, Mom? How did this happen to me? I don't want this addiction. I try so hard."

October 31, 2017, Clay became an uncle. He checked himself into a detox center and rehab that very day. This time was going to be different, he said. He had an unstoppable determination to beat his addiction so he could be the best uncle possible. During Clay's two-month stay at a short-term facility, we were desperately trying to find a long-term treatment center. By chance, I bumped into a childhood friend of my son's and he told me about a faith-based, long-term recovery program for men.

Reluctant and nervous but desperate to beat this demon of addiction once and for all, Clay checked into the recovery program on January 8, 2018. While at the recovery program, Clay flourished. His faith grew and he was full of hope and excitement. For the first time in several years, I had my son back! He wrote me, his dad, and his grandparents the most positive, upbeat letters. We were overjoyed. He called me just about every day and we visited on a regular basis. We talked about the future. His dream was to work at this recovery program. He wanted to help others who fought the difficult fight of addiction. The director wrote in one newsletter, "Clay is a special young man...He is full of joy and peace...When you see Clay, you see a big smile. He loves people and wants to show the love of God." That was my son. That is who he was.

Clay graduated from the program on August 4, 2018. He was accepted into their re-entry program, which allowed him to continue living there but gave him more freedoms. He remained determined to stay clean and continued to surround himself with the right people. He met a lovely young lady at church and almost immediately they were inseparable. They went to church together, bible study, and hiked. One afternoon, in early September, Clay and his girlfriend went on a hike. While hiking, they came upon a mailbox on the ground. Painted on the side of the mailbox were the words "A Box for Your Thoughts."

When they looked in the box, they discovered an array of poems, short stories, and inspirational thoughts. Clay opened his backpack, got out a piece of paper, jotted something down, and put it in the box. "We better get going," he said. When his girlfriend asked what he wrote, Clay simply replied, "Just something I hope will minister to someone someday," and kept on walking. It wasn't until she went back alone a few weeks later that his girlfriend found what Clay had written and put in the box: Matt. 11:28 "Come to me all who are weary and carry heavy burden and I will give you rest."

Toward the end of September, Clay had decided it was time to move from the "dorm" setting of the recovery program and into an apartment. We were so proud of him. We were so excited for his future. He talked about selling his house, so he could buy a house in Greensboro because he loved it there. We were overcome with joy that he had fought such a hard fight and won. So we thought. Clay found an apartment in Greensboro and was scheduled to move in Thursday, September 27, 2018. His step-mom arranged to bring him a bedroom set and my parents made plans to bring living room furniture the following week. I called Walmart and ordered him a TV. Everything was falling into place perfectly. His last night at the recovery program, September 26, 2018, Clay sent a group text to his father, stepmother, me, and my husband, and here is what it said:

"I was just lying in bed before I fall asleep and wanted to tell you all that I pray for y'all and love y'all so much! It means so much to me that you have stuck with me and never gave up on me, even when I fell so short, and I have the best parents and step parents anyone could ask for! A nighttime text doesn't do justice to the sincere gratitude and love I have, so thank you so much for all that all of you do for me and I love you so much!! Goodnight."

The morning of September 27, 2017, Clay signed a lease for his new apartment and picked up the keys. His stepmother met him there with his bedroom furniture. He moved all his personal belongings in. That evening, he went grocery shopping with his girlfriend. He sent me a Snapchat photo of the two of them in his new kitchen and the caption read, "New Life Begins." It warmed my heart and made me smile. Thankfully, I took a screenshot of the photo. We talked on the phone that night around eight p.m. He was excited about moving and thanked me again for believing in him. He told me he loved me. His girlfriend left around nine-thirty p.m. That was about the time I received my last text message from my son. It said, "Goodnight love u." I texted back, "Goodnight. I love you more."

I sent Clay a text message around lunchtime on Friday, September 28, 2018. He didn't answer. I wasn't concerned because I knew he was at work. I sent him another text at two p.m. Still no answer. I figured he'd call me after work. At 3:53 p.m., my cell phone rang from a 336-area code number, which I knew to be Greensboro. I laughed to myself, thinking it must be Clay calling from a friend's phone. It was not uncommon for him to let his phone die. I was wrong.

Instead, it was a stranger's voice on the other end and a call that would literally stop my world from turning. My son had not shown up for work that morning and no one could reach him. Some friends from the recovery program asked his new landlord to let them in his apartment for a "wellness check" because they were concerned. Their fear became reality. Clay was found at 10:10 a.m. He was gone. Forever taken from this world at twenty-nine-years-old. There was a needle in the bathroom and he was found slumped over on the floor of his walk-in closet. He was presumed to have died of a drug overdose. It wasn't until six months later when we received his autopsy report that we learned his cause of death was acetylfentanyl and fentanyl toxicity. Our son, like so many, was killed by fentanyl poisoning.

My life has never been the same. Through all the pain and grief, I knew I had to do SOMETHING. I knew there were other moms (and dads and family members) living the nightmare of having a family member affected by drug addiction or worse yet, who have lost a child or family member to the opioid drug crisis. My passion is to bring awareness and do what I can to help remove the stigma of addiction. But also, my desire is to offer support to other moms and families, so that no one who finds themselves in these shoes ever feels like they have to suffer in silence. I fight this fight and I share my son's story so people know addiction does not discriminate. It can happen to anyone. I know first-hand. It happened to my family. It happened to my son…my smart, handsome, athletic, successful, loving son. He was over-prescribed opioids and opioids later stole my son from me, from my family. He fell victim to this horrific drug crisis which is now a national epidemic. For him and all the others, I fight on!

Clay's Mom,

MICHELE R.
Waynesville, North Carolina

Vincent

FOREVER 23

What words does one begin with for a son's eulogy? How does a mom tell the world about her baby boy? These are the two questions I've spent every waking moment since "the phone call" came thinking about. How do you write about a life so short yet so important and full of life? Vincent had a huge kind heart. He loved to laugh. He was the best hugger. His love for his family and friends was without boundaries. He saw goodness in everyone and believed everyone deserved a second chance. He loved to be silly. He loved ramen noodles and cereal. There was never a phone call that did not end with I love you. He loved just being loved by his family. He loved to tell me, "Go get in the tub and wash away your crankiness Momma." He loved to be loved and to get love. Those were the things I thought only his family knew. But since his death we have received so many beautiful notes about his kind spirit and love for friends. Those notes and messages have helped put little band aids on the cracks in our heart.

Recently when Vincent was home, we spent the day together. Sitting outside at lunch, I asked him, 'Vincent, what's your best childhood memory?"As I'm sitting there trying to guess what his answer was going to be: some special gift, a day trip, a vacation, something big, he reached over and held my hand and laughed and said, "Do you remember when we were kids and you would put a blanket on the living room floor and have a picnic and put music on and we'd dance?" I looked at him and said yes, thinking (as anyone who knew Vin knows he took forever to tell a simple story) in Vincent's very, very long-winded way of telling stories eventually that this was somehow, at some point leading to his best memory, he squeezed my hand and said, "That's IT.' I laughed and said, "No, seriously it has to be bigger than THAT.' He said, 'Nope, Momma that was the best. You and I would sing Pink Floyd because Gab didn't know the words and Gab would make our plates on that blanket then I'd take turns with Gab dancing on your feet." And then a few minutes later, Vincent said, 'Wait, I've got a second best one…it is making homemade play dough with the Lyons." He laughed when he said it because I hated play dough and never let my kids have it. So, it was special to both Gab and Vin that they made it.

Picnics and play dough, that's who my Vincent was. Big things were not important but being with his family and having fun was. The memory of that conversation has passed through my mind a million times this week. He texted me after that day and said thanks for such a great date. He recognized that it was our first "adult" sober date and he thanked me for it. Something so small to one person can be so, so big to another. This past year, we lost a member of our family, Zach, to this disease. I talked to Vincent about the pain his parents (that my son loved) felt every single time he asked about his family, drilling into his head that Aunt Jean and Uncle Dave were left sitting there, hurting each day. Vincent loved them, he knew they hurt, which once again reminds me how powerful this disease is. And the powerlessness the addict must feel. We think in our hearts we know our children. Their good points, their flaws. But we do not REALLY know. We teach them as best we can and then we send them out into the world. So sure, they will all be the best and the brightest. We hope they make the best decisions they can. When they do, we as parents pat ourselves on the back and sigh with relief that we did a good job. When they make bad decisions, we as parents spend sleepless nights wondering where we failed. Vincent and I had THAT talk many times over the years. Where did I go WRONG as a parent? Why did you choose to do drugs? Why are you intentionally hurting us by doing drugs? If you loved us enough you would just say no and stop. Just stop Vincent. It's just that simple…or so I always thought. But I was so incredibly WRONG.

On my darkest night, I reached out to an angel on Facebook who writes a beautiful blog that by God's hand touched my soul. Someone had shared a blog post about her sister, Sarah, who died. I messaged her thinking I would simply air my heavy heart to a faceless stranger somewhere far away because I could never tell anyone about my son's battle. That far away stranger who I now know lives in Delaware reminds me with every beautiful word she writes that there is light at the end of every dark tunnel. And she has come to be one of the many angels I love as my friend. She wrote me back within minutes and I know she truly saved my life that night. Vincent and I many times talked about her Sarah like she was our friend. We talked about the pain Sarah's death caused her family because I thought if he knew about the pain, he would choose to stop. That night then sent another person into my life who asked me why I was donating a basket to Attack Addiction and before I even thought about it, said the words MY SON IS AN ADDICT out loud for the very first time. She sat across from me and without missing a beat said, "My daughter Ashley is dead and addiction sucks." There was no judgement on her face that day. It was like taking a deep breath after holding your breath for so, so very long under water. The day I got the call, she asked what I needed and I said, "I need a hug and to see your face." She hugged me with the fierceness only someone who loves you can. She brought me into the Attack Addiction family with Don and Jeanne and through the angels in that group, I've learned addiction is not a choice but rather a disease.

Addiction is a disease that is as real as cancer or diabetes. Listening for the first time to a young lady tell her story of recovery, I remember thinking she's baring her soul here hoping just one kid listens, and with her organization Hope Street, she is trying to educate and make a difference. Just listening to people in recovery tell their stories made me realize they were addicts not because their parents made mistakes, or were bad people, or they themselves did not love their parents or families enough to stop, or some life crisis made them choose to do drugs or drink. No one wakes up and says I'm going to start down the fire-filled agonizing road to hell by choice. But because like any DISEASE they become affected. Vincent finally had a job he loved, a good life, he was happy, but the disease crept in one final time for him. Vincent's addiction taught me it takes a village and our village was led by a brave woman who buried her own two babies but chose to step up even in her own unimaginable pain. It's sitting in your darkest moments laughing and feeling love so big and strong and powerful your mind can't understand why you can't see it…that something this big and powerful must be visible and it is. It's the hugs, it's the meatballs, it's the wine, the candy bars, the calls, the texts; it is the things we do because we can't just bake. Life is not always great but it is made up of people who are angels that carry us some days, and some days we have to carry them. I will never allow MY Vincent's life to be defined by the disease of addiction but by the smile ever present on his face and in his heart, by his love for his family, by his all-encompassing hugs, by the smile on Gianna's face for her Prince, for the middle of the night texts to say, "I love you Momma," and by the love of old movie lines with his dad. THAT is who my Vincent was.

I hope in my lifetime we figure out how to cure the disease of addiction. And I hope today everyone leaves here with a little bit more kindness in their heart. I hope the next time you think to use the word "junkie" you remember it's someone's kid, or Mom, or Dad, or that someday it could be your kid, your  Mom, your Dad, or brother or sister. I hope you all leave here today with a little less judgement in your heart for every person affected by addiction, not just the addict but the entire family. Thank you to everyone who has supported me as I've co-founded Face the Facts and The Vincent Tambourelli Family Assistance Fund that pays for funerals of addicts who have lost their battle.

Vincent's Mom,

PennyAnne R.
Wilmington, Delaware

Stephen

FOREVER 24

Stephen struggled with drugs on and off throughout his teenage years. Addiction had a hold of him in ways I would never understand. In July 2019, Stephen had a fishing accident where he required hospitalization and surgery on his hand. While in the hospital, he was given morphine for pain and pain killers once released. His addiction took control and he wanted and needed that high.

Once Stephen realized how hard it was to get pain pills on the street, his drug dealer introduced him to heroin. It was cheaper and easier to obtain! Little did I know, that drug was going to take my son less than three months later. In August, Stephen told me he had "a problem" and was dope sick from not having the heroin for twelve hours. I immediately sought help for him at an intensive treatment center in California (we live in Texas). I thought he was going to beat it. He was doing well and was transferred to a sober living facility and outpatient treatment. The insurance company would only pay for three weeks of treatment at a time in each facility so they would transfer him to another one. It became very frustrating.

During his time of sobriety, I got to enjoy my son again. It had been a while since he had been so clean. He had hopes and dreams that he hadn't had in a long time. He was going to go to school, he was excited about his future.

Well, he came home on October 14. We were out of time and resources in California. This was a Monday night. He promised he was going to go to Narcanon and continue treatment and find a sponsor. Six days later I found him on my couch dead! He died of an overdose of heroin and cocaine. I found him! I screamed! I called for help! I did CPR...I prayed! But it was too late. I lost my youngest son.

Stephen's Mom,

KIMBERLY R.
Conroe, Texas

Aidan

As a young boy Aidan, loved to dig in the dirt, watch big trucks roll down the street, and dirt bikes. It seemed that he loved anything that was fast and made lots of noise. But he had a gentle side, the little boy who loved to cuddle and read books, to sit quietly with me as we built Lego sets together.

As Aidan got ready to go to elementary school, I knew he was ready both socially and academically. Unfortunately, this was at a time when little kids were being tested for ADHD/ADD. Parents were made to believe that there was something wrong with their child if their child had trouble sitting or processing information the way the standardized test wanted them to. I was asked to have Aidan tested along with a host of other parents of young boys and girls. Aidan's tests all came back negative, but here is where I feel something went wrong. All these young and impressionable children were made to feel that they were somehow different, less than.

601

Aidan grew up playing sports, riding his bike, and skateboarding, spending summers at the beach and just being a kid. He struggled in school because he hated to write. I said he was my "Irish Story-Teller" because he would tell you everything about a subject in great detail until he had to write it down. That is when you would get one sentence. "The sun is orange." I grew very close with Aidan because I saw the gentleness of his heart. I knew the silent tears he would cry because everyone made a fuss over his sisters and he felt he was just annoying to everyone.

Aidan loved spending time with family and friends. On weekends, I would often play host to many boys at my house. Since we had three cleared acres of land, the boys would ride dirt bikes and build a big bonfire at night. I never worried because a few of the kids were junior firefighters. He cultivated friendships and built strong bonds. Upon his high school graduation just days after turning eighteen, Aidan flew off to Texas to start an internship with a construction company. It was hard work; he was gone for two months and my heart was heavy with missing him. Aidan came home for two weeks and left for three years for trade school. Between my husband and I, we took turns going to visit or flying him home. He loved coming home. Looking back on that time, I knew I made the mistake of allowing him to leave for so long. We talked almost every day and I knew he was missing us. Aidan was always so worried about disappointing his dad.

Aidan graduated in December 2016 and finally moved home. In March 2017, he got into some trouble and a car accident. He told me he needed help because he had started taking Xanax. Within days, I rushed him to the ER because he came home and could not stand and was not making sense. He was released after eleven hours and I took him home. The next day, I asked Aidan what he thought he should do and he said he wanted to go to rehab. I worked day and night interviewing rehabs and narrowed it down according to insurance and looking for a duel-diagnosis facility, because there must be an underlying reason for depression and addiction. Kids don't just wake up one day and decide to do drugs. Aidan spent a few hours talking to each facility and chose the one he felt was the best fit. We dropped him off a week after the car crash and ER visit. Aidan was gone for three months, two weeks in Pennsylvania and the rest of the time in Florida.

Aidan turned twenty-one while he was in Florida and I got permission for my family to fly down to surprise him. He was so happy! We spent three days together! Aidan was strong in his conviction to beat this addiction. He looked amazing physically, and seemed to be doing amazingly well mentally. Then something happened. I received a phone call from one of his group therapists who needed to talk to me. She informed me that she felt that Aidan was replacing his Xanax addiction with shopping. I told her that was not possible. Aidan had spent his whole life not feeling good about himself. I bought his clothes, told him when he needed a haircut, and bought him new shoes all because he did not care. He was finally getting his self-esteem and finding his value and worth. It did not matter what I said to this woman, she embarrassed him in front of everyone in group therapy. Within days, Aidan had hit rock bottom. He was going to drive to Miami and be homeless, but I convinced him to come home. It took days of begging because he did not want his dad to be disappointed. Aidan came home. He was here for Father's Day.

Aidan died on a Sunday, two weeks after coming home in a hotel room with two people he met one week before on a Sunday. They robbed him of his money, his watch, and his necklace. They refused to perform CPR. I know all this because the man who oversees the 911 call center was Aidan's football coach. He loved him like a son. The young man who was in the ambulance grew up with my son and the doctor in the ER worked tirelessly for over two hours trying to revive him. The investigator watched my son grow up and will not retire until he can prove foul play in my son's death.

What I found out after my son died was really who he was. The lessons he took with him in his short life, the relationships he formed all the years he was gone. My son was an amazing young man. Aidan gave his time and tough advice to people. He had friendships with real connections. Some he had never physically met because their friendships started on social media. The first comment I received via FB messenger was from a young man. His first line was, "Your son saved my life even though we had never met." Then there were more messages that would lift my heart. A few more just like the first, "I wouldn't be who I was today if I had never met your son."

In the last three years, I've met his friends from Texas, Florida, Pennsylvania, West Virginia, Tennessee, and New York. I have heard stories filled with fun and a lot of laughs. I have seen young men cry and girls sob. They all say the same thing...they have lost a brother. I have been to a wedding and one young man named his first-born son after Aidan. What is strange is that not one of these kids ever knew Aidan to do drugs. They said he really was not a drinker either. He did like to smoke pot.

I know that I did not have years of struggle and for that I am grateful. Unfortunately, it does not have to be years of struggle to have the same ending. My son overdosed one time and died. There are things I wish I had done differently. I will forever carry that guilt. I did not have enough  time with my son, but I know my son fulfilled his purpose. He was caring and compassionate. He treated you like you were the only person in the room while talking to you. He made you feel like you mattered by giving you his time and his heart. He had an amazing sense of humor but also knew disappointment. God knew my son was tired and needed to take him home. I know I will see him again.

Aiden's Mom,

Patricia R.
Monroe, New York

Christina

FOREVER 24

No mother should have to hold her 120 pound daughter in her arms one moment & hold her 7 pound bag of ashes the very next week. I HATE DRUGS!!!!!!!!

Your journey on earth started, Sept 6, 1992, at Riverside Hospital. We both fought hard together to bring you into this world. You wouldn't move your tiny fist from your mouth, so you could have an easy entry. They couldn't find the anesthesiologist to do a cesarean section. We both were in serious shape. You were supposed to be, Kyle Garrett, but after 24 hrs. of trying, I didn't care if you came out Dumbo the elephant. Doc, you can just get "it" out & sew me up for good after that battle. Little did I know, this was only the beginning of our fight for your life.

You were the sweetest little girl! Always with your blanket and/or dolly. You loved to test the boundaries though. We were on the 2nd story & you repeatedly were caught stacking anything you could find, styrofoam blocks, games, boxes under the window so you could go "exploring". Much to the amusement of our neighbors, your other pastime was running out of the house without clothes on. Couldn't take our eyes off you for a minute. One of my favorite photos, is you at about 3 yrs old, in a blue & white striped dress. You stuck 2 nerf balls up to the chest area, walking around giggling & grinning ear to ear. You looked like a top heavy little old lady with a way too perky rack! You loved making us laugh even back then.

In school, you were an obedient student. You loved school, your teachers & friends. You got good grades, enjoyed cheerleading, playing the flute, soccer, & collecting rocks. It wasn't until we hit the teen years that the problems begin to take off with you and your sister, Ashley. I couldn't keep you in school. Skipping classes, then just skipping the day to drink, smoke weed, hang with "friends". 3 years of 8th grade, trying 3 different school districts. Keeping up with you girls & chasing you down was one rough marathon. You both decided you knew what was best for yourselves & that was that. As an adult you were charismatic, stunningly gorgeous, feisty, in-your-face outspoken, had a robust, contagious laugh, would do anything for a friend & always lit up a room with your smile, energy & crazy sense of humor.

Then you fell in love with the sweet talking bad boy that taught you how to break into people's homes & take what you could to sell, then stealing from stores, whatever you could to get money for weed, percocets, cocaine then soon heroin. Once the drugs took over, my Christina was gone...it was the addiction running your life. From attending rehabilitation classes with you to you going to juvenile jail, jail, recovery centers & cold turkey tries at getting sober. I can't count the phone calls & visit you made after you had been beaten up, destroying every holiday by not showing up or showing up & causing a scene, the night the police came to our house at 2am to tell me your body was reported in the trunk of a car & not knowing it wasn't true til 10 hrs later, evicted out of one apartment after the other, the day I came over to the crack house you were living at to find bodies strewn everywhere & poor Lyla with a diaper so full she could hardly walk, rummaging around with a bottle of hard sour milk looking for something to drink, you quit or were fired from so many good job opportunities, using Lyla as a pawn to try to get what you wanted, when you started dancing in men's clubs I knew you had reached a turning point you might never come back from, totaling

3 vehicles, the last car accident causing you to go into labor & having Lyla at 17. At this point, I have Ashley & her 9 mth. old son, Keegan, you & Lyla & myself in a tiny 934 sq. ft. home. The night "prince charming" busted out our back door window, pulling you by the head, over the jagged pieces of glass, tearing your neck up badly. Tearing his own arm up as well, while screaming, "I'm gonna kill everyone in your house!", is a memory that visits me way more often then I care to admit. I called 911 immediately, but with how often the police had to visit our house, I thought we'd be killed for sure. They arrived quicker then they ever had before, in time to hear for themselves how he was going to kill us all. But you dropped the charges &, even with a previous record, he got off with being ordered to pay for my window. So many terrible memories that no child, daughter, mother, grandmother...no one, should have to live with, yet the worst was about to come.

May 20, 2017 my biggest nightmare came true. Lyla's paternal grandma was banging hard on my door. I awoke, went to the door to hear her say, "Christina OD'd, I think she's dead." I was in shock, no they are going to save her, I thought. She & a friend drove us to the house you were at. The policeman on duty, who gave you CPR was, Michael. A friend of our family. His mom was in my wedding & he went to school with you & Ashley & knew you both well. He was the first to greet me, "I did everything I could, I'm so sorry". He hugged me. I still was in disbelief. This wasn't Michael's normal beat to cover this side of town. He was covering for a fellow officer on vacation. I knew then God arranged for Michael to be there so I knew you weren't alone & everything that could possibly be done was. I wasn't leaving there without seeing you & it seemed to take an eternity. They brought you on the gurney & uncovered you. I couldn't touch you due to the investigation, but they let me kiss you on the forehead. You were still warm. You looked like a movie star, the beauty you always were. Like I could just shake you & wake you up & scold you for scaring me half to death. I'd give anything now to not have listened to them & just grabbed you and held you til they pried me away. Time of death 1:11 am.

I should have let you deal with all your irresponsibilities & mistakes way more. I wish I would have spent more time on healthy coping skills with you girls instead of studying so hard for excellent grades. It didn't help at all that I had a bad picker when it came to men either. I, also, thought just because I practiced things in my life that helped me immensely, so would you. I didn't take into account...your STRONG free will.

Your addiction was almost a 10 year battle. I was a terrible enabler for too long with you and Ashley. I tried to hide it. I didn't want anyone to know. Once I read, "Don't Let Your Kids Kill You" by Charles Ruben & Ashley took me to my 1st FAAD meeting (Families after addiction & death) I became woke" to the manipulations & lies. I did the tough love, old school way & never looked back. Thank the Lord, Ashley is still fighting the beast.

I know you are so very sorry for all of this now. Lyla & I have forgiven you. I know you have forgiven me for my failings to you. I know your soul loved Jesus, but your addiction was just too powerful. You left Lyla & I living in the aftermath of it all & though we keep the good memories in the forefront, there are times the pain gets the best of us. You are at peace, free from the chains that bound you, being held & loved by our Savior. I picture you running carefree through fields. I see you getting all the other mama's kids together and shaking your heads, laughing & cheering us on down here.

I will never see you graduate, go to college or marry, but I was honored to be your mommy for the time you were on loan from God. I could own a mansion on a small island with the money & possessions that both you girls stole from me, along with setting you up with vehicles, places to live, apartment furnishings, food, clothing, rehabs, providing for your babies. But you each gave me a beautiful grandchild who are both more precious then  anything else I can imagine. Lyla & I sing songs, talk about you & look forward to our reunion with you. In the twinkling of an eye, babygirl.

Christina's Mom,

PJ S.
Toledo, Ohio

Caleb

FOREVER 25

Caleb was our sixth attempt at getting pregnant. I was going into surgery to have my tubes tied because I couldn't bare to lose another child to a miscarriage. That is when we found out I was pregnant. We waited until the fifth month to announce our pregnancy.

At six months, he came into the world. He was so precious and perfect. His names were picked from our favorite people in the Bible. From a young age, we could see that Caleb was different from most kids. He always stuck up for the kids others bullied or made fun of. In kindergarten, he won an award for his kindness and helpful attitude. He was the first kindergartener to be awarded this at his school. He never understood why people made fun of others.

He decided at seven he wanted to be an evangelist and made sure everyone he met knew this. He loved people and helping them gave him purpose and joy.

Caleb would light up a room when he walked in with his infectious smile and laugh. He was respected by his friends and family. If he saw someone upset, it became his mission to change that to joy. He wore his heart on his sleeve and would get it easily broken.

Caleb was so much more than his addiction and the world lost a precious man on July 26, 2019.

Caleb's Mom,

KIM S.
Richmond, Virginia

Maya

My name is Rosa, and I lost my only child, a precious daughter, to an accidental drug overdose. I need to write about it because I am feeling so lost in this world without her. I need to write, talk, and tell my story, my child's story. I want to have her voice heard. First, I want to talk about her. Maya Noemi was born on September 12, 2001. She was the most perfect, healthy, and beautiful baby. She was born with such beautiful great big eyes. Everyone was there the day she was born. I just don't know how I am going to go on without her. It's excruciating pain. I miss her so much.

Maya was a fun and loving, sweet child. Her father and I were not married but raised her together. She always lived with me; my mom helped me in raising her always. Maya was so very loved. She had the absolute perfect as can be childhood.

Never did I think my daughter would get addicted to opioids. She is now a statistic of this horrible epidemic. Maya lost her battle to addiction on March 2, 2020. She was only nineteen years old! She was just a child. She had her whole life ahead of her and it was taken from her. We tried so hard to get her help. I have found out so many things after her death about her drug use. I seriously feel that I missed some things and have enormous regret about what I could have done better or differently and maybe she would still be here with me.

When she was younger, she did go through several rehab programs and years of therapy. She seemed like she was better when she was seventeen. She managed to graduate from high school with a 3.5 GPA; we were all so very proud of her. Things went wrong the summer after high school. Maya seemed to be stuck in the "party life." I remember having continuous conversations with her about making good choices and how bad choices always will have consequences. She would always say what I wanted to hear and blow me off most of the time. I feel this drug had her. She was excellent at manipulating me.

Maya also suffered from depression and low self-esteem. Looking back, I feel she took drugs to "fit in," peer pressure like most teens experience. During that time, I thought she would eventually shake it off and move forward into adulthood. She just seemed to stay stuck in the party mode. Maya was the sweetest and nicest friend to everyone. Generous and just plain sweet. I feel this may have been part of her downfall. She would let  people take advantage of her. I miss her so much with every day and I hope that parents, siblings, and just people overall can be aware of addiction in their loved ones before it is too late. Learn about the dangers of addiction. The pain I have will forever be with me. Mommy loves you forever, Maya.

Maya's Mom,

ROSALBA S.
Long Beach, California

Dephon

Forever Loved

I lost my beautiful son, Dephon Forever 19, to carfentanyl, a result of the horrible disease of addiction and murder. My son fought so hard through his addiction.

Dephon was in a couple of programs up in Boston and Weymouth, Massachusetts. I am from Boston but am in Florida now. Dephon had a heart of gold. He ran in the addiction marathon in Boston twice. He was so proud of helping all the other guys from relapsing. He thought of others more than himself. He talked in schools, always participated and spoke up in the meetings. Dephon was the one that showed more love for me than anyone. He was very well liked, and had the prettiest blue eyes and smile. He lost his life to addiction. He would cry to me, "Mom, it's like I've got the devil on one side and God on the other and the devil kept tugging me down.

My son lost his battle on September 7, 2018. Dephon had just graduated from his program. He got on the Greyhound bus in Boston to come down to Florida to start his new life over. So, so excited, he called me an hour before to tell me he loved me so much and couldn't have asked for a better mom. I called Dephon to say, "I can't wait to see you. Seven hours until you're here."

A Virgina state trooper picked up my son's phone to tell me my son passed. They found him in Virginia; he got as far as Virgina, didn't make it to me in Florida. The autopsy said no drugs were found on Dephon. Had a pin drop of carfentanyl in his system, nothing else. They called it murder.

Supposedly, the cameras weren't on; I know better. Dephon was just another person dying of an overdose. Where is our justice?

I will never be the same. I will hold Dephon so tight in my heart until I can hold him in heaven. God bless all you beautiful angel mammas and daddies, I love you all. Thank God for this wonderful group family.

Dephon's Mom,

Lisa S.
Bradenton Beach, Florida

Raymond

Raymond was thirteen years old when he slipped on ice and slammed his kneecap into a trailer hitch and split it in two. Surgery was needed, Oxycontin was given, he struggled ever since. He was a baseball player, and a good one, made all stars every year. He was a fisherman by trade, also a very good one. Won a striped bass tournament with older experienced fisherman when he was twelve years old; his competitors were not happy!

He did not need to be given Oxycontin at thirteen. If I had known what it was, it would not have been given. He did well off and on until he was 29. Then all it took was a bad night and Fentanyl. He was a great kid. He was a beautiful boy, a talented young man that people sought out to help them fix their boats, cars, and teach them how to fish. He was a beloved son, fiancé, father, brother, and uncle. He mattered.

615

Raymond's Mom,

Dawn S.
Staten Island, New York

> *A mom who's lost a child, doesn't think about today or tomorrow,*
> *she's just holding on minute by minute.*
> *~ Jolene C.*

Anthony

This is just a portion of my son's life... which I refer to as Anthony's Acknowledgment...

My youngest son, Anthony, forever 27, gained his angel wings on September 26, 2017, after a long battle with chemical dependency/substance use disorder. Our Heavenly Father took him Home…to end his battle with opiates. As his mom, my heart is forever shattered...but I am so thankful and blessed to have had him for twenty-seven years and to now know that he is no longer suffering. I have faith that I will see him again one day, in the Kingdom of God.

Anthony was a wonderful son, brother, grandson, and friend. To know him is to love him. Travis (my first-born son), Anthony (born fifteen and a half months after Travis), and I lived in a small city in rural Indiana, where I continue to live to this day. Their father and I divorced when they were two (Anthony) and three (Travis) years old. Although their dad and I lived in the same city, and he was always a part of their lives, I was, and still am, a single mom.

Anthony graduated from high school in 2008 and through the ten-plus years of his addiction, he was always a loving, caring, and hard-working young man. After high school, he worked, several years, for a roofing company, traveling around the US and spending several months in the New England area, where his addiction really took a turn for the worse. After returning home, he told me he felt lucky to be alive after the challenges and altercations he had while there, including an incident where he was nearly car-jacked! He admitted that most of the incidents were drug related.

For the last three years of his life, Anthony was employed by a steel manufacturing company where he operated a 10-torch oxy burner, which is used to cut extremely thick steel. For the last few months of his life, he frequently worked fifty-plus hours a week, including swing shifts and split shifts. His supervisors and co-workers loved him and continued to contact me for over a year after he gained his wings, acknowledging what a great employee and hard worker he was and how much they missed him.

Anthony was a lovable AND likable guy. He was fun to be around and had a heart of gold. He had a love for his family and little ones. He never married and did not father any children. He was one of MY best friends and there wasn't much that he didn't share with me. If I was feeling down or apprehensive about anything, he was always there with a shoulder to cry on or to cheer me up and remind me of his confidence in me. He was my number one cheerleader and always gave me that boost of confidence that I tried SO HARD to give him.

My sweet boy was extremely handsome and had a perfect build; yet somehow, he lacked self-confidence and typically didn't feel "good enough" in so many respects. He didn't want others to know about his addiction because he was embarrassed by his disease and felt even less worthy of anything good. I learned from him that the opioids and anti-anxiety meds gave him the confidence that he otherwise lacked. He tried so hard to hide his substance use disorder from his family and friends, and for the most part, he did a pretty good job of it. Sadly though, hiding his disease eventually led him to self-isolate, which was destructive for him. Watching him go from having friends around all the time to having none was heartbreaking.

Initially, Anthony didn't understand substance use disorder, which was then referred to only as addiction as a disease, but I truly hope that during his last rehab stay that he might have realized the seriousness of it. I think that he thought of it more as a character flaw, rather than a disease.

Anthony was diagnosed with ulcerative colitis at age sixteen. He tried to hide the pain associated with ulcerative colitis. He also tried SO hard to control the substance use disorder. He used to tell me, "I'm getting better, Mom. I've slowed down quite a bit...and pretty soon I'll stop." During this time, I prayed every day for him to be delivered from his addiction and I did my best to keep his addiction a secret... that only he and I...and God knew.

Anthony's addiction started with prescription pain medication that was given by a doctor when he broke his ankle playing football his freshman year, 2004. His ankle injury healed without surgery, but was soon followed by a broken hand requiring a bone graft, wisdom teeth removal, ulcerative colitis, and the list goes on and on.

Knowing that alcohol addiction runs in both my family and their dad's, I tried to teach my boys about the hereditary gene associated with addiction, so they would be armed with the knowledge if they ever chose to try alcohol or drugs. The cards just seemed to be stacked against my baby. My older son Travis didn't have any issues with addiction, which I don't find surprising as their personalities were quite different.

Anthony attempted rehab a couple of times during his addiction. When he was eighteen (in 2008), my ex and I agreed to let him go to a facility in California, in hopes of giving him the new start that he so desperately wanted. After two weeks, he came home to attend the funeral of his best friend's mom who overdosed. He returned to California, only to come back home a week later. He said he was "better." I can't tell you how many times I have heard those words, and how desperately I wanted to believe him. I knew in my mind that he wasn't, but I could not force him to stay in rehab and did not want to leave him in California to be "thrown to the wolves. So, his dad and I brought him back home and the saga started over once again.

The years between 2008 and 2017 were full of ups and downs, hopes and disappointments. I tried to mentally prepare myself for what might happen if he didn't get better, but couldn't even stand the thought. I talked and talked to him about the endless health problems that could stem from his drug use, but at that time, I didn't even realize how powerful the disease was.

In July of 2017, while trying to detox himself at home over the 4th of July holiday, Anthony got extremely sick. When he came out of his room, I was seeing many signs and symptoms of a stroke victim. I was so scared that I was going to lose him. He agreed and I took him to the ER where he was diagnosed with severe dehydration. He was re-hydrated, referred to a drug detox/rehab facility, and released to come home. For the next week, he got all the pieces in place to take family medical leave so he could go to detox/rehab and finally be free of this horrendous disease. He got all the plans finalized and was admitted to the detox/rehab facility on July 17, 2017.

Anthony completed the detox and intensive therapy of his rehab and then graduated to the sober living apartment associated with the program in August 2017. For the next few weeks, I really felt like I was getting my son back. Anthony and I had many phone conversations, went to dinner together, shopping, and shared other outings. I had not seen his eyes so clear, nor had I heard his true compassionate drug-free voice for years. He apologized to me and others in his life for hurting them while he was using.

My heart was so full; my prayers were finally being answered!

I had no idea how much temptation there is for someone in recovery from opiate addiction. It is unimaginable to those that have never suffered from this horrible disease that literally alters the brain. My sweet son gave in to the temptation "one last time" on September 26, 2017. That evening, my baby was found unresponsive by one of his sober living roommates, after the roommate returned to the apartment from an NA meeting. He told me that he did everything he could to try to resuscitate my son but his efforts, and those of the EMTs were fruit-less. It was his time to go Home. God had come to take my beautiful son away from his demons…to a place where there would be no more pain and struggling.

This pain has to be the WORST PAIN EVER for a mother to suffer. Some refer to me as, 'The strongest woman they know," but what they don't see is that inside, my heart is completely and forever shattered. I am broken and a part of me died with my son on September 26, 2017.

I am so very thankful for the twenty-seven years that God loaned Anthony to me. In his honor and memory, I am trying to live my life in a way that is pleasing to God, Anthony, and Travis. I try to smile and be the mom that my sons have always loved. And even with a shattered heart, God has helped me to occasionally find my smile and glimpses of happiness, even if just for a moment or two. I have faith that I will see him again, one day in the Kingdom of God. Today, I am not one day further away from my son, but rather, one day closer to him.

Since his passing, it is my sincere belief that with the hundreds of lives being lost to addiction every day, it would be Anthony's desire to help others by ACKNOWLEDGING his substance use disorder and to ACKNOWLEDGE it loud and proud. One of the first choices that I made was to start advocating to stop the stigma associated with overdose and addiction. I believe that if others come to realize that addiction is a disease and not a choice, more will reach out for help, rather than trying to hide their disease from their families and friends.

So, in memory of my beautiful son and in hopes of stopping the stigma and saving a life: This is ANTHONY, and the above is ANTHONY's ACKNOWLEDGMENT.

Anthony's Mom,

JILL S.
Alexandria, Indiana

Philip

FOREVER 23

My beautiful boy, Philip, was born in July 1995. He was a miracle. He had a brother and sister who adored him, as well as his dad. The whole family loved him. We still do. He was my best friend, my biggest supporter, my whole world. We spent his younger years back and forth from basketball to football to baseball. I was certain he was destined for greatness. My boy was well liked, popular, and a lady's man. He was so handsome. Not in a regular way, in an angelic way. He always shined.

Philip became an addict around the age of twenty. That's when I first noticed the signs. He would always deny everything, and I believed him. He would swear to God and on everyone's life that he was not an addict. And I believed him. When it became apparent my boy needed help, I enlisted the assistance of the court system in Cape Cod, Massachusetts. After a gut-wrenching hearing in September of 2018, my request to have my son committed was denied. The court doctor said that although my son had track marks, they were at least a week old. She stated my son was handsome, didn't look like an addict. They released him. My son later told me he had ten grams of heroin on his person in the court that day. He wasn't even searched.

On May 15, 2019, I received the dreaded call. My boy was in an ambulance on the way to the hospital on Cape Cod. I lived in Virginia Beach. The twelve-hour ride is a blur, as well as the next few days. When I arrived at the ICU, I knew my boy was gone. How could this be? I spoke to my Philip EVERY day. A LOT. Now he's gone. Somewhere in the corner of my mind I remembered he was an organ donor. So, with the help of my family and husband, we began the process with donor services in New England.

The whole time in the hospital, my sister was there with my children and family. I remember she rubbed lotion on his feet and cut his hair for me. I collapsed into my father's arms, cried with my mother, and children. Thank God my husband had the strength to tend to everything. I don't even remember when I said Philip was angelic. He was. He is. His organ donation helped two people and saved their lives. My family will never recover from the loss of our Philip, and we will never forget our hero. He had a heart bigger than the world and was loved by anyone he met. He was selfless, giving, kind, handsome, sweet, and the All-American boy. If this can happen to my baby, it can happen to anyone's. Please remember our children with love. They are someone's everything.

Philip's Mom,

STEPHANIE S.
Cape Cod, Massachusetts

Joshua

FOREVER 31

"NOT ONE MORE TIME" has become the motto for a lot of us mothers. If you think, "Not my child," think again. My son didn't get his addiction start from prescription drugs. He partied moderately through his late high school years, was not a heavy drinker, and did not have an addictive personality.

Joshua went to a weekend party with friends who were camping out, listening to many bands, and enjoying life. They decided to purchase heroin to snort and all pitched in. They thought there was no harm in snorting it and doing it once. The heroin they purchased was a higher grade and could not be broken down to snort, so they decided to shoot it up instead. No harm doing it once, right? That one time began his addiction. The next two days, he was sicker than he had ever been. He compared it to having the worst flu, times twenty.

His body hurt so bad that he just wanted to stop the pain and the only way to stop it was to use again. He kept his addiction at a low level, just enough to make it through work and to not throw up, have diar-

624

rhea, and to be able to eat. He came to me and begged for help and we were lucky enough to get him started on Suboxone.

He kept his job and insurance and did wonderful. He then lost his job, his insurance, and could not afford the Suboxone. Shortly after, he picked it up again. I called his father, begged him to come get him and help him. He needed to get away from the familiar surroundings and the people he dealt with.

Joshua thrived in his new sobriety, had a wonderful job, made good money, and survived through the death of many friends. In October and November 2016, we went through six weeks in a row of overdoses, five of which he died. I hugged Joshua, who was my only child, and said, "This could be me and you right now, but it is never going to be us, right?" And he said, "No, Mom. I love you". He got promoted to head of his department, was training his whole company on a new computer system, and was succeeding in his recovery.

We celebrated his thirty-first birthday and four years of sobriety on October 18, 2017. Six days later, on October 24, 2017, at 7:15 a.m., the knock on my door came. I first asked what happened. Since he worked until 3:00 a.m., I thought it was an accident. The sheriff lowered his head and tears flowed.

I said, "Please don't tell me it was an overdose," and he said, "It appears so; he was found with a band on his arm and a needle in his hand." My heart and my world stopped at that moment and stayed there for six months.

Looking back, I don't know how I went back to work two weeks later. I remember very little. I was blessed with a husband who did everything for me during that time. It took all I had to make it through the day.

One thing I do know; a friend got me connected to the Not In Vain group. PJ S started this page on the day my Joshua gained his wings and it has been my lifeline. I have read stories of great horror, sadness, smiles, and laughter.

For those who have lost their beloved children before me I say, "We made it. We have survived together." For those who have lost children after me and for those who will lose children if this epidemic is not stopped, we will be here for you to help you though this long hard journey.

And for those who may be fighting addiction with their child or with anyone, Fight Like Hell to save the ones we have left. Love you Mammas. I love you, Joshua. Until we meet again, my sweet baby boy.

Joshua's Mom,

TERI S.
Dalton, Ohio

Bradley

Bradley was a different child from the time he was very little. By the time he was eighteen months old, I had taken him to the doctor and told the doctor there was something "wrong." The doctor didn't believe me. By the time he was five years old, the doctors at a Chicago children's hospital diagnosed Bradley as bipolar. I never thought the bipolar label was correct, but I knew he struggled with "something." He was depressed often; he was very quick to anger and also very quick to make smile. We would always joke and ask, which Bradley did we have?

In school, Bradley had the same problem. He started getting into trouble in kindergarten. We switched schools in first grade and moved to Corbin, Kentucky. Bradley's first day of school, I went to the principal's office and told him about Bradley's problem. I told him I was scared he would create the next "Columbine" if we couldn't find him help. Bradley had a wonderful teacher and principal. In first, second, and third grade, they worked with us and we were able to get him on a 504 plan. Bradley was extremely intelligent and didn't otherwise qualify for an IEP.

However, in fourth grade, Bradley went to a new school, as that was the way his school district worked. Bradley got into trouble almost every day in school in the fourth grade. The principal would not work with us and refused to use known techniques to help Bradley. We pulled Bradley out of school in March of his fourth grade year and homeschooled him. He went back to school in fifth grade, but we pulled him out only two months into the school year, because of issues we had at the school with Bradley's behaviors. It was a horrible, sad time for Bradley. He had no one at home to help with his homeschooling and much was put on his shoulders. When we could help, we were not prepared.

When Bradley went into sixth grade, he went to middle school. What a beautiful, wonderful change. He was placed in restrictive classes, so he could study on his own, with a wonderful teacher. He was able to be mainstreamed for many of the technical classes, as he was smart as a whip.

In eighth grade, Bradley still had horrible anger issues and became mad at lunchtime. Bradley had never, ever hurt or got physical with anyone, but he was angry and threw a milk container across the lunch-room. The milk container hit a girl in the eye and caused a tear in her retina. The principal, who had always worked with Bradley, was talking to the local judge about what to do. The judge sent it to court. Bradley was charged with terroristic threatening and assault and battery. It was such a horrible and scary time.

We had no idea what was going to happen and there were so many sleepless nights. Bradley was ordered to do community service. However, during his community service he yelled at the office manager at the animal shelter and they let him go. Eventually, he finished his community service at the local library and his life started to turn around. Bradley loved books and while at the library, he was treated with respect and given duties to accomplish and not just busy work.

Bradley got into trouble one more time in high school. His principal called me and told me that Bradley was in trouble and I would have to come pick him up or they were going to call the police on him. At breakfast, the entire school got into trouble and were told when they came in for lunch after they sat down, they would not be allowed to get

628

back up. Bradley, being Bradley, and playing the game by the letter of the law, got his lunch and refused to sit down to eat. If he didn't sit down, then he wouldn't be stuck in his seat. He principal wanted to call the police because Bradley wouldn't sit down. He was not being loud, obnoxious, or causing trouble, but he did refuse to sit.

There were also so many happy times. During high school, he finally made friends for the first time in his life. There were two private schools in the area that only went to eighth grade. All these kids from the private schools came to his school for high school. New kids who didn't know Bradley from his years of negative behavior at school now got to see this kid as someone else. These were also some really smart kids who Bradley fit right in with. Bradley found a wonderful girlfriend, made the honor roll, became part of the Beta Team, the National Honor Society, and a member of the debate team. Bradley was also an Eagle Scout and completed his Eagle Scout project for the library, the same library that helped him.

Bradley's senior year, the family moved from Kentucky to Washington State. Bradley was asked if he wanted to stay in Kentucky to graduate, but he was ready to move and leave his old life behind. When we arrived in Washington, Bradley took advantage of a program they have there and he went right to college to finish his senior year of school. He seemed to be doing great in Washington, made friends, and found a girlfriend. He was still shy and very socially awkward, but he was growing. My husband and I never thought that Bradley would be able to hold a job or support himself, but he did get a job. He worked for more than two years at Burger King.

Bradley went away to college in January of 2017. He didn't want to go, but I wanted him to spread his wings, to be on his own. He had spent more than three years at the community college and needed to sprout. Bradley's life fell apart and by the end of the year he would be gone and the family would never be the same.

Bradley left for the university in January. It was a wintery, snowy day and there were so many cars in ditches that we took photos of them. The girls in the dorm room directly across from Bradley had rolled their car on the way to campus. I should have known to bring him home.

I don't know what happened or when, but by all accounts, before Bradley's birthday, in March, he had been charged with theft of a check, which he cashed into his own account, and smoking marijuana on a college campus. It was legal for him to smoke marijuana, but not on the campus. Bradley pled guilty to both charges, instead of telling me. When I found out months later, he said, "Mom, you always told me, if I did the crime, I had to do the time."

Around this time, I did know that Bradley was smoking marijuana. I told him that if he was smoking, he was not allowed to come home on spring break, so he didn't. He would tell me later that he went two days without eating because he had no money and no food. I was not giving him money while he was at college, since he had previously worked for more than two years at Burger King, but he had nothing left to show for it. I thought he was spending most of his money on computers and his girlfriend. He was excellent with computers and was always buying parts for them and he was never good with a dime. If he had money, he spent it before it could reach his pocket.

What was I thinking giving him no money to live on? How I wish I could go back and change what I did and how I did it. Bradley would be picked up one more time for smoking marijuana on the campus, which he would plead innocent too, but was found guilty. I would find out about all these charges in the summer. Bradley came home from school on the last day of classes.

Somewhere around this time, I found out about the marijuana charges. I'm not sure when I found out about the theft. It was by accident. I saw it online at mugshots.com. Bradley had to enroll in an outpatient treatment, ordered by the court. It took a while to find treatment and get in, according to Bradley, but he did finally get in and start going.

In August, Bradley was back in court, because it took him too long to find treatment and he had to spend a few days in jail. Bradley got out of jail and was able to go right back to work. He had found himself a great job, making good money, and things were looking pretty good for him. At the end of September, Bradley got very angry with someone he worked with. I don't know what happened, but he got himself fired from the position he had. He went back to his temp agency and they were able to get him another job, but he absolutely hated it.

The third week at that job he called in sick. He told me that it was "weird;" he went down an aisle to pick up a part. He was a picker. By the time he got down the aisle, he had forgotten what he was going to get. After two days of this, he called in sick because he thought he had the flu. On October 10, he had to go back to court. It seems that he was supposed to be doing AA classes and he had not. Bradley claimed he didn't know he was supposed to go to AA and when he found out he started going, but it was too late. He was being held as out of compliance. I thought he was doing good so I called and paid for an attorney to go to court with him. Bradley was spared going back to jail.

By Friday the 13th of that same week, I was in Kentucky with my other son, when Bradley called me and said, "Mom, should my fingers and toes be numb?" We had a talk about it. I told him that if he was sick, he needed to go to the doctors. He told me that he couldn't drive. I told him to have Destiny drive him. He told me that Destiny was going out with her boyfriend. I then told him Dan could take him to the doctors when he got home from work. Bradley didn't go to the doctors on the thirteenth, but on the fourteenth when he woke up, he could hardly walk and it was time to go.

The doctor's office turned him around and told him to go straight to the hospital. Bradley had signs of ataxia. He could not walk straight, he could not talk straight, and to a stranger, appeared drunk. Within a few hours, he was diagnosed with Miller Fisher syndrome. By the fifteenth, he was intubated, on a respirator, strapped to his bed, heavily sedated, and mostly paralyzed. I was still in Kentucky. I flew home two days later and realized just how sick he was. I never realized what "intubated" meant. I knew he was in ICU, but I didn't know the severity of his illness or I just denied it. I had started a message list to let family and friends know how he was doing.

My first post seeing him: "I can't begin to tell you what I saw today. A 22-year-old restrained to his bed because he can't control his movements. Breathing tubes. While we were there, they had to suction his lungs and say they are going to start cleaning his lungs every two hours. We were asked to leave the room when the respiratory therapist came in because his oxygen dropped to low. He can respond only with a yes or no shake of his hand. There were other symptoms I want to ask the doctor about. It's not pretty. Please keep praying for him. The only bright spot I told him, the next time his allergies are bothering him, I'll let the nurses clean his lungs. As best as he was able, he gave me a flicker from his middle finger. That's my Bradley, he is a fighter."

A day later, "Small blood clot in his arm. They say it's tiny and nothing to worry about. Today is the last day of the IVIG. They are going to put him on stronger pain medication but NOT opioids." Bradley would soon have pneumonia and a small blood clot. He would be moved to morphine or heavier drugs as he got sicker.

The doctors started talking about giving him a tracheotomy, telling me his recovery would be long, he would need to learn to walk again, eat, and tie his shoes. It was pretty grim. It was being discussed that he may have to be moved to an acute hospital once he was more stable, than a long-term rehab hospital. This is a twenty-two-year-old young man, my boy. He had pneumonia once before, but besides that, he had never been sick, not really sick.

A week later, Bradley, still sedated, got very angry with the nurses. I'm not sure why, but he was able to use his hands and one arm to let them know. He was having issues with the pneumonia, and was unable to hold his own oxygen. My son was fighting for his life and we just weren't sure he was going to win.

I remember walking into his room one day and just losing it. I thought he was dead, his head was hanging down, he was drooling, and was just not the person I remember. During this entire time, they kept increasing Bradley's pain medication. I remember when the physical therapist came in one day and Bradley was at the edge of the bed attempting to stand. He could only move about four inches, but it was so wonderful to see. He had movement. He still had muscles. He was going to make it!

Bradley was put in a regular hospital room while awaiting a rehab hospital opening. The first day in the regular room, Bradley was not able to eat, I had to feed him. It hurt, but I was so happy he was able to eat; he was going to make it. I came back the next day and he was feeding himself. OK, he was wearing a lot of the food too, but it was so rewarding to see. The doctors and nurses were even helping him move to a chair to sit. I put in my message updates, "Most certainly a Pellegrini moment. Bradley mad. I didn't bring him a chocolate shake. Told me to stand up for a minute. So, I oblige setting off the loudest alarm I've heard in a long time. New note, both his bed and chair are rigged to go off if he tries to get up on his own."

After three weeks in ICU, Bradley was released to a rehab hospital.

He did so well in the rehab hospital, he was able to come home after just a week there. Almost a month in the hospital our world was flipped upside down and inside out. The last post in my "Bradley updates" was the following: "2 days since the last post, wow life changes. Bradley is doing good. His eyes are still in a fixated position, but getting better. He had a new release of his favorite book come to the house to realize he can't read. Not like you and I. He still has double vision and his eyes can't move from left to right as you need to do to read.

On the other hand, he may only need occupational therapy a couple of times and physical therapy for a month or so. That's nothing compared to the day I walked in the ICU and thought he was dead. There will never be a day in my life that I won't thank the Lord that all my children are alive, breathing, and able. Thank you all for your support. I know who my real family is." The next post would be begging someone to tell me he was still alive, but I'm jumping ahead of myself. You see the very best day of our lives was yet to come.

On November 20, 2017, my husband, Daniel, adopted my sons Dale and Bradley, and we adopted our daughter, Destiny. Dan and I had been married since Bradley was seven, but he had never adopted the boys. This was my dream come true. Destiny had been our foster daughter for over a year, and what better way to make the family whole then by adopting all three children at once. It was a joyous occasion. Bradley still had fixated eyes. He was a little wobbly, but he was out of the hospital and walking.

On December 18, 2017, Bradley was flying to my mom's house in Illinois to celebrate the holidays. Bradley and I had had a talk the night before. He told me that he didn't want to stay at his grandma's over Christmas and that I never let him stay for Christmas. I told him that he was a big boy and that he could make the reservations if he wanted to be gone over Christmas.

Bradley gave me a huge hug in the kitchen. He held on a little tighter and a little longer than he had before. It was so wonderful he was getting back to normal. He had just started driving again the previous week, as his eyesight was getting so much better. On the morning of the 18th, I went into Bradley's room about 4:45 in the morning; I told him that he had better get up or he was going to miss the plane. I told him I was leaving for work and couldn't stick around to make sure he got up.

He said, "I'm awake. It's cold, I'll get out of bed in a few minutes." I had no way to know I would never see Bradley alive again.

Bradley caught his plane and was in Illinois with his grandma and many family members. I talked to him often. A few things happened and we got into a heated discussion. Bradley told me that he was having problems with his eyesight again and asked if I would take him to eye therapy when he returned home. I told him of course I would. Bradley then told me this crazy story that he had gone shopping very late at night and got really tired. Tiredness is an ongoing issue for people with Miller Fisher syndrome. He told me that he went to the van and proceeded to fall asleep in the parking lot of the Walgreens store.

A few hours later, the police and an ambulance came knocking on the door of the van. He told the officer about his Miller Fisher and how he was so tired and that it was not safe to drive, so he took a nap. The paramedics did a blood test and he tested negative for whatever they tested him for. The police officer then drove him back to his grandma's house and he said he would get the van the next day when he felt better.

That was December 22. December 23, as a Christmas tradition, the family in Illinois went to the shooting range to fire guns and have a little fun. Bradley did not feel well and he stayed home. He did talk my mother into giving him the combination to her gun safe. He claimed he wanted to look at the pretty guns since he couldn't go shooting. Dan and I were extremely upset and very scared.

Bradley had never hurt anyone, but he had been suicidal in the past. He had never attempted suicide, but his depression and anger issues have always kept us from letting him around guns unsupervised, and here he is alone with the combination to the gun safe. At one point, Dan and I actually considered calling the police, but were afraid of what the outcome would be if they thought he was unstable and had guns. He could have been killed, so we did nothing.

On Christmas Eve, Bradley called me crying. He begged me to let him come back home. He told me that he wanted to be home. He didn't want to be at his grandma's anymore. He asked me to let him come home and hold him. I told him that he couldn't come home before Christmas, but if he wanted to come home after Christmas, we could change his tickets and he could come home early. I had no way of knowing it then, but I would never speak to Bradley again. The last time

I saw him, he didn't want to stay so long at his grandma's, and the last time I talked to him he begged me to come home early. Both times I told him no. What I would give now to let him come home.

On Christmas Eve, just before dinner, Bradley told his great uncle that he was feeling suicidal. His uncle offered to, and did smoke a joint with him, to try and help him feel better. At dinner, it is said that Bradley was trying to cut his meat, but he was unable to "find it" and he kept stabbing the napkin. Sometime during dinner, it was suggested that Dale help Bradley to bed. As Dale was walking Bradley to bed, he fell asleep walking. One of his cousins thought it would be funny to take a picture of Bradley sleeping.

By the time he got the camera, Bradley woke up, but he took a picture of Dale trying to help Bradley to bed. Dale got Bradley into the bedroom and Bradley started doing all these stretches. Dale told him to just lay down in bed. Bradley never got out of bed. The next morning, Christmas morning 2017, Dale tried to wake up Bradley so they could open gifts. Bradley would not wake up. Dale asked his uncle to help him get Bradley up. His uncle walked into the room, slapped him on the head and said, "Get up." He would say the moment he slapped him, he knew Bradley was gone. I flew to Chicago immediately, but it was too late. My baby was gone.

Eventually, Dale would go through Bradley's bag and find two of my mother's pill bottles in his bag. Most of the pills were still in the bottle. Dan and I had no idea how or why Bradley died. We thought maybe it was a relapse of the Miller Fisher, although that didn't seem likely. Dan and I stood over Bradley and made a promise to each other and to Bradley, that if he had committed suicide, we would understand and not be angry with him. Bradley had so many ups and downs in his life and he had a long way to go to be stable. He was lonely, scared, and had very few friends. His girlfriend had broken up with him a few months prior and with his social awkwardness, he was having a hard time meeting anyone who could understand.

We had a viewing for Bradley in Joliet, where he lived as a young child and where he passed away, as he had many friends there. We had a viewing and funeral service in Michigan for him, where his half-siblings lived and where he was going to be buried. When we went back to Chicago for the very last night, I went through his bag just to hold his belongings and just to feel him closer. It was at this time I found morphine mixed in with his Aleve.

We would find out the morphine was my mother's and it had been locked in her gun safe. Did he know it was there? I don't know, but he knew what he had when he found it. I was able to look through his phone and Christmas Eve at 2:13 p.m., he looked up escitalopram, his antidepressant. He then looked up recreational doses of morphine followed by, "What's a recreational dose of morphine sulfate?" I'm sure this probably was not his first time using drugs, but it was his last.

My son passed away sometime overnight between Christmas Eve and Christmas morning. My hell will live forever. His nephew will never remember his Uncle Bradley whom he loved dearly. His brother will never go out for their traditional Thanksgiving evening movie. Dan was a father to Bradley for seventeen years, but only officially for thirty-five days. Destiny left the family shortly after Bradley's passing and went back to her biological family. Bradley had one foster sister at the time, Aiyanna aka Julian, who will always love him and miss him but wasn't able to say his last good-bye. "Where your treasure is, there will your heart be also." Matthew 6:21. "The last enemy that shall be destroyed is death," 1 Corinthians 15:26.

Bradley's Mom,

CASSANDRA S.
Nashville, Tennessee

Shane

FOREVER 20

My grief journey started on May 13, 2018. It was Mother's Day and my son Shane was supposed to be in treatment. We decided his treatment should be out of town, thinking it would be best for him to be somewhere he couldn't get distracted from his recovery or be around bad influences.

I'm so thankful Shane talked me into letting him go to treatment otherwise I probably wouldn't have seen him one last time. His dad and I went to Asheville in February 2018; we took him shopping for clothes and his hygiene stuff; then we went to eat. Little did I know that day would be the last time I ever saw him. I hugged Shane tight that February day. I kissed him and told him I loved him. I begged Shane to not put that poison in his body.

In the end it was fentanyl and opioids that killed him; they found him in a motel on the floor on a day meant for celebrating my mother-hood. We are aware of the events that occurred on the awful night of

Shane's death. Surveillance footage showed three people going into the motel room but only two leaving. I continue to wish for charges to be filed against the people who were with my son in his last moments, however there is no legal recourse.

I deeply regret giving him extra money in April; I didn't know his dad had also given him money. For a long time, I thought if only we hadn't given Shane money, it wouldn't have happened. A person will drive themselves crazy with the what-ifs. There is no way to know what's really going on in another person's mind; that's why we don't realize they are only acting as if things are better. It was a long time before I saw the whole picture and understood it was bound to happen. There are simply things we have no control over.

Shane's Mom,

MARY S.
Raleigh, North Carolina

Andrew

FOREVER 33

Andrew was born May 12, 1986, and was seven and a half weeks early. He weighed four pounds, fourteen ounces at birth and came home two weeks later, weighing four pounds, three ounces. Andrew was diagnosed with ADHD at age five and was put on Ritalin at age six. He was very hyper, but never destructive. I was a single mom, but always made sure Andrew saw his dad and had a relationship with him.

He went to a private high school and never felt like he fit in because a lot of the other kids had money, their own cars, and went on trips. During his junior year of high school, he started experimenting with a classmate, abusing Ritalin. I found out and put a stop to it, but that was the beginning. By age eighteen, Andrew was using heroin and had overdosed in our kitchen, with his friend.

Andrew was in and out of detox and what were considered long-term (fourteen to thirty days) facilities often. He would do well for a few months, but inevitably end up back on heroin. I tried to kick him out a few times, but he would not leave.

He finally got sober when his girlfriend got pregnant. He did well for about a year, but started getting high again and his girlfriend broke off the relationship. I had him sectioned a couple of times, the last time was in 2017. He did good for eight months, then went back.

He finally went to detox again in January 2018 and did really well. He was friends with the mother of his son, Jameson, and finally got to spend lots of time with him. He went to a sober home and even had Jameson overnight, every Wednesday. He was sober eighteen months. I was so happy for him.

Then, there were two overdoses at the sober house and Andrew decided he needed to leave because he was afraid of relapsing, and if his son was there when someone overdosed, he could lose his visits. He found a small place to move to and did well for two months.

Then one night, after work, he used, and unknown to him it was fentanyl and it took his life. He was at the morgue listed as John Doe; his wallet and phone were stolen. We finally found him on Tuesday morning, after calling hospitals and detox facilities all night Monday when we could not reach him or find him. He died September 22, 2019, at 5:03 p.m.

I miss Andrew every minute of every day. He was my one and only and I know he didn't mean to overdose. He loved his son way too much to leave him. Jameson is now six, has autism, and misses his daddy, but knows he is gone.

It breaks my heart to know Andrew will never be here to play with him, take him to his first baseball game, or to teach him all the things Dads teach their sons. I have Jameson every other weekend and we have a great relationship.

He is what keeps me going. I just found out I have another grandson. Andrew had another child from another relationship. He told me before he passed that he thought he was the dad and was going to do a DNA test.

He never got the chance. The mother reached out to me, just a few weeks ago. I did a DNA test and it came back that Andrew is the dad. I have another grandson, Declan, that is fifteen months old...Andrew's final gift to me.

Andrew's Mom,

SANDRA S.
Saugus, Massachusetts

Ginger

FOREVER 34

One day, I saw an official letter in the mail addressed to Ginger. Something told me to open it, and I read she was arrested for having a CD. What the hell is a CD? So, I called the police, pretended to be her, and found out it was a controlled substance. I was livid!! She knows better!!!

I'm waiting for her to come home so I can confront her. She, of course, broke down and told me she was doing coke!! I hired her a lawyer so we could try to salvage her life. They reduced the charges and Ginger received a second chance!Sometime later she met and moved in with a boy, and she was so happy, although they were struggling. We did what we could to help. In 2014, I was diagnosed with breast cancer and had to receive chemo treatments. One day, she showed up at my door and told me she wanted to stay with me to help, and that the boy had put her out. Ginger stayed with me for a while.

My husband told me there was something wrong; I told him no way she would do that. One night, there was banging at my door in the wee hours in the morning. I looked and there was a cop outside. I let him in and he told me Ginger had been found passed out in my car, with a needle in her arm! Once again, I went with my daughter to court, and discovered she had really never stopped the drugs. She was sentenced to outpatient rehab. I took her to meetings, trying to support her as much as possible.

My husband caught her stealing from us, and told me we had to put her out!! No way was I putting my child on the street! We fought for months over her! She met yet another boy, who seemed a little too clean cut, but who am I to judge? We had him over a few times for dinner and she met his family. I prayed all would be well.

My husband gave me a choice: either Ginger went or he did! Jesus, really? So, Ginger moved in with the boyfriend once again. We went over to Philadelphia to visit them, bring food or whatever, had them over for holidays and such. One day I received a call, "Ginger is missing!" I left work, ran home, called the police, and made a missing person report. A few hours later, she was found in jail, once again. Once again, I offered to take her to meetings and such...but she insisted she had to do this on her own.

The next call, I was not so fortunate. Her boyfriend called and told me he had found her in the bathroom, called 9-1-1, four doses of Narcan: "Get to the hospital." I had just got out of the hospital for heart surgery, but went to the hospital praying the whole way. Doctors and nurses all in the room...waiting...waiting. Moved her to ICU. "Let me spend one minute with her." I knew then there was nothing more they could do, but I prayed anyway. I don't remember much after that... just no brain activity...relieve the pressure.

Gift of Life people showed up, and told me she was an organ donor. I waited by her beside for what seemed like months, had a priest come and give her Last Rites, then made the decision to take her off life support. They confirmed brain death.

Ginger's Mom,

DEBORAH S.
Blackwood, New Jersey

Kathy

FOREVER 37

I'd like to tell you a little bit about my daughter, Kathy. She was born on January 10, 1980, in St Louis, Missouri. My labor was hard, but it was quick, and she was a beautiful baby. Big, blue eyes, she was so quiet and so good as a newborn, and as she continued to grow, she was still always so beautiful and that is something that people admired about her. But she was also so loyal and loving and funny and kind and smart. So really, she had a lot going for her. When she was nineteen, she met a guy and they started using drugs socially. I had no idea until one day, I saw her walking up the steps and I could see what appeared to be mosquito bites all over her ankles. It was then that she told me she had a drug problem. I was devastated; how could this happen to my little girl? I blamed myself. It must be because I left her dad.

Anyway, the years went by and Kathy met an older guy named Tim.

She married him and they had a beautiful baby girl who they named Hailey. I know she tried her best to be a good mom, under the circumstances. Her husband kept her supplied with her drugs, as much as she wanted, until it started affecting her emotionally. She began overdosing, so he took my little granddaughter and he moved away. Kathy was never to see her again. This devastated her and she began using drugs even more, all day long, every day. She got to the point that she stole for those drugs. She ended up going to prison.

When she was a toddler, my ex-husband and I had dedicated her to the Lord and when she was a teenager she got saved. But Kathy started using drugs before she grew in the Lord and didn't have the faith that she needed to overcome the abuse. None of us really knew how to help her, so I guess we distanced ourselves from her. Her emotions had become explosive. She was in and out of prison, all her life. She once told me that she would get herself in trouble in prison, so she could go to the hole, to be alone and read the Bible, hoping to get stronger and healthy. It never happened. My little girl was no longer somebody I recognized.

Two years before she passed away, I was in hospice with a heart condition, which God healed me from, so I couldn't let her live with me; my landlord wouldn't allow it anyway. However, she would come over and do my nails, comb my hair and rub my back; she said it made her happy to do things for me because she knew it made me happy. That was the kind of woman she was, however scared and worn she was from her drug abuse. For so many years she used men who would buy her drugs and buy her the things she needed, but as the years went by, life began to age her; she began selling her body for drugs and that threw her into a deep, deep depression and she hated what she had become. She had nothing, she had no one, her daughter was gone, her life was ruined, it would never be good. She told me that she would beg God to take her. She and I both knew that He would have to because she could never take her own life because of her faith, which actually gave me a lot of hope.

Kathy would come to visit me every Sunday. This particular Sunday, on October 22, 2017, she didn't come. Her boyfriend later called me and said, "Mom, Kathy's gone." I thought, she's only thirty-seven, how could she be gone? I began screaming and crying, asking, "Why God, please don't let this be true !!!!" As I hung up the phone, I received a call from her doctor telling me that while she was brain-dead, she was still alive physically, on life support, if we wanted to come and say our goodbyes.

I called my other daughter and my son. We went to the hospital together, met by other family members, and I kissed her all over her beautiful little face. It broke my heart, Kathy just lying there. But part of me thought, at least her mind isn't torturing her anymore. Her boyfriend told me that they went to bed, then she woke up and said she had to go to the bathroom. Later that morning he realized she had not returned to bed and he went to the bathroom and there she lay. It appeared that she had been dead for hours.

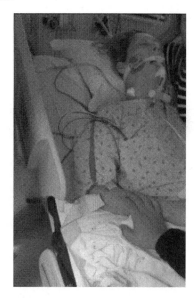

After several hours by my daughter's bedside, as I lay beside her singing to her, praying for her, kissing on her, my son on the other side of her, my oldest daughter standing by the bed crying, we went ahead and let them turn life support off. We were with her as she took her last breath; my daughter went home to be with Jesus. My life would never be whole again.

But the story doesn't end there because, as time went by and I would spend time in prayer and worship with the Lord, almost always begging Him to answer "Why?" I heard in an almost audible voice the Lord saying, "Kathy cried out to me and I took her."

Kathy's Mom,

SUE S.
O'Fallon, Missouri

Eric

FOREVER 37

Ever since the loss of my two kids, at times I just feel devastated with sadness and today is one of those days. I'd like to talk about my son, Eric. Today is his birthday he would have been thirty-nine. He passed away at the age of thirty-seven, almost two years ago. He was born on July 28, 1981, and man did I have a hard labor with him. But you know what they say: sometimes the hardest things bring about the greatest joy and that he did. My husband and I already had two girls and we were trying to have a boy. When we did, we were both mesmerized by every single thing he did. He was a boy's boy. He knew instinctively that he didn't like the toys his sisters played with; he liked trucks, guns and cars, baseball and eventually girls. Eric was a very witty young man; he had a lot of wisdom and he was captivating at times, well at least he was to me. He could always make you see the logic in anything and he always cared about the underdog. He was well-liked by everyone. He could walk into a room and it would light up with his smile.

He and his sister, Kathy, were very close. When she passed away October 22, 2017, of a drug overdose, it was hard for him to cope with her death. I didn't realize, but he had started dabbling in drugs himself. When I found out I could not believe it and I was furious. I called him and I said, "Eric what are you doing? Why would you use, when you know that that's what killed your sister? Why?" I went on to say I couldn't take it if he were to go too. He would look at me with his mischievous little smile and say, "Mom I'm not using drugs." I knew all along he was, but I invited him to move in with me. I told him that it would be easier for him to get back and forth from work, because it was closer and that way, he wouldn't be around all of his friends. As a mom you think you can help your child; the fact is I could never help Kathy, but maybe, I thought, I had learned something from Kathy's death. If I could keep him from going down that same path...I only needed to try, I thought. He could focus on work and his relationship with his girl-friend, and everything would be fine. But, that's not how it all went down.

Ten months and seven days after my daughter's passing, on September 1, 2018, my baby brother passed away. He had been on OxyContin for injuries he sustained and my son was really close to him, like a brother that he never had. So, between the death of my daughter and my little brother, I think my son just kind of lost hope. In hindsight, it didn't seem like he wanted to continue trying. On September 3, 2018, two days after my brother's passing, I didn't wake up until around noon because I'd been crying over my daughter all night, and my air condi-tioner went out, so it was hot. I really couldn't sleep. I came out to the living room. My son, he looked really bright and he was being very, very, loving to me.

He said, "Mom I'm making your favorite meal." He likes to cook, and so of course I would let him. Anyway, he made dinner and I ate, but he wasn't hungry. I guess he put his away for later. He and his girl-friend went outside to smoke after dinner. They were looking through their phones. I know because I could see them from the screen door and all of a sudden, my son came in and asked, "Mom can I take this fan in my room? I need to lay down for a minute." Of course, I said yes, because I could sense that something wasn't right. I asked him, "Eric, are you using again?" He looked at me with his beautiful, mischievous smile and he said, "No mom, I'm not using heroin."

But I had a feeling; I had a horrible feeling. He took the fan and went to his room. I couldn't hear his television go on or anything. It was awfully quiet. His girlfriend was still sitting out on the porch, which I found odd because she was the type of girl that followed him from room to room, even into the bathroom. That feeling just kept gnawing at me. Finally, after maybe ten minutes she came inside. She started washing a cup over and over and over again, and I asked her, "Amber, are you guys using again?" and she said, "No Mom." I told her, "I just have a horrible feeling. Will you please go in and check and see if Eric's okay? I haven't heard a sound in there."

So, she rinsed her cup and she went into the bedroom and again, I heard nothing. She did not come back out for maybe five minutes. I got up and Eric's dog Max ran ahead of me and he pushed open my son's bedroom door, and there he lay on the floor, and his lips were purple his girlfriend was sitting on top of him giving him CPR. I said, "Oh, no God, no," and she said, "Get out of here." For some reason I listened to her. I walked out of the room and I picked up the phone and I called 9-1-1. The police came and the ambulance came. I said, "Oh my son is dead. Please help, please!!!!" They took him from his bedroom and pulled him into the living room and were doing CPR.

I was commanding him in the name of Jesus to get up and walk. "Get up," I said, "Eric in the name of Jesus, honey, please don't do this to me." They made me and his girlfriend leave the house and I called my daughter, Shanna, and she came over. I called my boyfriend; I had to keep myself busy. I couldn't think about what they were doing inside my house. But how could I think of anything else? That was my son in there. Then a lot of my family members showed up. We all sat outside crying and praying, but it was all to no avail. There was no bringing Eric back. After a couple of hours, they brought my son out zipped up in a body bag. We all stood in a long line as they passed by us. We wanted to say our goodbyes.

The cops questioned each of us; they took his girlfriend aside and they questioned her. When they did, they found out something that infuriated me. They told me that earlier that morning his girlfriend said Eric had overdosed and she revived him with a can of Narcan. I was so angry that she didn't tell me so that maybe, I could have stayed with him, not let him go in that room. She said she was afraid I would make her move out and so I said, "No, I wouldn't have, but now I am. You have to go." I had no respect for her anymore. She may have saved his life had she told me. She was also a drug user, but she always tried to pretend like she wasn't. My son told me she was.

The day I went to visit my son's body for the first time after his death, for the last time as my baby boy, I was terrified to see him dead. Once I did, I couldn't help but hug him continuously. That whole night I never ever left the side of the casket. I couldn't. I didn't even want to leave when it was time to go because he was going to be cremated. I knew that would be the last time I would ever see my baby boy.

Eric was born on July 28, 1981. He left this Earth a grown man, at the age of thirty-seven on September 3, 2018. I kept his dog, Max, because he only adopted him the month before. He brought him home to my house and asked if he could keep him.

God would later show me that Max was a gift to me, because that dog and I stayed in my house all winter by ourselves. I even moved all of my things out of my bedroom and moved them into my son's bedroom. I slept on the very bed that he died in because I needed to feel close to him. I know that may seem strange to some people, but trust me, it's not. I still sleep there to this day. And I still have his dog, Max. He brought me such comfort, as I grieved my son's passing. I still grieve today; it comes in waves...I love you baby boy. Happy Birthday in Heaven...

Eric's Mom,

SUE S.
O'Fallon, Missouri

651

Brian

FOREVER 42

We should have known when this boy came into the world on November 24, 1976, in a mere thirty-seven minutes, weighing in at nine pounds, four ounces, and "baptizing" the delivery-room nurse, that we were in for the ride of our lives...and Brian didn't disappoint!

As a toddler, Brian was lovable, inquisitive, strong willed, challenging at times...always into some kind of mischief. We have a treasure trove of stories of crazy, funny things he said and did while growing up. He tested limits and was the first to try anything and everything, setting a not-so-great example for his older brother. He was colorful and lively...a unique little guy who won the hearts of everyone.

In high school, he played football and was an average student for the first two years. After meeting and dating the love of his life, who maintained a 4.0 GPA, he was inspired to raise his to the same level, graduating with honors. Brian tended to live life with "one toe over the line." He possessed inexhaustible energy and enthusiasm, a sometimes frustrating, inquisitive mind, and an unbridled passion to experience everything life had to offer. His smile and laughter were contagious, and he had a magnetism and charm that drew others into his circle (including children and animals).

He was the guy that lit up a room the moment he walked in. He was gifted with a sense of humor and ability to tell a story that were unmatched by anyone, and his compassion for others was beyond measure. If anyone needed help, Brian was there, no matter the hour of the day or night. He went above and beyond, from helping a friend at three a.m. with an on-line class, to driving 100 miles round trip twice a week during the summer to tutor a friend in calculus and physics.

He was always available with a kind heart, listening ear, unquestioning support, and helping hand. He would sit down on a curb next to a homeless person, listening to their every word, handing them everything in his wallet before leaving. He made certain that no one was ever left empty-handed or feeling alone, without a friend. Brian was not a thug, not uneducated, did not grow up with an abusive past, was definitely not lazy, and was certainly not unemployable (which is sadly some people's vision of an addict). This was not "karma" for a shady past... not something he "deserved." He had a wonderful childhood, with a loving family, including an older brother and younger sister, and several pets. He dated several girls and had a few long-term relationships over the years but never seemed interested in settling down.

He began experimenting with recreational drugs in high school and college (of which his dad and I had no knowledge; only his older brother and sister were aware). When we found out (via a phone call to my daughter from a friend of Brian's) that heroin had made its entrance into his life in 2010, we were all shocked and I was absolutely devastated; "not my child" immediately came to mind. Brian was in his 30's, blessed with an extremely good income at a very lucrative tech company in San Diego. He owned real estate, was a graduate of the University of Colorado with a degree in computer science, owned a nice car, joined a gym, worked out and biked regularly, and had a solid group of friends. He was kind and cared deeply about the welfare of others. We never once heard him speak ill of anyone. He believed in God, was a Christian, and attended church. He was extremely intelligent, requesting math books for Christmas and reading books about quantum physics for fun. It seemed he should have been "smart enough" to beat it.

These young people whose lives are hijacked and being taken far too soon by substance addiction are some of the kindest, most caring, generous, intelligent, and compassionate people ever created. I believe it's their highly sensitive nature that makes them easy targets when life gets too difficult. Brian respected, and enjoyed a close relationship with, his dad. They worked together for several years.

When his dad passed away in 2008 of a massive coronary, Brian spiraled downward and was never the same. Although we didn't have a clue, he had become addicted. Two years later, once we were aware, we tied it closely to his extreme sense of loss. We believe he turned to heroin to numb the intense pain, in the hope that life would be easier to bear. He was also unable to forgive himself for mistakes he had made, and his self-esteem plummeted. He became detached emotionally, stopped working out, and went "off the radar screen" for periods of time. He lost his job, was homeless for an extended period of time, and tried to take his life, but was miraculously spared. As a family, we tried everything to save him and help him rebuild his feelings of self-worth in the form of love and support, followed by lengthy periods of tough love. We then ultimately provided him with money and rehab.

We invited him into our homes to live (paying his airfare more than once to and from Colorado). We took him to doctor and therapy appointments, paid his rent for a couple of months, bought him groceries, and more than one cell phone. There was even a close friend who offered him landscape work until he could find another technical support position. Truthfully, we all enabled him to varying degrees, but I can honestly admit I would do the same thing all over again…he was my child and never seemed strong enough to seek the help he so desperately needed through the means of "tough love." Although it is highly effective with some, it just wasn't with Brian.

The most agonizing times during his addiction (for us and for him) were the weeks and months when we wouldn't hear from him, when he didn't show up for the job he loved, and no one had any idea where he was or that he was homeless, living in a park, eating who knows what, and to what degree he suffered with anxiety and depression. On one occasion when he had been out of touch for an extended period of time and hadn't reported for work, I was frantic, didn't sleep or eat, struggled with severe anxiety myself, and eventually filed a missing person's report.

After several weeks, I finally received a brief email from him, telling me where he was and that he was "NOT OK." I immediately flew to Colorado, had him admitted to the hospital, and after three days, he had detoxed and recovered. I brought him home with me to Texas. We spent time with my daughter and family. The Brian we knew emerged once again, and we felt confident things were headed in the right direction. After a month, he insisted on returning to Colorado to pursue work. Knowing that I couldn't force him to stay here, I paid his airfare back home. He temporarily did some landscape work for a friend, was then hired by a reputable financial institution in Denver, had found a place to live, and was ready to move forward.

He had been on Suboxone for a period of time, then qualified for an experimental, longer-lasting drug (a monthly injection of Sublocade) that would supposedly eliminate the craving for heroin, which thankfully it did for him, and he was eventually able to give it up. We felt he was on the right path…finally. Unfortunately, the start date for his new job was pushed back a couple of weeks. During that time, he turned to alcohol (which ultimately proved to be a fatal choice). We knew he was drinking heavily, but felt confident that as soon as he started the new job, he would feel a sense of purpose once more and give up the alcohol. He could rally at the drop of a hat if he was motivated, and we genuinely felt he was. We were out of touch for the three weeks leading up to his death. I thought he was preparing to move and getting settled prior to his start date for the new job and didn't want to bother him or "hover."

But on March 5, 2019, at one thirty a.m., I got that call no parent ever wants to receive. Brian had been found in his hotel room, appearing to have simply fallen asleep. The coroner's report indicated there were no illicit drugs in his system, only alcohol, caffeine, and a very small trace of an antidepressant. Over time, his drug and alcohol abuse had severely damaged his heart and liver. The COD was listed as "acute alcohol abuse."

Brian's story is not just about heroin. It's about addiction. Addiction is devastating, no matter what the substance may be. It heavily impacts and scars every member of the family, each and every day in ways and to a depth that cannot adequately be described. Every family member dies a slow death, along with their loved one, which is agonizing to witness and experience. As a mother, I believe that losing a child is the greatest tragedy and pain no one should suffer.

I miss Brian every day, but with a strong faith and the support of this wonderful Not In Vain support group of parents, who genuinely care and understand, I have managed to keep moving forward these past seventeen months, doing my best to live my life the way Brian lived his...for others, with compassion and generosity, without criticism or judgment. Yes, I have regrets...I wish we would have encouraged Brian to remain in rehab longer and that I had been in closer touch with him during his final three weeks. I even questioned for a long time if Brian had paid the ultimate price for my own past mistakes. But a quote I recently read from a book on grief provided some measure of peace. It was written as God's answer to the question, "Is God punishing me for my sins?" It reads, "I did not take your loved one to punish you, my child; I took them because it was best for them." I have been able to let go of that nagging question and am so thankful that Brian is no longer suffering on this earth, taking comfort in knowing I will see him again. I've always said I would gladly suffer in my children's place, and now...I am.

It's absolutely crucial that we all realize and take seriously the severity of this problem of epidemic proportions so that more lives can be saved through greater awareness, stricter laws, and harsher conse-quences for those who contribute to this cruel disease of addiction. I strongly feel that convicted dealers should be mandated to donate their illegal gain to funding affordable rehab facilities and sober homes that are so desperately needed. If Brian was here and could write his own story, I believe his message to those out there who struggle with addic-tion every day (or who are being tempted) would be:

YOU ARE NOT WORTHLESS OR ALONE. SAY NO TO A LIFE
YOU CAN NEVER GET BACK. ABSOLUTELY NO ONE IS
IMMUNE. DO NOT BE ASHAMED TO SEEK HELP NO
MATTER HOW MANY TIMES IT TAKES. DON'T GIVE UP.
DON'T EVER TOUCH IT. EVER. DON'T LET THE DEVIL WIN.

Brian touched each of our lives in unique ways that have been chiseled in our hearts and minds, to be cherished forever. I am incredibly thankful for the countless, priceless moments and experiences we all shared throughout his, all-too-brief, forty-two years on earth. And above all, I thank God for the priceless honor of being chosen as his mother. May he and all of our precious children, who have gone on before us, rest in peace until we see them again.

Brian's Mom,

Kathleen S.
Floydada, Texas

Morgan

FOREVER 25

Morgan suffered with anxiety around middle school. She was very shy. We discovered she was cutting herself and began therapy and some medication. The doctors started with an anti-depressant and then later began adding medications. I believe they just weren't educated enough on this issue. We saw a therapist for a couple of years.

When she began high school, Morgan would find people that shared their pills with her. Most were found in their parents' cabinet. It really scared me. It continued. We changed schools. She began to hide it well. Later, she met someone that provided it for her and she moved out. And it got worse. She turned to meth and heroin, as it was cheaper. I would have never even begun to think she would use a needle to shoot anything up.

Beyond what I thought about my daughter, Morgan was a beautiful, blonde-haired, green-eyed girl. Beautiful, inside and out. She came back home for help and began taking Suboxone. It changed her life. She had a beautiful baby boy and was healthy for a year and then she and the boyfriend started taking pills again. She quickly spiraled back to heroin.

After shutting the door on Morgan a few times, she checked herself into detox and then rehab, dragging herself all the way, but checking herself in. After six weeks, she was missing her baby and wanted a life for her family. She began getting lonely and wanted to meet new friends. She left the house for a few days and we got a knock on the door that she had died of a heart attack. What?! She wanted recovery. We thought we were into a new life and future.

The report came back; it included fentanyl. I never thought it would happen to my child. She was too smart. Six years of watching her struggle mentally and using drugs.

I miss those years of the real Morgan.

There needs to be more detox treatments. The pharmaceutical industry needs more research on mental illness. Six weeks isn't long enough in rehab. We need more awareness. We need to stop the stigma. Our children don't want to live that way. We need better, affordable programs. To the Addict: 1000's of beautiful lives have been lost. Families are left heart broken. We watched as our children slowly deteriorated as a person.

Many loved ones left suffer with trauma from battling their disease with them. Just don't try it. It will control you for the rest of your life. The addict slowly loses all hopes and dreams of reality, along with losing the ones that care the most about you. It's the hardest life I have ever seen. Addiction is hell on earth. Love, a broken-hearted mother.

Morgan's Mom,

KELLY S.
Acworth, Georgia

Brendon

FOREVER 26

Brendon was born on March 15, 1989 and passed on February 13, 2016, while withdrawing from heroin. He was only in jail three days, but he started withdrawing on day one.

While in jail, Brendon became sick. He wasn't able to eat, drink, or keep anything down. Brendon's hands started to become like claws from the withdrawal. He was taken to the nurse many times, but she would just have him taken back to his cell. On day three, he was really sick. He had diarrhea and tried to stay on the toilet. He soiled his pants, and had to take them off, but the nurse who watched him on the monitor told him to put his pants back on. He was so sick that he fell off the toilet twice, hitting his head on the ground. The second time he fell off, he rolled around a few times and died. He also lost a lot of weight in the three days he was there.

They chose not to help him at all. All Brendon needed was an IV!! They could have saved him, but they didn't. The hospital was only about three miles away. No doctor or other medical person at the jail cared about my son.

Brendon left behind two little girls, who at the time were two and nine years old; a niece who loved him; a girlfriend; a brother; mother; father and grandparents; the mother of his oldest daughter; aunts and other family members; and friends. The day after he got arrested, he was to start rehab, but chose to have one more fix.

Brendon was born in Front Royal, Virginia. He was just a delightful little boy, cute and lovable. Brendon and his brother were very close growing up. I am not sure when he started using drugs or what he started with. I do know that in his late teens, he was stealing my pain pills and money. He wouldn't stay in school. He was a landscaper by trade and proud of his work. Brendon was a loving and caring father and son.

His death has been really hard on his oldest daughter. She is now fourteen, and it just about killed her too. She has had counseling and has talked about wanting to die/kill herself. He'll never be here for birthdays, graduations, weddings, or grandkids.

Yes, Brendon, was an addict, but he was still a human being. And his life mattered. If it weren't for drugs, who knows how his life might have turned out. It's not just the addict who is affected by the drug usage.

Seeing him in the casket was unreal; it didn't look like him at all. He had lost so much weight. If it wasn't for some marks on his face or tattoos, I would not have believed it was him.

Getting the phone call was difficult. I had just driven sixteen hours through a snowstorm on the way to Myrtle Beach, had to turn around and drive back, and felt like the officer didn't care that my son had died, because he just blurted it out. He didn't even ask if I was driving or by myself.

It's been four years and it still seems like yesterday. The first year you think he's going to call or show up, out of the blue. The second year it became more real, but at the time I was working on getting justice for Brendon. Finally, after three years, we did get some justice for him. The nurse is still working somewhere and so are the jailers. The jail is still having problems with their employees.

All I can say is, drugs hurt everyone, not just the addict. They are human and addicts need help, not jail. Channel 9 out of Washington, DC, contacted my lawyer and wanted to do a story about Brendon. You can look it up! I haven't watched it. My lawyer asked me not to. It was hard enough sitting with my lawyers in court, hearing some of the things he went through, also seeing pictures and reading a report they had. It was a minute to minute account of his three days of hell. Please watch the video.

Brendon's Mom,

JOANIE S.
Linden, VA

Amber

FOREVER 25

Who can truly tell her story, but Amber? I can do my best to put together the pieces.

Amber is my youngest, of three kids. She has two older brothers. Amber was born by natural childbirth. She came into this world January of 1992 in Toledo, Ohio. She was a happy baby, who loved tons of attention. She had a dislike for sleeping alone. As a toddler, she escaped her bed often. We would find her sleeping at the end of her brothers' beds many nights.

Amber often escaped the back yard. She would climb the fence as a toddler. We ended up putting in a privacy fence, to keep her in the yard. She was not a frilly girl. I often joked, she dressed like a clown. She loved loud colors. Everything about them was a comfort for her. She took a brief interest in dressing up when she watched *The Little Rascals*. That was an adorable phase.

Amber's personality ran hot and cold. Her dad and I used to joke that she had split personality. She was either happy or mad; no in-between. She always gave it to people straight. She was incapable of running warm. We spent a lot of time shopping in her teen years. If I couldn't decide between two items, I'd just ask Amber. She always told me the truth. Both items are ugly, or "you dress like an old lady" was my favorite. Sometimes she liked an item and later borrowed it. Shopping became unbearable after her passing. How do I choose the right one now?

Amber played a lot of sports all through grade school. She played softball for four years. She played soccer for three. She was really good at sports, which was a surprise, since she could trip on air. Amber was a very clumsy girl. Amazingly though, she had complete control over a soccer ball and a softball.

Amber was a very loyal, loving girl. Amber had an enormous heart. She spent a lot of time helping her friends and family. She loved animals. We had a Chihuahua, Chewy, when she passed. That dog would growl at me if I told her to do something. Amber would laugh and say, "Tell her, Chewy." Chewy would steal her food while she played on the phone. The dog would also spend his evenings going back and forth between her bed and mine. Chewy would growl at you when you moved at night. So, Chewy got kicked out of bed a lot. He'd get kicked out of my bed and move on to Amber's.

Chewy would never leave her side when she was sick. A few times while Amber was detoxing herself she told me she was just sick. She would be in bed sick for a week. That dog laid right with her. He always knew when she was dope sick.

When Amber passed, Chewy looked for her for exactly sixty days. He was hit by a car out front, looking for her. I had to carry his dead body to his dog bed. I literally had a nervous breakdown. We buried Chewy under Amber's window, by the wild onions. He loved to roll in those wild onions. My baby wanted her dog. Chewy is home. Amber has her dog now. I imagine Amber and Chewy walking along the beach. This is my new reality. This is my baby's home, a beautiful white home by the beach.

Her smile, pure sunshine. Amber had a big, full smile. Her smile ran from her eyes all threw her body. She lit a room up. I used to joke I could have bought a car for what that perfect smile cost me (braces). It was so worth it.

School was always easy for my daughter. She excelled in math and science. Her reading skills were phenomenal. Academics were never a struggle for Amber. She graduated from high school in the spring of 2010.

Her senior year was a challenge. She became defiant and crossed many lines, skipping classes and going in late. She had different friends. She took little interest in school; A's and B's went to C's and D's. I chalked it up to, "I'm 18 now." I realize, now, it was the beginning of depression.

Amber loved being with the family. She always came to holidays and birthdays. For one thing, the girl never missed a free meal. She also adored all her cousins. We had a lot of little ones in our family. Amber told me the last month of her life that all she really wanted was to be a mom and wife. She could be anything, but this was her heart's desire. It amazed me that in a time when my daughter had the world at her feet, she picked the most important job. I raised a beautiful soul.

I became aware my daughter had a pill problem in the spring of 2015. She would be dead by summer of 2017, from fentanyl. Amber started using pills, Percocet, at the age of twenty-three. She was addicted. Her personality took on different traits. She became angrier, less attentive to her grooming. She let her bills go months without payment. This was so out of character for my daughter. This behavior went on for close to a year.

The fighting was horrible between us and Amber's family. She started to lie and steal from the entire family. The spring before she passed, she stole her brother's car while he was sleeping. She was pulled over that night. Her brother was told he would have to file charges on his sister or be charged himself for allowing an unlicensed driver to drive his car. She would, in the end, be sentenced to ten days, which she would never serve. She died the day she was due to report to jail.

She continued to receive traffic violations in every small community surrounding us. Amber was in a car accident her senior year. She was in the hospital for a week. This was Amber's first long-term exposure to pain medication. I asked if this was the start for her. She always told me no. This was the start of her behavior change from my view. These traffic violations added up to a point suspension. Amber would have no driver's license the last year of her life. She was pulled over and charged with speeding in the Spring of 2015, and this is when we first learned of her using. She had a Percocet on her. I was called at work, by the Toledo police, who informed me that my daughter was being arrested for possession of a controlled substance and I needed to go get her car.

I arrived and a very kind detective informed me of the place she came from and person she was with. This was all drug related and we're not talking some marijuana. I'm not even sure what half the drugs are that this detective was telling me are being sold. I thought I knew something.

Later, I picked up my daughter from jail. Amber informed me she has a pill problem. She continued to inform me that she isn't dumb enough to do white china. She also informed me she will not be getting help; she doesn't need it. All I'm thinking is, "What the hell is white china?" GREAT, my kid is addicted to pills and she's fine with it. She's twenty-three years old. I have no damn control over her. She was put on probation. I was so happy. I thought finally she has to face all this. She did. She played the game. Her next drug charge, an overdose of fentanyl/heroin, December 14, 2016. She survived. Life is good. SHE is getting help. She's doing it for real. This is real. Is it real? Please GOD, is it real? My God, my baby is using heroin.

I will never forget the ride home from the ER. Amber is sitting next to me; her dealer is in my back seat. I'm taking him home. He called the ambulance. He went to the hospital with her. He was offered a treatment program also. I drop off the drug dealer; we drive to the expressway. I ask my daughter, "Does she believe Jesus died on the cross for her sins." I need to know. If anything happens to her, I need to know she's home when I die. She answered, "Yes." My soul was at peace.

Amber overdosed in December at the hospital I work at. I clocked out early that day. I told my boss the truth. He knew my daughter had a problem. I had to leave work earlier that year. Interestingly enough, there were other co-workers in my situation. The first thing I did when I saw my daughter was hold her. I told her, "Nowhere to go but up baby." She just cried. I held her. It had been almost a year since she had let me touch her. She was in so much pain. This addiction runs so deep. Everyone is screaming with pain in total silence with the fear and shame this disease brings. Time to find your voice; speak your words of pain.

The last few years of Amber's life she spent helping her friends. She got involved with guys that were addicted to pills and heroin. They would end up in jail. Amber would try to keep in contact, put money on books at jail. I think she tried harder than the guys did at times. I felt it beat her down. It was disappointing and a lot for a young adult to handle. Her pain was pouring out of her. We have this great intervention unit, instead of jail. It's called the Dart Unit. They step in. Amber is offered help. It's amazing. She is guided in all the right directions.

Amber actually did seek treatment on her own during the summer of 2016, before the December overdose. She was turned away from many treatment facilities. Amber made too much money for state insurance. My health insurance actually covered nothing in this area.

Amber was actually functioning in her addiction. She worked a lot. Her job didn't offer insurance. This was Amber's saving grace. When Amber had the Dart Unit open doors for her, she went to detox the night she overdosed. We were never charged for this. It was her first blessing. Amber left detox and at first it seemed liked we lost her again. She came home and stole her roommate's mom's car. She was gone for a week. She finally brought that car back. The next week, she takes her roommate's car to pick up her check. She is speeding and gets another ticket. This turns into a felony. You ask why? She took her handcuffs off in the police car. This is interfering with an investigation. She will now spend the last six months of her life fighting a two-year charge.

I sold our home in the Spring of 2017. My hope was to move Amber with me. Amber came to live in the new home the last ninety days of her life. Amber's last summer, she started drug treatment. She was doing better. She had a private counselor that seemed to help a lot. We were talking about everything. I told her I looked for her on those streets. I told her, "I made your friends tell me what was going on." I took care of some of them. I called on them to return a favor. She was relieved, I think, that I still adored her. Nothing could stop me from loving her. We seemed to be finding her again.

Late April of 2017, Amber started dating a new guy. He was a drug dealer. He had just got out of jail. My daughter was under the impression he was recovering. This guy was turning his life around, as she was.

In June of 2017, my daughter had come home to live with me. She

667

had left her roommates. She did steal his car, twice. She was staying with the new guy. The new guy is not trying to turn his life around. He is still selling dope. He has now hit her. He tore up a purse he gave her. She was actually using the purse when he did this. My daughter brought her things home in a little garbage bag. He also picked a fight with her public defender, so now she has no lawyer. This is for her felony case.

Amber needs a $5,000 lawyer. Oh, he has got her a lawyer. He is trying to buy her. Amber is sick over all of this. She is not a girl to take money from a guy. She earns her own money. She tries calling the public defenders' office, with no luck. She tells me this guy has filed a complaint against her public defender. She ends up using the boyfriend's lawyer, with the agreement to pay him back. Amber's last summer, she served two five-day jail sentences, one for driving without a license, the second for violation of probation, smoking marijuana.

She spent her summer in outpatient treatments. She was so proud. The beginning of July, she announced she was six months clean. Amber asked if I was proud of her. "Yes," I answered; I was so proud. In fifty-two days, she would be dead. I never stop thinking of that day.

Amber spent her summer dating this guy on and off. She always came home at night. I asked her about this one day. She stated he sold dope in the evenings and she could not be around it. They had a horrible fight about this in July. I received a call from this guy to come get my daughter before he hurt her. When I arrived, my daughter was cut, bruised, and bleeding. He, of course, was nowhere to be found. I had to pick my daughter up at the corner gas station. He took her belongings. I wanted to take her to the ER, but she refused. A police report was taken at the gas station. The police saw her injuries, took a report, but couldn't do anything without her going down and filing charges on him. She refused; she was afraid. This was July 21, 2017. All I can think is, this guy is not right. This is a big problem. He's going to kill her. She's afraid. What is going on here? She will be dead in thirty days.

June and July of 2017, there would be many more occurrences with the new guy. He would bring flowers, a dozen roses, for Amber. Cards and dinners would follow his angry outbursts. I remember receiving a call in July from Amber to come pick her up at the new guy's house. We were doing yard work, so I ordered her a ride home. The new guy sends the ride away. He calls to tell me he isn't letting her come home. We have to pay him a hundred dollars because he paid a court fine of hers. He wants this money for her. I inform him he can have his money, but I'm not buying my daughter. I will be sending the police. He agreed to let her go home.

It's the end of July; I realize my daughter is using pills again. I talk to her about this. She listens to me, no response. A few days later she tells me she would like to look into inpatient or outpatient drug treatment. She would like to enter when she finishes her ten-day jail sentence, which is coming up soon. I let my daughter know I will support and help her with this decision.

August 2017, the last twenty-one days of my daughter's life were spent in our new home. She told me if anything ever happened, to look to the new guy. Never believe the new guy! She talked about a lamp she broke and blamed a young toddler named Kevin. She told me about her favorite Disney movie, *Aladdin*. She talked about who she was before the addiction. She talked about her traumas. Talked about all her friends. She talked about boyfriends. She told me to start being a mom again to her ex-boyfriend. He was in trouble, and needed someone. She was setting the world right. I felt her life was in danger. I also felt so close to her.

The week before Amber died, the new guy came to my home, August 16, 2017. He and Amber were talking in her room. My daughter runs into the living room, I hear glass break. The new guy breaks the dresser mirror. He has her phone that was just fixed. He broke her phone a few weeks ago. I reach for it but he pulls it out of my hand. He has blood dripping all over his hands. My daughter is standing in a corner. The new guy has a friend in a car outside. I now have to calm this guy down. The new guy shouts threats to her, me, and my family. I focus all on him. Big ego, I understand this guy. I need to get him out of here. It takes about an hour of listening to his nonsense to get him out of my home. After he leaves, Amber and I head straight to bed. We agree to talk about it later. Thursday morning, we both head to work.

We both came home Thursday evening. She tells me the new guy wants to pay for her mirror. I end up ordering it that day. We are unable to talk that day. Amber wants to sleep. She has to work early. I agree we will talk tomorrow. This entire day, the new guy has been calling her. She has been ignoring him. He even called me while I was working to say he was sorry. He hoped Amber would forgive him. I only told him I stand with my daughter, whatever she decides. I hoped she would get out before he killed her, were my thoughts.

Friday afternoon, my daughter ends up working with two of her aunts and her grandma. She works for a cleaning company. It's a big job today. At lunch, my daughter accidentally locks her grandma's keys in the car, so her grandpa has to come get the keys out. This would be the last time any of them would see her. They were all so glad for this day, small mistakes we're so thankful for. I remember my aunt dropping her off that day, laughing about the keys. I was in her room still cleaning up glass. I had to pick up the new mirror that day, and put the replacement piece in. We lied to her aunt, because I didn't want to explain the new guy just yet.

Amber was to begin serving her jail sentence on Monday. I did not want to cause too much stress with her. She still was not talking to the new guy. She was going to drug rehab, after jail, so I felt like she was making some good choices.

Amber had dinner, watched some T.V., and went to bed around ten p.m. that evening. She was sad and nervous. How I wanted her to get past this. I was thinking, "Next summer baby, you will be so happy." Next summer she would be dead.

On Saturday morning, the new guy drops off a dozen roses and a card. She loves the flowers. Just great…all I can think is, "I'm throwing them in the trash as soon as I drop her off at jail on Monday." She says to me, "I almost threw them away." She says they're pretty, and that no one has ever given her so many flowers. I think, "Yes they have," then I think she must mean boyfriends. Now I'm sad. This new guy gives her all these beautiful flowers. But the cost is way too high.

Later, that evening we have a bonfire out back. I invite my daughter to join us. She declines.

I find her later that evening, about nine thirty p.m. in the driveway sitting in a car, talking with someone. I assumed she was talking to the new guy. She went in the house around ten thirty p.m. and went to bed.

Sunday is the big day. Amber has jail tomorrow. She requested sausage and gravy. We make her this big meal. She also informs me the new guy is picking her up today. I say okay. What can you do? I remind her she has a job today at four p.m. She tells me to meet her there today. I help her on Sunday. I agree to meet her at four p.m.

Later that day, I meet up with Amber. She requests to be dropped back off with the new guy when we're finished; I agree. I tell her, just call tonight or tomorrow for us to pick her up for court, unless the new guy would be taking her, but I never counted on him.

I drop her off, make a little joke about *Forrest Gump*, we had just watched that. I watched her walk up to the door, do this little hop, skip. I had an overwhelming need to go back to hug and kiss her. This is the last time I would see her alive.

Sunday, August 20, 2017. How I wish, every day, I turned that car around and hugged and kissed her.

When I get home, her brother is waiting to see her. He knows she has jail tomorrow. He wants to spend some time with her. He hangs out till around one a.m. I go to bed around eleven p.m. We expect, maybe, Amber will call for a ride.

Around midnight, I have this overwhelming need to call her. Keep in mind she has no phone. I have to call his phone. I'm thinking, "No, she will call." So, I fall asleep.

I wake up at five a.m. for work. Amber stayed at his house. I'm not sure I like this. Should I go over there; should I make sure he's taking her to jail? Will they answer the door this early? What can I tell work? If I'm late, it will be a problem with work. Great!! So, I go to work. I feel something is not RIGHT.

I arrive at work Monday, August 21, 2017.

I text his phone around seven thirty a.m., asking if he's taking her to jail. I hear nothing. I get busy at work. She is very heavy on my mind.

Around 1:40 p.m., my phone has a bunch of texts on it. I was working up front and didn't have my phone. I respond to my phone at 1:45 p.m., The new guy tells me Amber is hurt and to come to the hospital. I ask what hospital. He tells me. I already know, it's bad. My body has been screaming for hours. I know she's gone.

Its forty-five minutes to get to her. I go alone; I call no one. I arrive in the ER parking lot and there is the new guy. I get out of my car. He walks up to me, says she died, and they have kicked him out. I start punching him, then I walk right for the ER. I have to get to her. My baby is alone. There must be a mistake. She just needs her mom.

I walk into the ER and he follows me. I'm shaking, I want to run through there and find her. I ask the lady at the desk for Amber. She asks me to wait. I'm taken to a waiting room, he follows me. The doctor asked me to step into a private room to talk. They ask me what I know. I state she had drug issues. I need to know what happened today! It appears she overdosed and went into cardiac arrest. They couldn't save her. She passed at 1:44 p.m. They are waiting on toxicology reports. She was given Narcan four times. It revived her for a minute. She never woke again. She did receive last rites with the pastor. I just wanted to see her.

I was taken to the far end of the ER. Here, my daughter lays on a silver bed with a white sheet draped over her body. The tubes still in her throat, her hands at her sides, tucked in the white sheet. Her hair flowing back behind her. She was not sleeping. She was gone. Amber was gone. How I wanted to rip off that sheet, pull her up, and wrap her in my arms.

It's in investigation now. Your child is evidence now.

I could feel her spirit was gone. I could also feel my grandfather with me. I walked up to her and touched the part of her hand that was exposed. It was warm, lightly cool. She had been gone an hour.

I wanted to fall on the floor. I did not want to stand; I wanted to lay in a ball and die with her. I could not move from her. I had to stand. I just cried why, why, what happened? There were nurses, doctors, pastors, and the new guy surrounding me.

I caught the nurse, out of the corner of my eye, crying. I felt bad, in that moment, for her. She was not much older than my Amber. I can't imagine the trauma this must put on your soul to try and save so many drug overdoses.

I asked the pastor to pray with me. We prayed over my dead daughter. I stood over her crying for thirty to forty minutes.

The ER doctors kindly informed me they would need the operating room she was in. I would need to decide what funeral home to move her to, or keep her at the morgue. This is way too much. I cannot have her at a morgue. This makes me crazy. I have her at a funeral home in one day, thanks to family.

I'm also told I will need to talk to the police. I tell the doctor I'm eager to speak with police. Seems police were searching the new guy's house. Amber overdosed at his home. The ambulance was called at one p.m., she died at the hospital at 1:44 p.m. No drugs were ever found. The new guy claims that he just got home and found her that way. You see, the new guy was in jail. He was arrested at midnight due to a warrant. He claims the police bumped into him at his carryout and asked who he was.

The rumor, I hear, was that the police were called out to his home for fighting, and loud noises. Then, they picked him up for his warrant. The new guy claims she was dead when he got home Monday. He said she overdosed during the night. The detective on Amber's case called me a few days later. He stated she overdosed shortly before the ambulance came, not that night. The detective also told me he believed it was a fentanyl overdose and he is waiting on toxicology reports. Since the new guy's house was clean, they cannot prove where the drugs came from. They do know the new guy's history with drugs, but will not discuss the case with me.

Amber's celebration of life was on August, 26, 2017. This was my cousin's birthday. She died on my other cousin's birthday. Her grandma's, my mom's, birthday is August 27. I was having a birthday that year on the twenty-sixth, the day of Amber's funeral. It's a day my family will remember. Dates are a funny thing; they can bring joy and grief. Just numbers on a calendar.

Amber was cremated. Her remains were put in a zebra urn. She loved zebra prints. Her urn is in her room with her pipi, my dad, her dad, and her niece. People joke it's a little cemetery. My dad passed away six months after Amber. He died of cancer. Amber's dad died fourteen months after she passed. He had a heart attack in his sleep. Her niece passed at nine days, three years before her. She also has a nephew that passed five years before her.

The service was nice. I was numb. I have no idea how I made it. I honestly believe God carried me. My feet did not touch the ground that day. The worst part was leaving at the end of the service. This was the last time I would see her. I could not stand leaving her at the hospital. Now I have to leave her for good. When I return, she will be in an urn. GOD, why! Where is my daughter???

I leave, I take a balloon, I release it with her friends. Now go to dinner. You can do this. Make your baby proud. The dinner is at my old elementary school and church. Amber went there for a while. I go swing on the swings; my brother joins me. We don't talk, just swing.

I finally go into church for dinner. I see the pastor. I have to go speak to him. I need to know, why? I speak with the pastor. Asking the question we all want answers to, why?? His response was Jesus saw that she was ready, so he took her. He said he feels Jesus knows when the time is right. I will know more when I meet Jesus. This of course didn't make me happy. He only gave me twenty-five years with her. But I am so thankful for those twenty-five years.

I cannot imagine a world without Amber. My heart cries out every day for you.

Amber, I hope in writing this, your passing was not in vain. I hope that others fighting addiction will be sparked by you. I hope if you're fighting addiction, you know how incredible you are. You, my friend, are a hero. You are valued. I pray for each and every one of us fighting addiction.

I pray no parent will stand over the coffin of their child. I know you always think it's not your child. For me it was less than a year. My daughter was functioning and appeared to be healthy. For a while she even seemed happy.

Amber's toxicology report came back in October. It showed Amber was killed with fentanyl. It's called an overdose in Ohio. The new guy Amber was dating died thirteen months after Amber. He was shot in the leg in front of his home. He bled to death. He was thirty years old. No one was charged with Amber's death. All we know is she used it before p.m. on Monday, August 21, 2017. She was with the new guy and no drugs were ever found.

I have learned a lot over the past five years. The system is not set up to help addicts. A lot of Amber's arrests were drug related, drug seeking. She could have spent her time in drug units, not in jail doing nothing. I believe in education and reform. Amber was very smart. You want to help her, address the addiction. Seems to me jail does not address addiction, drug reform, or help with job skills. Instead, we have people like the new guy leave jail, and remain a dope dealer and user.

New guy is dead now too. But only after he sold poison.

There needs to be more drug counselors added into the judicial system. I feel this would lead to more success.

Honestly, as a parent, I do not know what to tell another parent. I just loved her. Amber always needed to be looked at. That was her thing as a baby. So, I gave her the thing she needed most. You know what your child needs. So that's how you handle it.

We openly talked about addiction in my family. Amber and I talked about her addiction. She said she prayed I never felt this sick when she withdrew. I knew it was bad. Amber did not complain about much. She said she could not live like this. It was bad. It was painfully clear.

It was a surprise to all of us when she overdosed. I knew she started using pills in July. To this day, I do not know what happened. The truth died with the new guy.

What I do know is that I live without my SUNSHINE every day. Her name is Amber...

Amber's Mom,

DAWN S.
Toledo, Ohio

Mitchell

FOREVER 24

Mitchell had been struggling with addiction since he was fifteen. I would convince him to go to rehab and then the next day, he would exit himself out.

In February of 2019, he called telling me he couldn't walk and said that he was going to the hospital. After he talked to the doctor, he found out it was serious and he was scared.

They needed to do surgery on his leg or else he was going to lose it. His organs were also shutting down. They were able to save his leg.

He spent eight days in critical care, and five days in a "regular" room. That was a very scary time for me. He went over a year being clean from that scary episode, and then on May 6, 2020, I got the worst news ever. It was my youngest son.

"Mitchell's dead, Mitchell's dead." He did CPR on him until the paramedics showed up. He then went in the bathroom and threw up.

This isn't anything we should have to be going through. This is so painful for all of us. I'm back to work now and it's hard. I just pretend that I'm fine, but deep down I am hurting. I just want this pain to go away.

Mitchell's Mom,

Louise T.
Bellevue, Michigan

Melissa

FOREVER 33

If walking over hot coals would have saved my daughter, I would have walked over those coals. If I could have robbed a bank to save her, I would have robbed all the banks. That's not how life, and especially addiction, works. There is pain and suffering mixed with laughter and tears. Melissa loved hard, was a faithful, helpful, compassionate friend who cared deeply, was a lot of fun, and had a great sense of humor. She got stuck in addiction. The fallout is pain, suffering, loss, death, and grief.

My story of loving a drug addict began on May 26, 1985, when my daughter was born in Hartford, Connecticut. It was Memorial Day weekend, Sunday, and she was the most beautiful baby I have ever seen. At birth she was placed on my belly and promptly pooped on me. I think this was an omen! I was a nervous new mother, and I truly believe she picked up those "vibes" before birth and they manifested more deeply as she grew. Two and a half years later, her baby brother joined us. She adored him, helped with him, and looked out for him, until she was about eleven or twelve, when the sibling rivalry kicked in.

Melissa was my sidekick, my "Mini-Me," and I took pride in that. She was a little nervous and always wanted to be with me and help me. She was a sweet, sensitive, caring girl who got lost while trying to have fun and be strong. She always liked music and dancing, reading, and had a soft spot for all animals. Stressors grew as her alcoholic father and I divorced when she was five years old. We parted amicably and lived near each other. I am sure that change contributed to a sense of fear and instability in Melissa. Yet, she excelled in elementary school, received recognition for academic achievements, and was an altar server in our local church. Despite her nervousness, she was quite strong-willed.

There were times of hardship and loss that would upset any sensitive young girl. In 1995, on Melissa's tenth birthday, we lost a dear friend, who was a second mother to me and very close to Melissa, from ovarian cancer. In December 1996, we lost Melissa's paternal grandfather. In May 1997, her maternal grandfather died and we learned her maternal grandmother had dementia. Blessedly, Melissa was still very close to her paternal grandmother, a warm, loving, picture-perfect Grandmother! In 1998, the kids and I moved from their hometown eighty miles away to be closer to my disabled sister and mother. This was particularly hard on Melissa, as she was just turning thirteen and entering middle school.

Shortly before we moved, I became aware that Melissa had been stealing mail from mailboxes looking for money. I found several checks hidden in her room. I demanded she write letters of apology to those people and return the checks with her letters, which she did, begrudgingly. Our move turned out to not be a positive one. The man I had planned to marry, with whom we lived, disregarded my parenting rules, and taught the kids to undermine me. At the end of 1999, the kids and I moved to our own condo, in the same town, keeping them in the same schools. Melissa was a very bright and sensitive girl, and had difficulty finding the right group of kids for her. She ended up with the one group that reached out to her and befriended her: The Misfits. This group accepted her, enjoyed her sense of humor, and opened the door to risky behavior. At fifteen, Melissa came home from a party drunk. We discussed the dangers of alcohol, and more importantly, the need for a young lady to always maintain control over her own body, so no one else would gain that control. I believed she understood. I would be proven wrong.

In high school, Melissa made some new, less risky friends, and was a life guard. She drank a little on weekends, but I didn't over worry about it. I drank through high school and college and I didn't become addicted. She was "Mini-Me," she would be okay too. She did well in her classwork. Her moods were challenging at times. She could talk her way out of a paper bag…and I fell for a lot of her stories. Heading into junior year, Melissa asked to go to a private, Catholic, all-girl high school. I was surprised, but she explained that she could learn better because classes were smaller, no "boy" distractions, and her best friend was going. It made sense to me. (I learned twelve years later the move to this school was because her girlfriend's boyfriend had raped Melissa.) During this time, she was also in psychotherapy (which she stopped at age eighteen). She did well at the private school, starting their first Dance Club, and graduating with good grades. Then it was off to college. She was a resident student for the first semester.

Then the world started to crumble. December 2003, at age eighteen, Melissa was first arrested on a drug charge. I was shocked, devastated, scared, and heartbroken. I had no idea she was so deep into drugs that she could be arrested. She was very good at hiding things from me and letting me know only enough to keep me satisfied and to not look bad in my eyes. (Years later, she told me about the popular, influential business people she partied with in our town. To say I was appalled is a total understatement.) January 2004, she went to her first of nine rehab programs. She was broken and swore she would do better. She cried about a lady in her forties who was there and lost everything: family, children, home. Melissa said, "Oh Mommy, I don't want to be like her." I told her it was up to her to NOT be that woman, and I believed she could do it. It was that rehab that encouraged me to find an Al-Anon meeting. This program, based on the 12 Steps of Alcoholics Anonymous, truly saved my life, and helped me through the many stages and fears of my daughter's addiction. It taught me excellent life lessons, the most important being that I could NOT save my daughter, despite my love for her, and that I didn't cause her addiction, I couldn't control it, I couldn't cure it, but I could contribute to it. And I did, unknowingly.

The next fifteen and a quarter years saw my daughter sink into the world of drugs, strip clubs, ER visits, arrests, multiple rehabs, two abortions, and prison. Her behavior forced my son to move out of the house when he was sixteen because she and a boyfriend threatened to hurt him. I lived in constant fear of more arrests or her dying. I felt like a failure and totally responsible for her outrageous behavior, and at one time I was truly afraid to be alone with her. The last time I posted bond for her (2008), the bail bondsman told me my daughter was very smart. I felt proud…until he said, "She's too smart for her own good and that will be her downfall." Those were very prophetic words. The arrests and rehabs continued. Her primary drug of choice became heroin. She kicked it while in prison for two and a quarter years. After prison, she relapsed, recovered, and then turned to alcohol. With a very high tolerance for alcohol, she could drink a lot and not appear drunk, however, it was destroying her body. In December 2018, she returned to heroin.

Her final dose was laced, illegally, with fentanyl. She died alone in her car a block from her home on the evening of Wednesday, April 3, 2019. I learned of my daughter's passing at 11:32 that night when I received the call I had feared for fifteen years. The ER doctor told me my daughter had been brought in to the hospital unresponsive. Efforts to revive her were unsuccessful and her heart failed. Autopsy results showed a .285 alcohol level, anti-depressant medication, heroin, fentanyl, and carfentanyl. It was the latter that killed her. She did not want to die. She just wanted to feel better, ease her pain, and silence her demons. She didn't want to use, but she couldn't stop. It owned her.

Melissa's addiction was a nightmare: from the wild, always changing behaviors; to the manipulation, the lying, and the regret. Yet, she continued to teach me and I continued to love her. And there were also moments of enlightenment: through her addiction I learned that my father, her paternal grandfather, aunt, and uncle were all alcoholics. I do wish I had understood the depths of my daughter's psycho- emotional condition and her genetic predisposition to alcoholism in the beginning. I did what I thought was right. I tried to help her, to support her in health, but not in addiction…sadly, that can be a fine line. I believed in my daughter and that she would overcome this…she did several times, but was always pulled back. She was very strong, but not strong enough. I always believed in her potential. During periods of sobriety, she received an associate's degree, became a certified drug and alcohol rehab counselor (she wanted to help other people like her), and was one semester away from achieving a bachelor's degree in psychology, her dream since high school.

I was naive. Addiction is bigger than my love for her and her love for herself. Addicts are amazingly sensitive and very good at manipulation. They know what to say and how to act, so no one suspects they're using...until they can't any more. I lived with the pain of helplessness, heartache, and frustration every day. That heartache continues today. Migraine headaches, sleepless nights, hopelessness, anger, self-recrimination, and constant worry were a way of life. I was living to help her. Once I learned I cannot save my daughter from her addiction, I became stronger and more aware of what I needed to do to save myself. No one can save an addict. They need to save themselves. That sounded so selfish in the beginning, but is very true. The hardest thing to accept was that I could NOT save my beautiful baby girl, and letting go to let her follow her path was what I had to do. It is the hardest thing I've ever had to do. Yet, I stood by and helped where appropriate, and loved her through it all.

Some of my experiences with Melissa are beyond horrifying: the car wrecks, the arrests, the stealing, breaking house rules, the lies, the manipulating, the anger, the name-calling, prison, nine different rehabs, and the truly horrible things she said to me that no parent should ever hear from their child. Fifteen months after her death, I am still brought to my knees from the pain, helplessness, and regret. Until I gained the strength to stand up and say, "No more," I was always there. Even then I was there, but not directing her. Yet, she was more than just an addict. She was my daughter with an innate wisdom that was far beyond her years. She helped me learn and become a better person. She pointed out some of my questionable behaviors, which taught me a better way to be. I changed my behavior in an effort to teach my kids better and to build healthier relationships based on love and respect than I had been taught. In many ways, she was my alter ego.

Addicts are very complicated and sensitive people. Melissa did NOT choose to become an addict. She merely wanted to ease the emotional pain embedded in her mind. No one wakes up and decides, "I think I'm going to become an addict." It just happens. It's something people slip into by accident…some people are just "wired differently" and Melissa's physiology didn't allow her to be a casual user. Instead, the drugs quickly ruled her. Some people are more susceptible to addiction, just like some people are more susceptible to other illnesses. She was a good, loving person with a disease, substance abuse disorder.

Addiction is a disease, not only of the mind, but of the spirit and of the body. It not only affects the individual with the disease, it also affects everyone who cares about that individual, and everyone that individual cares for. It's a magnet, and we, as parents, think we have the power to break that magnetism. The sad truth is we don't. We can only save ourselves. We have to let our children find their own way to save themselves. I believed, and had faith, she would overcome this. And she did a few times, for various lengths of time. We all have choices in this world. Some people, like my daughter, make poor choices. Having a child die is against the law of nature and losing a child to addiction is devastating and horrifying. No parent should ever have to endure it. There is no pain greater.

Grief is a process and we each experience and process it in different ways. It is not something one "gets over." It lasts as long as we last. Watching your child go down this path of self-destruction is the most excruciating experience a parent can imagine…let alone live through. It is a roller coaster ride not for the weak of heart…and really NO parent should have to endure the pain, the helplessness, the struggle, the attacks, the ineptness of not knowing what to do. Reaching out for support, guidance, and understanding to those who have walked this path before you makes the journey a little bit easier. Knowing you are not alone is soothing and comforting. Walk away from those who say, "Get over it," or "This too shall pass," and connect with those who know and have preceded you on this journey. Only those who experience a death of an addicted child know or understand the deep all-encompassing grief, the range of emotions, the thoughts, the regrets, hurt, resentment, blame, shame, "Woulda-coulda-shoulda, what if, and if only," all of these really disastrous thoughts that eat away at me.

My biggest regret is not recognizing and understanding her deep sensitivity as a child. Had I understood, things may have been different. Many people have given me advice as to what I should do or should have done. Nobody knows until they walk in another's shoes. I know

Melissa did not intend to die from that last dose of heroin. She did not know it was laced with fentanyl. She just wanted to feel better, to feel "normal." Still, the result is the loss of a beautiful girl with untapped potential. I had feared "that call" for so long; to actually receive it was, in a very weird way, a relief. She is at peace. Her struggles against the demons that lived in and controlled her mind are over.

Now, fifteen months after she transitioned, I try to focus less on the pain and more on the beautiful, happier memories we shared. I honor her and the lessons she taught me. I know she is the lucky one in a much better place, and that we will be together again. Sometimes she comes to me in meditation and dreams. One of her messages was "Mommy, don't be sad." I know she is happy, joyous and free on the other side, and she wants me to live my life to its fullest with joy and gusto. And then, when it's least expected, that wave of grief comes along, and knocks my feet out from under me, fully enveloping me in its murky water. The pain is like nothing I've ever felt before…and it doesn't ever go away completely, it's just around the corner waiting for another moment to catch me off guard.

Thankfully, I have the #NotInVain Facebook support group for mamas who have lost a child to the drug epidemic, and some other in-person and on-line supports, as well as my Al-Anon groups. My daughter spiritually guides me in my business. She is with me always, and I am grateful. When I "see" her smile, or "hear" her voice, I feel the love and wholeness she brings me, and I feel full and at peace. Then, there are the times of emptiness, darkness, despair, overwhelming pain, and hopelessness that suck the breath right out of me. Journaling (I keep a Grief Journal) has also helped me cope with this horrific experience that no parent should ever have to endure. But endure we do; I do.

I have no advice to give to any parent reading this, other than to do your best. Honor your child's strengths, weaknesses, and feelings. Love your child unconditionally. And find support from those who have walked this path before you. We are all willing to help. Do not be ashamed to ask for help. If you suspect your child is using drugs, do not delay in talking with them, giving them facts, and taking a hard line. Don't believe everything they say. Assure them of your love and willing-ness to help them appropriately, as long as they are willing to work on sobriety and healing. And be firm; you cannot do it for them. They have to do the hard work (with your support). And love them always. I wish you well, much luck, and Peace, Joy, Love, and Harmony always.

Melissa's Mom,

ROBIN T.
Apollo Beach, Florida

Cassandra

FOREVER 25

It took a year to conceive this beauty, and her challenges began in my first trimester of pregnancy. I almost lost her, but she hung on and was born into this world on September 30, 1992, thirty-one days early. Again, clinging to life, she prevailed. Cassandra was extremely clingy, high maintenance (lol) and extremely dramatic, yet she had the biggest heart and a compassion in her, like no other.

Cassandra was, one hundred percent, an old soul. She had a wisdom about life that I never even had, and she helped hundreds of people whom she crossed paths with. We knew from the time she was about ten years old, that she had something mentally imbalanced.

She knew as well, so we began seeing a psychiatrist immediately. We saw her counselor for years, but Cassandra was never treated for an actual diagnosis. We ended up going to another facility for counseling and, again, she was never given a diagnosis.

She made it through high school (she did great), yet every day was a challenge. She was working full time at our local hospital, as a CNA (certified nursing assistant) and they absolutely loved her. She received multiple Angel awards.

While working, she was going to college to be a nurse. Cassandra's life was amazing, or so I thought, but she was struggling with demons that absolutely no one diagnosed her with during all of her years of therapy. She hit her early twenties and fractured her foot. Pain meds seemed to be endless for her, until they stopped prescribing them. She then hit the streets for pills.

This went on for a couple years and I was completely clueless. How? I don't know, but she never seemed different, other than the weight loss. I then started finding odd-shaped packages in her bedroom. When confronted, she admitted that she was snorting heroin.

I don't remember how we got on the subject, but a patient in our office and I began talking about it (her daughter is a recovering user). She connected me to a local group, where I reached out for help.

Cassandra, without hesitation, was placed in a local inpatient facility. It was a two-week program and we were not allowed to see her. I picked her up at the end of her program and she was doing great. I sold my home and relocated to a different town. A new beginning.

Six months later, she relapsed. This time she was injecting. I started noticing my valuables disappearing and now I'm afraid. I found a facility three hours away that would take her.

After two weeks, she called me to pick her up. She said it was only a two-week program. What did I know? I was clueless about addiction. Later, I would learn that she left the program early. It was, I think, a matter of weeks before I again noticed more of my jewelry missing. Car accidents and tickets were unbearable.

At this point, she hadn't been going to work for months. Again, something I would learn later, as she left every day in scrubs. She was angry, agitated, and sick ALL the time. I found a local three-month inpatient program and, again, she went.

You see she never fought me on it, because she was fighting for her life. I got to visit her every Sunday and she seemed happy and herself again. I was so incredibly proud of her and so hopeful that my baby would have her beautiful life back.

After three months, instead of the facility transferring her to the same controlled living housing as the rest of the girls that she had become so close to, they wanted to send her to a half-way house again. She would have to start over with none of those whom she had grown so close to and depended on for support. She wasn't having it, so she came home with the hopes that outpatient treatment would be just as successful.

At first, it was working out well, but I had to work full time. We had taken her car away, so she got a ride from her grandfather, until it became too much, since he was also caring for his terminally ill wife.

Cassandra applied for transportation help, but was denied. She had no means to get back and forth and the bus stop was so far away from our home. As far as I knew though, she was getting back and forth. Again, I was clueless.

She quickly relapsed and later I found out through her journals that she overdosed in our bathroom and survived it. She describes the needle still in her arm and how when she came to there was blood everywhere.

She, again, came to me for help. She wanted to go back to the facility that she just came home from. We called immediately and every single day after, until they could place her.

In the meantime, I took her to Buffalo, where they kept her so she could detox. She was so sick. We continued to call every day for two and a half months, begging for placement. It was an absolute joke.

Finally, a friend of mine got her in by going over the facility coordinator's head and miraculously they could place her. The coordinator did not hide the fact that she was upset that we went over her head. I nicely thanked her for saving my daughter and left.

Seven weeks into the three-month program, I received a call that she needed to be picked up. When I picked her up (on a Friday afternoon no less) she was desperately calling other facilities to take her right away.

You see, two weeks prior to this day, July 20, 2018, a resident snuck a drug in. Cassandra was one of the three girls to participate in taking it. The girl who brought it in left the house, Cassandra got kicked out two weeks later on a FRIDAY AFTERNOON, and the other girl got to stay. I feel like it was a lesson for going over their head to get her back in.

Everyone absolutely loved Cassandra in that facility. She was a great patient and a great friend. But I had brought her home before...Of course, you can't get placed on a Friday afternoon, and I had to run out for a bit. She was in great spirits and just lectured me on how she wanted her life back and never wanted her parents to have to bury their child.

I asked her if she was okay, said, "I love you" and left. I came home to find her dead in her bedroom. Needle and drugs on her nightstand. They (EMS) tried extensive measures to revive her, but she was gone. My beautiful baby girl, who was fighting for her life, was dead at twenty-five years old. If I had known about addiction…If someone would have helped me understand, she'd still be here. I was involved in a group for help on what to do, but not one single person helped me understand the severity of addiction. The facility, as far as I'm concerned, killed her.

If I had known, I would have taken a leave from my job to help my child; I would have reached out to my family for help (she didn't want anyone to know); I would have had her involved in this huge community of recovery that I didn't know existed. I would have found every possible resource available. If I had known... Rehabs need to change. They didn't say a single thing to me when I picked her up. Later on, I was told that she was making comments to people in the rehab facility that they were sending her home to die... not a single person told me this. I never would have left her alone. My goal now is to make sure that every parent struggling with a child in addiction knows what I didn't. I have opened a resource center in the very town my daughter grew up in. I will not stand by and let a parent do this alone.

Cassandra's death has taught me that the stigma of this disease needs to end. These are beautiful people that are so sick and so desperate to have their lives back. They do fight and they fight hard, but there are so many broken links in our system. I will go to  my grave fighting for change. She deserves, at least, that much, as all of our children do.

Cassandra's Mom,

Christina W.
Rochester, New York

Ryan

FOREVER 27

My son Ryan was born in the spring of 1988. He was my second child. We had been trying for several years to have another baby and I had suffered a miscarriage just a year prior to his birth. To say he was so wanted is an understatement. He was my beautiful, red-haired boy. We did go on to have two more children after him. My family of a daughter and three sons was complete.

We had the perfect life. We attended church and the kids played recreational sports through our city parks program. We enjoyed trips each summer to the Destin, Florida, area and when the kids were younger, we used to drive from Memphis to Peoria, Illinois, to bring my husband's grandparents to Memphis for Christmas. Grandma called Ryan her sunshine boy because of his sweet smile that brightened her day and all of our days.

Like all the other Moms I have met over the last five years, I spend many days wondering what happened, where things went wrong, where I failed my child. I remember the bullying he endured about his curly, red hair. I remember the first job where he spent time with older kids and was introduced to drugs. I remember my sweet, sensitive, insecure child who wanted more than anything to be accepted and to have friends and I firmly believe this was the base of the problem. Ryan would tell me later that when he was high he was funny, he could dance, the girls liked him and he was part of the group. He wanted to be the guy everyone liked and he wanted to be remembered.

Remembered. That word still haunts me. It has been five years. Do they remember? I never knew what we were dealing with until Ryan had been involved with drugs for a few years. Of course alcohol and pot to start with and then Bars and Tabs. (Xanax and Lortabs). Looking back, I realize that some of the erratic behavior and mood swings were probably in a large part from the Xanax. I never, ever dreamed heroin would be part of Ryan's world. I never considered that my child could be prone to the brain disease of addiction. Not my child.

A few years after high school, Ryan went to live in North Carolina. He would be working for my brother there and would live with him and his wife for the first year. This was his plan to get away from the Memphis crowd that he admitted was not good for him. But it was not long before Ryan was lonely; he missed his friends and he missed being the 'fun guy." An old friend from high school moved to North Carolina and moved into the apartment Ryan was living in. Ryan told me after a few months that he had kicked the roommate out when he found evidence the guy was using heroin. I have never known the exact truth behind that story but within a few months I discovered Ryan had used heroin as well. He had relapsed. Relapsed to a drug I didn't know he had ever used to begin with.

He entered rehab for the first time and he loved it. He loved sharing his story and he loved counseling others. He would have stayed forever but after a few months it was time to take the next step and get back to earning a living. He lived for a while in a sober living house and spent the next few months working and going to meetings. He met a girl at an NA meeting and fell pretty hard, pretty fast. A few weeks after he met her, she reunited with an old boyfriend and overdosed on heroin. She spent many days in ICU but survived...that time. Ryan came home. I think he needed his family and I needed him back with me.

For about a year, things were pretty good; the more time that passed though the more he returned to his old friends and eventually his old demons. He met a girl who also had a history of addiction. I am still not sure if Ryan loved her or loved the idea of her. He often told me he wanted a wife and a family. He wanted kids and he wanted to raise them just like he had been raised. He really thought he could do it.

On April 4, 2015, I received a call that would start the final downward spiral for my beautiful boy. Ryan had overdosed and was in the emergency room. He was revived with several doses of Narcan. The doctor told me and my husband to take him straight to an NA meeting when he was discharged. We did. Before leaving the hospital that afternoon, Ryan got a call from the girlfriend. Turns out she had been with him and had also overdosed. She was taken to another hospital and released but not until she was given a pregnancy test. I could hear her through the phone telling my son they were pregnant. He was so happy. This was the answer, he said. This was his cure. His dreams were coming true and he was going to get healthy for this baby.

For the next few weeks, he went to NA meetings almost every night. His girlfriend went along to one but told him she was tired and pregnant and didn't want to go anymore. He continued to go without her for a few more weeks. Again, he loved sharing at those meetings. He told me he wanted to help others with this battle. He proudly told all who would listen he was going to be a father and he was going to get healthy and provide the best life for this child. A few nights later, I heard him on the phone with his girlfriend's sister saying his girl had informed him that if he continued going to meetings instead of spending time with her she would get an abortion. He was devastated and determined not to allow that to happen. That was the end of meetings.

When Ryan was not at work he was with her. Together, they thought they could get better on their own. They would quit using for a few days, get sick from withdrawal, use again to feel better, quit, get sick... This continued for the duration of the pregnancy. Of course, their unborn child also used every time his mother did and went through the same withdrawal and stress on his body and brain when she didn't use.

I was not supposed to ever find out this baby had survived another of his mother's overdoses in August, the same day they saw him for the first time on ultrasound and were told they were having a son. I had brought up the topic of neonatal drug exposure to my son and his girl-friend several times during the pregnancy.

Each time, she grew angry and insulted that I would suggest she would do anything to hurt her baby. She insisted they were not doing drugs. I bought them groceries and offered to take them to prenatal doctor visits. Her mother, who they were staying with, told her she didn't need ongoing prenatal care, that she was a nurse who knew better than I did. (She was a nurse who lost her nursing license when she was caught stealing medication from her patients at a nursing home.) I was only successful in getting her back to a doctor two more times. I prepared myself for what I knew was coming. I arranged to host a baby shower. I had guided her to make a baby registry with what I knew I would need to care for him. All the while she pretended to be having a healthy, drug-free pregnancy but I knew this wasn't the case.

My son was wasting away before my eyes and other than making sure they ate, I was helpless. I had no idea what to do for them or where to get help for them. Any progress I ever made in trying to convince him to go to rehab was soon shot down with the excuse that he had to work to support his family. (He did and he also had no insurance which further complicated things.) Ryan's son, Carter, was born in October, just short of six weeks premature. After the birth, the baby was whisked away to be evaluated. He appeared healthy but within a few hours my concerns were all confirmed. He was diagnosed with Neonatal Absti-nence Syndrome. He was treated with small doses of morphine for the next five days before being fully weaned off of it and then finally discharged after two weeks. Child Protective Services (CPS) was called in and the baby was released to my custody. Mommy and Daddy were ordered to get help.

I began caring for a sick baby. I barely saw my son and his girlfriend. He would call me every day to tell me he was doing as directed by CPS and was looking for inpatient treatment but if he found a place to take him, he couldn't find a place to take her and they were not going to go unless they were both going at the same time. Every day, he was told call back in the morning to see if there were beds available. He would make calls every morning and they would use heroin every afternoon. I don't know where they got the money for this or where they were living. I saw them just a few times when they would come visit the baby. They attended a few meetings. During these weeks, my son would survive another overdose. While in the emergency room, barely conscious, he mentioned the baby and the nurses informed the police had called us to determine the baby was safe.

Things were only getting worse. Finally, just a week before Thanksgiving they found openings at local treatment facilities. I took Ryan to get some clothes and toiletry items and dropped him off at treatment. His girlfriend was to enter another facility that afternoon but things changed and she ended up at the same place he was, about a week later, but in the woman's building. On December 15, Ryan was discharged after about thirty days in treatment. His girlfriend was due to get out the next week. He insisted he had been there long enough even though one of the counselors asked him to stay. He had been a model patient. Again he thrived in the rehab environment and talked about returning to work there one day as a counselor. But first he had some things to figure out.

He had to secure a place to live for him and his girl and start saving some money. He again had big plans. He had to take the needed steps to regain custody of his child. Since I had custody of the baby, CPS said he could only stay with us the first night or two then he would need to stay somewhere else. Their reasoning was it wasn't fair to Mommy if Daddy was with baby when she could not be. I should have fought that, but I was terrified of the baby being taken from me and put into the foster care system. I had to follow the rules. Ryan checked into a hotel in a bad part of town but it was close to where he needed to be picked up for work. He assured me if he was going to use he could use no matter where he was. He said, "I have no more saves in me. I have to stay clean or I will die." He was right.

A few nights later he was gone. I got a call from his girlfriend around noon on Sunday asking if I had spoken to him. I will never forget her words. She told how she had spoken to him the night before and it sounded like he was partying. She said she heard voices and what sounded like ice in a glass and beer cans opening. She said, "I think he is dead. He isn't answering his phone." I had not spoken to him the night before. The baby was having a really bad time with what I assume were lingering withdrawal symptoms and some stomach issues.

Normally, I would have called and texted nonstop until I reached

Ryan, but I was exhausted and didn't that night. My husband rushed to the hotel and found Ryan dead from a heroin overdose. I believe the dealer had been at the hotel. I read a message my son sent her inviting her to bring her grandchildren swimming at the hotel's indoor pool. I believe she was in the room with him and left him to die. I will never know for sure.

I do not want Ryan to be remembered for how he died or for the disease that took him from us. I want to remember my sweet, red-haired boy. I want to remember his laugh and his love for his family and for his dog. I want to remember all the happiness he brought me and others. I hope he knew how much I loved him. I think he knew I would always take care of his child. I am so thankful to have his child and to now be Mommy to this sweet part of my son. (His girlfriend basically deserted the baby and we were fortunate that she agreed to terminate her rights, allowing us to adopt him before he turned one. He has never been away from us. We have no contact with her. Carter continues to have some delays and medical issues from his drug exposure and it seems we are always waiting for the next health issue to arise.)

I sometimes hear from people who knew Ryan and they tell me stories of how they knew him and how much they valued his friendship. Some were "friends" that used drugs with him. I have been approached by some of them who are sober at different addiction and overdose awareness events I take part in. I must admit I always wonder why they survived and he didn't. One of them told me about Ryan's drug use with his twelfth grade English teacher and the huge part this man had in Ryan's struggles. I can't help but hate this man even though I know he struggles with the same disease. I have heard from friends Ryan made in rehab and they have told me how much he helped them during their journey.

Sadly, some who have contacted me are now gone too. I spend my days caring for Ryan's child…now my child. I don't know how or when I will explain things to him. I still struggle with blaming myself and blaming others. I still have days when the grief hits me so hard I don't want to get out of bed but I have to get up and take care of "our" little boy. Life is about taking care of Carter now and giving him the happy childhood he deserves and that Ryan so wanted for him. I have joined some addiction and overdose awareness groups and work when I can to promote the idea of harm reduction services and Narcan distribution. I help when I can to connect those suffering with potential treatment resources, though openings in recovery and the detox needed to enter those facilities are so hard to come by. I no longer have to worry about where my son is or if he will survive another day, but I am doing my best to make sure he is remembered.

Ryan's Mom,

SHARON W.
Germantown, Tennessee

Elizabeth Dallas

FOREVER 20

 My daughter, Dallas, came into this world a beautiful, happy, smiling baby. She grew up loving animals, cheering, and her baby sister. She was my social butterfly, always making new friends, even on beach vacations. Her childhood was pretty typical. Dance, cheerleading, and friends. At the end of her tenth-grade year, the drama in her life began to take a toll. She seemed overly anxious and showed signs of depression. I took her to counseling, but she refused to talk to strangers about her problems.

I took her to a doctor to see about medication, but she wouldn't take it. I eventually withdrew her from school and she began a homeschool program, finishing a year earlier than her peers. Now, she had time on her hands, without school or cheering. She became bored and began to socialize with the wrong kind of people. She met the majority of these friends on Facebook. She was a typical teenager going out on the weekends and growing a little more distant from me.

She had my granddaughter, Madelyn, at seventeen and I had never seen love in someone's eyes as much as hers when she held her baby. Soon after, she moved in with her boyfriend and his mom. I knew it wasn't a great situation, but I also knew the more I objected, the more I would push her away. It was during this time, I suspect, she began using some form of drugs. Maybe she went straight to heroin; I don't know exactly.

She began attending community college during the day and taking care of the baby at night. She began losing weight and looked ill, most of the times I saw her. She kept excusing it, as being tired from all she was having to do. She fell ill and was misdiagnosed by four different doctors, here in our home county. From bronchitis (with no chest x-ray) to autoimmune disease to arthritis. I had taken Madelyn home with me when Dallas became too sick to care for her.

Dallas came to visit Madelyn at my house on December 4, 2014. She looked very sick and could barely walk. She told me she had been using a walker to finish up her semester classes at school. I arrived home December 5, to find her barely conscious and unable to move. I drove her to the closest hospital and again she was misdiagnosed as having an autoimmune disease. They sent us to a larger hospital, but with no ambulances available, I had to drive her myself. Little did I know my baby was literally dying in the seat beside me.

When the doctor saw the lab work from the previous hospital, she was immediately rushed to ICU and placed in a medically induced coma. All of her organs were failing and I was told for three nights to prepare myself for the worst. Doctors told me it was endocarditis, caused from a MRSA infection and it was a very common occurrence in IV drug users. WHAT? My daughter sure didn't use drugs, much less IV drugs. I had no idea any of this had been taking place. No warning signs then, but in hindsight, the signs were everywhere. Spoons missing, wearing long sleeves in warm weather, always seeming sleepy, etc.

The heart doctor said as soon as they could, Dallas would need to have her heart valves replaced and a pacemaker put in place. He gave her a twenty percent chance of coming off the heart lung machine. She was in ICU for twenty-one days and in the hospital for over fifty. She had to relearn how to walk from being in the bed so long. She also had to have a skin graft done for two places on her foot that the infection had destroyed. They had just been blisters from some boots she wore on Thanksgiving. They were so bad, you could see her bones and Achilles tendon.

She made it through all of this and was a true miracle in everyone's eyes. We went home with IV antibiotics daily, but by June the infection had returned. She had continued using, without my knowledge, even after almost dying. Again, the doctor performed open heart surgery and replaced her pacemaker. Again, she made it off the heart lung machine and became a walking miracle. This time home from the hospital, she refused to even take the antibiotics. She lasted only a few days, at my house, before she was back using again.

The drug had taken over her brain a long time ago and she just couldn't beat it. In October of 2015, the infection returned for the third time. This time all the valves were infected, not just two. Only now she was sent home with hospice care because no doctor in the entire United States would agree to open her chest for a third time in less than a year. My family and friends had called every hospital we could think of that had a reputation for helping heart patients. As soon as they heard the words drugs, addict, etc. they quickly turned us down.

At nineteen, my daughter was told she had six months to live. I refused to believe it, but Dallas and I had many late-night talks about her future. She wanted me to know her wishes for her funeral and afterwards. I listened and made many promises. Yellow casket, sunflowers, certain songs, doing her hair, make-up, and nails, writing and reading her eulogy. I kept a strong face, but was so broken inside. How does a nineteen-year-old face their death? Mine used drugs more than ever. Why not numb the pain, if she's going to pass away anyway?

She began even using at home and I had to make the heartbreaking decision to make her leave. A so-called friend called DHS on me, and they told me they would take my younger daughter and granddaughter away, if I didn't put her out. How do you put your dying child out on the street alone? You look into the eyes of her eight-year-old sister and two-year-old child and know you must choose them over her.

A friend later found her living under a bridge in a horrible part of town. We got her into what would be her last rehab. She wanted to be clean for her last months and be with Madelyn. She was clean for forty-five days and we talked every night on the phone. God knew what was coming, because he gave me that time with my daughter. The one I knew before the drugs took over. She came home from rehab on Mother's Day and stayed clean for a total of three days. Once again, she would have to leave and go house to house living with friends. We would text every now and then, but by this time she had no ID and no phone. See, she had stolen every valuable I had long before this, including my car. She wrecked three cars total. She sounded bad on the phone when we talked, but she told me she knew she wasn't in any shape to come home and be around the girls.

I found out through Facebook messenger that my daughter had gone to be with the Lord at ten a.m. on July 17, 2016. She died alone in someone's house, trying to detox one more time for Madelyn. Detoxing for a healthy person can be deadly and her heart just couldn't take it. She made it three months longer than the doctors had given her. I kept my promises to her and sharing her story is one of the biggest of those. Never letting her  memory die and never letting her death be in vain. I'd like to close with her favorite verse:

"She is clothed with strength and dignity. She laughs without fear of the future." - Proverbs 31:25.

Dallas's Mom,

Debbie W.
Hernando, Mississippi

David

FOREVER 30

David was born on March 30,1990, nine pounds, ten ounces, a healthy baby boy...all ten fingers and toes. That is what all the mothers told me to look for. His father was adopted, so we didn't have any insight into a family history, other than my side, who show only signs of heart disease and aneurysms. What they didn't tell me was there would be an illness that I would never see, the silent killer...addiction. Besides bed wetting until age six, David started acting strange at about eight years old. I never could pinpoint what it was exactly.

He did this thing where he would ask me a question and repeat it with just his lips. It was like he was making sure it sounded right. I watched that strange activity for about a year and even asked him why he did that. He didn't know it was even happening. By ten, we were in therapy because of his behaviors. He was bigger than all the kids for three grades up! He found a way to get in trouble every school year from kindergarten on up, from cutting little girls' hair to breaking a boy's arm, a move he learned in karate. I kept him busy with things to work out his aggressiveness. He loved karate, but had to quit; we can't break people's arms just because we can!

At age thirteen, still no diagnosis of mental illness, yet we were smack dab in the middle of this horrible end. Alcohol consumed David's life from then on. It was a race to save his life! We worked together through the "system" and we tried everything. Teen groups, boot camps, boy's schools, filed through the court for incorrigibility which, with evidence, locked him up. I had to save his life! Nothing helped.

Finally, we received a diagnosis from a doctor who said he was "dual." Well, dual diagnosis only means substance abuse and mental health disorder together at the same time and we were already doing our part. It didn't work. The more I paid, the worse he got. Something in him couldn't change. My job was to simply keep him alive until he was an adult. That's when David went in deep and I could only love him and support him and encourage him to make healthy choices. There were times he did! They never lasted long enough.

By nineteen, David was put in prison for home invasion. At twenty-one, he was released to a drug treatment center which kicked him out for coming in late, causing a parole violation. Six months later, he was released into a halfway house, which kicked him out for co-mingling with another resident, causing another parole violation and back into lock up. The system institutionalized him. He was on excellent medications, but once he felt good, he would take himself off. He would say he was fine now...time and time again. Finally, yet another parole violation put him back in prison for six months where he got honest and they put him back on his meds. He was doing great! Focused. Then, once again the system let me down. He was released without a prescription or a follow up plan. I reported within hours of his release that they let him leave, without his medication, to his social worker and her reply was, "I'll look into it," and I never heard back from her.

David's goal was to beat his alcoholism. He pushed through for a few weeks and then it happened. Misery loves company, as we all know. He ran into a friend from high school, who showed him that you didn't have to drink to get high. That friend showed him how to shoot heroin. It wasn't but a few weeks later that he sent me a long text message telling me all about it and how he can't live like this. So, I brought him to yet another detox center, who did a fine job of letting this pass through his system, but the rest was up to him. He was twenty-nine years old now and here I was, still the only person who reached out to try and help him. His last chance staying at our house, the rules were simple: don't bring drugs or alcohol into this house, no friends over, and no uniform visited for any reason. He was such a hard worker, but the more money he made, the worse he would get.

Three months later, I came home from work to hear this horrible snoring sound coming from my bathroom. I knew to open the door right away. Sure enough, blue, barely breathing, needle on the floor, heroin bag on the counter. I called 9-1-1; EMS came and administered Narcan and took David to the hospital. Then I called his social worker and parole officer and told him where he was and if they didn't hurry, he would be gone again. Their response was a message to have him report by the following Monday. They released him the next morning. He never went back to his parole officer. He stayed running. He would call looking for money and I would offer him gas or food instead. Then I got the ugliest text from him ever. How I was the worst person for reporting him? The system has never helped us out ever yet I still called them. He was right. They never did help him. They never sought the treatment he needed, even when I put the right phone number in their hands. Just herd them in and out of that revolving door, collect their paychecks, and call it another day.

My son had an illness that only he could treat, but he needed better tools. No one could do it for him. I knew those words were not my son talking. I knew, but it hurt anyway. One week more he would survive. He died. He finally settled on a spot where I believe he knew no one could save him with Narcan. Smack dab in the middle of Detroit, on an abandoned porch, with a cell phone and his wallet. First responder said he was DOA. Second report said he had been there at least ten to fifteen hours. I knew. I KNEW! My heart was mimicking an anxiety attack. I sent him what would be my last message to him, at that time, and told him, "I am praying so hard for you David. Please know that." That was November 4, 2019, at 5:35 p.m. They found him on November 5, 2019, at 9:30 a.m. Going through his things I found a note. It read:

I just got tired. I couldn't go back to my alcoholic abyss. It's just no fun anymore. I love you so much Mumma!...Your #1 son, David.

Me? Well, I cry. I do miss my son so much. I break down with a song or a picture or the wind. But I also can smile and laugh and remember his funny self. Man, was he funny...the infectious laugh he had...the cool stories he would tell...the hugs that made me pee my pants...the quiet talks by the fire. He was proud of me and he loved me unconditionally. That is one of the blessings through our journey. Over half his life was spent at war. Now, he is at peace and I can sleep again. I can see again. My horrible headaches are gone. I have money again. I didn't realize how much of myself I gave up for him... and... I'd do it all over again. My #1 son, David.

David's Mom,

Mary W.
Wixom, Michigan

Ian

FOREVER 23

How does a smart young man with a bright future at twenty-three years old end up dead from fentanyl poisoning on the floor of his college apartment his senior year of college? The answer to that question is a Wendy's straw and four small bags of a white powdery substance found by police at the scene. Through a thorough investigation by police that handled this as a crime scene from the onset, the dealer was found, convicted, and is serving a prison term. As a family, this is a minimal consolation because, in reality, nothing will bring our beloved son and brother Ian Michael back to us. Justice, in the eyes of the law, was served. We had our "how" questions answered.

"Why?" remains our question and the reason I write our family story. I say "our" story because Ian is not here to tell his story. I'm sure he saw things from a different perspective. He saw many things from a different perspective than mine. Ian was very much his own person. He wore a leather bracelet that read, "Think for yourself. Question everything," ironic to me now yet indicative of his independent personality. If you are struggling with a child with a substance use disorder, perhaps you may see some similarities and intervene in a different manner with a positive outcome. I've had several years to examine 'why." I have written this from the heartbreaking perspective of 20/20 hindsight. It's difficult opening up our lives to examination by the public. We are very private people. Our family has given me permission to open up in the hopes that, with insight to another, Ian's life is #NotInVain.

I feel it's important to discover not only WHAT a parent may be dealing with as a medical disorder but WHO is this child as a person and HOW to intervene appropriately. My husband and I have been together over forty years. I am a nurse, my husband a physician. We live in a quiet suburb in the same house for thirty years. A great, safe place to raise a family. We have a calm, stable, drama-free home life. Our daughter Abby was born in 1989. I became a stay at home mom. I loved it. After much difficulty and medical intervention, Ian was born four years later. This pregnancy was difficult and I spent eight months on bedrest. Out of necessity, I was very tuned in to nuance during this time. In utero, Ian startled easily. A noise or motion set him jumping. This was different from my previous pregnancies.

Ian arrived June 14, 1993 via a scheduled C-section. Vivid strawberry blonde hair and bright blue eyes, he was stunningly gorgeous. When asked, "Who does your baby brother look like?" my daughter appropriately responded, "He looks like himself." He was, indeed, very much his own person. Ian relaxed best in my arms. He was difficult to breastfeed but adapted with my persistence. He was reactive to noise and responded to calmness, and self-soothed with his constant companion security blanket. He was a healthy baby. Walked at one year but was hesitant to speak and preferred gesticulating to communicating verbally other than mama, dada, sissy, and such until two. His first sentence came unexpectedly as he grabbed the TV remote, pointed at his sister, and said, "Turn Abby off." He took his bottles out to the curbside trash can at two at my suggestion. He was done with them and wanted a cup, finally. Ian was a picky eater and never had an appetite. He potty trained himself in a day at age three in exchange for a "big boy"bicycle. Most developmental milestones were hurdled on his terms.

Ian relished choices. I wouldn't describe him as confident. He was hesitant, resistant, introspective, extremely sensitive, and ANXIOUS. Ian challenged me to think from a different approach to parenting as he was resistant to instructions that he didn't understand. Seams in socks, arches in shoes, fabric textures, tags in clothing, newly cut fingernails and hair, smells, sunlight all seemed to be a reactive sensitivity for him. I don't believe in "breaking" a person's spirit. I believe in working with the spirit. Ian attended preschool at three and four years old. He enjoyed it, interacted well with other children, abided by the teacher's authority, and thrived. Ages five and six were half-day to all-day kinder-garten. This was the norm in our school district. I noticed he was intel-lectually bright but lacked a grasp of recognizing letters of the alphabet when taken out of order. I knew he could be obstinate but I felt some-thing past his personality may be a problem. I took him to a child psychologist for an evaluation. He was diagnosed as gifted intellect with a correctable reading disorder and mild performance anxiety attributed to his intellect with a reading issue. He was privately tutored, mastered reading, and his anxiety level dropped to a very manageable level through high school.

Ian was very social, had many friends, and did honors level classes in school. He was sinewy built, athletic, and agile; loved downhill skiing, snowboarding, and soccer. He lettered in varsity in soccer all four years and ran track. He volunteered in Appalachia as a service project, held a job at a tuxedo store, and even modeled a bit. Ian graduated from high school with honors.

Ian was handsome, charming, and very quick witted. He had a lot of girlfriends. Ian was meticulous about his appearance and a fashion-ista. He loved a good debate and could be relentless in his opinions and cunning with his dialog. He never had a disciplinary action in school nor with the law. We shared a love of music, metaphysics, and politics. He was involved in a website application development while in high school. This site never materialized due to some shady business actions with betrayal and he was devastated. I didn't know the depth of his devastation about this until a few years later. He never got over it. He had no clear career plan but college and law school were discussed.

Ian chose a university five to six hours away from home. I was surprised as he never expressed a desire to explore far from home. His sister had graduated from the same university and perhaps this played a factor in his choice. When it came time to begin, he seemed reticent but off he went, with a few friends attending the same college and a familiarity through his sister. In hindsight, I should have encouraged him to stay closer to home. I feel his performance anxiety really reared its ugly head at this time. He was out of our sightline and private about his insecurities. He was assigned a private single dorm room, a huge mistake as he expressed isolation. He joined a travel soccer team on campus and in his sophomore year, a fraternity. He moved into a frat house his third year, another big mistake as this was party city. Because of the distance between the campus and our home, he managed to keep us as separate and uninvolved as possible. I would ask to visit, he countered with a visit home within two to three weeks and travel soccer as an excuse.

Ian was always very convincing with explanations. We are not stupid nor naive parents. He was an incredibly artful dodger. His first year of college felt rocky to us as parents. It didn't, at the time, feel unordinary with growing pains of a college student. We asked questions, he gave believable responses, we gave options, he chose, and that's how his first few years went. What we knew and now know about his drug use from high school through his first three years of college: we know he smoked marijuana and drank some beer, never at home but with high school buddies. It didn't seem to interfere with his grades, sports, job, ambition nor demeanor. As parents that grew up in the seventies, we didn't find it out of the ordinary but discussed alcohol and drug use routinely in our home and around the dinner table. He began attending outdoor music festivals the summer after high school and dove deeply into the electronica music genre as escapism. I think that's where the heavier drug dabbling began to take a more significant role in his recreation. I didn't know about it until I discussed it with his close friends after his death. I now know he was dabbling in MDMA (Molly) Adderall, Percocet, and Xanax. I believe the Xanax started out as experimental but became self-medicating for anxiety. I believe they were originally acquired from a friend's parent's medicine cabinet. We, his parents, did not know this was going on. Never underestimate exactly how secretive a teen can be. I was a stay at home mom with the personality of a cop and yet could be artfully dodged. I suspected something was wrong but never found much to substantiate my suspicions. Ian never stole money from us.

Most of his expenses were explained in what felt to be reasonable terms at that time.

Life unraveled rather quickly and abruptly the summer of his third year at college. His grades were failing. He was placed on academic probation. He looked physically and mentally awful. Ian insisted on returning to complete college. He said he was nervous and let it get the best of him. After extensive discussions, he returned. He moved into a lovely apartment with his girlfriend whom he described as the love of his life. She had graduated college the semester before him. She was smart, ambitious, and shared his music festival hippie trippy lifestyle. He met his intellectual match. We liked her. She swears she had no idea at the time the extent and type of drug use Ian was involved in; we definitely didn't. They attended a party on the 4th of July 2016 where Ian collapsed and had a seizure.

An ambulance ride and ER trip prompted a call from Ian to us on July 5. I jumped in the car and drove to bring him home. He was a total mess. Longest car ride of my life. He was nodding off and incoherent the whole way home. It was five to six weeks since we had seen him last and a dramatic change of everything about him. I called an 800 help number for inpatient drug rehab as Ian finally admitted to heavy Xanax use that he stopped on his own hence the seizure. We had minimal choices for rehab as beds were full and were given one near us so we took it with minimal knowledge and in shock terror for our son's life. It was an abstinence AA-based twenty-eight-day program with seven days of medically supervised detox. We dropped him off and went through the paces. This was the biggest mistake of our lives. It was not a good fit for him. A horrible fit. He was put in a generalized box of one size fits none treatment type. It had no psychiatric evaluation nor treatment for co-occurring mental disorders nor MAT for opioid addiction.

We were told, "This program is not a failure but a client can fail the program." Yes, a direct quote. I asked about what exact drugs my son was using. We were told, "That's not important and he'll share with you what he chooses." It was important and my son didn't choose to share ever. We had no idea what we were dealing with and were ill prepared to deal with it. We own that. Ian spent his twenty-six of twenty-eight days and we, as parents, paced and cried. We knew no one that had a child with SUD (substance use disorder). We were frightened as well as embarrassed by the stigma and judgement rendered upon people in this situation. We stayed private about it. My son asked us to be private. He was embarrassed about his situation. We respected his privacy. We own that too. We attended the facilities parents session. It was basic and was heavy AA and alcohol focused. Ian hated this place. I didn't blame him. It was a terrible fit with his personality. We were called on day twenty-six to pick him up. Told to clear the house of all alcohol and he was to attend twenty AA meetings in twenty days. That's it. That's all we had. Ian looked clear and healthy.

AA was not going to be a fit for Ian. "Mom, I'm not going to identify myself as Hi. I'm Ian and I'm a drug addict for the rest of my life. It doesn't define me." I set him up with a psychologist to treat his anxiety and SUD. They met three times a week for the month of August 2016 and he insisted on his desires to "pick up the pieces of his life," return to his college apartment, complete his final year of college, and move forward. He was convincing enough. We said ok. We watched every single penny. Accounted for every dime spent. His sister jumped into academic support and assisted with an organized study schedule that she presented weekly to decrease his anxiety and get him organized. His girlfriend was supportive.

We feel, in hindsight, he relapsed back to Xanax by January 2017. He couldn't afford the Xanax. He got his hands on heroin to snort. It was cheaper and he felt easier to titrate and control as per a drug friend's recount and Ian's text messages recovered after his death. Ian came home for spring break. He looked shaky. He voiced "total crippling anxiety." I spent four days looking into a psychiatrist that specializes in co-occurring medical disorders of anxiety and SUD in the city where he attended college. I concurrently researched inpatient rehab centers that handled both diagnoses. I found only one I felt suitable. He was given an appointment for March 27, 2017, two weeks away. He returned to college for midterms at his insistence. He called daily and asked if there were any quicker appointments. He was on a wait list. We were all hopeful, as Ian was not in agreement with any type of rehab resembling his first experience. I happen to agree to this very day about that. They tried to "break" his spirit.

March 22, 2017, three p.m. I got a call from his girlfriend. Ian was found dead on the floor of their apartment. The police and 911 were called. I only remember the sound of my screams and hitting the kitchen floor. Everything else went to nightmarish blurry after that. We buried Ian on March 27, his scheduled appointment date. Fentanyl got him first. No second chance for an appropriate fit for rehab. Hindsight is 20/20. I wished for a better rehab fit for my son.

These are some things I've learned along the way, unfortunately too late for our family but #NotInVain. Anxiety runs in both my husband's and my families. We have parents, siblings, nieces and nephews that struggle with this diagnosis. Two members have been treated for SUD (substance use disorder). Privacy can be respected. Silence due to stigma shouldn't happen. Rehabilitation should include treatment for all medical diagnoses. Over 90% of all people with SUD have an underlying mental health diagnosis, whether or not it has been identified. If your gut feeling is "something isn't quite right," it most likely isn't.

It's impossible to think as a clinician when the client is your child. The chaos and fear with SUD rendered both my husband and I to our knees. Good sound medical treatment helped bring Ian into this world: improper medical treatment helped take him out of it. We own that too. Ian Michael Forever 23. Forever loved. Forever missed. Never forgotten. Your life mattered.

Ian's Mom,

CATHY W.
Clarks Summit, Pennsylvania

Michael

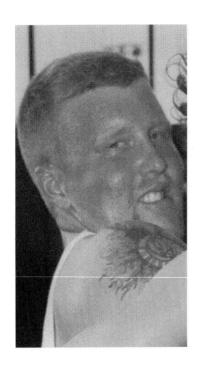

Where do I begin when my whole world has gone crashing to pieces as I lie on the floor screaming NO over and over!!! Later that night after the reality of the dreaded phone call sank in, I could not deny the increasing discomfort in my chest. A trip to the ER and a cardiac catherization and discussion of possible broken heart syndrome then ultimately the diagnosis of a mild heart attack...but through all of this my thoughts were focused on the loss of my first-born child, my son Michael. I always felt in my heart and soul in the years before his death that this was going to happen, but nothing prepares you for it when you stare at it at that horrible moment!

Michael was a beautiful boy growing up, probably like all our children. He was the oldest of my three children; very intelligent, shy, loved the outdoors, and was very close to his grandfather, my father. Unfortunately, in his teens, my marriage started to fall apart, and his youngest brother had obvious drug and alcohol problems. I was engrossed in dealing with his legal and mental needs as Michael watched from the sidelines. I was unaware of how far Michael's drug abuse was progressing. He was very secretive and elusive.

As the years progressed, I divorced and moved from the area. My son continued to keep me at a distance unless he needed money. He would spin quite a tale every time and be quite convincing as to why he needed my help. He would even promise to stay in touch more often. His father was an active enabler in his life, but he never notified me of any important issues. Michael was homeless at times, but he lived with a girlfriend sporadically. While living with her towards the end of his life he would call me occasionally and spin a story of how they needed money for some basic needs and I would fall for it out of desperation and my love for my son. I had no family contact or resources to back up his information so I sent him the money reluctantly knowing I would never see it again and suspecting it might be to buy drugs. It was a horrible feeling...

There were many other times Michael would reach out especially while he was in the hospital. Our phone conversations would start out okay but would always escalate. Either he was depressed or angry. He had recently woken up and found his girlfriend dead next to him. She was a drug addict too. That really upset him a lot! He said he kept seeing her dead face every time he closed his eyes. My son was dead of his overdose five months after his girlfriend. I have always accepted the fact that God took my son home because he was suffering and in so much pain. It was time for him. But this is the worst pain I have ever experienced...to live with this loss every day the rest of my life.

My son, Michael, died alone in a motel room and was discovered by the motel staff the next day. My heart breaks that my son died alone or did he....so many of our children are left to die as others panic and run! But I believe he probably bought his drugs and really was alone. Which continues to haunt me along with all the questions all of us parents have running through our minds. Did they suffer, how long did it take, what did they see and feel...it continues to seep into a parent's heart and soul.

I asked the detective how my son looked when he found him, and he told me he looked like he was peacefully sleeping.

Well I bought that pretty picture for a while until I thought about my options as I was going to travel back to the state where my son had been born and died. I contacted the detective and asked if I could have a copy of the photos that I knew had been taken at the scene. I was told by law that was not possible. That angered me that I had no right to see my son on his death bed!

The more I thought about it I called back and asked if I could come in and see the photos. They agreed to that. It was the most difficult heart wrenching experience I will ever have! My son was not peacefully sleeping!!! He fell back on the bed almost immediately DEAD! Fentanyl sucks!!! Our children are being murdered......I realize the detective was trying to spare me heartache and pain, but my gut kept pushing me on.

God help our children.

Michael's Mom,

ROBIN W.
Lake Havasu City, Arizona

Shannon

FOREVER 39

Her name was Shannon Jean. She was a beautiful thirty-nine-year-old woman. She was also my baby girl. How could this have happened? Doesn't this always happen to other people...not your own child? I knew she was doing drugs, but I really didn't want to believe it could happen to her.

We did rehab; didn't work. She would tell me she was doing better, but it was all a lie. She had a boyfriend she was getting serious about and a new life to look forward to, but that wasn't enough. She still needed that high. I don't understand it and I probably never will. I miss her terribly. Her one-year angelversary will be coming up next month and I hope I can make it.

Shannon's Mom,
CHRISTINE W.
Girardville, Pennsylvania

David

My son David was born in 1984, my second son and much-loved little brother to Chris. He was a beautiful blue-eyed towhead that was always ready for fun. That's what people remember about him, his smile and laughter.

Both boys were close to their dad, but we divorced when they were eight and three. Davey took it harder as time went by as he didn't have as many memories as his brother did because he was younger.

I had to work two or three jobs to keep us afloat, and I blame myself for not seeing the signs sooner, but I believed my boys knew better than to try drugs as we do have addictions in our family and openly talked about the consequences.

By the time he graduated high school, he had been smoking pot and did cocaine with his friends. His best friend passed away one and a half years before Davey, and gave him his first taste of opiates.

From that point forward, he was a hardcore user. Davey was living with his girlfriend and I didn't see him as often as I liked, but I could accept he was growing up. He was a concrete finisher and worked so hard but gave away every penny to the dope boys.

A friend of his from work got in touch with me and let me know what was going on with him. I thank God he cared enough to tell me, and I tracked my son down and got him into rehab, his first one at nineteen. I stupidly thought this is it, my kid knows better, he will go there, get better, and never do it again.

That was my wishful thinking. He started using again within six months of getting out. He continued to use, he kept working unless he was dope sick, then started stealing to support his habit. He got arrested for stealing, probation violations, possession charges, and spent some time in county jails, but never got or accepted the help he needed. Davey always thought he was stronger than IT until he realized he wasn't.

At twenty-two, his girlfriend had their son, Devyn, and all was going well. He was in a methadone program and successfully completed it in two years time. Then his girlfriend wanted her freedom when she turned twenty-one and left with the baby. Davey was crushed and within six months he was strung out again. This time, a cousin showed him how to shoot heroin and he never came back from the ledge.

Years followed with arrests for stealing, looking like a homeless person, losing everything he worked for, and not being much of a father to Devyn. He stole from us all. His brother has a construction company and he tried so many times to help him out with work but he became such a liability he couldn't let him drive his vehicles. It became so hard to watch him slip away, and we always talked honestly about his drug use.

He always said, "Mom, I'm doing ok, I will be fine, things are getting better." But I always saw the sadness in his eyes and the disappointment he had with himself.

In 2013, he got an eighteen-month prison sentence and I really hoped this would be the time away from people, places and things he needed. He got out in 2015 and came to stay with me. He got back to work, was happy and healthy; he looked the best he had in a long time.

A year later he moved out, got his own place, and was proud of himself. He was seeing his son and paying child support, times were good, and we all had such hope for the future. In 2016, he met another girl and he went back down the slippery slope.

I don't believe she did hardcore drugs, but she sold weed and was a true party girl. She had money, so David had a steady source to buy heroin. She thought she could be his savior and kept him isolated from all of us. I don't think he cared because he could stay high and not face any of his family.

In May of 2018, I spoke to my son for the last time. Just a conversation about how he was doing, and that he was trying to stay away from the police as he was heading back to jail for another probation violation. He sounded so tired, and the last thing we both said to each other was I love you.

When he did get arrested, I asked his girlfriend where he was and how he was doing. She told a stack of lies about how she hadn't talked to him, didn't see him, wasn't sending money, and on and on with the lies. When she said she was moving out because she was tired of being his bank account, I said maybe that's the best thing to do for yourself right now.

Little did I know she told my son that I said that, and when he got out of jail in July, he didn't want anything to do with anyone in his family because of what she was telling him. I tried calling him, she got him another phone and changed the number.

I went to his house many times pounding on the door when both of the cars were there. He cut himself off from all of us and began using heroin again.

On September 19, 2018, I got a call at work from my mom saying she had bad news. My sweet boy was gone. I don't remember much about the following days, and his girl-friend was never honest about what happened that night. She said they got into a fight because he was high and she left.

Sometime later he got a fatal hit of fentanyl and when he didn't show up for work, she went back to the house to find him on his knees, long gone from this world.

The police treated it as just another overdose, another junkie thief they don't have to worry about. But he was my son, my baby and His Life Mattered. Rest in Heaven, Davey Bell. Thirty-four years with you was not long enough.

David's Mom,

TRISH W.
Hartford, Ohio

Patrick

I was a young nineteen-year-old having multiple issues with labor and was put in the hospital a week before my due date. It was a cold, cloudy morning in St. Louis, Missouri, and I had been laying in the hospital for three days with nearly twelve hours of hard labor. I had chosen to have a natural birth with no epidural, and frankly by the time I was begging for it, we were told it was too late and I needed to deliver immediately or I would be prepped for a Caesarean section.

The doctors said the baby needed to come out, so I asked my mom who was in the room with me to turn on the music hoping to get me relaxed enough to deliver. Music has always been an integral part of my life and during my pregnancy every night at seven p.m. I would sit and play classical music on my cassette player and put the headphones on my belly, hoping my baby could hear it. I would play Mozart, Beethoven, and Kenny G.

It took five pushes and I heard the most beautiful cry. Overjoyed, I squealed on December 18, 1993, "Happy Birthday Baby!" I heard the doctor and nurse say, "Congratulations it is a boy," and he was born to *What Child Is This* playing on the radio. As they were weighing my boy, they were talking about how incredible it was that my son was born to this Christmas song about the birth of Jesus.

My mom was the first person to hold my sweet baby boy. She was walking my new bundle of joy who was crying over to me and I said, "There's my baby boy," and he threw his head as if searching for my voice. As I held this baby boy, I said, "Welcome to the world." He was absolutely perfect, with ten toes and ten fingers, his lips were red, and he had a little layer of dark hair. Not many people know, but I had originally named him Tyler for several hours after birth. That all changed when I went to the nursery and asked to see Tyler and the nurse said, "We have nine Tylers that have been delivered in two days." Must have been the popular boy's name of the week at the hospital. Later, as I was holding and feeding him, I was touching his face looking down. I said, "You are not a Tyler; you my Irish son are Patrick," and he looked at me with a little smile. I knew without a doubt I made the right decision naming him Patrick. While I held this beautiful baby, no one told me I only had twenty-two years before he would die from an overdose.

If you walked up to my house and opened my roof you would find a normal family life. We were happy, loving, and filled with laughter. We would cry, laugh, and play Yahtzee and Rummy and the Old Maid cards. A very competitive family game night was always a weekend fun time. We would root for each other, and fight like hell. We had feelings, we would yell, we would high five. Our house was filled with love and support. My kids and I had my parents who were gushing over their grandkids. My parents never missed a game of Patrick's and his sports teams would adopt them as the team grandparents.

Patrick as a young boy enjoyed cars, animals, board games, music, sports, and being outside! He also had to know how things worked. On Patrick's third birthday, we bought him a Hot Wheels set with 100 cars. He lined those up in the living room and down the hall. When Patrick was not looking, my dad took one car and adjusted the line so you couldn't tell. That afternoon, Patrick was intently looking at his cars and he said, "Mom, what happened to the red car that was right here?" I had no idea my dad moved it so I told Patrick I didn't know (truthfully, I didn't even know there was a red car). So, Patrick asked my dad and my dad giggled and said yes indeed, he had moved it. Patrick at age three would take apart the remote control and put it back together.

My dad taught Patrick at about age four to play chess. They would sit for hours and play chess. Patrick was fascinated with my parents' piano. He and my mom would sit for hours playing the piano. No wonder Patrick begged me for a guitar or drums at about six years old. I am not musically talented, but it is in my blood, and I find music to always be healing and I had a wide range of music influence Patrick as he grew up. I finally took him to the music store and Patrick connected to the young man who was educating us on which guitars and drums to choose from. This young man took his time with Patrick and we actually picked out a small set of drums.

Patrick's little face was glowing and he could not hardly wait to set it up. It only took a week. My neighbor had given Patrick a microphone and a Karaoke speaker. He was all set and he would play the drums pretty much all day and I didn't mind as he played in the basement. He would say, "I want to be like Ringo Starr." I liked the Beatles but truly had no idea who their drummer was! Patrick and one of his friends had unbeknownst to me moved the drum set upstairs. One Saturday morning early I hear, "Wake up Momma we would like pancakes" coming out of the speakers and then the beat of drums almost like an opening of a concert with the drum roll. Needless to say, that was the last time the drums were allowed upstairs to the bedroom and the speaker and microphone were banned upstairs too!

A little while later, we purchased a guitar and the love and passion of singing and playing guitar became our family time and we all enjoyed it so much. Patrick was able to hear a song and play it. His love of music covered a wide range of genres. One Friday night, I came home to find all the middle school kids hanging in my front yard and sitting on the front porch was a drum set, and Patrick was entertaining these kids with his guitar. Melted my heart and then I said, "I am going to start charging admission fees."

Patrick had such a kind, tender heart. He would rescue all baby animals, loved his dogs, guinea pig, birds. One day, I had just purchased a new couch and prior to moving my old set out, I kept it in the garage. That evening, I was searching for Patrick, calling his name, nothing. I opened the garage door and Patrick was sitting on the new couch putting something behind the pillows. He looked up at me and said, "Mom please don't be mad, I saved a baby bird that had fallen." I said, "And what are you doing?" He slowly stood up and I saw the pillow fall and the baby bird laying there. So, we made a nest and before we could move the baby bird, it had died.

In school, Patrick was always well liked and always having and invited to sleepovers. His teacher and coaches were fond of him and knew he went the extra mile. He always carried good grades and loved school, especially lunch and PE. Most of his friends played sports on several teams with Patrick. These boys grew very close and so did the parents. One afternoon walking with two of his friends, a new boy who had moved into the neighborhood was making fun of one of his friends for being chunky. Patrick without hesitation stood up for his friend. He was always the kind of heart that rooted for the underdog. What upset Patrick as he grew was the sometimes meanness of the world. He forever would give you the shirt off his back never expecting anything in return. Here is a quote from one of Patrick's first coaches who knew Patrick since he was four-and-a-half-years old:

> Some of the best experiences I've ever had were coaching, especially the fiery Patrick who was always respectful of his coaches and would accept any roll and bust his butt for the team. I loved him and his character and loyalty. Great parents and families were the other part of the puzzle. Thanks for your total support and backing always Kate as well as that of your parents.

Another friend Tony said one of his favorite stories was when they were playing soccer or football at a fellow friend's house and everyone couldn't have been more than eleven or twelve years old. Something happened and when everyone was telling each other they sucked, Patrick was the positive one, encouraging everyone to keep their heads up and that it was okay.

When Patrick was nine and a half years old, his little sister was born. He absolutely adored Khloe. He really enjoyed it as she grew and was eligible for "time out." He was so eager to record our family moments or Khloe cutting her dolls or horses hair after being told not to. Khloe was always included by all his friends; she was also their little sister. As Khloe grew, she struggled with math. I am not the greatest at math either but for Patrick, math came easily. He used her textbook to create math problems for Khloe to solve, then worked with her to solve these math questions. To this day, she hasn't struggled with math because of Patrick's tutoring.

Patrick had pretty normal teenage years, skateboarding, drawing and journaling things, writing music, playing music. He would say, "Mom, it's more than just the lyrics, you actually feel it in your soul. The vibration of music is deep. I dream of writing music and it comes to me all the time, my brain doesn't shut down, it just constantly gives me music."

High school came and as usual things changed. One teacher pulled me aside and said Patrick is bored. He's doing work just enough to pass, however he's acing tests. He comprehends the class, it's just too easy for him. He was dating a young lady in high school and one time after either an argument or break up she fired up his locker and burned his books. Who would know years later that both would overdose within eleven months of each other and the burning of books would be a cherished memory for both her mom and I?

May of 2012, Patrick was injured on a ranger utility vehicle at a friend's house. I can't disclose much regarding this. He had a severe concussion and broken nose which led to several years of doctors. One neurologist gave him a four-hour test for short and long-term memory, along with an IQ test. When the testing was over, the doctor came out and said, "I don't always get to say this to parents, but the results of the IQ test are in; you got yourself a genius." We were blown away and I even giggled and said, "Well don't most parents want to think their kid is a genius, but mine actually is." What a sweet memory.

What we didn't know is that not all doctors have your best interest in mind. Patrick was about eighteen years old and he was having debilitating issues that manifested from the accident. He did see several doctors but only one of those doctors started the journey we feel led to addiction. I am not a pharmacist and not a doctor, but I was always taught to listen to the doctors. If a doctor felt you needed medicine, then you took it as prescribed. I never questioned doctors. This might have been a fatal mistake on my part. I trusted this doctor who had studied the body and medicine and knew the dangers of opioids, yet wrote scripts like he was handing out candy. Then one day the doctor moves on and stops writing scripts and by this time it's too late.

I am not going to say Patrick was innocent, he smoked pot. Do I feel this encouraged his addiction? No, I do not think marijuana led to his addiction. To be honest with you, I wish that was the worst he did. I was not ok with him smoking pot and I lectured him and grounded him, restricting his rights as parents do. I had no idea what bigger issues lay down the road, but pot led only to him having the munchies and being completely relaxed. He was able to function, he was able to work. I did notice that when he smoked pot his health complications improved. I kept a journal of his injuries from the accident. I actually wrote that it seems the doctor after three years felt it's time for him to not need the prescriptions any more. I had no idea what this meant at the time. I didn't know the hell that was about to change our lives.

In the spring of 2014, Patrick was twenty and I noticed his guitar playing had slowed down and he wasn't wanting to hang out with his friends as much. He was aloof to doing family things, which caused us to have more family fights. We went to lunch and Patrick said, "Mom, I tried heroin." My heart jumped out of my chest. I was speechless. He said, "It's ok, I won't do it again. A friend of mine gave me Subutex and I take these when a craving happens and I won't be sick."

I was devastated and lost and very confused. How does this happen to a normal boy who is slated to have the world at his feet? He's in college and doing extremely well with high honor grades. How could he slip up and just try heroin? I kept opening my mouth but I couldn't catch my breath as I felt those words, "Mom, I tried heroin," like it wasn't a big deal and it would never happen again. I have never known anyone who did heroin or drugs for that matter. Maybe I was naive, which is completely possible. But my son, the son who had everything and could do or be anything had tried heroin. I didn't know the depth of what "trying heroin" was. I barely took Tylenol. I knew enough to know heroin was deadly and knew it was the worst drug ever. Little did I know it actually hijacks their brains and the person they are is no longer.

What I didn't know is that this devil would be a beast to slay but I was willing to do anything to have my boy back. The only thing I could think was, "Not My Family," and I also believe those are fatal words. He promised me he wouldn't do it. Then came the loss of all things he loved.

No one told me, "Buckle your seat belt, you are in for a ride." Heroin not only was in my backyard, it had crept its ugly ass up my stairs and hijacked my sweet boy. It stripped away all the joys of every aspect of Patrick's life. It sped up the manipulation side of his brain, he was nodding out, he overdosed at least four times. I took away his car, his cell phone, and wouldn't allow him to work. We did outpatient rehab; we did local rehabs which are deplorable to this day, sadly. We had one center say, "We are the experts, he needs outpatient;" we were like, 'We are the parents, he needs inpatient." He was fully insured and we still had issues with finding a good, decent rehab center. How in the world can I save my boy and help him get better and back on track? I didn't know how hard this would be. It literally tore our hearts out. You will hear tales of tough love, those who lock them away, those who know what they would do if they were in this situation. I didn't know anyone who walked this dangerous path. We felt alienated and alone and yet fought to save my son. How did this happen?

The most dangerous words said, "Not My Family." Why not your family? Is it because you have a job, career, you have a house and car, and plenty of money in the bank? Is it because your household provider's income allows you to stay at home? Is it because you home-school your kids, or your kids go to a private/public school? Is it because your kids play sports, is it because you don't know anyone in your family who has an addiction? Is it because your kids are on honor roll, they have jobs, and are responsible adults? Is it that your kids are too young to understand addiction or drugs? Is it because your zip code is marked "Safe" in your head? As I suddenly found, there's no excuse for "Not My Family."

Addiction doesn't discriminate. It doesn't care about your house, your income, your car, it doesn't care where your kids go to school, or if your kids play sports; it certainly doesn't care about your grades or your zip code. It doesn't care about your race, religion, or sexual preference. It doesn't care about your family or destruction of the path it will take you on. Your social status means nothing. Addiction is in your backyard, on your street, in our schools, in our zip code, at our jobs, at our kids sporting events. It's usually swept up under your welcome mat and that's mostly where you try to leave it. Addiction comes in different forms, such as and not limited to food, alcohol, sex, gambling, shopping, video games, plastic surgery, and behavioral addictions such as substance abuse and substance dependency. There is sadly an endless list to the many different addictions. How gullible I was to believe "Not My Family."

Once the dark path has entered your home, all forms of denial need to be shot out the window. Stop thinking about where you went wrong; at this point, you are in the fight of your life to save your loved one.

Over twenty million Americans over the age of twelve have an addiction. This doesn't include tobacco. Daily, 201 lives are lost to overdose and this has skyrocketed in the past ten years. Prescriptions are abused at higher rates; painkillers are the most common.

I wanted so much to believe my love would cure all. If love cured all we wouldn't be battling addiction. Parents wouldn't be saying goodbyes to their children and lowering them in the ground or having them cremated.

After several attempts with rehabs, Patrick was finally sober and for about eight months. We were starting to take our guard down. Still watching as if the finger was on the pulse constantly. I would hold my breath with calls and I lived in a panicked state of mind. I was working full time, battling my son's addiction, trying to keep normalcy for my daughter, and wasn't talking to many people other than those close to me about what I was battling to save him. He was enrolled in college and doing extremely well. Things were looking up and we felt our lives getting back on track. We learned at Patrick's Celebration of Life that he had stopped by the GED office. One of his favorite teachers was teaching and there were four elderly people working on their GED. Patrick helped them with math as they struggled to understand it. They came in honor of Patrick helping them pass the GED just a mere week prior to his passing. They were extremely emotional and shocked to learn he had been fighting addiction, yet were so grateful for his kindness in helping them.

Just three weeks before he passed, we noticed a change immediately. He started dropping weight like crazy and hallucinating, his pupils were little dots. He was pale and frail. We struggled to get him help; he truly was lost in the failed system we battle to this day. Hugging him was like hugging a skeleton, just bones. We were in the hospital twelve times the last three weekends he was alive. He had taken many Xanax. We found a bag and he told us there were 100 in it and when we counted, only sixty were left. We were scared that he was overdosing. We rushed him to the hospital. I saw the same doctors in the ER who would say, "Oh, just let him sleep it off" or "Once he sobers up, he will be fine." It was explained to us that with Xanax, it is easy to take a pill and several minutes later they don't think they took it so this continues until they pass out or are rushed to the hospital.

On the last Thursday night prior to him passing, I heard his cell phone ring at ten p.m., then heard his door. He went outside and I looked out to see this large man hand him a bag. I quickly threw on my shoes and ran out and Patrick was screaming at me that he is a dangerous drug dealer. I asked him what he gave him and he said weed and showed me a bag of weed. I had a bad feeling, but after he showed me the bag, I chose to believe that it was weed and even if I called the police, they wouldn't do anything because it was weed. I let it go. It was unsettling and I did second guess myself.

It was abnormally warm the last weekend of January 2016. Tim, my boyfriend, and I had made plans that evening. Patrick had been up all night from what it sounded like and this was completely normal. Tim and I went looking for houses while he slept, and then planned to have dinner and meet up with friends. We had not been out with friends in months because I couldn't bear to think, what if Patrick overdosed and we weren't home to save him? However, we went to dinner. I peeked in on him while he was sleeping (or what we thought was sleeping).

We went to dinner and about seven p.m.; I said to my significant other, "Something feels off like in the pit of my stomach." He calmed me by saying it's the first time we have been out and Patrick will be fine if he sleeps because he needs it from being up all night. We finished dinner and met friends that night. About ten p.m., I was growing anxious and my legs wouldn't stop moving under the table. I was shaking and the pit in my stomach grew worse. We finished up with our friends and made our way home about eleven p.m. I kept saying in the car, "Something is wrong and I am worried sick."

We pulled up and went in, then noticed that Patrick hadn't been up or eaten anything the entire time we were gone. Tim asked me to stay in the living room while he checked on Patrick. I heard him say Patrick's name three times and I knew this wasn't good. He asked me to take the dog outside. I was sitting in the car and could hear the sirens. I physically couldn't get out of the car; after a few minutes there were police and EMS flooding our home. I kept asking if he was alive and no one would answer me. I could tell by my significant other's face it was not good. He was pale and said, "We are headed to hospital," and I said, "I have the dog with me." He said, "Bring her to the ER."

I kept saying, just tell me, I know he passed. I could feel it. Those two minutes it took to get to the hospital felt like we drove eighteen hours. I kept looking at the stars and the moon praying for my boy to find peace. I prayed for peace; whatever peace is, I was praying for him to have it. After sixty minutes, they came into the quiet room and the same doctor in the ER who had seen Patrick at least twelve times in the past three weeks had to look me in the eye and say, "I'm sorry, we tried everything. I am so sorry, Miss, your son has passed".

January 31, 2016, I lost my sweet boy. No more hearing his infectious laughter, no more of his beautiful smile, no more hugs, kisses, no more of his kindness and hearing him say, "Momma, I love you." No more singing our lungs out in the car as a family together, no more Patrick playing the guitar. No more texts or calls all ending in love you Mom. My heart will remain completely shattered until we meet again. One thing is sure, our bond of mother and son will never be broken not even through death. Patrick continues to show me and encourages me to fight for others. The rest of that year was a complete blur and I refused medication as I saw this as exactly what got my son onto this deadly path.

I continue to this day to be a huge pain in the ass dealing with doctors. I research everything and question them on everything. I know this won't bring my son back, but I know enough now to help others.

If love cured my son he wouldn't be on the shelf, he would likely be still in college pursuing his dream of neuroscience.

We have turned to honor Patrick

729

with Wyland Wolfpack educating and spreading awareness. Our coined theme which I feel he sent us "Be A Kind Human" on all our T Shirts. I miss my son more each day, but I draw strength in helping others.

Patrick's Mom,

KATE W.
St Louis, Missouri

Donny

FOREVER 21

My boy! He was born February 26, 1999, after I spent forty-five days in the hospital while pregnant with him. I had fallen down, bleeding internally, instantly throwing me into labor. After forty-five days in the hospital, given Demerol four to five times a day, maybe more, I was literally addicted to this medication when I came home from having him. If it was a medication I knew I could get on the streets, I probably would have.

Thank God I survived it. Anyway, I had an eight-pound, ten-ounce, bouncing, jumping, and running baby boy! He was born a month early. He was due on my momma's birthday, March 26.

Donny was a relatively healthy baby! At two years old, I worked for a dental office and he needed dental work. We used to sedate little ones with Demerol. I brought him into the office, the doctor gave him the meds, and Donny was wired!!! It did not work on him.

She could not complete the procedure. She told me to bring him back next time and try just giving him over the counter Benadryl and then she would try. About two weeks later we did just that, which was a success. He was out for the whole procedure! Never thought anything of it.

Donny was a very active boy! I was a football lover, and I was going to have the next running back of the NFL! He tried so hard, and he tried for me! He was so little. One day his coach came to me and said, "We are going to get him hurt." Okay I get it, it's okay. So, then he tried band! We all knew he was an amazing guitar player, but he played by ear. He had no idea how to read music!

This is where he thought he would excel! He gets into band class, and they tell him he will play the trombone! He tried! Then he tells me, "This is dumb, Mom." Okay, I get it! It's okay! He then tries track and field! He runs all the time! I'm get him to the track or wherever they are running at five a.m.! I am not a morning person, but hey, whatever it takes! He loses every race, but he's not giving up! He finishes them all!

He then tries long boarding! (Different than skateboarding, I was corrected.) He LOVED IT! He was AMAZING AT IT! We took him to competitions, where he did so well! In the meantime, of all these long board competitions and practicing, around the house, through his teenage years, he had fourteen broken bones! Yes fourteen!!!

Every time he would say, "Mom, it's okay, don't take me to the doctor, it will cost too much!" I didn't care! He found something he loved and was good at. I took him to the doctor, and as a mom, that is what you do. The doctor would put a cast on the broken bone, send him home with a prescription of pain pills, and say, "See you in six weeks!"

When Donny got to high school and started driving, I was so scared; but he was always respectful to us and had a job! I knew Donny started smoking marijuana. One thing my son never did was hide things from me or lie. Yes, I know I didn't know everything, but for the most part I did.

Once he graduated high school, he didn't have any ambition. He was smoking marijuana more and we thought we needed to play "tough love,' so we told him to get his stuff together and join the military or he needed to go. Looking back, was it the right thing to do? We don't know! However, we do believe the navy saved his life for two more years.

Donny obviously got clean long enough to join the navy. February 26, 2018! (The day he turned nineteen) I never thought in a MILLION years he would graduate boot camp! He did!!!! Well, not without being remembered as the "Rice Krispy Kid!"

At graduation (April 27, 2018), his dad (my husband) looked at him and said, 'Son, look at you! Aren't you so glad you are off that stuff?" Lil D said, "Dad, I think about it every day!" (He had gained thirty pounds in boot camp.)

Then he went to "A" school where he graduated second in his class! I thought, "Heck yes, we got this!"

He came home for fourteen days after "A" school, where he was still doing well!

June 14, 2018, his first duty station was on the John C. Stennis in Bremerton, Washington! He left, went off, and was having the time of his life! Donny was an ABE, and loved every minute of it! He immediately left for deployment in October 2018! Again, doing great, loved his job, and traveling the world! Oh, the stories he would tell!

Once he got to Virginia in May 2019, it all went downhill! We could see it. Even though we could not physically see it. We knew! He called me up one day in September of 2019 and said, "Momma, I'm coming home!"

Without hesitation I said, "Okay, come on!" Donny came home the very next day and told us he had a problem! I said, "What kind of problem?" He said, "Momma, I'm an addict!" I said, "An addict to what?" He said, "Heroin." I about fell over!

Yes, I knew there was something wrong, but NEVER IN A MILLION YEARS did I think it would be heroin! He said, "Momma, you thought high school was bad, I can get it anywhere I want!" He also told me he went to heroin because it was much cheaper than pills on the streets.

For the next nine days (that's all he was home for), I watched my baby go through withdrawals! It was the hardest thing I've ever had to see! I called people trying to find out what I needed to do, when I needed to take him to the hospital, etc…I had no clue!

He was not raised this way! We did not do drugs nor did we allow him around people that did! He was still owned by the United States government! What could I do? NOTHING! I had to sit and watch him, and talk to him, and beg him once he got back to please self-report and get the help he needed! HE DID! He did just as I asked!!!! October 9, to be exact, is when he self-reported! They wanted to make him an informant, but he told them no! He was there to get the help he needed. He was still able to come and go as he pleased! To a mom, that was awful! I was so mad! I was angry! It wasn't until I believe October 28 when the Stennis went underway, I called a JAG and asked if they were going to chalk this up to another suicide if something happened to him.

Now please, do not take that wrong! I was so upset! He needed help! Well, they flew him off the ship to rehab! I was so happy! He was so happy! YES, WE DID IT! He was getting the help he needed! He got out of rehab December 9, 2019. Totaled his car December 10! Donny was discharged by the Navy December 28. I get it! Zero tolerance! He got it too!

He bought a brand-new car January 5! Totaled that car January 10! At this point, we are asking him to stay home on the tenth, for sure! January 15, Donny overdosed for the first time! Luckily, his navy buddies were there and could call for help! However, they had no idea about his problem! It's not something he advertised! I then asked him what he was going to do and he said he did not know.

Well, Momma had a plan! I told him he could come home, but before he did, I wanted him to go to a sixty-day rehab in Kentucky! He WOULD NOT GO! I had the means for him to go for FREE! HE WOULD NOT GO! He's twenty years old at this point! I cannot make him! I told him, "If you do not go to rehab you cannot come home." (I have two granddaughters that I had to think about.)

Donny called me every day and we still had the same awesome relationship! He was doing great! He finally got a job at a local hotel in Virginia and he loved it!

March 16, 2020, Donny calls and says, "Momma I'm coming home. We are getting furloughed because of COVID-19." Heck yes, come on home! I never mentioned drugs, never mentioned rehab or anything. He got home at six-thirty a.m. on March 18. We spent all day together! He was great! We were in the process of moving to our new home and after his dad got home about three-thirty p.m., he went to our old house to get his guitar.

Little did we know he met with a guy who gave him the fatal dose of methadone during that time out. Donny was looking for heroin, according to the text messages on his phone. Also, on those text messages were instructions on how much of the methadone to take! He came back home, played guitar for us, and even sang for us that night! We hugged him, told him we loved him. His dad even told him he didn't care how long this lasted, we had enough money to take care of his car payment, for a while. We all went to bed.

Donny's dad and I did not see him on the nineteenth. He was gone visiting his sister and nieces, one whom he had never met. He also visited other family members that day. He got home about nine-thirty p.m. His dad and I were already in bed, as we get up at four-thirty a.m. every morning. Donny texted me to let me know he was home.

I thanked him and told him I loved him and said, "I just wanted to make sure you were ok," and he knew what I meant by that. I even have a text message on my phone to this day that says "Momma I love you! I'm the best I've ever been!"

March 20, 2020, our worst nightmare came true. Donny had passed away in his room. My baby was gone! He was told to take four TIMES A LETHAL DOSE.

My goal is to help get these drug dealers off the streets. Some people may disagree with me, and that is okay. If there were no drug dealers, my son would still be here today. He did not want to die. He had a problem and did not know how to fix it. My point of telling his story is that this can happen to anyone!!! As parents, we are learning way too much, too late. We are all one broken bone, one surgery, one tooth extraction, etc., away from becoming an addict! Addiction does not discriminate! We buried my baby one day after my momma's birthday, March 27, 2020! Please, if I can help or talk to someone you love, please let me know! My mission is to save one person since I was unable to save my sweet boy! I will also make sure NOBODY forgets my son!

Donny's Mom,

Kim Y.
Splendora, Texas

Brandon

My beautiful blond-haired, green-eyed only son Brandon lost his struggle with addiction on April, 23, 2020. Brandon was the light that lit up a room. His goal in life was to make everyone smile and laugh. He was the funniest, most loyal, compassionate son, brother, and friend that anyone could ask for! We are all so fortunate to have known him and loved him and to have felt that love in return. His kindness and big heart are the legacy he leaves behind. He will be tucked safely in our hearts forever!

Brandon was a beautiful boy; his white blond hair and green eyes captivated all who met him. He had such a zest for life and as he grew, he became sweeter by the minute! He was my little boy and I always called him my little Bubba. His older sister Amber and he were insepa-rable, being only two-and-a-half years apart. They loved to sled ride, play with our neighbors, and fly down our hill in their homemade derby cars! That was her little brother and she loved him so much! He looked up to her and just loved being around her...even during his last days on earth, he said how much he admired his Amber.

Then in 1999, I had twin girls, Carly and Cristy. He was six and when asked how he liked his new sisters, he said he wanted to "throw them back up to God!"But as the years went on, their bond grew deeper. I had four beautiful children...I was blessed!

Brandon loved deck hockey and baseball and was a great part of all the teams he was on. Fast forward to Brandon being around fifteen. He was caught up with marijuana and suspended for two weeks. We had him go to a local outpatient program trying to "nip this in the bud" so to speak. He seemed to learn his lesson and then got his wisdom teeth out at seventeen. I feel this is when his addiction began. I noticed the bottle of pain meds they prescribed him was missing (I had them in my room to give to him as needed). When confronted, he said he took them as needed and I worry too much! But he would not provide me with the pills or the bottle. This opioid prescription was the beginning of an addiction we battled until his death at twenty-seven.

He started Xanax and cocaine at twenty and heroin at twenty-three. He had been in and out of rehabs and outpatient programs and constantly in trouble with the police. But it was always everyone else's fault, never his. Last year, we had a lot of hope. He was given a scholarship to go to a rehab program in Austin, Texas. He left November 15, 2019. He was the most at peace I'd ever known him to be...so spiritual and finally found the self love he had been searching for all these years. He would call me and tell me how much he loved it there and how he felt a "thump" on his heart when doing a freestyle "rap prayer."

I said, "That tap on your heart you felt was from Jesus, Brandon!" Unfortunately, he felt he had to come back to Pittsburgh on March 6, 2020, to face some upcoming DUI hearings. We begged him to stay but he didn't want a warrant out for his arrest, so he said he wanted to come home, face the music, and go back to the sober living house in Texas where he was staying. Sadly, he never got that chance. He relapsed soon after coming home and marched himself into two local rehabs one-and-a-half months. Two days out of the second rehab, he used and overdosed on April 23, 2020. Fentanyl poisoning...a drug delivered by his good friend...his grade school friend! Police could care less that I have names on his phone from that fateful night so I guess I'm not supposed to seek justice for my son's murder?

As I sit on my front porch while writing this, I hear the sound of a bat cracking a baseball at the field below and am reminded of what a great baseball player my Brandon was. And of all the games I attended and cheered him on! It is sounds like these that bring me to my knees...wishing I could go back in time and relive every single game and every pizza party after. I was his biggest fan then, and even during his active addiction, I rooted for him while he was in the cusp of his life... begging and pleading with God that he would hit that "homerun" and run around the bases of his demons and score the winning run of sobriety that would change the outcome forever for him. He wanted so badly to reach "home plate" and had every opportunity to do so, but he was too weak and never got the chance. He dropped that cross that weighed so heavily on his shoulders and now it's up to me...his loving and grieving Mom to pick up that cross that he dropped, keep saying his name, and march forward in his legacy!

Brandon wanted nothing more than to get clean and stay clean but the demons kept coming back to haunt him. He tried time and time again to love himself, find God, and to find a way out of this life that we knew he didn't want for himself or for the family that he knew loved him so very much. He fought harder than anyone I know and for that I'm forever proud of my beloved son.

He is forever brave..forever kind. I'm beyond blessed that God chose me for Brandon to call "Mama, Mommy, Mom, and Ma" for the last twenty-seven years. My world is shattered beyond belief and I am forever broken! But we thank God for giving us the life of Brandon Michael that we will love and cherish until the end of time. "I'll love you forever; I'll like you for always as long as I'm living, my baby boy Brandon you'll be!"

In closing my chapter in this book on my beloved son, I'd like to share his last entry in his HOPE recovery journal that I found after he died. It speaks volumes of how he struggled so hard in trying to reach "the peak." He titled it "Treacherous Mountain".

Treacherous Mountain

I'm climbing up this mountain to success
Cutting off luggage to make it to the next ledge.
It seems the higher I get, the thinner the air gets
Now I'm starting to get tired, feels like life is suffocating me until I expire.

But now I get inspired because I see the peak
So I cut the last line and make it in time to see the light that SHINES.

I recently set up a scholarship in Brandon's name for those suffering as he did. I call it "Brandon's Light" because he was, and will always be, the light of my life!

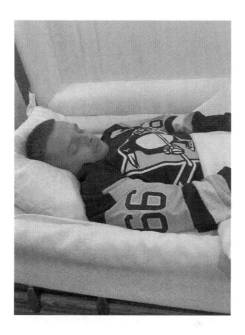

Brandon's Mom,

LYNNE Z.
Pittsburgh, Pennsylvania

Jason

FOREVER 23

On July 31, 2018, Jason brought a pizza home for dinner. He put it down, ran upstairs to get his bong, and went into our backyard to smoke and make a phone call. About fifteen minutes later, I went outside to see what was taking him so long. His phone was on the table. His bong was not lit. Jason was sitting on a chair...his head tilted back...his lips were purple with foam and blood oozed out of his mouth. I knew he was dead.

I remember being calm and just staring at him. I called 9-1-1. I was told to place him down flat on the ground. I was asked if I could perform CPR. I couldn't. I could only see the foam and blood. I was told to do heart compressions. I did the compressions, but kept saying that my son was dead. I remember the ambulance and police arriving and my dogs running upstairs to hide. I remember calling my husband, who was at a wake, and telling him to come home because Jason was dead.

I called my brother, who lives about an hour away. He came and brought my daughter, who lives closer to him. She was hysterical and kept saying that we were good parents and didn't deserve this. He also brought our mother. Jason was close to his grandma. I remember going outside to the "crime scene" and staring at Jason's dead body. A police officer went through Jason's room and his wallet and found packets of heroin. I would later learn that Jason had died from heroin laced with fentanyl.

The funeral was two days later. Then we sat shiva. We are Jewish, not at all religious and even less so after Jason's death. I remember seeing his dead body before the service and just kept thinking how is this happening...how did we end up here.

Jason had a perfectly normal childhood. He was born on August 30, 1994, in Brooklyn, New York. His sister was born eighteen months later; we then moved to Freehold, New Jersey. Jason was a quiet, sweet, and easy-going kid. He loved video games and roller coasters. He did well in school, had friends, had parties, went to parties, went on family vacations, went to day camp, to travel roller coaster camp... got what he wanted...I never in a million years thought that drugs would be something he would want.

Jason's personality changed when he started high school. He became more private, even a little moody. His group of friends had changed as well. I thought it was just normal teenage behavior. I also knew that he was occasionally smoking pot with his friends. I didn't love that he was doing this and when he got caught by local police officers, we enrolled him in a local out-patient drug program for teens. Huge mistake...I would later learn that he did drugs at this facility and would lie through his teeth about his "false positive" drug tests. Still, I knew NOTHING about addiction and wanted to believe my son when he said he would stop. Of course, he didn't stop and the lies continued.

After his death, I attended GRASP meetings and have learned so much about this "disease." I don't know if my knowing sooner would have changed the outcome, but I do know that I would have been more understanding. I regret telling him to "get a life," and calling him a "loser." I had no idea that at some point this disease took over my boy's brain. He knew that I didn't understand. He also knew that I was always here for him and that he always had a loving family and home. I later knew that he didn't mean to lie to my face, to curse me out or to "use" me and make me feel like shit after I would give him money or pay his bills. How did this become our lives?

In April 2017, after three car accidents, court appearances, and many trips to the ER, (which were all a waste of time, as they did nothing for Jason and they always sent him home), Jason agreed to go to rehab. He was in a nice facility in Texas. His counselor told me that he was "a poster child for addiction." Again, I couldn't believe or understand this, but I was confident that he would get better there. After all, you go to rehab and then you're better...Boy, was I wrong. Our insurance ran out after two weeks, and I really missed Jason and thought he was better so he came back home. He lived with his girlfriend at this time and promised that he wasn't doing "bad" things. I still, to this day, cannot believe that MY son used and knew where to buy drugs...opioids, pills, things I've never heard of. I remember seeing white powder, foil, and cut up straws in his room... was I really that naive?

In April 2018, Jason went to rehab for the second time. He had always loved California and chose a detox and sober living facility recommended by a "friend." Looked perfect from what I had read on the web. It was actually horrible. Jason was using drugs while in sober living. My insurance company, along with us, were paying for his treatment, so they looked the other way and allowed Jason to stay. He finally decided to come home in June.

Jason came home on June 17. He was nodding out and falling asleep at dinner with our family that evening. I, of course, said he was tired from his trip home. The next morning, I found vomit all over the backyard and heroin packets in his bedroom. Jason ended up in the ER once again. While waiting for him, I received a phone call from the rehab center that he had just left. The woman was telling me how fabulous he was doing and asking for more money and for Jason's Social Security number. She had no idea that Jason wasn't even there anymore.

I apologize for my thoughts being all over the place. There are so many details and things that I just can't remember. In conclusion, Jason later admitted that he had been using drugs since "childhood." He didn't think he had a problem. I tried to focus on positive things and not always harp on the drugs. It was difficult for me. His behavior and appearance began to disgust me and I would be angry with myself for feeling this way. I was angry at Jason for "ruining our good lives." I would always say "we aren't drug people, just stop already."

On July 20, 2018, Jason and I went to Great Adventure together. It was great until I realized that whatever he was "on" was wearing off. He was gone eleven days later. I still can't believe it. I love and miss him so much. I have cried at some point every day since his passing.

Jason's Mom,

HOLLI Z.
Freehold, New Jersey

Ryan

FOREVER 25

Let me introduce you to Ryan. As a twenty-five-year-old, Ryan loved life and all it had to offer. Ryan loved music, playing drums, and going to concerts, especially with mosh pits. His favorite band was A Day to Remember. He was caring, empathetic, and had the biggest heart. He had many new things in his life...his own apartment, a girlfriend, and a job cooking at a restaurant that he loved. He worked many hours, but said that was good because it kept him busy and gave him a chance to save some money. Ryan told me that he wanted to set up a weight bench in the basement, so that he could start working out again. Working out made him feel good. Ryan did not have much in his apartment, but what he had I know meant a lot to him. Ryan was working hard on being an adult and being independent.

As his mom, I was so proud of him, but I was also scared. Having a child that suffers from substance use disorders and had been to rehab more than once leaves you cautious. I did not ask the hard questions to my son, because I was scared of the answers. Now I live with the guilt of those unasked and unanswered questions. I never sent Ryan money. I was afraid that he would buy drugs or alcohol. Instead, I sent care packages. In early December 2018, I sent Ryan a care package. Ryan lived in Connecticut, while I live in Florida. Ryan texted me on Sunday, December 16, that he received the package and loved the blanket. We said that we loved each other.

At four p.m. on Monday, December 17, 2018, my life forever changed. I got the call that Ryan was dead. My youngest son was gone. He died alone in his apartment. It was ruled an accidental overdose (heroin with fentanyl), but I call it drug-induced homicide. No one was ever charged with his murder.

The bright and promising future for my son is gone. Ryan's addicted brain won the battle and he lost the fight on December 17, 2018, at only twenty-five years young. I found out after his death that he was going into rehab that day. I will never see my son married, become a father, go to college, or become an uncle to his brother's children. I miss his smile. I miss his laugh. I mostly miss his hugs. There are no more new memories to be made. All I can do is make sure that Ryan did not die in vain. He was too special to this world to be forgotten. Opioids killed my son. I am forever changed because I am forever heartbroken. I am Forever Ryan's Mom. Remember his name.

Ryan's Mom,

MaryBeth Z.
Davenport, Florida

That One Last High

That one last high…

That one last high destroyed everything good..

That one last high sounded like a good idea at the time I guess... just one last time turned into forever.

That one last high led to two detectives ringing my doorbell at 3:44 am. Telling me my baby is gone.

My precious little girl, my first true love.

That one last high led to me explaining to her brother and father and aunts and uncles that she had died.

That one last high led me to a funeral home. Only 12 hours after being told the life-altering news. Staring at my sweet girls face, her body half covered by a sheet, hospital gown draped over her to hide the autopsy incisions.

That one last high led me to holding her face and crying…kissing every part of her I could. Wanting so bad to pull down the sheet and look at her birthmark on her leg or the birthmark on her finger I had kissed each night since she was a baby.

That one last high led me to a room, brain in a fog, staring at caskets trying to decide which one my little girl should be buried in.

That one last high led to writing an obituary, planning a funeral and a house full of flowers from grieving friends and family.

That one last high left me going through her closet. Picking out a dress. Buying a cardigan of her favorite color for her to be buried in. I was careful to cut out the tags because I know she didn't like the way they made her itch.

That one last high led me to going through countless pictures from her first breath til her last. Making memory boards and slideshows... trying to fit 18 sweet years into 10 minutes.

That one last high led me to my knees in front of her casket at the viewing. Pleading with God to take me instead. Demanding him to rewind time. Yelling if he is so almighty why can't he take it back.

Staring through a haze saying thank you for coming repeatedly and comforting her friends.

That one last high led us to the church at 11am.

Where I watched her 15 year old brother help carry her coffin. Where I looked at her for the very last time. Where I wore a matching outfit to what she would be buried in. Where I leaned into her casket and kissed her cold lips and tucked her hair behind her ear one last time.

That one last high left me staring at her casket for an hour after everyone had left the graveside. Scared to leave my baby girl alone.

That one last high led to me sleeping on her grave so she didn't have to be alone, contemplating suicide so I could hold her hand on her way to heaven.

That one last high resulted in months of laying on the floor crying, clinging on to anything that reminded me of her or had her scent. Regretting not wrapping her in a blanket because I know she hates the cold.

That one last high has turned my hair white and added 10 years to my face. That one last high has left empty days and dreaded nights. Mornings that turn into evenings with no memory of the day.

That one last high led me on a search for her ghost everywhere.

I am a broken mother because of one last high.

~Angee Penner mother of Ashlyn Cannon (Forever 18)

Drug Promises

I have some promises I'll make to you,
if you will do what I want you to.
The more that you consume of me,
the more then will your losses be.
Here are the promises to you I make and I promise,
the promises to never break.
I promise to take your money,
your home and all you can get in way of a loan.
I'll take your character, your reputation, your good name.
I'll take from you too your friends.
I'll take from you one day,
your family from you I'll turn away.
I'll take your car.
I'll take your wealth.
I'll take your job.
I'll take your health.
I'll take your watch.
I'll take your chain.
I'll cause you to stand out in the rain.
I'll take your credit.
I'll take your bail.

748

I'll make you sleep in a dirty jail.
I'll cause you regret, remorse, and pain.
I'll cause your name to go down in shame.
I'll bring you misery.
I'll bring you woe.
I'll bring you trouble more than you know.
I'll take your clothes, and pawn them too.
The necessities of life, I'll take from you.
I'll take from you days,
I'll take from you years.
I'll double the flow of your bitter tears.
I'll take your heart, give you one of stone.
I'll cause you to walk through life alone.
I'll take away your desire to live alright.
Your light of day, I'll turn to night.
I'll cause you to dishonor your mom and dad.
I'll take all the pleasure you could have had.
I'll turn all your love for your friends to hate.
Your desire to repent will come too late.
Your road to despair for you I'll pave.
I'll cause you to fall in a pre-mature grave.
I'll put you in an institute for the insane.
Your normal thinking, I'll not let you gain.
I'll cause you to murder your best friend.
I'll trouble your mind to the very end.
I'll bring you contention.
I'll bring you strife.
I'll finish you by taking your life.

Alecia C. written 3/18/11
January 5, 1991 to September 23, 2015
Forever 24

Life as a Mother of an Addicted Child

If I were to describe the life of a mother with an addicted child, my best description would be like being on a roller coaster ride. The emotions I experienced were fear, hope, anxiety, worry, anger, doubt, anguish and shame.

Fear after every payday that I would find him after an overdose.

Hope after every apology and promise that he wants to be clean and enter into a treatment program.

Anxiety when you plan a trip without him that you will get a call that he has overdosed.

Worry constantly about how he is truly doing and if he is lying to me so that I don't worry.

Anger, that he is lying to me and won't seek help to overcome the addiction.

Doubt, that I am making the right decisions and my ability to keep him safe. Knowing there is a fine line between safety and enabling. Knowing that tough love is society's acceptable answer but also doubting if that is the best choice when factoring other things like Autism and coping skills.

Anguish that accompanies all these other emotions. The pain that I feel every day because of his choices.

Shame is probably the biggest emotion I experienced. I questioned what I did wrong and how could I, or why wasn't I able to prevent the addiction. Shame in that I perceived others as judging me in my inability to stop this. This shame is real, but it is misplaced. Addiction has reached epidemic levels and is touching all levels of society low, middle and higher incomes. If your family hasn't been touched yet the tragic reality is that in time it will in some way. The shame and fear of judgment has many riding this roller coaster alone. There is strength in unity. It is time to start having the conversation and realize the shame has no place on this ride.

And then one day the ride ends. And there is *relief*. All the emotions that I experienced on this ride has stopped. It is over and there is so much relief. But as I walk away from the ride this path is now filled with guilt and grief.

Guilt that I didn't do enough, didn't love enough, didn't pray enough. Guilt, that I'm relieved the roller coaster ride has ended. Guilt, that I would prefer this path over the roller coaster ride.

Grief that accompanies me every day. Grieving the missed opportunities. Never being able to meet his future wife. Never being able to hold his future babies. Never being able to see his smile and hear his laugh. Never being able to experience life with him (like the holidays). And never being able to hear him say "I love you."

But there is one last emotion that I experience along this path. It is *peace*. As hard as it was for me to experience the roller coaster ride, it was harder for him, the addict. The ups and downs and upside-down loops… It can only be described as a living hell for us both. He wanted the ride to stop even more than I did. He didn't want death because he knew that meant grief for me even though it meant peace for him. And that one day when neither of us expected the ride to end, it did. And as he is now at peace, I can also experience his peace.

GLORIA ATCHESON
Terra Haute, Indiana

751

New Normal

Somewhere in between the love you have for your child and the deep agonizing pain of their death, you will find your new normal.

Do not try to find the you that you once were. You are different now.

You have experienced the worst emotional pain a human can experience.

Pain so deeply rooted that it causes physical distress.

You will long for the old you, but she is long gone. She died with your child.

This is a terribly hard concept for some to grasp. You will long for your old life, the normality of it all.

Truth is, the normality died when your child first tried drugs.

It's an inconceivable concept of carrying on a life without your child. I promise you will, just as you attempted to carry on life during active addiction.

I remember the first few days after my child died repeating over and over "how do I do this?" One person in particular kept saying to me "you ARE doing it, this IS you doing it."

I didn't understand at the time and I'm sure you don't as you read these words. This IS the new normal they talk about. This is OUR new normal.

"One wakeup at a time", I always tell fellow grievers of children. One wakeup at a time you will learn to honor your child in the things you do.

Love and grief coexist. Happiness and sadness coexist as well.

You will learn to carry the weight of your pain while preserving your child's memory.

I promise, sweet mama, you will live again. Look how far you have come already.

You thought you would never survive the wake or funeral but here you are.

Think of how hard you fought for their sobriety. Remember the painful nights not knowing where they were. The nights you cried yourself to sleep worrying about your baby.

You have been through so much. When you feel your weakest remember whose mother you are and acknowledge your strength.

You will forever be your child's mother; death does not change that.

Written by Angee Cannon, Ashlyn's Mom

A Glimpse of an Addict's Mom's Loss

They mean well, but when friends ask, "How are you?" I dread it. I say "God's got me or I'm okay, considering." Truthfully, I'm usually just keeping my head above water.

A mom who lost a part of her heart.

I watched heroin and crack cocaine take your light, your sanity, your friends, your family, your health and your own child from you. I watched you slowly die in front of my eyes while fighting with you, begging you to get help. You tried so hard quite a few times and once right before you died, I'd actually got my hopes up again.

I thought I could finally get some sleep. But an addict's mom's bottom can drop out at any time. We don't rest. We panic every time we get a text or hear the phone ring. We wait for the phone call that usually comes in the middle of the night. We get sick to our stomach when we see your name come up on our cell. We have anxiety attacks every time an ambulance siren goes off.

We lose our health, our retirement, our friends, our jobs, our peace and our sanity. We begin to pray for God to take us or you home because we can't bear to see you destroy yourself and all we love around us. Especially your own child! But then who would be here for you or for them? We are lost in a black pit of despair and it seems like there is no way out.

Meanwhile, you are numb and escape into your drugs to cope, but I am left to deal every minute of the day with the reality of not only trying to save you, but myself, your children, our relatives and friends that are all impacted by this. And then comes that gut feeling I cannot ignore. It's not the nagging feeling I've had for years that you're going to die someday. It is a without a doubt, 100%, gut wrenching silent voice: "Christina's time is up, be ready."

I told three close friends you were dying soon. I prepared your funeral. There is NOTHING that could have prepared me for the day every addict's parent dreads. You overdose, they try to revive you. But this time it doesn't take. I'm making guttural noises that I didn't know existed. But you don't wake up. My baby girl on the floor with a needle in her arm, lifeless.

Next my nightmare on a gurney, in a body bag, in a strange house. When they unzipped the body bag to allow me to kiss your forehead, I felt a chunk of my heart leave me for the rest of my earthly life. I have to break the news to your daughter. 2nd worse thing I've ever experienced, as she screamed: "Nooooo" and kicked her legs and flailed her arms in the air and fell into my arms like a ragdoll.

The funeral is a blur.

Everyone is there for you one moment and soon no one is there and I must deal with the excruciating fact you aren't walking through my door with the most beautiful smile and contagious laugh God ever created. Friends have no clue of the magnitude of the bomb that exploded in my world and how emotionally destroyed I am. I put on the smile as they could never deal with the raw, cold, hard, ugly truth of my daily new normal. The silence is so loud its deafening. I do all the things I thought were creepy when I heard others do them. Sleeping with clothes that still had your scent on them. Making a Christina corner in the living room so you are still with us and keeping a lock of your hair. Holding on to your ashes rather than burying you in the ground. The triggers are the worst. I hear a certain song, see something you would have wanted at the store, watch your daughter do something you would be ecstatic over and if the grandchildren are not with me. I am reduced to a blubbering mess in the parking lot.

I know I will be with you in the blink of an eye. But the emptiness is beyond anything I could have ever imagined.

Why couldn't you see how much we loved you? You were so loved by so many! You just couldn't overcome the beast. I hate drugs!

In Loving Memory of *Christina Marie Westfall*

PJ CHAMPION SALLIE
Toledo, Ohio

Delaney's Poem

Funny, I don't remember no good dope days.
I remember walking for miles in a dope fiend haze.
I remember sleeping in houses that had no electric.
I remember being called a junkie, but I couldn't accept it.

I remember hanging out in abandons that were empty and dark.
I remember shooting up in the bathroom and falling out at the park.
I remember nodding out in front of my sister's kid.
I remember not remembering half of the things that I did.

I remember the dope man's time frame, just ten more minutes.
I remember those days being so sick that I just wanted to end it.
I remember the birthdays and holiday celebrations.
All the things I missed during my incarceration.

I remember overdosing on my bedroom floor.
I remember my sister's cry and my dad having to break down the door.
I remember the look on his face when I opened my eyes, thinking today was the day
that his baby had died.

I remember blaming myself when my mom decided to leave.

757

I remember the guilt I felt in my chest making it hard to breathe.
I remember caring so much but not knowing how to show it, and I know to this day
that she probably doesn't even know it.

I remember feeling like I lost all hope.
I remember giving up my body for the next bag of dope.
I remember only causing pain, destruction and harm.
I remember the track marks the needles left on my arm.
I remember watching the slow break up of my home.
I remember thinking my family would be better off if I just left them alone.

I remember looking in the mirror at my sickly complexion. I remember not recognizing
myself in my own damn reflection.
I remember constantly obsessing over my next score,
but what I remember most is getting down on my knees and asking God to save me
because I don't want to do this no more!
- Delaney Farrell

July 13, 1993 - July 1, 2017
Forever 23

Noticeable Behavior Changes from Drugs

The following includes what mothers on the #NotInVain Grieving Mothers Support Facebook page shared regarding the behaviors they noticed their children displaying while on drugs:

"My son Aj age 23 was diagnosed two months ago with Stage 3 Kidney Disease. We were shocked and didn't know why. We found out weeks later he was using Ketamine street name "K" and his kidneys were shutting down from the use of this drug meant for a 1500lb horse not a 180lb man. We had no idea. He lived on his own. This is used more as a club drug but is becoming more known on the street." Wendy B.

"Marijuana, red eyes. Stimulants, staying up all night, mood swings" Tina B.

"With Xanax "my son also got a little violent, definitely not his personality. My son in law is a disabled vet and it also made him violent. I always noticed my son scratching but Xanax made him do that. Later when he got into heroin, I also noticed the scratching and the head bobbing" Laurie C.

"Xanax-extremely noticeable slowed speech!" Shelly G.

"Benzos made her paranoid and scared to be alone in the house. When the opiates became noticeable, so did the lack of self-care. She was always dressed well, makeup and hair done prior to that. She was sick to her stomach a lot of the time with heroin, always complaining that she was constipated too. Alcohol brought on horrible arguments either saying terrible things. I used to tell her she was a very nasty drunk. Sometimes she would be very "up" and happy and positive, but mostly the last couple of years she spent a lot of time sleeping and isolating." Janet G

"Heroin makes their skin crawl and a lot of times it gets worse in the shower, my son used to let the shower run to make me think he was taking a shower when he was actually using." Terri S.

"Marijuana - eating everything and anything, red eyes, good mood. Pills - mood was totally opposite, snippy, very irritated. Heroin – stumbling and spending a lot of time in bathroom - hemorrhoid meds needed, cold and hot flashes, sick to stomach, throwing up, beads of sweat on face, falling asleep anywhere (on the bathroom floor, in the shower, in the convenient store bathrooms, in the car while driving, outside on the porch, in the yard)." Judy P.

"My son's VOICE would change... He had a heroin voice, a too much alcohol voice, an LSD voice... Sometimes he would drift off mid-sentence. The voices were just different. The alcohol voice was really smooth...The LSD voice I couldn't hear through all the laughter. The heroin voice would struggle to remain on topic, and sometimes stop altogether as he would nod off in mid-sentence. SOMETIMES, there were no distinguishing voice changes. He was clean. Sometimes I got to hear HIS voice." Shannon S.

"I can also remember the heroin voice from my daughter. It was raspy. I could always tell when she was using." Patrice B.

"My son at 16 started with Marijuana, then acid, then mushrooms, then cocaine, then crack, then LSD, then prescription pills, then Xanax, then methadone, and then heroin. He was hyper on cocaine, then sleeping while on pills and heroin. While on crack he became combative and on LSD he was out of it. On marijuana he was sleepy. I also notice sleeping nonstop and not eating whenever he combined Xanax, methadone and heroin" C.C.

"Klonopin made her act drowsier. I always seemed to ask her what was wrong when she was on those. Adderall she never ate and had bound- less energy." Rachel C.

"My son's drug of choice was meth (we call it ice in Oz) His behavior was really nice, and chatty. He was normally very shy and anxious, and this just disappeared. If he was on a bender the bad behavior would set in because of the lack of sleep after a couple of days. Because he was so lovely it took me a while to notice the pattern. I was so naive. It was heroin that got him in the end. He was a polyuser, and just hated being in his own head." Polly H.

"Marijuana- dilated pupils, opioids- sleeping all the time, fentanyl- was clueless until the police told me." Patty L.

. . .

"Marijuana- mellowed out, munchies, giggly (I did not mind him using it as he was able to work, be responsible, and it kept him focused).When he used heroin, totally the opposite, weight loss, eyes that had no soul, no holding a job, bank account overdrawn, a lack of caring about anything." Teri S.

"My son's drug of choice was benzos! We noticed extreme slowed speech and darkness under eyes! He also could not complete (or sometimes even start) simple tasks we asked of him! It's like his mind could not figure out how to do them-simple things like putting clothes up or organizing things. After his death we found many bottles of Imodium (yes-anti diarrheal med) it was also found in his system! If taken in large quantities, it's like an opiate!" Shelly G.

"Opiates. Her face would be pale but red on her cheeks." Kelly S.

"My son Kyle drug of choice originally was any opiates. He told me once it got to difficult and expensive, so he found out fentanyl was cheap and easy to get. Then his addiction was full on. If he was on it, he was mostly pleasant, head bob occasionally, didn't care about hygiene. I never noticed scratching. When he'd try to stop, he'd be sick to his stomach, throwing up a lot, mean, miserable. He held a job for a year like that. His boss found him snorting fentanyl off his phone at work one morning. His boss and coworkers had no idea he was addicted to fentanyl. Got him to go to Florida for rehab. He detoxed mostly at home. He would lay on couch, take a shower, sit outside, throw up, lay on couch, take a shower, sit outside for 3 days until he got on the plane. He only stayed 35 days. When he got home, he did great for a few weeks. He relapsed 6 weeks later and died. I saw signs the last few days before. Moody, erratic, loving then hateful then back to loving." Cory F.

"Pot: squinty eyes, no motivation, grades hit rock bottom, belligerent and defiant. Left paraphernalia out, forgetfulness. Heroin: missing spoons and the ones I had were bent and had been burnt on the under-side, filthy bedroom, blood stains on his socks, nodding, immediate with-draw from contact with family or meals, locked bedroom door, quick anger and profanity, TV and lights left on 24 hrs. a day. Eventually needles were left out, cooking tins, tourniquet. A bag of clean needles with packet alcohol wipes." Sandie B

"Meth- face sores, not wearing short sleeves despite warmer weather. I think he interacted with us more when he was high on meth." Leona K.

Signs and Symptoms to Look For

We've collected this list from what our grieving moms shared in the Facebook support group #NotInVain when recognizing the signs and symptoms of drug abuse and the behaviors associated with it.

- Appetite: Changes in appetite, such as a decreased appetite and associated weight loss
- Attitude: Less considerate, without care for things they usually care about. Dramatic change, overly emotional, irritable, angry, outbursts, confusion
- Behavior: Altered behavior, such as an increased desire for privacy. Suddenly lose interest in their hobbies they loved. Fidgety, paranoid and/or anxious. Frequently avoiding eye contact. Defensiveness when asked about substance use
- Belongings: Selling or pawning their own valued possessions that they once loved including even clothes
- Body Temperature: Always wearing socks and/or long sleeves/hoodies even in the summer
- Damage to Property: Burned areas on furniture and/or rugs. Black residue on floor, counters or furniture
- Dental Hygiene: Teeth begin to deteriorate, refuses to go to the dentist

- Digital payments: to people such as Venmo, CashApp, Bit Coin, etc.
- Driving: Getting into random accidents and claim it was not their fault
- Excessive Sweet Eating: Sugar, lots of candy and/or sweets
- Excessive use: of nose spray for chronic stuffy nose
- Eyes: Dilated, small pupils, droopy, bloodshot eyes
- Falling Asleep: during normal activities such as eating/cleaning/conversing.
- Fatigue: Nodding out, dozing off, sleeping all day, up all night. A noticeable lack of energy when performing daily activities and appearing tired or run down
- Health: Changes in physical appearance, such as wearing inappropriate or dirty clothing and a lack of interest in grooming. Rapid weight loss, frequently sick, vomiting for days, body aches, frequent visits to the ER (usually for pain meds or relief for detox).
- Hygiene: Not showering. Wearing cologne/body sprays to cover smells. Females always in need of tampons so male/female can use the plastic applicator
- Job: Poor work performance, being chronically late to work, appearing tired and disinterested in work duties, and receiving poor performance reviews. Never has any money to show for it.
- Leaving during the night: while everyone else is sleeping
- Loss of Interest: Missing events both with family and friends, always being late
- Menstrual Cycle: Lack of or very inconsistent
- Missing: steel wool pads, screens off faucets, screens from windows. Money/checks missing, unaccounted for, claiming their money was lost or stolen, valuable or non-valuable items in the home or garage.
- Spending: more money than usual or requesting to borrow money. Issues with financial management, such as not paying bills on time
- New Friends: Begin to hang out with people they never did before. Disregarding their old friends

- Nose: Sniffles and/or rubbing their nose constantly; nose always itching and/or red
- Pawn receipts: From pawning any valuable or invaluable item by stealing it even from their loved ones and friends.
- Personal Property: Pawning valuable or invaluable items
- Phone: Not answering phone calls or texts for long periods of time. Text messages don't make sense or unusual wording and acronyms; will not share his password with you. Frantically on their phone either texting or walking away on a call
- Privacy: Door locked or blocked, spending excessive time in bathroom. Carrying a backpack/purse everywhere with them, even to bed, without letting it out of their sight
- Reasons/excuses: Explanations that don't make common sense but difficult to disprove
- Receiving Packages: From India/Indonesia/China/Mexico
- Relationships: Drastic changes in relationships
- School: disinterest in school-related activities, and declining grades
- Skin: Picking face and skin; scratching, itching, having wounds that they can't explain or remember. Unusual acne. Bloodshot eyes, poor skin tone. Diagnosed with sepsis on skin blaming it on a pimple/bug bite or unexplained skin rash.
- Smell of chemicals: in the home or garage. Smell of vinegar
- Smoking: Tearing cigarette filters in half for more nicotine.
- Speaking/Voice Changes: Speech is slurred or delayed, groggy, raspy or hoarse. Speaking in a loud or softer voice than usual and/or nonstop
- Splatter: On bathroom mirror/walls/ceiling/floor of blood droplets
- Tolerance: Wanting higher alcohol content

SIGNS OF OVERDOSE

- DEATH RATTLE: A GURGLING SOUND WHEN NO LONGER ABLE TO SWALLOW OR COUGH. SALIVA BUILDS UP IN THE BACK OF

THE THROAT AND THE AIRWAYS CAUSE A "RATTLING" SOUND WHEN AIR PASSES THROUGH.

- SEIZURE
- NON-RESPONSIVE, UNCONSCIOUS OR PASSING OUT
- FOAMING AT THE MOUTH
- VOMITING
- PALE OR BLUE TINGED SKIN
- LOSS OF COORDINATION
- CONFUSION

PARAPHERNALIA

- ALUMINUM FOIL: IN UNUSUAL PLACES, MISSING FROM YOUR PANTRY.
- BOTTLE TOPS
- CANS: SQUEEZED WITH HOLE CUT OUT AND RESIDUE, PIECES MISSING, CUT UP PIECES LAYING AROUND WITH RESIDUE
- CIGARETTE PACK CELLOPHANE
- COTTON OR TISSUE PAPER: BROWN COTTON BALLS, TWISTED UP TISSUE PAPER FOR NOSE.
- EMPTY CIGARETTE PACKS
- EMPTY PEN BARRELS
- FOLDED UP LOTTERY TICKETS
- LACES: MISSING FROM SHOES AND CLOTHING
- LIGHTERS WITH THE TOP REMOVED
- Q-TIP HEADS
- ROLLED UP DOLLARS, FOLDED DOLLARS
- RUBBER BANDS/TINY RUBBER BANDS
- SCENTED ITEMS: INCENSE, CANDLES, EXCESSIVE USE
- SCISSORS: MISSING, FOUND WITH UNFAMILIAR RESIDUE ON THEM
- SMALL TINY BAGGIES, BAGGIES CUT AT THE CORNER
- SPOONS: MISSING, BENT, BURNT, HAVING BLACK SMUDGES
- STRAWS: CUT IN HALF, FOUND IN UNUSUAL PLACES
- SYRINGES, ORANGE NEEDLE CAPS
- TINY BALLOONS

Questions to Consider When Researching Rehab Facilities

1. Are you a co-occurring mental disorder treatment facility? Please define.
2. Do you provide medically assisted detox? If so, explain your protocol in great detail and what is your supervision?
3. What is your specific admission procedure?
4. Is there a complete medical examination done by a physician to include blood work, urinalysis, drug screening, cardiac and lung evaluations, vital signs, EKG completed and within how many hours of admission?
5. How soon after admission will they receive a psychiatric evaluation and by whom?
6. What professionals and their certifications comprise a client's treatment team? Please define all degree initials, length of employment in the field.
7. Is your clinical director full time and onsite?
8. How long has the director been with the program?
9. What is your staff turnover?
10. What is your facility's license?
11. What treatment therapies do you offer? Led by whom?
12. Are the primary counselors licensed and certified?
13. Do they have a master's degree in counseling?

14. What is the daily/weekly treatment schedule?
15. How often is a client/treatment team/family meeting and can it include a cyber conference?
16. Can a family speak directly with physicians? I
17. s there 24/7 medical supervision and at least an RN onsite at all times?
18. Do you encourage a client to place a family member on their HIPPA?
19. How often can family expect feedback on a client's progress: What is your policy if a client wants to leave?
20. What physical exercise do you incorporate?
21. What is your criteria in assessing progress?
22. What type of billing and expenses can I expect?
23. What is your facility's association with laboratories and outpatient care?
24. How often is lab work drawn, billed?
25. What are the average costs incurred?
26. Where do you commonly suggest sober living or further follow up and why?
27. What percentage of clients repeat readmission and is the fee different?
28. Do you offer any program scholarships for treatment?
29. How soon do you address discharge planning and with whom?
30. What determines the length of stay and is it insurance driven?
31. What is the policy/procedure with phone contact?
32. What is the procedure if extended stay is deemed necessary?
33. What is your family therapy?
34. What is your discharge follow up and for how long post discharge?
35. Are you willing to work with a client's outpatient therapist for a smooth transition to home care? Please define.
36. How do you handle a poor fit between a client and a treatment team member?
37. Is changing a treatment team member an option?
38. How individual is a treatment plan tailored and adapted?

39. What is the chain for handling a dispute?
40. Do you have a list of previous clients that are willing to discuss/share their personal experience with your facility?
41. How do you define a successful outcome?
42. Can you break it down by diagnosis?
43. Has any client died while receiving treatment at your facility? Explain the circumstances.
44. Has your facility been convicted in court? If yes, can you define why?
45. Are you coed and if so how mingled?
46. What percentage of your staff is in recovery?
47. Tell me about your food/menus and dining experience.
48. How do you handle medical illnesses and emergencies?
49. When a client is left alone, what is your procedure to check on them? How often?
50. Who addresses disputes between clients?
51. What is your disciplinary process?
52. What are some of your scheduled recreation activities?
53. What security measures are in place?
54. Do you provide any life skill classes?
55. Does discharge include MAT if deemed appropriate? How is this arranged?
56. Breakdown your policy of discharge planning to the next level of care and the long-term treatment plan. Does it include about eighteen months over all step-down levels of care? This seems to be the single greatest predictor of long-term recovery.

Questions created by Cathy W. Ian's mom, who is a nurse and her husband a doctor.

Grieving Moms Share Advice

"I'm not sure I could offer any advice, the only thing I'd say, and have said, is keep them close. Unfortunately, I was happy when my son started socializing at around 13 as before this, he was a real homebody.

My son was much like me when I was young, give anything a go, invincible.

His underlying poor mental health (severe anxiety) meant that when he tried, he liked, and way more than the next kid, it made him feel the way he wanted to feel when not on drugs.

I believe most kids try mind altering substances even if just alcohol. It is the disease that gets some and not others, I think it can be about what is going on in their lives. If they're not happy and have poor mental health, bad self-esteem, a bad home life then it's probably the escape they are looking for.

Keep them close, is all I can offer." Polly H.

"Keep them busy and limit social media. Once they express interest in a sport, music, art, etc, fully support and encourage it. Allow only supervised times to spend on their phones." Janet G.

"I think we need to work on getting our kids to communicate about their mental health at the earliest possible age. My son was picked on by teachers and I never knew until way after the fact. It is more than a just say no campaign that they need. We need to work with kids' acceptance

771

of each other so fewer kids feel left out and have the feelings of not belonging. I believe fewer kids would try drugs to begin with if they didn't have the need to mask their pain." Brenda R.

"What advice would I give to other moms, I am going to make it my mission to change some laws so we parents can help our kids over 18 or at least feel like we could have tried to help them. Nothing here in ILLI-NOIS to help with this." Wendy B.

"My son told me that a babysitter introduced him to marijuana when he was 9. Talking to him about drugs at that age was not even on my radar. Schools started drug education programs in junior high. Mark went through DARE and I remember talking to him about drugs when he was 14 and a freshman in high school when it was covered in a health class. Much later he told me they taught you about drugs but not about ADDICTION. Our suburban high school had a huge drug problem but I believe they tried to keep it under the rug. Not my school, not my community. My son's behavior changed. I thought he just needs a little help from counseling. Long story but he ended up out of control, ER, Psyche ward. He was 16 referred to what was supposed to be a highly regarded adolescent outpatient program that was highly shame based. We were advised in another program that they have to reach rock bottom. All things that I now believe are wrong." Terri Z.

"Little kids need to be SCARED of drugs. They need to be exposed to someone that is established in their addiction, that knows the goal of the encounter in order to personalize it. Its key to do this BEFORE they are offered any stuff, from kids at school, the neighborhood, etc. Then you tell your kid after the person leaves... Well, if you want to have your life ruined, like theirs, just accept that joint or pill you are going to be offered soon. And you WILL be offered something. If you want all the problems THAT person has, then feel free to try that pot, or snort that line. . . maybe you will be ok... b ut you may end up exactly like this person. This way you have a better idea what drugs can offer your life.

I did this with my daughter. It worked like a charm. She even thanked me when she was in her early twenties. She was not ever curious or pressured or tempted because she had made up her mind ahead of time. Sadly, I didnt do the same performance with my son. Get to them BEFORE the free samples are provided...Or offered. Or given. Or found." Shannon S

"I sadly don't feel like an expert in this topic. As a graduate from ULE (University of Life Experience) with a MGM (Master in Grieving Mom), I have had several friends with younger children message me for advice. My "thesis" was in loving a child with undiagnosed learning disabilities, ADHD, and Autism. My first observation would be that these learning challenges don't resolve on their own. You may choose to not medicate, like I did, but early diagnosis and treatment like helping them learn coping skills is vital. Without these coping skills, chances of the child self-medicating is high. Social anxiety is real and extremely difficult and challenging for the child that experiences it.

When a parent confided with me about her child smoking two cigarettes, I was able to share my personal experience about my son. The key question is to find out why did they smoke? Many times, it is stress, often it is to help with social anxiety. It might be peer pressure, but usually the true reason is a little beneath the surface; like they don't feel accepted because of their social awkwardness and this helps relieve the stress and anxiety. Cigarettes are the gateway to harder things. Eventually the anxiety is not relieved by just the cigarettes and the next step is Marijuana, and the progression continues.

My suggestion beside the above, is to also be very involved with your child. Know their friends, and their friends' parents. Do activities together that your child enjoys. Learn their interests in different activities and help them get involved. Be a safe place for them to come to and talk to you about anything. Yes, you may be freaking out inside. If they don't think you can handle the truth, then they will protect you with lies.

I hope this knowledge will save someone from the same pain as mine."

Gloria A.

Resources

For information about understanding drug use and addiction, visit:

- www.drugabuse.gov/publications/drugs-brains-behavior-science-addiction/drug-abuse-addiction
- https://teens.drugabuse.gov/drug-facts/brain-and-addiction
- https://easyread.drugabuse.gov

For more information about prevention, visit:

- www.drugabuse.gov/related-topics/prevention

For more information about treatment, visit:

- www.drugabuse.gov/related-topics/treatment

To find a publicly funded treatment center in your state, call 1-800-662-HELP or visit:

- https://findtreatment.samhsa.gov/

National Institute on Drug Abuse (NIDA) Resources

- Heroin (overview)
- Prescription Drugs and Cold Medicines
- Blog: What can we do about the heroin overdose epidemic?

Substance Abuse and Mental Health Services Administration (SAMHSA)

- www.samhsa.gov

SAMHSA Blog Posts

- SAHMSA Blog on Recovery Month
- SAMHSA Blog Posts

White House Office of National Drug Control Policy (ONDCP) Resources

- A Comprehensive Approach to Drug Prevention

#NotInVain for Private Support Group is available to help grieving mothers through their most challenging loss, their child.
Public website: www.notinvainmoms.com

About the Author

Bobbie Ziemer is an Ohio native living just outside of Columbus. She's the mother of three incredible children and she has had a very successful as well as reputable career in telecom sales working for all the major world-wide providers.

Bobbie lost her oldest child, Madison, forever 22, on October 10, 2017.

Although she is not able to share her own story due to a pending lawsuit, she has made it her mission to help spread awareness, open dialogue around a topic that is extremely taboo while creating a space for those struggling as well as grieving to know they are not as alone as she felt during and after the battle to save her daughter's life.

About the Publisher

After losing my oldest daughter, Madison, I couldn't help but want to do something to alert and prevent other parents in any way I possibly could from ever feeling the loss of losing a child. Even more important to me was helping the families who have lost their children understand that they are not alone and the things that happen to their minds, bodies and relationships are normal. When a person loses a child, there is nothing that can prepare you for the roller coaster of grief and survival.

I've raised all of my children to believe that they are capable of being someone who can change or at least leave a mark that they were here in this world. This is my gift back. If this book helps save even one life, the energy put into this painfully raw piece of work will be worth it all. These beautiful mothers opened their hearts, shared their pain and through writing their stories experienced some healing although there is nothing that will ever truly take away the heartbreak we all now carry.

I pray that God uses this book as he has all who have contributed to it to help, educate and assist in breaking the stigma that our children carried as well as the one we now do as the mothers of children lost to the drug epidemic. All proceeds of this book are being donated back to the #NotInVain Mothers Nonprofit Support Group to continue being a light in helping these mothers navigate this unimaginable loss.

For more information or inquiries, please email notinvainbook@gmail.com

For the latest updates on the Not In Vain Book Book Series, "like" and "follow" the "Not In Vain Book" public Facebook page.

Volume 2 of the *Mothers Share their Journey through their Child's Life and Loss to the Drug Pandemic* will be the next volume.

You may also "Follow the Author" on Amazon under "Bobbie Ziemer".

Future *Not In Vain* book series and volumes will include:

Not In Vain: The Aftermath. After the Flowers have Dried and the Impact on the Remaining Family

Not In Vain: Siblings Speak. Often Forgotten within the Midst of the Battle and the Loss

Not In Vain: What About the Children? A Nation Now Raising the Parentless Child

Made in the USA
Monee, IL
29 April 2021